Neanderthals in the Levant

New Approaches to Anthropological Archaeology

Editor-in-Chief

Thomas E. Levy, University of California, San Diego

Series Editors

Guillermo Algaze, University of California, San Diego
Paul S. Goldstein, University of California, San Diego
Augustin F. C. Holl, University of Michigan, Ann Arbor
Joyce Marcus, University of Michigan, Ann Arbor

Anthropological Archaeology offers a methodologically refreshing approach to the study of cultural evolution. It recognizes the fundamental role that anthropology now plays in archaeology and also integrates the strengths of various research paradigms which characterize archaeology on the world scene today, including new or processual, post-processual, evolutionist, cognitive, symbolic, marxist, and historical archaeologies. It does so by taking into account the cultural and, when possible, historical context of the material remains being studied. This involves the development of models concerning the formative role of cognition, symbolism, and ideology in human societies to explain the more material and economic dimensions of human culture that are the natural purview of archaeological data. It also involves an understanding of the cultural ecology of the societies being studied, and of the limitations and opportunities that the environment imposes on the evolution or devolution of human societies. Based on the assumption that cultures never develop in isolation, Anthropological Archaeology takes a regional approach to tackling fundamental issues concerning past cultural evolution anywhere in the world.

This new series welcomes proposals from 'intellectual foragers' whose interests combine field research with theoretical studies of issues of cultural evolution in the past and in the ethno-archaeological present. The series differs from much theoretical discourse in archaeology today in that it is dedicated to publishing work firmly grounded in archaeological fact, while also venturing to explore more speculative ideas about how cultures evolve and change.

Published titles in the series:

West Africa During the Atlantic Slave Trade: Archaeological Perspectives, edited by Christopher R. DeCorse

Egypt and the Levant: Interrelations from the 4th Through the Early 3rd Millennium B.C.E., edited by Edwin C. M. van den Brink and Thomas E. Levy

Landscapes, Rock-Art and the Dreaming: An Archaeology of Preunderstanding, Bruno David

Early Urbanizations in the Levant: A Regional Narrative, Raphael Greenberg

Neanderthals in the Levant

BEHAVIORAL ORGANIZATION AND THE BEGINNINGS OF
HUMAN MODERNITY

Edited by

Donald O. Henry

BLOOMSBURY ACADEMIC
LONDON • NEW YORK • OXFORD • NEW DELHI • SYDNEY

BLOOMSBURY ACADEMIC
Bloomsbury Publishing Plc
50 Bedford Square, London, WC1B 3DP, UK
1385 Broadway, New York, NY 10018, USA
29 Earlsfort Terrace, Dublin 2, Ireland

BLOOMSBURY, BLOOMSBURY ACADEMIC and the Diana logo
are trademarks of Bloomsbury Publishing Plc

First published by Continuum in Great Britain 2003
This Paperback edition published by Bloomsbury Academic 2023

Library of Congress Cataloging-in-Publication Data
Neanderthals in the Levant: behavioral organization and the beginnings of
human modernity / edited by Donald 0. Henry
p. cm. — (New approaches to anthropological archaeology)
Includes bibliographical references and index.
ISBN 0-8264-5803-3
1. Neanderthals–Middle East. 2. Mousterian culture–Middle East. 3. Tor Faraj Cave Oordan)
4. Human evolution. 5. Social evolution. 6. Middle East–Antiquities. I. Henry, Donald 0. 11. Series.
GN772.3.M6 N43 2003
569.9–dc21 2002067341

ISBN: HB: 978-0-8264-5803-2
PB: 978-1-3503-4399-3
ePDF: 978-1-4411-6719-4

Series: New Approaches to Anthropological Archaeology

Typeset by BookEns Ltd, Royston, Herts

To find out more about our authors and books visit
www.bloomsbury.com and sign up for our newsletters.

Dedication

In memory of Harold "Hal" Hietala (1940–2010)

Contents

Summary

List of Figures

Appendices

List of Tables

List of Contributors

Teresa L. Armagan, self-employed archaeological contractor, 2005 N 50th St., Omaha, NE 68104 USA (t_armagan13@hotmail.com). Ms. Armagan has designed and developed databases for management of archaeological sites for the Tulsa District and most recently the Omaha District, U.S. Army Corps of Engineers.

Yuri E. Demidenko, Crimean Branch of Archaeological Institute of National Ukrainian Academy of Sciences, Yaltinskaya St. 2, Simferopol 95007, Crimea, Ukraine (ydemidenko@svitonline.com). One of Dr. Demidenko's research foci is on tracing technological changes for industries related to the Middle-Upper Paleolithic transition in central Europe and the Near East. He is currently involved in investigations of Micoquian and Aurignacian industries in the Crimea.

Thomas M. Harris, formerly Associate Professor, Department of Chemistry and Biochemistry, University of Tulsa, Tulsa, Oklahoma; presently Catalyst Development Chemist, Delphi Catalysts, Tulsa. While at the University of Tulsa, Dr. Harris provided a variety of chemical analytic services to archaeological researchers.

Donald O. Henry, Professor, Department of Anthropology, Harwell Hall, University of Tulsa, Tulsa, OK 74104 USA (donald-henry@utulsa.edu). Professor Henry has led several research efforts focused on understanding the ecology of prehistoric groups living in the Levant. He is currently investigating an Early Neolithic village in southern Jordan.

Harold J. Hietala, Professor, Department of Anthropology, Southern Methodist University, Dallas, Texas 75275-0336 USA (hhietala@mail.smu.edu). Professor Hietala, a specialist in archaeological statistics and spatial analysis, has conducted studies of numerous Paleolithic sites in Israel, Egypt, and Jordan.

Arlene Miller Rosen, Institute of Archaeology, University College London, 31-34 Gordon Square, London WC1H 0PY UK (a.rosen@ucl.ac.uk). Dr. Rosen is a geoarchaeologist and phytolith specialist researching the responses of ancient societies to climate and environmental change. She is currently working on research projects in the Levant, Turkey, China, and Central Asia.

Vitaliy I. Usik, Museum of Archaeology, Archaeological Institute of National Ukrainian Academy of Sciences, B. Khmelnitsky St. 15, Kiev 02030, Ukraine. Dr. Usik is known for his refitting studies on Central European Levallois-Mousterian and Early Upper Paleolithic industries. Presently, he is studying some Middle and Upper Paleolithic industries in the Ukrainian Transcarpathian region.

Preface

In assembling *Neanderthals in the Levant* it would have been difficult to imagine that the focal site of Tor Faraj and those nearby would have still been providing vital evidence for understanding Neanderthals and their relationship with modern humans over twenty years later. The volume not only offers a detailed description of the broad array of findings over multiple seasons of excavation at Tor Faraj, it also sets out a framework for evaluating the degree to which the occupants of the site organized their behaviors along the lines of modern humans.

This effort was made possible largely by the remarkable preservation of stratified living floors within the rock shelter that, in turn, prompted a research design focused on a high resolution spatial analysis of the behavioral residuals across the floors. Especially noteworthy was the large number of hearths exposed in the excavation in that these proved to provide a key element in tracing the ways in which the residents of the shelter spatially structured their hearth centered activities. The piece plotting of chipped stone artifacts (almost 3,000 > 2.5cm) along with rocks and hearths, coupled with the spatial distributions of micro-debitage, phytoliths and sunlit heated areas furnished data-sets for exploring the positioning of various activities (e.g., food preparation and processing, social congregation, primary lithic production, sleeping, and refuse disposal) within the shelter. The refitting of many lithic artifacts into numerous constellations offered a better understanding of the specific technical aspects of the particular Levallois reduction strategy employed at Tor Faraj and, perhaps more important, the study offered a means of following the spatial paths of artifacts across the living floors as they travelled along their reduction streams.

From a broader perspective, the insights gained from the research at Tor Faraj highlight the conceptual use of space by the occupants of the shelter showing that they recognized specific places for doing certain things. In arranging their activities in this manner, they organized their occupation of the shelter along the lines of modern humans. Rather than a *simple* site structure in which many overlapping activities were undertaken around a central hearth, a pattern traditionally thought to characterize Neanderthal encampments, the residents of Tor Faraj created a *complex* site structure with spatially discrete places for particular activities. This complex site structure, common to modern human occupations, is shown in the site plans of archaeological and ethnographic rock shelter sites, presented in the volume, that offer an uncanny resemblance to that of Tor Faraj.

Many of the research findings presented in the volume have also served as a springboard for several subsequent research efforts largely having to do with Tor Faraj and neighboring Late Levantine Mousterian and Upper Paleolithic occupations in the Jebel Qalkha area in southern Jordan. Professor Seiji Kadowaki of Nagoya University has been the lead investigator in many of these (Kadowaki, et al., 2022, 2021, 2019a, 2019b, 2019c). Additionally, several studies building and refining the initial investigation's focus on intrasite patterns have been undertaken (Henry, 2019,2011, 2010; Henry et al., 2004) as well as ones examining intersite connections (Henry et al., 2017, Henry, 2011, 2007). The chert sourcing study introduced in the volume has also inspired subsequent research (Ichinose et al, in press, Kadowaki et al, 2022; Henry and Mraz, 2019; Suga et al., 2022) employing more elaborate technical approaches as well as expanded field investigations. Data-sets from the analysis of the Late Levantine Mousterian lithic assemblages from Tor Faraj have also contributed to subsequent studies of the site's stone tool assemblages (Kadowaki, et al., 2022, 2021; Groucutt, 2014). All in all, the

volume provides a wealth of information that is useful to understanding the behavioral organization of Neanderthals in the Levant.

Donald O. Henry

References Cited

Groucutt, H.S. (2014) Middle Palaeolithic point technology, with a focus on the site of Tor Faraj (Jordan, MIS 3). *Quaternary International* 350:205-226

Henry, D.O.(2019) High resolution spatial analysis with different objectives and scales. In S. Nakamura, T. Adachi and M. Abe (eds.), *Beyond the Fertile Crescent: Essays on Western Asian Archaeology in Honour of Sumio Fujii*, pp. 43–66. Tokyo, Rokuchi Shobo.

Henry, D.O. (2011) Late Levantine Mousterian spatial patterns at landscape and intrasite scales in Southern Jordan. In J-M. Le Tensorer, R. Jagher and M. Otte (eds.), *The Lower and Middle Palaeolithic in the Middle East and Neighbouring Regions*, pp. 115–130. Liege, Etudes et Recherches Archéologiques de l'Université de Liège (ERAUL).

Henry, D.O. (2010) The palimpsest problem, hearth pattern analysis and Middle Paleolithic site structure. *Quaternary International* 194: 1–21.

Henry, D.O. (2007) Searching for Neanderthals and finding ourselves. In T. Levy, M. Daviau, & R. Younker (eds.), *Crossing Jordan*. London, Equinox Publishing Company.

Henry, D.O., Belmaker, M., and S. Bergin (2017) The effect of terrain on Neanderthal ecology in the Levant. *Quaternary International* 435, A-12:94–105; http://dx.doi. org/ 10.1016/ j.quaint.2015.10.023.

Henry, D.O., Hietala, H., Rosen, A., Demidenko, Y.E., Usik, V.I. and T. Armagan (2004)

Human behavioral organization in the Middle Paleolithic, were Neanderthals different? *American Anthropologist* 106:17-31.

Henry, D.O. and Mraz, V. (2019) Lithic economy and prehistoric human behavioral ecology. *Journal of Archaeological Science, Reports* (Special Issue – Fall 2019), In C. Delage and J. Webb (eds).

Ichinose, N., Suga, E., Kadowaki, S, Tsukada, K., Bayart Nadmid, B., Umeda, K., Manchuk Nuramkhaan, M., Massadeh, S. and D.O. Henry (Submitted) Petrographic and geochemical characterization of chert artifacts from Middle, Upper, and Epi-Palaeolithic assemblages in the Jebel Qalkha area, southern Jordan *Archaeometry*

Kadowaki, S. and Henry, D.O. (2019) Renewed investigation of the Middle and Upper Paleolithic Sites in Jebel Qalkha, Southern Jordan. In S. Nakamura, T. Adachi and M. Abe (eds.), *Beyond the Fertile Crescent: Essays on Western Asian Archaeology in Honour of Sumio Fujii*, pp. 23–41. Tokyo, Rokuchi Shobo.

Kadowaki, S., Kurozumi,T. and D.O. Henry. (2019) Marine shells from Tor Fawaz, southern Jordan, and their implications for behavioral changes from the Middle to Upper Paleolihic in the Levant. In Y. Nishiaki and O. Joris (eds.) *Learning Among Neanderthals and Palaeolithic Modern Humans*, pp.161–178. New York, Springer.

Kadowaki, S., Suga, E., and D.O. Henry. (2021) Frequency and production technology of bladelets in Late Middle Paleolithic, Initial Upper Paleolithic and Early Upper Paleolithic (Ahmarian) assemblages in Jebel Qalkha, southern Jordan. *Quaternary International*, 596, 4–21. https://doi.org/10.1016/j.quaint. 2021.03.012

Kadowaki, S., Tamura, T., Kida, R., Omori, T., Maher, L., Portillo, M., Hirose, M., Suga, E., Massadeh, S. and, D.O. Henry. (2022) Lithic technology and chronology of Initial Upper Paleolithic assemblages at Tor Fawaz, Southern Jordan. *Journal of Paleolithic Archaeology* 5,1:1-59. https://doi.org/10.1007/ s41982-021- 00107-3

Kadowaki, S., Tamura, T., Sano, K., Kurozumi, T., Maher, L. Wakano, J.Y., Omori, T., Kida, R.,Hirose, Massadeh, S. and D.O. Henry. (2019) Lithic technology, chronology, and marine shells from Wadi Aghar, southern Jordan, and Initial Upper Paleolithic behaviors in the southern inland Levant. *Journal of Human Evolution* 135:2–25. https://doi.org/10.1016/j.jhevol. 2019.102646.

Kadowaki, S., Tsukada, K., Hirose, M., Suga, E., Massadeh, S. and Henry, D. O., 2022. Survey for chert outcrops in the western Hisma Basin, Southern Jordan and its implications for paleolithic raw material procurement. *ORIENT* 57: 3-20.

Suga, E., Ichinose, N., Tsukada, K., Kadowaki, S., Massadeh, S. and Henry, D. O., 2022. Investigating changes in lithic raw material use from the Middle Paleolithic to the Upper Paleolithic in Jebel Qalkha, southern Jordan. *Archaeological Research in Asia 29:1–11*. https://doi.org/10.1016/ j.ara.2021.100347.

Acknowledgements

I owe a great number of people a hearty thanks for helping in so many different ways to bring the Tor Faraj Project to completion. Following the excavation seasons over the summers of 1993 and 1994, the analysis and write-up phases stretched over seven, sometimes it seemed grueling, years through the summer of 2001. Beyond energy and intellect, archaeological research depends on funding. In this case, grants from the National Science Foundation and the Office of Research, the University of Tulsa provided generous support for the study.

I would like to thank the directors and staffs of the American Center of Oriental Research (Pierre Bikai, Director) and the Department of Antiquities of Jordan (Dr. Safwan Tell, Director in 1993 and Dr. Ghazi Bisheh, Director in 1994) for their invaluable assistance. The personnel of both organizations did much to make our work in Jordan an enjoyable experience. In this regard, a special thanks is offered to Sawsan Alfakhry, Director of the Aqaba Office of the Department of Antiquities, and Mohamed Friehat who served both seasons as our Department of Antiquities Representative. My thanks are also extended to Mr. Faraj Suleiman Jadaylat for the hospitality he showed us while we worked in his rockshelter. The countless pots of tea he prepared for our morning breaks and tent visits will long be remembered.

1993 research team in Jordan

Yuri Demidenko, Bill Dickens, John Dockall, Matthew Elliott, Mohamed Friehat, Rita George, Steve Hall, Nancy Henry, Hal Hietala, Steven Mack, Chris Miller, Holly Owens, Pat Thomas, Vitaliy Usik, and Greg Walwer.

1994 research team in Jordan

Jesse Benton, Jeremy Forstadt, Mohamed Friehat, Thom Golden, Steve Hall, Ruth Ann Hargus, Nancy Henry, Hal Hietala, Clare Leader, Laura Longo, Connie Murray, Holly Owens, Stephen Phillips, and Erin Schirtzzinger.

1995–2001 laboratory analysis and write-up

Teresa Armagan, Jesse Benton, Yuri Demidenko, Hal Hietala, Seiji Kadowaki, Kris Kerry, Chen Shen, Travis Taverna, Vitaliy Usik, Joel White, and John Williams. Special analyses: Steve Hall (geology), Tom Harris (geochemistry), Gif Miller (amino acid dating), and Helene Valladas (thermoluminescence dating). The artifact illustrations were skillfully drawn by Seiji Kadowaki, Chen Shen, and Vitaliy Usik.

I also want to express my appreciation to Tom Levy, Editor-in-Chief of the New Approaches to Anthropological Archaeology series, and Janet Joyce, Valerie Hall, and Sandra Margolies of Continuum Press for their good advice and able assistance in bringing the volume to print.

I would like specifically to thank my wife Nancy for enduring two seasons of managing the field station in Mureygha and most of all for her encouragement over many years, to complete 'the book.' Finally, I dedicate this volume to my three sons, Heath, Matt, and Zachary, each of whom had great experiences in Jordan.

Introduction

1 The Emergence of Modern Humans: Issues and Debates

DONALD O. HENRY

Arguably, the most controversial issue in paleoanthropology today involves the various questions having to do with the emergence of modern humans. These center on alternative views of human evolution during the Late Pleistocene, as encompassed by competing 'continuity' and 'replacement' models, as well as the question of the degree to which the behaviors of archaic and modern humans differed. Within this debate, modernity is defined and contrasted with archaic patterns across biologic, cognitive, and behavioral realms.

The large view: bio-cultural evolutionary models

The prevailing view among researchers is that sometime after about 200,000 years ago, humans spilled out of Africa following a much earlier wave of dispersion. But unlike the earlier exodus that led to the spread of Homo erectus groups throughout the Old World, this putative second expansion was composed of hominids that had evolved physical, as well as cognitive and behavioral, traits very similar to those of modern humans. Moreover, according to the replacement model, the adaptive advantages held by modern human groups enabled them to out-compete and ultimately supplant indigenous populations of archaic humans throughout the Old World. Thus, intertwined with this notion is the idea that modern humans were able to achieve greater success in competition with indigenous archaic populations because of their advantages in cognition and behavioral organization. Most advocates of the replacement model do recognize how early misconceptions have come to depreciate our views of archaic behaviors as, for example, in the negative connotation of things Neanderthal. But many researchers nevertheless point to a wide array of archaeological data as evidence of what is thought to represent real cognitive and behavioral differences between archaics and moderns.

An alternative view among paleoanthropologists holds that while modern humans may have evolved in Africa, they did so elsewhere as well. This continuity model argues for regional evolutionary successions leading from Homo erectus to Homo sapiens sapiens. Although seen as geographically distinct, these successions are thought to have occurred at a roughly similar pace due to some amount of gene flow throughout the Old World. In contrast to the replacement model, cognitive and behavioral differences between archaic and modern populations are not emphasized by continuity advocates. They acknowledge cognitive and behavioral differences along an evolutionary continuum, but do not see a sharp break between archaic and modern patterns.

These two intellectual camps, as described, are ideal, polar types. In reality, the views of many scholars fall somewhere between these extremes. Perhaps the most common centrist position is represented by the supporters of the hybridization model. This model holds

that while modern humans may have originated in Africa and expanded over the Old
World, they did not simply replace local
populations, but enveloped them to varying
degrees both culturally and genetically. This
supposedly would have resulted in instances
of shared behavioral patterns and some
genetic hybridization.

Biologic domain

From a biologic perspective, recent analysis of
mitochondrial DNA recovered from the original (Feldhofer Cave) Neanderthal skeleton
indicates ·that Neanderthal and modern
human lineages diverged before 317kya
(Krings *et al.* 1997; Krings *et al.* 1999, Fig.
1.1). This, coupled with DNA findings, that
show living humans to have held a common
ancestor in Africa about 200kya, furnishes
strong support for the phylogenetic aspects of
the replacement model. Also, finds of anato-

mically modern humans in Africa (120 to
70kya) and the Levant (120 to 90kya), which
significantly pre-date the latest Neanderthals,
furnish fossil evidence consistent with biologic
replacement. Similarly, fossil finds and archaeological materials falling within the period
from *ca.* 40 to 28kya across Europe have been
interpreted as an expression of a modern
human expansion, encompassing a period of
co-existence with Neanderthals, that ultimately led to outright replacement (summarized by Mellars 1996: 412-17; Bar-Yosef and
Pilbeam 2000: 84-5; Boquet-Appel and
Demars 2000). During this period of co-
existence, some hybridization may have
occurred between modern groups and late
surviving Neanderthal populations as has
been suggested for fossil finds from Portugal
(Duarte *et al.* 1999; Holden 1999; *cf.* Tattersall
and Schwartz 1999) and eastern Europe
(Bräuer 1992). Such inter-breeding would
not be ruled out by the genetic findings
(Klein 2000: 30).

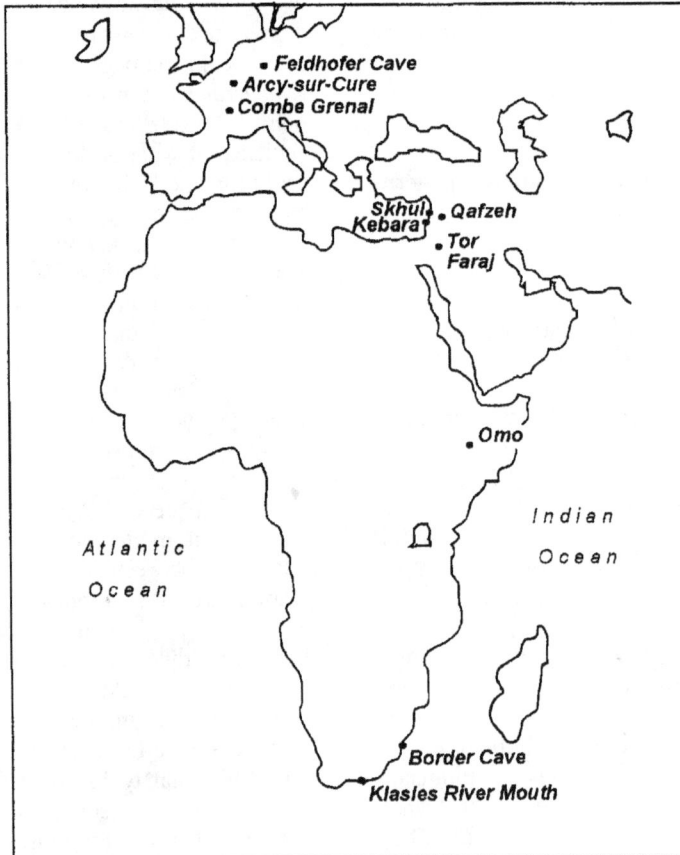

Figure 1.1 Map showing locations of sites discussed in the chapter

While the combined DNA and fossil evidence appears to furnish a strong case for the biologic part of the replacement model in Europe, there is greater diversity of opinion regarding the evolutionary successions of Africa and the Near East. Fossil finds from Omo Kibish in Ethiopia and the Klasies River and Border caves of South Africa are often cited as evidence for the presence of anatomically modern humans prior to 40 to 50kya (Stringer and Gamble 1993: 129-30). But, as pointed out by Klein (2000: 26), the fossil sample is actually quite small and most of the skulls are highly fragmentary. Moreover, dating of the specimens is only really secure for the Klasies River material (Stringer and Gamble 1993: 129-30).

Although the Qafzeh-Skhul skulls from the Levant are much more complete, they display considerable variability in features attributed to both modern humans and archaic forms, causing them to be labeled 'near-modern' (Klein 2000) or 'proto Cro-Magnon' (Vandermeersch 1981). Regardless of the extent to which the Qafzeh-Skhul specimens are viewed as modern, there is no real reason to see them as evidence for a population dispersion from Africa in that they are more securely dated to an interval as early as that of the South African material. Moreover, as suggested by Klein (2000: 27), the Qafzeh-Skhul material 'does not reflect a true Out-of-Africa event' in that biogeographic evidence indicates that Africa had expanded ecologically to incorporate the adjacent reaches of southwest Asia at this time (Tchernov 1992, 1994).

When the Qafzeh-Skhul specimens are compared to Near Eastern fossils classified as Neanderthals, *sensu lato*, researchers have regularly viewed both groups as part of a single, highly variable population (McCown and Keith 1939; Clark and Lindly 1989; Corruccini 1992; Simmons 1994; Wolpoff 1996; Arensburg and Belfer-Cohen 1998). Other researchers, however, interpret the Near Eastern fossil record as reflecting two distinct populations (Vandermeersch 1992; Trinkhaus 1995; Trinkhaus *et al.* 1998), but even here there is a lack of consensus on the degree to which the more archaic forms can be viewed as Neanderthals, at least as they are recognized in Europe. The variability of the Near Eastern archaic population and the presence of more progressive, modern features observed for some specimens are variously explained by hybridization (Hovers 1997) or local evolution (Kaufman 1999). Both explanations assume an immigration of European Neanderthals into the region as a consequence of cold, deteriorating conditions in the higher latitudes of Eurasia (Bar-Yosef 1994, 1995).

In summary, the biological data and interpretations, especially as they relate to the hominid fossils, have not produced agreement, even on such basic issues as continuity between the early near-moderns and fully modern humans appearing some 35 to 40kya. Questions tied to the proposed hybridization of late surviving European Neanderthals and fully modern humans also remain unresolved. Researchers still remain undecided upon the biologic relationships of the large group of Late Pleistocene hominids from the Levant.

Cognitive domain

Although ideas that Neanderthals were cognitively inferior to moderns are rarely explicitly defined (Mithen 1994), they are implicit within proposals of inferior linguistic (Lieberman 1975; Whallon 1989; Klein 2000), planning (Binford 1973; Soffer 1989), artistic (Chase and Dibble 1987; Gargett 1989), motor (Dennell 1985), and symboling (Gargett 1989, 1999) abilities of Neanderthals. Studies specifically devoted to cognition are largely theoretical. Based upon notions of different domains of intelligence (Fodor 1983), Mithen (1994) proposes that the Middle to Upper Paleolithic transition was precipitated by changes that enhanced the flow of information between the major cognitive domains. Following developmental psychological theory, especially neo-Piagetian ideas of control structures, Gibson (1988, 1990, 1993) suggests that neocortical changes in organization provided the capacity for new and more complex behaviors.

Empirical studies have relied upon various forms of stone tool analysis (Wynn 1979, 1985, 1991, 1993, 1995; Gowlett 1984; Belfer-Cohen and Goren-Inbar 1994). Although largely focusing upon Lower Paleolithic assemblages, they nevertheless suggest a relatively advanced cognitive level at this pre-

Neanderthal stage of human evolution. In applying neo-Piagetian concepts, analysis of the symmetry and complex production procedures associated with Levallois points from Levantine Mousterian sites shows that the knappers possessed a high degree of competence within an advanced conceptual domain, see Halford's (1987) multiple-system mapping (Kerry and Henry 2000). Along different lines, Hayden (1993) has observed anecdotally that few modern flint knappers are capable of producing Levallois points. Also, the variability observed in a technological study of Levantine Mousterian assemblages prompted Goren-Inbar and Belfer-Cohen (1998) to conclude that suggestions of Neanderthal cognitive inferiority are unfounded. When the empirical studies are coupled with neurological assessments of Neanderthals (Gregory 1984; Deacon 1990; Wilkens and Wakefield 1995), there simply is no compelling evidence upon which to claim that Neanderthals were cognitively inferior to modern humans.

The question of the cognitive capacity of Neanderthals is also related to alternative explanations advanced for the Châtelperronian tradition in western Europe. Châtelperronian occupations are unusual in containing a technotypological mixture of Mousterian and Upper Paleolithic elements in the lithic assemblages along with personal ornaments and bone tools—traditional signatures of the Upper Paleolithic. Moreover, the human fossils found in Châtelperronian deposits are exclusively identified as Neanderthals (D'Errico et al. 1998). The presence of essentially Upper Paleolithic artifacts in association with Neanderthals has been alternatively explained by post-depositional disturbance, trade/collection, acculturation, or autochthonous development (ibid.). In a recent detailed study of these issues, D'Errico et al. support the notion that Neanderthals were independently responsible for the modern elements of the Châtelperronian, yet other scholars (e.g., Mellars 1998; White 1998) remain convinced that some form of acculturation occurred between groups of indigenous Neanderthals and colonizing moderns. Although White (1998: 31) argues that the proponents of the acculturation argument do not necessarily claim that it was driven by the cognitive inferiority of Neanderthals, Mellars (1998: 26), in noting genetic evidence that

indicates a long separation of Neanderthals and modern humans, suggests that 'the possibility of genetically based divergences in brain structure, neurology, and cognitive capacities can in no way be ruled out.'

Behavioral organization

In efforts to understand how modern foraging patterns came to replace archaic ones independent of cognitive changes, scholars have focused on various aspects of behavioral organization, emphasizing the ways in which the archaic patterns may have been less effectual. Subsistence practices, land-use strategies, regional interaction spheres, and basic social organization have singly or in combination framed the research.

Subsistence: hunting versus scavenging

Some researchers have proposed that the basic subsistence strategies of archaic foragers differed from moderns in ways that put them at a disadvantage. Archaic groups are thought to have depended principally upon scavenging of large animals and the taking of small species on an opportunistic, encounter basis rather than concentrating on single species through pre-planned hunts, as seen among many modern foragers (Binford 1984, 1985; Soffer 1989; Klein 1994; but see contrasting opinions in Chase 1989; Hayden 1993; Grayson and Delpech 1994; Mellars 1996: 220–36). In a recent review of the issue, Kaufman (1999: 72) has outlined the expected configuration of a faunal assemblage produced by scavenging and encounter-based exploitation. He argues such an assemblage should reflect: (1) the full range of fauna available within a site's environs; (2) age profiles indicative of animals most susceptible to predation (i.e., very young or very old animals); (3) a preponderance of small- to medium-sized game with some large game obtained through scavenging; and (4) predominantly meat-poor bones for the scavenged, large game (i.e., crania and distal limbs). His examination of seven Middle Paleolithic faunal assemblages from Levantine sites shows that these are not configured along the lines of assemblages generated through scavenging and encounter-based hunting (ibid.: 92–3).

Using prey mortality profiles, Stiner (1994) has shown that while scavenging may have been a dominant pattern during the early Italian Middle Paleolithic, after *ca.* 55kya the later Neanderthals were clearly effective hunters. And following a similar analytic approach for the faunal assemblage recovered from the Mousterian occupation of Kebara Cave in the Levant, Speth and Tchernov (1998) have found that most of the ungulates were hunted, not scavenged. In light of these studies, the proposed differences between archaic and modern foraging subsistence practices are simply not supported.

Land-use strategies

Interwoven with the notion that Middle Paleolithic subsistence depended upon scavenging and opportunistic encounters is the idea that archaic groups organized their activities with limited foresight, planning depth, and flexibility in adjusting behaviors (Binford 1979, 1985, 1989; Chase and Dibble 1987; Soffer 1989). Archaeologically, these attributes of behavioral organization are supposedly reflected in Middle Paleolithic sites which are small, ephemeral, and largely redundant in artifact content (Farizy and David 1992; Stringer and Gamble 1993). In his detailed review of Middle and Upper Paleolithic occupations in southwestern France, Mellars (1996: 362-5) found the occupations of archaic foragers to be smaller and more homogeneous than the largest and richest of those of modern foragers, but he also noted a remarkable similarity in basic regional site patterns relative to placement, intensity of occupation, and diversity in artifact content. Along the same lines, Kaufman (1999: 77) describes various settlement-procurement systems reported in detail for the Levantine Middle Paleolithic (Marks and Freidel 1977; Marks 1981, 1988b; Hovers 1990; Henry 1992, 1995b) concluding that:

> the data presented here goes a long way in disproving the notion that Middle Paleolithic hominids were lacking in foresight and planning. Their most fundamental adaptive systems as described here meet all the criteria of those applied to hunter-gatherers of the following period and of the ethnographic present.

Another avenue used in assessing planning depth has been raw material aquisition as a component of lithic technology. Raw material sourcing and technologic studies in Europe (Geneste 1988; Féblot-Augustins 1993: 254-7; Kuhn 1995: 175) and the Near East (Hovers 1990; Henry 1995b: 114-17) show that archaic foragers acquired their raw material within the contexts of techno-economic strategies indicative of significant planning depth and foresight. Thus, in summary, the archaeological record of archaic groups reveals little to suggest a major disjunction in subsistence or settlement strategies from that of modern foragers. The evolutionary changes that did occur in these areas appear to be more of degree than kind.

Language, interaction spheres, symbolic expression, and social organization

Beyond subsistence and settlement practices, several researchers have pointed to a major elaboration of language and the appearance of symbolic expression as driving forces behind a 'social revolution' that was responsible for emergent modernity (Gamble 1986; Whallon 1989; White 1989; Stringer and Gamble 1993; Soffer 1994). At a regional scale, the proposed social changes are thought to have involved the formation of kinship systems, distant trade connections, and alliance networks, all of which are crucial to the exchange of information and resources among modern foragers.

In the Upper Paleolithic of Europe, the use of cherts from distant sources and the presence of ornamental shells from the Atlantic and Mediterranean coasts (Taborin 1993; Mellars 1996) have been cited as evidence for the presence of region-wide interaction spheres that previously did not exist. But chert from distant sources is also reported for Middle Paleolithic sites in Europe (Geneste 1988; Roebroeks *et al.* 1988; Féblot-Augustins 1993; Mellars 1996: 398-400) and the Near East (Henry 1995b), although not to the degree as noted for the Upper Paleolithic. These data again suggest that a change may have occurred between the Middle and Upper Paleolithic in the intensity of regional interaction by foraging groups, but they do not signify a major qualitative shift in such interaction.

Beads and pendants fashioned from animal teeth, bone, ivory, shell, and stone are common to artifact inventories of the European Upper Paleolithic in its earliest stages, whereas such items, although present, are generally rare in Middle Paleolithic contexts (Bednarik 1992; Kaufman 1999). An exception to this pattern is that discussed earlier for the Châtelperronian site of Arcy-sur-Cure where a rich assemblage of probable personal adornment items was recovered in association with Neanderthal remains (Hublin et al. 1996). But such finds are atypical and the far-reaching distributions of such items are without parallel in the Middle Paleolithic. This 'explosion' of items of personal adornment in the Upper Paleolithic is thought to signal the emergence of self-awareness and social complexity along with fully modern language (White 1989).

The emergence of a modern language with its capacity for communicating information about distant places in contexts of the past, present, and future is thought by many researchers to represent the central triggering mechanism for modernity (Binford 1987; Whallon 1989; Soffer 1994; Mellars 1996). Whallon (1989) and Soffer (1994) stress the importance of a sophisticated language in making available information about the distribution of essential resources and in the integration of the activities of individuals, immediate social units, and widely dispersed groups. Klein (2000: 27) also emphasizes the role of language in the emergence of modern behaviors, but unlike most others, he argues for a biologic linkage in the form of a neural mutation, which spread some 50 to 40kya by population movement from Africa to Europe. Although Mellars (1996: 390-1) questions the cognitive argument for the emergence of modern language, he underscores the propositions of noted linguists (Bickerton 1981, 1990; Chomsky 1986) that it occurred as 'a relative sudden, "catastrophic" event, rather than a gradual process of mental and linguistic evolution.' Arguments that the neural circuitry or laryngeal areas of Neanderthals differed from moderns have been refuted (Hayden 1993: 131-2), but this still leaves open the notion of a major language shift unconnected to a change in vocalization or cognition. Unfortunately, such an idea is very difficult to examine in the light of hard archaeological evidence.

Social organization

The proposed differences between archaic and modern social organization are much more amenable to testing. The most provocative suggestion is that the 'sex-based separation and division of labor as we know it from the ethnographic record, occurred around the Middle to the Upper Paleolithic transition' (Soffer 1994: 111). More specifically, Soffer (ibid.: 111) proposes that Neanderthal groups were not composed of a few nuclear families, but instead consisted of 'diurnal small-sized foraging and co-residential units of mothers with immature young, plus perhaps, a small number of related adult females, as well as small-sized all-male units.' Following this model, female units would be expected to have more restricted day ranges than male units and this should be reflected in their dietary patterns. Males would be expected to have consumed a greater number of large herbivores, whereas females would have exploited more locally abundant small species of plants and animals.

Binford (1992, 1996) also questions whether archaic groups were organized around nuclear family units and he supports his arguments with cross-cultural evidence and from his analysis of data recovered from the French rockshelter of Combe Grenal.

In stressing the importance of site structure as a means of tracing the behavioral organization of foraging groups in their occupation of campsites, Binford (1996: 234) finds that modern foragers partition their habitation space into largely redundant, modular areas that regularly consist of a sleeping facility and small hearth which serve a single family. This observation is quite important, for it may provide a means of detecting the basic building block of human social organization, the family, in the deep past. Binford (ibid.: 234) goes on to state that such site structures are unknown from the Middle Paleolithic.

Binford's (1992) analysis of data from the French rockshelter of Combe Grenal not only causes him to question the presence of a nuclear family component within archaic groups, it also prompts him to propose a social organization which resembles that envisioned by Soffer. He notes that successive occupation horizons in the shelter show a common structure consisting of a central area of irregularly scattered ashes where notched and denticulated tools are concentrated, along with faunal elements indicative of marrow and brain extraction (Binford 1992; Mellars 1996: 357-8). In peripheral areas, typically situated near the front of the shelter, he finds concentrations of side-scrapers and points in conjunction with bones left from inferred primary butchery tasks. Raw material sources also add to the dichotomy observed within the site structure. The lithic artifacts in the central area are fashioned mainly from nearby, poor-quality raw material, whereas those from the peripheral areas consist of greater proportions of higher-quality cherts from more distant sources. Binford (1992) thinks the site structure at Combe Grenal reflects a sexual division of activity areas: the central area for females engaged in the extraction of fats from bones and crania, and the peripheral areas used by males engaged in heavy-duty butchering of scavenged carcasses. The contrasts in utilized cherts are thought to be linked to the higher mobility levels and greater foraging ranges for the males. Perhaps the most provocative aspect of Binford's (*ibid.*: 50) interpretation of the Combe Grenal data is that males and females formed separate foraging groups who came together only for brief periods of mating.

In a critical review of Binford's interpretations of the Combe Grenal evidence, Mellars (1996: 259-360) suggests that the contrasting spatial distributions of artifacts (side-scrapers and points versus notches and denticulates) may reflect distinct activities that were not necessarily gender-specific. Mellars (*ibid.*: 360) also points out contextual evidence from other sites that is inconsistent with viewing the activity area tool-kits as being linked to gender. He notes, for example, that assemblages dominated by notches and denticulates occur in sites associated principally with the primary butchery of large animal carcasses. And he lists five sites dominated by side-scrapers and points, Binford's proposed male-linked tool-kit, where the burials of very young children occurred.

Although Binford's inferences may not be entirely convincing, they do underscore the potential of examining intra-site patterns for insights regarding the social organization of archaic groups. Relative to evidence for the presence of family units prior to the proposed social revolution, Yellen (1996) has recently

suggested that artifact distributions within a living floor of a Middle Stone Age site in Zaire trace a site structure resembling the nuclear family signatures seen in camps of modern foragers. The site of Katanda 9, dated to *ca.* 90kya, also produced a remarkable series of barbed and unbarbed bone points (Yellen *et al.* 1995); artifact varieties thought by many to signal modernity. Yellen's findings are consistent with notions of precocious bio-cultural modernity in Africa, but similar studies of Middle Paleolithic sites outside of Africa are few and, as far as I know, none have been devoted to understanding social organization.

Conclusion

Although biologic data suggest that Neanderthals were an offshoot of the human lineage, the question of the degree to which archaic and modern populations differed in cognition and behavior still remains crucially important. This is because such potential differences in cognition and/or behavior may hold the key to Neanderthal extinction. Cognitive studies have largely been theoretical, but the little empirical research so far conducted shows no real difference between archaic and modern cognition. Relative to behavioral organization, the notions that archaic groups were ineffective hunters who lacked planning depth and flexibility in their land-use strategies have been refuted by several studies undertaken in Europe and the Near East. Archaic groups do appear to have employed items of adornment much less extensively than moderns, at least in western Europe, and they commanded much smaller interaction spheres. Whether or not these differences can be attributed to the development of a more sophisticated language and attendant sense of self, and the emergence of alliance networks, remains to be determined. An emphasis on ornamentation, a pattern that is largely lacking from the Near Eastern Upper Paleolithic, may have been culturally specific. And the larger scope of interaction spheres may simply reflect the high population densities of the Upper Paleolithic in western Europe. In the Near East, for example, such far-flung interaction does not appear until Early Neolithic times.

But what of the arguments that Middle Paleolithic groups, independent of any cognitive impediments, were organized socially in a remarkably different way than modern foragers? Could it be that our basic assumption that archaic groups were organized around nuclear families is wrong? The problem in answering these questions is that we simply have not investigated Middle Paleolithic occupations with an eye to social organization. In reality, most Middle Paleolithic sites are not really suitable for such analysis in that they are small and lack living floors. But perhaps a more important obstacle to the examination of Middle Paleolithic behavioral and social organization rests in decoding site structure (Pettitt 1997). Research conducted by Binford (1991, 1996) and Whitelaw (1991) offers an overarching clue to the decoding process in the parallels that exist between *spatial distances* within a site's structure and the *social distances* between those responsible for the various elements of the structure. And imbedded in this is the notion that the degree to which Middle Paleolithic behavioral organization resembled that of modern foragers should be reflected in comparisons of site structures from archaic and modern contexts. Such comparisons are used in guiding the intra-site spatial study at the Jordanian site of Tor Faraj and developing the inferences concerning the behavioral and social organization of the Middle Paleolithic occupants of the shelter as described in Chapter 10 of this volume.

If research along the lines of that undertaken at Tor Faraj consistently shows Middle Paleolithic social and behavioral organization to differ little from that of modern foragers, it raises the likelihood that the archaic to modern transition was stimulated by technological innovation rather than social or cognitive differences. Other researchers have argued this point. Jelinek (1992: 87-8) suggests that 'increased sophistication in the preparation of artificial insulation in the form of tailored clothing and tents' may have offered an expanding tropical population a major ecological advantage in palearctic Eurasia. Hayden (1993: 139-40) has recently argued that improvements in resource processing, specifically in filleting, processing, and storing meat, may have been the technical advance that triggered the Middle to Upper Paleolithic transition. And Bar-Yosef (2000: 141) sees models of 'techno-cultural inventions and innovations' as best fitting the archaeological evidence when attempting to account for the changes from the Middle to Upper Paleolithic. Regardless of the specific nature of the innovation, the general notion that a technological advancement was responsible for the emergence of the Upper Paleolithic and the disappearance of Neanderthals is consistent with recent examples where indigenous populations with inferior technologies have been culturally and genetically swamped by technologically superior immigrants. In historic contact situations, we do not argue that indigenous peoples were somehow cognitively or behaviorally inferior to colonizing groups. So why should we exclude the possibility that Neanderthals had essentially modern cognitive and behavioral capacities, yet simply lacked the technological sophistication of immigrant groups composed of modern humans?

Although they were able to survive in a predominantly cold, harsh environment for over 100,000 years, several studies indicate that Neanderthals were under physical and dietary stress to a significantly greater extent than modern humans. Mortality profiles among Neanderthals show that 40 percent died before reaching adulthood and fewer than 10 percent survived beyond the age of 40 (Trinkaus and Thompson 1987). Soffer (1994) found similar mortality profiles for Neanderthals in her research and noted that sub-adult mortality among early modern humans was significantly lower, i.e., 30 percent. Research on signatures of nutritional stress, enamel hypoplasia, and Harris lines also has shown that their incidence among Neanderthals is substantially higher than among modern humans (Ogilvie *et al.* 1989; Soffer 1994). Additionally, Neanderthals appear to have experienced a higher incidence of trauma, as evidenced by bone fractures, than early modern humans (Trinkaus 1989). And from the perspective of energetics, Neanderthals would have to have maintained a high-calorie diet in order to sustain their bulky, cold adapted bodies (Trinkaus 1983). In contrast, early modern humans could have survived on lower calorie levels due to their more gracile form.

Various technological innovations such as hearth banking, tents, tailored clothing, specialized tools of chert, bone, and antler, and perhaps use of the atlatl or even bow and arrow would have given modern humans a decided adaptive advantage over Neanderthals. Simulation models indicate that if Neanderthal mortality levels had exceeded those of moderns by even 1 or 2 percent, their extinction would have occurred in only 30 generations, less than 1000 years (Zubrow 1989). In recent, historic times, when waves of technologically advanced groups expanded into new territories, the population levels of indigenous groups often dwindled dramatically to a point where they were genetically and culturally swamped by the colonizers. A similar replacement phenomenon may well have followed expanding groups of modern humans across Europe some 30,000 to 40,000 years ago.

2 The Levant and the Modern Human Debate

DONALD O. HENRY

The Levant figures heavily in our understanding the emergence of modern humans for two reasons. First, intensive research of the region has produced an unusual array of fossil hominids in conjunction with a reasonably well-understood archaeological succession for the Mousterian. When these data are compared with evidence from the succeeding precocious Upper Paleolithic, there is cause to suspect *in situ* development of, at least, behavioral modernity some 40 to 50kya. Second, because of its geographic position as a land-bridge joining Africa with western Eurasia, the Levant provides a field laboratory for testing propositions concerning an African origin for modern humans and their attendant behaviors.

In examining the Levantine Mousterian and Upper Paleolithic, it is ironic that we have a much fuller understanding of many of the behaviors (e.g., settlement and procurement strategies and even ideology) of Middle Paleolithic groups than those of the earliest phases of the succeeding Upper Paleolithic. This disparity primarily stems from the larger sample of Middle Paleolithic sites coupled with the recovery of a greater diversity of evidence from their deposits. But even with comparisons largely limited to chipped stone assemblages, it is possible to evaluate notions of indigenous as opposed to external origins for the Upper Paleolithic.

The Levantine Mousterian

Sites of the complex are concentrated along the coastline of Lebanon and northern Israel, but extend inland across the Negev to southern Jordan in the south and into eastern Syria in the north (Fig. 2.1). Traditionally, Levantine Mousterian sites have been recognized by their lithic assemblages which display an intensive use of the Levallois technique in shaping cores for flake, blade, or point production.

The Industries

The deep deposit in Tabun Cave, one of the Carmel sites of northern Israel, furnished a long sequence stretching from the Lower Paleolithic (Tayacian/Tabunian, Upper Acheulean, and Acheulo-Yabrudian) to the end of the Middle Paleolithic, i.e., the late Levantine Mousterian (Jelinek 1982). Within the Mousterian layers at Tabun, three different types of assemblages were recognized corresponding to Layers C, B, and D (Copeland 1975). These three assemblage types, based upon differences in application of the Levallois technique and in emphasis on certain end-products, have come to be used to order the Levantine Mousterian into three assemblage groups or Industries (Copeland 1975; Jelinek 1981; Bar-Yosef and Meignen 1992; Marks 1992b; Bar-Yosef 1998). While the Tabun sequence does serve as a general organizational framework for the Levantine

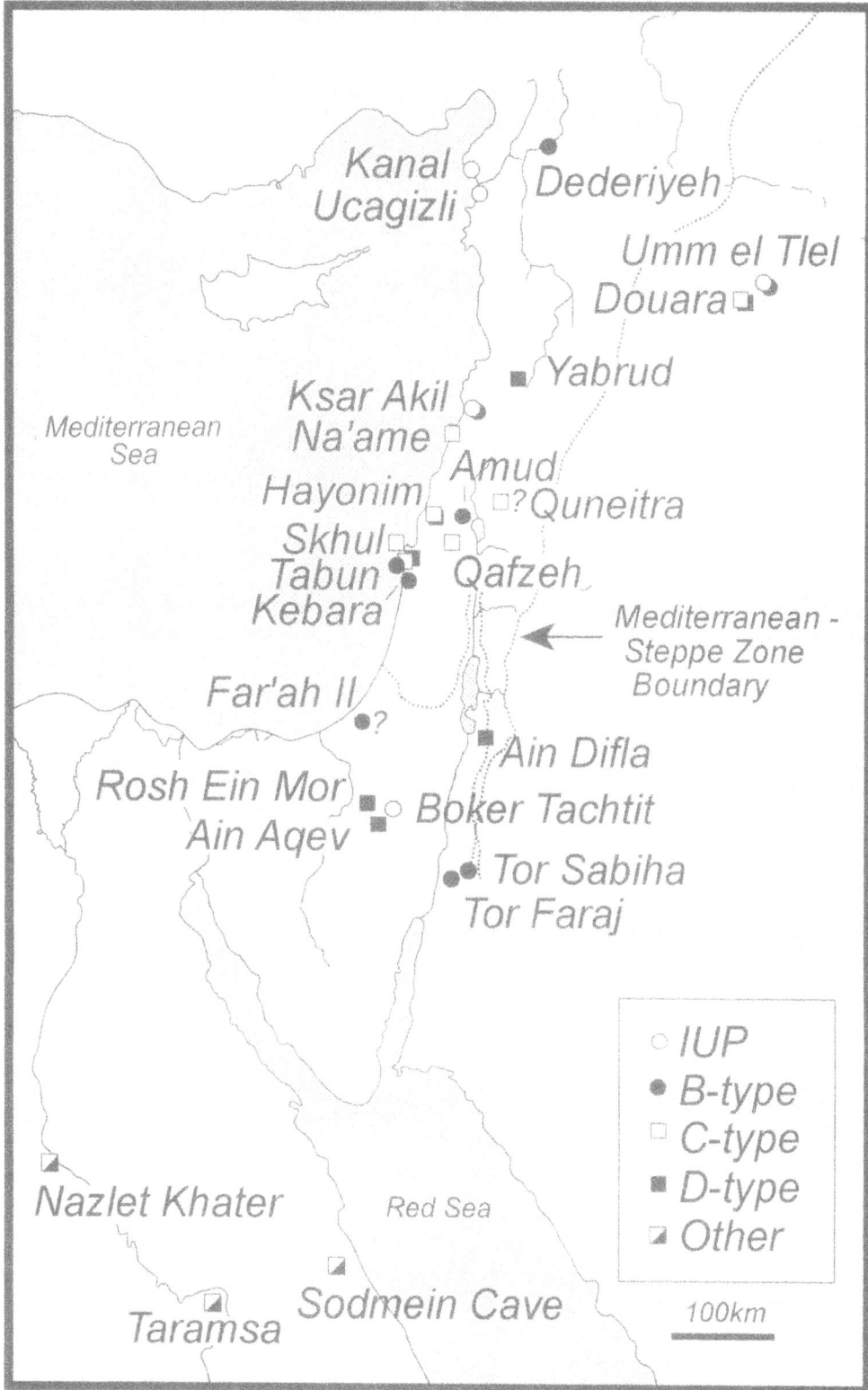

Figure 2.1 Map showing the locations of major sites in the Levant and northeast Africa

Mousterian, researchers often disagree on its application (see Hovers 1997 for a comprehensive review of the issues). Three general issues attract the greatest controversy. These include the specific placement of certain assemblages (e.g., Far'ah II, Bezez B, Quneitra, Amud), the integrity of the succession to all areas of the Levant, and the degree to which the Industries represent diachronic phases as opposed to synchronic facies. The reason that understanding the cultural-chronology of the lithic assemblages is so important is that the chipped stone artifacts represent the only means by which to examine the relationship of all the Levantine Mousterian assemblages.

D-type or Abu Sifian Industry

D-type assemblages exhibit a dominant use of unidirectional Levallois core preparation in the generation of blades and elongated points, although bidirectional preparation tended to be employed for the production of flakes and shorter points (Crew 1976; Munday 1976). Ovoid, radially prepared cores also appear in D-type assemblages, but to a lesser extent.

Besides the Levallois method, another approach to blade production has been recognized in many D-type assemblages. This 'laminar system' (Meignen 1998: 176) conceptually resembles that of latter Upper Paleolithic Industries, but it appears to lack the more refined techniques of core shaping, platform regularization, and soft-hammer percussion necessary for the removal of very thin blades. In contrast to the Levallois method in which a core's working face is typically organized along a single flat surface with removals oriented parallel to the plane, in the 'laminar system' the working face wraps the volume of a core, and removals are oriented along its maximum length. Beyond a distinctive core morphology, blades with keel-shaped cross-sections and crested blades provide signatures of the laminar method of blade production.

From a typological perspective, Marks (1992b: 232) observes that D-type assemblages generally have 'few side-scrapers, moderate numbers of denticulates, and significant numbers of Upper Paleolithic tool types' and Meignen (1998: 177) notes that retouched pieces consist mainly of retouched points and blades (Fig. 2.2).

D-type assemblages are widely distributed in the Levant and include: Hayonim Cave lower Layer E in the western Galilee of northern Israel (Meignen 1998), Tabun Cave D (Jelinek 1982) in the Carmel, Abu Sif and Sahba (Neuville 1951) of the Judean Desert, Rosh Ein Mor and Nahal Aqev in the highland Negev (Marks and Monigal 1995), Ain Difla in west-central Jordan (Lindly and Clark 1987; Demidenko and Usik 1993d; Clark et al. 1997), Douara Layer IV (Akazawa 1979; Nishiaki 1989), and Jerf Ajla (Schroeder 1969) in eastern Syria. Meignen (1998) has noted the presence of the laminar system at Hayonim Cave lower Layer E, Rosh Ein Mor, Ain Difla, and Douara IV. Abu Sif with its pronounced elongation of points and thick blades should also be added to this list. Ironically, the laminar method is not evident at Tabun D (ibid.).

Bar-Yosef (1998: 44) suggests that the D-type Levantine Mousterian be renamed the Abu Sifian Industry, after the Judean Desert type site. He feels this is needed in order to distinguish these assemblages from those of the Hummalian, centered in the El Kowm basin of Syria, which employ the laminar system but lack the Levallois method (Copeland and Hours 1983; Boëda and Muhesan 1993; Meignen 1995).

C-type Industry

In contrast to the blade and point dominant D-type assemblages, C-type assemblages are characterized by classic, radially prepared Levallois cores used in the delivery of ovoid flakes (Fig. 2.3). Elongated blanks appear, but rarely. Unilateral side-scrapers represent the most common tool type and at lower frequencies, notches, denticulates, burins, and perforators round out the tool-kits. Triangular points are present, but in small numbers, and they occur concentrated in specific horizons such as the top of Layer C at Tabun and Layer XV at Qafzeh (Bar-Yosef 2000: 116). Common tool types include unilateral side-scrapers, notches, denticulates, and a few burins (Hovers 1997).

The C-type Industry, confined to the northern and central Levant, is known from Tabun C, Skhul Layer B (Bar-Yosef 2000), Hayonim upper Layer E (Meignen 1998), Qafzeh (Boutié 1989; Hovers 1997), Ras el Kelb

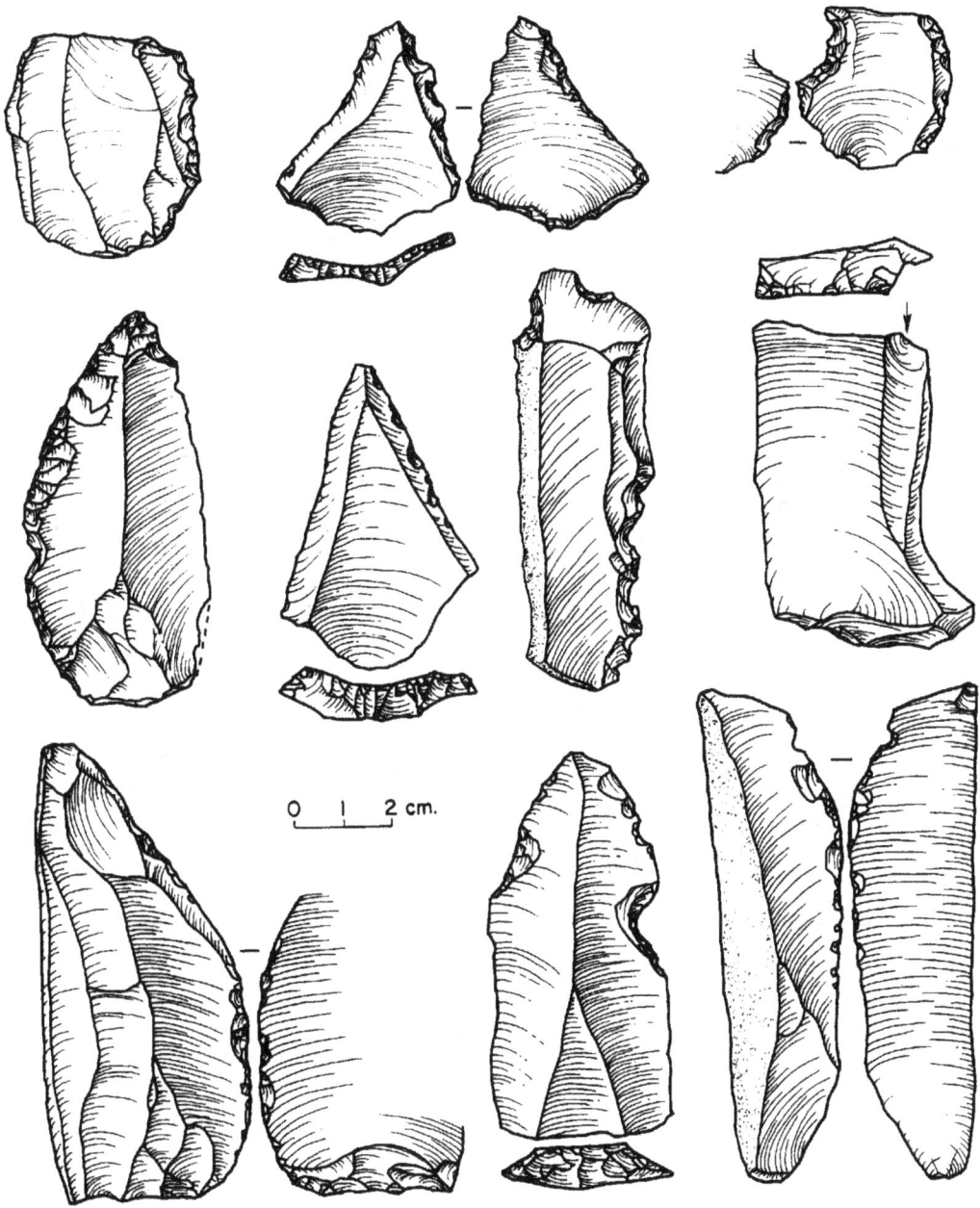

Figure 2.2   Illustrations of artifacts representing Levantine Mousterian D-type Industry (modified after Crew 1976)

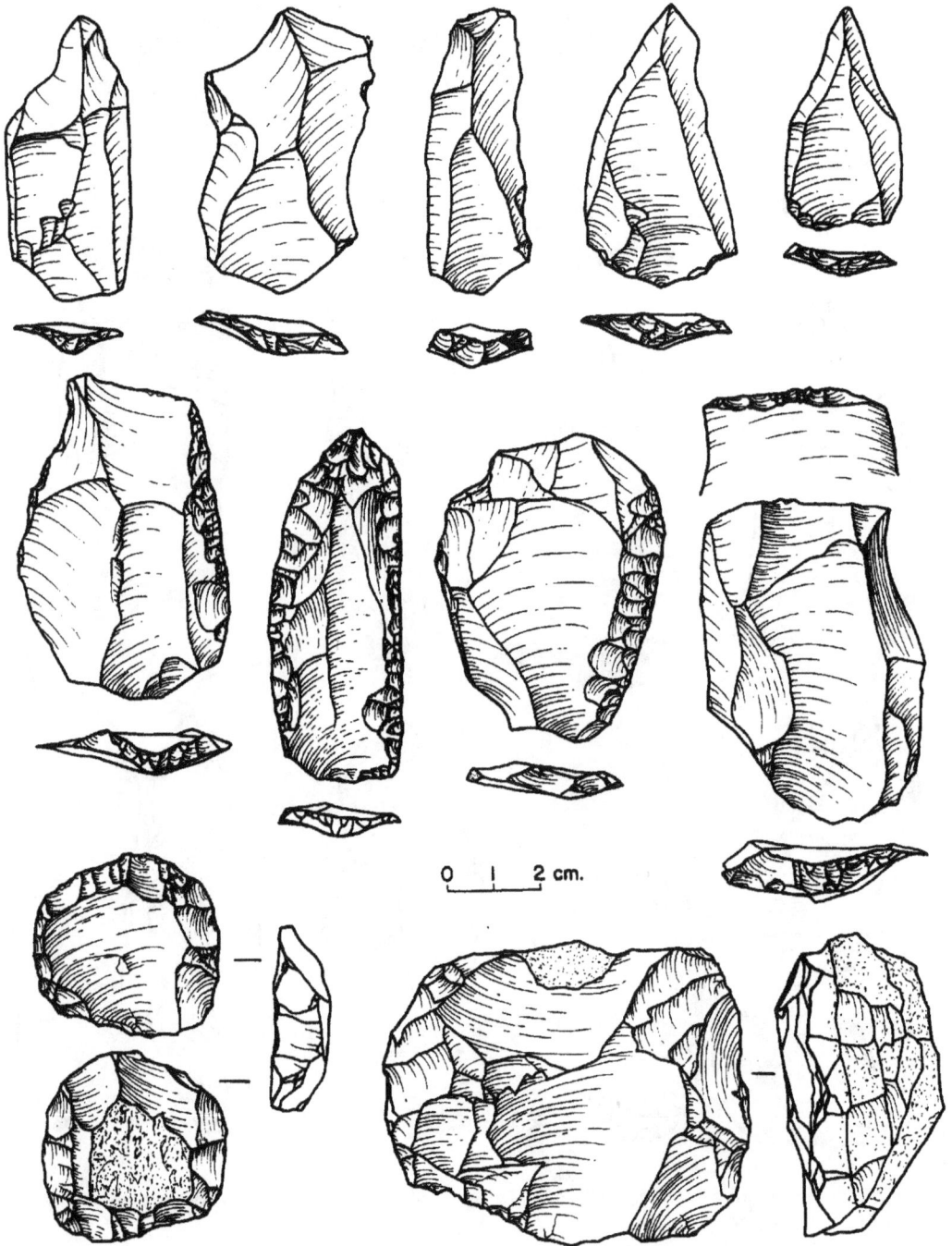

Figure 2.3   Illustrations of artifacts representing Levantine Mousterian C-type Industry (modified after Bar-Yosef 2000)

(Copeland 1998), Na'amé (Fleisch 1970), Ksar Akil Layer XXVI (Marks and Volkman 1986), and Douara Layer III (Akazawa 1979). Based on technology, Quneitra may also be included in the Industry (Meignen 1998, but cf. Goren-Inbar 1990).

B-type Industry

B-type assemblages are known mainly by the use of unidirectional, convergent Levallois cores for the promulgation of broad-based triangular points (Fig. 2.4). These Levallois points typically display a thick, heavily faceted, gull-wing platform (classic *chapeau de gendarme*) and lateral *Concorde* silhouette (Meignen 1995) with a diagnostic down-tilted nose. Blades vary in frequency reaching levels of 25 percent or more in sites primarily within the arid zone. Other than the Levallois points, side-scrapers, denticulates, notches, and burins form the tool-kits.

Although the Industry's geographic distribution includes most of the Levant, it is conspicuously absent from the Negev. This is surprising given the presence of several sites with B-type assemblages in nearby southern Jordan (Henry 1998b). Sites belonging to the industry include Tabun B, Kebara (Bar-Yosef et al. 1992), Amud (Hovers 1998), Sefunim (Ronen 1984), Erq el Ahmar Layer H (Neuville 1951), Ksar Akil XXVIII (Meignen 1995), Bezez B (Copeland 1983b), Keoue Cave (Nishiaki and Copeland 1992), and Tor Faraj and Tor Sabiha (among others) in southern Jordan (Henry 1997, 1998b). Bar-Yosef (2000: 116) would also include the Syrian site of Dederiyeh (Akazawa et al. 1995) within the Industry.

The Levantine Mousterian sequence at Tabun suggested a relative cultural-chronology, but it has only been over the past decade that we have gained a sense of the absolute ages of the sequence and even more recently the validity of the succession as a region-wide phenomenon. These insights largely have come from the use of relatively new chronometric techniques—i.e., electron spin resonance (ESR), thermal luminescence (TL), uranium series (Th/U), and amino acid racemization (AAR)—in establishing the ages of Levantine Mousterian deposits. However, the discovery of Levantine Mousterian sites in the Negev, Jordan, and Syria has allowed

evaluation of the regional applicability of the Tabun sequence.

Chronometry

Although the use of new chronometric techniques has enabled us to date Levantine Mousterian deposits which fall beyond the ^{14}C dating range of about 40kya, some of the results have been controversial. Discrepancies in the dates stem from several factors including their statistical overlaps, occasional lack of time-depth agreements, potential conflicts with environmental and archaeological proxy chronologies, and different results from different dating techniques (Jelinek 1992). Relative to differences between techniques, the 'long' TL (Mercier et al. 1995) and 'short' ESR (Grün et al. 1991) calendars for the Tabun sequence have drawn special attention. However, recent ESR (Schwarcz and Rink 1998) and TL dates (Valladas et al. 1998), coupled with an older Th/U date (Schwarcz et al. 1980), from Hayonim Cave provide support for the 'long' calendar.

In his recent review, Bar-Yosef (2000: 144-50) adopts the 'long' calendar in placing the D-type Industry between 270 and 170kya, the C-type between 170 and 90/85kya, and the B-type between 90/85 and 46/47kya (Fig. 2.5). Regarding the chronometry of the D-type Industry, there are problems beyond the differences seen between the 'short' and 'long' calendars of Tabun and Hayonim E. The D-type assemblage of Ain Difla has recently been linked to ESR dates (88.3 to 185.6ka) that, when viewed with an earlier TL date of 105 ± 15, mostly fall too young for its industrial placement (Clark et al. 1997). Other D-type Industry assemblages that are associated with younger than expected dates include Nahal Aqev (Th/U 74 to 85kya, but cf. 191 to 258kya; Schwarcz et al. 1979; Schwarcz et al. 1980), Rosh Ein Mor (49kya; Schwarcz et al. 1979; Schwarcz et al. 1980), and Far'ah II (ESR 45.6 ± 2.7 to 72 ± 4.9kya; Schwarcz and Rink 1998). Where Nahal Aqev and Rosh Ein Mor are typical of D-type assemblages, the industrial placement of Far'ah II is problematic (Gilead and Grigson 1984). And from a different perspective, the Rosh Ein Mor dates are not directly associated with the site's deposit, but instead are derived from a nearby spring deposit. Even with these cautions, it is

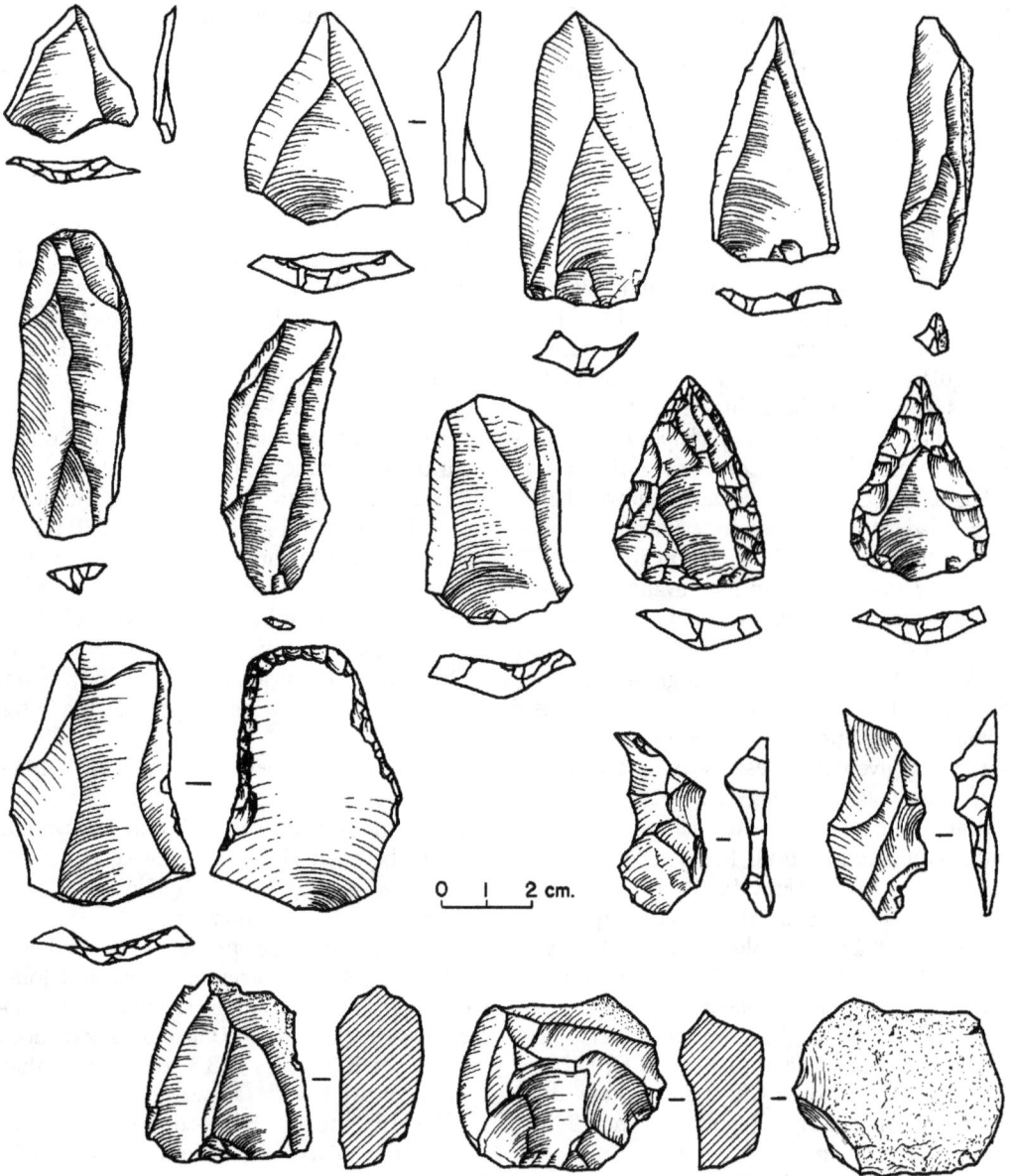

Figure 2.4 Illustrations of artifacts representing Levantine Mousterian B-type Industry (modified after Bar-Yosef 2000)

interesting that all the dated D-type assemblages from the arid zone yield younger-than-expected ages, when compared to the dates of Tabun D and Hayonim E. Whether the arid zone dates are spurious or the D-type Industry simply persists for a much longer period in the south remains an open and especially vexing question.

Dates for the C-type Industry come from Tabun C, Skhul, Hayonim Upper E, and

Qafzeh (Bar-Yosef 2000: 46-7). They range from *ca.* 92 to 171kya and tend to furnish stronger agreement across the various dating techniques than seen for the earlier, D-Type Industry. Only the TL (*ca.* 171kya) and ESR (*ca.* 102 to 119kya) dates from Tabun C show great variance, yet, even these fall within the range of dates shown by the other assemblages.

The chronometry of the B-type Industry comes from six sites: Tabun B, Kebara Cave,

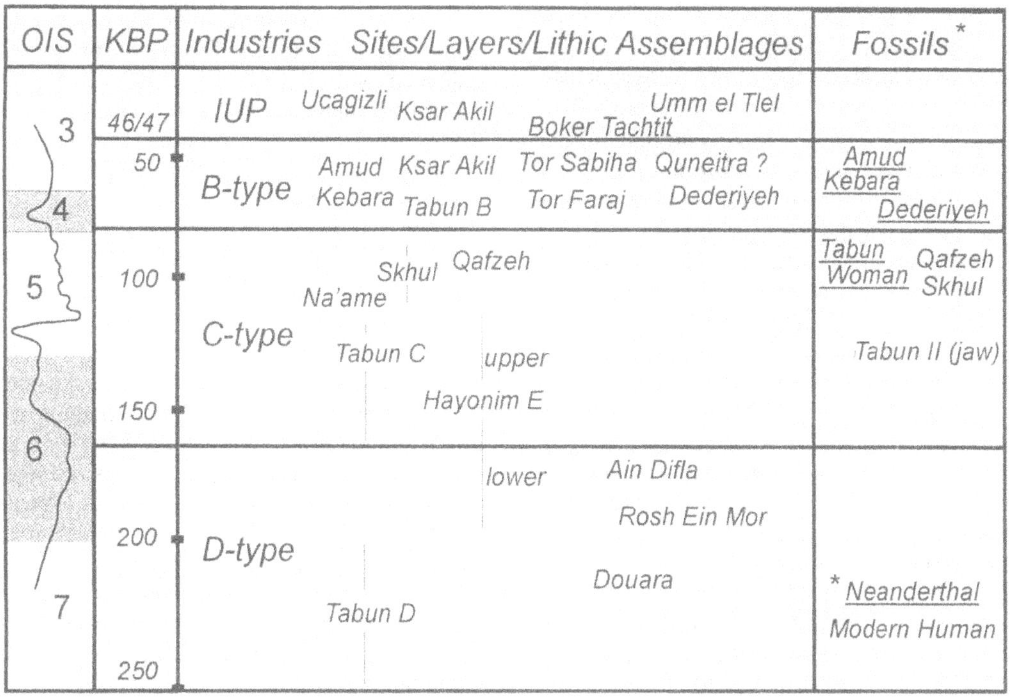

OIS	KBP	Industries	Sites/Layers/Lithic Assemblages	Fossils*
3	46/47	IUP	Ucagizli Ksar Akil Umm el Tlel Boker Tachtit	
4	50	B-type	Amud Ksar Akil Tor Sabiha Quneitra ? Kebara Tabun B Tor Faraj Dederiyeh	Amud Kebara Dederiyeh
5	100	C-type	Skhul Qafzeh Na'ame Tabun C upper Hayonim E	Tabun Woman Qafzeh Skhul Tabun II (jaw)
6	150		lower Ain Difla	
7	200 / 250	D-type	Rosh Ein Mor Douara Tabun D	* Neanderthal Modern Human

Figure 2.5   A synthesis of chronometry, archaeological units, hominids, and paleoenvironments of the Levant during the Late Pleistocene

Ksar Akil, Amud Cave, Tor Faraj, and Tor Sabiha. Kebara (48 to 64kya), Ksar Akil (44 to 47kya), Amud B1-2 (42 to 70kya), Tor Faraj (44 to 69kya), and Tor Sabiha (69kya) furnish very similar dating ranges across ESR, TL, Th/U, AAR, and ^{14}C techniques. The earlier ESR dates (86 to 103kya) for Tabun B and Amud B4 (68 to 113kya) represent outliers that will be best understood when additional dates from other techniques are available. Although the earliest dates for B-type assemblages remain somewhat unclear, the latest dates form a relatively tight cluster near the middle of Oxygen Isotope Stage 3, some 42 to 48kya.

The fossil hominids

Fossil hominids in association with assemblages of the Levantine Mousterian Complex have been recovered from the deposits of Amud, Kebara, Tabun, Dederiyeh, Ksar Akil XXV (individual KA-2), Skhul, and Qafzeh caves (Howell 1998: 10–11). Within these finds, many authorities recognize two groups of *Homo sapiens* composed of Neanderthals, represented by the Amud, Kebara, Tabun (woman), Dederiyeh, and Ksar Akil XXV

(individual KA-2) finds, and anatomically modern humans, represented by those from Skhul and Qafzeh, perhaps along with the Tabun C2 mandible (Vandermeersch 1992; Trinkaus 1995; Howell 1998; Rak 1998). Given this view, the Levantine Neanderthals, however, are distinguished from the *Classic* Neanderthals of Europe by certain progressive features. The presence of two populations in the Levant is explained by a Neanderthal intrusion (Bar-Yosef 1994) or the less well-developed notion of the region being at 'the boundary of Neandertal distribution' (Bar-Yosef and Pilbeam 2000: 185).

An alternative view of the Levantine fossils rejects the idea of two distinct populations, but instead argues that the fossils represent a single population of *Homo sapiens* with highly variable morphometric traits (McCown and Keith 1939; Corruccini 1992; Simmons 1994; Wolpoff 1996; Arensburg and Belfer-Cohen 1998). Recently, Arensburg and Belfer-Cohen (*ibid.*: 320) have proposed that:

> Instead of the regionality or migration hypotheses offered for the presumed origins of 'Neandertals' in this region, we advocate the view of a regional evolution … features observed

among Near Eastern hominids may be interpreted as synapomorphic characteristics that evolved parallel to those of 'classic' Neandertals.

They go on to point to the declining gradient of Neanderthal traits from Europe to the Near East and Africa, and suggest a stronger African than European influence on the composition of the Levantine Middle Paleolithic fossils.

The Levantine Mousterian Industrial associations with fossil hominid remains are not particularly relevant to the regional model, but they do figure heavily in ideas of dual populations and especially in notions of a Neanderthal intrusion. A number of researchers have used the apparent association of Neanderthals with the B-type Industry and anatomically modern humans with the C-type Industry as evidence for a proposed Neanderthal intrusion (Bar-Yosef 1994; Tchernov 1998). Other scholars have employed such associations as a basis for behavioral comparative studies (Shea 1989, 1998; Lieberman 1993; Lieberman and Shea 1994). Among the advocates of a dual-population model, there is no debate as to a linkage between the B-type Industry and Neanderthals, but there is a question of hominid associations with the C-type Industry (Kaufman 1999; Bar-Yosef 2000). The controversy, centering on finds at Tabun Cave, primarily involves: (1) the questionable stratigraphic placement of the partial skeleton of a female Neanderthal (Tabun I); and (2) the taxonomic status of a mandible (Tabun II) undeniably associated with a C-type assemblage.

Given the stratigraphic position of the Tabun I skeleton near the top of Layer C, where the deposit could not be distinguished from Layer B, and other considerations (Bar-Yosef 2000: 113), Garrod and Bate (1937) viewed the fossils as intrusive from overlying Layer B. Kaufman (1999: 41–2) notes other evidence that indicates the Tabun women, as well as other fossil remains in Layer C (Trinkaus 1993), are, in fact, attributable to that layer and were not intrusive. Although many specialists (Howell 1998; Quam and Smith 1998; Rak 1998) accept the early modern human designation for the isolated mandible (Tabun II), recovered about 90cm below Tabun I, this issue remains largely unresolved. Regardless of the mandible's taxonomic status, the presence of Neander-

thal remains in Tabun Layer C shows that the Levantine Mousterian C-type Industry was affiliated with both Neanderthals and early modern humans. This has important implications relative to the timing of a putative Neanderthal intrusion, the length to the interval of possible co-existence for Neanderthal and anatomically modern humans, and the degree to which there were direct links between hominid taxonomy and material culture.

Beyond taxonomic issues, fossil remains from the Levant have contributed to our understanding of Neanderthal prenatal development and capacity for speech. A study of the fragmentary remains of pelvises was thought to show that the pelvic inlets of female Neanderthals were substantially larger than those of modern females (Trinkaus 1984). This information prompted Trinkaus (*ibid.*) to propose that Neanderthals would have given birth after a year or more's gestation, thus making their offspring much less altricial than the newborn of modern humans. The social and behavioral implications of these findings would be far-reaching. Recently, however, the discovery of a complete right pelvis of a male at Kebara Cave has provided new insights into Neanderthal pelvic anatomy (Rak 1990; Bar-Yosef *et al.* 1992). And this, in turn, has shown that Neanderthal babies would have been proportionately no larger than those of modern humans (Tague 1992). Analysis of the basicranium of Neanderthals was used to reconstruct Neanderthal vocal anatomy. The form of the reconstructed vocal tract was thought to have severely limited the capacity of Neanderthals to make the range of sounds required by speech in modern humans (Lieberman 1984; Crelin 1987).

The discovery of a hyoid bone, resembling those of modern humans, in association with the Neanderthal skeleton at Kebara Cave indicates that Neanderthals were fully capable of human speech (Arensburg *et al.* 1990; Bar-Yosef *et al.* 1992).

Paleoclimate and environment

Following the 'long calendar' Levantine Mousterian chronometry, the complex persisted for some 220ky from near the end of OIS 8 to the middle part of OIS 3. In concert with global climatic changes, significant climatic shifts took place in the Levant over this long period. But in the context of these changes, evidence indicates that the Mediterranean climate common to the area today was the prevalent pattern for the interval. During interglacial times, however, a monsoonal pattern may have penetrated the extreme southern reaches of the region (Hovers 1997: 223). Cumulative paleoenvironmental data also indicate that the modern environmental zones, typically correlated with the phytogeographic zones of the region, were present over this long interval, although their distributions fluctuated with shifts in climate (Bar-Yosef 2000). The topographic features of the region also were much like those of today, except for episodic transgressions and regressions along the Mediterranean shoreline and the shrinking and swelling of inland lakes. These topographic differences would not only have significantly influenced the availability of resources, they would have played an important role in the creation of physiographic barriers (e.g., the Lisan Lake) or, conversely, environmental corridors (e.g., the inland lakes along the eastern desert periphery—Jafr, Hasa, Azraq, el Kowm) attractive to humans.

Several obstacles stand in the way of our environmental reconstructions. Perhaps the most important of these relates to the integrity of our chronometry and the extent to which different chronometric techniques and interpretations can be cross-referenced. In the absence of a reliable means by which to establish the relative ages of deposits and their paleoenvironmental inclusions, we are unable to develop region-wide reconstructions. The depositional sources of paleoenvironmental indicators also vary in the degree to which they furnish representative signatures of the surrounding landscape. For example, many of the thick cave deposits that have typically yielded Levantine Mousterian assemblages are known to have accumulated mostly through anthropogenic or biogenic activities (Goldberg and Bar-Yosef 1998). Such deposits would not be likely to contain the same range of evidence as similar settings with mostly natural sedimentation. Another problem facing regional environmental reconstructions stems from the latitudinal lag-times that may have created different local environmental expressions to a common paleoclimatic shift. While this phenomenon is not

well understood relative to the Levantine Mousterian, largely because of the coarse-grain of our paleoenvironmental and chronometric data, it nevertheless needs to be recognized.

The following paleoenvironmental synthesis is drawn largely from the recent reviews by Bar-Yosef (1992, 2000). These involve efforts to correlate deposits in the core Mediterranean zone with those situated in drier steppe and desert settings on the basis of chronometry and various paleoclimatic indicators.

OIS 6

During this stage at Tabun, Layer D was formed from loess thought to have been derived from the Negev and Sinai. The lack of a significant influx of sand suggests that the shoreline was positioned some distance from the cave and is perhaps evidenced by a *kurkur* ridge situated 2km west of the site. Formation of a *hamra* soil and pollen from Layer D suggest a woodland landscape. Humid conditions are thought to have formed a small spring inside the cave and caused erosion that truncated the top of Layer D at the end of Stage 6 and early 5e (*cf.* Jelinek 1992, however).

For Stage 6, evidence from the arid zone principally comes from the highland Negev and the Wadi Hasa of west-central Jordan. In the Negev, spring activity in the vicinity of Nahal Aqev combined with relatively high (25 percent) arboreal pollen from the sites of Rosh Ein Mor and Nahal Aqev (Horowitz 1976) point to moister conditions than those of today and environmentally equivalent to a marginal Mediterranean setting. Moister than modern conditions are also indicated for the Jordanian site of Ain Difla (Clark *et al.* 1997). Although the pollen assemblage from the site is poorly preserved, the reconstruction suggests a cool steppe dominated by shrubs and grasses. Trees were present, but only as localized elements occurring along drainages and other better watered settings. A fossil spring near the site was also active at the time of the occupation.

OIS 5

Within the last inter-glacial, warm-water-loving West African molluscs were able to reach the eastern end of the Mediterranean basin, leaving evidence of a signature species, *Strombus bubonius*, in the Enfean II transgressive shoreline along the Lebanese coast. Following Gvirtzman *et al.* (1985), Bar-Yosef (1992: 202) places this during Stage 5e and suggests that subsequent transgressions labeled by Sanlaville (1981) as Enfean IIb and Naamean correlate with Stages 5c and 5a, respectively.

Although wet periods are indicated at Tabun by the opening of a 'chimney' in the roof of the cave and an in-filling of *terra rossa* soil, the second half of Stage 5 appears to have been dominated by warm-dry conditions. This interpretation is, of course, contingent upon the dating of the Qafzeh deposit, an issue that has been debated for a long time (Bar-Yosef and Vandermeersch 1981; Jelinek 1982, 1992; Bar-Yosef 1998). The impressive faunal assemblage recovered from Qafzeh Cave is thought to show a major turnover in microfauna from earlier assemblages recovered from Hayonim and Tabun (Tchernov 1998). Earlier Pleistocene fauna, principally of Palearctic mammals, is replaced by an assemblage dominated by Afro-Arabian elements. Tchernov (*ibid.*: 85) notes that the microfauna from the Mousterian layers at Qafzeh is composed mainly of open-country, steppe, or savannah species, although the site presently rests within the Mediterranean woodland zone. Further support for this interpretation comes from the megafauna including African antelope, African ass, a North African equid, as well as camel and ostrich.

OIS Stage 4 and early Stage 3

The generally dry-cold conditions of Stage 4 appear to have brought about another faunal turnover, as seen in the return of Palearctic and European elements within the assemblages of Kebara, Amud, and Tabun Layer B (*ibid.*). The drying and erosion of the deposit in the main chamber at Kebara may also have been linked to the drier conditions and the drop in sea level.

Evidence from the arid zone for Stage 4 and early Stage 3 also points to dry conditions as seen in erosional terraces in the Negev (Goldberg 1984) and the influx of drift sand in the B-type Mousterian deposits in several rockshelters in southern Jordan (Henry 1997).

Although this was a predominantly dry interval, the environment appears to have been somewhat more verdant than that of today in southern Jordan (Henry 1995c, 1998b; Chapter 3 of this volume). Pollen, phytolith, and sedimentary evidence retrieved from the sites of Tor Faraj and Tor Sabiha indicate a steppe setting, but with seasonally standing water, isolated patches of trees, and C3 (cool, moist environment) grasses, all uncommon today. A return to moister conditions in early Stage 3 may also be indicated by the accumulation of silts at the site of Far'ah II (Gilead 1988) and the deposits underlying Boker Tachtit (Goldberg 1983).

Population and paleoenvironments

Although the paleoclimatic oscillations of OIS 6-early 3 were accompanied by shifts in the distribution of the region's major environmental zones, Levantine Mousterian occupations appear to have been tethered to Mediterranean woodland and nearby steppe settings. Such settings furnish the highest biomass in the region because of their relative high densities of browsing and grazing herbivores. Bar-Yosef (1992) has argued that it was only with the Early Upper Paleolithic and attendant higher residential mobility levels that full steppe and desert settings were inhabited.

From another perspective, when we find evidence for Levantine Mousterian occupations in the arid zone accompanied by paleo-environmental data, these data always indicate conditions moister than those of today. Sites of the D-type Industry in the Negev and west-central Jordan are associated with marginal Mediterranean or moist steppe settings. And even during the cold, dry conditions linked to the B-type Industry, sites in southern Jordan contain evidence of a moist, cool steppe environment. These correlations may explain why C-type Industry sites are confined to the better watered, northern and central Levant during the warm-dry conditions of OIS 5. Although the faunal turnover of this interval points to an intrusion of Afro-Arabian elements specifically adapted to arid habitats, the southern reaches of the Levant may have simply been too dry to support human habitation dependent upon Middle Paleolithic adaptive strategies. The Afro-

Arabian faunal influx of Stage 5 has prompted Tchernov (1992) to suggest this as proxy evidence for a human population movement from Africa, but if this were the case, we should expect to find sites of the C-type Industry in Sinai, the Negev, or southern Jordan.

Climatic change also has been suggested as a mechanism that triggered a population intrusion into the Levant during Oxygen Isotope Stage 4, but instead of modern humans, this proposed expansion relates to Neanderthals. The cold conditions of OIS 4 are thought to have caused Neanderthal populations to have been pushed southward by deteriorating conditions in the higher latitudes of western Eurasia (Bar-Yosef 1992; Tchernov 1992). As evidence, Tchernov (1992, 1998) points to an influx of European and Palearctic fauna into the area at this time. However, if the Tabun I woman is correctly associated with Layer C and OIS 5, then Neanderthals would have been in place in the Levant before the colder conditions of Stage 4. This has prompted Kaufman (1999) to suggest that there occurred two pulses of Neanderthal expansion.

Inter-site patterns: settlement and procurement strategies

Studies of Levantine Mousterian settlement and procurement strategies have emphasized differences in residential mobility, seasonality, and provisioning of resources. Various models have typically recognized a dichotomy between radiating (logistical) and circulating (opportunistic) modes of settlement and procurement (Henry 1994, 1995b). These have been applied to site distributions in the Negev (Munday 1976; Marks and Freidel 1977; Marks 1988b), southern Jordan (Henry 1994, 1995b, 1998a), and northern Israel (Lieberman 1993; Lieberman and Shea 1994; Shea 1998). Hovers (1990) has also used this settlement dichotomy as a basis for studying the site of Quneitra's settlement structure on the Golan Plateau. The studies in the Negev and Jordan emphasized local adaptive strategies, whereas Lieberman and Shea have explored adaptive differences between modern humans and Neanderthals. While not engaged in a settlement study, *per se*, Hovers (1997) examined the fit between

various adaptive models and expectations in Levantine Mousterian artifacts.

Given the wide ranges of specific environmental and topographic settings of these studies, it should not be surprising that no one model appears to hold for the region. Logistical and opportunistic provisioning appears to have been employed in conjunction with multi-season and seasonal occupations. These appear to have occurred both diachronically (Negev) and synchronically (southern Jordan, northern Israel). Large long-term base camps (e.g., Qafzeh, Kebara, Rosh Ein Mor, Tor Faraj) and more ephemeral hunting (Far'ah II, Quneitra) or collecting camps appear to have been used. In combination, the settlement-procurement studies indicate that Levantine Mousterian groups maintained a repertoire of highly flexible, diverse strategies for dealing with the range of environments and unique resource distributions they were likely to encounter. Within this, it would appear that lower resource densities, whether brought on seasonally or through longer-term climatic change, did induce higher mobility levels. And in topographically diverse areas (e.g., southern Jordan, northern Israel), there does seem to be good evidence for transhumance. The proposed lower residential mobility levels and greater emphasis on hunting by Neanderthals than modern humans (Lieberman 1993, 1998; Lieberman and Shea 1994; Shea 1998), however, lack general support (*cf.* Hovers 1997, 1998; Kaufman 1999: 100-2).

Studies of Levantine Mousterian subsistence practices show the exploitation of a wide range of large mammal species. These include aurochs, hartebeest, gazelle, red deer, fallow deer, roe deer, ibex, hippo, rhino, camel, and several species of equid. Also, small mammals, such as fox and hare, ostriches (and their eggs), and sessile animals (e.g., tortoises) appear to have contributed to the diet. Although scavenging may have played some role in the acquisition of meat, Levantine Mousterian groups appear to have been effective hunters of medium (wild boar, red deer, hartebeest, equids) to large (aurochs) sized mammals (Gilead and Grigson 1984; Speth and Tchernov 1998; Kaufman 1999). Gilead and Grigson (1984: 93) suggest that late Levantine Mousterian groups at Far'ah II concentrated on hunting large congregations of ungulates attracted to nearby water during the dry season within the arid Negev. Based upon their study of small animal remains from Hayonim Cave, Stiner and Tchernov (1998) have found that Mousterian groups also exploited sessile animals, especially tortoises, over more hard-to-catch prey (e.g., hares). While this may have been attributed to technological deficiencies (e.g., nets, traps), it could also have been a result of a low population density in the Mousterian and a corresponding lack of pressure on available resources (ibid.).

We have just recently begun to appreciate the wide range of plant foods that were exploited by Levantine Mousterian groups. Nearly 4000 specimens of charred seeds and kernels were recovered from the ashy deposit of Kebara Cave. Among the edible species were legumes, cereals, acorns, nuts, and fruits. The fruits of *Celtis sp.* were retrieved from Douara Cave (Akazawa 1987) and phytoliths recovered from the Tor Faraj deposit (Chapter 7, this volume) suggest the consumption of dates, pistachio, and seeds.

Intra-site patterns: living floors

Our understanding of intra-site patterns comes from the examination of 'living floors' at only a few sites (Far'ah II, Quneitra, Kebara, and Tor Faraj). Burials accompanying Levantine Mousterian occupations at six sites furnish additional intra-site information, although of more limited scope and tied to a specific activity.

Refitted and conjoined artifacts along with animal bones have been used to identify living floors at the open-air sites of Far'ah II (Gilead and Grigson 1984; Gilead 1988) and Quneitra (Goren-Inbar 1990; Saragusti and Goren-Inbar 1990). Far'ah II is located in a thick silt deposit of alluvial origin adjacent to the Nahal Besor about 22km from the Mediterranean shoreline in the lowland Negev. Excavation revealed distinct concentrations of chert and limestone artifacts and animal bones, the densest of which were associated with a large hearth. A refit study, involving 225 removals tied to 15 cores, showed most of the removals to fall within 2.25m of their parent cores. This suggests an occupation of limited duration, coupled with limited recycling of artifacts. In

that the stream cobbles of the nearby Nahal Besor provided a source for raw material, there was little need of economizing measures in the lithic technology. Gilead and Grigson (1984) concluded that the large herd animals (aurochs, equids, hartebeests) found on the site were killed while watering nearby, then butchered and consumed on-site by a small group of ten or so persons who occupied the location for no longer than a few weeks.

A refit study was also undertaken at Quneitra which was situated at the edge of a lake on the Golan Plateau. Unlike Far'ah II, most of the refits (conjoins) were derived from flexion fractures of relatively small lithic specimens. But as at Far'ah II, the conjoined specimens were in very close proximity (Saragusti and Goren-Inbar 1990). This likely points to extensive reduction, an economizing measure necessitated by the distance (9 to 13km) to preferred chert sources (Hovers 1990). Quneitra is thought to have been a short-term, exploitation camp representing one segment of a logistically organized settlement–procurement strategy (Goren-Inbar 1990; Hovers 1990).

Intra-site studies of sheltered sites include those of Kebara (Bar-Yosef et al. 1992) and Tor Faraj (Henry et al. 1996; Henry 1998a; Chapters 8, 9, and 10, this volume). At Kebara, hearths and ash were recorded near the entrance to the cave, while most of the lithic artifacts and bone were dispersed toward the rear part of cave (Bar-Yosef et al. 1992). A living floor consisting of hearths and concentrations of lithic artifacts and bone was traced over an area of *ca.* 12m^2 in the central part of the cave. The hearths, formed by shallow, oval, scooped-out depressions, contained little bone, although burnt lithic artifacts were common. Charcoal identification and experiments in replication indicate that hardwood, mainly Tabor Oak, and grass were used for fuel. None of the hearths were stone-lined for warmth banking. Bar-Yosef (1998) has noted that the artifact density against sedimentation rate at Kebara (*ca.* 1000 specimens per 1m^2 over 3ky) is *ca.* ten times greater than that recorded for the Mousterian deposit at Hayonim Cave. He suggests that this greater occupational intensity of Kebara and the more ephemeral use of Hayonim were likely linked to a 'central placed foraging' settlement pattern.

Tor Faraj is located over 300km from Kebara in a substantially different environment, yet the two chronometrically synchronous occupations share many characteristics beyond their artifact assemblages. The most apparent of these is the presence of numerous, small oval hearths (Henry *et al.* 1996; Henry 1998a; Chapters 8, 9, and 10, this volume). At Tor Faraj, stratified living floors were exposed over large areas (*ca.* 67m^2) and these revealed 19 hearths. Based on associated artifacts and other evidence, the hearths appear to have tethered a wide range of activities (e.g., sleeping, cooking and general communal tasks, primary lithic processing, and butchery) within the shelter. Although the large living floor exposures at Tor Faraj provide an unusual glimpse of such hearth-centered activities, hearths have also been reported from Levantine Mousterian excavations at Amud, Qafzeh, Ain Difla (Clark *et al.* 1997), and Douara Cave IV (Akazawa 1988). With the exception of a large hearth recorded at Douara Cave (5m diameter), hearths from Levantine Mousterian occupations tend to be small, oval, shallow depressions.

Burials and grave goods

Burials were discovered in the excavations of Skhul (McCown 1937), Qafzeh (Vandermeersch 1981; Tillier *et al.* 1988;), Kebara (Bar-Yosef *et al.* 1992), Amud (Suzuki and Takai 1970; Rak *et al.* 1994), Dederiyah (Akazawa *et al.* 1995), and Tabun (Garrod and Bate 1937; Tillier *et al.* 1988). Despite claims to the contrary (Gargett 1989), there is overwhelming evidence that Levantine Mousterian groups intentionally buried their dead (Bar-Yosef 1992; Belfer-Cohen and Hovers 1992; Kaufman 1999: 85-92). Finds of numerous skeletons, often in positions of anatomical articulation, can be explained only by purposeful inhumation. Without burial, the slow rates of sedimentation in most of these sites would have left a corpse accessible to disturbance by scavengers as well as other humans that are known to have regularly visited the caves (Bar-Yosef 1992).

Although inhumation in its own right is a symbolic expression, there does appear to be ample evidence for more concrete symbolism in the form of grave goods and in post-burial intervention. Kaufman (1999: 86-90) has recently reviewed the evidence for grave offerings within the Levantine Mousterian. These consist of a wild boar mandible within the arms of the Skhul V burial, the antlers of a fallow deer on the chest of a child in the Qafzeh 11 burial, and the maxilla of a red deer found against the pelvis of a Neanderthal infant at Amud. Additionally, within the artifactually sterile fill of a grave at Dederiyah Cave, an infant's skeleton was found with a limestone slab just above its head and a flint flake on its chest. At Kebara Cave, a nearly complete, articulated skeleton was found in which the skull was missing. The positions of the mandible, hyoid bone, and right upper third molar (which had fallen from its socket and rested near the lower third molar), indicate that the skull was deliberately removed after the corpse had decomposed within the burial (Bar-Yosef *et al.* 1992), a practice reminiscent of much later Near Eastern Neolithic burial customs.

Other symbolic expressions

Beyond burials and grave goods, several items have been found in Levantine Mousterian deposits that point to the presence of symbolic expression. Red ochre (iron hematite) was identified at Kebara and a scraped lump of ochre was recovered from Qafzeh (Bar-Yosef 1992). These may have been used for any of a number of decorative purposes (e.g., body adornment, painting of hides) that constitute art or symbolic behaviors. Perforated marine shells (*Glycymeris*), reported from Qafzeh and Skhul (Bar-Yosef 1992; Kaufman 1999), are often noted as evidence of personal adornment and a 'sense of self,' but typically in the context of the Upper Paleolithic (White 1989). Although rare, the shells nevertheless suggest that such qualities of behavior and even emotion were likely to have been extant in the Levantine Mousterian. Other, more direct examples of artistic expression come from the sites of Quneitra and Qafzeh (Kaufman 1999). These are in the form of flat, cortical surfaces of relatively large chert specimens that have been extensively engraved. The Quneitra example displays two sets of engravings: a group of four nested circles and another composed of several long, parallel lines. The specimen from Qafzeh, a core fragment, shows 27 parallel lines. The Quneitra example has been interpreted as an abstract depictive image (Marshack 1996) and other researchers have underscored the commonalities between the two specimens (Hovers 1997; Kaufman 1999).

Artifacts and features that are linked to nonutilitarian behaviors and symbolic expressions in the Levantine Mousterian are uncommon, but they are present. And when taken as a whole, they are consistent in showing that many of the signatures that are attributed to the emergence of modernity occur well within the Levantine Mousterian.

The Initial Upper Paleolithic or Transitional Industries

Only a handful of sites are known from the period immediately following the Levantine Mousterian and these have produced a relatively narrow range of behavioral evidence which is mainly limited to lithic artifacts. Traditionally, this interval was known as the Emiran, named after the type site of Emireh Cave, but the term 'transitional Industries' also is commonly used to designate the assemblages that are thought to bridge the Levantine Mousterian–Upper Paleolithic boundary. Recently, a new term 'Initial Upper Paleolithic' (IUP) has been proposed *in lieu* of 'transitional' based upon the argument that our terminology should remain neutral and not suggest an evolutionary connection that in many ways remains unresolved (Kuhn *et al.* 1999).

Three widely separated sites, Boker Tachtit, Ksar Akil, and Umm el Tlel, contribute most to our understanding of the interval (Fig. 2.1). These sites have yielded assemblages that contain a high proportion of typical Upper Paleolithic tool types in conjunction with technological traits common to the Levantine Mousterian. At a more detained level, however, each of the assemblages contain certain unique typological and technological features. At Boker Tachtit (Marks 1983; Marks and Volkman 1983a), a comprehensive refit study revealed how Levallois-like points were produced through bidirectional preparation of cores that were shaped volumetrically. Moreover, the traditional typological signature of 'Transitional Industries,' Emireh points, were recovered in substantial numbers.

Layers XXV to XXIV at Ksar Akil, although poor in artifacts, yielded opposed platform cores with parallel sides (Ohnuma 1988). Higher in the stratigraphy, Layers XXIII to XXI/XX produced triangular-shaped cores with convergent scar patterns associated with blades and Levallois points with similarly convergent patterns on their dorsal surfaces. Given that the points greatly outnumbered cores, Ohnuma and Bergman (1990) suggested that as at Boker Tachtit, many of the points may have been produced from prismatic cores. Emireh points were also found at Ksar Akil, along with chamfered pieces. At Umm el Tlel, Layers IIbase and III2A, the Levallois concept was followed in the production of unidirectional, convergent points and blades (Bourguignon 1996). The points differ from classic Levallois points in lacking thick *chapeau de gendarme* butts and 'Y' *arretes*. Instead, they display multi-faceted convergent dorsal faces, prompting the designation of Umm el Tiel points. Emireh points have not been recovered at Umm el Tlel.

Beyond lithic artifacts, we know relatively little of IUP material culture. However, at Ksar Akil a bone awl (Newcomer, in Bergman 1987) and hundreds of marine shells, some perforated (Altena 1962), were recovered from the IUP horizon. Recent research along the coast of southeastern Turkey at Üçagizli and Kanal caves has identified a blade-oriented industry with Upper Paleolithic tool types and Umm el Tlel points associated with marine shells (Kuhn *et al.* 1999). Dates of *ca.* 39 to 40kya (^{14}C AMS) for Üçagizli place it late in the IUP or very early Upper Paleolithic timeframe. In commenting on these finds, Bar-Yosef (2000: 127) notes that this shows the earliest Upper Paleolithic in the Levant to have 'incorporated one of the cultural components considered critical for characterizing modern behavior.'

A review of the radiometric assays for the earliest IUP assemblages (*ibid.*: 129-30) indicates ages of *ca.* 46/47kya at Boker Tachtit (Marks 1983a) to perhaps 50kya at Ksar Akil (Mellars and Tixier 1989). Given the latest dates for the Levantine Mousterian of 42 to 48kya at Kebara, Amud, Ksar Akil, and Tor Faraj, the latter of the IUP dates seems more reasonable. Although an evaluation of the dates is complicated by their large standard errors and the unknown degree to which TL and ^{14}C years correspond, the dates, as we know them, are not inconsistent with an autochtonous development of the Upper Paleolithic in the Levant.

The question of African connections

The putative origin and subsequent expansion of modern humans from Africa were prompted largely by genetic studies. The conclusions of these studies, however, have been inconsistent, especially with regard to age estimates that have ranged between 300 and 100kya (Bar-Yosef and Pilbeam 2000 and references therein). The fossil and archaeological evidence from Africa when compared to the Levant offers independent lines of evidence upon which to evaluate the Out-of-Africa model. The fossil evidence from the African sites of Omo Kibish, Border and Klasies River Mouth caves are interpreted as early examples of modern humans dated to 120 to 70kya (Klein 2000). Also, a Middle Paleolithic burial thought to be representative of a modern human was recently recovered from the Egyptian site of Taramsa 1 (Vermeersch et al. 1998). A series of optically stimulated luminescence dates on the burial fill range from ca. 50 to 80kya. While these data are all consistent with the Out-of-Africa model, equally early dates for the fossils from Skhul and Qafzeh in Israel do not rule out a biologic origin for modern humans in the Levant (Arensburg and Belfer-Cohen 1998) which for Klein (2000) was simply a biogeographic extension of Africa at the time. Regardless of whether modern humans first emerged in Africa or the Levant, there was a considerable time-lag (20 to 80kya) between the earliest behavioral manifestations of the Upper Paleolithic, dated to 40 to 50kya, and the ages attributed to the earliest biologically modern humans.

If Africa was the source of the Upper Paleolithic revolution, whether spread by population expansion or cultural diffusion to Eurasia, we should expect to see traces of this in the archaeological records of northeast Africa and the Levant. For the critical time-frame of the Late Pleistocene, these records are principally limited to stone tool assemblages. Several studies have specifically addressed the question (Crew 1975; Marks 1992b; Van Peer 1998).

Two archaeological complexes (Nubian and Lower Nile Valley) have been identified that are thought to have co-existed along the Nile for much of the last 160ky (Van Peer 1998). The Nubian Complex appears to represent intrusive groups from the south into northeast Africa during the later part of the Middle Pleistocene. Blade production is common to the earliest stages of the complex, as seen in refitted cores from the site of Taramsa 1, and becomes fully developed by 35kya, as seen at the site of Nazlet Khater 4. Whereas the Nubian Complex would appear to support notions of sub-Saharan African origins of modernity, the indigenous Lower Nile Complex also shows a dramatic technological change toward blade production ca. 40kya or earlier, following tens of millennia of technological stability. This situation prompts Van Peer (ibid.: 130) to suggest a model similar to that proposed for Europe where in situ evolution of the Middle to the Upper Paleolithic took place in isolated areas alongside an Aurignacian intrusion. In northeast Africa, however, Van Peer (ibid.: 130) suggests that the transition took place after a very long period of co-existence.

Beyond evidence for pulses of population intrusions into northeast Africa, are there indications in the archaeological record that these extended to the Levant? In Van Peer's (ibid.: 136) review of potential connections between northeast Africa and the Levant, he stresses that 'there are similarities only at the broadest level of comparison.' He points to the problem of viewing certain type fossils (e.g., truncated-faceted pieces found in both Nubian and Levantine Mousterian) as evidence of a cultural connection, when their specific techno-functional contexts (chaîne opératoire) have not been considered. With respect to trucated-faceted pieces, for example, one could also argue for long-term Levantine cultural continuity on the basis of the type's presence in a Late Acheulean context at Joubbata in the Golan (Goren 1979; Marks 1992b).

In another detailed study of the northeast African and Levantine Paleolithic successions for the interval from 150 to 50kya, Marks (ibid.) found no archaeological support for the Out-of-Africa model. He notes disjunctions in the Levantine record with the appearance of the Mugharan Tradition (150 to 100kya) and later with the B-Type, Late Levantine Mousterian (*ca.* 60kya), both of which are thought to indicate cultural intrusions into the region. Apparently neither of these can be traced to northeast Africa, however. Instead, they have more logical connections to the north and east (Bar-Yosef and Vandermeersch 1981; Bar-Yosef 1987; Marks 1992b).

Bar-Yosef (2000) has recently presented an alternative scenario to an autochthonous development of the Upper Paleolithic in the Levant. He appears to lean toward a Nile origin and suggests that certain elements indicative of 'transitional' assemblages (such as Emireh points, Levallois points with bidirectional scar patterns, and chamfered blades) are best explained as intrusive techno-typologic features. Moreover, he argues that some tools (e.g., Emireh points) may have been newly invented by the African colonizers once in the Levant and thus should not be expected to be found in the original homeland. Here, it is worth noting that two Emireh-like points have been reported from the 'Middle Paleolithic level 1' occupation of Sodmein Cave in the Red Sea Mountains of Egypt (Mercier *et al.* 1999) and bidirectional Levallois production is seen in Nubian Type 1 cores found in assemblages (Van Peer 1988, method group N) stretching from Nubia to central Egypt. But Marks (1992b: 243) argues that although the cores resemble Levallois point cores, they rarely resulted in points as seen in the Levant, but instead produced 'pointed Levallois flakes which are otherwise rather ovoid.' Moreover, refitted cores from Tor Faraj not only confirm bidirectional preparation of cores for Levallois point removal in a Late Levantine Mousterian context, they also indicate that the method was employed as a measure for extending core production in a chert-poor setting (see Chapters 4 and 6). Chamfered blades are also known from coastal Libya and Egypt, but in recalling Van Peer's cautions concerning context, we know little of how they fit into the *chaîne opératoire* of their respective industries.

Conclusion

The Late Pleistocene biocultural record of the Levant differs from that of Europe in several important ways. Modern humans appear in the Levantine record much earlier than in Europe and are associated with Middle rather than Upper Paleolithic artifact assemblages. Moreover, the early modern humans of the Levant share similar cultural dimensions (artifact inventories, stone tool uses, burial practices, and varieties of sites) with Neanderthals recovered from mostly later, but nearby deposits. Whereas early modern humans reported from Africa fall as early as the Levantine fossils and are found in the context of Middle Stone Age artifacts, the absence of Neanderthals in Africa precludes the kinds of behavioral comparisons that are possible in the Levant.

From the perspective of artifact inventories, the Levantine Mousterian differs substantially from the Mousterian facies of Europe. Perhaps the most important of these differences rests in the greater emphasis upon the production of blades in the Levantine Mousterian. Although blades traditionally have been viewed as a technological feature linked to both biological and behavioral modernity, there is really no clear association between blades and hominid biology or behavior. Blade production occurred sporadically over much of Europe, western Eurasia, and Africa tens of millennia before becoming synonymous with the Upper Paleolithic expansion into Europe (Bar-Yosef and Kuhn 1999: 333). The reason that an emphasis on blade production in the Levantine Mousterian is so important is that it immediately precedes the blade-rich assemblages of the Initial Upper Paleolithic (IUP) in the Levant. Thus, unlike Europe where the blade technology of the earliest Upper Paleolithic is thought to denote a cultural intrusion, the blade technology of the Levantine Mousterian provides a reasonable precursor for that of the Levantine Upper Paleolithic. Moreover, detailed examinations of the technical steps in blade production observed in assemblages from sites in the Negev (Boker Tachtit, Marks 1983a) and coastal Lebanon (Ksar Akil, Ohnuma and Bergman 1990) show a change in which a Levallois approach is replaced by series blade production. Other 'transitional' assemblages, while showing continued use of the Levallois method (although substantially modified) in point and blade production, reveal resultant blanks that were retouched into traditional

Upper Paleolithic tool types, e.g., end-scrapers and burins (Bourguignon 1996).

Thus the kinds of marked changes in artifact assemblages thought to denote a cultural intrusion by modern human groups in Europe are not evident in the earliest Upper Paleolithic in the Levant. In contrast, the Middle to Upper Paleolithic progression in the Levant is relatively smooth across chronological, spatial, and material culture boundaries. From a chronological perspective, the cluster of terminal dates (42 to 48kya) obtained from Late Levantine Mousterian (B-type Industry) occupations fits nicely with the earliest IUP dates of *ca.* 46/47kya. Spatially, the Late Levantine Mousterian shows a similar geographic distribution to that of the IUP sites. This is a wide distribution stretching from the Mediterranean coast inland to eastern Syria and south to southern Jordan and the Negev. The techno-typological configuration of the late Levantine Mousterian shows an emphasis on point production from Levallois cores that were principally shaped through unidirectional, convergent preparatory removals. However, it is also important to recognize that, as part of the primary core shaping and rejuvenation, blades were habitually removed to form the lateral ridges of the classic 'Y'-*arrete*. Blades, therefore, often form a substantial portion of debitage and tool blanks in Late Levantine Mousterian assemblages. With the emphasis on convergently prepared points and blades in IUP assemblages, it thus seems reasonable to view the Late Levantine Mousterian as the precursor. Even the tendency toward bidirectional point preparation seen at Boker Tachtit is present in a Late Levantine Mousterian context. Not only is bidirectionality confirmed on the dorsal scar patterns of points at Tor Faraj, the refit study shows this to be an economizing behavior for the production of points from small cores and cores-on-flakes (see Chapter 6, this volume). In my mind, the most parsimonious way in which to interpret the chronological, geographic, and material cultural evidence is that it is an expression of the *in situ* emergence of the Upper Paleolithic from the Late Levantine Mousterian.

An autochthonous development of the Upper Paleolithic in the Levant is further indicated by the apparent absence of cultural connections between the Levant and north-east Africa during the Late Pleistocene (Crew 1975; Marks 1992b; Van Peer 1998). The putative expansion of modern humans from Africa to Europe and Asia between 200 and 50kya would be expected to have left cultural tracks across the Levantine land-bridge. Although the Late Pleistocene archaeology of both northeast Africa and the Levant have been intensively investigated, clear cultural connections have yet to be identified. From a different perspective, Tchernov (1992, 1998) has identified a faunal turnover, represented by an intrusion of Afro-Arabian elements into the Levant during the exceptionally warm-dry conditions of OIS 5, which he sees as proxy evidence for modern human expansion. Not only do we fail to find artifactual similarities between the Levant and northeast Africa at this time, this arid interval would appear to have made the drier southern Levant inhospitable to human habitation as evidenced by the restriction of C-type Industry sites to the better watered central and northern Levant. While forming an environmental nexus with northeast Africa, these arid conditions also may have created a barrier to human movement across the Eastern Desert and Sinai Peninsula. As stressed by Bar-Yosef (1992), human adaptation to dry steppe and desert conditions does not appear to have emerged until the Upper Paleolithic.

The Levantine Late Pleistocene record, then, has several important implications relative to the emergence of modern humans. First, the apparent similarities in the behaviors of early modern humans and Neanderthals indicate that biologic and behavioral modernity may not have necessarily been linked. Second, the autochthonous emergence of the Upper Paleolithic in the Levant some 40 to 50kya would be less consistent with a biologic-stimulated change than one based on technical innovations or inventions. Rather than a population movement Out-of-Africa at this time, there may simply have been a population expansion from the Levant into Europe, stimulated by one or more technical innovations such as series blade production (Hayden 1993; Bar-Yosef and Kuhn 1999), bone tool innovations (Jelinek 1994), or more efficient propulsion of projectiles, e.g., atlatl or bow and arrow (Bar-Yosef 2000).

In many ways, the modern human expansion into Europe may have resembled that which occurred later, during Neolithic times. Bar-Yosef (1994, 2000), in fact, has suggested that the spread of agriculture from the Near East through Europe be used as a model for organizing our understanding of the emergence of the Upper Paleolithic and modernity. Conceptually, this is a useful observation, but unlike the unambiguous signatures left by the Neolithic expansion, those of modernity are less apparent and sometimes open to debate. The time-space distributions of assemblages containing an abundance of worked bone and shell items along with evidence of series blade production should point to the origin or origins of cultural modernity. Studies of impact features, edge-wear, and breakage patterns on

pointed tools from Middle and Early Upper Paleolithic assemblages may also provide evidence for innovations in propulsion devices (e.g., Shea 2001). The geographic distributions and ages of the latest Middle and earliest Upper Paleolithic sites across Eurasia and Europe suggest that the Upper Paleolithic emerged substantially earlier in the Levant than elsewhere (Bar-Yosef and Pilbeam 2000: 184-5). Whether or not such technological innovations were tied to biologic modernity remains open to question. Although it is widely assumed that the earliest Upper Paleolithic (IUP) assemblages were produced by *Homo sapiens sapiens*, the rarity or absence of associated fossils leaves even this as an untested notion (*ibid.*).

Case Study

3 A Case Study from Southern Jordan: Tor Faraj

DONALD O. HENRY

The case study reported upon in this volume centers upon reconstructing the way in which the late Middle Paleolithic occupants of a 50 to 70kya Jordanian rockshelter site, Tor Faraj, organized their behaviors when using the shelter. The research is especially relevant to understanding the degree to which the archaic behaviors of the shelter's residents may have differed from those of modern foragers in parallel settings. Notions of a behavioral revolution leading to modernity some 40 to 50kya have prompted a number of researchers to suggest that Middle Paleolithic groups organized their behaviors in profoundly dissimilar ways from those of modern foragers (Binford 1983b, 1985, 1989, 1992; Chase and Dibble 1987; Simek 1987; Whallon 1989; Soffer 1993; Stringer and Gamble 1993). Analysis of the site structure of two, stratified living floors buried within the deposit of Tor Faraj provides an unusual opportunity to evaluate many of these ideas.

The definition of prehistoric living floors is uncommon within shelters, especially over areas as large as those exposed at Tor Faraj (67m^2) and for Middle Paleolithic occupations in general. The research described here is also unusual in that it integrates the intra-site evidence of the current study with local, inter-site data acquired through earlier work (Henry 1994, 1995b). This integrative effort then not only allows an understanding of the activities that were undertaken in the shelter and how these were segregated, it provides for these behaviors to be placed in the larger

context of local Middle Paleolithic land-use practices as expressed in settlement-procurement patterns followed in this mountainous region of southern Jordan.

The fundamental adaptive strategy of the Middle Paleolithic foragers of the area is thought to have involved transhumance, a pattern that continued through the terminal Pleistocene into the Holocene and even modern, historic times. This involved seasonally scheduled and elevationally governed movements from near sea level in the Rift valley to high elevations, reaching 1700masl, on the Ma'an Plateau. Embedded in the seasonally scheduled migrations were shifts in the residential mobility and sizes of foraging groups. These demographic shifts also corresponded to changes within procurement strategies. This was expressed in (1) long-term, winter encampments in which groups coalesced into larger social units that were supported through logistical provisioning; and (2) ephemeral, warm season camps in which groups dispersed into small social units that were sustained through opportunistic provisioning. Within this pattern of transhumance, the occupations at Tor Faraj are thought to have been associated with long-term, aggregated, winter encampments.

As suggested in earlier publications (Henry 1994, 1995b, 1998a), the presence of such essentially modern land-use practices in the Middle Paleolithic runs counter to many of the notions concerning a behavioral revolution that ushered in modernity and the Upper

Paleolithic. The research at Tor Faraj therefore provides an opportunity to test such notions in a couple of ways. First, it allows for checking the integrity of the local land-use model by comparing the site structure of the occupations at Tor Faraj with the complex structure predicted by the model for long-term, aggregated, winter encampments. Second, the site structure defined within the living floors at Tor Faraj can be compared directly with archaeological and ethnographic examples of occupations of rockshelters by modern foragers. If the Levantine Mousterian occupants of the area did not organize their behaviors in an essentially modern fashion, we should not expect the site structure identified at Tor Faraj to meet the expectations linked to the local settlement-procurement model nor should it resemble those site structures that are common to modern foragers.

Regional physiography and environment

Tor Faraj (the Shelter of Faraj) is a large rockshelter located about midway between the towns of Ma'an and Aqaba in southern Jordan. The site is situated in a range of mountains that parallels the eastern flank of the Aqaba-Dead Sea Rift (Wadi Araba) and stretches from the southern edge of the Ma'an Plateau, defined by the Ras en Naqb Escarpment, to near the head of the Gulf of Aqaba (Osborn and Duford 1981; Hassan 1995, Fig. 3.1). The region exhibits a striking diversity in its

Figure 3.1 The location of Tor Faraj and the major land-forms of southern Jordan landscape, climate, and environment that is due largely to the extensive faulting along the Rift.

Within a radius of 20km from Tor Faraj, five major physiographic settings are represented: the uplands of the Ma'an Plateau, the piedmont of the Ras en Naqb Escarpment, the broad plain of the Hisma Basin, the eastern flanks of the Rift, and the floor of the Rift (Fig. 3.2). The climate of the region is predominantly Mediterranean and defined by a short winter wet season and a long dry season, both accompanied by relatively mild temperatures. Elevation is the single most important variable governing the local temperature and precipitation patterns (Shehadeh 1985), thus there is considerable variability from the high reaches of the Ma'an Plateau to the floor of the Rift. These climatic belts, coupled with local edaphic conditions, largely govern the zonation of the region's distinct biotic communities. Although the specific elevational parameters of these belts would have differed from today's during the Middle Paleolithic occupation of Tor Faraj, the relative order of the belts would have been much the same.

Uplands of the Ma'an Plateau

Reaching elevations of 1700m near Ras en Naqb, the rolling limestone, hill country of the plateau is dominated by shrubs and low bushes of Garigue and Batha Mediterranean vegetation (Zohary 1973; El-Eisawi 1985). Relics of former Mediterranean woodlands are seen as isolated trees or small stands of juniper (*Juniperus phoenicea*) and pistacia (*Pistacia atlantica*). Extensive overgrazing is thought to have degraded the woodlands and induced massive erosion of the uplands as evidenced by rocky, flint regolith or hammada surfaces (*ibid.*). The notion that the high reaches of southern Jordan were recently forested, however, has been challenged by Harlan (1988). In reviewing observations of nineteenth-century visitors to the region, he concluded that the plateau was covered mostly in grassland. Woodlands would have been restricted to well-watered areas at very high elevations or seeps adjacent to acquifers (*ibid.*). These would have included pine (*Pinus halepensis*), oak (*Quercus calliprinus*), laurel (*Laurus nobilis*), maple (*Acer syriacum*), and cedar (*Cedrus libani*) in addition to juniper

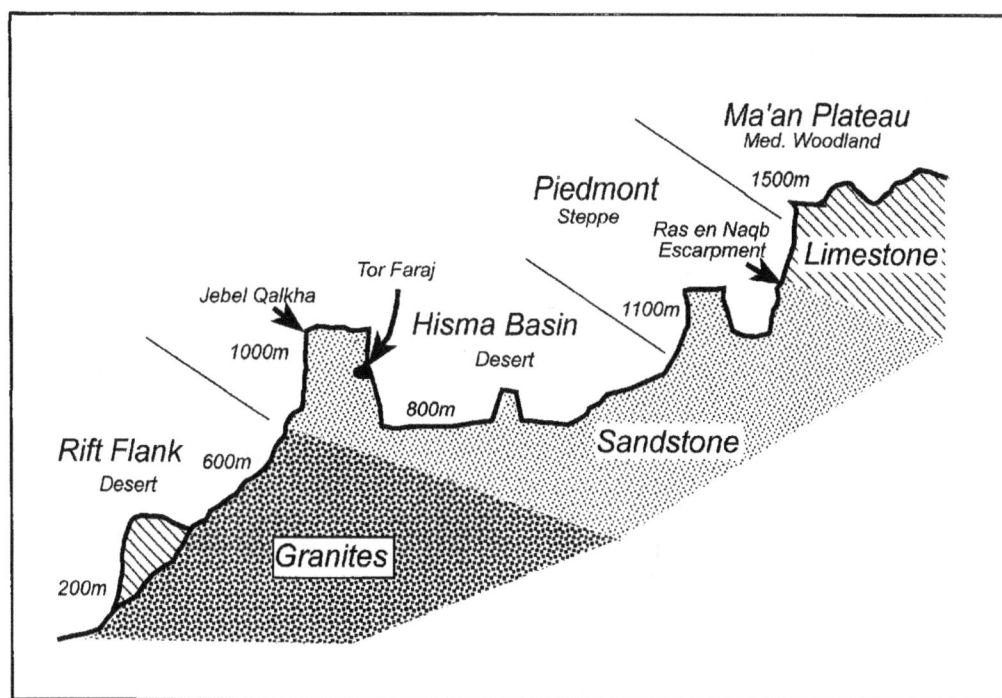

Figure 3.2 Schematic cross-section of the region around Tor Faraj from northeast to southwest showing the topography, environment, and bedrock lithology

and pistacia. Understory vegetation would have consisted of shrubs, grasses, bulb, and tuber plants common to Mediterranean woodlands. Recent efforts at reforestation have been launched with the planting of pines and cedars near Ras en Naqb and the establishment of fruit tree orchards north and west of the village. Much of the uplands is cultivated in wheat.

Remnants of *Terra rosa* soil indicate mean annual precipitation levels of over 300mm. With mean annual temperatures for the uplands ranging from 12 to 17°C, the climate falls within the 'Cool Temperate Rainy' climate of the Koppen Classification (Shehadeh 1985) and the 'Arid Mediterranean (Cool Variety)' bioclimate of El-Eisawi (1985). Mean minimum temperatures for January range from 0 to 3°C with precipitation often coming as snow. July temperatures average about 22°C; thus, transpiroevaporation rates are relatively low, leaving sufficient soil moisture to sustain green grasses and shrubs long after they have died back at lower elevations. The clayey soils of the uplands further enhance moisture retention.

Piedmont of the Ras en Naqb Escarpment

A series of high basins formed between the Ras en Naqb Escarpment of the Ma'an Plateau and sandstone outliers create a piedmont at elevations between 1000 and 1300m. Alluvial fans drape the steep flanks of the basins at the foot of the 600m high escarpment and coalesce to form broad, nearly level floors up to 3km across. Steppe vegetation, characterized by small shrubs and bushes, dominates the piedmont. Sage (*Artemesia herbae-albae*), saltwood (*Haloxylion articulata*), bean caper (*Zygophyllum dumasum*), white broom (*Retama raetam*), and *Anabasis articulata* are the most common species. Better-watered areas along wadis and shaded settings beneath cliffs support denser vegetation occasionally accompanied by pistacia, the principal tree of the steppe zone. It should be noted, however, that such trees represent remnants or relics of earlier distributions during moister intervals, for nowhere in the area have seedlings or young trees been reported (Zohary 1962).

With mean minimum temperatures in January ranging from 3 to 6°C and rainfall measuring some 200 to 300mm annually, the

piedmont falls within the 'Cool Steppe' of the Koppen Classification and the 'Arid Mediterranean (Warm Variety)' bioclimate of El-Eisawi (1985).

The Hisma Basin

The broad Wadi Hisma, resting between 800 and 1000masl, runs southeast, parallel to the edge of the plateau, for about 80km. The floor of the basin is some 10km wide at its western end near Tor Faraj and narrows to the east before joining a maze of narrow sandstone canyons and inselbergs. The southern edge of the valley is defined by granite mountains.

The nearly level floor of the basin contains numerous mud flats, the remnants of Pleistocene lakes, and is occasionally punctuated by sheer-walled jebels. These spectacular sandstone inselbergs rise 200 to 300m above the basin floor and often attain elevations of over 1000m. Surface sediments within the Hisma form a mosaic of talus scree from the inselbergs and granite mountains, silty-sand of the lake beds, and extensive fields of drift sand that in some areas form prominent dunes.

The sparse plant cover of the basin is associated with desert vegetation of the Saharo-Arabian and Sudanian phytogeographic zones (*ibid.*). The Saharo-Arabian vegetation is composed mainly of shrubs such as sage (*Artemesia herbae-alba*), saxual shrub (*Haloxylon persicum*), *Calligonum comosum*, and *Archillea fragrantissima*. This vegetation dominates the valley with the densest stands occupying areas of drift sand and the shorelines of mud pans. Sudanian species, typified by acacia (*Acacia sp.*) and thorn (*Zizyphus spina-christi*) trees, are more common to the lower, drier settings that are covered by granite scree along the southern edge of the valley.

The daily temperatures of the lowlands average some 3°C higher than the piedmont and over 6°C higher than the uplands. With minimum January temperatures averaging 5 to 8°C and annual rainfall measuring less than 50mm, the Hisma Basin falls mainly within the 'Cool Desert' classification of Koppen and the 'Saharan Mediterranean (Warm Variety)' bioclimate of El-Eisawi (*ibid.*). The lower (near 800masl) southern edge of the basin, with higher average annual temperatures of 20 to 22°C, would be included within the 'Warm

Desert Climate' of the Koppen Classification. The meager rainfall of the area is restricted to the winter and many years can go by without measurable precipitation. Water sources are limited to springs along the valley's southern margin and to the lake beds which are charged for a few weeks by run-off from the uplands during abnormally wet years.

The flank of the Rift

The headwaters of streams draining to the Rift are found only 1 to 2km west of Tor Faraj along an escarpment formed by the Jebel Qalkha Fault. These drop away precipitously to the northwest, falling almost 1200m in 14km, and create a complex landscape composed of deeply incised canyons and high buttes. Many of the canyons have formed *siqs* or extremely narrow defiles through sandstone where they often measure only a meter or so in width and have nearly vertical walls that reach upwards of 30m.

Although the bedrock geology of the flank is varied and complex due to the extensive faulting along the Rift, an east–west transect largely shows Cambrian sandstones occupying the upper part (500 to 1200m) of the Rift Flank (Rabb'a 1988; Ibrahim 1990). These give way to Late Proterozoic–Early Cambrian rocks (e.g., rhyolite, granodiorite, and volcanoclastic) of the Aqaba Complex at lower elevations (200 to 500m). Chert-bearing Cretaceous limestones are also found within this lower elevation belt, although these are not as extensive as the rocks of the Aqaba Complex. Extensive bedrock exposures and slopes covered in scree dominate the highest elevations of the flank, but alluvial terraces, alluvial fans, dune fields, and even lacustrine deposits become increasingly common at elevations beneath 600m.

As elsewhere in the region, steppe vegetation is found at elevations above 800m. Lower on the flank of the Rift, desert plants of Saharo-Arabian (dune fields) and Sudanian (rocky areas) varieties are dominant. At very low elevations (200 to 300m), springs and seeps become common and these support small patches of oasis vegetation.

The floor of the Rift

The floor of the Rift or Wadi Araba forms a nearly level alluvial plain that measures some 10 to 12km in width and reaches an elevation of *ca.* 150m in that segment west of Tor Faraj. The landscape consists of the toes of alluvial fans, dune fields, and mud flats. Vegetation resembles that found on the lower reaches of the Rift flank.

Quaternary geology of the region and Middle Paleolithic deposits

Studies of the quaternary geology of the region mainly have been prompted by prehistoric archaeological investigations. These have centered on the Judayid Basin of the higher piedmont (Henry et al. 1983; Hassan 1995), the Jebel Qalkha area of the lower piedmont (Hall 1996; Henry et al. 1996; Henry 1997, 1998b), and the wadis of Nukheileh and Gharandal in the lower flank of the Rift (Henry et al. 2001). Sediment cores have also been collected from Pleistocene lake beds located near the center of the Hisma Basin, but these remain undated (Hall 1996).

These studies indicate that cycles of aeolian activity, forming region-wide sand or silt deposits, separated by erosional intervals, have been the dominant processes of landscape modification during the Late Pleistocene. When compared to ancillary evidence (pollen, phytoliths, faunal remains), it would appear that episodes of drift sand accumulation were linked to dry conditions (although rarely as dry as today), whereas area-wide silt deposition occurred under conditions considerably more moist than today (Henry 1997). Widespread erosion marked changes in the sedimentary cycles, regardless of whether silt or sand was being deposited. This would suggest that erosion was triggered principally by climatic changes that induced a situation in which groundcover was inadequate to retard sheet erosion. Thus the direction of the change (i.e., moist-dry or dry-moist) was not as important as the disequilibrium it produced.

Jebel Qalkha area

Of the four study areas in which geologic investigations have been undertaken, the one in the vicinity of Jebel Qalkha has yielded the most complete results. The Late Pleistocene

Jebel Qalkha

▲ J433
MP/UP Transitional

Q3 Red Sand

▲ Tor Faraj 49-69Kbp
Lev. Mousterian

▲ J403, J412, J431,
J432, J444, & J447
Lev. Mousterian

Q4 Yellow Silt

● 8m
Paleosol B / **Terrace**

Nari

● Isolated Mousterian
Artifacts

Judayid Basin

Sabiha Formation

▲ Tor Sabiha
69Kbp
Lev. Mousterian

Member I Alluvial Fan Fill

Wadi Gharandal

Quasi-Lacustrine Deposit / Upper Sand

Isolated Mousterian Artifacts

▲ J602
MP/UP Transitional

●

▲ J603
Lev. Mousterian

Lower Sand

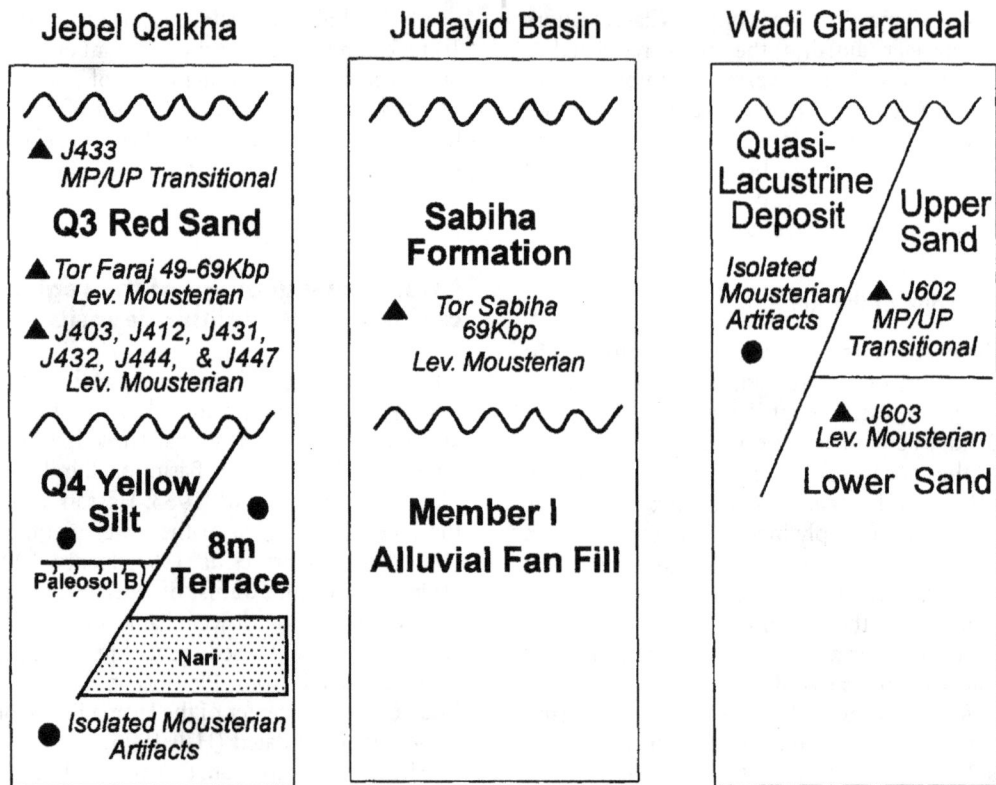

Figure 3.3 A comparison of depositional successions and archaeological evidence from three localities in southern Jordan in the vicinity of Tor Faraj

deposits that accumulated during the prehistoric occupation of the area are composed primarily of aeolian sediments. These consist of alternating light brown-yellow silt (loess) and red sand deposits that form valley fills which in the Wadi Humeima measure over 10m thick (Fig. 3.3). Two calcic paleosols appear within this succession, that are both associated with silt deposits. Although eroded, their calcic B-horizons reveal *Stage III* carbonate concretions and nodules, a degree of development that indicates each of the soils required 10 to 20k years to form, at least when compared to rates of development known from the North American southwest (Hall, in Henry et al. 1996).

Most of the surfaces surrounding the Jebel Qalkha are covered with a talus scree (5 to 10cm thick) of sandstone rubble that declines in size and density with distance from the jebel's escarpment. It is noteworthy that rubble lenses defining screes on paleosurfaces buried within the silt and sand deposits never

show the thickness or density seen in the scree on the modern surface.

The uppermost of the red sands, the Q1 Red Sand, has been identified only within the Wadi Humeima where it extends from the surface to reach a thickness of ca. 2m. Exposures in archaeological excavations and natural erosional cuts reveal a massive, coherent red sand (2.5YR4/5) occasionally containing thin lenses of small, angular sandstone detritus. The lenses, representing talus scree, define much gentler valley slopes than exist in the area today. Culturally, the Q1 Red Sand contains Epipaleolithic assemblages from five sites (Early Hamran and Qalkhan) that should date from ca. 15 to 20kya, based upon cross-reference dates (Henry 1997; Byrd 1998).

Underlying the Q1 Red Sand is a yellow silt (7.5YR6/4–10YR6/6), the Q2 Yellow Silt, that not only appears in extensive exposures within the Wadi Humeima, it fronts most of the eastern escarpment of the Jebel Qalkha extending well into the Hisma Basin. The unit, over 2m thick, is associated with a calcic paleosol (Paleosol A) that developed during the early accumulation of the silt. Stratigraphically, the yellow silt is seen to underlie the Q1 Red Sand in an erosional exposure on the southern bank of the Wadi Humeima just east of the Epipaleolithic Qalkhan Site of J407. A sharp, unconformable contact joins the two units. Culturally, the Q2 Yellow Silt contains Upper Paleolithic (Early Ahmarian, Non-Ahmarian) and/or Middle Paleolithic (Late Levantine Mousterian) assemblages at five sites. Stratified Upper-Middle Paleolithic sequences have been defined at four of these (Henry 1997).

A lower red sand (2.5YR5/6), the Q3 Red Sand, is occasionally exposed within the Wadi Aghar and Wadi Humeima valley fills, but it shows extensive exposure within the area north of Jebel Qalkha where it measures some 3 to 4m thick. Exposures in the upper reaches of the Wadi Humeima reveal unconformable contacts between it and the overlying Q2 Yellow Silt as well as the underlying Q4 Yellow Silt. Similarly, the archaeological deposits of the rockshelter sites J403 and J412 show the Q3 Red Sand, resting on bedrock, to underlie Q2 silt deposits. Culturally, the Q3 Red Sand contains Late Levantine Mousterian assemblages at five sites and a likely *transitional* Middle-Upper Paleolithic assemblage at another.

A lower silt, the Q4 Silt, is found underlying the Q3 sand in exposures within the upper reaches of the Wadi Humeima. The unit is *ca.* 1m thick and contains a calcic paleosol (Paleosol B). Artifacts have not been found within this lowermost unit.

Our understanding of the alluvial geology of the Jebel Qalkha area is derived primarily from a study of the Wadi Aghar drainage basin undertaken by Hall (Henry *et al.* 1996). The drainage displays a single high terrace and two lower inset terraces. The high terrace is predominantly composed of gravels and contains numerous Levantine Mousterian artifacts, while the lowest two terraces appear to date to Chalcolithic and recent times, respectively. An alluvial fan and nari carbonate deposits also contain numerous Levantine Mousterian artifacts.

An alluvial terrace, situated 6.5 to 8m above the present channel, forms the principal feature of Wadi Aghar. The terrace consists of poorly sorted red (2.5YR5/6) to reddish-yellow (7.5YR6/6) sandy gravels derived from local sandstone. The imbricated gravels, with individual clasts up to 40cm, occur in weakly defined beds alternating with a few sand-dominated zones measuring less than 20cm thick. Paleosols were not observed within the terrace deposit. The terrace gravels contain Levantine Mousterian artifacts presenting no apparent stratigraphic pattern. Given that artifacts recovered from the terrace are restricted to those of Levantine Mousterian age and that artifacts of Upper Paleolithic, Epipaleolithic, and Chalcolithic sites located within the wadi are not found within the terrace, it seems most likely that the terrace dates to the Middle Paleolithic.

A lower terrace, inset against the 8m-terrace, is preserved in only a few sections of the wadi where about a meter of the deposit is exposed. The lower 40cm is composed of imbricated, sandstone gravels overlain by *ca.* 60cm of light-red gravelly sand. Only three artifacts were recovered from the 3-m terrace. Two were non-diagnostic and the third was tentatively classified as Chalcolithic in age. Remnants of an even lower, 1-m terrace were observed in only two localities within the Wadi Aghar. These show about 1 meter of reddish-yellow (7.5YR6/6), silty, fine sand with scattered granule gravels and occasional lenses of small gravels. The deposit contains the *in situ* remains of more than 20 small hearths similar in structure and content to numerous other Bedouin hearths found on the sandy surface of the terrace. Diagnostic artifacts were not found in the terrace deposit.

Deposits of a remnant fan of the prehistoric Wadi Aghar are exposed near the present-day mouth of the wadi. The fan sediment is a reddish-yellow, gravelly sand, massive with some cross-beds, with zones of imbricated small sandstone gravels, carbonate coats on gravels, and carbonate nodules in the lowermost massive sand horizon. Paleosols do not occur sedimented within the deposit. A Levallois point, diagnostic of the Levantine Mousterian, was recovered within the fan 1.7m above its base. Hall (*ibid.*) noted that although the alluvial fan and the 8-m terrace appear to have accumulated synchronously, the fan is composed primarily of sand while the terrace consists mainly of gravels. Given these sediment differences, Hall suggests that the discharge of Wadi Aghar was insufficient to transport gravels out of the canyon as far as the fan. The wadi today carries only sand as far as the fan remnant.

Nari, a variety of travertine-like carbonate cement, has developed in the Wadi Aghar through the dissolution and secondary precipitation of carbonate from the calcareous sandstone that forms the canyon walls of the drainage basin. It occurs as carbonate crusts on sandstone outcrops, cements colluvial gravels that cover the canyon slopes, and cements basal gravels of the 8-m terraces where they contact bedrock. The occurrence of nari carbonates is related primarily to proximity to bedrock.

Hall (ibid.) observed that the nari is most likely to have originated during a period of wetter climate, not just one of greater effective moisture, but of actual increased precipitation sufficient to cause the dissolution of carbonate cement from the Cambrian sandstone. Moreover, the nari within the Wadi Aghar appears to result from a single period of formation. Four nari localities yielded diagnostic artifacts, all attributed to the Levantine Mousterian.

The Judayid Basin

A line of sandstone hills joins the base of the Ras en Naqb Escarpment to create the Judayid Basin, the headwater of Wadi Judayid. Hassan's (1995) study showed the dominant Late Pleistocene deposits in the basin to consist of alluvial fans. These have coalesced to form a bajada that is dissected by more recent gullies which are eroded toward the center of the basin. Hassan identified two units within the fans. The lower unit (Member I) is composed of hard compact sand with carbonate nodules and colors ranging from light brown to strong brown-reddish yellow. The upper unit (Member II) consists of friable sand, reddish-yellow to light brown or pink in color. Archaeological evidence was not recorded for the lower unit, but the upper unit contains numerous Epipaleolithic occupations that suggest that its deposition encompassed the period from ca. 16 to 13Kb.p.

A deposit of relict drift sand was found to overlie the Member I alluvial fan unit in a small embayment high on the southwestern edge of the basin. A Levantine Mousterian site (Tor Sabiha) was discovered eroding from the sand and dated to ca. 70Kb.p. The age of this overlying drift sand may indicate that the formation of Member I alluvial fan took place in the early part of the Late Pleistocene or earlier. The Member I sands are cemented by carbonates, including zones rich in carbonate nodules, that are thought to indicate a subarid environment, moist and warm with rainfall perhaps in the magnitude of 300mm (ibid.). The development of the reddish-yellow color is suggestive of the warm, moist conditions that were sufficient to mobilize iron oxides. Seasonal dryness is also suggested by the precipitation of carbonates, which were presumably introduced during the rainy season.

Erosion of Member I followed, along with the accumulation of drift sand from freshly weathered sandstone under dry, cool conditions. This deposit contains the Levantine Mousterian occupation of Tor Sabiha in association with faunal and pollen evidence pointing to steppic conditions (Emery-Barbier 1995; Henry 1995c). Amino acid racemization dates of ostrich eggshell place the occupation at ca. 70Kb.p (Henry and Miller 1992).

The following alluviation of the Member II fan denotes warm and somewhat moist conditions. In the lower parts of the basin, finer sediments accumulated and thin crusts of calcium carbonates were developed. Hassan (1995) interprets the lack of carbonate concretions and the presence of thin crusts to indicate a drier climate than that which prevailed during the alluviation of the lower unit (Member I) of the fan deposits. He speculates that the climate was probably similar to that under which yellow steppe soils are formed. Also, frequent cut-and-fill structure, rapid lateral and vertical changes in facies, and frequent occurrence of large stone blocks and boulders suggest occasional torrential rainfall. Late Epipaleolithic (Middle Hamran Industry, Geometric Kebaran Complex) sites, located in situ in the top part of the upper unit of the fan, confirm that alluviation lasted until ca. 14 to 13Kb.p.

Since that time geomorphic processes for the basin have been mainly erosional. A series of seven cut-terraces were established along the Wadi Judayid with the lowest visible terrace at .5m above the modern wadi floor. Following the formation of the highest terrace, the early Natufian settlement of Wadi Judayid was established. This provides a limiting date for the termination of the episode of erosion as determined by radiocarbon dates for occupation of *ca.* 12.5Kb.p. The erosional period then would appear to have lasted from as early as 14Kb.p to as late as 12.5Kb.p.

Cooler, drier conditions followed, leading to intensive mechanical weathering and aeolian activity. This interval is likely to have corresponded to the late Natufian arid phase, correlated with the Younger Dryas and dated to *ca.* 11Kb.p. The dune sands covering the artifact horizons at the site of Wadi Judayid are evidence of this interval. Continued aridity and accumulation of drift sands during the early to middle Holocene are indicated at early Neolithic and Chalcolithic occupations in the basin.

Correlation of Middle Paleolithic deposits

A comparison of the geomorphic successions recorded in the Jebel Qalkha and Judayid Basin areas suggests that the Middle Paleolithic occupation of the region bridged a climatic-environmental transition from moist to drier conditions (Fig. 3.3). Although the age and stratigraphic correlations of deposits associated with the moist interval are problematic, much more information is available for understanding the subsequent drier interval.

The presence of Levantine Mousterian artifacts imbedded within nari at several localities in the Jebel Qalkha area confirms very moist conditions during the Levantine Mousterian. Moreover, the absence of artifacts of later archaeological periods within the nari (despite the abundance of such later period sites in the area) indicates that such high moisture levels have not been reached since that time. Also, the fact that nari was not found to cement Late Levantine Mousterian horizons at Tor Faraj and five other excavated sites further suggests that the moist episode preceded the Late Levantine Mousterian and the accumulation of the Q3 Red Sand. Although stratigraphic correlations between the nari and the Q4 silt have not been observed, the presence of isolated Mousterian artifacts eroding from the Q4 Silt in the Jebel Qalkha area

implies that the silt is of an Early Levantine Mousterian age and therefore may have formed contemporaneous with the nari. Alluviation along drainages is also associated with this moist interval, as evidenced in the Wadi Aghar by an 8-m terrace that contains Mousterian artifacts, some of which are embedded in nari at the base of the terrace. Correlations with the depositional sequence in the Wadi Judayid are much more tenuous. While it is tempting to tie the earliest (Member I) fill of the basin to this moist interval in that it is known to underlie drift sand containing the Late Levantine Mousterian site of Tor Sabiha, it could of course date to an even earlier episode. Unfortunately, organic evidence for paleoenvironmental reconstruction is unavailable for this interval.

The nari, that has cemented gravels at the base of the 8-m terrace in the Wadi Aghar, is an indication of moist conditions. But the nari disappears toward the top of the terrace deposit, a sedimentary change that likely corresponded to a progressively drier setting. Such aridity ultimately would have triggered the erosional hiatus that terminated alluviation and led to downcutting. This drier interval also was probably associated with the Late Levantine Mousterian occupation of the area and the formation of drift sand deposits in the Hisma (Q3 Red Sand) and Judayid (Sabiha Formation) basins. Seven Late Levantine Mousterian sites have been found within the Q3 Red Sand of the Jebel Qalkha area and another (Tor Sabiha) has been excavated from drift sand in the Judayid Basin. The dates from Tor Faraj and Tor Sabiha indicate that the drift sand was accumulating between 49 and 69Kb.p. Moreover, the presence of a transitional Middle/Upper Paleolithic site (J433) in the Q3 Sand in the Wadi Aghar and another transitional occupation in the Upper Sand Unit (Henry *et al.* 2001) in the nearby Gharandal Basin point to continuation of aridity and sand mobilization following 49Kb.p. In that the Q3 Red Sand (and also the Q1 Red Sand) accumulated along the western and northern margins of the basin, prevailing winds must have blown from the east and south. This is in striking contrast to the modern situation in which dune fields form on the eastern and southern margins of the basin in response to predominantly northwestern winds (Henry 1997).

Environmental data for the arid interval come mainly from the excavations of Tor Faraj and Tor Sabiha. These data are consistent with a generally arid climate that was cooler and moister than that of the area today and most likely corresponding to that of the modern Arid Mediterranean (cool variety). Although pollen was not preserved in the Tor Faraj deposit, a rich phytolith assemblage was recovered (Rosen 1995, and Chapter 7 of this volume) and this was dominated by Festucoid C3 (cool environment) grasses. Rosen (Chapter 7) notes that C3 grasses favor conditions receiving over 300mm precipitation annually. Moreover, the phytoliths of canes, reeds, palms, and rushes confirm the presence of nearby standing water. The poorly preserved faunal remains from the deposit include equid teeth, gazelle, and ostrich eggshell fragments; all of which are consistent with a predominantly open, arid setting.

At Tor Sabiha, the sedimentary sequence suggests that the occupation began following a cold-dry episode represented by the weakly weathered, almost white sand of Layer D. The angularity of grains and light oxidation of the sand argue for less moisture and possibly lower temperatures than today. The overlying Layer C sands contain Tor Sabiha's archaeological horizon and are pinkish-gray in color. This sharp contrast in the color of the sand layers suggests the site was first occupied during an episode of slight climatic amelioration associated with an elevation of temperature and precipitation as indicated by the greater weathering of Layer C.

Pollen (Emery-Barbier 1988, 1995) and faunal evidence from Layer C are consistent with a generally arid environment, but moister and cooler than the area today. Specifically, the nearby Judayid Basin and hilly uplands are likely to have supported grassland with pockets of woodland in protected, well-watered areas and along major streams. Alder and elm pollen in Layer C suggest that the wadis on the basin's floor were lined with stands of trees and flowed for much of the year. The pine pollen denotes some woodlands, most likely in the uplands of the plateau and along the basin's sandstone rim. Pollen fluctuations within Layer C may denote a rise in temperature as reflected in the rise of the thermophilous Cheno-podiaceae type *Noaea* and the attendant rise of grasses (*ibid.*).

Faunal remains are poorly preserved in the deposit of Tor Sabiha and, as at Tor Faraj, include gazelle, equid, and ostrich eggshell fragments. The only additional species is *Bos*. These fauna point to a generally open, relatively arid environment, but the daily water requirements of *Bos* also would suggest that standing water was available within the site's catchment.

Evidence from both Tor Faraj and Tor Sabiha for the presence of ostriches (*Struthio camelus*) in the area is helpful in reconstructing the Middle Paleolithic environment, especially paleotemperature. This, of course, assumes that the modern and prehistoric habitats required by ostriches are similar. Ostriches are adapted to arid settings and need dunes or drift sand for nesting. They are not cold-tolerant and enjoy a modern range of 15 to 35°C (Brown 1982). Given that the modern annual mean minimum temperatures for the piedmont and uplands range from 15 to 12°C, the presence of ostriches in the area suggests that temperatures are unlikely to have been depressed much beyond 3°C during the deposition of Layer C. When the paleotemperatures associated with a high resolution chronostratigraphy developed by Martinson et al. (1987) are reviewed, there are two intervals with temperatures that are depressed by 3°C or less between 49620 and 72640B.P. These fall between 51620 and 59980B.P. and at 68990B.P.

When comparing the paleoenvironmental succession as presently understood for the Middle Paleolithic of southern Jordan to the Levant as a whole, it is tempting to correlate the moist-dry sequence to a similar sequence widely thought to characterize the Levant. In this, the Early Levantine Mousterian is typically linked to moist, even pluvial conditions, whereas the late Levantine Mousterian is associated with drier conditions (Bar-Yosef 1992: 202-3).

Our understanding of the Levantine Mousterian paleoenvironmental succession comes from several lines of evidence. These include pollen studies of prehistoric occupations (Horowitz 1976, 1979; Leroi-Gourhan 1980; Emery-Barbier 1988, 1995; Jelinek 1992; Clark *et al.* 1997), and lake cores (Horowitz 1979; Bottema and van Zeist 1981; Wienstein-Evron 1988), geologic investigations of depositional sequences in cultural and natural contexts (Farrand 1979; Goldberg 1981, 1986; Bull and Goldberg 1985; Schuldenrein and Clark 1994; Hassan 1995; Henry *et al.* 1996; Henry 1997), and faunal analyses (Garrard 1982; Tchernov 1992, 1994). Collectively, this evidence has been interpreted to show that pluvial conditions prevailed during early Mousterian (D- and C-type) times, followed by a drier and colder setting during the Late Levantine (B-type) Mousterian (Bar-Yosef 1992: 202-3).

This generally accepted notion of an early Levantine Mousterian wet phase followed by drier conditions during the Late Levantine Mousterian has been questioned, however. Wienstein-Evron (1988), for example, finds evidence for pluvial conditions in the pollen diagram of her Hula Basin core in the northern Jordan Valley, that she attributes to Early Levantine Mousterian times, but she fails to see indications of a subsequent arid interval. In contrast, Leroi-Gourhan's (1980) detailed pollen study of the Lebanese cave deposit of Nahr Ibrahim, containing C- and B-type assemblages, reveals two cycles of fluctuations between cool, moist forest and dry steppic settings. Fish's (reported in Jelinek 1992) pollen investigation of Tabun Cave (limited to Layers D and C within the Levantine Mousterian succession) suggests a relatively stable setting characterized by steppic conditions. While the pollen from the Early Levantine Mousterian deposit of Ain Difla in the Wadi Hasa of west-central Jordan shows more mesic conditions than indicated by an earlier study, the sample is nevertheless representative of steppic conditions (Clark *et al.* 1997).

These studies indicate that the paleoclimatic succession of Levantine Mousterian times is not as well understood as generally believed. The ambiguity in the paleorecords of the archaeological and natural deposits is likely to stem from three major factors: (1) data tied to a low resolution chronometry; (2) data associated with limited points of reference in both time and space; and (3) real differences in climate across the region. It seems unreasonable to expect that the climate remained stable over such huge spans of time as encompassed by the Levantine Mousterian, especially the early phase that may have stretched over 100k years or more. Thus with only a handful of reference points, most of which are undated, it is not surprising that there is a lack of agreement in paleoclimatic data. Moreover, even at the same points in time, environmental expressions across the region are likely to have varied. Latitudinal, marine, and orographic factors create complex meteorologic patterns for such a small geographic region. This is true today and is becoming increasingly well defined for earlier periods, such as the terminal Pleistocene, because of relatively precise chronometries coupled with more and wider spread paleoenvironmental data (Henry 1983, 1989b, 1998b; Baruch and Bottema 1991; Baruch 1994). The terminal Pleistocene, in particular, provides a model by which we might examine earlier climatic shifts such as those of the Levantine Mousterian.

Site setting and access to resources

From a regional perspective, Tor Faraj rests at the lower edge of the piedmont of the Ma'an Plateau at an elevation of ca. 1000m. It is situated on the north wall of the Wadi Aghar, a steep canyon that has formed within a Cambrian sandstone upland, the Jebel Qalkha (Figs 3.2, 3.4, and 3.5). This upland is the most prominent of several sandstone outliers that join the Ras en Naqb Escarpment to a range of granite mountains and create the western margin of the Wadi Hisma (Osborn and Duford 1981; Hassan 1995). This range also separates the Hisma basin from the Rift Valley, the floor of which is located about 15km to the west. The Jebel Qalkha is drained mainly to the southeast by the Wadi Aghar and Wadi Humeima. These feed into the Wadi Qalkha, the major drainage of the western Hisma, close to where it skirts the western edge of the jebel before turning eastward into the central part of the basin. The western slopes of the Jebel Qalkha run along a major fault and drain to the west-northwest to meet the Wadi Aheimir as it drops westward to the Rift. In many ways, Tor Faraj rests along one of the few natural passageways that connects the Ma'an Plateau with the Hisma Basin and Rift Valley.

Site catchment analysis and site territory

A catchment analysis is employed here in an effort to reconstruct the variety and distribution

Figure 3.4 Looking at Tor Faraj from the west side of the Wadi Aheimir opposite the shelter

Figure 3.5 Looking out from Tor Faraj to the outlet of the Wadi Aheimir and the Hisma Basin. Note the east block (*left*) is being mapped and artifacts recorded by laser theodolyte, while the west block (*right*) is under excavation

of resources that would have been available to the Mousterian inhabitants of Tor Faraj. In developing site catchment analysis, Higgs and his colleagues defined a *site territory*, the area around a site that is habitually exploited, as encompassing an area that typically falls within 5 to 10-km radius or about two hours' walking distance from a site (Vita-Finzi and Higgs 1970; Higgs and Vita-Finzi 1972; Higgs and Jarman 1975). The shape of a site's territory, however, might vary greatly, dependent upon local topography and other factors affecting travel time. Unlike site territories, *annual territories* were defined by the Cambridge researchers as comprising the area exploited by a group over the course of a full year and often consisting of two or more site territories.

A sometimes overlooked detail and potential source of confusion in the analysis is that a *site catchment* does not necessarily correspond to a *site territory*. A site catchment is seen as incorporating those settings inclusive of and also beyond a site territory. Extension beyond that part of the catchment that was habitually and intensively exploited (the *site territory*)

would occur, for example, when a group exploited distant resources through occasional forays. But how is this to be addressed when a group habitually and routinely used resources beyond the physical limits (two hours' walk or 10km) of the site territory? In many ways, Binford's (1980) model which contrasts polar types of settlement-procurement strategies clarifies the issue. In his classification, a *foraging strategy* involves the opportunistic exploitation of a catchment that largely corresponds to a site territory, whereas a *collecting strategy* entails the exploitation of an immediate catchment in addition to the logistical acquisition of resources from distant points.

Examination of the area encompassed within a 5-km radius of Tor Faraj shows the extreme ruggedness of the terrain to the north and west of the site (Fig. 3.4). In particular, west of the prominent escarpment created by the Jebel Qalkha Fault the landscape is heavily dissected by deep canyons that fall some 800m to the Rift. To the south of the site, the landscape primarily consists of low ridges and hills cut by west-east oriented drainages.

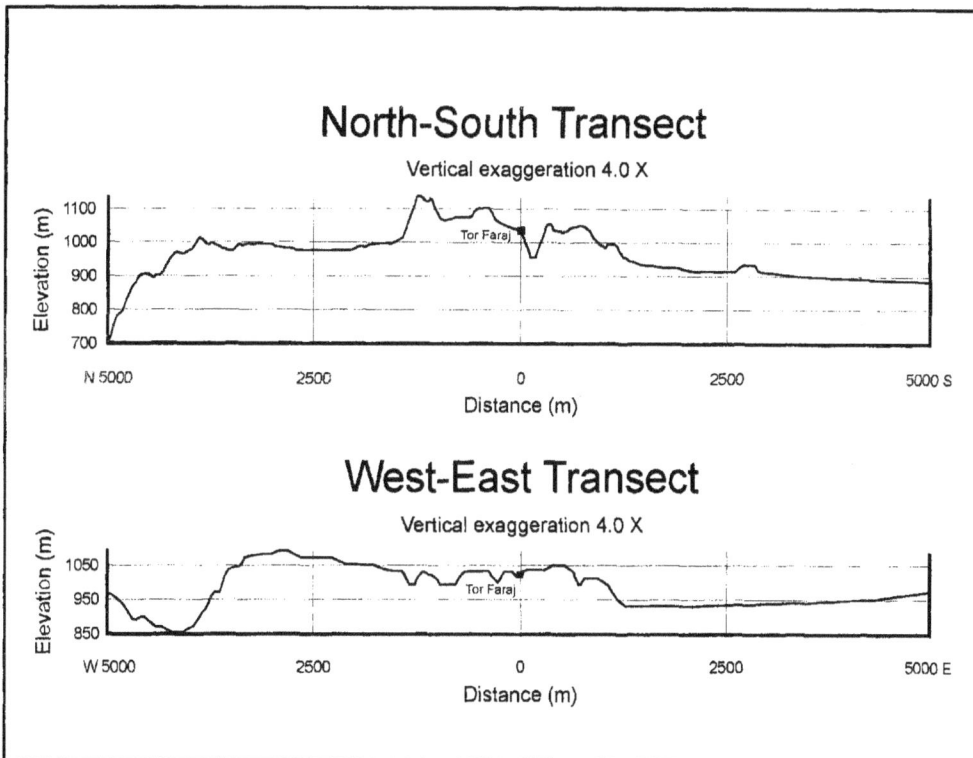

Figure 3.6   Elevational transects of the area within a 5-km radius of Tor Faraj

Although much less rugged than the territory to the west of the Jebel Qalkha Fault, foot-travel directly south of Tor Faraj is impeded by two steep-walled canyons. Access to this area is likely to have involved following the Wadi Qalkha south and then turning westward up any of the drainages. In contrast to the broken terrain to the north, west, and south of Tor Faraj, the Hisma Basin provides a gently rolling to nearly level floor that is easily accessed from the mouth of the Wadi Aghar, just east of the site.

Because of the varied topography surrounding Tor Faraj, the shape of its catchment is likely to have differed significantly from an idealized circular form. The broken terrain to the north, west, and south of the site would have increased travel-time greatly, thus shrinking its territory in these directions. The western boundary of Tor Faraj's site territory can be estimated from the daily 40-minute travel-time from our 1988 camp at the mouth of the Wadi Aghar to the site of Tor Hamar, located about 2km, straight-line distance and 3km upstream. Using the two-hour rule, the western margin of the territory then would fall about 6km away, just beyond the Jebel Qalkha Fault. This estimate is based upon the most efficient means of traveling in the area, i.e., walking the wadi beds. When traversing the canyon systems, travel-time is greatly increased and probably doubled. It is noteworthy in this context that the local Bedouin rarely climb 'up-and-over' the drainage divides that separate the canyons of the area. They typically follow the inter-connecting drainages even though this greatly increases walking distances. Therefore, an average straight-line distance for a two-hour walk from Tor Faraj to the north, west, and south is estimated at 3 to 4km. Moreover, the 150- to 200-m-high escarpment of the Jebel Qalkha Fault creates a prominent topographic barrier that would have further reinforced this boundary to the west and north. Reconstruction of the eastern portion of the site territory is based upon a travel-time of *ca.* 5 to 6km per hour. This is consistent with the time it took to walk from our camp at the mouth of the Wadi Aghar to excavations along the eastern edge of the Jebel Qalkha in 1983 and 1984. Once leaving the Wadi Aghar canyon, the Mousterian occupants of Tor Faraj would have been able to travel rapidly over the nearly level landscape of the western Hisma Basin to the north, east, and south. Thus, an average straight-line distance of 10 to 12km from the mouth of Wadi Aghar is used to trace the eastern margins of the site territory of Tor Faraj.

Resources within the site territory

Water, the most important of resources, would have been most extensively available during the winter, wet season from run-off collected in pools formed in the sandstone bed of the Wadi Aghar and lateral drainages. Today, during normal years such pools hold water from December through February, but during wet years they may contain some water into the late spring. During the occupation of Tor Faraj, the temperature depression of *ca.* 3°C alone is likely to have extended the normal availability of seasonal water through the spring. Beyond seasonal water, a seep or spring that was active during Roman times is located *ca.* 1.5km northeast of the site on the south wall of the Wadi Humeima, the next canyon north of the Wadi Aghar. Within the site territory of Tor Faraj, both perennial and seasonal water sources would have been limited to the sandstone formation of the Jebel Qalkha (i.e., the more restricted western portion of the territory). East of the site within the Hisma Basin, surface water would have been limited to short periods during the wet season when the Wadi Qalkha was flowing.

Animals forming the principal food sources for the occupants of Tor Faraj are likely to have consisted of those common to a steppe environment such as wild goats (and perhaps sheep), equids, gazelle, *Bos*, hare, chukar partridge, ostrich, tortoise, and various large lizards. Of this list, only gazelles, *Bos*, equids, and ostriches are confirmed through the recovery of faunal remains, but the other species have been found in nearby Middle Paleolithic deposits and later Epipaleolithic horizons. Of the megafauna, caprines would have preferred the canyons and cliffs of the Jebel Qalkha, but equids, wild cattle, gazelles, and ostriches would have favored the open habitat offered by the nearby Hisma Basin. Pools found within the canyons of Jebel Qalkha, however, are likely to have attracted animals out of the basin for regular watering.

Given the environmental setting, plant foods available to the occupants of Tor Faraj are likely to have included various nuts, tubers, leafy vegetables, and dates (see Zohary 1962; Evenari *et al.* 1971; and Scott 1977, for discussions of plants from the Negev). Direct evidence for plant exploitation, however, is limited to the results of Rosen's (Chapter 7 in this volume) study of phytoliths, spores, and starch grains recovered from the shelter's deposit. She notes the presence of phytoliths of the date palm (*Phoenix dactylifera*) and fossil spores of horse-tail rush (*Equisetum sp.*) and points out that both would have offered potential food sources. Rosen also identified starch grains, one matching the form of pistachio, and suggests that they were derived from nuts, tubers, and roots brought into Tor Faraj. From the perspective of the site territory, the highest density of plant foods would have been found around pools and within the protected, better-watered canyons of the Jebel Qalkha.

Beyond foodstuffs, fuel and chert probably represented the most important resources to the occupants of Tor Faraj. Today, Bedouin tent-groups living in the area rely on shrubs and brush for fuel. Within the site territory of Tor Faraj, these are concentrated in the Jebel Qalkha area because of the higher density of moist settings. For that part of the site territory located on the Hisma Basin, plants for fuel are restricted principally to the Wadi Qalkha. While the modern distribution of fuels provides a hint of where the occupants of Tor Faraj would have gathered their fuels, the moister climate would have contributed to a wider availability of fuels and even have supported some woodland near the site within the Jebel Qalkha area. This is evidenced by Rosen's recovery of concentrations of phytoliths of dicotyledon (woody) plants from hearth samples and other areas of the site.

Chert sources within the site territory are limited to two areas. An *in situ* source comes from a cluster of three small hillocks located *ca.* 3 to 5km northeast of Tor Faraj near the ancient Roman/Nabatean site of Humeima. The hillocks represent remnants of Turonian (Amman Silicified) and Cenomanian (Shuieib and Na'ur) limestones that contain nodular and bedded cherts. Non-chert-bearing Cambrian sandstones form the remainder of the site territory. Chert from the Amman Silicified Limestone, referred to in an earlier study as the Humeima source (Henry 1995b:

114-17), is of fine quality for knapping, but occurs in small nodules that are difficult to extract. The small sizes of the nodules (60 to 70-mm maximum dimension) also would have reduced their attractiveness, given the size demands for raw material to be incorporated into a Levantine Mousterian technology. For example, primary elements from Tor Faraj average about 60mm in length and many exceed 100mm. The Cenomanian cherts, also of excellent quality, occur in beds that, once exposed, become brittle with numerous microfractures and break into small chunks.

Another chert source is found in cobbles eroded from the Cretaceous limestones of the Ma'an Plateau and transported downstream in the bed of the Wadi Qalkha, presently situated *ca.* 2km east of the site. The cobbles show a distinctive water-worn or gravel cortex and rarely exceed 50mm maximum dimension.

A comparison of the chert varieties identified within the Tor Faraj assemblage with those recorded in a 1985 field study of the region shows that neither of the two nearby sources, those near Humeima or in the bed of the Wadi Qalkha, were extensively utilized (*ibid.*: 119). Cherts coming from beyond the site territory on the Ma'an Plateau were those most commonly exploited. Of those varieties from the plateau, the rarity of cores and primary elements with gravel cortex points to the chert as having been collected at or near its *in situ* locations and not from the nearby bed of the Wadi Qalkha. Another out-of-territory chert was identified in the study, but rather than coming from the Ma'an Plateau, the source of this distinctive black chert is the flank of the Rift Valley. This Rift Valley chert never accounts for more than 20 percent in the Tor Faraj assemblages.

Seasonality, settlement pattern, and site selection

In a previous study it was proposed that Tor Faraj was occupied during the winter, wet season by Levantine Mousterian groups who followed a strategy of transhumance (Henry 1994, 1995b: 125-7). This strategy is thought to have involved annual, scheduled movements from the Rift Valley to the Ma'an Plateau along connecting drainages. Following this model, groups would have inhabited the highest reaches of their annual territories during the hot, dry season on the plateau and upper piedmont. Winter would have triggered a downslope migration across the lower piedmont and Hisma Basin, ultimately bringing groups to the flank and floor of the Rift. With the onset of the warm season, groups would have moved upslope again for a return migration to the plateau.

Tor Faraj, positioned in the lower piedmont, would have occupied a central position in this proposed settlement model. Most likely, it would have been inhabited during the downslope migration in the early winter and then perhaps again during the upslope migration in late winter to spring. The precise determination of the season of occupation of the site simply cannot be made with the data at hand, but from the evidence available, all indications are that Tor Faraj was occupied during the winter, wet season and perhaps the early spring. Water is not likely to have flowed in the Wadi Aghar beneath the site beyond the wet season, although the bedrock pools may have frequently held water into the early spring. The shelter's exposure to the south is also consistent with a winter occupation. In facing south the natural shape of the shelter allows sunlight to bathe most its floor from morning to late afternoon, while still offering protection from the elements. The most direct evidence for seasonality comes from Rosen's (Chapter 7, this volume) phytolith study. She found among the single-celled phytoliths a small, but consistent proportion of dendritic long-cells derived from the floral parts or seed husks of grasses. From this she concludes that Tor Faraj was probably occupied between February and June, given that these are the months in which grasses flower and produce seeds. The evidence of phytoliths and starch grains, pointing to the consumption of dates and pistachio nuts, is also indicative of a winter occupation, although earlier in the season.

An additional clue to the seasonality of Tor Faraj comes from the apparent exploitation of ostrich eggshells for food and perhaps even for use as water containers. In Africa, ostriches lay their eggs in sand optimally at the end of the dry season just before the coming of the rains (Brown 1982). A caveat to this interpretation, however, has to do with the possibility that at Tor Faraj the ostrich shells were used as water containers and thus carried about (and broken) long after they were collected.

Site selection

In attempting to understand why Middle Paleolithic foragers would have selected Tor Faraj for occupation, we first need to establish the degree to which natural forces played a role in preserving the residuals of their encampments in the shelter. Rock overhangs and shallow cavities are common to the steep cliffs of the Wadi Aghar and other canyons within the Jebel Qalkha. They typically form along the contacts of sandstone formations that experience different rates of weathering. The underlying formation, weathering at a more rapid rate, undercuts the overlying more resistant unit, creating a brow or overhang. At Tor Faraj, blocks falling from the collapse of the brow over time have created a series of natural terrace walls on the bedrock floor of the shelter and these, in turn, have entrapped aeolian sediments along with Mousterian residuals. Most of the rockshelters in the area, however, lack such sediments and generally exhibit bedrock floors. These, of course, rarely contain any archaeological evidence, but almost always hold some indication of a Bedouin presence such as a small hearth, sardine can, or odd plastic sandal. The overhangs also are subject to collapse. From virtually any viewpoint in the Wadi Aghar, for example, one can see many areas where sections of the canyon's walls have given way. These observations suggest that Tor Faraj was probably only one of many sites that were inhabited by Mousterian groups within the canyon. Thus, it seems unlikely that the shelter was particularly special, other than forming in a way that entrapped sediments and archaeological evidence and in resisting collapse for 70,000 years or so.

But what would have attracted Mousterian groups to Tor Faraj other than the obvious protection from the elements? The answer probably lies in a combination of factors. In forming a natural passageway between the Ma'an Plateau and Rift Valley, prehistoric foragers probably used the Wadi Aghar to gain access to the Wadi Aheimir and the Rift Valley below much in the same way as do modern Bedouin herders. If the seasonal interpretations are correct, the wadi also would have provided one of the few, dependable sources of water in the area and this would have been especially so following the rainy season when surface water would have been limited to bedrock pools. Beyond providing water for drinking, the pools would have drawn herd animals from the Hisma Basin into the narrow canyon for easy hunting. Tor Faraj also would have made an ideal base camp from which to launch hunting forays out onto the basin of the western Hisma because of its commanding view and easy access. The bedrock pools and generally more mesic settings around the site in the Wadi Aghar also would have furnished a range of plant foods not generally available in the Hisma. The one important resource that would not have been readily available near the site is chert. But, ironically, through time this may in itself have made the shelter an attractive place for Mousterian foragers to revisit. In knowing that remnants of chert remained from earlier encampments in the shelter, the site would have progressively become a kind of *cultural quarry*. The extensive economizing behaviors that we see within the technological and refitting studies

(Chapters 4 and 6) are certainly consistent with this notion.

Excavation plan, stratigraphy, and chronometry

The shelter, formed at the contact of Salib Arkose (early Cambrian) and Umm Ishrin (early to middle Cambrian) sandstone, is fronted by a narrow terrace that drops away to the bed of the wadi some 22m below. The roof of the shelter extends out 5 to 6m along some 20m of the cliff which, at this point, forms a gentle arc following a general NE-SW orientation (Fig. 3.7). The deepest part of the shelter is at its eastern end where a vertical fissure extends from a bedrock bench, located *ca.* 3m above the shelter's floor (Fig. 3.8). The fissure holds a small solution cavity that may well have initiated the formation of Tor Faraj. Near its western end, soft sediments on the floor give way to bedrock and here a Bedouin storehouse has been constructed (Figs 3.7 and 3.9). In vertical profile the shelter's brow rests *ca.* 13m above the floor and even at the shelter's back wall, its ceiling is still some 10m high.

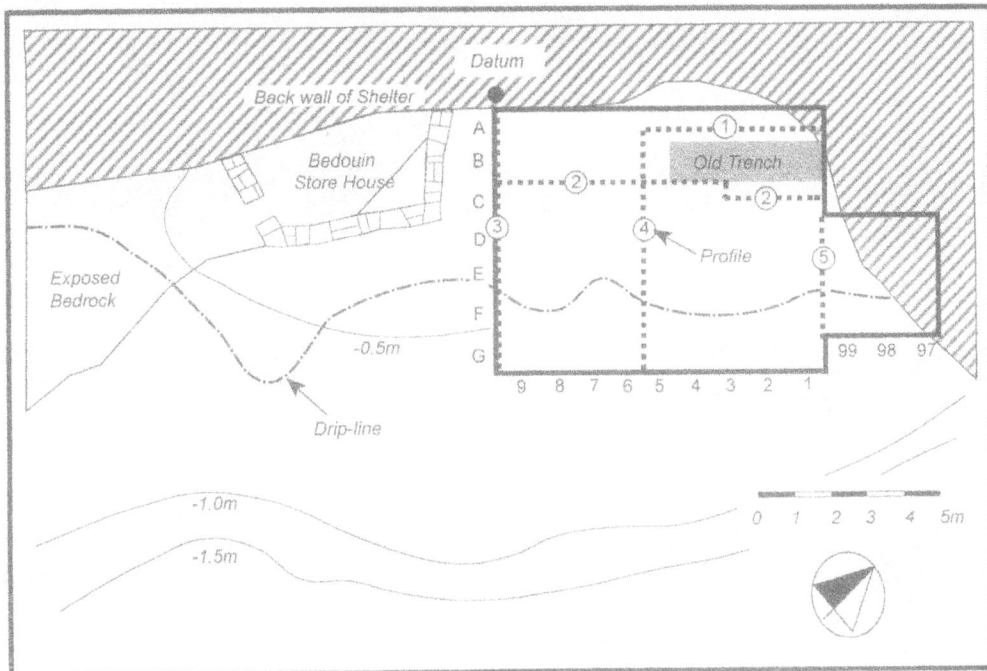

Figure 3.7 Plan of Tor Faraj showing location of excavation block relative to Bedouin storehouse and back wall

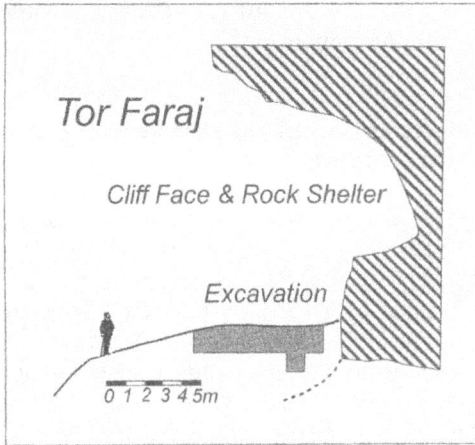

Figure 3.8 Cross-section profile of Tor Faraj showing the location of the excavation block

General stratigraphy

Before about 1977, the stratigraphy of Tor Faraj was reasonably simple, in that the depositional processes mainly had involved successive brow collapses behind which aeolian sediments became entrapped. With the construction of the storehouse and associated leveling of the shelter's floor in 1977 by the Faraj tent-group, the stratigraphy became much more complicated.

Prior to these Bedouin construction activities in the shelter, the floor gently sloped away from the back wall to the terrace (Fig. 3.11a). The surface, at that time, would have displayed a fine, dark gray powdery sediment composed of silty-sand mixed with dung and ash. In approaching the back wall the dung layer thickened. Cultural evidence from this old surface consisted of the remnant of a plastic sandal and a few small, shallow hearths containing partially charred twigs and dung. Chipped stone artifacts, all heavily patinated, were also recovered from this old surface layer. In constructing the stone-walled *gorfu* or storehouse, the floor of the shelter was leveled through the removal of a wedge of sediment (and accumulated dung) that ran along the back wall, extending out about 2m (Fig. 3.11b).

Figure 3.9 A view of the excavation during the 1994 season. Note the dry-stone storehouse beyond the far corner of the excavation block, the large blocks of roof-fall in the SW corner, and the old, 1983–84 trench adjacent to the back wall of the shelter

Figure 3.10 Mr. Faraj Suleiman Jadaylat, for whom the shelter is named

A line of dung-stain and artifacts cemented to the wall clearly defines the extent of the old surface. This excavation appears to have deepened to the west toward the *gorfu* and presumably exposed what is now the bedrock floor of the structure. Units B8-9, C8-9 revealed a portion of the 'ramp' dug to the storehouse, reaching a depth of 80cm below datum on the western edge of the excavation block. A wooden handle of a shovel, presumably used in the construction, was exposed at the contact marking undisturbed sediments. The backdirt from this activity was pitched out on the terrace, leaving four large backdirt piles composed mostly of the bright-red sand of Layer C and high densities of Levantine Mousterian artifacts. Erosion of these piles after *ca.* 1977 then mantled the terrace and shallowly in-filled the area toward the back wall concurrent with the renewed accumulation of dung (Fig. 3.11c).

When I discovered the site in December of 1983, my initial objective was to establish the degree to which it had been disturbed. During work at the site that December and the

following January and July, a 1 × 4m trench was excavated running parallel to the back wall where the wedge of deposit had been removed. The trench was dug in steps with the deepest reaching 1.5m below surface (Henry 1995c: 55). It revealed 20 to 30cm of thinly bedded layers of sand, ash, and dung (Layers A and B) that represented the post-1977 in-filling of the Bedouin diggings. But more importantly the trench exposed a much more compact red silty sand (Layer C) that contained a high density of Levantine Mousterian artifacts. These were unpatinated and displayed very fresh edges. Moreover, an unquestionable hearth (Feature 21) was exposed at a depth of 70cm below the surface.

Excavation plan 1993-94

Work was not resumed at Tor Faraj until 1993/94 when a large block excavation was undertaken. The focus of these two, eight-week seasons of research was on defining intra-site patterns in artifact distributions, but a more detailed understanding of the stratigraphy of the deposit was also a major goal of the work.

When work was started in the summer of 1993, our first task was to remove the Bedouin backdirt piles and overburden. In an effort to maintain some sense of provenience, each of the piles was excavated and screened independently. Once the piles had been removed, a grid was established and the remainder of the overburden from the Bedouin backdirt (5 to 40cm thick) was excavated down to the contact with the pre-1977 surface. The grid, consisting of a 7 × 9m rectangle, was initially excavated in two contiguous blocks (east block Units D1-G5, west block Units B6-G9) concurrent with the cleaning and wall straightening of the old 1983/84 trench in Units B1-B4 (Fig. 3.7). During the second season, the entire grid was excavated in addition to adding *ca.* 5m^2 in the southeastern corner of the shelter (Units D99-F97).

Excavation methods

The grid was established in 1m^2 units that were subdivided into quadrants. The excavation proceeded by quadrant in 5-cm-thick levels unless natural stratigraphic changes were encountered. Wooden ramps and flour

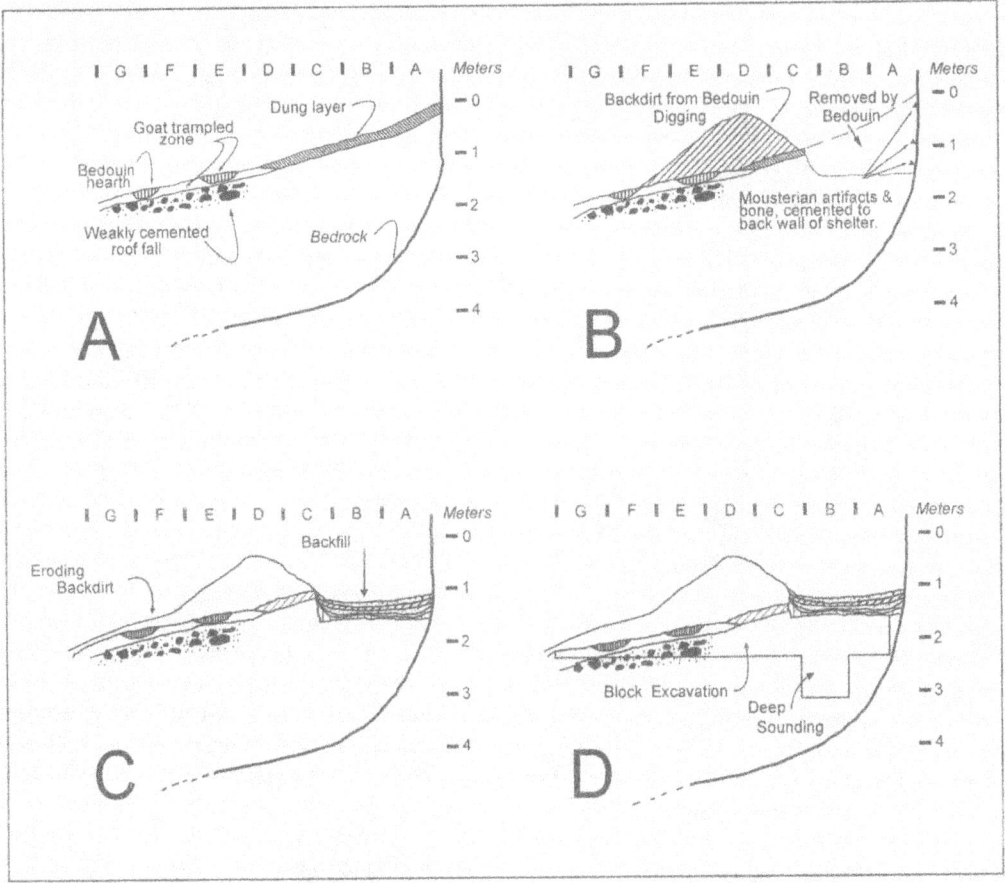

Figure 3.11 The evolution of the Tor Faraj deposit from: (**A**) immediately before the Bedouin leveling activities; (**B**) immediately after the leveling activities; (**C**) the 1983/84 test excavation; and (**D**) the 1993/94 block excavation

sacks filled with screened backdirt were used to support excavators and protect excavation levels once exposed (Figs. 3.12 and 3.13). Artifacts measuring 30mm or greater (long axis) were left in place or 'dropped' in place to the floor of the 5-cm excavation level. Each such artifact was labeled with a discrete number and drawn to scale and orientation on a level record for each $1m^2$ unit. Each of these was also plotted three-dimensionally with a laser theodolite (Sokkia Set 6 Total Station) and given a preliminary field classification (e.g., point, core, flake, blade, other). Features (hearths), large rocks, ostrich eggshell fragments, and bone fragments were similarly recorded on unit level records and with the laser theodolite. Artifacts smaller than a 30-mm-long axis were collected by quadrant.

The perimeter of the excavation block was outlined with a wooden frame secured to vertically imbedded metal rods. The frame was then covered with one to two courses of sand-filled bags. Beyond stabilizing and protecting the walls of the excavation, the procedure created a level perimeter for entering and exiting the excavation block. The wooden frames also provided permanent surfaces on which to place clearly visible coordinate markers. The excavation was conducted with trowels, micropicks, and bent screwdrivers. All of the matrix was dry-screened through 2-mm wire mesh. Sandbags and 0.5m × 2m wooden palettes were used to elevate excavators above the grid and protect the excavated surfaces. In general, an entire level was excavated for the east or west block before beginning the other. This practice allowed for artifacts to be left in place over large areas and to be recorded with

Figure 3.12 A view of the excavation from the north, out of the alcove. Note the use of wooden ramps and sandbags to protect the excavated surfaces from trampling

Figure 3.13 The eastern part of the excavation viewed from the back of the shelter. Note the large manuports of tabular sandstone in the foreground. These are thought to have been used as 'tables' for food processing

Figure 3.14 Stratigraphy of Unit A3 south face. Note the hearth and ash-lines and their horizontal bedding

the laser theodolyte without the interference of excavators.

Detailed stratigraphy

Tor Faraj, resting at the contact of two sandstones, formed as a result of the more rapid rate of weathering of the underlying unit (Salib Arkose). This undercut created structural weaknesses and attendant small solution cavities in the overlying, more resistant Umm Ishrin sandstone and led to the occasional collapse of the leading edge of the overhang. Thus, the evolution of Tor Faraj followed that typically described for rockshelters formed in a retreating face of a cliff (Laville *et al.* 1980; Waters 1992: 246). What is so important about the formation of Tor Faraj is that it not only entrapped predominantly aeolian sediments, it did so in a manner as to create nearly level bedding planes (Fig. 3.14).

Near the end of the 1993 season an effort was made to plot the configuration of the

bedrock floor of the shelter by driving a small diameter level rod through the soft sediments of the shelter to bedrock. These probes show the shelter's bedrock floor to fall away steeply from the back wall out for about 5m at which point it levels out, or perhaps even rises slightly, over the distance of another 5m before falling away steeply to the bottom of the wadi (Fig. 3.8). Running perpendicular to this line and roughly parallel to the back wall of the shelter, the bedrock falls away steeply toward the center of the shelter. The topography of the bedrock floor of the shelter is consistent with the expected evolution of the floor during the progressive retreat of the cliff face (Fig. 3.6). The presence of a shelf just beyond the modern dripline indicates that this portion of the floor would have been subject to weathering and therefore exposed for some period of time prior to the accumulation of sediments in the shelter. The creation of the shelf also would have encouraged the build-up of rock-fall from the retreating brow of the shelter. This rock-fall would then have formed a natural wall behind which sediments would have been entrapped. This succession of brow collapse, rock-fall build-up, and sediment accumulation produced the continued in-filling of the shelter (Fig. 3.15).

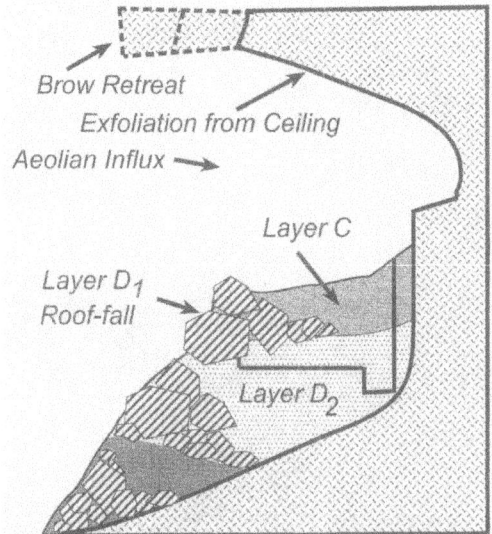

Figure 3.15 Schematic cross-section of the Tor Faraj deposit showing successive brow collapse and in-filling episodes

The excavation revealed six stratigraphic layers within a 165-cm-thick deposit (Table 3.1). The overall maximum thickness of the deposit is estimated to be some 3.5 to 4m. Layers A and B, some 20 to 35cm thick, represent natural and anthropogenic (dung and ash) sediments that accumulated following the Bedouin leveling activities. Most of the excavation occurred within Layer C, but Layer D_1 rock-fall was found to protrude through and rest beneath Layer C sand in the SW corner of the grid. This cemented rock-fall layer was found to overlie another sand, Layer D_2, around the periphery of the cemented rock-fall at *ca.* 180cm below datum. The Layer D_2 sand differs only slightly from Layer C, but appears finer and redder. In the deep sounding dug in Unit B2, Layer E was encountered. This consisted of a red sand, but much more heavily cemented than that of Layer D_2. The contacts between layers C, D_2, and E are diffuse and gradational. Levantine Mousterian artifacts were recovered throughout the deposit.

The stratigraphy of the deposit indicates a series of brow collapses that formed rock-falls behind which sediments were entrapped, but the excavation only really exposed one of these brow collapses as represented by the D_1 rock-fall. It rests on what was a sand-filled floor (Layer D_2) at the time when the brow retreated. This rock-fall created a new sediment trap that accumulated windborne sands and material exfoliated from the ceiling of the shelter forming Layer C. Interestingly, artifacts recovered from the sands of Layer C and Layer D_2 are rarely patinated and almost always resting flat, whereas those excavated from the D_1 rock-fall are almost always patinated and were typically resting on edge or end. This suggests that the rock-fall remained unburied for some time, thus allowing artifacts to find their way into crevices between rocks and remain exposed to the atmosphere. In contrast, those artifacts discarded behind the rock-fall on the aggrading sandy floor of the shelter typically would have assumed nearly level planes and experienced relatively rapid burial.

Given that the major objective of the research centered on the definition of horizontal spatial patterns of artifacts, features, and related evidence, a critical stratigraphic question concerned the identification of bedding planes. While the initial work at Tor Faraj clearly showed bedding planes to run nearly horizontally, this work was confined to a small area near the back wall of the shelter (Henry 1995c). The question remained as to whether

Table 3.1 Description of stratigraphy of deposit at Tor Faraj. Munsell readings are on dry sediment

Layer	Description
A	Loose, light-red (2.5YR6/6) silty sand with lenses of sand and organics, decomposed dung; 2–35cm thick; contains sparse Levantine Mousterian artifacts; sharp boundary with Layer B
B	Friable, red (2.5YR5/6) silty sand; ash, burnt twigs and dung, finely bedded pockets, and clay laminae; 3–20cm thick; contains sparse Levantine Mousterian artifacts; sharp boundary with Layer C
C	Coherent, reddish-yellow (5YR6/6) medium quartz sand, very-fine, fine, to coarse sand, subangular to subrounded, silty, occasional granule, strongly clacareous, sandstone rock fragments; 30–75cm thick; contains abundant Levantine Mousterian artifacts, hearths; sharp boundary with rock-rubble Layer D_1, gradational boundary with sand of Layer D_2
D_1	Partially cemented weathered sandstone rubble containing fist- to boulder-sized clasts; 10–35cm thick; contains abundant Levantine Mousterian artifacts; sharp boundary with Layer D_2
D_2	Coherent, light red to red (2.5YR6-5/6) medium quartz sand, very-fine, fine, to coarse sand, subangular, moderately sorted, silty, finer texture than Layer C, carbonate cemented root casts 1mm diameter; 30–75cm thick; contains abundant Levantine Mousterian artifacts, hearths; sharp boundary with rock-rubble Layer D_1, gradational boundary with sand of Layer D_2
E	Reddish-yellow (5YR6/6) silt and very-fine quartz sand, subrounded, moderately sorted, strongly calcareous, granule-sized fragments of carbonate cemented sand, sandstone rock fragments, +45cm thick; contains numerous Levantine Mousterian artifacts

or not the remainder of the shelter's deposit was similarly bedded. In that the contacts between Layers C, D_2, and E are gradational, they offer little help in tracing bedding planes over an extensive area. Indirectly, however, the diffuse contacts between layers does indicate that while each of the sedimentary pulses responsible for the layers may have differed somewhat environmentally, there apparently was no prolonged period of interruption in sedimentation. In short, during this interval of the Late Levantine Mousterian, the fills entrapped behind the rock-fall were deposited continually and relatively rapidly.

Although bedding planes could not be traced between layers, the numerous lenses or laminae within Layers C and D_2 allowed for the estimation of bedding planes. Ash lenses from the numerous hearths in the shelter assist in tracing paleosurfaces as do laminae from decomposed sandstone tablets fallen from the ceiling of the shelter and laminae from carbonate precipitates. When examined along a line parallel to the back wall, hearths, ash lenses, and carbonate laminae show that

the layers (at least as revealed by exposures of C and D_2) were nearly level or slightly (1 to 3 percent) inclined to the W (Profiles 1 and 2, Figs. 3.7 and 3.16). Similar evidence indicates that these layers were inclined some 2 to 5 percent to the S (i.e., from the back wall to the terrace), although the gradient seems to have been steepest near the back wall, becoming nearly level toward the terrace (Profiles 3, 4, and 5, Figs. 3.17 and 3.18).

Nineteen hearths were recorded in Layers C and D_2 (Table 3.2). One of these (Feature 21) was recorded in the 1983/84 sounding. Initial field designations included 21 hearths, but subsequent evaluation grouped two sets of hearths (features 10 and 13, 16 and 17) that are thought to represent a hearth and an adjacent hearth cleaning or extension.

Sedimentary analysis of layers C, D_2, and E shows subtle, yet perhaps significant changes within the stratigraphic succession. With depth, sediments become finer with greater rubification and carbonate cementation. In general, these attributes would indicate greater available moisture with depth. This trend is

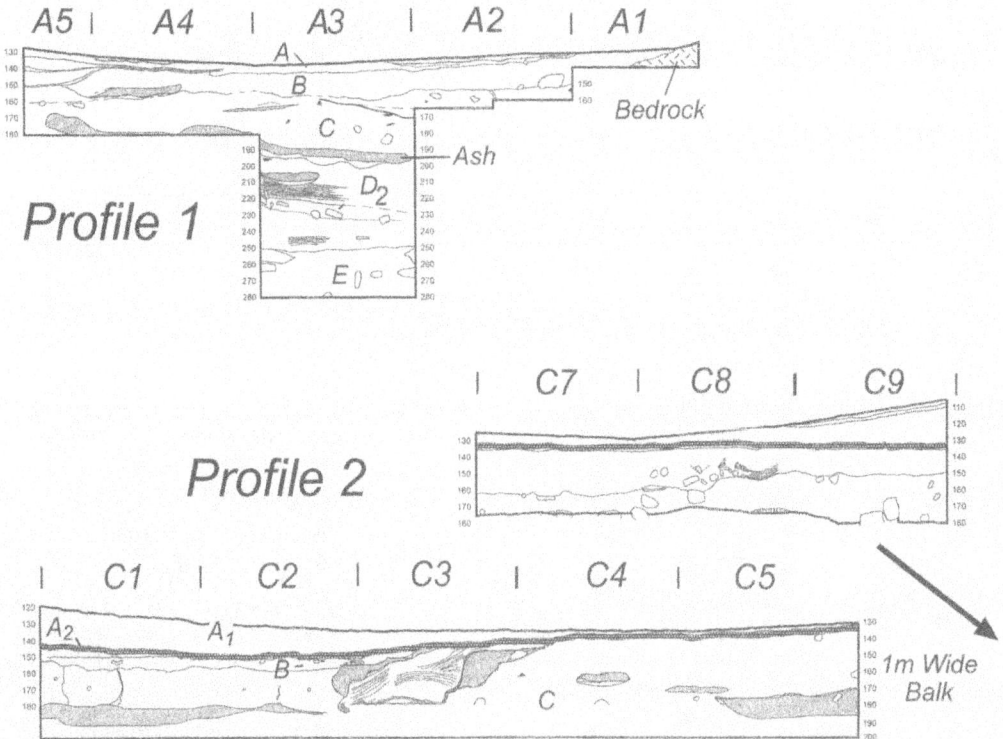

Figure 3.16   Stratigraphic Profile 1 (south face) and Profile 2 (north face). See Figure 3.7 for location within the Tor Faraj excavation plan

Profile 3

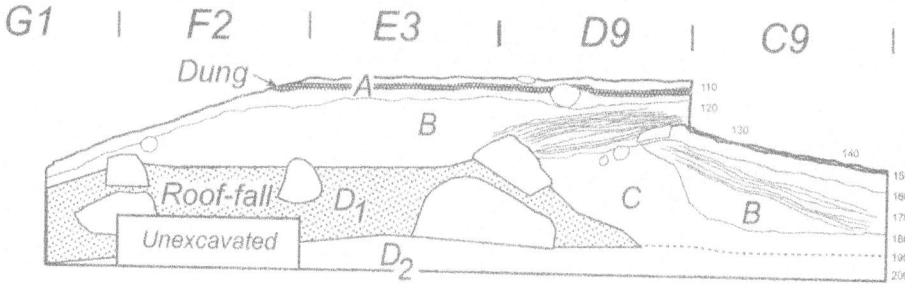

Profile 4

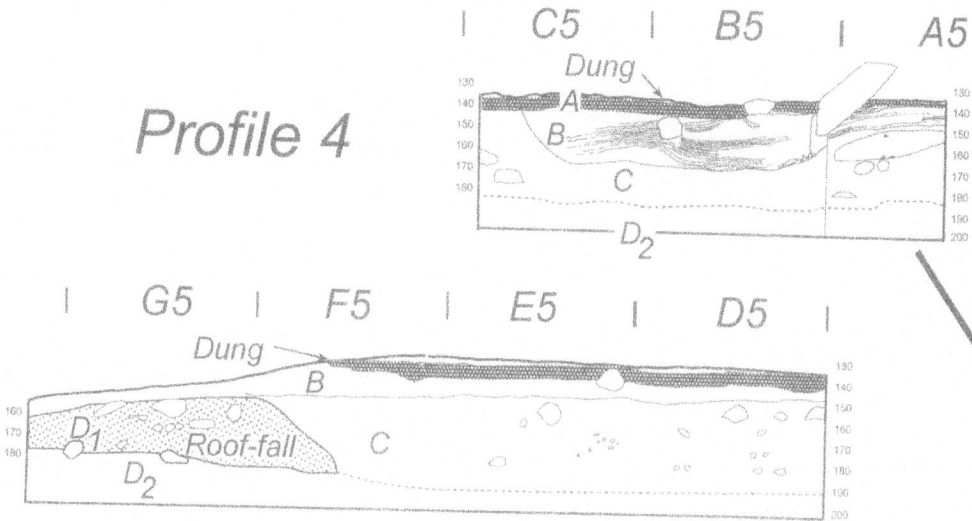

Figure 3.17 Stratigraphic Profile 3 (east face) and Profile 4 (east face). See Figure 3.7 for location within the Tor Faraj excavation plan

Profile 5

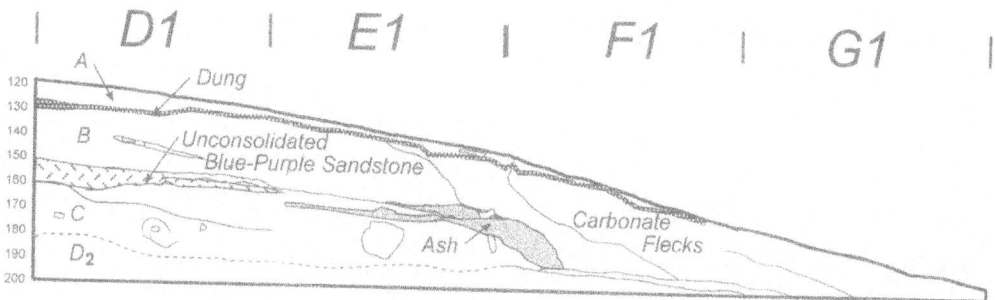

Figure 3.18 Stratigraphic Profile 5 (west face). See Figure 3.7 for location within the Tor Faraj excavation plan

Table 3.2 Locations and descriptions of hearth features. Features originally designated Numbers 16 and 17 were combined with Features 10 and 13, respectively, after review. Feature 21 was recorded in 1983-84

Feature number and floor	Unit/Level	Maximum thickness	Comments
1-II	C2b–C1a/185	6	Light gray ash
2-I	A3c–d/170	9	Dark gray ash, cemented sand
3-I	A4c–A5d/170	2	Dark gray ash, non-burnt artifacts
4-II	C5b, c–d/180–5	3	Dark brown-gray mottled ash
5-II	A4c/180	5	Gray ash, soft sand
6-I	C4c–C5d/170	5	Gray ash, compact sand, carbonate
7-I	C4d/165	?	Carbonate Layer
8-I	E1a, b/175	3	Dark gray ash, loose-compact red sand
9-II	A3a/180	5	Gray ash, loose sand
10-II	B9d/B8c/190	?	Light brown ash, loose red sand
11-II	A4d/A3c/190	?	Gray ash, mottled, burnt rock and artifacts
12-II	A3b/190	4	Dark gray ash, red sand
13-II	C9d-C8c/190	?	Light brown ash, reddish sand
14-II	C3b/195	?	Gray ash, fine sand
15-II	C3a–b–C4b/195	5	Gray ash/reddish fine silty sand
18-II	C1d/200	?	Gray ash/firm sand
19-II	A5b/185–90	?	Gray ash, charcoal, burnt chert
20-II	D99c/180	?	Gray ash, red compact sand
21-I	B1–B2/170	4	Dark gray ash, burnt red sand (1983–84)

consistent with the age of the deposit (49 to 69Kb.p) and the notion that moister conditions dominated the interval immediately preceding the accumulation of Q3 sands locally and the Late Levantine Mousterian regionally. Bar-Yosef (1989), for example, suggests that the moist interval associated with the Early Levantine Mousterian stretched from Oxygen Isotope Stage 5d/e to 5a (118/115 to 73KA), followed by colder and drier conditions during Stage 4 (73 to 61KA).

Chronometry

The chronometry (Table 3.3) of the deposit, extending from 49 to 69Kb.p, comes from three lines of analysis: amino-acid racemiza-tion (Henry and Miller 1992), uranium series (McKinney, personal communication, in Henry 1995c), and thermoluminescence (Valladas, personal communication, 1990). Given the overlap in the stratigraphic locations of the dated materials and the geologic indications of a relatively rapid, uninterrupted accumulation of sediments in the shelter, it is unlikely that the dates accurately define the length of time it took the deposit to form. Instead, it seems more likely that the dates simply define a bracket of time which has a duration that is largely a factor of the imprecision of the dating techniques. When compared to the chronometries of other Late Levantine Mousterian (B-type) deposits, the chronometry of Tor Faraj shows remarkable similarities (Table 3.4).

Table 3.3 The chronometry of the Tor Faraj deposit. TL-thermoluminescence (Henry 1998b), AAR–amino acid racemization (Henry and Miller 1992), U-series–uranium series (McKinney, personal communication; Henry 1995c)

Layer/Provenience	Material	Technique	Age (KBP)
Layer C	Burnt chert	TL	43.8 ± 2
Layer C	Burnt chert	TL	47.5 ± 3
Layer C	Burnt chert	TL	52.8 ± 3
Layer C	Ostrich eggshell	AAR	69.0 ± 6
Layer C (backdirt)	Ostrich eggshell	U-series	62.4 ± 14
Layer C	Ostrich eggshell	U-series	28.9 ± 3.9

Table 3.4 Comparison of chronometries for Late Levantine Mousterian sites

	Tor Faraj[1]	Tor Sabiha[2]	Kebara[3]	Amud[4]	Quneitra[5]
Age range (KY)	43.8–69.0	69.0	48.3–64.3	44.1–75.9	39.2–53.9
N of dates	5	1	9	19	2
Techniques	TL, AAR, U	AAR	TL, ESR	TL	ESR

[1,2]Henry and Miller 1992; Henry 1995c; [3]Valladas *et al.* 1998; Schwarcz *et al.* 1989; [4]Valladas *et al.* 1998; [5]Ziaei *et al.* 1990

Conclusion

Tor Faraj is located in a topographically and environmentally diverse region of southern Jordan. Situated in the lower steppe zone, the shelter rests roughly midway between the Mediterranean wooded uplands of the Ma'an Plateau and the desert zones of the Hisma Basin and Rift Valley. Paleoenvironmental evidence points to the site having been occupied under cooler and moister conditions than persist today, yet still within a steppic environment. Seasonal data indicate cold, wet season occupations of the shelter. These were likely tied to times when Levantine Mousterian groups used the Wadi Aghar, a natural passageway connecting the plateau to the Rift, in their seasonal migrations tied to transhumance.

The shelter appears to have followed a typical evolution in its formation. This involved differential weathering and creation of an undercut in stratified sandstone bedrock, episodic weakening and collapse of the overhang, and entrapment of predominantly windborne sediments behind the rock-fall. The stratigraphy revealed in the upper part of the 3.5- to 4-m-deep deposit shows no evidence of an interruption of sedimentation. Four strata associated with the Levantine Mousterian occupation were identified. These include three layers of aeolian sand (C, D_2, and E) and a layer of rock-fall (D_1). Subtle changes in grain size, color, and degree of carbonate cementation suggest that sedimentation occurred under increasingly moister conditions with depth. A suite of chronometric determinations (AAR, U-series, TL) brackets Layer C of the deposit to 49 to 69KA. This age range is consistent with the chronometries of other Late Levantine Mousterian (B-type) occupations.

4 Human Behavior and the Stone Tools from Tor Faraj

DONALD O. HENRY

The artifact inventory derived from the pre-historic occupations of Tor Faraj consists almost entirely of chipped stone specimens belonging to the Levantine Mousterian Complex. Several reports have been published on the assemblages of Tor Faraj. These focused on the material recovered from the initial test excavation of the site (Henry 1988, 1992, 1995b, 1995c) and the preliminary findings of the renewed investigations under-taken in 1994 and 1995 (Henry 1998a; Henry et al. 1996). The report presented here builds upon previous descriptions of the assemblages in several ways. It (1) enlarges and spatially expands the artifact sample; (2) provides a more comprehensive view of the technological reduction stream; (3) specifically examines the technical role of truncated faceted specimens; and (4) reassesses the taxonomic placement of the assemblage within the Levantine Mousterian Complex. And beyond the tech-notypologic study presented here, studies devoted to small debris analysis (see Chapter 5), refitting (see Chapter 6), and microscopic wear and polish (see Chapter 8) of the lithic artifacts from Tor Faraj are described later.

Earlier technotypologic descriptions of the Tor Faraj assemblages were based upon materials recovered from Layer C in the 1983/84 test excavation (Henry 1995c). These included stratified assemblages from 'Lower C, Mid C, Upper C and Top C.' Of these, only the 'Top C' assemblage yielded a sample of adequate size (200 tool specimens and 1168 total artifacts) for statistical analysis.

Unfortunately, the Top C assemblage was recovered from the Bedouin backdirt piles. Although the assemblage's general strati-graphic position and even horizontal location could be determined, it was not recovered in primary context. Beyond enlarging the in situ samples from Layer C, the recent excavation of Tor Faraj expanded the scope of artifact recovery both stratigraphically and spatially. In addition to materials from Layer C, the underlying strata of the D_1 rock-fall and D_2 sand yielded sizeable assemblages, numbering over 13,000 artifacts. And whereas the earlier test excavation encompassed only 4m^2, the 1994-95 investigation involved a block exca-vation of 67m^2. These questions of sampling within a site are especially important when considering local and regional inter-site com-parative studies. Small and spatially restricted investigations at sites with substantial internal spatial variability in artifacts, such as Tor Faraj, have the potential of confusing attempts to detect region-wide artifact patterns (Henry et al. 1996). Therefore, the quantitative profiles of data from the large block excavation of Tor Faraj should prove more useful in regional comparisons than those data from the earlier test excavations.

Although certain technotypologic features (e.g., high frequencies of cores and primary elements; point to primary element dimen-sions) identified in the initial analysis of the assemblages allowed for tracing the reduction stream in some detail (Henry 1992, 1995b, 1995c), the much larger artifact samples obtained from the recent excavation have contributed to an even more refined understanding of the *chaîne opératoire* followed by the occupants of Tor Faraj. Moreover, relative to understanding the technological processes associated with the Tor Faraj assemblages, this new research benefited immensely from the refitting study undertaken by Demidenko and Usik (see Chapter 6). In particular, their work helps to clarify the role of Nahr Ibrahim retouch or truncated faceted specimens as resulting largely from the use of flakes as cores in an effort to maximize the productivity of chert at the site.

In the summary report (Henry 1995b, 1995c) of the earlier work at Tor Faraj, I viewed the assemblages as a late representative of the D-type Industry of the Levantine Mousterian largely because of the high proportions of blades and points and the significant amount of bidirectional preparation for removals. Although the typological similarities of the broad-based Levallois points from Tor Faraj and other B-type Industry sites (e.g., Kebara) were noted, it was thought that these might simply represent a horizon marker derived from late Levantine Mousterian B-type groups inhabiting the Mediterranean woodlands. In short, I gave greater weight to the technological differences than the typological similarities in classifying the Tor Faraj assemblages.

Subsequently, it has become apparent that the production of blades is technically tied to the preparation of cores for point removals. Moreover, the production of points appears to have been environmentally linked, probably because of a greater emphasis on hunting (Henry 1995b; Shea 1998). Those sites in the arid zone show a much higher proportion of points, regardless of taxonomic affiliation. Also, the technological and refitting analyses of the Tor Faraj assemblages (Henry *et al.* 1996; Demidenko and Usik, Chapter 6 this volume) show that bidirectionality in core preparation is related to attempts to extend the productive lives of cores, especially cores on flakes. Therefore, as in the cases of blade and point proportions, bidirectional preparation does not appear to be a very useful guide to chronological or taxonomic placement of an assemblage. Given these considerations, I now view the Tor Faraj assemblages as belonging to the B-type Industry, although

with significantly higher point and blade proportions than typically described for the industry (Henry 1998b).

Technological overview

Stone tool production at Tor Faraj centered on the manufacturing of broad-based, triangular Levallois points. These were struck from cores that predominantly had been unidirectionally prepared in the formation of convergent ridges to guide point removals. An important feature of the technology was the deliberate selection of ovate chert nodules for point production. The natural shape of the nodules, especially their convex faces, enabled Mousterian knappers to initiate the delivery of a point after only minor initial preparation. This often involved striking off no more than 4 to 5 preparatory flakes (Demidenko and Usik, Chapter 6 this volume).

Beyond the ease and efficiency by which point production could be initiated, the refit study also showed that subsequent point removals from the same core required only minor rejuvenation of platforms and flaking surfaces. For example, one of the refitted constellations traced six point removals. Although some scholars have argued that a Levallois technology is inherently wasteful, this was not the case at Tor Faraj. In part, the general efficiency of lithic reduction procedures undertaken at the shelter were driven by the paucity of knappable chert in the area (Henry 1992, 1995b, 1995c). This required the occupants of the site to import ovate chert nodules from outcrops on the Ma'an Plateau some 22km distant and some 500 to 600m higher than the site. But the natural convexity of the nodules reduced incentives for trimming and forming rough cores at the outcrops. The relatively high proportions of primary elements and cores within the Tor Faraj assemblages can thus be explained even though the site is distant from raw material. This initially presented a puzzling phenomenon, for assemblages distant from raw material sources generally show little evidence for primary reduction (e.g., decortification and initial core shaping).

Another aspect of the technology's efficiency is related to the useful by-products that were generated in the production of points.

Converging and often elongated edge elements were struck off to form the classic Y-arrete scar pattern that guided the removals of points. These often were of blade or, at least, elongated flake proportions and the initial removals were partially covered with cortex (Bordes' naturally backed knives). And because of the converging pattern developed on core faces, these preparatory removals typically display pointed terminations. Thus given these attributes, it is not surprising that these 'by-products' were often employed as tools as evidenced by the results of Shea's (1995) wear pattern analysis. The points themselves were also remarkably efficient tools for two reasons: multiplicity of uses and durability. As shown in edge-wear studies (Lee 1987; Shea 1995), points were principally used for tipping spears, but they also served a wide range of other functions such as those related to butchery, scraping, and even working wood. Levallois points at Tor Faraj, as elsewhere, also appear to have been remarkably durable as evidenced by the small proportions of broken points. Whether this durability was a consequence of the design of the points or the manner in which they were hafted (Henry 1995b) is difficult to determine, but it nevertheless would have been an important aspect of a technological system employed in the chert-poor area around Tor Faraj.

Another important feature of the lithic technology of Tor Faraj relates to the use of cores on flakes. Although proportionately much less common than point production from cores formed from chert nodules, the practice of using thick flakes to form cores for Levallois point production is another clear indicator of the overall efficiency of the technology. The ability of the knappers at Tor Faraj to squeeze another small point or so from cores fashioned on flakes has several ramifications. First, it provides additional support to the notion that Nahr Ibrahim retouch is principally tied to core preparation (Solecki and Solecki 1970; Goren-Inbar 1988). It also shows that the very small points were, in fact, intentional final removals and not misstrikes or preparatory removals. The production of small points from cores on flakes using a different method, but achieving points with similar proportions as those produced from nodular cores, also underscores the technological flexibility of the knappers at Tor Faraj.

Description of the assemblages

The assemblages that have undergone detailed technotypologic attribute analysis and are reported upon here come principally from Floor I (160 to 170cm BD) and Floor II (180 to 195cm BD). Less intensive analysis was conducted on the intervening horizon represented by Level 175cm BD, the underlying Level 200cm BD, and the $1m^2$ deep sounding that reached 230cm BD. These assemblages are only briefly discussed.

Table 4.1 shows how the arbitrary levels and natural stratigraphy, as described in the 1995 report (Henry 1995c: 53-4), correlate with the new level designations and stratigraphy of Tor Faraj as now understood. Floor I largely corresponds to the 'old' Upper Layer C designation and Floor II correlates with the upper part of what was previously described as Middle Layer C. While Floor I does fall in Layer C (the lower part), Floor II is now known to actually rest within a different natural stratigraphic unit, Layer D_2. The difference between the arbitrary levels of the earlier 1983/84 sounding and the 1994/95 excavation results from re-establishing the datum. The datum was repositioned (+150cm) in the recent work to facilitate referencing the laser theodolyte each day during excavation.

Table 4.1 The correlation of natural layers and excavation levels observed in the 1995 report (Henry 1995c: 52-5) and the current study

1995		1999
Layer	Below datum (cm)	Layer below datum (cm)
Top C	Bedouin backdirt	
Upper C	10-30	Floor I, Layer C, 160-70
Middle C	30-70	Floor II, Layer D_2, 180-95

Technology

The lithic technology at Tor Faraj is reconstructed through a comparison of various data sets associated with raw material usage, traditional technological indices, debitage frequencies, and technical attributes linked to loading and reduction stages. When interwoven, these data furnish a means of better understanding how occupations, such as at Tor Faraj, fit into areal settlement-procurement strategies (Henry 1995a, 1995b). And at a finer scale, such data-sets also can be employed to define intra-site variation.

Raw material

Following a field-based classification of cherts, described in an earlier study (Henry 1995b: 114-19), seven chert varieties and a 'catchall category' were recognized for the assemblages (Table 4.2). These come primarily (81 to 82 percent) from the Cretaceous limestone (Amman Silicified Limestone) exposed on the Ma'an Plateau. Another distant chert is represented in the assemblages by a black variety found along the flanks of the Rift Valley (most likely derived from the Eocene Um Rijam Chert Limestone), but this source accounts for only about 5 percent of the utilized cherts. A nearby chert coming from a small remnant of Amman Silicified Limestone was also used although not as extensively as might be expected given its proximity to the site. The source, located on a hillock near the Nabatean town site of Humeima, consists of small nodules that are difficult to remove from the limestone. This may explain why the source accounts for only 5 to 10 percent of the utilized cherts in the assemblages. The

Table 4.2 Utilization of different chert varieties by floor at Tor Faraj

Chert variety - source	Floor I	Floor II
Ma'an Plateau - 1	18.5	25.7
Ma'an Plateau - 2	12.9	9.3
Ma'an Plateau - 3	40.3	34.4
Ma'an Plateau - 4	6.6	7.1
Ma'an Plateau - 5	3.9	4.2
Rift Valley	5.3	4.8
Humeima	7.3	10.2
Catchall variety	5.3	4.3
Total	100.0	100.0

'catchall variety,' accounting for 4 to 5 percent of utilized cherts, includes those cherts within the artifact assemblages that could not be identified as to a specific source. Given the distribution of chert bearing limestones in the area, it is likely that most of this variety comes from the Ma'an Plateau, but from unidentified sources other than the five that were most commonly exploited. Comparison of the chert utilization between Floors I and II fails to show a significant difference.

Technological indices

Comparisons of blade (Ilam), faceting (IF), and Levallois (IL) indices show little variation between floors (Table 4.3). And, with exception to the IF values, the indices for Floors I and II closely resemble those computed in the earlier study for Top Layer C of the shelter (Henry 1995c: 60).

Table 4.3 Technological indices for Tor Faraj

Indices	Floor I	Floor II	Top C
IL	17.9	14.9	13.8
IF	42	60.5	46.5
ILAME[a]	25.9	22.4	36.4

[a]Limited to complete specimens and inclusive of unretouched Levallois points

The Levallois indices are relatively low for Levantine Mousterian assemblages and especially so it seems for sheltered sites (Hovers 1997: 234). However, the low Levallois indices at Tor Faraj are somewhat deceiving in that technological, typological, and refitting studies are all consistent in showing Levallois point production to have dominated lithic processing at the site. The low Levallois indices may well be a consequence of flakes, which compose almost half of the debitage, not being a central element in point production and thus less often exhibiting the characteristics of Levallois products. Another important factor affecting Levallois indices is the variability in which Levallois products are recognized by different lithic analysts (Bar-Yosef and Dibble 1995: 93). Whereas the recognition of Levallois points is relatively straightforward, the classification of Levallois flakes and blades is more problematic. In this study, a Levallois product was identified on the basis of a combination of characteristics that included a multi-faceted platform, a convex lateral profile, and a converging or centripedal dorsal scar pattern. Given the focus on point production at Tor Faraj, *chapeau de gendarme* butts also were commonly used to define Levallois products.

The high-faceting indices underscore the importance that the knappers in the shelter placed upon carefully preparing striking platforms. Platforms were heavily faceted regardless of their sizes or the accompanying dorsal scar patterns (i.e., Levallois or not). Blade indices for the assemblages are high and again this is thought to be directly linked to the

importance of elongated preparatory removals in Levallois point production.

Debitage proportions and characteristics

The relative proportions of different debitage classes vary little between Floors I and II (Table 4.4), thus suggesting that a similar range of lithic processing activities was undertaken in the two occupations.

Cores

Cores, accounting for only a small part of the debitage, are principally represented by orthogonal and opposed platform and amorphous-indeterminate varieties (66.1 percent). Levallois cores make up the rest. Of these,

Table 4.4 The distribution of artifact classes for Floor I and Floor II assemblages of Tor Faraj. Tables based on laboratory identification and field provenience

Artifact classes	Floors combined		Floor I		Floor II	
	Number	Percentage	Number	Percentage	Number	Percentage
Tools						
Levallois point – ret.	23	5.41	7	4.22	16	6.18
Levallois point – unret.	77	18.12	43	25.90	34	13.13
Side-scraper	13	3.06	4	2.41	9	3.47
End-scraper	5	1.18	3	1.81	2	0.77
Burin	54	12.71	18	10.84	36	13.90
Truncated piece	5	1.18	2	1.20	3	1.16
Notch	31	7.29	6	3.61	25	9.65
Denticulate	10	2.35	3	1.81	7	2.70
Retouched piece	194	45.65	74	44.58	120	46.33
Varia	13	3.06	6	3.61	7	2.70
Subtotal	425	100.00	166	100.00	259	100.00
Debitage						
Core	59	2.18	32	3.03	27	1.64
Primary element	320	11.85	119	11.26	201	12.23
Core trimming element	76	2.81	38	3.60	38	2.31
Blade	508	18.81	213	20.15	295	17.94
Flake	1307	48.39	488	46.17	819	49.82
Levallois flake	236	8.74	96	9.08	140	8.52
Levallois blade	78	2.89	32	3.03	46	2.80
Burin spall	36	1.33	12	1.14	24	1.46
Truncated-faceted pc.	81	3.00	27	2.55	54	3.28
Subtotal	2701	100.00	1057	100.00	1644	100.00
Debris						
Chips	9302	91.56	3531	87.57	5771	94.17
Chunks	858	8.44	501	12.43	357	5.83
Subtotal	10160	100.00	4032	100.00	6128	100.00
Grand total	13286		5255		8031	

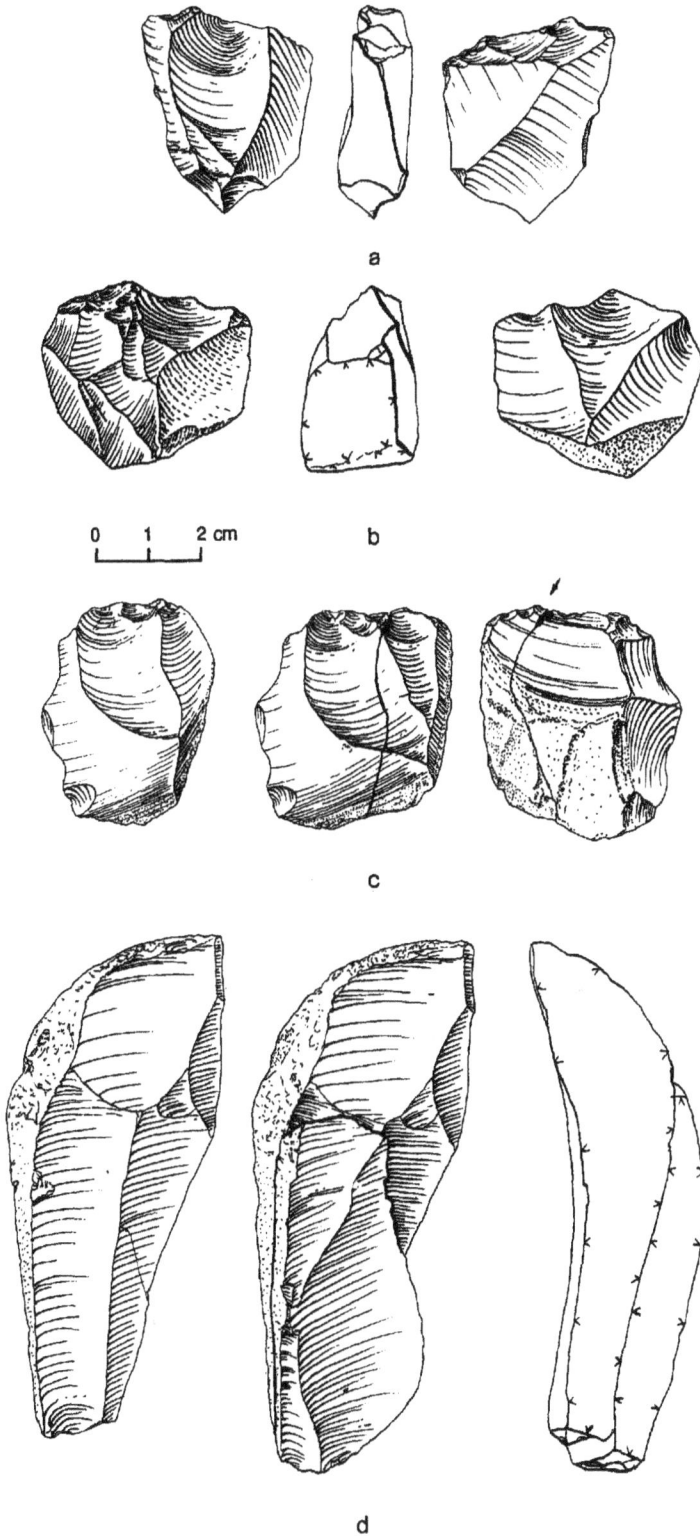

Figure 4.1 Illustrations of cores and refitted artifacts from Tor Faraj: **a** and **b**, small Levallois point cores; **c**, refitted core on flake; **d**, refitted edge element

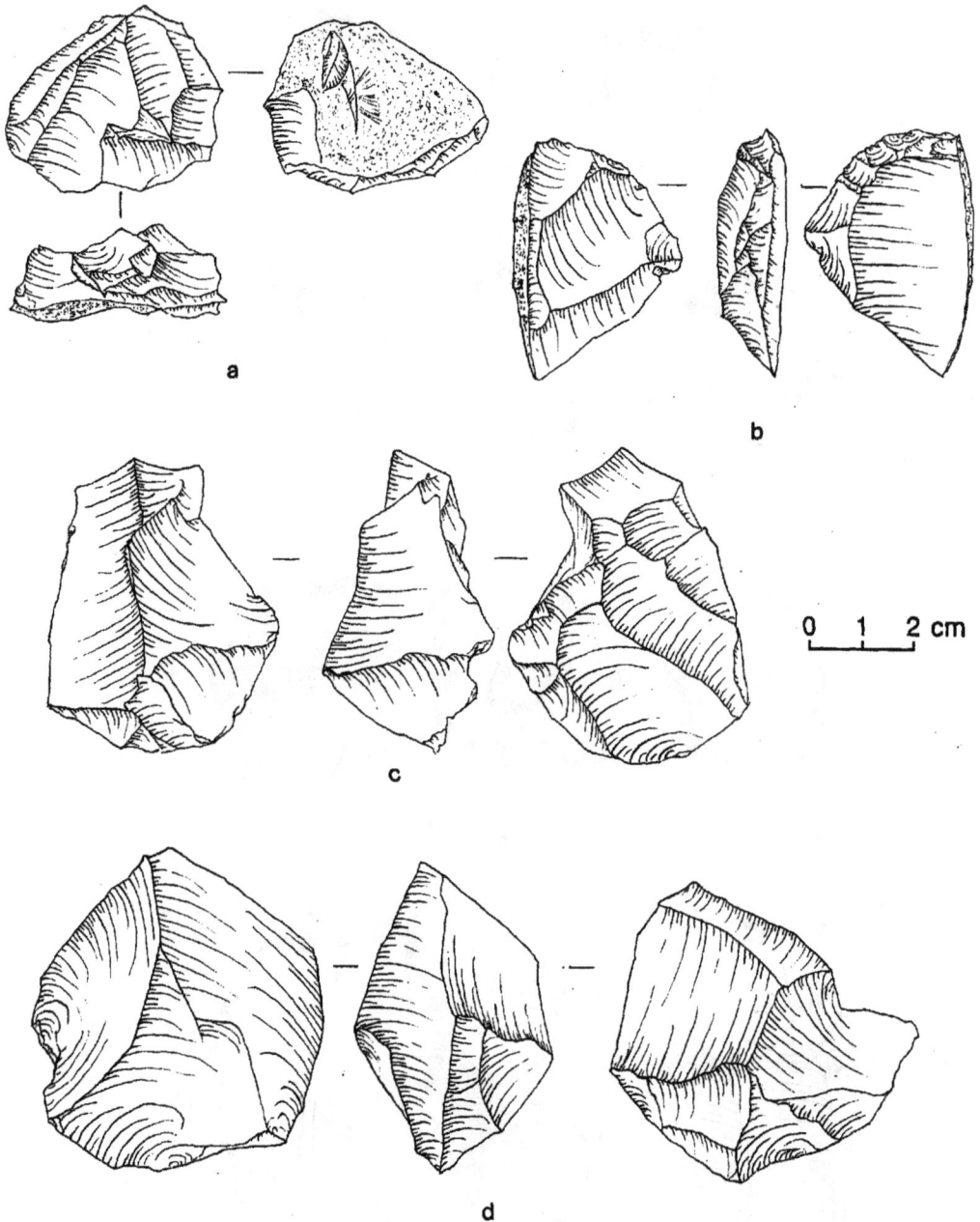

Figure 4.2 Illustrations of cores and core fragments on flakes from Tor Faraj

Nahr Ibrahim or cores-on-flakes constitute some 3.4 percent of the class (Figs 4.1 and 4.2). The dominance of irregular varieties is an expression of the overall exhaustion of cores when they were abandoned. This is also underscored by the small dimensions of cores. Levallois cores average *ca.* 52mm in length, 50mm in width, and 24mm in thickness. The irregular varieties are substantially smaller, averaging only *ca.* 38mm long, 24mm wide, and 10mm thick.

Primary elements

Primary elements, those specimens displaying one-third or more cortical coverage, represent about 12 percent of the debitage. Given the considerable distance to raw material sources, this is unexpected. Typically when raw material was imported from beyond a site's catchment, the cortex was trimmed away to improve the efficiency of transport. In the case of Tor Faraj, however, it may well have been that the natural convexity of the chert nodules allowed for Levallois point production with only minimal core preparation. This would have reduced the incentive for cortical removal at the source of the material.

Although some of the removals of primary elements likely were related to initial, early stage core shaping (e.g., splitting nodules), there are clear indications that many of the removals actually set up cores for the delivery of Levallois points. In their refitting study, Demidenko and Usik (Chapter 6) trace the removal of such primary elements as guides for point production, i.e., edge elements. Examination of the scar patterns on the dorsal surfaces of the primary elements show ca. 25 percent are parallel, converging, or Y-shaped and ca. 43 percent of their platforms are dihedral or multi-faceted. These attributes are consistent with the preparation of a core's platform and the shaping of its face for the subsequent removal of a Levallois point. A large proportion (61.5 percent) of the primary elements also display curved lateral profiles, an attribute consistent with knappers having used the rounded surfaces of the chert nodules to generate convex working faces on cores even with the first removals. About 21 percent of the primary elements are laminar in form and some 66 percent show unidirectional preparation; again characteristics consistent with initial preparation of cores for point production.

Over 80 percent of the bulbs on primary elements are unlipped and pronounced; and about half of these display prominent bulbar scars. Less than 5 percent are lipped. This configuration of bulbar attributes would indicate that hard-hammer percussion was the dominant loading variety used in primary production, but some soft-hammer percussion likely was employed. Whereas none of these attributes alone are definitive of specific loading states (Hayden and Hutchings 1989), lipping does occur at higher frequencies with soft-hammer and lipping does show strong inverse co-variance with bulbar scar-

ring, an attribute linked to hard-hammer percussion (Wiseman 1993). Armagan's (Chapter 5 of this volume) study of the loading characteristics of small debris also determined hard-hammer percussion to be the dominant loading variety.

Primary elements show a wide range in their sizes with some measuring over 100mm in length, but mean length is only ca. 46mm, just slightly less than that of the Levallois cores.

Core trimming elements

Core trimming elements or core management flakes represent slightly less than 3 percent of the debitage. The class includes specimens that display a significant portion of a striking platform beyond that from which an element was struck and specimens which exhibit lateral and/or distal cortex (i.e., edge or overpassed flakes) indicative of early core shaping flakes (Fig. 4.1). Overpassed or edge flakes bearing cortex in many ways form a continuum with morphologically similar forms classified as primary elements, but with less (< one-third) of their surface covered with cortex. A large proportion (71.2 percent) of core trimming elements show curved lateral profiles, some 30 percent exhibit converging or parallel scar patterns, and 7.5 percent show the tell-tale Y-pattern linked to Levallois point preparation. Also, 54 percent of the platforms reveal dihedral or multiple faceting, an indication of the degree to which platforms were prepared for blank removal.

Core trimming elements show a wide range of lengths with some specimens reaching > 100mm, but mean length registers 52.5mm. About 28 percent of the core trimming elements are of blade proportions.

Blades

Blades include those specimens that display maximum dimensions that are ⩾ twice as long as they are wide and if they exhibit cortex, it covers < one-third of the dorsal surface. Although Levallois blades were distinguished from other blanks with lamellar proportions for computation of Levallois indices, blades were considered *in toto* for computation of all other blade related attributes (e.g., metrics, platform facets, distal profiles, etc.). Blades account for 19.3 percent of the debitage.

Most of the blades are curved (55.7 percent), but a substantial proportion (22.3 percent) are twisted. Their platforms are predominantly multi-faceted (68.2 percent) with 'v'- or 'u'-shaped platforms (28.4 percent), although diamond-shaped, triangular, and lenticular-shaped platforms also are common. Dorsal scar patterns are dominated by Y-*arrete* and converging (46.5 percent) and parallel forms (41.9 percent). Distal shapes are mostly pointed and oblique (59.7 percent). The direction of removal is mainly unidirectional (42 percent), but a good number of blades were removed bidirectionally (24.1 percent). As discussed earlier, most of these dominant attributes are consistent with blades having been produced as part of preparing core faces for the propagation of Levallois points.

The bulbs of percussion on blades are primarily pronounced and unlipped (82.3 percent) and about 40 percent display bulbar scars. With only 7.8 percent of blades showing lipped bulbs, it is likely that the great majority were delivered with hard-hammer percussion. In that blades are dominated by feathered distal terminations (82.6 percent), it appears that this was accomplished with considerable efficiency. The blades from Tor Faraj exhibit moderate elongation (L:W ratio = 2.26) and a mean length of 50.8mm with a range stretching from 12.9 to 97.8mm.

Flakes

Flakes include those specimens that display maximum dimensions that are < twice as long as they are wide and if they exhibit cortex, it covers < one-third of the dorsal surface. Although Levallois flakes were distinguished from other blanks with flake proportions for computation of Levallois indices, flakes were considered in *toto* for computation of all other flake related attributes (e.g., metrics, platform facets, distal profiles, etc.). Flakes account for just over half of the debitage.

Most flakes display curved lateral profiles (60.7 percent) and their platforms are mainly multi-faceted (61.6 percent) with 'v' or 'u' shapes (37.2 percent). Dorsal scar patterns are predominantly converging or Y-*arrete* (33 percent), but parallel scars account for 23.6 percent. Flakes display distal shapes that are largely pointed or oblique (43.8 percent) and these typically end in feathered terminations (79.8 percent). In combination then, these dominant attributes furnish clear signatures that most flakes were produced as by-products of a lithic technology that was principally focused on the production of Levallois points from unidirectionally prepared, convergent cores.

Examination of the loading attributes of flakes shows the large majority (80.7 percent) to have unlipped, pronounced bulbs of percussion and 37.5 percent of these display bulbar scars. This coupled with a very low frequency (6.4 percent) of lipped bulbs indicates that hard-hammer percussion was the dominant loading variety in flake propagation. Feathered distal terminations occur on about 80 percent of the flakes. Flakes average about 40mm in length with a range from 9 to 89mm.

Truncated faceted or Nahr Ibrahim elements

Elements that have been struck from cores and that have subsequently been modified through additional retouch technically come under the classification of tools. However, analysis of truncated faceted elements has shown that most, if not all of such specimens, are related to their use as *cores on flakes* (Solecki and Solecki 1970; Goren-Inbar 1988; Henry 1995c). And the refitting of truncated faceted pieces from Tor Faraj (Demidenko and Usik, Chapter 6) provides additional support for their having been used as cores. Most of the truncated faceted specimens found at Tor Faraj, however, are not cores, but merely the by-products of the process of shaping and delivering blanks from cores on flakes. Of all the truncated faceted pieces, only a little over 25 percent appear as cores. The rest occur on a variety of blanks, most often on flakes (54.3 percent).

An examination of the technological attributes of Nahr Ibrahim elements reveals a considerable contrast with those described for the other debitage classes. Curved lateral profiles (39 percent), multi-faceted platforms (45.2 percent), 'v'- and 'u'-shaped platforms (9.5 percent), pointed and oblique distal shapes (21.7 percent), unidirectional removals (11.4 percent), and Y-*arrete* and convergent facet patterns (20.7 percent) all occur at substantially lower rates than seen in the other debitage classes. Given that these attributes are signatures of a Levallois technology, specifically a unidirectional convergent approach to point production, then it would appear that those blanks (generally flakes) selected for subsequent 'recycling' as cores were largely not part of the initial Levallois reduction stream. Preference for these essentially non-Levallois blanks for use as cores may have stemmed from their being less likely to display ventral curvature and their being thicker on the average. In that the working faces of truncated faceted cores were formed predominantly on the ventral surfaces of flakes, flakes with strong ventral curvature (a dominant characteristic of Levallois products) would have been avoided. Similarly, thick blanks would have been selected for preparation into cores over thin ones.

Levallois signatures and reduction

Studies focusing on the Levallois technology, that is, the special way in which a core is formed in order to control the production of a blank with a predetermined morphology, have typically emphasized three concerns. These include: (1) establishing the degree to which the Levallois technology was employed; (2) defining variability in the specific manner or method that the technology was implemented; and (3) tracing the primary reduction strategy that was utilized from initial raw material modification to blank production.

In his review of the alternative 'systems' used in the study of Levallois technology, Van Peer (1992: 63-6) traces three major approaches. These consist of: (1) a traditional approach emphasizing a morphological typology and most strongly associated with the work of François Bordes; (2) an approach largely inspired by experimental results which focuses on the assessment of a *volumetric conception* linked largely to the research of Eric Boëda (1986); and (3) an approach concentrating on the definition of certain artifact attributes that are tied to specific reduction strategies (and stages) which often have been observed in refits. When interwoven with refit studies, this last approach is best identified with the works of Marks and Volkman (1983, 1987) and Van Peer (1992, 1995), but several other researchers have

utilized attribute studies alone to understand Levallois technology better (Crew 1975; Munday 1977; Fish 1979; Goren-Inbar 1990; Henry 1995a, 1995b, 1995c; Kuhn 1995; Hovers 1997).

Although seemingly objective and quantifiable, the indices originally developed by Bordes fail really to define different Levallois methods or changes that may occur within a reduction sequence (Bar-Yosef and Dibble 1995). Moreover, the indices simply do not differentiate morphologically similar end-products that result from different reduction strategies. In contrast, the experimental approach advocated by Boëda has produced various models in which alternative reduction strategies or methods can be traced within the overarching Levallois concept and by which non-Levallois technologies may be distinguished. And these *chaînes opératoire* are linked to specific morphological and technological artifact varieties as both end-products (e.g., Levallois point) and preparatory products (e.g., edge element). This approach relies more on qualitative than quantitative comparisons, however.

In this study, I have largely followed Van Peer's approach, but with a much expanded attribute analysis. Many of the attributes are those that were employed in the earlier study of Tor Faraj (Henry 1995c), but others have been adopted because of additional technological questions and insights gained in the ancillary refitting analysis conducted by Demidenko and Usik. The attribute analysis provides an opportunity to trace variability in Levallois methods and reduction sequences in addition to easily quantifying the results (Table 4.5).

The predominantly unidirectional convergent method of shaping cores for Levallois point propagation generated a series of distinct attributes for the lateral profiles, platform facets, platform shapes, distal shapes, removal directions, and scar patterns of those elements produced in the process. This cluster of *signature attributes* can be identified on end-products (e.g., Levallois points) as well as on preparatory products (e.g., edge elements) and refitted constellations. Specifically, within the range of attributes for each of these categories, *curved* lateral profiles, *dihedral* and *multiple* platform facets, 'v' and 'u'-shaped platform silhouettes, *pointed* and *oblique* distal shapes, *unidirectional* removals, and *convergent*

Table 4.5 The percentages of Levallois signature attributes as they appear on different classes of debitage and Levallois points

Signature attributes	Primary elem.	Core trim: elem.	Blade	Flake	Lev. point	Core on flake
Curved lateral profile	61.5	71.2	55.7	63.2	82.9	46.8
Dihedral-multiple facets	42.9	53.9	68.2	63.3	100.0	17.4
V–U-shaped platforms	14.1	19.2	28.4	39.9	88.9	8.2
Pointed-oblique distal shape	36.2	42.3	59.7	48.6	90.8	18.2
Unidirectional removals	78.4	68.0	63.5	67.6	51.4	29.6
Y-convergent scar patterns	34.9	66.6	46.5	51	95.9	12.5
Bulb forms						
Lipped	4.5	5.8	7.8	6.5	5.1	3.8
Not lipped	40.5	53.8	42.3	46.0	46.5	26.4
Not lipped with scar	40.5	30.8	40.0	38.4	43.4	28.3

Note: The artifact classes are arranged in an order of stage reduction (left to right), progressing from primary elements through cores-on-flakes

and *Y-arrete* scar patterns provide signatures for the method. Therefore, the degree to which the method was employed in the production of elements is reflected directly in the proportionate representation of these attributes in an assemblage. Furthermore, in comparing the proportionate representation of these signature attributes along a reduction stream, it is possible to determine the manner in which the method was employed within the overall lithic technological repertoire in evidence at Tor Faraj. Here, I believe it is worth emphasizing that numerous studies show that different lithic technologies were often employed simultaneously by Middle Paleolithic groups (Marks and Volkman 1986; Goren-Inbar 1990; Boëda 1995; Kuhn 1995; Marks and Monigal 1995). In analyzing Mousterian assemblages, it seems important that we not only attempt to tease apart the alternative lithic technologies that were utilized, but to understand under what specific conditions they were employed.

In the Tor Faraj assemblage, examination of lithic attributes along a reduction stream defined by traditional morphological characteristics (e.g., cortical coverage and flake scar-platform orientation) shows the intensity of the Levallois signatures progressively to increase from primary elements to Levallois points (Table 4.5). Primary elements rank lowest in the intensity of Levallois signatures, but even at this initial stage of production five of the six signatures occur at rates of 34.9 to 78.4 percent; only *platform shape* (14.1 percent) falls lower. This indicates that a Levallois technology was employed regularly, at least one-third or more of the time, in the early decortification of chert nodules. Several refitted constellations show this process (Demidenko and Usik, Chapter 6), but with refitted constellations alone, we are not informed of the extent to which the practice was followed because of the small and potentially biased artifact sample. However, the attribute analysis, based upon a much larger artifact sample, clearly shows that Levallois point production was regularly interwoven with decortification at Tor Faraj.

When compared to primary elements, core trimming elements show a rise in the percentages of Levallois signatures in all but *unidirectional removal* (Table 4.5). At this stage in reduction, half of the Levallois signatures occur at rates over 66 percent and two others are present in over 42 percent of the sample. Only the signature of *platform shape* remains weakly represented (19.2 percent).

Further along the reduction stream, blades and flakes show increased proportions of Levallois signatures for three attributes (*dihedral* and *multiple* platform facets, 'v'- and 'u'-

shaped platform silhouettes, and *pointed* and *oblique* distal shapes), but display reduced proportions for the other three (*curved lateral profiles, unidirectional* removals, and *convergent* and *Y-arrete* scar patterns). But even with the moderate declines in values for these attributes, Levallois signatures remain relatively high for both flakes and blades. When flakes and blades are compared, neither debitage class is consistently dominant in the proportions of Levallois signatures.

As end-products of the technology, Levallois points furnish quantitative baselines for the Levallois signature attributes. And as might be expected, most of these signature attributes display very high percentages, ranging from 82.9 to 100 (Table 4.5). One attribute (*unidirectional removal*) presents an exception to this pattern, however. Not only does it occur at a relatively low percentage (51.4 percent), it shows a quite different trend when compared to the other attributes. While the other signature attributes largely exhibit progressive rises in their percentages along the reduction sequence, the percentages for unidirectional removal progressively decline. Given the refitted constellations and other technological evidence that indicate a unidirectional, convergent method of producing Levallois points, how can such a trend be explained? In part, the explanation was observed in the refitted constellations when it was noted that when points were produced on small cores, especially cores on flakes, the knappers at Tor Faraj often departed from unidirectional preparation and adopted more opportunistic, bidirectional preparatory removals. Such a technological shift then would mean that proportionately, unidirectional preparation for point removal would have decreased as elements declined in size along the reduction stream. This is confirmed when removal directions are compared for points above and below the mean length of 35mm. Whereas 61 percent of the sample of longer points were unidirectionally prepared, only 41 percent of the shorter point sample show unidirectional preparation.

Another, but more substantial departure from the unidirectional, convergent method was adopted when flakes were recycled into cores. In this case, as evidenced by Nahr Ibrahim or truncated faceted pieces, the

Levallois technology appears to have been largely abandoned. Refits show some attempts to utilize a Levallois technology, even in point production, but when all truncated faceted specimens are examined Levallois signature attributes are found to occur at very low levels (Table 4.5). In fact, none of the signature attributes, recorded for Nahr Ibrahim specimens, reach the percentages recorded for any of the other debitage classes. Thus, it would appear that, at least at Tor Faraj, Middle Paleolithic knappers adopted a largely non-Levallois technology when attempting to maximize the productivity of cores formed on flakes. Not surprisingly, dimensional data show that unusually thick flakes (over 1.5 times thicker than other flakes) were selected for further processing as cores, yet the planar dimensions of Nahr Ibrahim specimens are only slightly larger than other flakes.

Dimensional data are also informative when compared along a reduction stream. Length (measured along the striking axis) is perhaps the dimension most sensitive to reduction. On the average, blanks would be expected to decline in length with progression along the reduction stream. Examination of data on the lengths of different classes of debitage and Levallois points from Tor Faraj shows the mean lengths of core trimming elements, blades, and Levallois points to be quite similar as would be expected given their inter-related generation in point production (Fig. 4.3). Surprisingly, primary elements display mean lengths that are substantially less than end-product points as well as core trimming elements and blades. A combination of factors may account for the lower than expected mean values of primary element lengths. The initial preparation of a striking platform involved decapitation of chert nodules and attendant production of rather short primary elements. The same is true for the initial production of a central plane which would have produced a relatively short wide primary element.

When compared to the lengths of Levallois points, the much shorter lengths of cores and core facets indicate a significant degree of core exhaustion. Moreover, this indicates that many of the smaller cores were employed in the production of non-Levallois blanks.

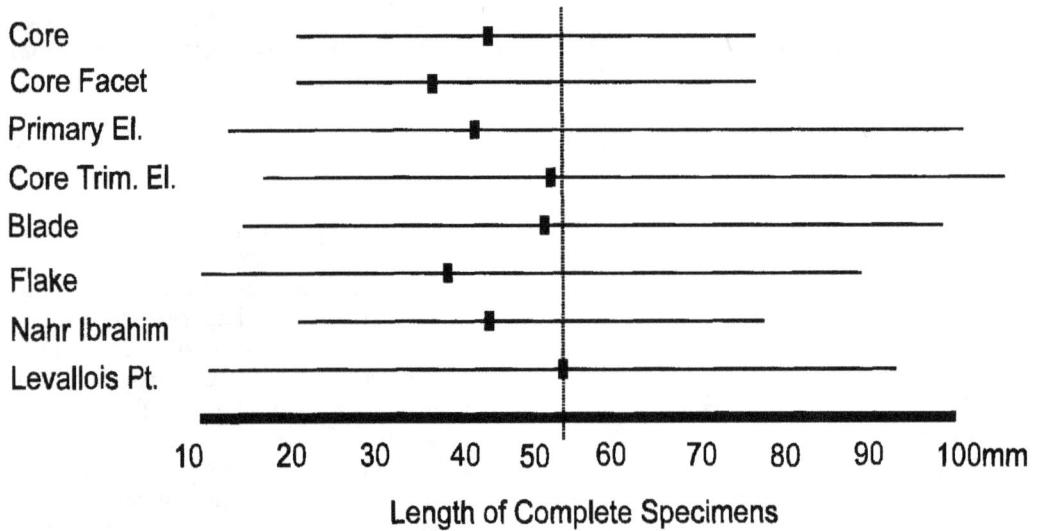

Figure 4.3 Comparison of the lengths (mean and range) of debitage and Levallois points recovered from Tor Faraj

Typology

Of the 425 tools recorded for the two floors, about 61 percent come from Floor II (Table 4.4). In comparing the relative proportions of tool classes from the two floors, the only significant differences relate to the higher percentages of unretouched Levallois points from Floor I and notches from Floor II. The proportions for the other classes are remarkably similar and there also appears to be little typological variability between floors. Because of the general lack of variability between floors, the typological description of the artifact assemblage is presented for the combined floors.

Levallois points

Given the preceding discussion of the technology of Tor Faraj, it is not surprising that Levallois points (Figs 4.4 to 4.11) dominate the type-list , accounting for *ca.* 24 percent of the tools (Table 4.4). Unretouched Levallois points are included here with the tools, along with retouched points. This departs from traditional Bordesian systematics, where unretouched points are included with other Levallois products in the type list, but excluded (along with other retouched and inversely retouched pieces) in the computation of restricted indices. In order to facilitate

standardized comparison with other Mousterian assemblages, Bordesian systematics have been followed in the computation of traditional indices. In all other computations, however, unretouched Levallois points have been included in the tool category. This issue has importance beyond classificatory semantics, for in assemblages dominated by points as at Tor Faraj, their placement in tools or debitage strongly effects various quantitative measures (e.g., tool:debitage ratio, tool:core ratio) that help to identify prehistoric activities.

The logic for categorizing unretouched Levallois points as tools stems from two observations. First, unlike the other Levallois products, Levallois points could have served specific predetermined and rather standardized functions without any additional modification through secondary retouch. While one might argue that the same holds true for other unretouched tools (e.g., naturally backed knives), such tool forms do not display characteristics that trace a complicated set of steps of core shaping designed to control the form of the end-product precisely. Additional support for including unretouched Levallois points in the tool category comes from edge-wear studies that show points to have been used to a proportionately far greater extent than any class of debitage (Shea 1995).

Points appear mainly on blanks displaying

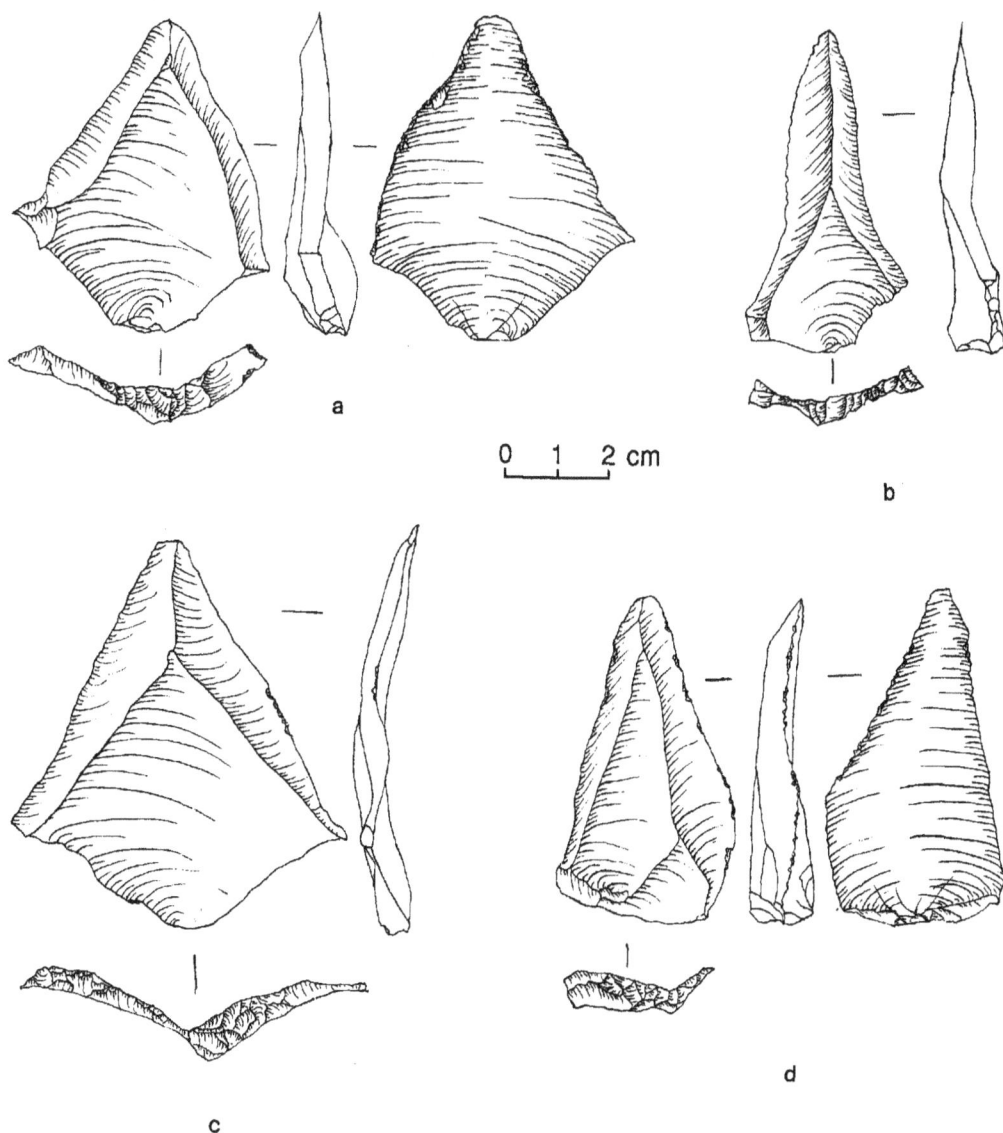

Figure 4.4 Illustrations of Levallois points from Tor Faraj. Note classic *chapeau de gendarme* platforms and Concorde silhouette on specimen **c**

flake proportions, a pattern that is most strongly pronounced among unretouched points (Table 4.6). Aside from retouched points being more elongate (L:W 1.6 compared to 1.4) and heavier (15gm compared to 12.7gm), the metric characteristics of retouched and unretouched points are nearly identical (Table 4.7). Patterns of breakage and the presence of impact spalls also show strong parallels between retouched and unretouched points. Few of either point variety are broken (76 to 78 percent complete) and of those that are, proximal ends are some 4 to 6 times more common than distal ones. The presence of impact spalls, found on 65 to 70 percent of the specimens, is very high for both point varieties.

For the retouched points, obverse retouch is dominant (62 percent), but a substantial portion of the points show inverse retouch (38 percent). The position of the retouch, relative to its location along the edges of points, shows

Table 4.6 The relative proportions by which tool classes occur on different blank varieties

Tool class	Core	Blade	Flake	Cr. tr. el.	Prim. el.	Bur. spl.		Total
Lev. pt. retouched		39.13%	60.87%				100.00%	23
Lev. pt. unret		12.99%	85.71%			1.30%	100.00%	77
Side-scraper		38.46%	61.54%				100.00%	13
End-scraper			100.00%				100.00%	5
Burin		27.78%	62.96%	1.85%	7.41%		100.00%	54
Truncated piece		20.00%	80.00%				100.00%	5
Notch		35.48%	58.06%		6.45%		100.00%	31
Denticulate		60.00%	30.00%		10.00%		100.00%	10
Retouched piece	1.03%	27.32%	60.82%	4.12%	3.61%	3.09%	100.00%	194
Varia		38.46%	61.54%				100.00%	13
Total	2	115	278	9	14	7		425
	0.47%	27.06%	65.41%	2.12%	3.29%	1.65%	100.00%	

Table 4.7 Comparison of metric data for unbroken retouched and unretouched points

	Unretouched Levallois points				Retouched Levallois points			
	N	Range	Mean	Std. Deviation	N	Range	Mean	Std. Deviation
Maximum length (mm)	59	22.9–90.2	51.9	15.5	18	30.6–97.8	57.6	15.4
Maximum width (mm)	59	7.5–56.7	36.6	10.1	18	19.8–54.6	35.2	10.2
Width at mid-length (mm)	59	12.9–48.3	28.8	8.2	18	13.4–46.1	28.3	8.6
Maximum thickness (mm)	59	2.4–20.3	8.2	3.1	18	4.2–12.9	8.3	2.8
Max. platform thickness (mm)	58	2.1–15.0	7.4	2.9	18	3.3–12.9	7.6	2.8
Weight (grams)	59	1–44.4	13.4	9.6	18	3.8–40.4	14.8	10.4
Mean L/W ratio	1.44				1.41			

no strong patterning. This finding contrasts with that of the earlier study where retouch along the basal margins was found to be dominant (Henry 1995c: 69). The different results of the two studies may be linked to the much larger sample for the current study, which contains three times the number of points of the 1995 study.

Side-scrapers

The tool class, accounting for a little over 3 percent of the tool-kit, is composed mainly of simple, convex side-scrapers (Figs 4.5, 4.8, 4.9, 4.10, 4.11) that show moderately invasive retouch. The majority of the retouch is located on the obverse face (61 percent), but there is no distinct pattern in edge position. Although less common than obverse scrapers, those appearing on the inverse face are consistently present (39 percent) and thus not a rare form as designated in the Bordesian typology. Side-scrapers are restricted to blade (38 percent) and flake (62 percent) blanks.

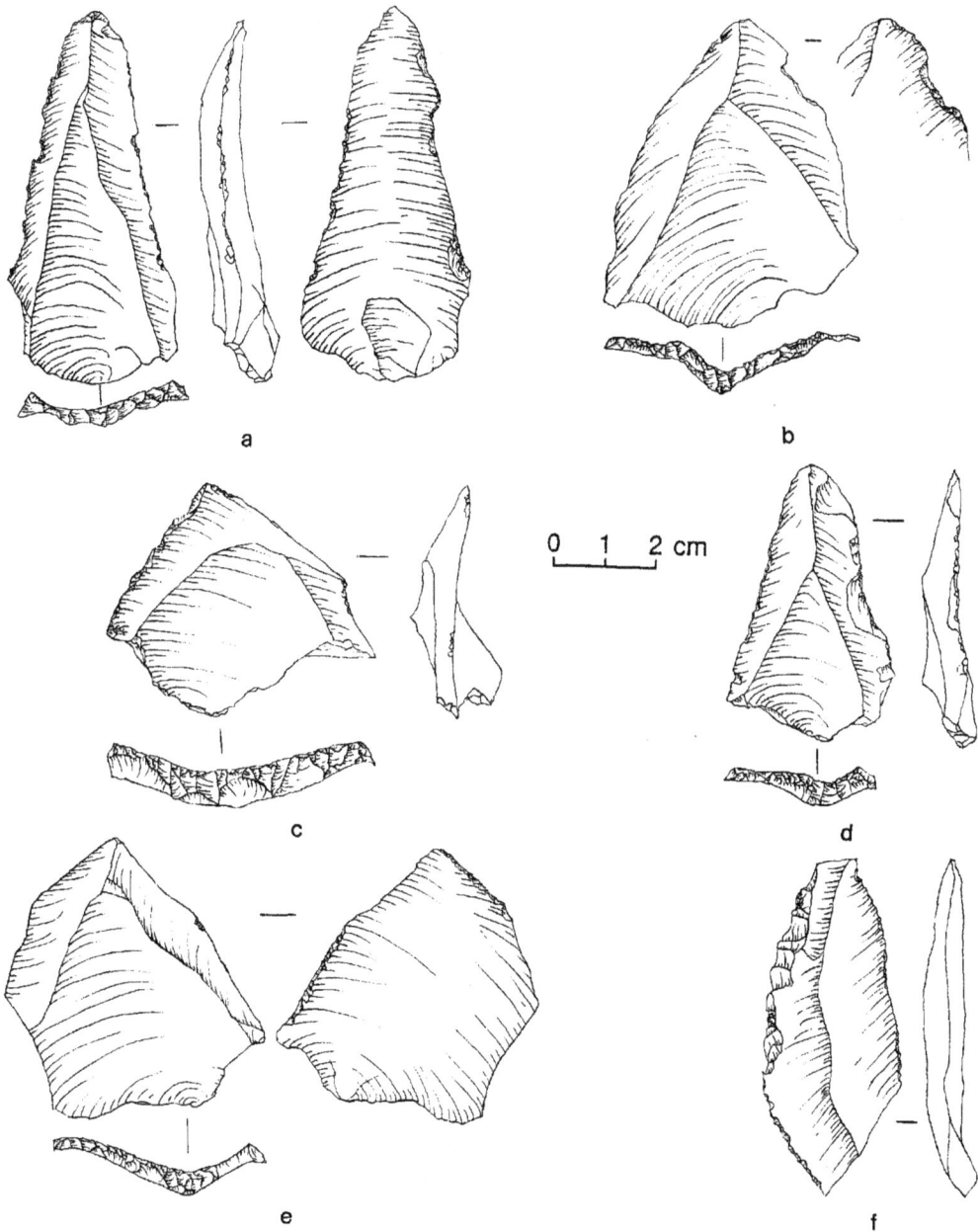

Figure 4.5 Illustrations of lithic artifacts from Tor Faraj: **a**, **b**, **d**, retouched Levallois points; **c**, **e**, retouched rejuvenation flakes; **f**, side-scraper on blade. From Donald O. Henry, *Prehistoric Cultural Ecology and Evolution*, Plenum, 1995. Reproduced by permission of Plenum

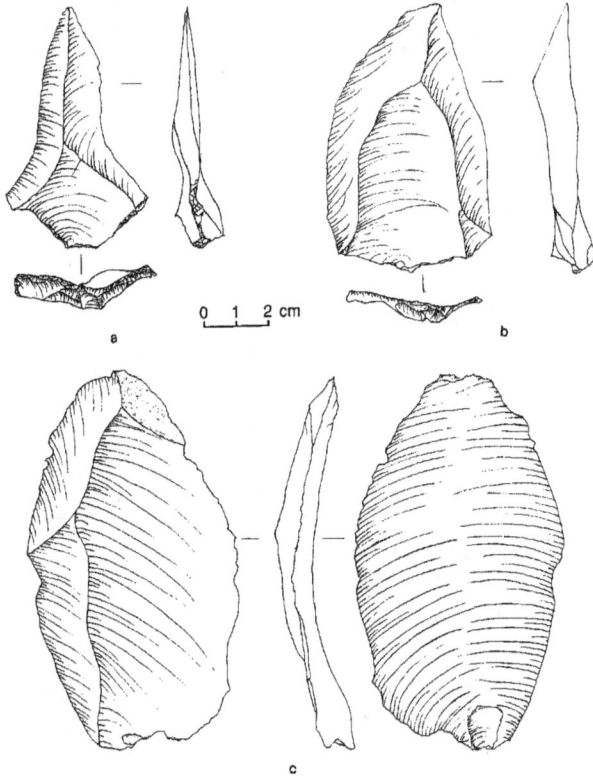

Figure 4.6 Illustrations of lithic artifacts from Tor Faraj: **a**, Levallois point; **b**, **c**, Levallois flakes

End-scrapers

End-scrapers (Fig. 4.10), representing slightly over 1 percent of the tools, occur only on flakes. All are retouched on their obverse faces and the retouch forms simple, rounded scarper bits.

Burins

Angle burins (Fig. 4.12) struck on breaks and old surfaces dominate the class. Almost all display multiple blows. Most were formed on flakes (63 percent) and blades (28 percent), but over 7 percent were made on primary elements.

In their refit study, Demidenko and Usik found that flakes were often bisected with burin-like blows as part of the creation of truncated faceted pieces for use as cores on flakes (Henry et al. 1996: 45–6; Chapter 6, this volume). Their findings therefore would suggest that some specimens identified typologically as burins may not have served as burins functionally, although it is of course

also possible that burins generated in the process of developing cores on flakes may have subsequently been used functionally in the same ways as burins produced intentionally as tools. Two lines of evidence indicate that most, if not all, of the typologically identified burins served as burins functionally. First, in Longo's use-wear study, all the burins examined for the 180 to 185cm excavation level (Floor II) showed evidence of use. This represented six specimens or 11.1 percent of the burins in the tool assemblage. Second, a little more than half of the burins in the assemblage display multiple blows, a tell-tale characteristic of tools intentionally fabricated for use.

Truncated pieces

In representing only a little more than 1 percent of the tool-kit, truncations principally occur on flakes (80 percent) that have been retouched on their obverse faces (60 percent). In their discussion of truncations, Debénath and Dibble (1994: 102) note that truncations

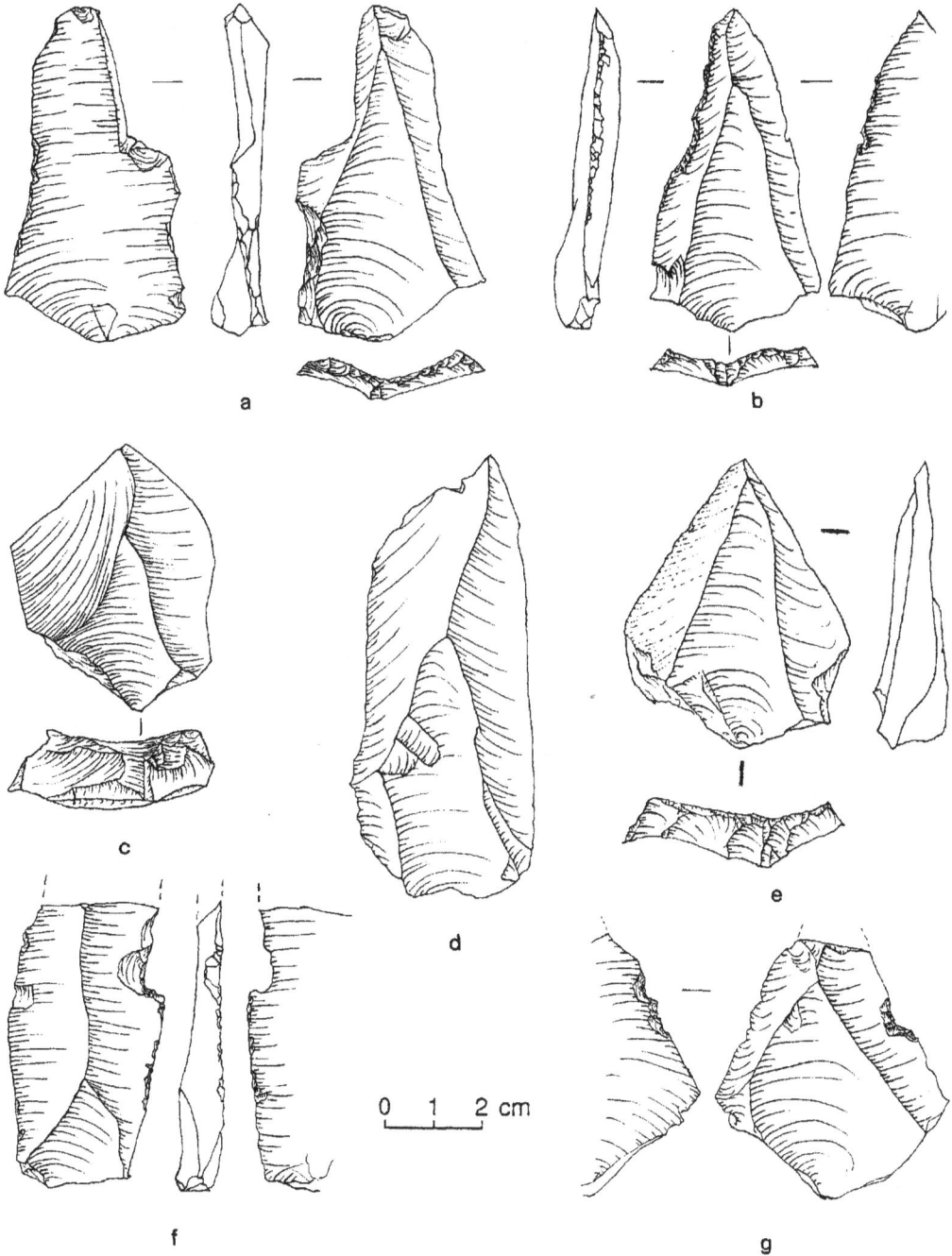

Figure 4.7 Illustrations of lithic artifacts from Tor Faraj: **a**, **b**, retouched Levallois points—note impact spall on **a**; **c**, **e**, core trimming elements or rejuvenation flakes; **d**, Levallois blade; **f**, notched blade; **g**, point. From Donald O. Henry, *Prehistoric Cultural Ecology and Evolution*, Plenum, 1995. Reproduced by permission of Plenum

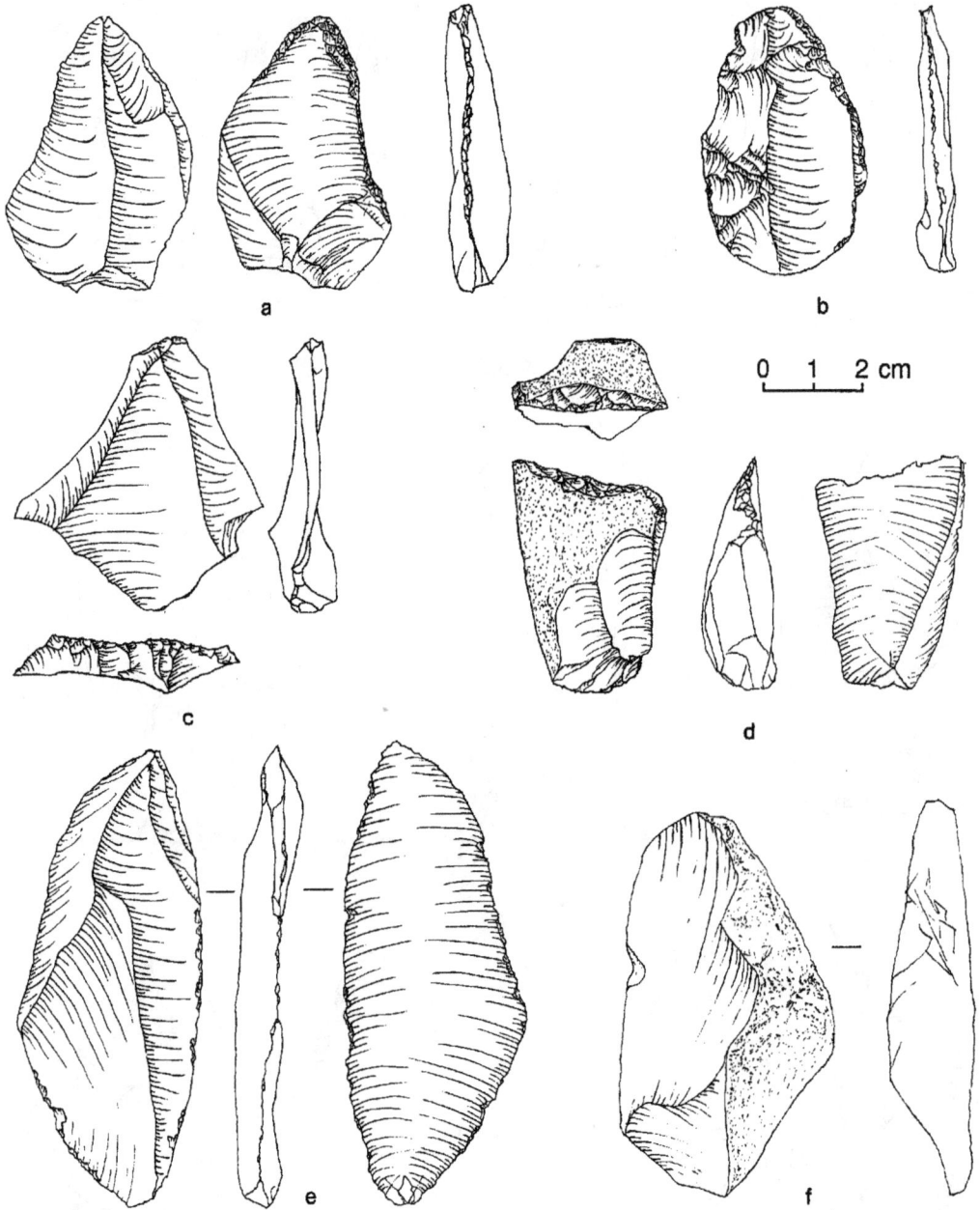

Figure 4.8 Illustrations of lithic artifacts from Tor Faraj: **a**, retouched truncated faceted flake; **b**, retouched flake; **c**, Levallois point with impact spalls; **d**, truncation on primary element; **e**, marginally retouched blade; **f**, naturally backed knife

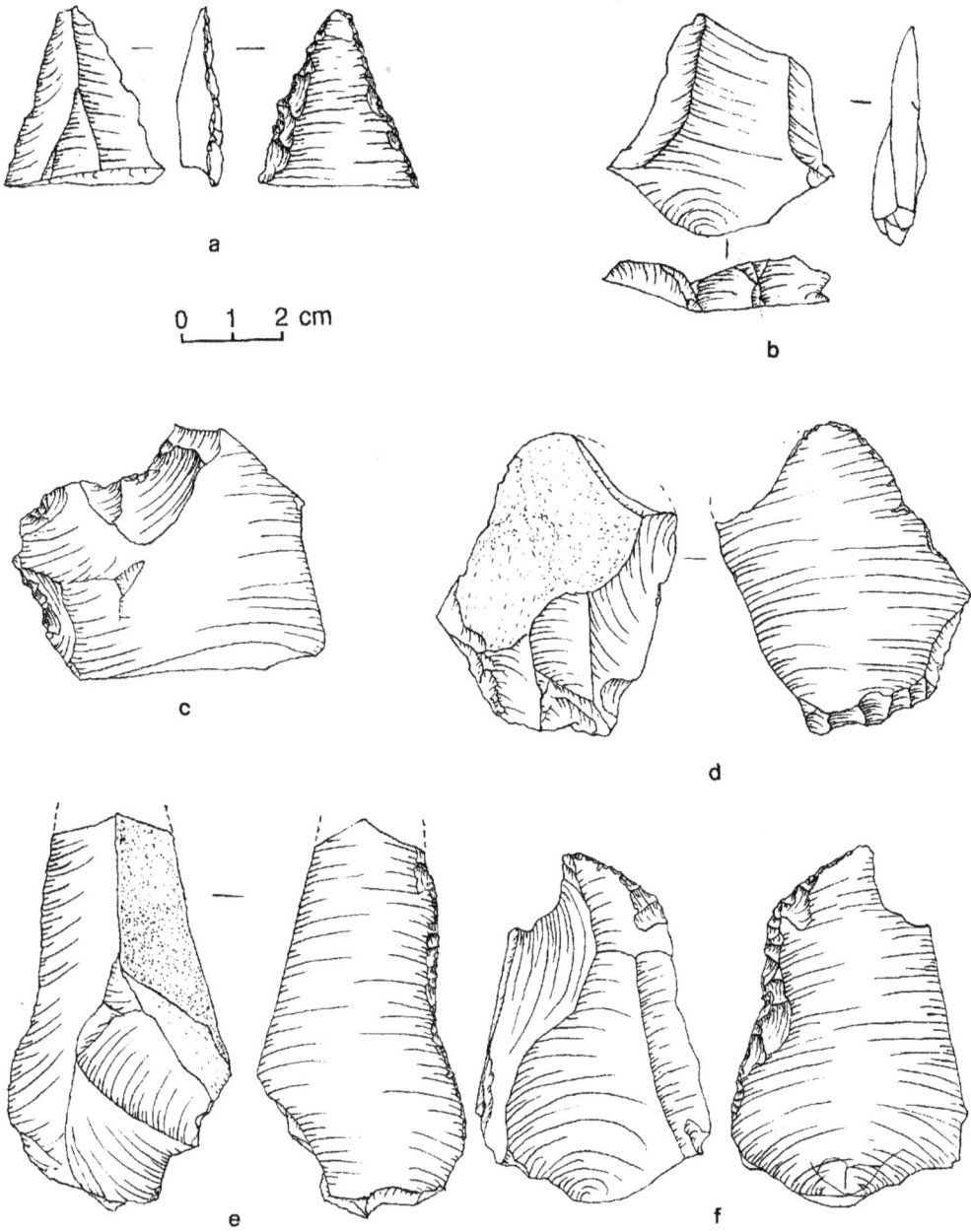

Figure 4.9 Illustrations of lithic artifacts from Tor Faraj: **a**, inversely retouched point tip; **b**, point base; **c, d**, truncated faceted pieces; **e**, inversely retouched blade; **f**, inversely retouched side-scraper. From Donald O. Henry, *Prehistoric Cultural Ecology and Evolution*, Plenum, 1995. Reproduced by permission of Plenum

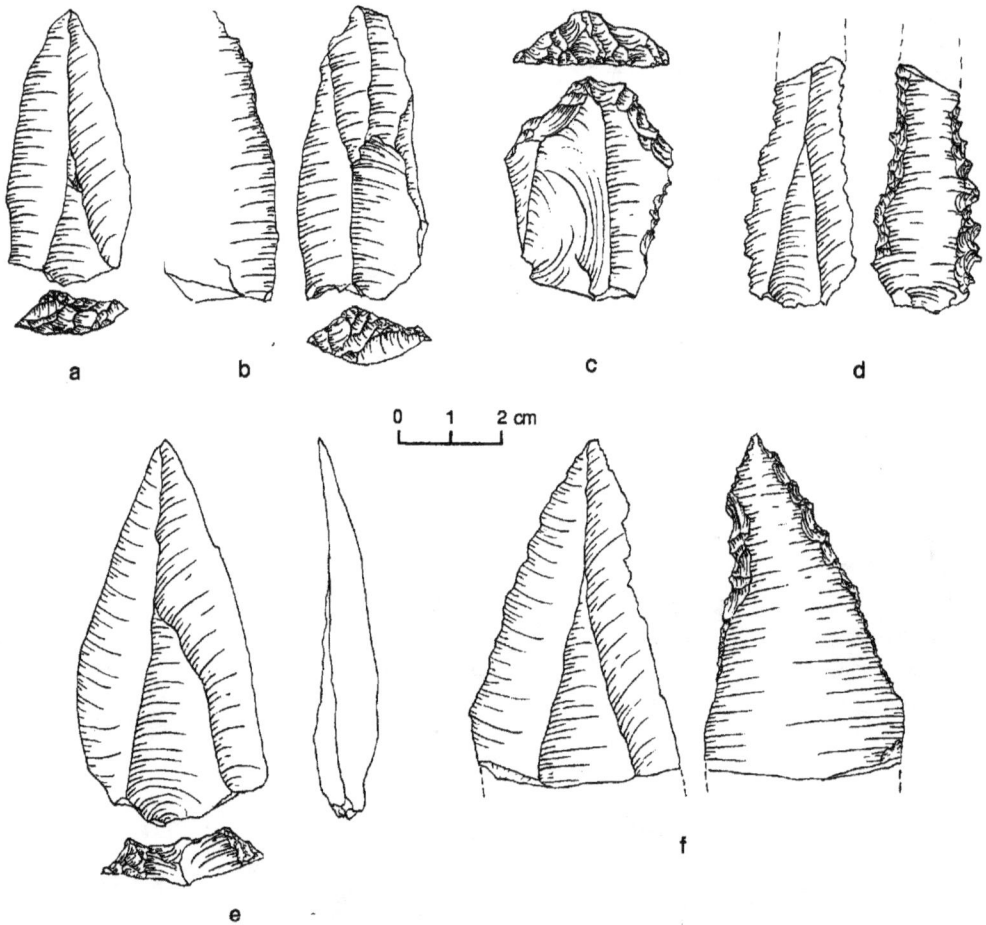

Figure 4.10 Illustrations of lithic artifacts from Tor Faraj: **a, e,** Levallois points; **b,** inversely retouched blade; **c,** end-scraper on flake; **d, f,** denticulate on inversely retouched point

would have been formed as an initial step in producing truncated faceted specimens or cores on flakes. Given the high frequency of truncated faceted pieces at Tor Faraj, one would expect greater numbers of truncations, especially inversely retouched ones, if the production of cores on flakes had been regularly aborted at the initial step. Apparently, the production of cores on flakes was rarely interrupted, but once initiated, undertaken as a continuous task that must have been completed in a manner of minutes.

Notches

Notches (Figs 4.5 and 4.7), representing 7.3 percent of the tools, are found principally on flakes (58 percent) and blades (35.5 percent).

Only complex notches, those with numerous overlapping flake scars, were recognized, i.e., single blow, Clactonian notches were not classified as tools. The class is composed mainly of single notches formed on the distal portions of lateral edges. Their position is relatively balanced between right and left edges. Multiple and distal (end of piece) notches are rare.

Denticulates

Denticulates (Figs 4.10 and 4.11), accounting for a small percentage (2.4 percent) of the tools, appear principally on blades (60 percent). In comparison with other retouched tools (e.g., scrapers, retouched pieces, etc.), denticulates show the most extensive retouch

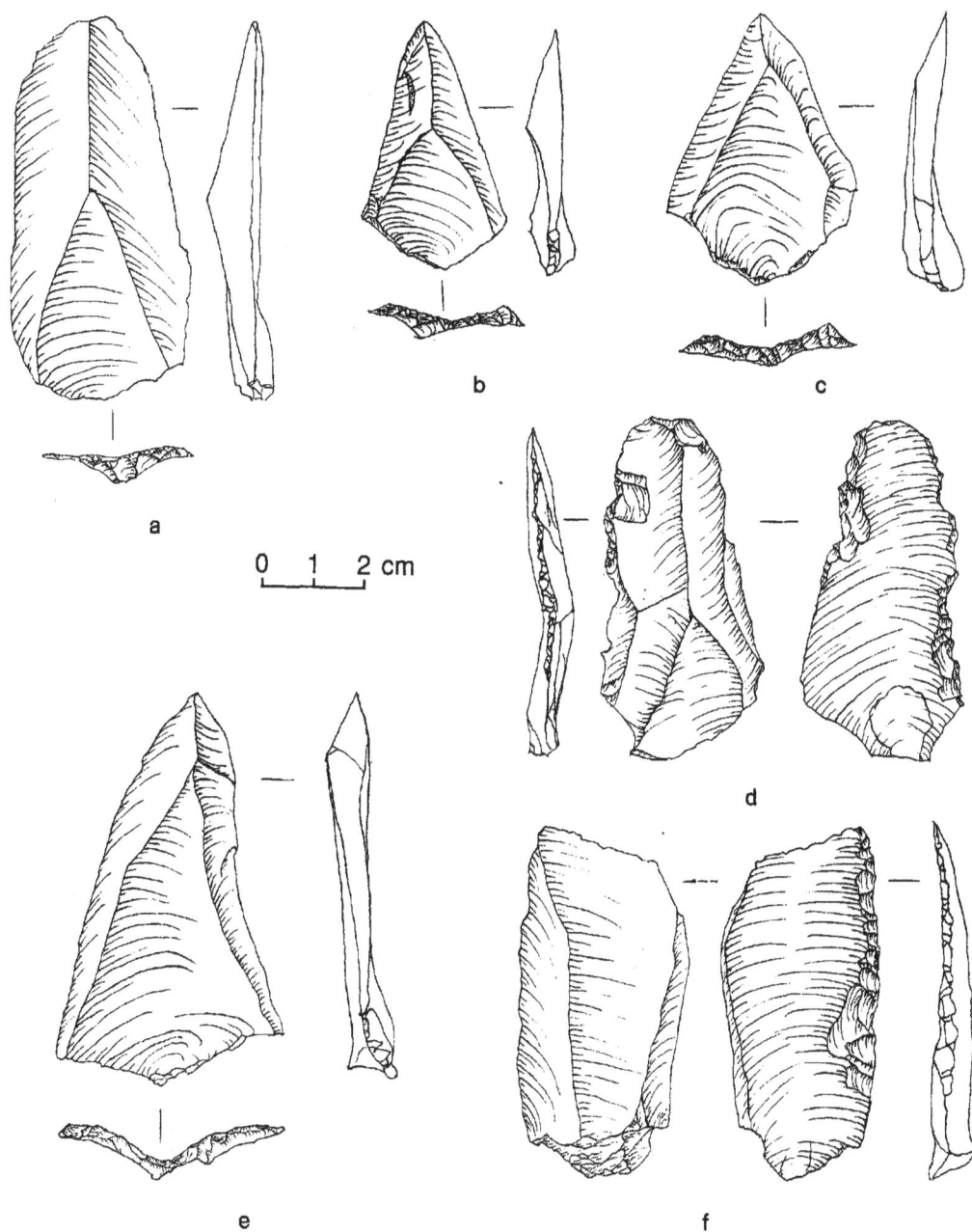

Figure 4.11 Illustrations of lithic artifacts from Tor Faraj: **a**, Levallois blade; **b**, **c**, **e**, Levallois points; **d**, denticulate on inversely retouched flake; **f**, side-scraper inversely retouched on blade

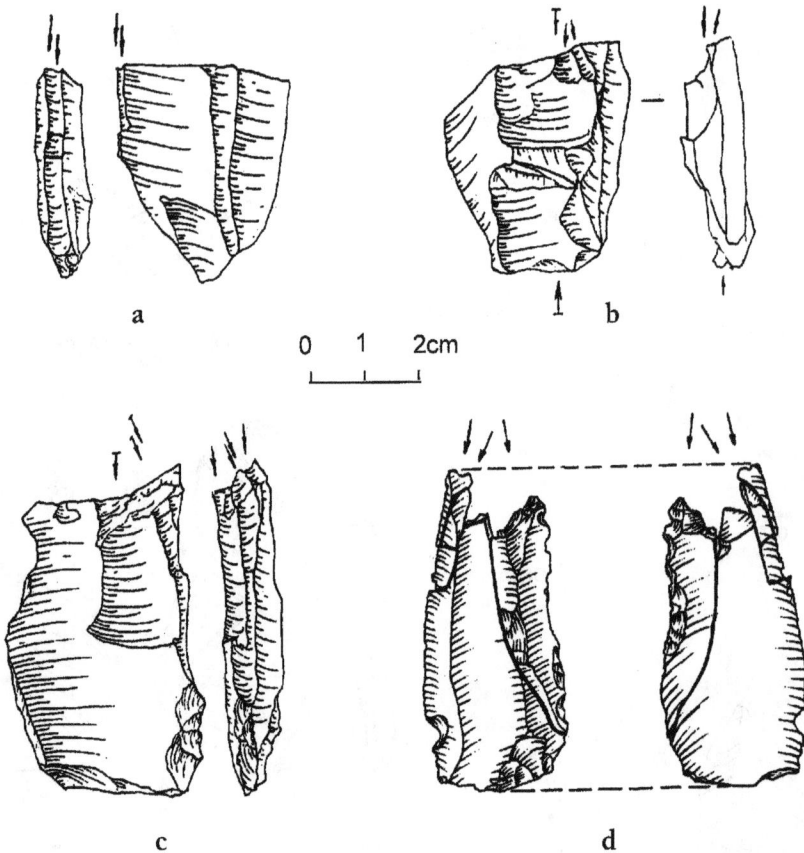

Figure 4.12 Illustrations of lithic artifacts from Tor Faraj: **a**, angle burin on snap; **b, c**, angle burin on truncated faceted piece; **d**, refitted dihedral burin on blade

and greatest degree of edge modification. The retouch is roughly balanced relative to position on inverse (53.9 percent) or obverse (46.1 percent) faces and there is no clear patterning in the location of retouch on lateral edges.

Retouched pieces

In representing 45.7 percent of the tool-kit, this is by far the largest class. Retouched pieces (Figs 4.4, 4.5, 4.7, 4.8, 4.9, 4.10, 4.11, 4.12) are found on all debitage classes, including burin spalls (Fig. 4.12d), but flakes (60.8 percent) and blades (27.3 percent) are the most commonly preferred blanks. Most specimens (49 percent) are retouched on their obverse surfaces, but substantial proportions also show inverse (24 percent) and both obverse/inverse (27.1 percent) retouch (Table 4.8).

The locations of the retouch along the lateral edges of blanks show a clear dominance of medial and distal over proximal positions for obversely retouched pieces, but for specimens with inverse retouch there is no discernible difference in lateral position. Similarly, there appears to be no real pattern in the location of retouch along the right or left lateral edges for either obversely or inversely retouched pieces.

Varia

The class, including about 3 percent of the tool-kit, is composed of a wide variety of specimens most often representing multiple tools. About 25 percent of the varia display burin blows in combination with other forms of retouch. Three of the 13 specimens are retouched bladelets (all from the same level

Table 4.8   The face that bears the retouch for different tool classes

Tool class	Retouch obverse		Retouch inverse		Both		Total	
	No.	Percentage	No.	Percentage	No.	Percentage	No.	Percentage
Lev. pt. retouched	10	43.48	5	21.74	8	34.78	23	100.00
Side-scraper	8	61.54	2	15.38	3	23.08	13	100.00
End-scraper	3	60.00	2	40.00	0	0	5	100.00
Truncated piece	3	60.00	2	40.00	0	0	5	100.00
Notch	12	38.71	12	38.71	7	22.58	31	100.00
Denticulate	1	10.00	4	40.00	5	50.00	10	100.00
Retouched piece	94	48.96	46	23.96	52	27.08	192	100.00
Varia	9	69.23	4	30.77	0	0.00	13	100.00
Total	140	47.95	77	26.37	75	25.68	292	100.00

and unit, B8) that are most likely intrusive. This is noteworthy, given the paucity of intrusive evidence for the site in general.

Conclusion

In previous reports, Tor Faraj (and Tor Sabiha) were placed *late* within Levantine Mousterian sequence, but continuity with earlier D-type assemblages was emphasized on the basis of technological considerations (Henry 1982, 1995c; Henry and Miller 1992). The relatively high proportions of Levallois points, blade indices, and incidence of bidirectional scar patterns were thought to indicate stronger affinities to D-type than B-type assemblages. It is now apparent, however, that these artifact patterns are not accurate indicators of an assemblage's position within the Levantine Mousterian sequence. Instead, Levallois point and blade indices appear to be more sensitive to environmental settings as high values for both indices are a hallmark of arid zone sites. And the degree of bidirectional core preparation reflected by an assemblage would appear to be strongly connected to economizing measures and thus indirectly related to the availability of chert. The artifact pattern that does appear to have strong chronological significance is tied to the specific technique employed in the production of broad-based Levallois points. The steps followed in production and the end-products at Tor Faraj are nearly identical to those described by Meignen (1995) for the B-type assemblages at Kebara. And the chronometry of the deposits is overlapping. Therefore, Tor Faraj is viewed as a B-type assemblage.

Dual technologies

Although the lithic technology of the inhabitants of Tor Faraj centered on the production of broad-based Levallois points struck from unidirectionally prepared cores, another technology was employed to maximize the productivity of the chert that for the most part was imported to the site from well beyond its catchment. This second technology, involving cores being formed on flakes, was introduced as a primary means of production, but only after raw material had been reduced to a size that a Levallois strategy could no longer be practiced, at least not along the standard lines as used in the broad-based point production. Although some cores on flakes were used to produce small Levallois points, most blanks displaying Nahr Ibrahim retouch were produced by non-Levallois flaking techniques. This is evidenced by the rarity of Levallois signature attributes on specimens with Nahr Ibrahim retouch (Table 4.5).

The specific way in which Levallois points were produced in the dominant technology (detailed by Demidenko and Usik in their refitting study in Chapter 6) also explains one of the unusual features of the Tor Faraj assemblage. This has to do with the relatively high proportions of cortical covered artifacts (primary elements) on chert imported from distant (> 22km) sources. Typically, in such circumstances, primary elements are uncommon because cortex is removed near the chert source. In the context of Tor Faraj, the natural convexity of the faces of the ovate chert nodules precluded extensive trimming or core shaping and thus enabled knappers to generate a Levallois point with as few as five removals (i.e., decapitation, formation of central plane, removal of two convergent edge flakes, and detachment of Levallois point). The importation of untrimmed or slightly trimmed chert nodules to Tor Faraj was therefore economic in the context of Levallois point production.

Occupational permanence

The importation and use of chert nodules denote the importance of primary production at Tor Faraj, but the presence of significant numbers of cores on flakes underscores efforts at recycling and secondary production. Moreover, tool fabrication and use are also confirmed by the presence of formally retouched specimens and microscopic evidence of use-wear (Lee 1987; Shea 1995). As noted in the earlier study (Henry 1995a, 1995b: 112), analysis of the full operational sequence of the assemblage along the lines suggested by Geneste (1985) shows a dominance of primary production activity, but also habitual tool use and maintenance. In that the length of the reduction stream reflected by an assemblage is often correlated directly with the residential permanency of the group that produced it, the occupation of the shelter would appear to have been more than an ephemeral one, most likely falling within Butzer's (1982) 'temporary' campsite category.

In discussing residential permanence, Butzer's (ibid.: 238-9) distinction between ephemeral, temporary, seasonal, and semipermanent camps is useful in defining specific points along a continuum of differing degrees of mobility. In giving primacy to spatial and temporal variables, Butzer (ibid.: 238) defines different camp types as follows: ephemeral

(several hours to a few days), temporary (several days to several weeks), seasonal (several months), and semipermanent (several months, repetitively over several years).

Other lines of evidence for establishing the duration of settlement at Tor Faraj comes from the degree to which tools were worked and from artifact density. Beyond marginally retouched pieces (45.7 percent), Levallois points (23.5 percent) form the dominant tool class, followed by notches (7.3 percent). Few of the formally retouched specimens show extensive edge modification, however. When compared to the small, higher elevation shelter of Tor Sabiha, the Tor Faraj assemblage does exhibit a higher proportion of retouched tools, an attribute thought to be connected with more intensive, longer occupations (Rolland 1981; Dibble 1984a), but the comprehensive data from the shelter indicate a middle range of occupational intensity. Artifact density, for example, averages about 78 specimens per $0.1m^3$ at Tor Faraj, whereas at Qafzeh, lithic densities range from low density layers registering > 50 specimens per $0.1m^3$ to high density levels where 200 to 250 specimens per $0.1m^3$ were recorded (Hovers 1997: 201). Hovers (ibid.: 252) also reports densities ranging from ca. 71 to 135 specimens per $0.1m^3$ at Amud Cave. Intra-site (and inter-layer) variability in artifact density coupled with potential inter-site variability in rates of deposition may significantly affect such comparisons, but at face value, the artifact density at Tor Faraj falls in the lower range of those reported for other sheltered sites in the region.

Beyond the artifactual evidence, the presence of relatively thin hearths preserved in compact, yet easily disturbed, sand suggests that the occupational episodes probably extended over a period of several days to a few weeks as opposed to longer periods as suggested for coastal sites in the Mediterranean woodlands (Lieberman 1993; Lieberman and Shea 1994). If such extended, seasonal encampments had been established at Tor Faraj, they would likely have dispersed hearths to the extent that they were unrecognizable, except as ash lenses. The number of hearths exposed on each of the floors is also more consistent with temporary as opposed to longer seasonal encampments. Additional evidence in support of a temporary occupation comes from the limited vertical displacement of refitted artifacts in which five specimens were found to exceed a vertical range of 15cm. An intensive occupation is more likely to have resulted in a greater amount of postdepositional vertical displacement of artifacts.

Technological data and implications for behavioral organization

In being able to trace the sequence of the generation of artifacts related to primary (cores from chert nodules) and secondary (cores on flakes) production, as well as their end-products (Levallois points, blade and flake blanks), we have the opportunity of partially understanding the relative timing and spacing of specific activities across the Tor Faraj living floors. The major sequence involved: (1) the importation of chert nodules to the site; (1a) the trimming and shaping of a nodule for the production of an initial Levallois point; (1b) the rejuvenation of a core's face for a subsequent point removal and the repeating of this process until a core was exhausted; (2) the selection of a large, thick, and relatively flat flake for use as core; (2a) the preparation of a core and the generation of blanks, both recognized by the presence of Nahr Ibrahim retouch; (3) the modification of Levallois points and blanks by secondary retouch (and burin blows); (3a) the use, rejuvenation, and abandonment of such tools.

If this sequence of activities is placed on a time-scale:

(1)   The time between importation and initial production cannot be determined.
(1a-1b) Primary production is likely to have been conducted continuously over a period of several minutes to hours.
(2-2a) The actual temporal relationship between the use of cores on flakes as opposed to nodules cannot be known, but at least in the initial processing, use of nodules must have preceded cores on flakes and these primary production events are likely to have been separated by a period of

hours or days. That is, some time would have had to have passed for nodules to become exhausted and secondary production from cores on flakes to have been required.
(3-3a) The use and maintenance of points and other tools are likely to have extended over several hours to days or weeks after production.

The sequence and its timing have important implications. First, there is no compelling reason why all these segments of production and use (with the possible exception of the secondary production) would have required more than a day in time and a single locus in space. In other words, nothing inherent to the technology would demand multiple activity loci. Therefore, if we find that these activity segments are spatially segregated, then we have to ask the question of why the occupants of the shelter would have undertaken different activities in different locations in the shelter.

Another important implication has to do with the use of cores on flakes. This secondary production, involving the recycling of flakes as cores, clearly indicates that the occupants of the shelter regularly experienced shortages of chert. This is not surprising since the most utilized chert sources were located outside their catchment some 22km away. From a temporal perspective, it is likely that after the importation of chert nodules at least a day or so would have passed before knappers would have had to recycle flakes for the production of points and other blanks. Given this, most flakes selected for recycling would have been gathered from various parts of the occupation floor. Again the most expedient production method would have been to establish a knapping area near the center of the distribution of such flakes. In contrast, if we find the same area was used for both primary and secondary production of blanks, then we have good evidence for a specialized activity area that was established for reasons other than simple expediency. These and other issues having to do with the spatial distributions of artifacts, features, and other evidence will be explored in Chapters 8, 9, and 10.

5 Small Lithic Debris Analysis

TERESA L. ARMAGAN

This study is unusual in that an often ignored category of artifacts, small lithic debris, was examined for what it could reveal about the prehistoric activities that occurred in Tor Faraj. Considering the great number of specimens of small lithic debris that were recovered, accounting for over 70 percent of the lithic artifacts, their analysis seemed important.

In not forming a common component of lithic studies, investigations of small lithic specimens are plagued by terminological ambiguity. In this work, the procedures and terminology employed in the earlier lithic studies at Tor Faraj are followed (Henry 1982, 1995c). Debitage refers to potential, but non-actualized tools, whereas debris applies to specimens that are too small to have been fashioned into tools, falling under 30mm in maximum dimension. For continuity's sake, the term 'small debris' is used here to designate artifacts measuring between 2mm and 30mm (maximum dimension), and 'microdebris' or 'microdebitage' for artifacts measuring less than 2mm. This study covers the examination of small debris, not microdebris.

Objectives of the study

The objectives of this study were: (1) to identify activity areas where certain lithic processing activities were taking place across the two living floors of the site; (2) to discern what types of loading techniques were being employed in each of the activity areas; and (3)

to trace the reduction sequence represented by each activity area.

Relevant to the first objective, there were areas at Tor Faraj where small debris was concentrated in association with hearths. Although some of these were most likely due to formation processes such as burning and thermal stress, others appeared to have been the result of lithic processing. Other debris concentrations were located away from large hearths, at the fringes of where most of the domestic activity seems to have taken place at Tor Faraj (Henry 1998a, Chapter 10, this volume).

The second goal of the study, that of identifying loading techniques, was based on the premise that certain attribute states expressed in the lithic material *have been shown* to be common to some manufacturing techniques and not so common to others (see references to Tables 5.1, 5.2, and 5.3). A comparative study undertaken by Wiseman (1993) which included Levantine Middle Paleolithic assemblages identified hard-hammer and soft-hammer percussion techniques, but Henry (1995b) suggested that some pressure flaking may have occurred at Tor Faraj. In this study, attribute states linked to all three varieties of loading were examined.

The final objective was to identify what parts of the reduction sequence were represented within each activity area. All reduction stages appeared to have been present in this assemblage; however, it was anticipated that small debris would help to identify initial versus final processing areas, because small debris would have been less likely than larger artifacts to have been carried off to another part of the site.

Methods

Each of the objectives listed above depended in part on some aspect of the first objective, i.e., identifying the activity areas. This consisted of isolating concentrations of small debris and then examining the concentrations for attributes indicative of certain lithic activities.

Establishing concentration areas

All of the matrix of the excavation was dry-sieved through 3-mm-square mesh and hand-picked. While some artifacts recovered were smaller than this, concretions and varying soil consistency mean there was some unknown degree of bias in the collection of very small debris. In addition, formation processes have distorted the number of small debris somewhat, especially through thermal fracture.

To identify the concentration areas, first artifacts were plotted by numbers of artifacts per quadrant (0.25m^2) per layer onto a Surfer (Golden Software, Inc.) generated contour map for each level of the site. Ambiguous layer designations, such as C/D$_1$, C?, and D$_1$/D$_2$, were evaluated as D$_1$, since this layer had an uncertain field designation relative to Layer C. Once maps were generated for each layer and each level, comparisons were made to determine the locations of artifact concentrations. A concentration was defined by the close nesting of those quadrants with the highest numbers of recovered small debris.

Small debris samples used to identify areas of concentration came from Levels 160 to 195. These samples represent those levels that largely correspond to Floor I (160 to 170) and Floor II (180 to 195) as followed in this volume. But inclusion of Level 175 in Floor I and exclusion of Level 195 from the study cause the overall samples of the small debris study and the other lithic-based studies to differ in absolute numbers of specimens reported.

The areas with the highest densities of small debris across the excavation block showed remarkable uniformity with four concentrations of artifacts occurring in similar

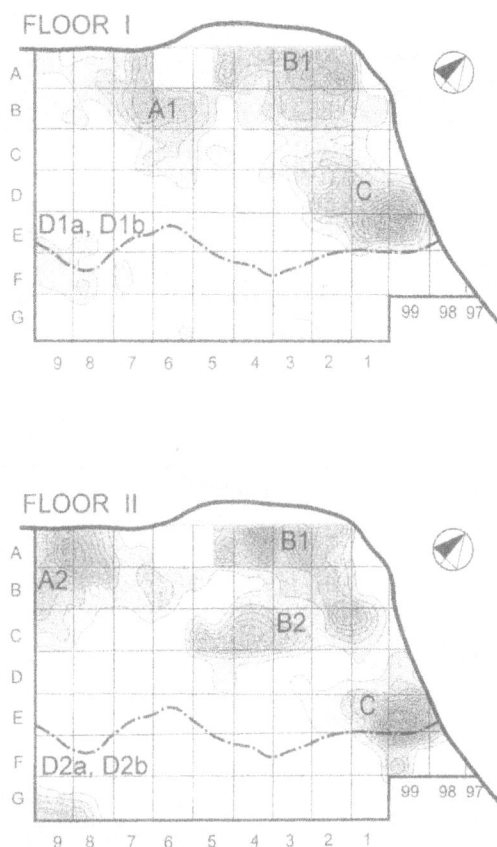

Figure 5.1 Maps of Floor I and Floor II at Tor Faraj showing the locations of small debris concentrations. Floor I (N = 3918 specimens) and Floor II (N = 6604 specimens) are plotted with density contours of 10 specimens

locations for both living floors (Figs 5.1a, b). In this study, each of these concentrations is referred to as a *cluster*. *Subcluster* labels were used to designate specific density peaks observed within clusters, but at different loci or layers.

Sampling techniques

Once general concentrations were established, samples were taken within each concentration for each floor. The samples consisted of those quads with 10 or more artifacts. This was done under the premise that artifacts cannot be typed individually because even the most distinctive attribute state can occur in low incidence from most of the loading techniques and during most or all of the reduction stages. Percentages of quads sampled were based on number of artifacts needed to ensure a large enough sample size of artifacts for both intra-cluster analysis and intra-site analysis in general.

In addition, there was some intentionally programmed bias in the sampling procedure. Within each concentration, quads with 10 or more artifacts were numbered, then a percentage of quads was chosen using a random number table. If, for example, the number for

Quad E9a, Level 165 was chosen, the numbers for Quad E9a on other levels of the floor could not be chosen. This was to ensure a sample with a large spatial distribution based on both horizontal and vertical planes.

Hypotheses for each objective

The hypotheses for the three objectives are listed in Tables 5.1, 5.2, and 5.3. For each one

Table 5.1 Intra-site attribute state predictors for possible explanations of small debris concentrations at Tor Faraj

	Formation processes				Lithic processing activity areas		
	Hearth area location	Other thermal formation processes	Chemical formation processes	Trampling and other mechanical processes	Lithic processing/ activity area location	Heat treatment area location	Dump area location
Raw material	high relative number of particular type(s) with burning	high relative number of particular type(s) with 'other' heat alteration	high relative number of type 6 (with heavy patination)		high relative number of particular type(s) without heat alteration	high relative number of particular type(s) with heat treatment	mixed types
Artifact class	more shatter and 'other' class (from burning)	more shatter and 'other' class (from 'other' heat alteration)	more broken flakes with heavy patination	more broken flakes (especially without thermal alteration)	more complete flakes	possibly a higher amount of shatter and 'other' class	fewer complete flakes; more shatter?
Thermal alteration	more burnt artifacts	more 'other' heat alteration			more artifacts without heat alteration	burnt, heat-treated, and 'other' heat alteration	mixed
Patination degree	more patination in general		more heavy patination			more patination in general	
Cortex amount					clustering by amount category		mixed
Cortex type	clusters of same type(s) per raw material	clusters of same type(s) per raw material			clusters of same type(s) per raw material	clusters of same type(s) per raw material	mixed
Artifact size				generally smaller			generally larger/ larger platforms
Loading technique					one or more types		mixed types
Reduction sequence					one or both stages		mixed stages

Note: Blank cells denote instances where no particular attribute state is helpful in determining a reason for a debris concentration

Table 5.2 Intra-site attribute state predictors for loading techniques that were possibly used at Tor Faraj during lithic processing

	Loading techniques		
	Hard-hammer percussion	**Soft-hammer percussion**	**Pressure flaking**
Flake types	DEB and 'r' flakes absent (4)	DEB and 'r' flakes present (4)	
Residual striking platform	lower percent remaining (7)	lower percent remaining (7)	higher percent remaining (7)
Platform/bulbar crushing	more frequent (4) than PR (8)	less frequent (4); more frequent than PR (8)	less frequent than HH and SH (8)
Lipping	less frequent (3, 4, 5, 6, 10)	more frequent (3, 4, 5, 6, 10)	more frequent (3)
Bulbar scarring	present (3)	absent (3)	absent (3)
Point of impact features	more frequent (3, 4); present (10)	less frequent (3, 4); absent for flakes made w/non-stone hammers (10)	absent (3)
Multiple bulbs	present (9)	present (9)	absent (9)
Ventral rippling			low frequency (7)
Length	shorter (2, 10)	longer (2), for flakes made with non-stone hammers (10)	most are < 5.66 mm (1)
Width	larger (2); more variable (8)	smaller (2); more variable (8)	less variable (8)
Thickness	thicker relative to length (2, 4, 10)	thinner relative to length (2, 4), for flakes made w/non-stone hammers (10)	thinner (3); thinner at 4mm size-grade (5)
Platform width	larger (2)	smaller (2)	
Platform thickness	larger (2, 4)	smaller (2, 4)	
Platform size/weight or length ratio	larger (4, 10)	smaller (4), for flakes made with non-stone hammers (10)	
Weight	heavier (1, 2); slightly heavier than SH (5)	lighter compared to HH (1, 2, 5)	lighter compared to HH and SH (1, 5)
Bilateral symmetry	higher frequency of poor symmetry (6); low amount of symmetry (7)	lower frequency of poor symmetry (6); higher amount of symmetry than HH, but lower than PR (7)	medial amount of symmetry (7)
Cross-sectional symmetry	low amount (7)	medial amount (7)	high amount (7)

Notes: Blank cells denote instances where no attribute state for a particular attribute is helpful in determining a specific loading technique. Numbers denote references from which information has been derived for the hypotheses: 1) Ahler (1989a, b); 2) Amick *et al.* (1988); 3) Cotterell and Kamminga (1987); 4) Hayden and Hutchings (1989); 5) Henry *et al.* (1976); 6) Patterson (1982b); 7) Patterson and Sollberger (1978); 8) Sollberger and Patterson (1976); 9) Speth (1972); 10) Wenban-Smith (1989)
Key: HH/SH – hard-hammer/soft-hammer (percussion/flakes); PR - pressure flaking (flakes); DEB - distinctive expanding billet flake; 'r' - distinctive SH flake with an 'r'-like shape; (See Appendix A for definitions of DEB and 'r' flakes)

Table 5.3 Intra-site attribute state predictors for lithic reduction stages at Tor Faraj

	Initial processing stage	Final processing stage
Loading technique	more hard-hammer percussion (inferred from 5)	mixed loading techniques (inferred from 5)
Artifact class	fewer complete flakes (3, 6); fewer broken flakes (6); more shatter (3, 6, 9)	more complete flakes (3, 6); more broken flakes (6); less shatter (3, 6, 9)
Cortex amount	higher (1, 2, 4, 5, 9)	lower (1, 2, 4, 5, 9)
Dorsal scar count	lower (2, 4)	higher (2, 4)
Overall artifact size	larger (8, 10)	smaller (8, 10)
Weight	larger (5)	smaller (5)
Length	larger (5, 7, 9)	smaller (5, 7, 9)
Width	larger (5)	smaller (5)
Thickness	larger (5)	smaller (5)
Platform width	larger (5)	smaller (5)
Platform thickness	larger (5)	smaller (5)
Platform facets	fewer facets (9)	more facets (9)
Platform cortex	more frequent (inferred)	less frequent (inferred)

Note: Numbers denote references from which information has been derived for the hypotheses: 1) Ahler (1989a, b); 2) Amick *et al.* (1988); 3) Baumler and Downum (1989); 4) Mauldin and Amick (1989); 5) Odell (1989); 6) Prentiss and Romanski (1989); 7) Raab *et al.* (1979); 8) Stahle and Dunn (1982); 9) Tomka (1989); 10) Towner and Warburton (1990)

of these tables, the attributes are listed in the left-hand column, the hypotheses are listed across the top, and the predicted attribute states are listed in the cells underneath. For each of these, the null hypothesis is that there would be no statistical differences in frequencies of attribute states for each of the attributes, either within or between areas of the site.

• *Activity area hypotheses.* While identifying an activity area sounds like it should be simple, it must be remembered that, for the first objective, a debris concentration does not necessarily equate to an activity area. Table 5.1 lists the possible reasons for concentrations of debris found across Tor Faraj. In effect, each column of Table 5.1 constitutes the hypothesis of what attribute states must be found in order to identify the reason for the debris concentration. These reasons include both formation processes (hearth locations, other thermal

processes, chemical formation processes, and trampling and other mechanical processes) and activities (lithic processing activities, heat treatment, and dump area locations). Since activity area research has dealt mostly with larger artifacts or micro-debris, attribute states listed in Table 5.1 are largely inferred.

• *Loading technique hypotheses.* Table 5.2 lists possible loading techniques used at Tor Faraj. A loading technique is the way energy is delivered to a core or another flake for a removal. As mentioned above, three loading techniques were investigated: (1) hard-hammer percussion; (2) soft-hammer percussion; and (3) pressure flaking.

• *Reduction sequence hypotheses.* Table 5.3 lists those attributes linked to initial and final reduction stages. All studies referenced in Table 5.3 have attempted to break down the lithic reduction sequence into various stages. The most definitive stages, i.e., the ones associated with attributes that are found to be distinguished from the others statistically, are the initial and the final stages of processing. Although intermediate stages are undoubtedly present, these stages are continuous rather than discrete. Thus, I elected to view primary and final processing as end-points along a continuum by which to measure the emphasis on reduction within a specific concentration.

Measurement of attributes and attribute states

Speth (1972, 1974) has stressed the importance of evaluating the most informative, non-redundant attributes for the specific task at hand. To this end, the attributes listed in all three tables were measured for what they could reveal about small debris concentration areas at Tor Faraj. See Appendix A for definitions of attributes and attribute state codes used. Measurement techniques were taken from lab procedures employed for the Tor Faraj analysis and from definitions listed in small debris studies. In those instances where no adequate definition was given for an attribute state listed in the literature referenced in the previously listed tables, one was synthesized, particularly for the analysis of symmetry used to determine loading technique. These are discussed in detail within the individual definitions in Appendix A. When necessary, a Bausch and Lomb stereo microscope (1-7X) was used to observe attribute states.

Results

For each of the objectives of the study, attributes were examined for significant differences between subclusters for each of the two living floors (Figs 5.1a, b) and for significant differences between the floors themselves. Appendix B has the results for all the attributes. Examples of some of the attribute states found on Tor Faraj small debris are shown in Figures 5.2a to 5.2j.

Identification of loading techniques

Data tied to defining areas where hard-hammer percussion, soft-hammer percussion, and/or pressure flaking occurred are presented as tables for each attribute (Loading techniques attributes, in Appendix B) and statistical results are illustrated in histograms shown in Armagan (1998: Figs 4.2 to 4.17).

Direct percussion

Direct percussion (hard-hammer and soft-hammer) was found to dominate all of the subclusters of each floor (Tables 5.4a, b, c). Platform crushing, a clear signature of percussion, consistently occurs on a high percentage of specimens. Sollberger and Patterson (1976: 526) found that the highest amount of crushing for techniques that are not direct percussion was 11 percent (indirect percussion). Since the lowest amount within Tor Faraj subclusters is 23 percent, direct percussion is inferred. The presence of point of impact features and multiple bulbs of percussion in most subclusters also signals direct percussion.

While width measurements themselves do not directly indicate percussion over pressure flaking, greater width variability does. The high coefficients of variation for subclusters with smaller mean artifact dimensions indicate that they are more likely to be the result of percussion than of pressure flaking. And larger artifacts are more likely to be the result of percussion because of their size.

Hard-hammer percussion

For Floor I, hard-hammer percussion is indicated for every subcluster by the presence of bulbar scarring (Table 5.4a). For subclusters B1 and D1b, the absence of 'r' flakes may not necessarily preclude soft-hammer percussion; however, the significantly lower amount of good bilateral symmetry implies hard-hammer percussion. Subcluster D1a is more strongly linked to hard-hammer percussion. Not only are 'r' flakes absent, mean thickness for all complete flakes, mean platform width, and mean platform thickness are all significantly larger. Shorter mean lengths would seem to indicate hard-hammer percussion in subclusters B1, C, and D1b, but these shorter means could alternately be caused by clearing activities that would have removed larger debris from main areas.

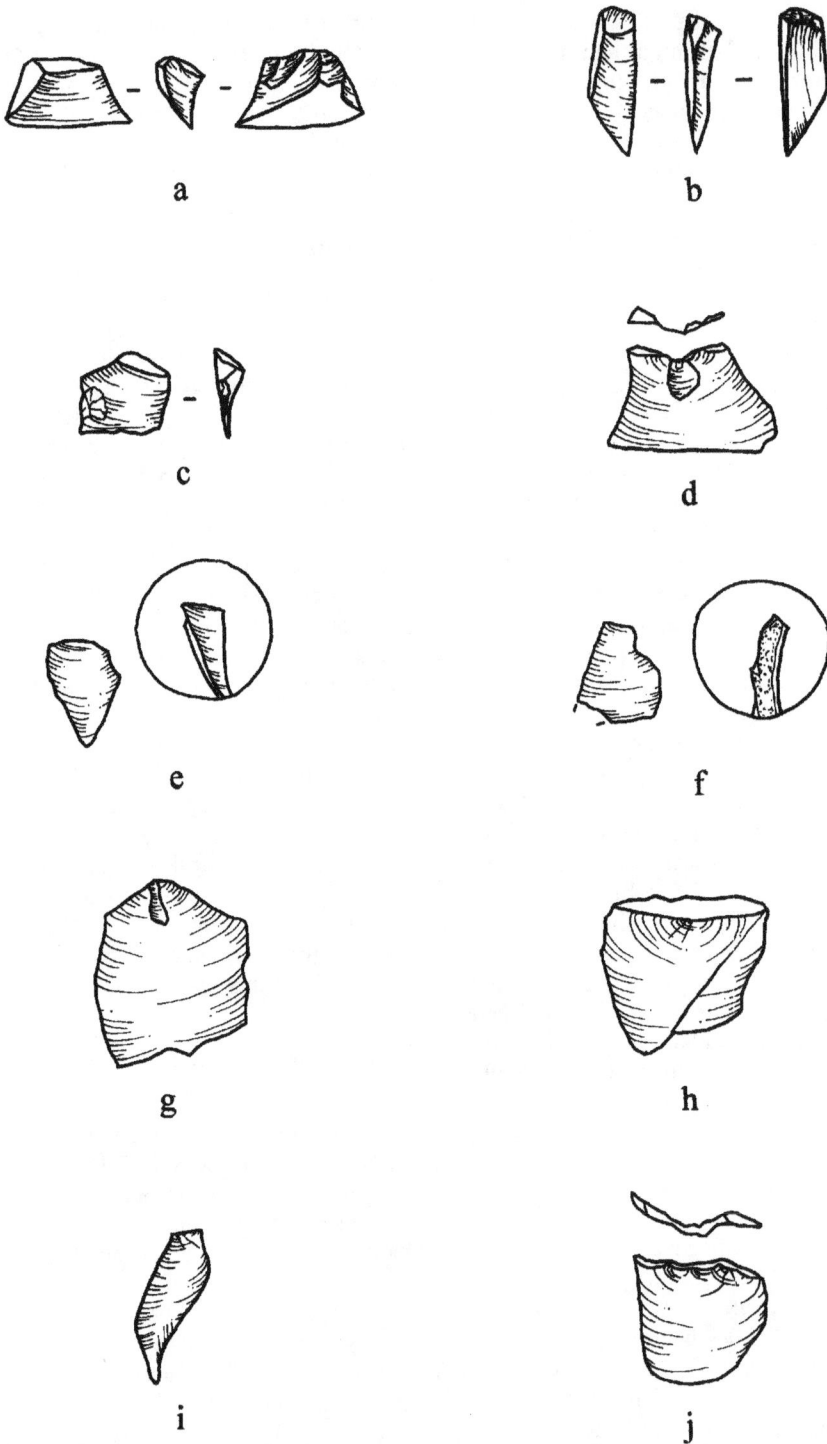

Figure 5.2 Examples of small debris attributes recorded for the Tor Faraj assemblage: a, 'r' flake - ventral, side, and dorsal views; b, 'r' flake - ventral, side, and dorsal views; c, 'r' flake - ventral and side views; d crushing and bulbar scar - ventral and platform views; e, lipping - ventral and side views, magnified 6X; f, lipping - ventral and side views, magnified 6 ×; g, point of impact features and bulbar scar - ventral view; h, point of impact features - ventral view; i, point of impact features - ventral view; j, multiple bulbs - ventral and platform views

Table 5.4

a. Loading technique indicators by each of the Floor I subclusters

Loading techniques	Subcluster A1	Subcluster B1	Subcluster C	Subcluster D1a	Subcluster D1b
Hard-hammer percussion	5	1, 5, 9,**† 20	5, 9,**† 19†	1, 5, 13, 17, 18, 19†	1, 5, 9,**† 20
Mixed hard- and soft-hammer percussion	3, 4, 6, 7, 8, 9, 10, 11, 12, 13, 14, 15, 16, 19, 21	3, 4, 6, 7, 8, 10, 12, 13, 14, 15, 16, 19, 21	3, 4, 6, 7, 8, 12, 14, 15, 16, 21	3, 4, 6, 7, 8, 9, 10, 11, 14, 15, 16, 21	3, 4, 6, 7, 8, 10, 11, 13, 14, 15, 16, 18, 19, 21
Soft-hammer percussion	1, 17, 18	11,† 17, 18	1, 11,† 17, 18	20	17
Mixed soft-hammer percussion and pressure flaking			13, 20		
Pressure flaking	2,* 20	2*	2,* 10	2,* 12***	2,* 12***

b. Loading technique indicators each Floor II subcluster

Hard-hammer percussion	1, 5, 11	5, 9**	1, 5, 19, 20	5, 9,** 19	5, 11	1, 5
Mixed hard- and soft-hammer percussion	3, 4, 6, 7, 8, 10, 13, 14, 15, 16, 17, 18, 19, 20, 21	3, 4, 6, 7, 8, 12, 13, 14, 15, 16, 17, 18, 19, 20, 21	3, 4, 6, 7, 8, 9, 10, 11, 12, 13, 14, 15, 16, 17, 18, 21	3, 4, 6, 7, 8, 10, 12, 13, 14, 15, 16, 18, 20, 21	3, 4, 7, 8, 10, 13, 14, 15, 16, 17, 18, 20, 21	3, 4, 6, 7, 8, 9, 10, 11, 13, 14, 15, 16, 17, 18, 19, 20, 21
Soft-hammer percussion	9**	1, 11		1, 11, 17†	1, 9,** 19	
Mixed soft-hammer percussion and pressure flaking					6	
pressure flaking	2,* 12***	2,* 10	2*	2*	2,* 12***	2,* 12***

c. Loading technique indicators by each floor

	Floor I	Floor II
Hard-hammer percussion	5, 9**	5, 11, 13,**** 17, 18
Mixed hard- and soft-hammer percussion	3, 4, 6, 7, 8, 10, 12, 14, 15, 19, 20, 21	3, 4, 6, 7, 8, 10, 12, 14, 15, 16, 19, 20, 21
Soft-hammer percussion	1, 11, 17, 18	1, 9**
Mixed soft-hammer percussion and pressure flaking	13, 16	
Pressure flaking	2*	2*

Notes: The attributes are as follows: 1) 'r' flakes; 2) residual striking platform; 3) platform/bulbar crushing; 4) lipping; 5) bulbar scarring; 6) point of impact features; 7) multiple bulbs of percussion, 8) ventral rippling; 9) length; 10) artifacts under 5.66mm; 11) width; 12) width variability; 13) thickness of all complete artifacts; 14) thickness of complete artifacts between 10 and 4mm; 15) thickness to length ratio; 16) weight; 17) platform width; 18) platform thickness; 19) platform area to weight ratio; 20) bilateral symmetry; 21) cross-sectional symmetry.

Table 5.4, *contd.*

*Residual striking platform may not be very informative as to loading technique.

**Other factors besides loading techniques may be influencing flake length for this subcluster/floor.

***Width variability may be too high to indicate pressure flaking.

****Thickness may merely indicate percussion with a stone-hammer (whether hard or soft).

†Attribute for this subcluster is not significantly different from other subclusters of this floor; however, it is comparable to a significantly different subcluster on the other floor

Floor II also shows the presence of hard-hammer percussion in every subcluster as evidenced by bulbar scarring (Table 5.4b). Subcluster A2 is more strongly associated with hard-hammer percussion by significantly larger mean widths and the absence of 'r' flakes. Subcluster D2a also has a significantly larger mean width. Subcluster B2 shows poor bilateral symmetry, an absence of 'r' flakes, and larger platform area to weight ratios. Subcluster D2b shows an absence of 'r' flakes, which could imply hard-hammer percussion. Subcluster C has significantly larger platform area to weight ratios. Finally, subclusters B1 and C show smaller mean lengths, resembling Floor I.

Both living floors appear to have resulted, at least partially, from hard-hammer percussion as indicated by comparable amounts of bulbar scarring (Table 5.4c). Floor II, however, has more attributes that show significant differences indicating hard-hammer percussion. Floor II artifacts have a higher mean width, thickness, platform width, and platform thickness. Floor I artifacts, on the other hand, have a shorter mean length, which could indicate hard-hammer percussion (though factors other than loading technique could also be affecting mean flake length).

Soft-hammer percussion

For Floor I, three subclusters had more indications of soft-hammer percussion than the others, subclusters A1, B1, and C. For each of these, the significantly smaller mean platform width and platform thickness indicate soft-hammer percussion. Subclusters C and A1 both contain 'r' flakes (a small number, but they are present nonetheless). And both subclusters B1 and C, though their mean widths are not significantly different from the rest of the Floor I subclusters, have means comparable to the significantly smaller mean widths of subclusters C and B1 of Floor II.

Subcluster D1a, while it has no artifacts that exhibit good bilateral symmetry, has only 57 percent with poor symmetry, which could indicate soft-hammer percussion. Subcluster D1b has a smaller mean platform width, comparable to subclusters A1, B1, and C.

Floor II has three subclusters that have more indications of soft-hammer percussion, subclusters C, B1, and D2a. All three contain 'r' flakes. And subclusters B1 and C have significantly smaller mean widths. In addition, subcluster C, while not having a significantly different mean platform width from other subclusters within Floor II, does have a mean comparable to subcluster B1 of Floor I, which was significantly lower among the subclusters of its floor. Subclusters A2 and D2a contain significantly longer mean lengths, which may either indicate soft-hammer percussion or, instead, the dumping locations of larger debris. Subcluster D2a artifacts possess significantly lower platform area to weight ratios and possess no point of impact features, which according to Cotterell and Kamminga (1987) indicates pressure flaking, but according to Wenban-Smith (1989) could indicate soft-hammer percussion.

Of the two floors, Floor I exhibits more indications of soft-hammer percussion in general. Both contain 'r' flakes, but Floor I artifacts have a smaller mean width, a smaller mean platform width, and a smaller mean platform thickness. Floor II, on the other hand, has a significantly larger mean length, which could indicate soft-hammer percussion. This may, however, point to other factors that will be discussed later in the chapter.

Pressure flaking

There are some attributes that might indicate pressure flaking, except that larger mean artifact dimensions seem to indicate percussion, rather than pressure flaking for the subclusters of both floors. For example, the frequency of residual striking platforms is uniformly high for all subclusters. Since so many other attributes indicate percussion, however, I infer that either this attribute is not as helpful a discriminator as Patterson and Sollberger (1978) believed, or I measured it in quite a different manner from them. Another attribute that indicates pressure flaking is a lower amount of width variability. Floor I subclusters D1a and D1b and Floor II subclusters A2, D2a, and D2b show lower amounts of width variability, but they had larger mean artifact dimensions, especially subclusters D1a, D1b, A2, and D2a. I would have liked to have compared my results to that of Sollberger and Patterson (1976), but they recorded their information with width ranges, rather than coefficients of variation, and did not list the standard deviations for experiments.

Another indicator of pressure flaking is small artifact size. Ahler (1989a, b) shows that most pressure flakes were under 5.66mm. In the samples tested for this study, only two subclusters even had complete flakes under 5.65mm, Floor I subcluster C (3 flakes) and Floor II subcluster B1 (2 flakes). These could have been the result of pressure flaking; however, it must be remembered that all loading techniques result in larger numbers of small flakes.

Floor I subcluster C has a significantly smaller mean thickness for all complete flakes, which could indicate pressure flaking; however, it is probably less reliable than the mean thickness to length ratio, which showed no significant differences between the subclusters of either floor.

Floor I subcluster A1 may have good enough bilateral symmetry to indicate pressure flaking. Patterson (1982b: 57) did not do experiments with pressure flaking; however, the symmetry frequencies he listed for soft-hammer percussion (7 to 12 percent good, 17 to 23 percent fair) are exceeded by subcluster A1 (and slightly exceeded by subcluster C). Patterson and Sollberger (1978) did do experiments with pressure flaking, but they listed bilateral symmetry as presence/absence. Pressure flaking was listed as 49 percent symmetrical; soft-hammer percussion as 39 percent symmetrical (*ibid.*: 108). If the frequency of good and fair symmetry for subcluster A1 is taken together,

it equals 50 percent, which could indicate pressure flaking.

The lower frequencies of rippling of some subclusters cannot be equated with pressure flaking. The lowest frequency of rippling is in subcluster C, Floor I. At 54 percent, it is well above the 29 percent that Patterson and Sollberger (*ibid.*: 106) found for pressure flaking in their experimental study. Most probably the differences in rippling frequencies are due to characteristics of the raw materials used on the site.

There were some attributes that may either indicate pressure flaking or soft-hammer percussion. One of these is lipping (Cotterell and Kamminga 1987). There were no significant differences between the relative frequencies of any of the subclusters, yet all had at least a 20 percent incidence of lipping, which would indicate a consistent use of either soft-hammer percussion or pressure flaking.

Another attribute that may indicate pressure flaking has already been mentioned in the soft-hammer section. Floor II subcluster D2a artifacts possess no point of impact features, which could either indicate soft-hammer percussion or pressure flaking.

Overall, Floor II as a whole does not show any indication of pressure flaking. Floor I has a significantly smaller mean thickness of all complete flakes and a significantly smaller mean weight, which could indicate pressure flaking, but which most probably indicate soft-hammer percussion.

Summary

Overall, both hard-hammer and soft-hammer percussion appear to have been used during the occupation of both floors, but soft-hammer percussion was used more during the later occupation (Floor I). Within Floor I, subcluster C shows more evidence of soft-hammer percussion, subclusters A1 and B1 show a mix, and subclusters D1a and D1b appear to be mostly from hard-hammer percussion. Within Floor II, subcluster C and possibly subclusters B1 and D2a appear to have resulted from relatively more soft-hammer percussion, while subclusters A2, B2, and D2b were the result of mostly hard-hammer percussion. Pressure flaking is possibly indicated for some of the subclusters (mostly from

Floor I subclusters A1 and C), but the results indicating pressure flaking are generally more difficult to interpret.

Identification of reduction sequence

Investigators have broken the lithic reduction stream into varying numbers of stages (see references listed for Table 5.3), but they have generally found significant differences only between the first and last stages. In this study, since stage distinctions are, in the end, somewhat arbitrary, only two stages are investigated: initial processing (i.e., core reduction) and final processing (i.e., tool production/maintenance). The section Lithic reduction stage attributes, in Appendix B, shows the results of attribute testing based on hypotheses made in Table 5.3. Results of statistical tests linked to the testing of hypotheses are illustrated in histograms in Armagan (1998: Figs. 4-10, 4-11, 4-18 to 4-23).

Initial processing

For Floor I, subcluster D1a has several dimensions indicating initial processing, all of them linked to larger artifact dimensions (Table 5.5a). Interestingly enough, those subclusters that have lower amounts of either dorsal scar counts or platform facet counts, indicating initial processing, also have the smaller dimensions which could indicate final processing (particularly subclusters B1 and C). Subcluster A1 does have a larger mean weight of artifacts and a mix of other size dimensions that would put it somewhere in the middle. Subcluster D1b also has some

Table 5.5 Reduction stages used at Tor Faraj, as indicated by attributes

A. Floor I					
Reduction stages	**Subcluster A1**	**Subcluster B1**	**Subcluster C**	**Subcluster D1a**	**Subcluster D1b**
Initial processing	4, 10**	10**	3,** 10**	4, 7, 8, 9	1*
Mix of stages	2, 5, 6, 7	2, 3, 7	2	1, 2, 5, 6	2, 3, 4, 6, 7
Final processing	1, 3,** 8, 9	1, 4, 5,† 6,† 8, 9	1, 4, 5,† 6,† 7, 8, 9	3,** 10**	5,† 8, 9, 10**

B. Floor II						
Reduction stages	**Subcluster A2**	**Subcluster B1**	**Subcluster B2**	**Subcluster C**	**Subcluster D2a**	**Subcluster D2b**
Initial processing	4, 5, 6, 8		4	10**†	4, 5, 6, 8	1,* 4
Mix of stages	1, 2, 7, 9	2, 3, 7, 10	1, 2, 3, 5, 6, 7, 8, 9, 10	1, 2, 3, 7, 9	2, 7, 9, 10	2, 5, 6, 7, 8, 9, 10
Final processing	3,**† 10**†	1,† 4, 5, 6, 8, 9		4, 5, 6, 8	1, 3**†	3**†

C. Comparison between floors		
Reduction stages	**Floor I**	**Floor II**
Initial processing		1,* 4, 5, 6, 7, 8, 9
Mix of stages	2, 3, 10	2, 3, 10
Final processing	1,* 4, 5, 6, 7, 8, 9	

Notes: The attributes are as follows: 1) artifact class; 2) cortex amount; 3) dorsal scar count; 4) weight; 5) length; 6) width; 7) thickness; 8) platform width; 9) platform thickness; 10) platform facet count.

*Results for artifact class are actually quite mixed for this subcluster/floor.

**Other factors may be influencing this attribute.

†Attribute for this subcluster is not significantly different from other subclusters of this floor; however, it is comparable to a significantly different subcluster on the other floor

dimensions that seem to fall between the stages. However, it also has a low amount of complete flakes, comparable to what Prentiss and Romanski (1989: 91) found for tool reduction both before and after trampling. (Note that in Appendix B the attribute state frequencies for artifact class for subcluster D1b is virtually identical to Floor II subcluster D2b.) This is mitigated, however, by the fact that overall rates of shatter are low for all subclusters, indicating final processing rather than initial processing.

Floor II shows initial processing to be likely in subclusters A2 and D2a, given the larger artifact sizes in these areas (Table 5.5b). Subclusters B2 and D2b show artifacts with larger weights that would indicate initial processing, but their other dimensions appear to put them somewhere in between the two stages. As stated above, subcluster D2b also has the distinction of having a low frequency of complete flakes, but a low amount of shatter mitigates anything that can be said about initial processing in this subcluster. Subcluster C artifacts display the lower amounts of platform facets that might indicate initial processing; however, other attributes indicate final processing or a mix of the two stages. Subcluster B1 is the only subcluster that does not show any indications of being the result of initial processing.

A comparison of the two floors suggests that more initial processing took place on Floor II. Every artifact dimension for Floor II has a larger mean than that of Floor I, but other indications of initial processing are missing. One would expect more cortex, fewer dorsal scars, and fewer platform facets for the artifacts of Floor II, but there are no significant differences between these attribute states for the two floors.

Final processing

For Floor I, subclusters B1 and C have the strongest indications of final processing (Table 5.5a). Each shows smaller overall artifact dimensions. Subclusters A1 and D1b show indications of final processing by their smaller platform dimensions, with subcluster A1 also showing a higher amount of dorsal scars, while subcluster D1b shows a higher amount of platform facets. For subcluster D1a, the only attribute states that could be interpreted

as indications of final processing are the high amounts of dorsal scar and platform facet counts. These could, however, also be more a function of the larger size of the artifacts in this subcluster, rather than indications only of reduction stage.

Smaller artifact sizes indicate that most of the final processing for Floor II appears to have been done in subclusters B1 and C (Table 5.5b). Subclusters A2, D2a, and D2b have high amounts of dorsal scar counts, but as discussed above, this could be a function of their larger size rather than only reduction stage. Only subcluster B2 shows no indication of final processing (and only one attribute indicating initial processing). It would appear to be the result of a mix between the two stages.

As mentioned in the initial processing section, Floor I has smaller overall artifact dimensions, which could indicate that, relative to initial processing, more final processing occurred during the occupation of Floor I. However, as mentioned above, the more distinctive indications of initial and final processing are missing.

Summary

The results of the attribute analyses show some interesting trends that were not really expected. Foremost, it was thought that dorsal scar count, cortex amount, and platform facet count would be more helpful in determining areas of initial processing. It was hypothesized that areas of initial processing would have the larger artifacts, lower dorsal scar and platform facet counts, and a higher incidence of cortex (Table 5.3). The above analysis shows that subcluster areas with larger artifact dimensions also have more dorsal scars and more platform facets, and cortex is not more evident. Not only did the incidence of cortex fail to co-vary as expected, cortical coverage is actually relatively low compared to experimental studies of core reduction (Ahler 1989b: 94; Mauldin and Amick 1989: 71; Tomka 1989: 138). In addition, artifact class attribute states show a relatively high frequency of complete flakes and low frequency of shatter overall, with some of the highest frequencies of shatter co-occurring in the same subclusters as the highest frequencies of complete flakes.

Table 5.6a Tor Faraj Floor 1 explanations for concentration areas as indicated by attributes

	Subcluster A1	Subcluster B1	Subcluster C	Subcluster D1a	Subcluster D1b
Raw materials (Armagan 1998: Appendix C)	Amounts of artifacts without burning or 'other' thermal alteration: **high** (15 and up): type 1 (35.0% cmplt; 25.0% ctx) type 4 (40.0% cmplt; no cortex)	Amounts of artifacts without burning or 'other' thermal alteration: **high** (15 and up): type 1 (26.1% cmplt; 4.3% ctx) type 2 (22.7% cmplt; 18.2% ctx) type 4 (33.3% complete; 4.8% shatter; 9.6% ctx)	Amounts of artifacts without burning or 'other' thermal alteration: **high** (15 and up): type 1 (31.8% cmplt; 9.1% ctx) type 4 (36.4% complete; 4.5% shatter; 9.1% cortex)	Amounts of artifacts without burning or 'other' thermal alteration: **high** (15 and up): none	Amounts of artifacts without burning or 'other' thermal alteration: **high** (15 and up): none
	moderate (10-14): type 2 (54.5% cmplt; 18.2% ctx) type 8 (60.0% cmplt; 30.0% ctx)	**moderate** (10-14): type 3 (50.0% cmplt; no cortex)	**moderate** (10-14): none	**moderate** (10-14): none	**moderate** (10-14): type 4 (no complete; no cortex)
	low (5-9): type 3 (40.0% cmplt; 20.0% ctx) type 5 (12.5% complete; 20.0% shatter; 37.5% cortex) type 7 (66.7% complete; 16.7% shatter; 66.7% cortex)	**low** (5-9): type 7 (33.3% cmplt; no ctx)	**low** (5-9): type 2 (50.0% cmplt; 12.5% ctx) type 3 (33.3% cmplt; 33.3% ctx) type 8 (no complete; 14.3% cortex)	**low** (5-9): type 1 (20.0% cmplt; 20.0% ctx) type 4 (40.0% cmplt; 20.0% ctx)	**low** (5-9): none type 5 (no complete; 40.0% cortex)
	very low/none: none	**very low/none**: types 5 and 8	**very low/none**: types 5 and 7	**very low/none**: 2, 3, 5, 7, and 8	**very low/none**: types 1, 2, 3, 7, and 8
Artifact class (Armagan 1998: Appendices C, D, E)	**Complete**: 24.5% **Broken**: 46.4% (53.4% not burnt or 'other') (6.7% of all artifacts are broken w/heavy patina) **Shatter**: 5.5% **Other**: 23.3% (esp. type 6) (60.5% burnt, 28.9% 'other' thermal alteration)	**Complete**: 21.2% **Broken**: 53.5% (64.2% not burnt or 'other') (9.4% of all artifacts are broken w/heavy patina) **Shatter**: 5.3% **Other**: 20.0% (esp. types 8, 6, and 2) (76.5% burnt, 5.9% 'other' thermal alteration)	**Complete**: 23.5% **Broken**: 57.4% (67.1% not burnt or 'other') (12.7% of all artifacts are broken w/heavy patina) **Shatter**: 4.4% **Other**: 14.7% (esp. types 8 and 3) (50.0% burnt, 46.7% 'other' thermal alteration)	**Complete**: 24.0% **Broken**: 66.0% (62.5% not burnt or 'other') (24.0% of all artifacts are broken w/heavy patina) **Shatter**: 6.0% **Other**: 4.0% (50.0% burnt, 0% 'other' thermal alteration)	**Complete**: 9.5% **Broken**: 73.4% (91.2% not burnt or 'other') (41.9% of all artifacts are broken w/heavy patina) **Shatter**: 2.7% **Other**: 13.5% (esp. type 6) (90.0% burnt, 10.0% 'other' thermal alteration)
Thermal alteration (Armagan 1998: Appendix D)	**Burnt**: 23.3% (esp. types 6, 8, and 2) **Heat treated**: 3.1% (esp. type 4 (12.0%)) **Other**: 12.9% (esp. types 1, 7, 3, 4)	**Burnt**: 21.8% (esp. types 8, 6, and 2) **Heat treated**: 1.8% **Other**: 2.9%	**Burnt**: 14.7% (esp. types 8, 3, and 2) **Heat treated**: 2.0% **Other**: 14.2% (esp. types 8, 1, 6, and 3)	**Burnt**: 10.0% (esp. type 8) **Heat treated**: 2.0% **Other**: 6.0%	**Burnt**: 21.6% (esp. types 8 and 6) **Heat treated**: 5.4% **Other**: 5.4%
Patination degree (Armagan 1998: Appendices D, E)	**Patinated**: 66.8% **Heavily patinated**: 24.5% (esp. type 6 (79.5%)) (57.5% burnt; 10.0% 'other')	**Patinated**: 64.3% **Heavily patinated**: 21.8% (esp. types 6 (71.4%), 8, and 4) (43.2% burnt; no 'other')	**Patinated**: 75.0% **Heavily patinated**: 20.6% (esp. types 6 (72.4%) and 8) (14.3% burnt; 28.6% 'other')	**Patinated**: 86.0% **Heavily patinated**: 38.0% (esp. type 6 (75.0%)) (21.1% burnt; no 'other')	**Patinated**: 89.2% **Heavily patinated**: 58.1% (esp. types 6 (85.3%), 8, and 4) (27.9% burnt; 2.3% 'other')
Cortex amount (Armagan 1998: Appendix D)	17.8% have cortex	11.2% have cortex	16.2% have cortex	18.0% have cortex	21.7% have cortex
Cortex type (Armagan 1998: Appendix D)	**Limestone**: 10.4% (esp. types 7 and 8) **Gravel**: 7.4% (esp. type 1)	**Limestone**: 4.7% **Gravel**: 6.5%	**Limestone**: 9.3% (esp. types 2 and 8) **Gravel**: 6.9% (esp. types 1 and 4)	**Limestone**: 6.0% **Gravel**: 12.0% (esp. types 1 and 6)	**Limestone**: 10.8% (esp. types 5 and 8) **Gravel**: 10.8% (esp. type 2)

Table 5.6b Tor Faraj Floor I explanations for concentration areas as indicated by attributes

	Subcluster A1	Subcluster B1	Subcluster C	Subcluster D1a	Subcluster D1b
Artifact size (Armagan 1998: Appendix B)	Somewhat **larger mean weight** for all artifacts. Significantly **smaller mean platform sizes**	Significantly **smaller mean weight** for all artifacts. Significantly **smaller mean platform sizes**	Significantly **smaller mean weight** for all artifacts. Significantly **smaller mean platform sizes**	Significantly **larger mean weight** for all artifacts. Significantly **larger mean platform sizes**	Significantly **smaller mean weight** for all artifacts. Significantly **smaller mean platform sizes**
Loading techniques (Table 5.4a)	Soft-hammer, Hard-hammer	Soft-hammer, Hard-hammer	Soft-hammer, Hard-hammer	Hard-hammer, Soft-hammer	Hard-hammer, Soft-hammer
Reduction sequence (Table 5.3)	Final stage, Initial stage	Final stage, Initial stage	Final stage, Initial stage	Initial stage, Final stage	Final stage, Initial stage?
Final explanation	**Probably processed:** type 1 (initial, final) type 4 (final) (heat-treatment)	**Probably processed:** type 1 (final) type 2 (initial, final) type 4 (final)	**Probably processed:** type 1 (final) type 4 (final)	Probably a **dumping area**	
	Probably some processing: type 2 (initial?, final) type 8 (initial?, final?)	**Probably some processing:** type 3 (final)			**Probably some processing:** type 4 (final)
	Probably very limited processing: type 3 (initial?, final?) type 5 (intial) type 7 (initial?, final?)	**Probably very limited processing:** type 7 (final)	**Probably very limited processing:** type 2 (final) type 3 (initial?, final?) type 8 (initial?)	**Probably very limited processing:** type 1 (initial?, final?) type 4 (initial?, final?)	**Probably very limited processing:** type 5 (initial)
	A **hearth** was probably located in this area	A **hearth** was probably located in this area	A **hearth** was probably located in or close by this area	Probably no hearth	A **hearth** was probably located in this area and/or it was used for **dumping**
	Very little thermal alteration may be due to heat treatment	Most, if not all, thermal alteration appears to be due to burning	Most, if not all, thermal alteration appears to be due to burning	Most, if not all, thermal alteration appears to be due to burning	Most, if not all, thermal alteration appears to be due to burning
	Most heavy patination is probably due to burning	Much heavy patination is probably due to burning	Much heavy patination is probably due to other thermal alteration and burning	Most heavy patination is probably due to weathering and only slightly to burning	Most heavy patination is probably due to natural processes and some burning
		Trampling or more probably cleaning activities	Trampling or more probably cleaning activities		Trampling?

Table 5.7a Tor Faraj Floor II explanations for concentration areas as indicated by attributes

	Subcluster A2	Subcluster B1	Subcluster B2	Subcluster C	Subcluster D2a	Subcluster D2b
Raw materials (Armagan 1998: Appendix C)	Amounts of artifacts without burning or 'other' thermal alteration: **high** (15 and up): none	Amounts of artifacts without burning or 'other' thermal alteration: **high** (15 and up): type 1 (22.7% complete; 9.1% cortex)	Amounts of artifacts without burning or 'other' thermal alteration: **high** (15 and up): none	Amounts of artifacts without burning or 'other' thermal alteration: **high** (15 and up): none	Amounts of artifacts without burning or 'other' thermal alteration: **high** (15 and up): none	Amounts of artifacts without burning or 'other' thermal alteration: **high** (15 and up): none
	moderate (10-14): type 1 (50.0% complete; 20.0% cortex) type 4 (23.1% complete; no cortex)	**moderate** (10-14): none	**moderate** (10-14): type 3 (36.4% complete; 27.3% cortex)	**moderate** (10-14): type 1 (30.8% complete; 15.4% cortex) type 3 (50.0% complete; 10.0% cortex)	**moderate** (10-14): none type 1 (70.0% complete; no cortex) type 3 (50.0% complete; 20.0% cortex)	**moderate** (10-14): none
	low (5-9): type 2 (40.0% complete; 20.0% shattr; 60.0% ctx) type 3 (22.2% complete; 44.4% cortex)	**low** (5-9): type 2 (37.5% complete; 25.0% cortex) type 3 (55.6% complete; 22.2% cortex) type 4 (14.3% complete; no cortex) type 7 (50.0% complete; 37.5% cortex)	**low** (5-9): type 2 (33.3% complete, 16.7% shatter, no cortex)	**low** (5-9): type 4 (14.3% complete; 14.3% cortex)	**low** (5-9) type 4 (nc complete, no cortex)	**low** (5-9): type 1 (20.0% complete; no cortex) type 3 (no complete; 33.3% cortex)
	very low/none: types 5, 7, and 8	**very low/none**: types 5 and 8	**very low/none**: types 1, 4, 5, 7, and 8	**very low/none**: types 2, 5, 7, and 8	**very low/none**: types 2, 5, 7, and 8	**very low/none**: types 2, 4, 5, 7, and 8
Artifact class (Armagan 1998: Appendices C, D, E)	**Complete**: 20.6% **Broken**: 68.7% (72.7% not burnt or 'other') (15.3% of all artifacts are broken w/heavy patina) **Shatter**: 0.8% **Other**: 9.9% (esp. type 3) (69.2% burnt, none of 'other' thermal alteration)	**Complete**: 23.5% **Broken**: 59.7% (63.3% not burnt or 'other') (5.0% of all artifacts are broken w/heavy patina) **Shatter**: 2.5% **Other**: 14.3% (esp. type 6) (82.4% burnt, 17.6% 'other' thermal alteration)	**Complete**: 12.8% **Broken**: 46.8% (72.7% not burnt or 'other') (10.6% of all artifacts are broken w/heavy patina) **Shatter**: 3.2% **Other**: 37.2% (esp. types 6 and 3) (88.6% burnt, 11.4% 'other' thermal alteration)	**Complete**: 19.8% **Broken**: 56.3% (63.9% not burnt or 'other') (13.5% of all artifacts are broken w/heavy patina) **Shatter**: 4.2% **Other**: 19.8% (esp. types 6 and 3) (52.6% burnt, 47.4% 'other' thermal alteration)	**Complete**: 32.2% **Broken**: 57.6% (55.3% not burnt or 'other') (11.9% of all artifacts are broken w/heavy patina) **Shatter**: none **Other**: 10.2% (esp. type 3) (83.3% burnt, 16.7% 'other' thermal alteration)	**Complete**: 11.7% **Broken**: 76.6% (77.5% not burnt or 'other') (58.4% of all artifacts are broken w/heavy patina) **Shatter**: 2.9% **Other**: 7.8% (100% burnt, none of 'other' thermal alteration)
Thermal alteration (Armagan 1998: Appendix D)	**Burnt**: 25.2% (esp. types 8, 2, 6, and 3) **Heat treated**: 10.7% (esp. types 4 (27.8%), 3 (11.1%), 5 (40.0%))	**Burnt**: 21.0% (esp. types 6 and 2) **Heat treated**: 7.6% (esp. types 4 (33.3%) and 7 (22.2%))	**Burnt**: 38.3% (esp. types 6, 7, 8, and 3) **Heat treated**: 2.1%	**Burnt**: 19.8% (esp. types 6, 2, and 3) **Heat treated**: 7.3% (esp. type 4 (38.5%))	**Burnt**: 11.9% (esp. type 3) **Heat treated**: 25.4% (esp. types 3 (22.2%), 7 (50.0%), 4 (28.6%), 1 (15.4%))	**Burnt**: 20.8% (esp. type 6) **Heat treated**: 5.2% (esp. type 4 (12.0%))
	Other: 13.7% (esp. types 3 and 4)	**Other**: 6.7%	**Other**: 14.9% (esp. types 3 and 4)	**Other**: 17.7% (esp. types 3 and 4)	**Other**: 3.4%	**Other**: 5.2%
Patination degree (Armagan 1998: Appendices D, E)	**Patinated**: 79.4% **Heavily patinated**: 24.4% (esp. types 6 (72.4%), 8, and 7) (37.5% burnt; 9.4% 'other')	**Patinated**: 64.7% **Heavily patinated**: 17.6% (esp. type 6 (94.1%)) (71.4% burnt; 9.5% 'other')	**Patinated**: 71.2% **Heavily patinated**: 22.3% (esp. types 6 (28.1%), 8, and 7) (47.6% burnt; 14.3% 'other')	**Patinated**: 73.9% **Heavily patinated**: 28.1% (esp. types 6 (80.0%), 7, and 2) (40.7% burnt; 18.5% 'other')	**Patinated**: 83.0% **Heavily patinated**: 22.0% (esp. types 6 (57.1%), 7, and 1) (15.4% burnt; no 'other')	**Patinated**: 89.6% **Heavily patinated**: 79.2% (esp. types 6 (100%), 3, and 1) (26.2% burnt; 3.3% 'other')
Cortex amount (Armagan 1998: Appendix D)	24.5% have cortex	17.7% have cortex	18.1% have cortex	14.6% have cortex	23.7% have cortex	24.7% have cortex

Table 5.7b Tor Faraj Floor II explanations for concentration areas as indicated by attributes

	Subcluster A2	Subcluster B1	Subcluster B2	Subcluster C	Subcluster D2a	Subcluster D2b
Cortex type (Armagan 1998: Appendix D)	Limestone: 12.2% (esp. types 1 and 7) Gravel: 11.5% (esp. types 2 and 3)	Limestone: 10.1% (esp. types 6 and 7) Gravel: 6.7% (esp. type 3)	Limestone: 12.8% (esp. types 2, 7, and 8) Gravel: 5.3% (esp. type 1)	Limestone: 4.2% Gravel: 9.4% (esp. types 1 and 6)	Limestone: 11.9% (esp. type 7) Gravel: 11.9% (esp. types 3 and 6)	Limestone: 18.2% (esp. types 3 and 6) Gravel: 3.9% (esp. type 1)
Artifact size (Armagan 1998: Appendix B)	Significantly **larger mean weight** for all artifacts	Significantly **smaller mean weight** for all artifacts	Significantly **larger mean weight** for all artifacts	Significantly **smaller mean weight** for all artifacts. **Smaller mean platform widths**	Significantly **larger mean weight** for all artifacts	Significantly **larger mean weight** for all artifacts
Loading techniques (Table 5.4b)	Hard-hammer, Soft-hammer	Soft-hammer, Hard-hammer	Hard-hammer, Soft-hammer?	Soft-hammer, Hard-hammer	Hard-hammer, Soft-hammer	Hard-hammer, Soft-hammer
Reduction sequence (Table 5.3)	Initial stage, Final stage	Final stage, Initial stage?	Some initial stage, rest is between stages?	Final stage, Initial stage	Initial stage, Final stage	Mostly between stages, some initial stage, some final stage
Final explanation	**Probably some processing:** type 1 (initial?, final) type 4 (final) (heat-treatment)	**Probably processed:** type 1 (initial?, final)	**Probably some processing:** type 3 (initial, final)	**Probably some processing:** type 1 (initial?, final) type 3 (final)	**Probably some processing:** type 1 (final) type 3 (initial?, final?) (heat treatment?)	
	Probably very limited processing: type 2 (initial, final?) type 3 (initial) (heat treatment?)	**Probably very limited processing:** type 2 (initial?, final?) type 3 (initial?, final?) type 4 (final?) (heat treat.) type 7 (initial, final?)	**Probably very limited processing:** type 2 (final)	**Probably very limited processing:** type 4 (initial?, final?)	**Probably very limited processing:** type 4 (initial?, final?) (heat treatment)	**Probably very limited processing:** type 1 (final) type 3 (initial)
	A **hearth** was probably located in this area	A **hearth** was probably located in this area	A **hearth** was definitely located in this area	A **hearth** was probably located in this area	Probably no hearth. Possibly an area for processing of heat-treated artifacts?	A **hearth** was probably located in this area and/ or it was used for **dumping**
	Possibly some heat treatment	Most, if not all, thermal alteration appears to be due to burning	Most, if not all, thermal alteration appears to be due to burning	Possibly some heat treatment	Possibly some heat treatment	Most, if not all, thermal alteration appears to be due to burning
	Most heavy patination is probably due to burning and other thermal alteration	Most heavy patination is probably due to burning	Most heavy patination is probably due to burning and other thermal alteration	Most heavy patination is probably due to burning and other thermal alteration	Most patination is probably due to weathering	Most patination is probably due to weathering and some burning
		Trampling or more probably cleaning		Trampling or more probably cleaning		

These trends suggest that the earliest stages of initial processing were infrequently undertaken at the site. The low relative frequency of cortex and the fact that there are no significant differences between the subclusters for this attribute suggest that a major portion of the material carried onto site may have been decorticated elsewhere. The relatively low incidence of cortex, however, may have been tied to the unusual primary processing technology used in Levallois point production at Tor Faraj. The technological reconstructions based upon debitage analysis and refits (Chapters 4 and 6, this volume) underscore how little a chert nodule was modified before an initial Levallois point was removed. This extraordinary efficiency in primary processing may explain the lack of co-variation between the incidence of cortex on small debris and the other expected attributes of initial processing.

Examination of concentration areas

Attributes of small debris were examined in an effort to determine the nature of the formation processes and the lithic-related activities that were associated with each of the concentrations (see Table 5.1, Tables 5.6a and b for Floor I, Tables 5.7a and b for Floor II; Debris concentration attributes, Appendix B).

In order to identify the nature of the lithic-processing activities that were associated with specific subclusters, it was first necessary to identify, as far as possible, the formation processes that had occurred in each of them. These include: hearth locations, other thermal processes, weathering, and trampling and other mechanical disturbances such as cleaning activities.

Tables 5.6a and b and 5.7a and b show both formation processes and lithic processing for each subcluster area as indicated by each of the attributes. Information for these tables was derived from data presented in Appendix B.

Hearth locations

Though in itself a hearth constitutes an activity, the presence of a high amount of burnt material means that artifact numbers, and therefore some attribute states (such as the number of broken artifacts), are artificially skewed for analysis of reduction stages.

In order to identify hearth areas, each raw material was looked at in terms of heat alteration, artifact class, and patination. (Cortex was not found to be useful.) Burnt and 'other' heat alteration constitute almost all of the 'other' artifact class, with burnt artifacts generally outnumbering the 'other' thermally altered artifacts. Also, heavy patination seems to be somewhat associated with heat-altered artifacts in a majority of the subclusters.

As can be seen in Table 5.6a, every subcluster of Floor I contains burnt artifacts; however, subclusters A1, B1, and D1b all have at least 20 percent burnt artifacts. In addition, subclusters C and A1 each have over 10 percent 'other' thermal alteration, which could indicate that either their artifacts were near a hearth or they were subject to some other kind of thermal processes. While these data are largely consistent with the exposure of hearth features in concentrations B and C in Floor I, hearths were not identified in the excavated areas of A and D.

For Floor II, subclusters A2, B1, C, and D2b all show frequencies of burnt artifacts at around 20 to 25 percent (Table 5.7a). Of these, both subclusters C and A2 show 'other' thermal alteration greater than 10 percent. Subcluster B2 shows the highest amount of burnt artifacts of any subcluster (38.3 percent) plus a high amount of 'other' thermal alteration (14.9 percent). Subcluster D2a, like subcluster D1a from Floor I above it, shows a fairly low incidence of burning (11.9 percent) and 'other' thermal alteration (3.4 percent). Excavation of Floor II revealed hearth features in the concentration areas of A, B, and C, but not D.

Other thermal processes

It was thought that other thermal processes such as rapid freezing and thawing could possibly have affected the artifacts of Tor Faraj, thereby causing 'other' thermal alteration. It appears, however, that this attribute state is more dependent on raw material type. For example, for both floors raw material types 1 and 4 are more likely to show 'other' thermal alteration than they are to show typical indications of burning such as potlidding. Types 3, 5, and 7 are mixed. The rest are more likely to show actual burning, especially type 8 of which just over half are burnt for both floors. Since so much burning seems to have taken place, it is concluded that burning, rather than other thermal processes, predominantly affected the artifacts at Tor Faraj.

Weathering

Overall patination rates are quite high for both floors, ranging between 64 and 90 percent, which is not really surprising, given the 70Kb.p. age of the deposit. Floor I overall patination rates are lower for subclusters B1 and A1 (64.3 percent and 66.8 percent respectively), mid-range for subcluster C (75.0 percent), and high for subclusters D1a and D1b (86.0 percent and 89.6 percent respectively) (Table 5.6a). This is not really surprising given that this is consistent with a small portion of subcluster C and a larger portion of subclusters D1a and D1b lying outside the dripline. The heavy patination rates for subclusters A1, B1, and C range from about 20 to 25 percent and appear to be affected mostly by thermal alteration, especially for subcluster A1. Subclusters D1a (38.0 percent heavy patination) and D1b (58.1 percent) appear to be only somewhat affected by thermal alteration; therefore weathering processes more strongly affect the artifacts in these areas. With the exception of subcluster A2, Floor II artifacts show a similar pattern of patination as seen for Floor I (Table 5.7a). Compared to subcluster A1, subcluster A2 has an increased overall patination rate (79.4 percent); this perhaps indicates other weathering processes not associated with the dripline or with burning.

Trampling and other mechanical disturbances

It is difficult, but important, to identify trampling and other mechanical processes, since they skew artifact sizes and class frequencies which are also the attributes used to identify loading techniques and reduction sequence. As is mentioned elsewhere in this volume, other than some disturbance in the northwest corner of the excavation which probably affected the size and location of subcluster A1, Floor I, the floors appear to be relatively unaffected by later trampling. Fragile hearths (at least those within the dripline) have been found intact in a sediment in which they would easily disappear. This does not, however, take into consideration trampling and cleaning activities of the past inhabitants of Tor Faraj.

As can be seen in Appendix B, the attribute length shows that run counter to expectations, given the rest of the dimensional attributes listed. For example, the shorter relative length of complete specimens in subclusters C and B1 of both floors indicate hard-hammer percussion, while other attributes such as smaller mean widths and platform dimensions indicate soft-hammer percussion (see also Tables 5.4a and b). If soft-hammer percussion had been occurring in these areas, as other attributes suggest, then some other factor (possibly trampling or cleaning activities) might account for short mean lengths and overall sizes of artifacts in these areas.

Table 5.6a shows that, of the broken artifacts for Floor I, subclusters D1b, C, B1, and A1 have higher rates of breakage for artifacts that are not burnt and do not have 'other' thermal alteration than the breakage rates for all artifacts. Since subclusters C and B1 have significantly smaller mean weights and platform sizes (while subcluster A1 has a larger mean weight), trampling or cleaning could have possibly occurred in these areas. Subcluster D1b also has a smaller mean weight and platform sizes; however, the area of subcluster D1b coincides with a rocky area that probably would not have been cleaned anyway. Here it is assumed that breakage rates and sizes coincide with lithic processing.

Floor II shows the frequencies of broken artifacts that are not burnt and do not have 'other' thermal alteration to be higher than the frequencies of broken flakes overall for subclusters B2, C, B1, and A2 (see Table 5.7a). Of these, mean artifact weights are significantly smaller only in subclusters C and B1, and mean platform width is smaller in subcluster B1, possibly indicating some trampling and/or cleaning of these areas.

Lithic activity areas

The three activities considered here and their attendant loci include: lithic processing areas, heat-treatment areas, and dump areas.

Lithic processing areas

By examining each raw material, especially

artifacts that are not burnt or show 'other' thermal alteration (the 'processed' artifacts), it should be possible to determine where lithic processing took place for any given raw material. This is not completely realistic, since at least some of the burned artifacts were in fact processed, but the procedure does largely distinguish small debris generated by thermal fracturing from that produced in manufacturing.

Tables 5.6a and 5.7a show the raw materials of each floor placed in groups of high, moderate, low, and very low/none, based on actual counts of complete flakes, broken flakes, shatter, and 'other'/indeterminate class artifacts (Armagan 1998: 160-7). As stated above, these counts do not include burnt or 'other' thermally altered artifacts, though they do include artifacts that have been heat treated and those for which thermal alteration or lack thereof was not discernible. The four groups into which the artifacts were placed were arrived at arbitrarily. Any raw material with 15 or more artifacts within a given subcluster is considered to be in the high category (and therefore more likely to have been processed) regardless of the total number of artifacts of this raw material that a subcluster has. The moderate category is considered to be 10 to 14 artifacts, the low category is 5 to 9 artifacts, and the very low/none category is from 0 to 4. For both tables, the frequency of complete flakes and shatter (if it was found) and presence of cortex are given also in order to give some idea of whether the processing might have been closer to the initial reduction stage or the final stage. These were used for the last row of Tables 5.6b and 5.7b, i.e., the final explanation.

For Floor I, subclusters A1, B1, and C furnish the greatest evidence for lithic processing and this was mainly related to chert types 1 and 4 (Tables 5.6a and b). Subcluster A1, given a higher frequency of cortex for the 'processed' artifacts (20.5 percent) as well as for all the artifacts in the subcluster (17.8 percent) appears to be where the majority of initial processing was taking place. Mainly types 1 and 4 were processed, with some processing of types 2 and 3. Subclusters B1 and C have lower incidences of complete flakes than subcluster A1 (30.5 percent and 31.6 percent of 'processed' artifacts respectively), but they also have lower frequencies of cortex as well (8.5 percent and 10.5 percent of

'processed' artifacts respectively). It appears that more final processing was occurring in both locations.

Much less processing appears to have occurred in subclusters D1a and D1b. In subcluster D1a, probably some very limited processing of types 1 and 4 was done. Since so few artifacts (24 by count) were examined as 'processed' artifacts, it is difficult to say what stage of processing was occurring, though the section on reduction stages indicates that it was probably more initial processing.

In Floor II, lithic processing was common to all of the subclusters with the exception of D2b. Although various chert types were used between subclusters, types 1, 3, and 4 predominate. From the data on loading techniques and reduction sequence, it can be inferred that initial processing with hard-hammer and some soft-hammer percussion was taking place in subclusters A2 (25.5 percent of 'processed' artifacts are complete flakes, 21.0 percent have cortex) and D2a (44.7 percent of 'processed' artifacts are complete flakes, 23.7 percent have cortex). More final processing with soft-hammer and some hard-hammer percussion was taking place in subclusters B1 (36.7 percent complete flakes, 18.3 percent cortex) and C (36.1 percent complete flakes, 16.7 percent cortex), and subcluster B2 (24.4 percent complete flakes, 18.2 percent cortex) is somewhere in between.

Heat-treatment areas

The locations described here are not necessarily where artifacts were treated, but where already treated artifacts were processed. Very little heat treatment occurred at all for Floor I and it seems likely that most heat-treated artifacts on this floor were just incidental to burning (Table 5.6a). For Floor II subclusters, heat-treatment frequencies are more variable, but only Subcluster D2a displays proportions of heat-treated artifacts (25.4 percent of all artifacts, 39.5 percent of the 'processed' artifacts) sufficiently high enough to suggest a 'heat-treatment' area (Table 5.7a).

Dump areas

The areas examined here are those related to dumping of lithic material. It is inferred that a dump area will consist of mixed amounts of many types of raw material, fewer complete flakes, mixed amounts of thermal alteration, and generally larger artifacts and platform sizes.

For Floor I, subcluster D1a provides the greatest evidence linked to a dump area. There appears to have been very limited processing of only two raw material types. There was a mix of thermal alteration, but not enough to state that a hearth was located in this area. Finally, artifacts have both a significantly higher mean weight and mean platform sizes. The only attribute that does not meet expectations is the high percentage of complete artifacts. Either this area was used for dumping, or there was lithic processing in this concentration area, and the smaller artifacts filtered down to layer D_1 (subcluster D1b). Subcluster D1b, the one that has been defined as layer D_1 artifacts, has some characteristics of a dump area, and in fact coincides with subcluster D1a. It has the lowest number of complete flakes, relatively less evidence for processing of any types but 4 and 5, and has a mix of thermal alteration (which actually indicates enough burning probably to infer a hearth location). The sticking point, however, is that the mean weight of all artifacts and the mean platform dimensions are significantly smaller than those of subcluster D1a, leading to the conclusion that, while artifacts may have been dumped in this same concentration area, those that fell between the rocks of the D_1 layer (to form subcluster D1b) were probably from processing and the effects of a hearth.

In Floor II, subcluster D2b exhibits the strongest evidence for dumping. It contains a low number of complete flakes (11.7 percent) and has a low incidence of processing of any types except small amounts of types 1 and 3.

Summary

The artifact concentrations at Tor Faraj are the result of both formation processes and lithic processing activities. Aside from lithic processing itself, which appears to have taken place in most of the subcluster areas, burning had the largest impact on the small debris of Tor Faraj.

For Floor I, subclusters A1, B1, and C

appear to be the main lithic processing areas, with more initial processing having occurred in subcluster A1 and more final processing and/or cleaning activities in subclusters B1 and C. All subclusters show evidence for both hard-hammer and soft-hammer percussion, but more soft-hammer percussion seems to have taken place in subclusters B1 and C. Subcluster D1a is either a possible dumping area, or it simply 'caught' larger artifacts, while smaller ones filtered down to the rocks below to form layer D_1, i.e., subcluster D1b artifacts. Hearths appear to have been associated with all subclusters, except possibly D1a. Possibly only raw material type 4 was intentionally heat treated. And finally, weathering processes most strongly affected the subclusters near the dripline, subclusters D1a, D1b, and C.

For Floor II, lithic processing activities appear roughly to coincide with the same subclusters as seen in Floor I. Subcluster B1 shows the most processing, followed by subcluster A2, then C and D2a, with an apparent mix of stages in each. As above, evidence for both hard-hammer and soft-hammer percussion occurs in every subcluster, but subcluster B1 and C show more evidence of soft-hammer percussion. Subcluster B2 shows some evidence of processing activities, but presence of hearths is so strongly indicated that processing is more than likely masked by thermally altered small debris. Subcluster D2b is more likely the dumping area of this floor. It shows only very limited processing of two raw material types, plus a low incidence of complete flakes. Hearths appear to be associated with subclusters A2, B1, C, D2a, and especially B2. And finally, as above, weathering more strongly affected the subclusters near the dripline, D2a, D2b, and C, and also strongly affected subcluster A2 for some unknown reason.

Conclusion

The results of the study of small debris at Tor Foraj have provided much useful information in support of intrepretations drawn from other lines of inquiry (e.g., areas of burning, initial and final lithic processing). But, perhaps more importantly, the study produced novel evidence for identifying activities in the shelter (e.g., cleaning and dumping) that would be difficult to detect through traditional lithic studies.

Small debris shows a mix of soft- and hard-hammer percussion, initial and final lithic processing, and extensive burning across all areas of the floor of the shelter. But Area D of Floor I and areas A and D of Floor II stand out as loci in which a greater emphasis was placed on hard-hammer percussion and initial lithic processing. Soft-hammer percussion and final processing dominate the other activity areas.

Small debris attributes also point to more extensive burning in those areas where hearth features were recorded during excavation, especially Area B of Floor II. This furnishes corroborative evidence for the identification of the hearths. An exception to this pattern was noted in Area D (subclusters D1b and D2b) where high frequencies of burnt small debris were identified even though a hearth feature was not encountered in the excavation of either floor. In conjunction with other attributes (i.e., size, breakage, diversity of chert types), the high proportion of burnt small debris in absence of hearths in Area D may indicate that ash and sediments from hearth cleanings, as well as other habitation refuse, were dumped there. From another perspective, the relatively smaller sizes of the samples recovered from areas B and C (for both floors) may reflect the intentional cleaning of that part of the shelter.

Area D also displays a very high proportion of patinated artifacts. This confirms that the rate of deposition and attendant burial of artifacts occurred much more slowly along and outside the dripline. This phenomenon, however, was also detected in Area A of Floor II which rests well inside the dripline and the reason for this is really not understood.

In the end, it appears that something very small can indeed make a large contribution to site analysis. Small lithic debris contain the marks of both activities and formation processes, which can help build a more complete picture of how a site was formed, even in the absence of other information.

6 Into the Mind of the Maker: Refitting Study and Technological Reconstructions

YU. E. DEMIDENKO AND V. I. USIK

Studies focusing on the articulation of artifacts through conjoins and refits have their historical roots in the late nineteenth century (Spurrell 1880a, 1880b; Smith 1984), but it has been only since the seminal work at the Magdelenian site of Pincevent (Leroi-Gourhan and Brézillon 1966, 1972) that the real importance of this approach has been recognized (Cziesla *et al.* 1990; Hofman and Enloe 1992).[1] The *refitting method* assists in solving three principal kinds of archaeological problems: stratigraphic, planigraphic, and technologic. The positions of refits within a deposit provide important information for understanding the deposit's stratigraphy and formation processes (Cahen and Moeyersons 1977; Villa 1982). Similarly, the planigraphic distributions of refitted artifacts allow for the reconstructions of their 'life histories' and the associated occupational structures of sites (Leroi-Gourhan and Brézillon 1966, 1972; Cahen *et al.* 1979; Cahen and Keeley 1980). Refitted artifacts also furnish a means of reconstructing core reduction sequences with great clarity and, in so doing, provide a wealth of information on the methods, techniques, and technologies of the primary flaked stone processes of sites and particular industries (Marks and Volkman 1983; Volkman 1983; Van Peer 1992; Sellet 1995). The approach taken here has been to employ the refitting method to address each of these objectives

with the materials from Tor Faraj , but it is the technological reconstructions that will be emphasized within this chapter. The implications of refits for the site's stratigraphy and structure are examined in Chapters 3, 8, and 10.

Background: technological implications of refitting method

While students at Kiev University, we were guided by V. N. Gladilin in the examination of the Middle to Upper Paleolithic transition of the Carpathian-Balkan region. This was done largely by tracing changes in primary flaking processes as reconstructed through the refitting method. Our research not only proved successful to better understanding the local Middle-Upper Paleolithic transition (Gladilin and Demidenko 1989, 1990; Usik 1989), it also led us to explore parallel changes within corresponding Industries of the Near East (Demidenko and Usik 1993c, 1993d, 1994, 1995). These changes include a progressive development of Levallois method from a radial flake technique to a unidirectional, pointed flake technique within the final phases of the Middle Paleolithic to a bidirectional, pointed blade technique during transitional times. Our research also highlighted the importance of defining the main technical features and peculiarities of *pointed* Levallois-Mousterian industries and establishing their potential evolutionary trajectories into the Upper Paleolithic.

Methodology of refitting analysis

Although it is not as yet commonly employed, the use of the refitting method is no longer a novel feature in the analytic programs of Paleolithic studies. Even with the increase in its use, however, the method largely seems poorly understood. There appears to be a general perception that the refitting method is simple in its application and relatively well defined in procedure. Unfortunately, neither is the case.

Numerous reports describe the application and results of refits, but few works describe the specific procedures involved in the method. Moreover, when such discussions occur, they tend to be cursory and specifically focused on methods as applied to particular artifact assemblages (Volkman 1983: 128-9; Saragusti and Goren-Inbar 1990: 173-4). In generally failing to examine the procedure as employed in other studies from a purely methodological perspective, the refitting method appears to lack the kind of analytic evolution and attendant refinement in applications as seen in other methods (e.g., edge-wear studies). Lacking a common set of principles by which to guide the refitting process, the procedure all too often is employed intuitively, dependent upon good luck in matching specimens or the 'magic hands' of an especially talented analyst.

Given these observations, a general methodology is presented here for undertaking a refitting analysis. This methodology is not only applicable to the study of materials from Tor Faraj, but to other Industries employing Levallois and blade technologies and, to a lesser extent, lithic assemblages in general. The methodology, focusing on primary core reduction, is based upon our studies of several Middle and Upper Paleolithic assemblages from the Ukraine and Near East (Usik 1989; Demidenko and Usik 1991, 1993a).

Important assemblage characteristics

The degree to which a refitting study is successful depends upon a number of conditions associated with the assemblage under analysis. These fall within the domains of (1) depositional setting; (2) excavation format; and (3) raw materials. Ideally, an assemblage needs to have been recovered from a relatively well defined cultural horizon, usually not more than 10 to 20cm thick and lacking any significant post-depositional disturbance. In deposits containing multiple occupations, cultural horizons need to be separated by thick sterile lenses. Otherwise potentially refitted specimens are likely to be dispersed throughout several layers (e.g., Terra Amata [Villa 1982]). Ideally, an assemblage should be recovered from a kind of 'living floor' produced from an ephemeral occupation associated with intensive primary and secondary stone tool processing. In such settings, artifacts should be associated with specific paleosurfaces. Examples of such sites include Boker Tachtit, levels 1 to 4 in Israel (Marks and Volkman 1983, 1987), Korolevo I, complexes 1a and 2b (Usik 1989; Demidenko and Usik 1994), and Kabazi II, levels of Unit II in the Ukraine.

The scale of the excavation is also important to a successful refitting study. In our experience, excavation blocks of at least some 30 to 50m^2 appear necessary to capture the minimum spatial distributions of artifacts dispersed from a few knapping loci. Also, excavations of this scale are normally required to generate the artifact samples needed for a successful refitting of specimens and reconstruction of the technology.

The characteristics of the raw materials of an assemblage also strongly influence the degree to which specimens can be refitted. In general, the probability of refitting specimens is directly related to an assemblage's variability in raw material, as visually recognized, but extreme raw material variability may interfere with the recognition of refits as well. Ideally, an assemblage should have several, roughly balanced, distinctive raw material varieties. The Khormusan Site 1017 in the Sudan (Sellet 1995) contains close to an ideal combination of raw material varieties represented by Precambrian rocks, chert pebbles, sandstone, quartz, and fossil wood. Assemblages exhibiting a single predominant raw material or a raw material with wide, internal variability present significant problems for a refit study.

Beyond raw material variety, the color, texture, and luster of cherts are also altered by burning and weathering. Accidental and intentional thermal alteration of chert may significantly alter its visual appearance and thus hamper refitting. Similarly, weathering of cherts induces patination or frosting of surfaces. For example, at the site of Kabazi V, Ukraine (Yevtushenko, 1998), several of the raw material varieties showed two to four different kinds of patination that apparently resulted from subtle differences in weathering.

While it is unrealistic to expect that all of the characteristics of an assemblage will be ideally suited for a refitting study, it is important to recognize that some assemblages may be deficient in so many areas that they are not suitable for large-scale refitting.

Background information for refitting

Before attempting to refit specimens, one should conduct a traditional morphological analysis of an assemblage in order to gain a general understanding of the technology and the primary flaking processes that were involved in its production. The background information obtained through traditional analysis serves the dual role of: (1) providing a broad technological framework within which to place the specific processes revealed by refits; and (2) guiding the methodology and certain procedures employed in recognizing refits.

Given that even very successful refitting studies will articulate only a portion of the specimens in an assemblage, information from refits alone is insufficient for a comprehensive technological reconstruction. Such a reconstruction requires information generated through a variety of analytic techniques (e.g., traditional morphological, attribute, experimental, and refitting analyses). Refitting seems especially useful in placing static artifact categories (e.g., cores, shaping and rejuvenating flakes or blades, etc.) within a dynamic sequence and revealing particular features and peculiarities of reduction.

The experimental method, based upon efforts to replicate lithic reduction processes, also has the potential to generate technological reconstructions with great precision, but it differs from refitting in a fundamental way. While the experimental method reveals possi-

bilities, the refitting method shows what actually occurred (Bordes 1972: 150; Marks and Volkman 1987: 11). A criticism of the refitting method, often advanced by proponents of the experimental method, questions the degree to which refits represent reduction patterns. Given that refits involving large constellations of artifacts and revealing long intervals in the reduction process are relatively rare in a refitting study, it is sometimes argued that attendant technological reconstructions are not truly representative. They are thought to represent manufacturing mistakes or exceptions rather than the norm. Such criticisms might be valid if, in following the refitting method, there was not a continual effort made to understand the refitting results in the context of other analytic procedures, especially traditional morphological analysis.

Understanding the linkage between the refitting method and the general morphological and techno-typological features of an assemblage is crucial to the success of the refit study. For example, it might be assumed that in blade-dominated assemblages of the Upper Paleolithic the refitting of specimens would be relatively straightforward, but this only rarely is true. The wide variability in core platform preparation (including core tablet, change of orientation, and others) alone requires that an analyst have a good general knowledge of the technology of an assemblage prior to organizing it for refitting. For example, some Aurignacian assemblages with a strong bladelet component show *Dufour* bladelets with twisted profiles to have been produced from carinated pieces (Bergman 1987). In recognizing this correlation, such assemblages are organized for refitting by distinguishing between right- and left-twisted bladelets and doing the same with the carinated pieces. Similarly in refitting Middle Paleolithic assemblages, one should be aware of the coexistence of several methods of primary reduction (e.g., Levallois radial and point, non-Levallois blade, non-Levallois radial flake) as well as bifacial reduction.

Preparing an assemblage for refitting

Spatial organization

After washing and labeling specimens, they should be arranged on large tables by provenience unit (typically $1m^2$) in a spatial order resembling the excavation plan. A refit study commands a great deal of table-space and while it may not be possible to lay out all of the material from a large excavation, specimens from as many adjacent squares as possible should be examined in one viewing. Unless there is a special interest in small specimens (e.g., carinated bladelet production, burin spalls, etc.), these are excluded from the analysis. As specimens from a block under study are refitted, they should be set aside within view on an adjacent table. These refitted constellations of artifacts are subsequently compared to each newly laid-out block of artifacts, such that an ever enlarging picture of refits emerges for the excavation. Beyond expanding the comparison of specimens in this manner horizontally (across an excavation level), the same procedure is followed in comparing specimens vertically (from different excavation levels).

Sorting

The initial sorting of specimens is intended to identify conjoinable, generally broken artifacts rather than to begin refitting constellations of specimens produced by multi-stage production. The sorting procedure follows a series of dendritic divisions, each resulting in the identification of specimens with more distinct sets of characteristics. Specimens are initially sorted by raw material, followed by a division of each raw material group into core-like specimens (pre-cores, cores, core fragments), flakes, and blades (including retouched ones), and additionally, 'special' or peculiar specimens such as Levallois flakes or points, plunged or hinge-fractured pieces, etc.

As outlined by Volkman (1983: 128), the third step in sorting involves separating complete from broken pieces, followed by separating broken specimens into distal, medial, and proximal segments. In refining this step, we suggest an additional division according to dorsal surface characteristics: cortical coverage (complete, almost complete, right, left) and scar pattern (parallel, convergent, bidirectional, radial, etc.). These early steps in sorting should assist in conjoining specimens along a 'flat, single-space' dimension and in turn prepare the foundation for subsequent refitting of con-

stellations of specimens in 'volume, multi-leveled-space' dimensions.

The next step in sorting forms the foundation for refitting specimens derived from multi-stage production (e.g., core shaping, blank removal, core rejuvenation, etc.). This involves arranging debitage (cores and blanks) in rows according to their degree of exhaustion. The arrangement of specimens in this manner essentially follows a lithic reduction sequence. For example, specimens that are completely covered by cortex are placed in the center of a row and to their right and left are placed specimens with cortex on their right and left lateral edges, respectively. In the same way, crested blades and flakes are placed in the center of a row and 'secondary' crested elements with remnants of crested facets on their right and left lateral edges placed accordingly. This procedure simplifies refitting by organizing the material spatially into a visual framework that corresponds to the sequence in which it was produced. This again underscores the importance of understanding the general technology of an assemblage in undertaking a refit study.

After completing the several steps of sorting and organizing the material, a refitting analyst should spend some time becoming familiar with the raw materials, particular aspects of the reduction technology, and certain spatial distributions of artifacts.

Making refits

The degree of difficulty in refitting cores with removals largely depends on the nature of the prehistoric occupation and the attendant distribution of reduction activities. Briefly occupied workshop areas or sites that yield early stage cores and blanks offer the most direct opportunities for discovering refits. In contrast, longer-term occupations accompanied by reduction strategies geared to economizing on raw material usage yield lithic assemblages that are much more complex to refit. This is because cores have very long use-lives in such settings and may undergo several transformations in form as well as technology before they are abandoned. In such cases, the refitting of cores with most blanks is very difficult, if not impossible.

When directly refitting blanks to cores proves difficult, one should attempt to articulate constellations of blanks and then search for refits between these constellations and cores.[2] Also, one should pay special attention to plunged (over-struck) and hinge-fractured (under-struck) blanks in that these often terminate a core's production and thus represent the last removals.

Conceptually, the refitting of blanks to a core might be viewed as reconstructing three concentric layers: (1) an outer 'cortex shirt'; (2) an intermediate layer generally lacking cortex; and (3) an interior layer consisting mainly of the core at some stage of exhaustion. Specimens forming the outer layer are defined by their cortical covers and refitted following the procedures as described earlier. The intermediate layer often presents the greatest challenge for refitting. Here a knowledge of the main features and peculiarities of primary reduction processes (e.g., Levallois method with convergent, radial, or parallel core preparation) is critical to making refits. The interior layer of course centers on the core and includes specimens that were removed immediately prior to the core's abandonment.

Only rarely is a single refitted constellation likely to show a full reduction sequence composed of all three concentric layers. Usually a reconstruction of a reduction strategy is made possible through studying a composite developed from several constellations representing different segments of a reduction sequence.

Technological interpretation of refits

Through the examination of numerous refitted constellations, one should be able to identify patterns in reduction that, in turn, can be compared with information gained from traditional morphological analysis of un-refitted cores and debitage. This procedure should assist in defining the range of variability of core reduction strategies for an assemblage. In general, the definition of such strategies should describe the desired end-products (e.g., Levallois points, blades, etc.), the steps or length of a reduction sequence, and the specific techniques employed in completing the sequence.

An especially important part of interpreting refits and conveying these interpretations to colleagues rests in the quality and style of the illustrations of refit constellations. We believe

that such illustrations should be presented in an 'unfolded view' where the reduction stages are shown step by step in the form of the progressive transformation of a constellation (Usik 1989; Demidenko and Usik 1995). We favor this style in contrast to the more traditional representation (Volkman 1983). Readers may also note that we favor a *technological orientation* in aligning our illustrations. Thus our refitted constellations are positioned such that the striking platforms are at the top of the illustration as opposed to the traditional style of lithic illustrations where striking platforms are placed at the bottom.

The definition of core reduction strategies not only assists in establishing the main features and peculiarities of an assemblage, as such definitions often form the very basis for designating Paleolithic Industries or periods, as well as examining diachronic change and inter-assemblage variability (Marks and Volkman 1987; Van Peer 1991, 1992; Demidenko and Usik 1993d; Sellet 1995). The refitting method thus offers a unique and important analytic approach to better understanding lithic technologies and reduction strategies within Paleolithic studies.

Analysis of the Tor Faraj assemblage

After a brief examination of artifacts from Tor Faraj in 1992, it was clear to us that a refitting study of materials obtained from the large block excavation planned for 1993 and 1994 would be worthwhile. Our studies of the assemblage were undertaken during two periods: (1) in Jordan during July and August 1993; and (2) at the University of Tulsa during March and April 1995.

Although our effort to refit artifacts while in the field during the first season was not very successful, the experience gave us a good feel for the site, excavation plan, and recovery techniques. A large part of this season was consumed with clearing the overburden from the Bedouin diggings in the back of the shelter and with the preliminary analysis and classification of artifacts along traditional lines. This left little actual time for refitting *in situ* materials, but even with such a limited time we were able to assemble several constellations and identify some interesting patterns in reduction (Henry *et al.* 1996). During the second and main period of analysis, we were able to devote a month to examining *in situ* material recovered over the two excavation seasons. During this study we were able to refit a great number of specimens, discover new reduction patterns, and generally clarify our understanding of the reduction strategies employed by the occupants of Tor Faraj.

Data set

The specimens examined for refitting were drawn from two samples. One included those artifacts that were collected from the deposit that had been disturbed by Bedouin digging and the other consisted of *in situ* specimens recovered from levels 155 to 190, excluding the roof-fall area in the southwestern part of the excavation block. The patination of artifacts in this area prohibited successful refitting. In lacking specific provenience, those refitted specimens from the Bedouin back dirt furnished little information on the spatial distributions of artifacts, but they proved to be quite helpful in providing insights for reconstruction of reduction strategies. In addition to examining specimens across each 5cm excavation floor, artifacts recovered from the level above and below the one under study were compared for refits. Altogether, the refits in the study included 251 artifacts.

Obstacles in refitting Tor Faraj artifacts

The two major complications for undertaking a refit study of artifacts from Tor Faraj revolve around the considerable diversity in raw materials and the great extent to which materials had been reduced. Because of the numerous color variations in the chert, the raw material sort proved less useful than the subsequent sorts based upon technological observations (e.g., cortex positions, scar patterns, terminations, etc.). The extensive reduction of materials at Tor Faraj also hindered refitting in a couple of ways. First, the kinds of simple articulations of blanks to cores that characterize the relatively early abandonment of cores are just non-existent. Not only were cores reshaped and rejuvenated through several phases of blank removals, the blanks themselves were occasionally transformed

into cores for additional removals. This strategy of *economizing* tool production through extending the reduction stream in the primary processing of blanks added greatly to the complexity of finding refits. And this economizing further complicated the refit study by enlarging the spatial distributions of artifacts, the further they traveled along the reduction stream. Thus, very few situations occurred where a large constellation of artifacts was found within a relatively small area.

Technological characteristics and peculiarities

From a technological perspective, the most striking feature of the Tor Faraj assemblage is the small sizes of the cores, typically less than 50mm in maximum dimension. They are greatly exhausted and often do not reflect the general unidirectional convergent technique thought to typify late Levantine Mousterian assemblages, but instead exhibit bidirectional and multidirectional scar patterns. Some even show bifacial flaking surfaces. There also occur numerous pre-cores and 'truncated faceted' pieces on flakes and blades. The abundance of these cores-on-flakes greatly complicates efforts to find refits within the assemblage due to their significantly modified forms.

The lithic technology at Tor Faraj clearly was focused on the production of broad-based Levallois points from cores bearing unidirectional convergent scar patterns, at least early in their early stages of reduction. In later stages of reduction, alternative scar patterns were used for point production perhaps as a consequence of the smaller flaking surfaces and the necessary greater flexibility in the design of scar patterns. Other debitage varieties that signal the use of the unidirectional convergent technique for point production are edge elements consisting of lateral blades and flakes that normally display steep cortical edges (Boëda *et al.* 1990: 67-73; Demidenko and Usik 1993b: 33-40, 44-7). It is noteworthy, however, that edge elements also accompany blade production within the Levantine Mousterian (Marks and Monigal 1995), perhaps suggesting alternative, early stage reduction strategies at Tor Faraj.

Descriptions of the refitted constellations and conjoined specimens

This segment of our study centers upon the descriptions of the refitted artifacts leaving discussions of the technology of the assemblage for the following section. No single constellation was refitted to the extent that it represented a complete reduction sequence. Thus rather than reconstructing the lithic technology at Tor Faraj on the basis of one or more constellations showing the whole sequence, the reconstruction was developed through linking several specific refit patterns to key points in the reduction sequence.

The description of 64 refits, numbering 209 specimens, is organized largely around the key issues of point production with a specific emphasis placed upon: (1) those constellations showing the Levallois point method with unidirectional convergent technique; (2) those showing the generation of small points from cores-on-flakes and their relationship to 'truncated faceted' pieces; and (3) those that reflect other primary flaking techniques. Following the descriptions of the refitted constellations, the conjoined pieces, accounting for 21 flakes and blades from 42 specimens, are briefly described.

Point removals from unidirectional convergent cores

The first group of constellations described here (numbers 1 to 8) consist of those that have a Levallois point fitted to debitage and in some cases to other points.

Constellation 1

This includes four pieces: two Levallois points and a preparatory flake and blade (Figs 6.1 and 6.2). The preparatory elements were used to create the Y-*arrete* scar patterns on two successive flaking surfaces for the two Levallois point removals. In order, the removals consisted of: (1) a preparatory, unidirectional flake with remnant cortex on the left lateral edge and plain butt; (2) a Levallois point with unidirectional convergent scar pattern and faceted *chapeau de gendarme* butt; (3) a preparatory unidirectional convergent blade with marginal remnant cortex on its distal

end and a *demi-chapeau de gendarme* (Boutié 1981: 51) or convex-faceted-fine butt (Van Peer 1992: 14); and (4) a Levallois point with a unidirectional convergent scar pattern, faceted *chapeau de gendarme* butt, and *Concorde* profile.

Given the removals' order, scar patterns, and butt characteristics, the following reconstruction was developed for the manner in which the reduction was undertaken. First, a central plane was created in shaping the core's flaking surface to guide the removal of the first point (Fig. 6.1: a). A Y-*arrete* pattern was then created by three lateral removals, directed convergently (Fig. 6.1: b and c). The first of these was on the right side followed by two flakes on the left side. The second removal on the left side, a hinge-terminated flake (Fig. 6.1: 1), was followed by delivery of the first Levallois point (Fig. 6.1: 2). The scar left by the point formed a 'new' central plane on the core's flaking surface and subsequent lateral removals again created a Y-*arrete* pattern. The right lateral removal is represented by the third refit of this constellation (Fig. 6.1: 3). After the Y-*arrete* scar pattern had been formed, the second point (our fourth refit) was struck off (Figure 6.1: 4; 6.2: 4).

The refit constellation clearly reveals an operational sequence that involved the successive removals of two Levallois points from a unidirectional convergent prepared core. The refitted constellation also has other technological implications. In each point production, the central plane of the Y-*arrete* pattern was formed first, and followed by convergent cutting by lateral removals for the creation of the 'interfaceting ridge' forming the lower parts of the Y-*arrete* pattern. The lateral removals were twice struck from the edges of already prepared *chapeau de gendarme* striking platforms (*cf.* the planes of the platforms of the preparatory flake and blade to those of the points, Fig. 6.1). This shows that at Tor Faraj the highly formalized, intensive platform preparation, associated with *chapeau de gendarme* butts, was undertaken immediately following the creation of a central plane. This contrasts with what we typically see in Middle Paleolithic Industries where the intensive platform preparation occurred very late in the sequence, immediately before point removal (Demidenko and Usik 1994: 46).

The refitted constellation also furnishes information on the shape and volume of the

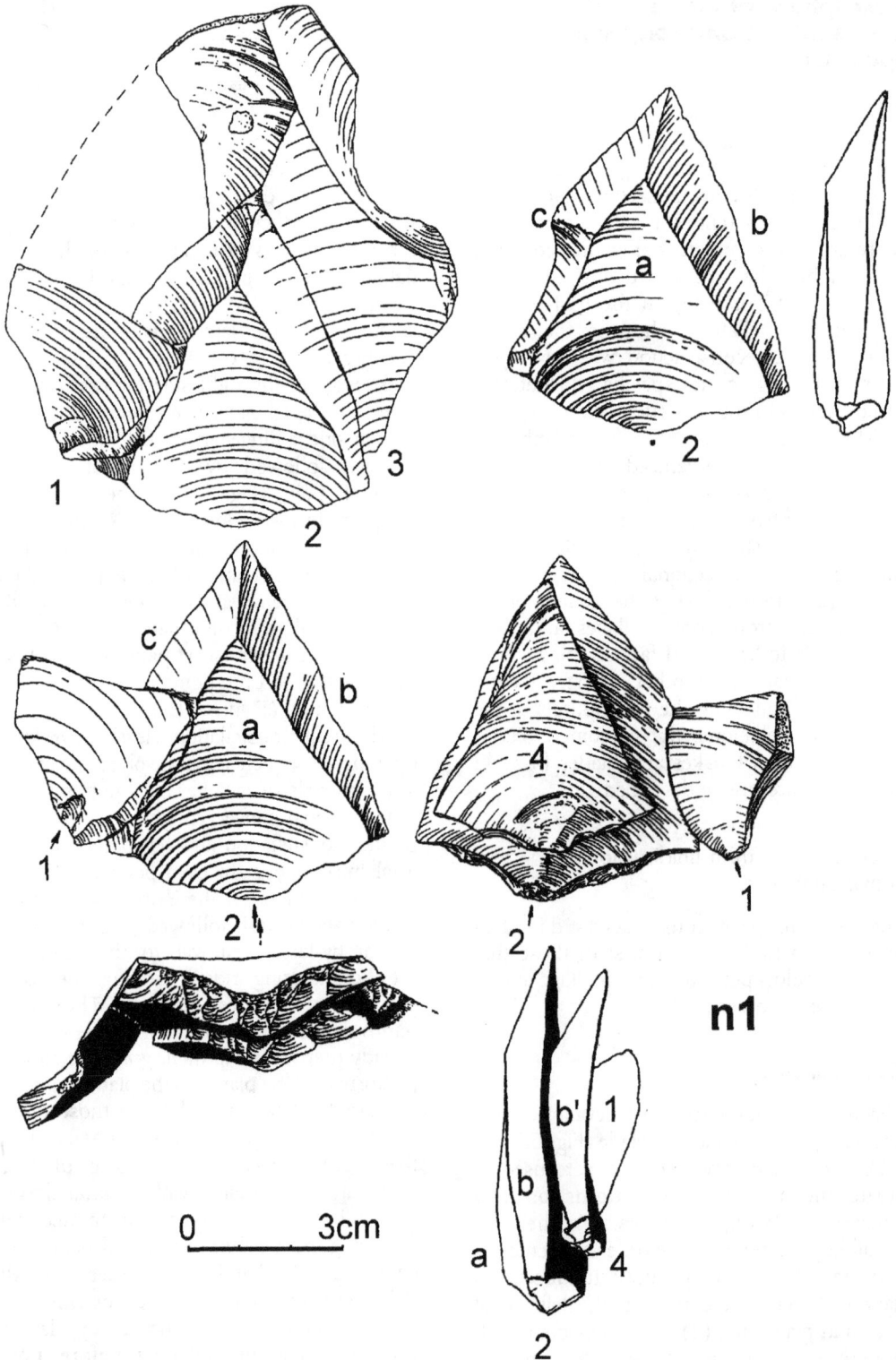

Figure 6.1 Illustrations of refitted artifacts from Tor Faraj: constellation 1: 1, preparatory flake; 2 and 4, Levallois points; and 3, preparatory blade

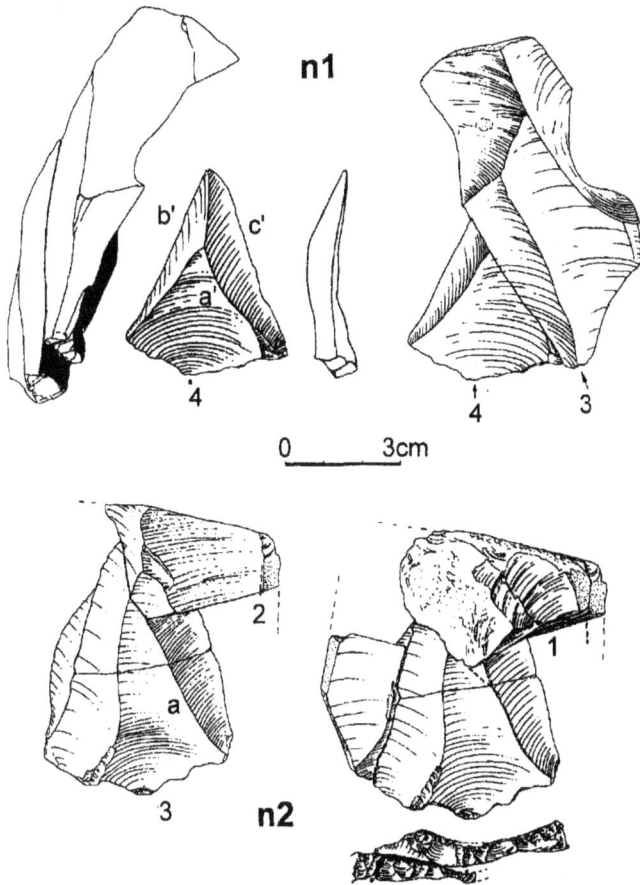

Figure 6.2 Illustrations of refitted artifacts from Tor Faraj: constellations 1 and 2. **n1**: 3, preparatory blade; and 4, Levallois point. **n2**: 1, primary flake; 2, preparatory flake; and 3, Levallois point

raw material as well as on general management strategies during its reduction. Although only minor remnants of cortex are present on the refits, these indicate that they were struck from a chert cobble with a long axis *ca.* 93mm in length. The presence of cortex on the preparatory flakes for both point removals indicates that points were removed after very little cortical trimming and consequently the shape and volume of the cobble had a strong influence on reduction strategies. For example, the Concorde arched profile of the second Levallois point was determined by lateral removals that beveled the edges of the core's flaking surface at acute angles. Such an orientation of the lateral removals is probably linked to the natural convexity and volume of the chert cobble.

Refits also provide useful insights for the technological interpretation of un-refitted debitage. For example, the scar pattern of the preparatory pieces (Fig. 6.1: n1, 3) shows clear triangular traces of the first point's negative. Therefore, preparatory or edge elements with such negatives can be considered as indicators of multiple Levallois point production from one side of a core. Also, as with many refits, this constellation provides a cautionary note. With most of the constellation having been refitted in Jordan, we interpreted the Y-*arrete* scar pattern as showing the right side to have been completed after the left one (Henry *et al.* 1996), but with the addition of the preparatory blade, it is clearly the opposite of this. Thus, we should be careful in trying to determine the sequence of preparatory removals related to Levallois point production as determined only by our 'fingers' through a relatively subjective examination of flaked surfaces (e.g., Crew 1976: 86-7; Boëda 1982; Meignen 1995).

Constellation 2

This constellation consists of six specimens: two Levallois points (one composed of two conjoined pieces), two preparatory flakes, and a blade (Figs 6.2 and 6.3). The specimens were removed in the order that follows: (1) distal part of a primary flake; (2) distal part of a unidirectional flake with remnant cortex on the right lateral edge; (3) Levallois point with unidirectional convergent scar pattern and *chapeau de gendarme* butt consisting of proximal and distal pieces; (4) proximal part of unidirectional blade with remnant cortex on left lateral edge and convex-faceted-fine butt; and (5) longitudinal part of Levallois point with unidirectional convergent scar pattern and *chapeau de gendarme* butt.

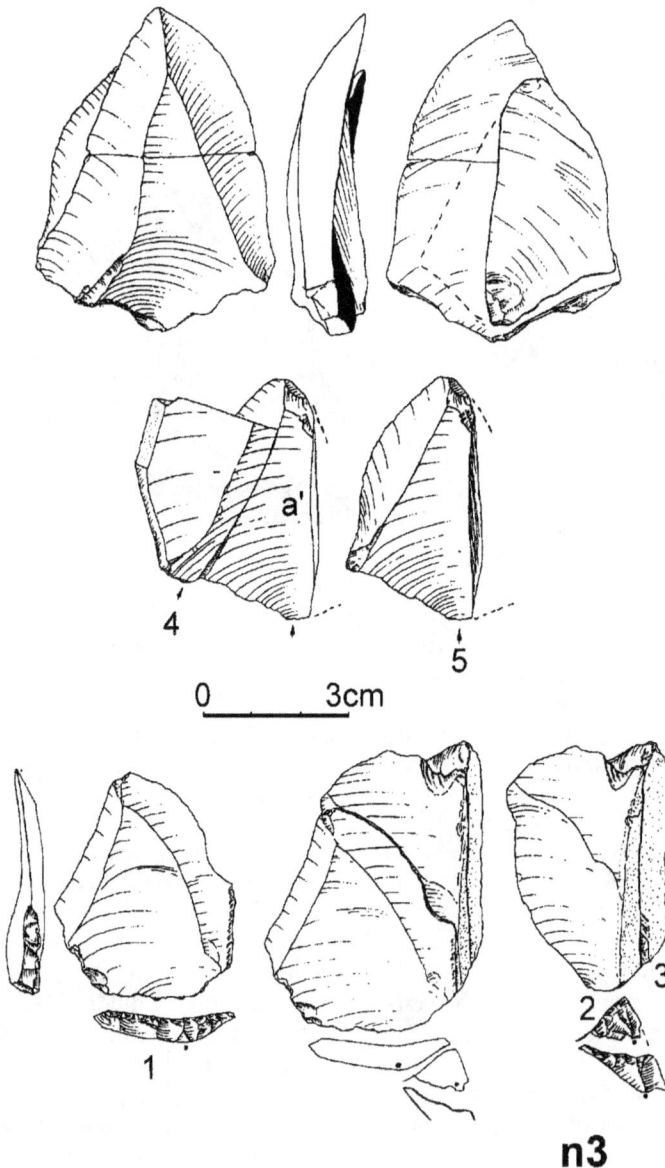

Figure 6.3 Illustrations of refitted artifacts from Tor Faraj: constellations 2 and 3. **n2**: 4, preparatory flake and 5, longitudinally fragmented Levallois point. **n3**: 1, Levallois point; 2, 3, lateral flakes with cortex

The constellation shows an operational sequence in which the first flake acted to clear cortex from the right side of the cobble along with other convergent removals. After detachment of this primary flake, the main part of the of the core's flaking surface was cleared of cortex and ready for systematic reduction. A central plane was then created (surface 'a', Fig. 6.2: n2) in the center of the core's flaking surface by a removal that is missing from the constellation. This central plane was then cut by lateral convergent removals to form a Y-*arrete* scar pattern. The preparatory element along the right lateral edge (Fig. 6.2: n2, 2) was the last removed before the Levallois point (Fig. 6.2: 3) was struck off. In its detachment the point broke into proximal and distal pieces.

The next phase of point production was initiated by lateral convergent removals that cut the central plane formed by the negative of the first point (Fig. 6.3: n2, a'). The lateral element (Fig. 6.3: n2, 4) shows such a removal forming the left margin of the second point (Fig. 6.3: 5). As with the first point, the second point broke during removal, but longitudinally. The high incidence of breakage among points and lateral removals implies that the chert cobble was exceptionally brittle.

Several technological parallels exist between constellations 1 and 2. Beyond the same approach to Levallois point production through unidirectional convergent core preparation, both constellations show a common, efficient method of rejuvenating the cores after the initial point removals. This pattern of rejuvenation is based mainly on the utilization of the negative of the first point removal as a central plane of a new flaking surface on which a Y-*arrete* pattern was formed by a new set of lateral convergent removals. It is noteworthy that as with the previous constellation, intensive platform faceting took place before the lateral removals.

Constellation 2 provides new information relative to decortification. The primary flake shows evidence of unidirectional convergent removals, even at this early stage of core preparation. And although only minor cortical remnants are present on preparatory flakes (Fig. 6.2: n2, 2 and Fig. 6.3: n2, 4), this allows for estimating the size of the chert nodule (length = 7.1cm and end width = 6.7cm).

Constellation 3

Three refitted pieces make up this constellation: one Levallois point and two lateral flakes (Fig. 6.3: n3). The order in which they were removed is as follows: (1) Levallois point with unidirectional convergent scar pattern and convex-faceted-fine butt and remnant cortex on the right lateral edge; (2-3) lateral flakes with cortex on right lateral edges and convex-faceted-fine butts.

Following the removal of the Levallois point (Fig. 6.3: n3, 1), two lateral flakes (Fig. 6.3: n3, 2 and 3) were struck along the right side of the core's flaking surface and from the same striking platform. The levels of the point and flake platforms vary less than 1 to 2mm and thus indicate very little platform rejuvenation between removals.

Although less complete than the earlier constellations, constellation 3 also suggests multiple Levallois point production based upon unidirectional convergent preparation. The two edge elements suggest an unsuccessful initial attempt at rejuvenating the core's flaking surface for a second point removal. Although the point lacks the thick, *chapeau de gendarme* butt and exhibits marginal cortex, it is a Levallois point and resembles similar Levallois points from other Levantine Mousterian contexts (e.g., Bezez Cave Level B, Copeland 1983b: pl. 2: 3 on p. 312).

Constellation 4

Three specimens were refitted into two Levallois points for this constellation (Fig. 6.4). The points consist of one with a unidirectional convergent scar pattern and *demi-chapeau* (convex-fine-faceted) butt and a second with a similar scar pattern and thick, *chapeau de gendarme* butt. This second removal was reconstructed through conjoining two longitudinal, thermal fractured parts.

The pattern of reduction generally follows that of the earlier constellations in which unidirectional, convergent points were successively removed from a core's face. In constellation 4, however, a single blade was struck off along the left side of the first point's negative to create a new Y-*arrete* pattern, whereas in the earlier constellations two or more removals were employed to rejuvenate the core for point production. The efficiency of this

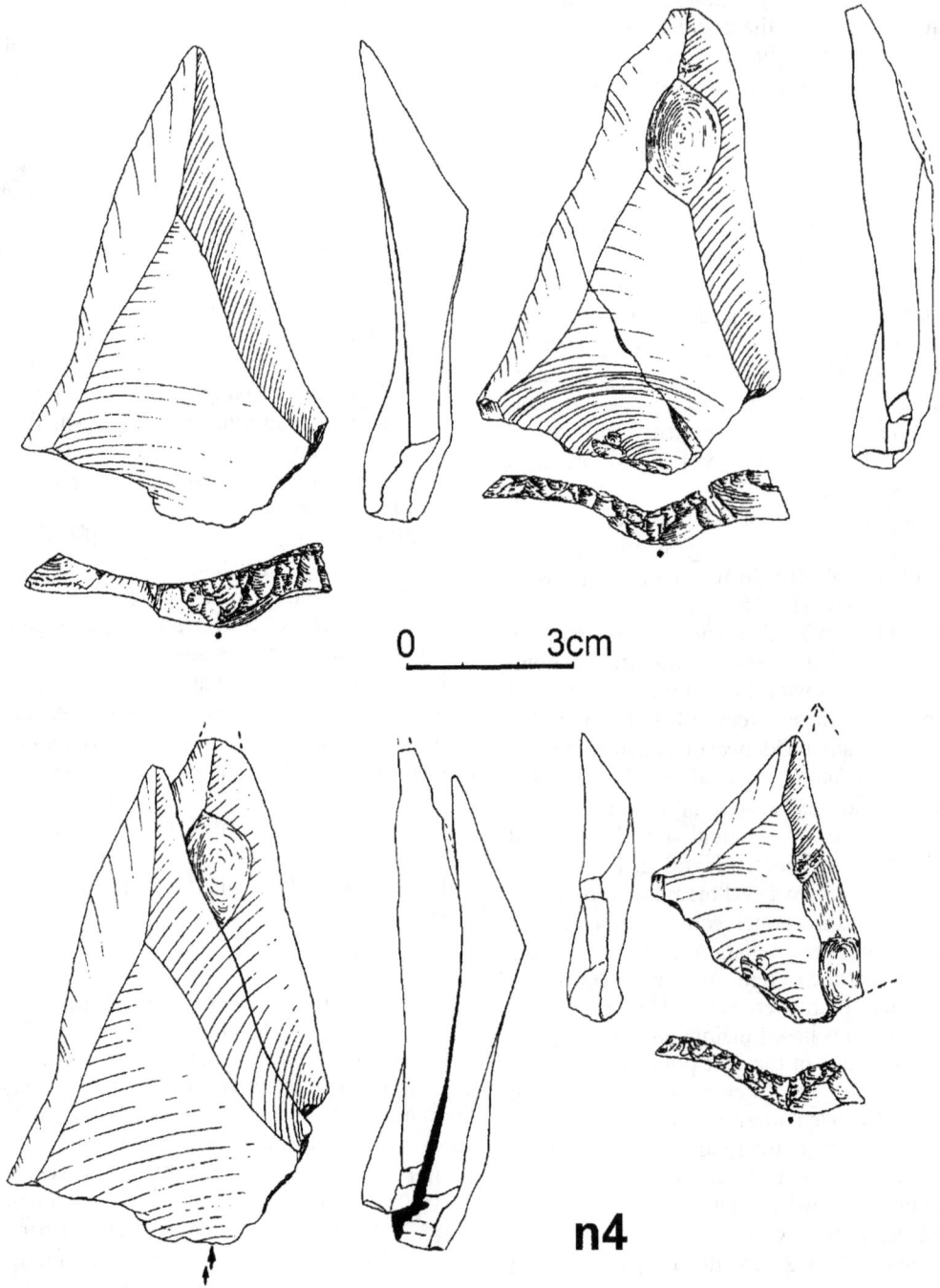

Figure 6.4 Illustrations of refitted artifacts from Tor Faraj: constellation 4. **n4**: Levallois points

approach to series point production is under-scored by their minor (5mm) difference in the butt levels.

Constellation 5

Two refitted pieces make up this constellation: (1) a Levallois point with unidirectional convergent scar pattern and *demi-chapeau* butt; and (2) a core bearing a unidirectional, convergent scar pattern (Fig. 6.5: n5).

After the Levallois point was removed, the core's *chapeau de gendarme* platform was rejuvenated with additional faceting. The previous point level of the platform was reduced by *ca.* 3mm at the 'pedestal' and significantly more along the right wing (Fig. 6.5: n5). Following the platform preparation, a single flake was removed along the right edge of the core, cutting the negative of the first point and creating a new Y-*arrete* pattern. Another point removal was then attempted, but failed when understruck.

Constellation 6

There are three refitted pieces in this con-stellation: a Levallois point and two prepara-tory flakes (Fig. 6.5: n6). In order of removal they consist of: (1) a unidirectional convergent flake with a *chapeau de gendarme* butt and a small amount of cortex along its right lateral edge; (2) a Levallois point with a unidirec-tional convergent scar pattern and a *demi-chapeau* butt; and (3) a unidirectional flake also with a convex-faceted-fine butt and a little cortex along its left edge.

The constellation shows that the first preparatory flake was convergently removed along the right side of the negative of the previously removed point near the right edge of that core's striking platform. The second preparatory flake, struck along the left edge, was not refitted. The constellation's point was then removed from the same striking platform as the first point. Another phase of rejuvena-tion was then initiated as evidenced by another preparatory flake (Fig. 6.5: n6, 3).

What is so interesting here is that with only three refitted specimens, three distinct phases of core preparation for point production are captured. The first two are unquestionable and the third is nearly identical to what is shown by the preparatory or edge elements of

other constellations linked to point produc-tion. The tiny remnants of cortex and the butt of the point also provide a means of estimating the core's flaking surface to be *ca.* 45mm long and 55mm wide.

Constellation 7

Two refitted pieces, consisting of a Levallois point and a preparatory flake, form this constellation (Fig. 6.6: n7). Their reduction and attendant scar pattern differ from those of the previously described constellations.

The sequence of removals involved: (1) a bidirectional flake with convex-faceted-crude butt, followed by (2) a Levallois point with a Y-*arrete* pattern created by three preparatory removal negatives and a *chapeau de gendarme* butt. While the dominant pattern of reduction reflected in the refitted constellations is unidirectional, constellation 7 shows bidirec-tional preparation for point production. Two preparatory removals were struck from the proximal end (Fig. 6.6: n7, c, b) and one from the distal end (a).

The constellation, in fact, shows that two removals were struck from the distal end of the core before the central plane was devel-oped with the removal of item 1 of the constellation from the proximal end. Another proximal removal then formed the left lateral edge of the Y-arrete. The *chapeau de gendarme* was then created leaving a butt's level difference between the point and preparatory flake of 5mm. This suggests a linkage between the directionality of the preparation of a core and the sequence in which the heavily faceted *chapeau de gendarme* butt is prepared. Whereas unidirectional preparatory removals utilize a platform common to the point, bidirectional removals are struck off prior to the creation of *chapeau de gendarme* butt for point removal.

Constellation 8

The two Levallois points composing this constellation (Fig. 6.6: n8) also display bidirectional removals. Two preparatory flakes were struck from the core's distal end along its right edge followed by four proximal removals from the center and left edge. The *chapeau de gendarme* butt was then fashioned and the first point removed. This was followed by the

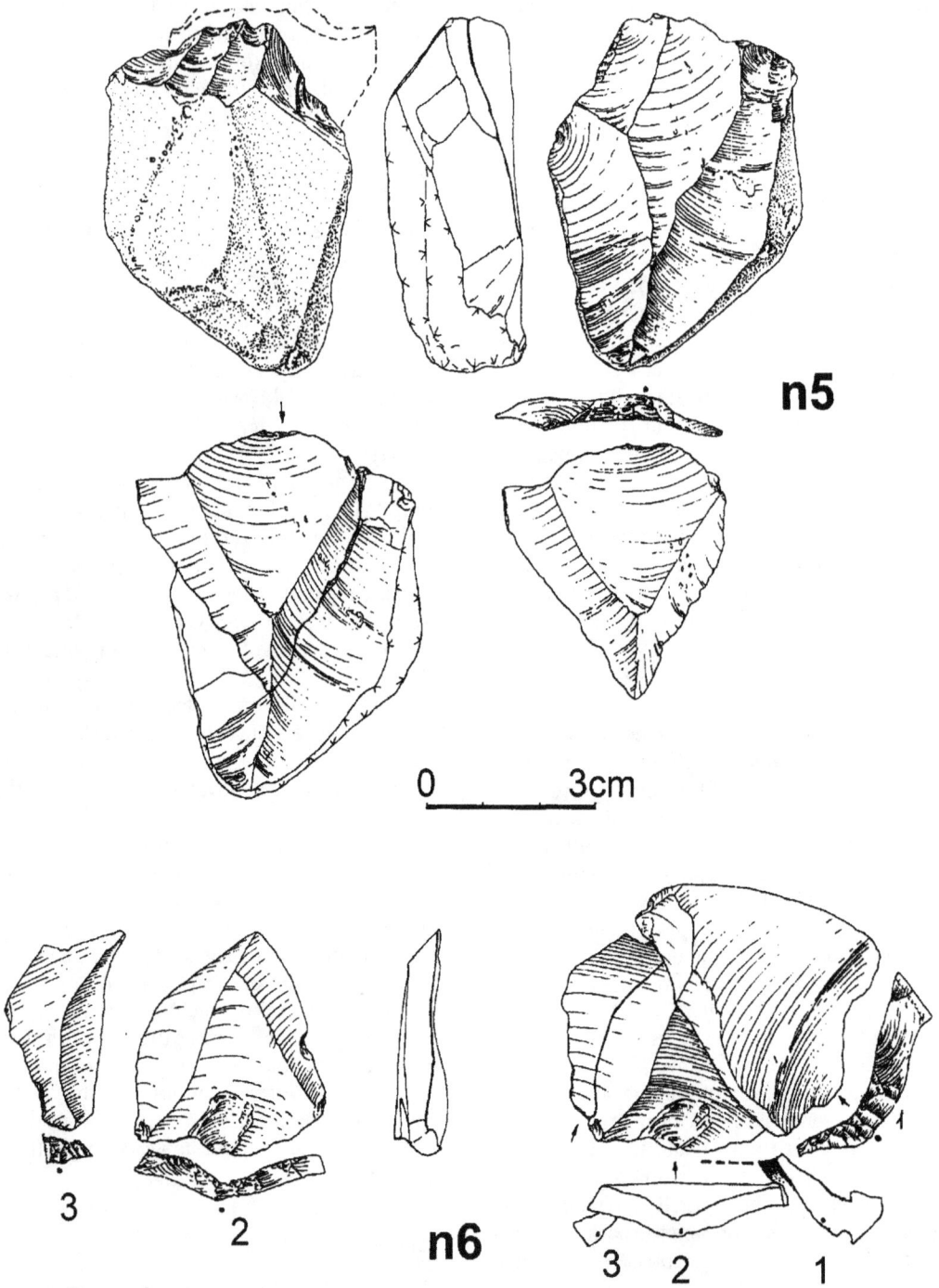

Figure 6.5 Illustrations of refitted artifacts from Tor Faraj: constellation 5. **n5**, core and Levallois point. **n6**: 1, 3, preparatory flakes; and 2, Levallois point.

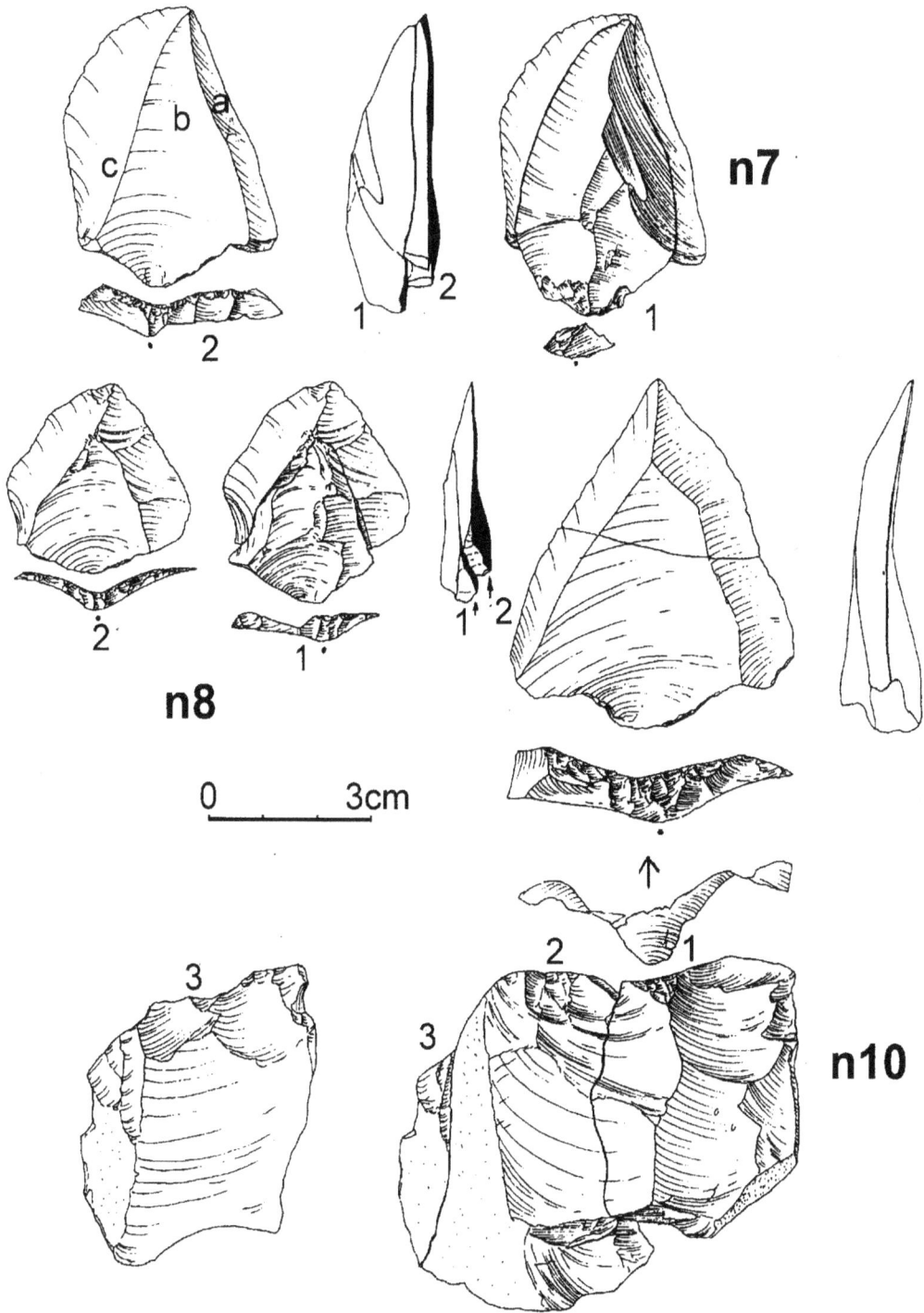

Figure 6.6 Illustrations of refitted artifacts: constellations 6, 7, 8, and 10. **n7**: 1, preparatory flake; 2, Levallois point. **n8**: 1 and 2, Levallois points; 2, preparatory flake. **n10**: 1, 2, 3, unidirectional, parallel flakes with cortex

rejuvenation of the platform, the core's face being left unmodified, before the removal of a second point.

This bidirectional pattern of preparation for point removal, coupled with the delivery of a second point without rejuvenation of the core's face, represents perhaps the most economical of the various strategies employed by the occupants of Tor Faraj. While this approach bypassed the reworking of the core's face in preparation for a second point removal, it substantially reduced the level of the striking platforms between removals (*ca.* 5mm). When the lengths of the two points are considered (26 and 32mm), such reduction amounts to some 16 percent.

One might argue that the initial point removal represents what Bordes (1961, 1980) described as a '*point Levalloisienne du premier ordre*,' but this is not the case. In contrast to constellation 8, the platform was left unmodified between the point removals in Bordes' hypothetical scheme.

The bidirectional pattern and the large number of preparatory flakes (six) appear to have been necessitated more by a very limited *operational space* than by a special tradition. With a flaking surface no longer than *ca.* 39mm, the core was most likely formed on a flake rather than a primary chert nodule.

Point removals from bifacial flaking surfaces

Constellations 9 and 10, containing 14 pieces, reveal point removals from opposite faces of a core.

Constellation 9

Nine specimens, four having been conjoined, make up this constellation of seven complete pieces (Figs 6.7, 6.8, 6.9). Following their order of removal they include: (1) a primary blade with about 50 percent cortical cover and a plain butt; (2) a convergent flake with a *demi-chapeau* butt which may represent an unsuccessful Levallois point removal; (3) a convergent flake with cortex bearing right lateral edge and convex-faceted-fine butt; (4) a convergent flake with cortex along its lower right lateral edge and a *demi-chapeau* butt (also a likely failed Levallois point removal); (5) a convergent blade with cortex along its left lateral edge and a convex-faceted-fine butt; (6) a conver-

gent flake with cortex along its left lateral edge and a convex-faceted-fine butt; and (7) a convergent flake with cortex along its lower right lateral edge and a convex-faceted-fine butt. Specimens 3 and 7 have been conjoined.

Specimen 1, a decortification element, is the only piece in the constellation that lacks platform faceting (Fig. 6.7). After this piece, there is a break in the series of refitted pieces, followed by specimens 2 and 3 which show primary reduction on the opposite face of the core. Specimen 2 appears to be an understruck Levallois point that failed to follow the complete Y-*arrete* scar pattern in its removal. The convergent scar pattern, faceted butt, and lateral position of specimen 3 suggest that it served as a preparatory element for resetting the core's face for another attempt to produce another Levallois point. Although additional specimens could not be refitted on this working face of the core, at least two phases of point production are indicated.

Returning to the opposite face, the removal of specimen 4 served to rejuvenate this flaking surface by clearing away the scars of hinge-fractured flakes and creating a new central plane (Fig. 6.8). This was followed by the removal of specimen 5, a convergent, preparatory flake that formed side 'B' of the core's Y-*arrete* pattern (Figs 6.7, 6.8, 6.9). After removal of a Levallois point (not refitted), specimen 6 was struck off to create yet another Y-*arrete* pattern to guide the production of a point (Figs 6.8, 6.9). The triangular negative appearing on specimen 7 reflects the point removal.

The series of removals displayed by the constellation denotes several distinct phases of reduction that after initial decortification are tied to the preparation and delivery of Levallois points. The refitted specimens alone indicate that six phases of point production (including failed attempts) were undertaken, two from one face and four from the opposite face. And, surely, given the size of the core as shown by the constellation, several more points could have been produced from the core before it was finally abandoned.

Constellation 9 clearly shows the high degree of efficiency achieved in point production by the occupants of Tor Faraj. While this pattern is reflected in previously described constellations, the early reduction stage and the number of refits represented in constellation 9 underscores the fact that the Levallois

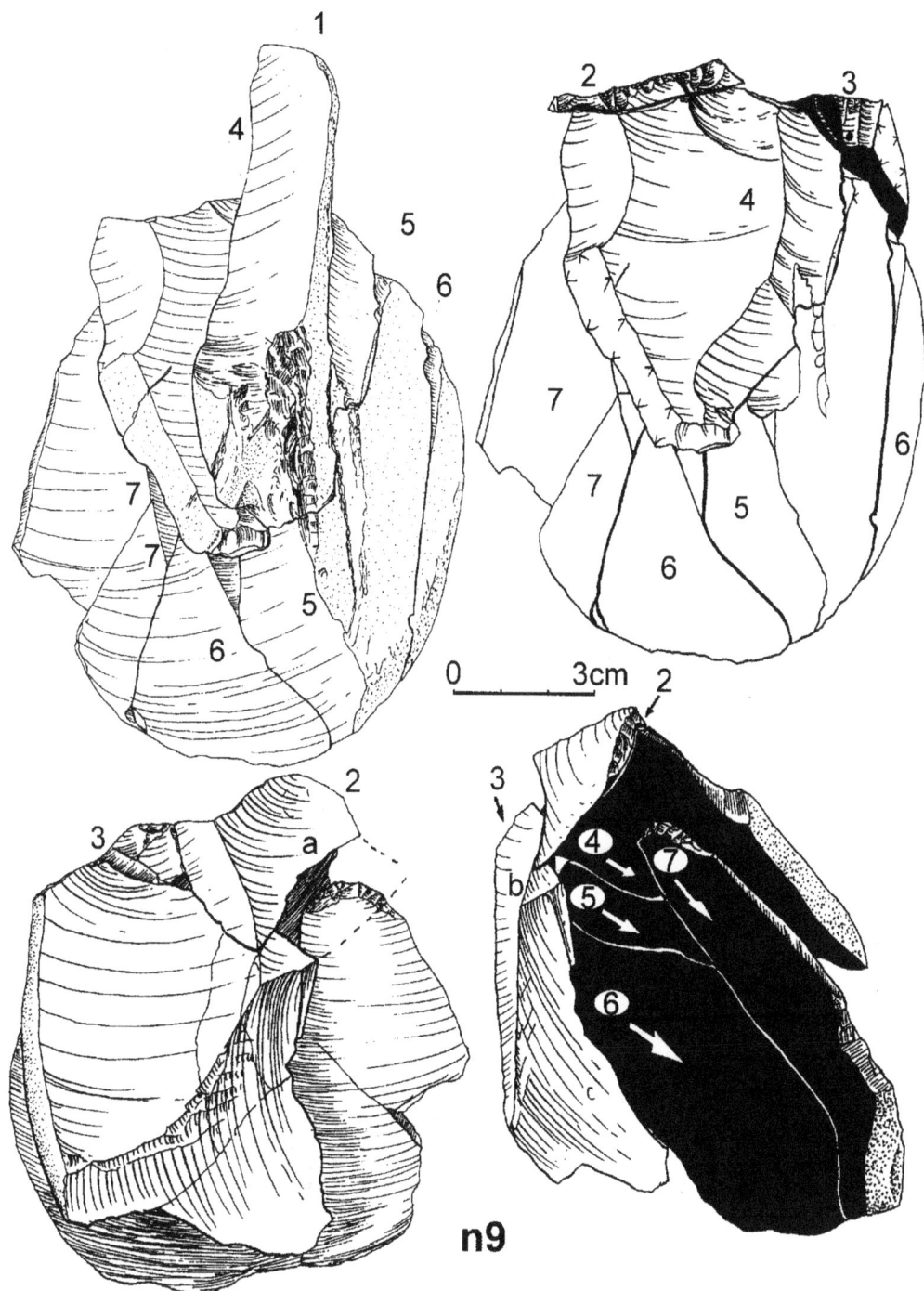

Figure 6.7 Illustrations of refitted artifacts from Tor Faraj: constellation 9, view 1, shows successive removals and the overall efficiency of point production

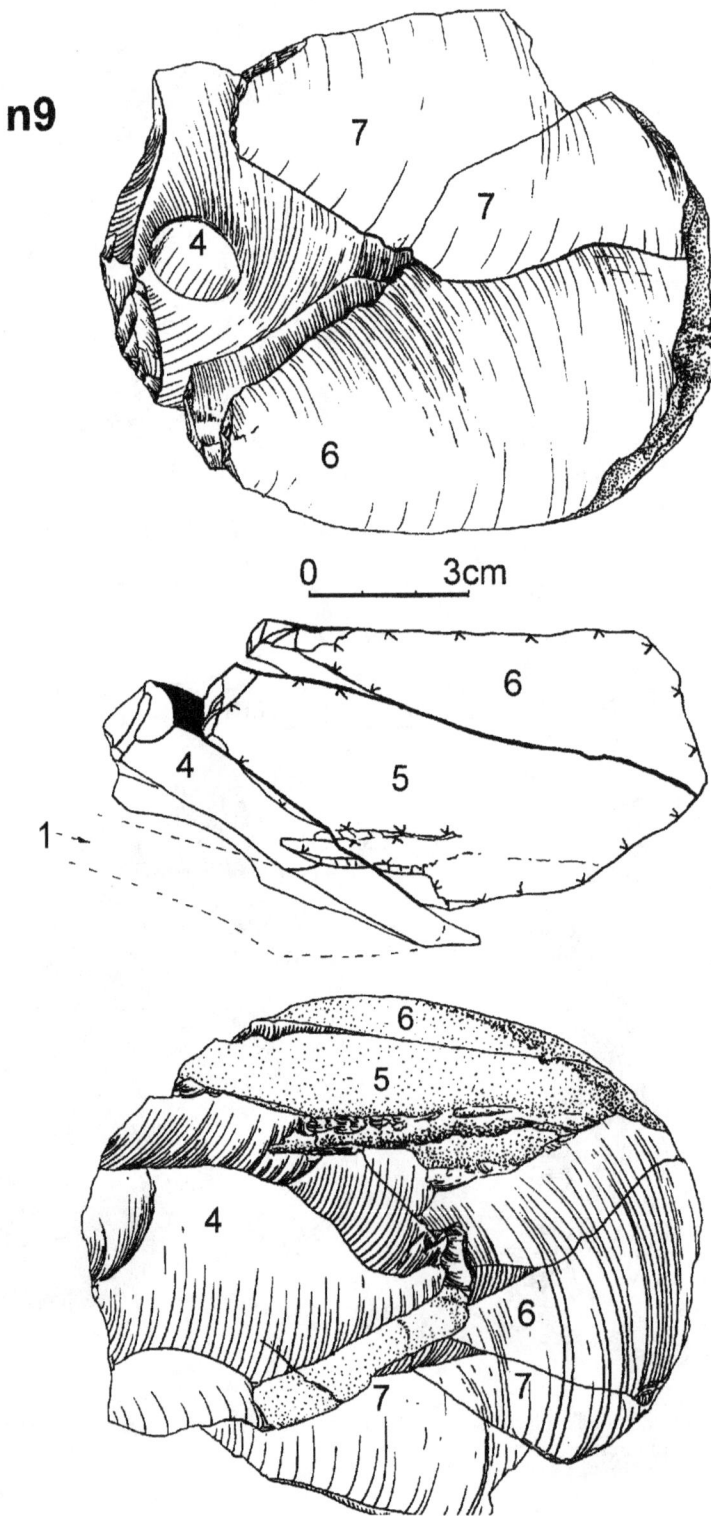

Figure 6.8 Illustrations of refitted artifacts from Tor Faraj: constellation 9, view 2, underscores the use of the natural convexity of the chert nodule

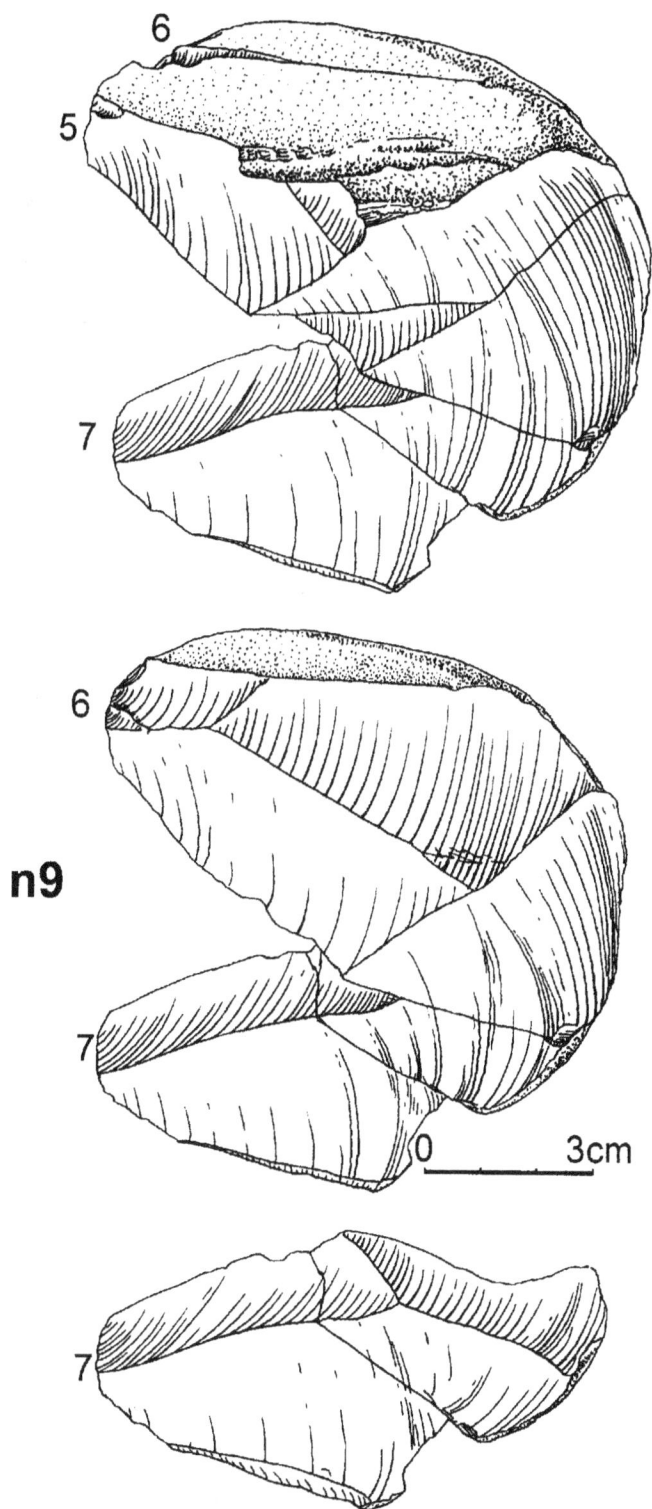

Figure 6.9 Illustrations of refitted artifacts from Tor Faraj: constellation 9, view 3, shows the successive removals for creating Y-*arrete* scar patterns

method of point production could be very economical. Several factors contributed to the efficiency of the method as applied at Tor Faraj: (1) choice of the shape of raw material; (2) use of bifacial flaking surfaces; and (3) minimal rejuvenation of a core's platform and face as required for subsequent point removals. The preferential use of nodular chert provided the natural convexity necessary for Levallois point production with very little preparation. Thus, as shown by constellation 9 and earlier constellations, decortification elements also served to establish the Y-*arrete* pattern and allowed for immediate point production without additional core shaping. The utilization of the opposite faces of a nodule further increased the efficiency of point production. The specific use of a unidirectional convergent pattern and a *chapeau de gendarme* butt also improved point production efficiency. The Y-*arrete* pattern typically required only one to two edge removals for rejuvenation, given that its central plane was created by the negative of the previous point removal. And the thick *chapeau de gendarme* butt not only provided a common platform for preparatory flake and point removals, it often could be reused with little to no rejuvenation. As noted in earlier constellations, constellation 9 clearly shows the minor degree of butt level reduction accompanying several phases of point removals. For example, Specimens 2 to 7 (accompanying the production of six points) show a butt level reduction of only 30mm!

Constellation 10

This constellation consists of three refitted unidirectional parallel flakes with some cortex. Superficially the constellation does not appear to offer much in the way of technological information, but closer examination reveals several negatives of small removals that trace the preparation of a striking platform for reduction of the core's opposite face. When refitted, the platforms of the three specimens resemble a *chapeau de gendarme* butt of a Levallois point (Fig. 6.6: n10). Although the point struck from the platform was not recovered for refitting, the constellation nevertheless provides insight on platform preparation for point removals. A point with typical morphological characteristics is used to illus-

trate the relationship of constellation 10 to the point's butt (Fig. 6.6: n10).

Lateral blades and flakes tied to unifacial point removals

Three constellations, containing nine specimens, show a remarkably uniform pattern of reduction that highlights the importance of the shape of chert cobbles in allowing for point production immediately following decortification.

Constellation 11

The three lateral removals (from five refitted and conjoined specimens) forming this constellation include: (1) a primary blade with convex-faceted-fine butt; (2) a convergent blade with cortex on left lateral edge, a convex-faceted-fine butt, and a clear triangular negative of a Levallois point removal (the specimen also bears inverse, marginal retouch); and (3) a convergent flake with cortex on left edge, a convex-faceted-fine butt, and yet another clear triangular negative of a Levallois point (Fig. 6.10: n11). Specimens 1 and 3 have been conjoined.

Constellation 12

Two lateral flakes make up the constellation: (1) a convergent flake with cortex along its left edge, a *chapeau de gendarme* butt, and a sub-triangular negative of a Levallois point; and (2) the distal portion of a convergent flake with cortex on its left edge and a clear triangular negative of a Levallois point removal (Fig. 6.10: n12).

Constellation 13

The constellation is composed of two preparatory blades that reshaped the Y-*arrete* patterns of a core's successive flaking surfaces following point removals. These include: (1) a convergent blade with distal cortex, a convex-faceted-fine butt, and a triangular Levallois point negative; and (2) another convergent blade with the same characteristics (Fig. 6.11: n13).

Constellations 11, 12, and 13 show initial preparation and subsequent rejuvenation of Y-

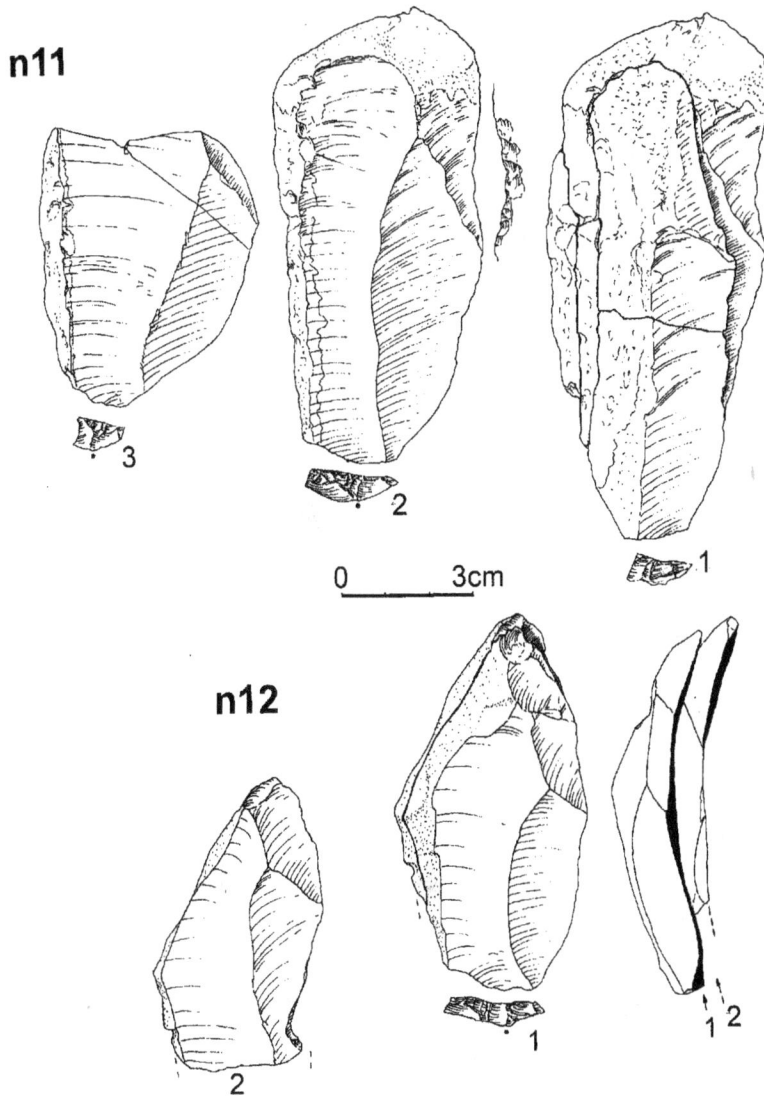

Figure 6.10 Illustrations of refitted artifacts from Tor Faraj: constellations 11 and 12. **n11**: 1, primary blade forming lateral removal in creation of Y-*arrete*; 2, blade with cortex on left lateral edge; 3, flake with cortex. **n12**: 1, 2, two lateral flakes

arrete patterns for controlling the removals of Levallois points. Consistent with the patterns seen in many of the previously described constellations, these three constellations indicate that heavy platform faceting occurred before, not after, preparatory removals. Additionally, the cortex-bearing edge elements of constellations 11 and 12 show that the chert nodules selected for processing were relatively narrow and ovoid. By guiding decortification along the natural edge of a nodule, elongated preparatory elements were

removed at the very beginning of core shaping and this allowed for point production after only a few initial removals from a nodule.

Constellations related to unidirectional convergent point production

This suite of constellations is composed of those that show Y-*arrete* formation accompanying initial decortification (constellations 14 and 15) as well as rejuvenation (constellations 16 and 17) and change in orientation

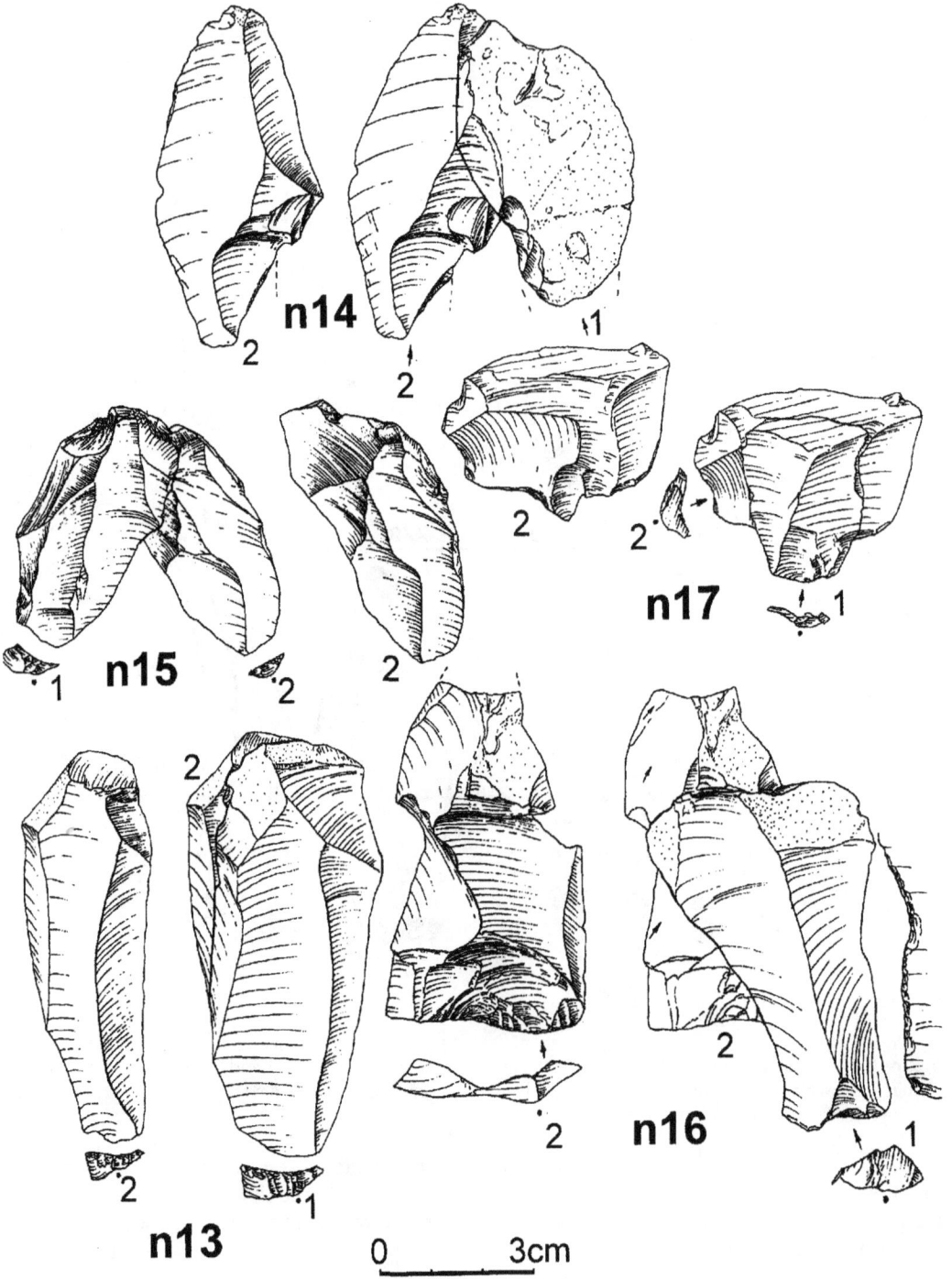

Figure 6.11 Illustrations of refitted artifacts from Tor Faraj: constellations 13, 14, 15, 16, and 17. **n13**: 1, 2, preparatory blades. **n14**: 1, decortification flake; and 2, blade. **n15**: 1, 2, convergent flake and blade. **n16**: 1, 2, convergent flakes. **n17**: 1, 2, convergent flakes

(constellation 18) of core flaking surfaces (Figs 6.11 and 6.12).

Constellation 14

The two refitted pieces in this constellation include: (1) a primary flake virtually covered with cortex; and (2) a convergent flake (Fig. 6.11: n14). Both of their platforms have been crushed.

Constellation 15

Constellation 15 consists of: (1) a convergent flake; and (2) a convergent blade; both with convex-faceted-fine butts and tiny remnants of cortex on their distal ends (Fig. 6.11: n15).

Constellation 16

The constellation includes: (1) a convergent flake with cortex near its distal end and a straight-faceted-crude butt; and (2) a convergent flake missing its distal end, bearing some distal cortex, and displaying a convex-faceted-crude butt. Specimen 1 also shows inverse retouch (Fig. 6.11: n16). Beyond showing a unidirectional convergent removal pattern accompanying the early stages of decortification, the constellation also suggests a rejuvenation stage following an unsuccessful attempt at producing a Levallois point (as indicated by the hinge fracture on specimen 2).

Constellation 17

The constellation is composed of: (1) a convergent flake with a convex-faceted-fine butt; and (2) another convergent flake with a concave-faceted-fine butt (Fig. 6.11: n17). The convergent removal pattern and faceted platform preparation trace those steps involved in Levallois point production.

Constellation 18

Eight specimens in this constellation were conjoined into five refitted pieces. They include: (1) a convergent flake with plain, partly cortex butt; (2) a primary flake with convex-faceted-crude butt; (3) the proximal part of convergent flake with a *chapeau de gendarme* butt; (4) a convergent flake with a convex-faceted-fine butt; and (5) the distal part of a convergent flake thought to be an unsuccessful Levallois point removal (Fig. 6.12: n18) with light dorsal marginal retouch. Specimens 2 and 4 have been conjoined.

After removal of specimen 1, decortification of the opposite face of the core was initiated with the removal of Specimen 2. This was followed by the creation of a central plane (Specimen 3) and its convergent truncation (Specimen 4). Another lateral, convergent removal (missing from the constellation) would have completed the classic Y-*arrete* pattern, before Specimen 5 was struck off. Its removal was flawed, as evidenced by the crushed, broken proximal end, resulting in a poorly formed point.

Constellations showing lateral reduction

Constellations 19 and 20, consisting of 11 specimens, represent lateral, decortification removals that acted to elevate the central portion of a core's flaking surface for point production (Fig. 6.13: n19 and n20).

Constellation 19

Constellation 19 includes: (1) a convergent flake with crushed butt; (2) a convergent flake with cortical left edge and crushed butt; (3) a unidirectional flake with cortical left edge and convex-faceted-fine butt; (4) a convergent flake with cortical left edge and convex-faceted-fine butt; (5) another unidirectional flake with cortical left edge but straight-faceted-fine butt; (6) a unidirectional flake also with cortical left lateral edge and convex-faceted-fine butt; and (7) a unidirectional convergent flake with distal cortex and 'punctiform butt.' The location of the cortex in the constellation indicates that the core was formed on an oval chert nodule about 80mm in length.

Constellation 20

Constellation 20 is composed of: (1) the distal part of a unidirectional flake with right, lateral cortex; and (2) a unidirectional convergent flake with right, lateral cortex and a dihedral butt. Based upon the location of the cortex, the core was fabricated from a chert nodule with a length of about 60mm.

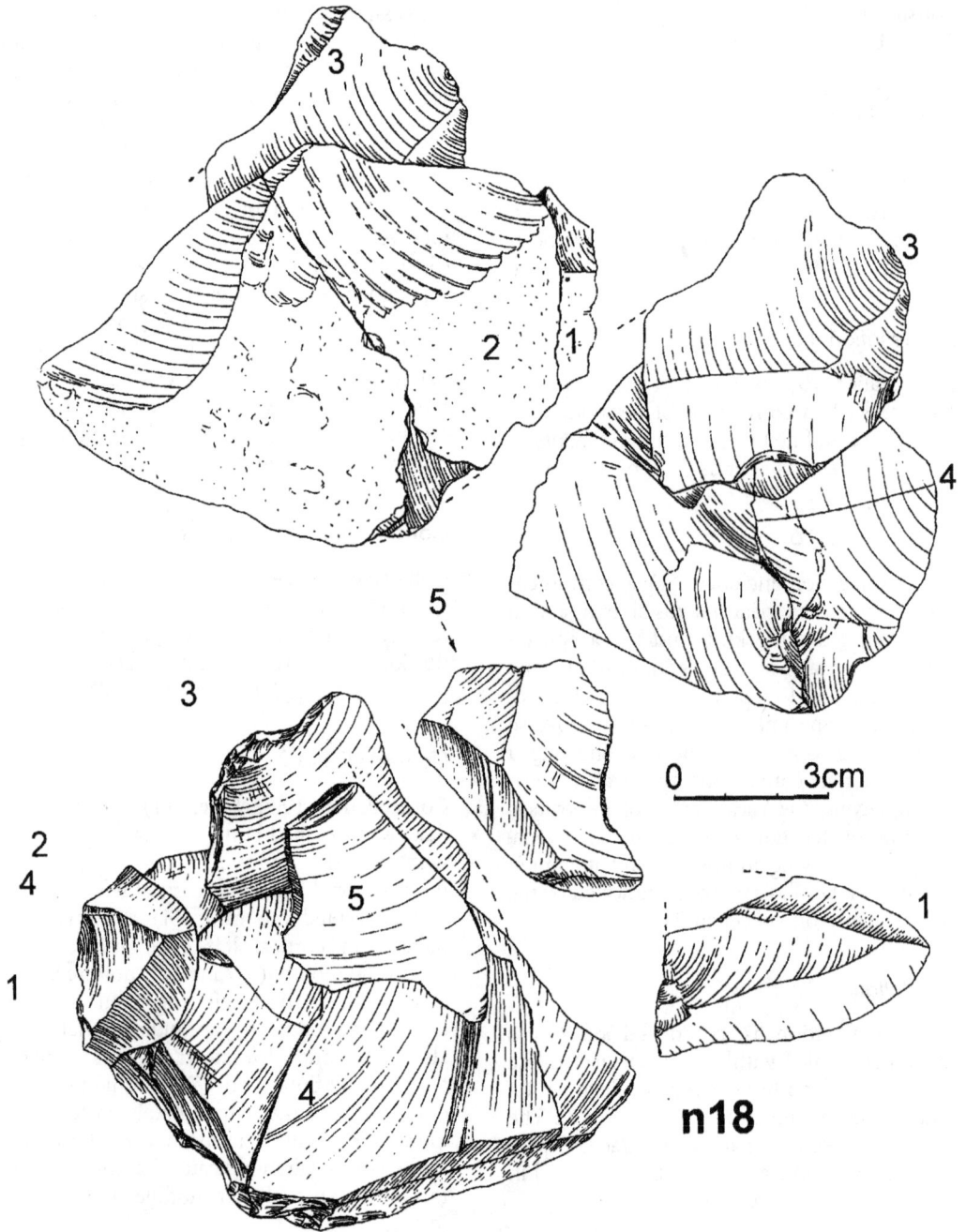

Figure 6.12 Illustrations of refitted artifacts from Tor Faraj: constellation 18. **n18**: 1, 3, 4, 5, convergent flakes; and 2, a primary flake

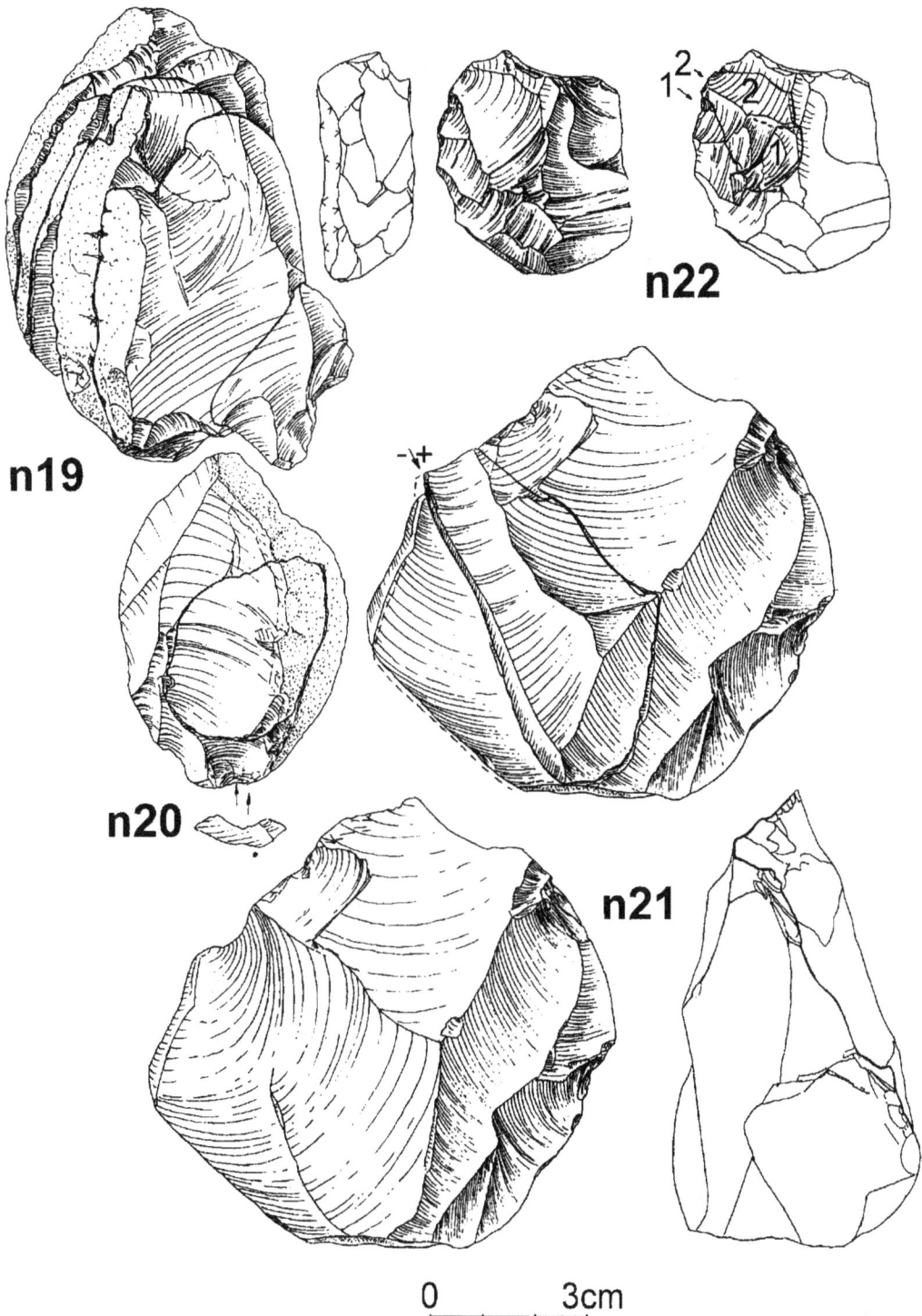

Figure 6.13 Illustrations of refitted artifacts from Tor Faraj: constellations 19, 20, 21, and 22. **n19**: seven lateral decortification removals; **n20**: unidirectional flake with cortex and convergent flake with cortex; **n21**: core with convergent flake removal; **n22**: two unidirectional flakes (1, 2) and a core

Constellations with cores showing different reduction stages

Constellation 21

Constellation 21 includes only two specimens: (1) the longitudinal part of a convergent flake; and (2) a core with a convergent scar pattern (Fig. 6.13: n21). Following the unsuccessful removal of a Levallois point, an initial attempt at rejuvenating the core's working face resulted in a small hinge-fractured flake to the right-of-center of the original striking axis. This was followed by a successful removal that split longitudinally, but nevertheless created a new Y-*arrete* pattern and removed some of the hinge scar of the first attempt at point removal. The core, 81mm long by 83mm wide and unusually large for Tor Faraj, was abandoned at this stage, however. This was most likely because of the central plane's great concavity.

Constellation 22

Constellation 22 consists of three refitted specimens: (1) the distal part of a unidirectional flake; (2) a unidirectional flake; and (3) a core with a unidirectional convergent scar pattern (Fig. 6.13: n22). The flakes reflect the last attempts to create a convergent scar pattern on a very exhausted core. Perhaps because of limited *operational space* many of the attempts resulted in understruck removals with hinge terminations.

Constellation 23

Constellation 23 is composed of nine flakes and a core (Fig. 6.14: n23). Following the order of removal, the constellation includes: (1) a unidirectional flake with cortex-bearing left lateral edge and convex-faceted-crude butt; (2) a unidirectional convergent flake with cortex-bearing butt; (3) a unidirectional flake with cortex remnants on left lateral edge and distal end and a plain butt; (4) the distal part of a unidirectional convergent flake with distal cortex; (5) a unidirectional convergent flake with convex-faceted-fine butt; (6) the distal portion of a convergent flake; (7) a bidirectional flake with cortex-bearing left lateral edge and plain butt; (8) the distal part of a unidirectional flake with cortex on its right lateral edge; (9) a unidirectional flake with

convex-faceted-fine butt; and (10) an atypical Levallois radial core.

Flakes 1 to 4 and 7 represent removals on the opposite side of those removals that led to the final shaping of the core. These flakes show the creation of a Y-*arrete* pattern that involved the production of a central plane (flake 2) and its subsequent truncation by lateral, convergent removals (flakes 3 and 4). Although there is a break in the refit sequence after specimen 4, at least one point was obviously removed. The difference between the butt level of specimen 7 and the core's end of 10mm implies that there were several removals that are unaccounted for in the constellation.

The next phase of reduction on the opposite face of the core is partly represented by specimens 5 and 6, and 8 and 9. The refitting of flakes 5 and 6 to flake 4 captures the technological transition from one core face to the other. The constellation thus shows a gentle, 'fan-like' rotation in which the removal of flakes 5 and 6 was intermediate between work on opposite core faces. Flakes 8 and 9, representing the last two removals on the opposite face, show the familiar attempt to generate a Y-*arrete* pattern for a point removal. The attempt failed, however, resulting instead in the removal of a hinge-fractured flake (specimen 9) and the abandonment of the core.

Constellation 24

Constellation 24 includes only two specimens: (1) a unidirectional convergent flake with cortex along its right lateral edge; and (2) a single platform core with parallel to slightly convergent scar pattern (Fig. 6.15: n24).

This constellation is very similar to the refitted sequence (including specimens 8 to 10) of constellation 23 which again shows the familiar lateral cutting of a central plane in formation of a Y-*arrete* pattern. And as in the previous constellation, the point removal failed, producing a hinge flake and terminating the core's reduction.

It is important to note that neither of the cores in constellations 23 and 24 would be viewed typologically as Levallois point cores, yet the refits show clearly that they represent failed efforts at point production. Such a discrepancy between an idealized reduction

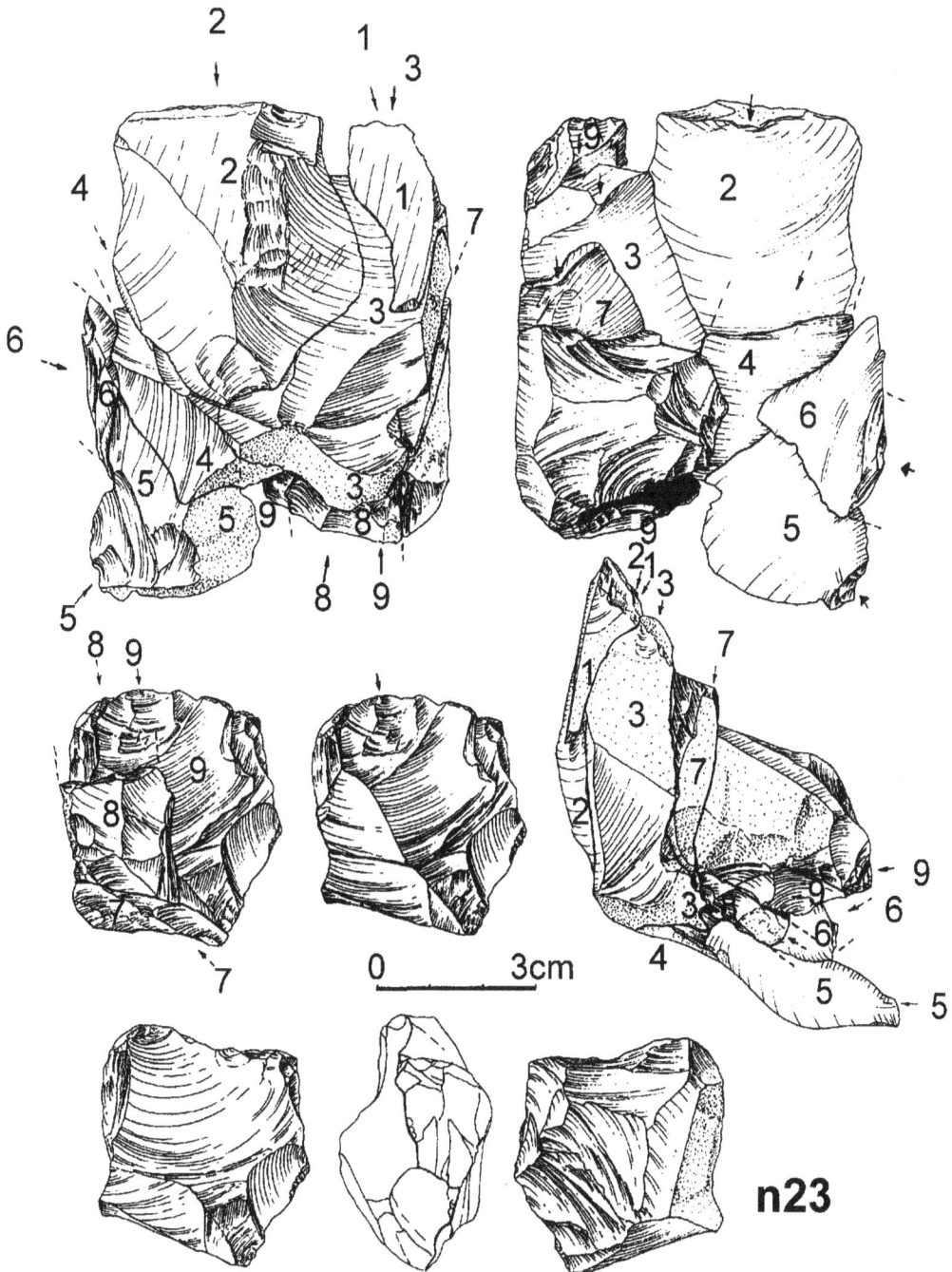

Figure 6.14 Illustrations of refitted artifacts from Tor Faraj: constellation 23. **n23**: 1, 2, 3, 4, 5, 8, 9, unidirectional flakes; 6, convergent flake; 7, bidirectional flake, and core

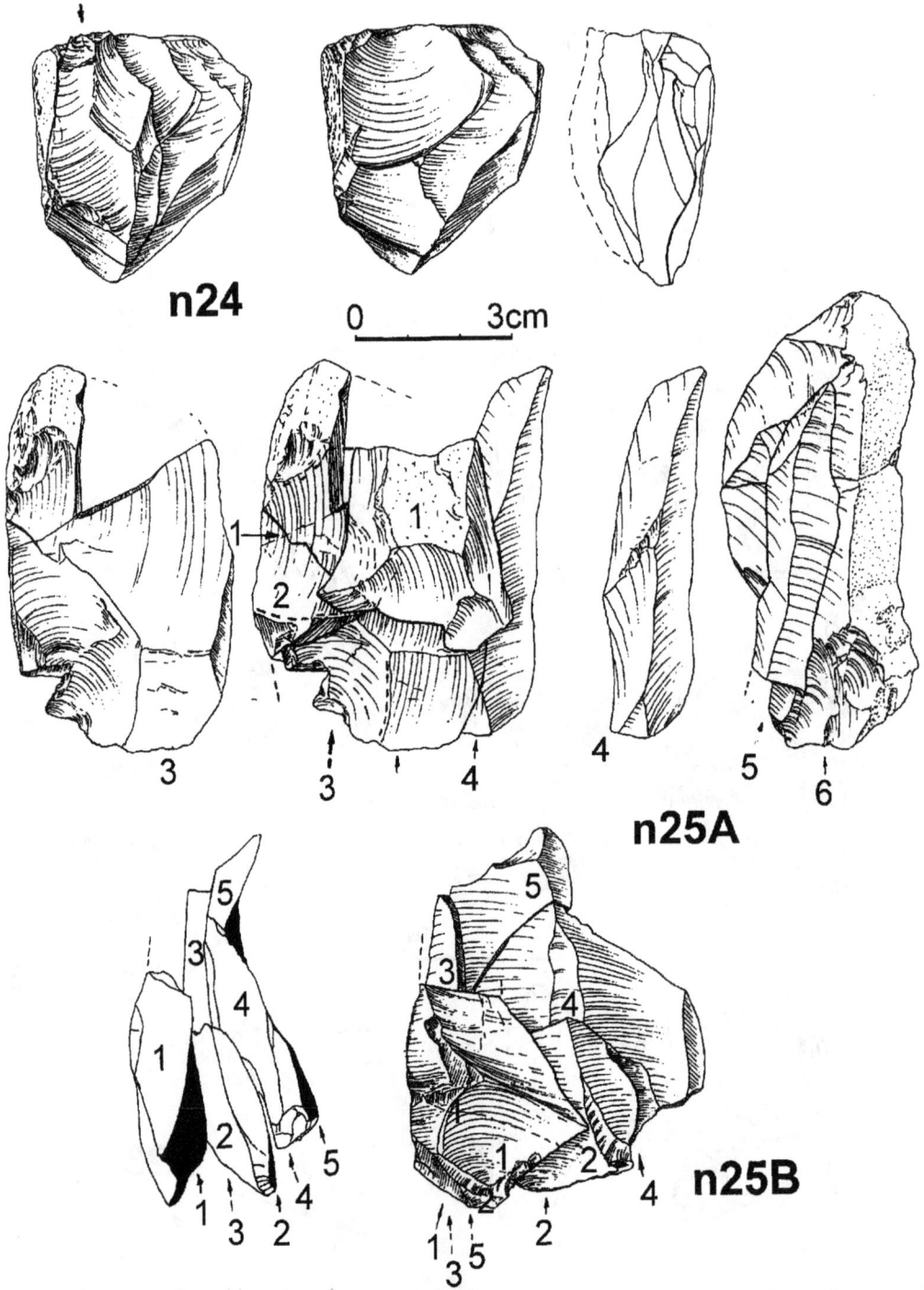

Figure 6.15 Illustrations of refitted artifacts from Tor Faraj: constellations 24, 25A, and 25B. **n24**: convergent flake and core. **n25A**: 1, 2, 3, flakes with cortex; and 4, 5, 6, convergent blades. **n25B**: 1, 3, flakes; 2, failed point removal; 4, atypical Levallois point; and 5, convergent flake

method and the final form of a core assumes should be kept in mind when developing typological definitions and technological interpretations of any industry's artifacts.

Constellation 25

Constellation 25 is an unusual one, for it consists of three different sets of refitted specimens that cannot be joined one to another, yet are clearly part of a common core. The color, cortex, and patination of the refitted sets of specimens show them to represent a common primary reduction effort and thus they are included in a single constellation (Fig. 6.15: n25A and 25B; Fig. 6.16: n25B and n25C).

Set A consists of: (1) the medial portion of a flake with some cortex; (2) the distal part of a flake with cortex; (3) an orthogonal flake with distal cortex and a convex-faceted-fine butt; (4) a convergent blade; (5) the distal part of a convergent blade; and (6) a convergent blade with right lateral cortex. The primary reduction represented by this set of refitted specimens involved the end of the core's decortification.

Set B includes: (1) the proximal part of a heat fractured flake; (2) a unidirectional convergent flake with convex-faceted-fine butt (a failed Levallois point removal); (3) the longitudinal portion of a flake broken during removal; (4) an atypical Levallois point with multi-convergent scar pattern and convex-faceted-fine butt; and (5) the longitudinal part of a convergent flake with crushed butt. The refitting hiatus between sets A and B masks the preparatory steps for point production in Set B. After the relatively unsuccessful production of two atypical points, specimen 5 represents a lateral removal in the next preparation stage.

Set C consists of only: (1) a Levallois point core; and (2) a unidirectional flake with left lateral and distal cortex, and a plain butt. The set shows the removal of a flake in formation of the striking platform of a Levallois point core. In this instance, the joining of parallel removals appears to have created a Y-*arrete* pattern, but the subsequent production of a point appears to have largely failed as judged by its negative on the core.

Constellation 26

Constellation 26 includes: (1) a primary blade with a convex-faceted-fine butt; and (2) a Levallois point core (Fig. 6.17: n26). The scar pattern on the face opposite the primary blade removal shows a unidirectional convergent pattern, but from the other end of the core.

Constellations related to truncated faceted pieces and small Levallois points

Our initial analysis of the assemblage led us to the tentative observation that the majority of the truncated faceted specimens served as cores. The light marginal retouch found on many specimens likely represents fine platform preparation and even apparent burin blows may have served more for core preparation than tool modification (Henry et al. 1996: 45-6). Now with a much larger and more comprehensive collection of constellations that address this problem (constellations 27 to 37 with 30 specimens), it is clear that truncated faceted specimens reflect economizing measures for extending Levallois point production to cores on flakes.

Constellation 27

Constellation 27 consists of: (1) a unidirectional flake with a convex-faceted-crude butt; and (2) a truncated faceted flake (Fig. 6.17: n27). The elongated flake was struck from the larger flake after preparation of a platform which formed the characteristic truncated faceted attributes of the core on a flake. The dorsal, left lateral edge of the removal also resembles a burin spall.

Constellation 28

Constellation 28 includes: (1) a plunged flake with crushed butt; and (2) a small core with a unidirectional scar pattern (Fig. 6.17: n28). The refit shows that a distal end of a primary flake served as a plain striking platform for a flake removal along its ventral surface.

Constellation 29

Constellation 29 is composed of four refitted specimens, but their removal order shows them to have been produced from the

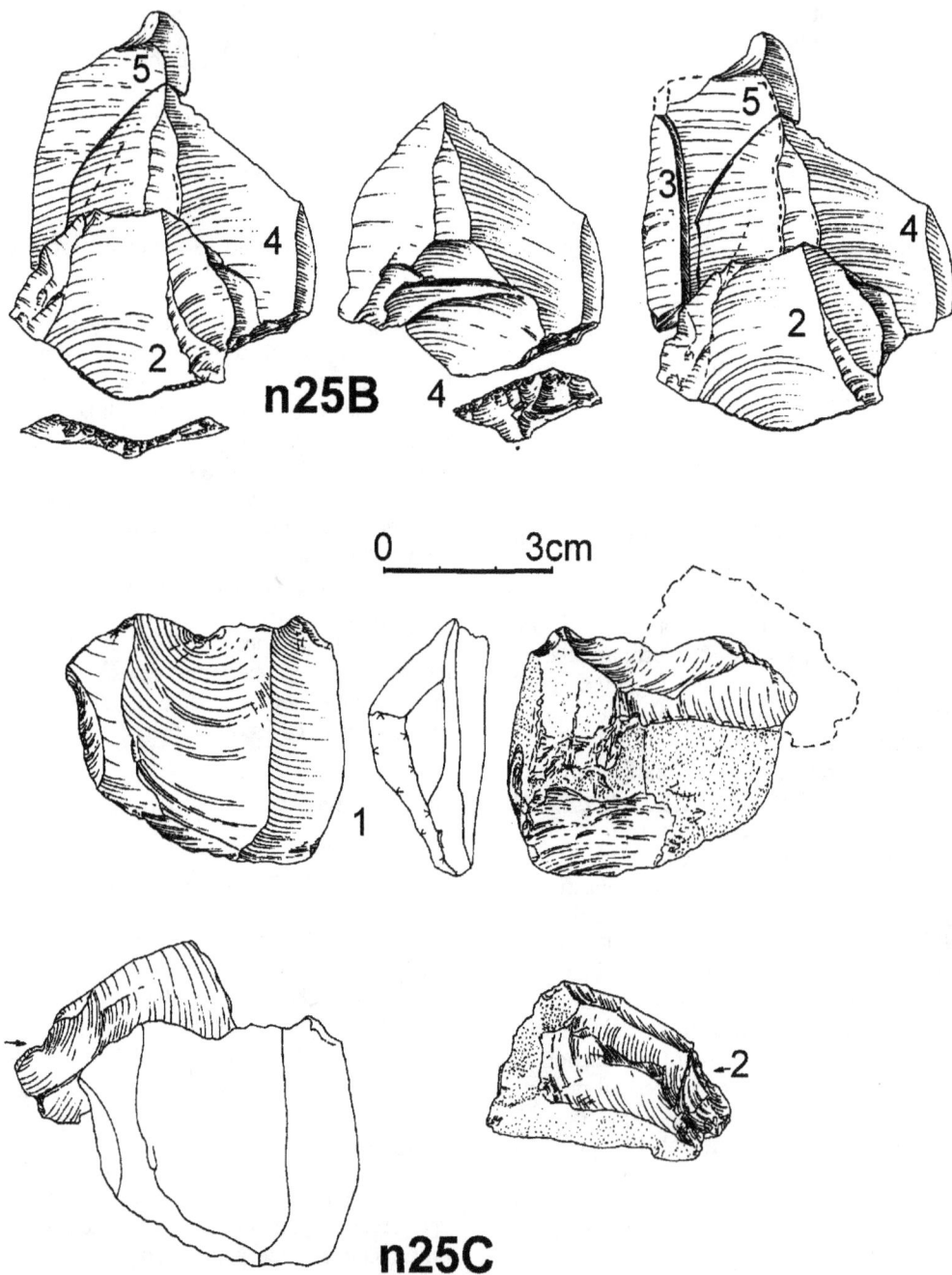

Figure 6.16 Illustrations of refitted artifacts from Tor Faraj: constellations 25B and 25C. **n25B**: second view. **n25C**: 1, Levallois point core; and 2, unidirectional flake

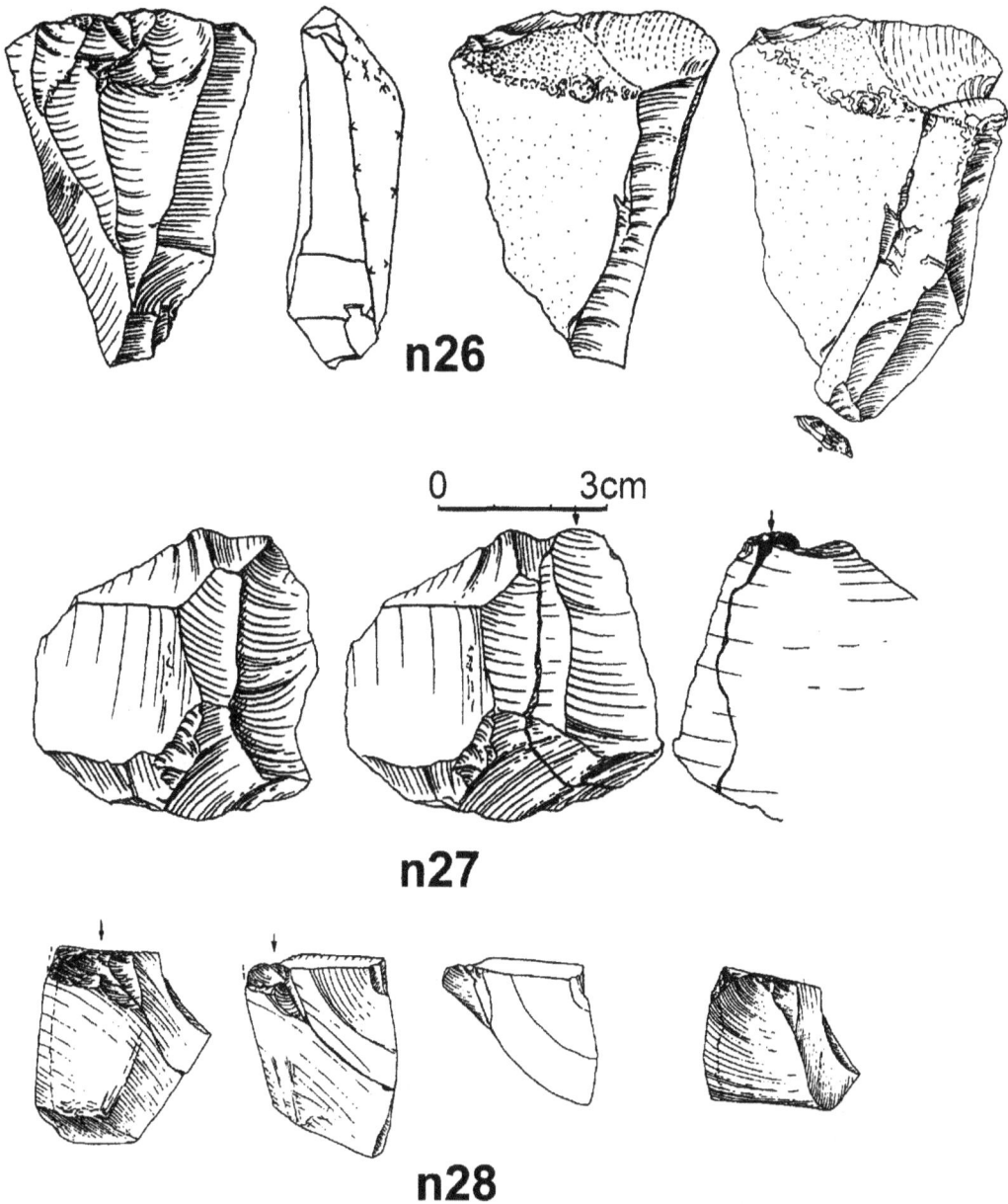

Figure 6.17 Illustrations of refitted artifacts from Tor Faraj: constellations 26, 27, and 28. **n26**: primary blade and Levallois point core. **n27**: unidirectional flake and truncated faceted flake. **n28**: plunged flake and small core

reduction of two cores on flakes (Fig. 6.18). Set A includes: (1) the distal part of a unidirectional flake; and (2) a core on flake with unidirectional convergent scar pattern, while Set B contains: (1) a unidirectional convergent flake with convex-faceted-fine butt; and (2) the distal end of a flake.

The constellation shows that a large (60mm-long) flake was selected for primary reduction and split. Each piece was then used as a core on flake from which a blank was removed from its ventral face.

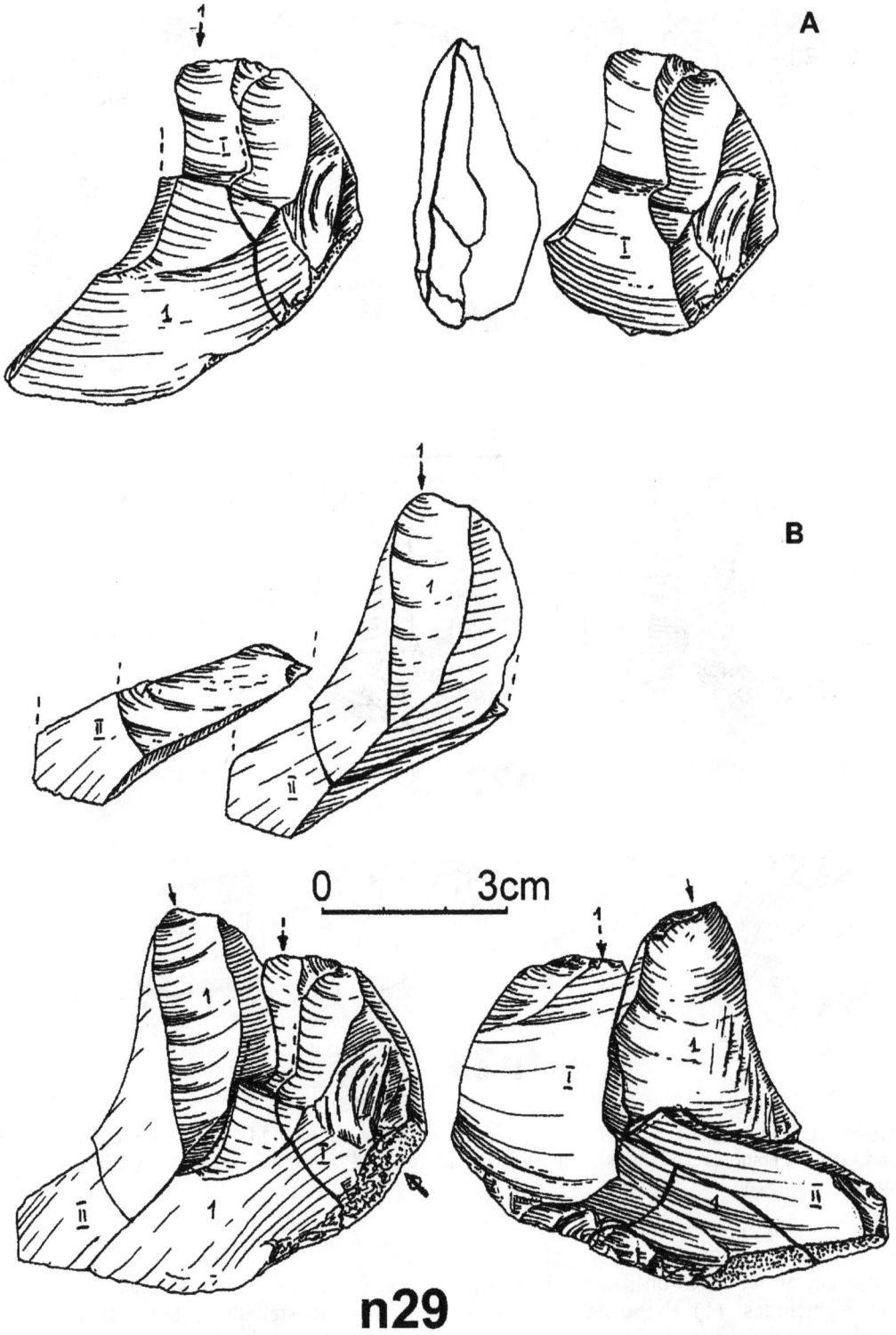

Figure 6.18 Illustrations of refitted artifacts from Tor Faraj: constellation 29. **n29**: two sets of cores on flakes

Constellation 30

Constellation 30 includes: (1) a unidirectional convergent blade with remnant, distal cortex and a convex-faceted-fine butt; (2) the distal part of a unidirectional convergent blade with distal cortex; and (3) a unidirectional convergent blade with remnant distal cortex and a plain butt (Fig. 6.19: n30). Specimen 3, broken transversely during removal, was conjoined from proximal and distal segments. The proximal segment had subsequently been modified by two burin blows.

At first glance, this constellation appears to represent a simple unidirectional convergent removal of three blades most likely connected to the production of a Levallois point. Specimen 1, however, was not removed from a core, but from the dorsal surface of specimen 2. The differences in butt levels of specimens 1 and 3 show that the blade with the lower butt level (specimen 1) had to have been struck from the blade (specimen 2), which served as a core/truncated faceted piece, after its removal from a parent core missing in the constellation.

Constellations 31, 32, and 33

Constellations 31, 32, and 33 all show a truncated faceted piece with attempts at two removals. Constellation 31 consists of: (1) a unidirectional convergent blade with left lateral cortex; and (2) a core on a flake (Fig. 6.19: n31). Constellation 32 includes (1) a unidirectional convergent understruck flake with a convex-faceted-fine butt; and (2) a truncated-faceted piece (Fig. 6.20: n32). Constellation 33 also includes: (1) a unidirectional convergent understruck flake with a convex-faceted-fine butt; and (2) a truncated-faceted piece (Fig. 6.20: n33). These constellations all exhibit convex-faceted-fine butts on their truncated faceted pieces, thus pointing to the care that was taken in platform preparation. They also have a common pattern in the removal of a central flake followed by the removal of a lateral one, ending the reduction sequence.

In many ways, the removal order and design of these constellations resemble those associated with Levallois point production from typical unidirectional convergent cores as previously described. With their smaller flaking surfaces, however, only one lateral

removal extending through the central negative was required to create the desired Y-*arrete* pattern.

Constellation 34

Constellation 34 includes: (1) a unidirectional convergent blade with remnant distal cortex and convex-faceted-fine butt; (2) the distal part of a unidirectional convergent flake with remnant distal cortex; (3) the distal part of a unidirectional convergent blade; (4) a small Levallois point with unidirectional convergent scar pattern and *chapeau de gendarme* butt; (5) the medial part of a unidirectional convergent flake (truncated faceted piece); and (6) a core with unidirectional convergent scar pattern (Figs. 6.20 and 6.21: n34).

This constellation shows a mixture of the familiar preparatory shaping of a Levallois point core (specimens 1 to 3 and 5 and 6) and the production of a small point from a core on flake or truncated faceted piece (specimens 4 and 5). The removals of specimens 1 to 3 and 5 and 6 follow the typical unidirectional convergent pattern of core shaping; specimens 4 and 5 show a different approach centered upon the production of a small point from a core on a flake (i.e., a truncated faceted piece). In that much of the proximal end of the truncated faceted piece was removed subsequent to the production of the point, the relationship of the point, truncated faceted piece, and parent core is complicated. A comparison of the butt levels of the point and parent core shows the point's platform to be some 2 to 6mm lower than the core; thus, the point could only have been removed from the truncated faceted piece after its removal from the parent core.

Examination of the small point and truncated faceted piece shows that unlike the highly structured core shaping followed on regular cores, preparatory removals for cores on flakes were more opportunistically selected. And as previously discussed, this was probably linked to the lack of operational space available for shaping the core's flaking surface (cf. n8). In this case, the Y-*arrete* pattern, guiding the delivery of the small point, was generated by the removal of a single central flake between the convergent negatives that already were present on the truncated faceted piece's dorsal surface.

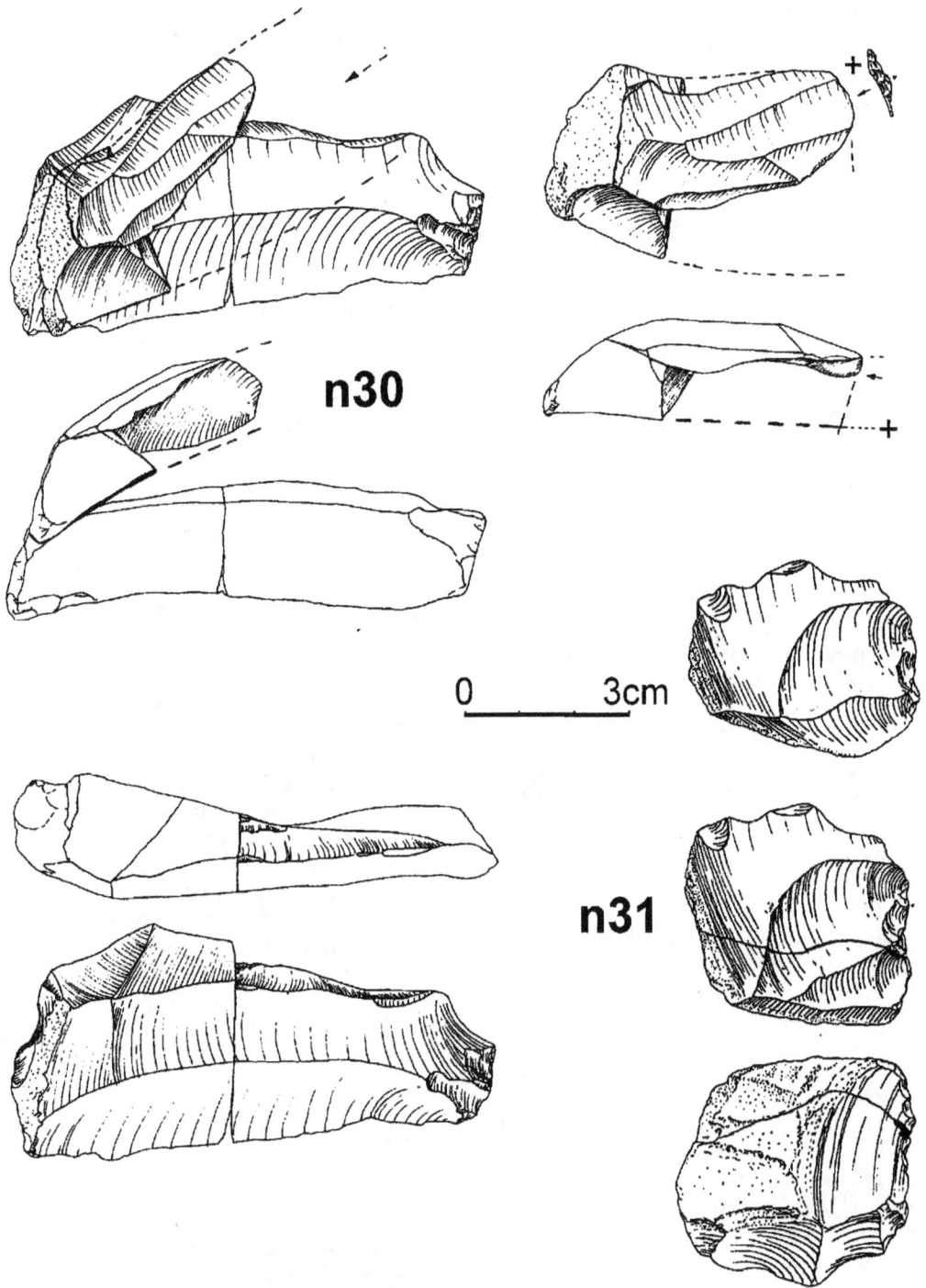

Figure 6.19 Illustrations of refitted artifacts from Tor Faraj: constellations 30 and 31. **n30**: unidirectional convergent blades. **n31**: blade and core on flake

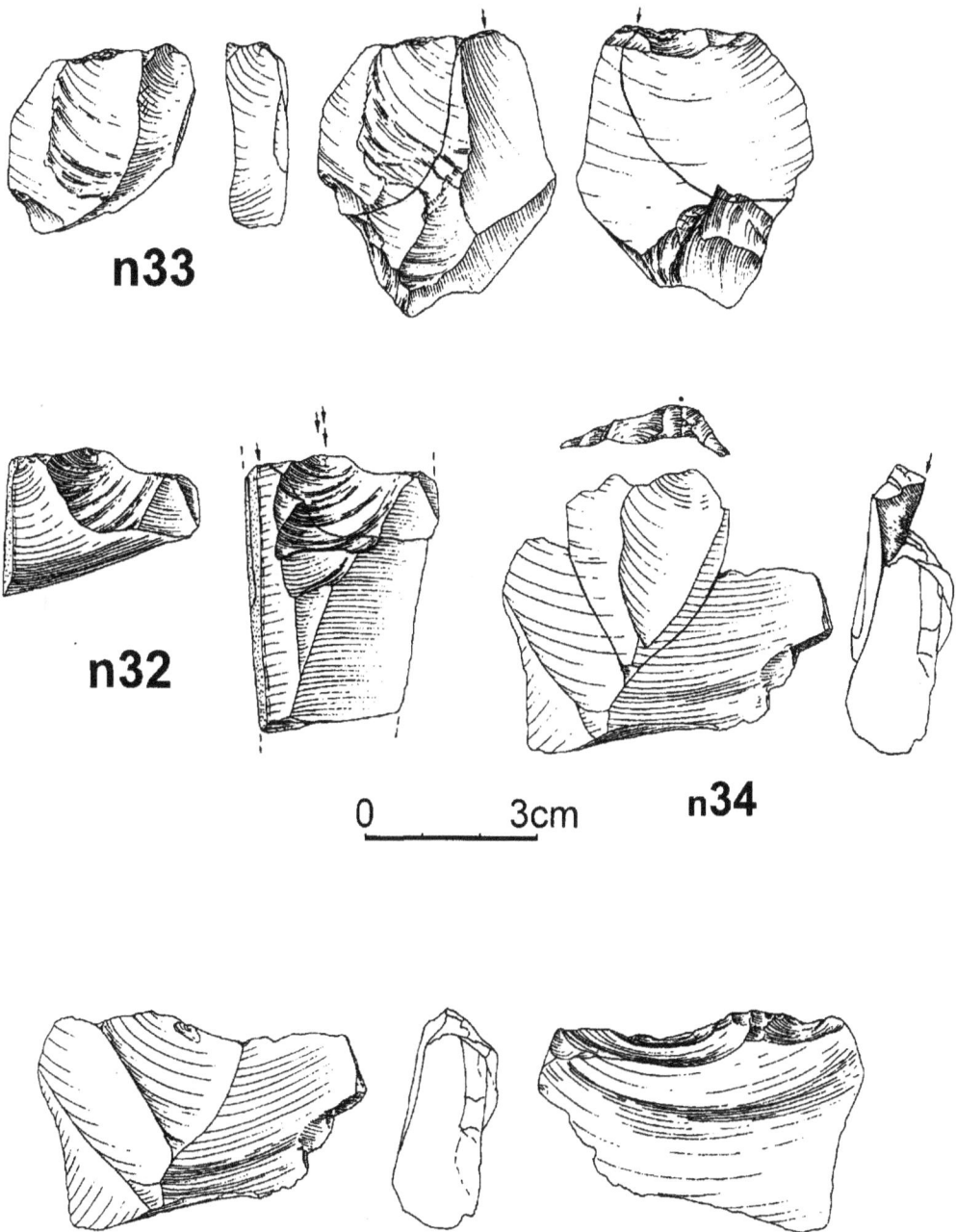

Figure 6.20 Illustrations of refitted artifacts from Tor Faraj: constellations 32, 33A, and 33B. **n32**: understruck flake on truncated faceted piece. **n33**: core on flake with lateral removal. **n34**: Levallois point struck from truncated faceted piece

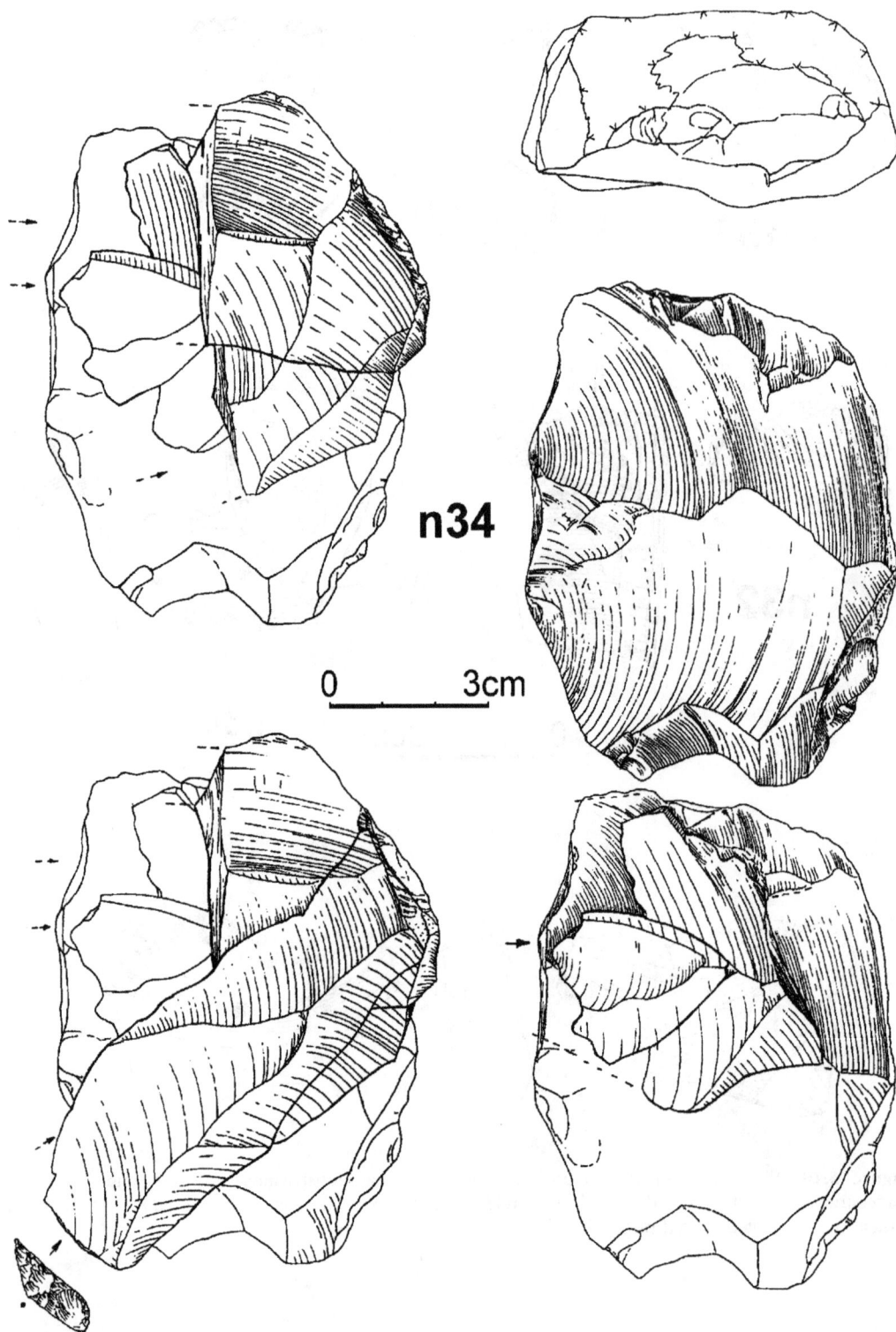

Figure 6.21 Illustrations of refitted artifacts from Tor Faraj: constellation 34. **n34**: core with convergent blade, flake, and small Levallois point removals

Constellation 35

Constellation 35 consists of a small Levallois point and a core on a flake, representing the last stages in the reduction process at Tor Faraj. Preparatory shaping, while again limited by the size and shape of this blank or operational space, nevertheless attempted to follow the same pattern of removals seen in larger cores. After creating a platform, a central Y-arrete was created by delivering two lateral blows to the right side of the core (Fig. 6.22: n35). These removals were successful in creating convergent negatives and no additional removals from the left side of the truncated faceted piece were required. After this, the small Levallois point was removed from this prepared surface.

The primary flaking of the core did not end here, however. The core's striking platform was rejuvenated through fine faceting and the removal of two new flakes from the right side, struck off in a convergent direction to the Levallois point's negative. But the removals of these rejuvenation flakes were too small because of their hinge-fractured character and after this the truncated faceted piece was abandoned as a core. The unsuccessful attempt to rejuvenate once again the core can be explained by the extremely small operational space afforded the prehistoric knapper.

Constellation 36

Constellation 36 (Fig. 6.22: n36) is unusual in that it includes the proximal end of a large Levallois point and a prominent removal similar to a burin spall. This burin-like removal appears to be the last in a series of removals. While this regularity of detachment and rejuvenation is commonly exhibited on typical burins, burins displaying serial burin blows are rare in the Tor Faraj assemblage. Similarly, this type of Levallois point/burin has not been recorded in any other Levantine assemblage.

Typologically, constellation 36 could commonly be classified as a burin, but may represent the utilization of a large, perhaps partial, Levallois point as a core. These serial removals, similar to burin blows, are analogous to the lateral removals used to create a Y-arrete on truncated faceted pieces. While no small Levallois points have been refitted to larger points, the presence of a chapeau de gendarme butt and a Y-arrete would make large points suitable for additional point production via the Nahr Ibrahim technique.

Constellation 37

Constellation 37 (Fig. 6.22: n37) consists of two conjoined truncated faceted pieces which represent a single primary element. Both the medial and distal part of this artifact exhibit ventral removals corresponding with other truncated faceted pieces at Tor Faraj. Whether these removals represent tool utilization or core preparation is difficult to discern. However, the location of retouch on the distal fragment demonstrates that several of these removals were removed after separation from the medial fragment. Unidentified truncated faceted pieces, such as this, are relatively rare in the Tor Faraj assemblage where the majority of such pieces represent cores-on-flakes.

Truncated faceted pieces at Tor Faraj primarily represent cores-on-flakes and core preparation. The majority of these illustrate a regular process of reduction, utilizing a similar unidirectional convergent technique employed in delivering Levallois points from more traditional Levallois cores. The utilization of flakes as cores tends to produce smaller points, reflecting the very end of the Levallois reduction sequence at Tor Faraj. Detailed technological interpretations of these small Levallois points and their corresponding truncated faceted 'cores' is discussed further in the concluding section of this chapter.

Constellations displaying rather non-Levallois reduction

Twenty-seven refitted constellations from Tor Faraj do not exhibit a Levallois method of reduction, but represent a more simple sequence. Eight of the more illustrative constellations are described below.

Constellation 38

Constellation 38 (Fig. 6.23: n38) is composed of a series of unidirectionally detached blades and primary elements with blade dimensions. These six blanks were removed with little platform preparation, exhibiting unfaceted or dihedral butts. Reduction required little primary

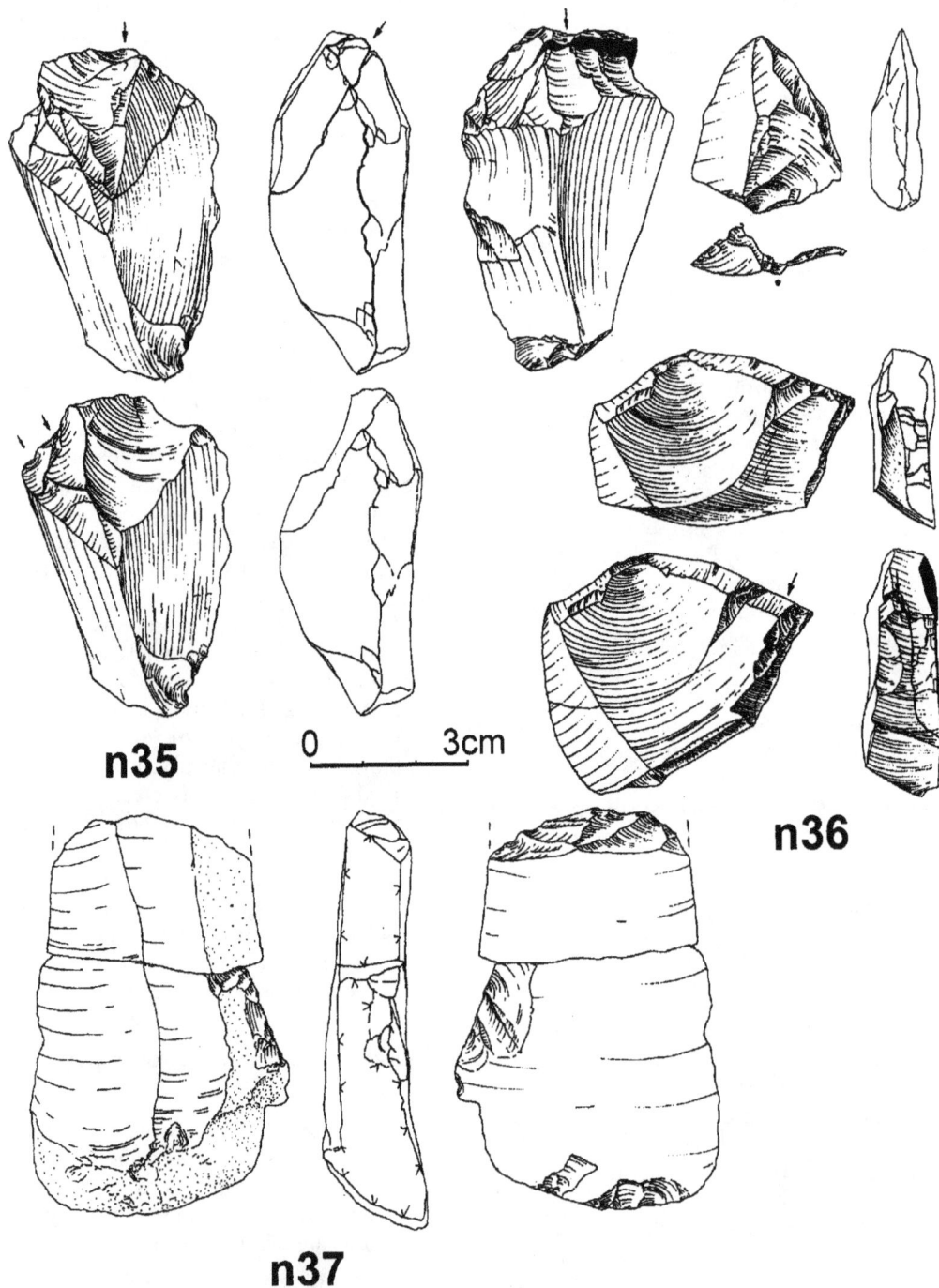

Figure 6.22 Illustrations of refitted artifacts from Tor Faraj: constellations 35, 36, and 37. **n35**: small Levallois point and core on flake. **n36**: burin-like spall struck from base of Levallois point. **n37**: conjoined truncated faceted pieces

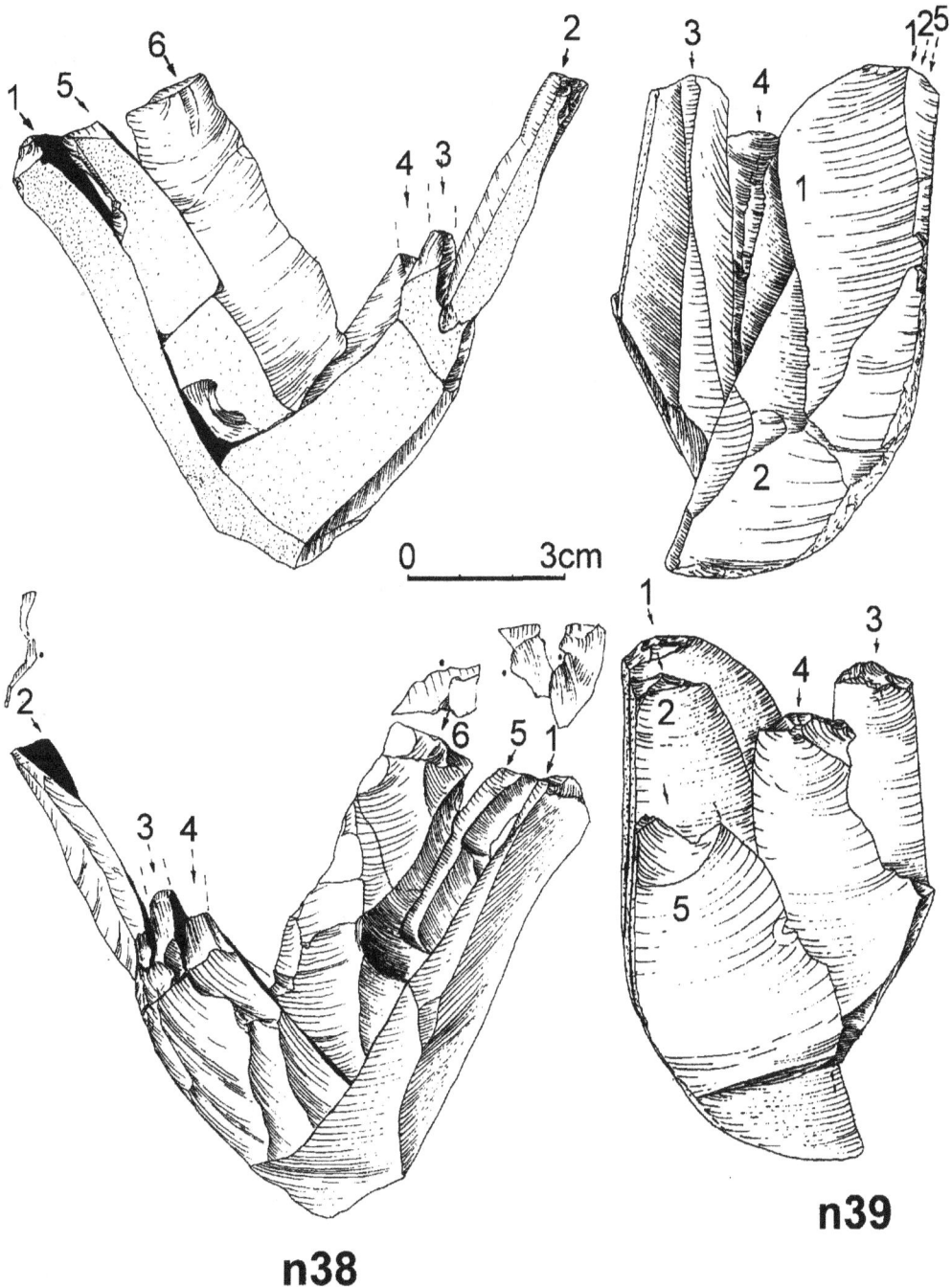

Figure 6.23 Illustrations of refitted artifacts from Tor Faraj: constellations 38 and 39. **n38**: a series of unidirectional blade removals. Note the lack of platform preparation evidenced by the unfaceted and dihedral butts. **n39**: a series of unidirectional blade removals. In contrast to **n38**, note the heavily faceted butts (even *chapeau de gendarme* platform) common to a Levallois technology

shaping and was dictated by the natural prismatic shape of the core. Platform rejuvenation was obtained simply by delivering another blank.

This constellation illustrates a reduction sequence quite distinct from the previously examined refits. Rather than utilization of the Levallois method, this particular constellation illustrates a method for detaching a series of elongated blade blanks from a single unfaceted platform. While not common in the late Levantine Mousterian, a similar reduction pattern has been found in the Negev at the sites of Rosh Ein Mor (Marks and Monigal 1995) and Level 4 of Boker Tachtit (Marks and Volkman 1983, 1987; Volkman 1983). A similar pattern also is associated with the northern Levantine transitional sequence at Ksar Akil Levels 25 to 21/20 (Ohnuma and Bergman 1990).

Constellation 39

Constellation 39 (Fig. 6.23: n39), like the previous constellation, is composed of a series of unidirectionally detached blades, but, unlike constellation 38, these five blanks are more suggestive of Levallois reduction. Three of these blanks exhibit fine, convex-shaped platforms, and a fourth blank has a *chapeau de gendarme* butt. Cortex on the outside lateral edges of these blanks illustrate a rather narrow, ovoid-shaped cobble. The narrowness of this cobble may have hindered the creation of a well prepared Y-*arrete*, and specimens 4 and 5 may represent an unsuccessful Levallois point removal and an additional removal in attempt to prepare the core for subsequent blank delivery, respectively.

Constellations 40 and 41

Constellations 40 and 41 (Fig. 6.24) represent perpendicular, or orthogonal, reduction. Since this type of reduction is not well represented at Tor Faraj, these examples may represent attempts at correcting mistakes in order to continue the methods of reduction discussed above.

Constellation 42

Constellation 42 (Fig. 6.24) appears to follow a similar reduction pattern seen in Constellation 39. Two of the blanks exhibit fine, convex-shaped platforms similar to those seen in Levallois blank preparation, yet there is an absence of a Y-*arrete*. While it appears Levallois reduction was being attempted, the lack of a recognizable Y-*arrete* makes the possibility of a unidirectional reduction equally possible.

Constellation 43

The two refitted pieces constituting constellation 43 (Fig. 6.24: n43) appear to represent reduction focused on producing elongated blanks. Unlike Levallois reduction, both blanks exhibit long, parallel flake scars and little, or no, platform preparation, similar to the reduction seen in constellation 38 and at Rosh Ein Mor (Marks and Monigal 1995), Boker Tachtit (Marks and Volkman 1983, 1987; Volkman 1983), and within the transitional sequence at Ksar Akil (Ohnuma and Bergman 1990).

Constellations displaying decortification and initial core shaping

Constellations 44 to 64

Constellations 44 and 45 (Fig. 6.25) both display primary removals, which are all of blade dimensions. Blank platforms within constellation 44 are unfaceted, while constellation 45 comprises a blank with a fine, convex-shaped butt, a blank possessing a platform suggestive of punctiform removal, and a blank with a cortex platform.

Relatively little information may be gained from the other refits displaying initial core shaping. The 19 other constellations, while including 41 flakes and blades, typically consist of only two refitted pieces. Nevertheless, attributes of many of these constellations allowed for the recognition of four reduction subgroups: (1) initial core shaping via lateral decortification removals (constellations 46 to 54); (2) unidirectional convergent reduction (constellations 55 to 60); (3) unidirectional reduction with either convergent or parallel removals (constellations 61 to 63); and (4) one example of indistinguishable core shaping reduction (constellation 64).

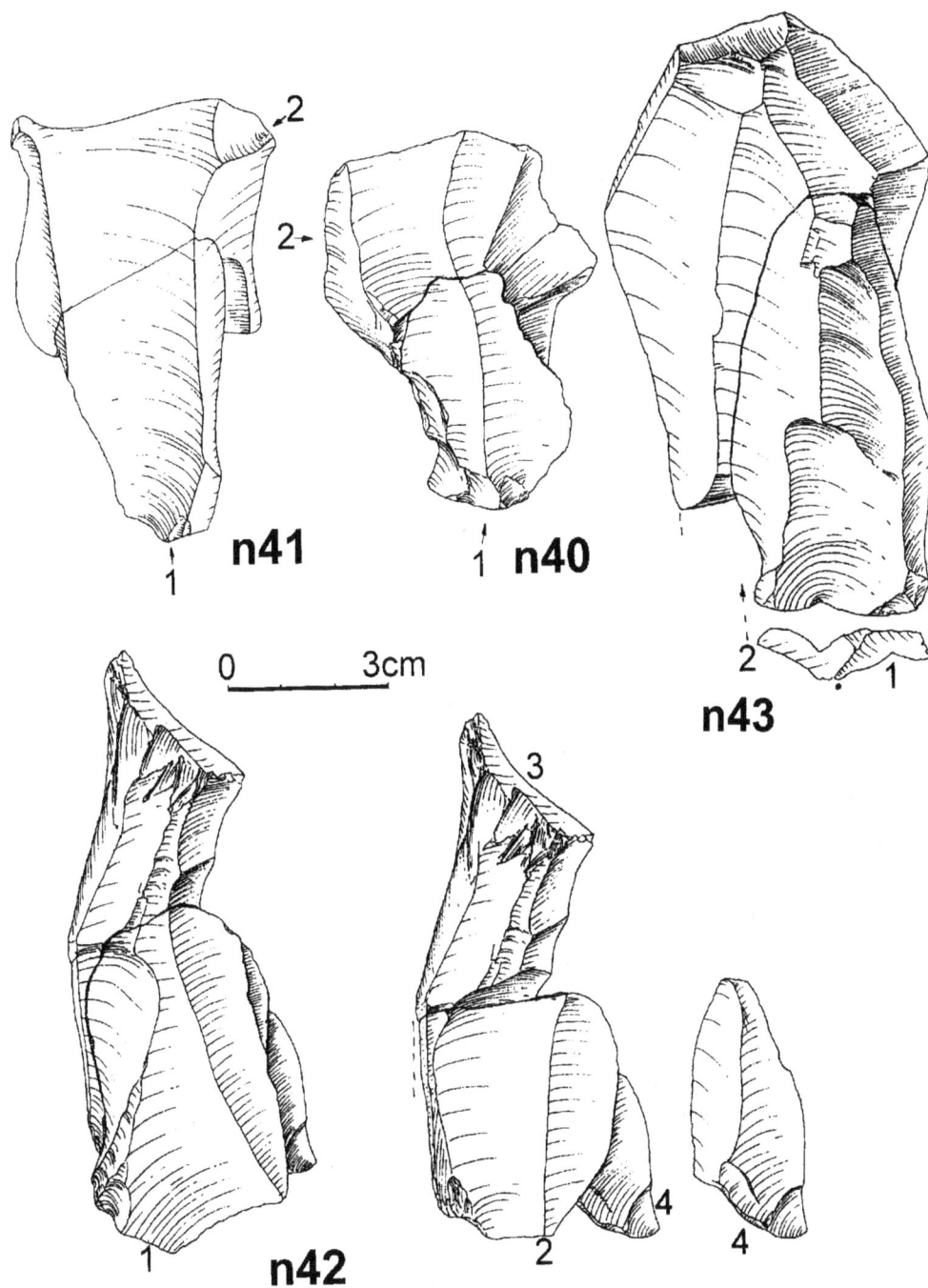

Figure 6.24 Illustrations of refitted artifacts from Tor Faraj: constellations 40, 41, 42, and 43. **n40** and **n41** are examples of perpendicular or orthogonal reduction. **n42** and **n43** are unidirectional convergent removals

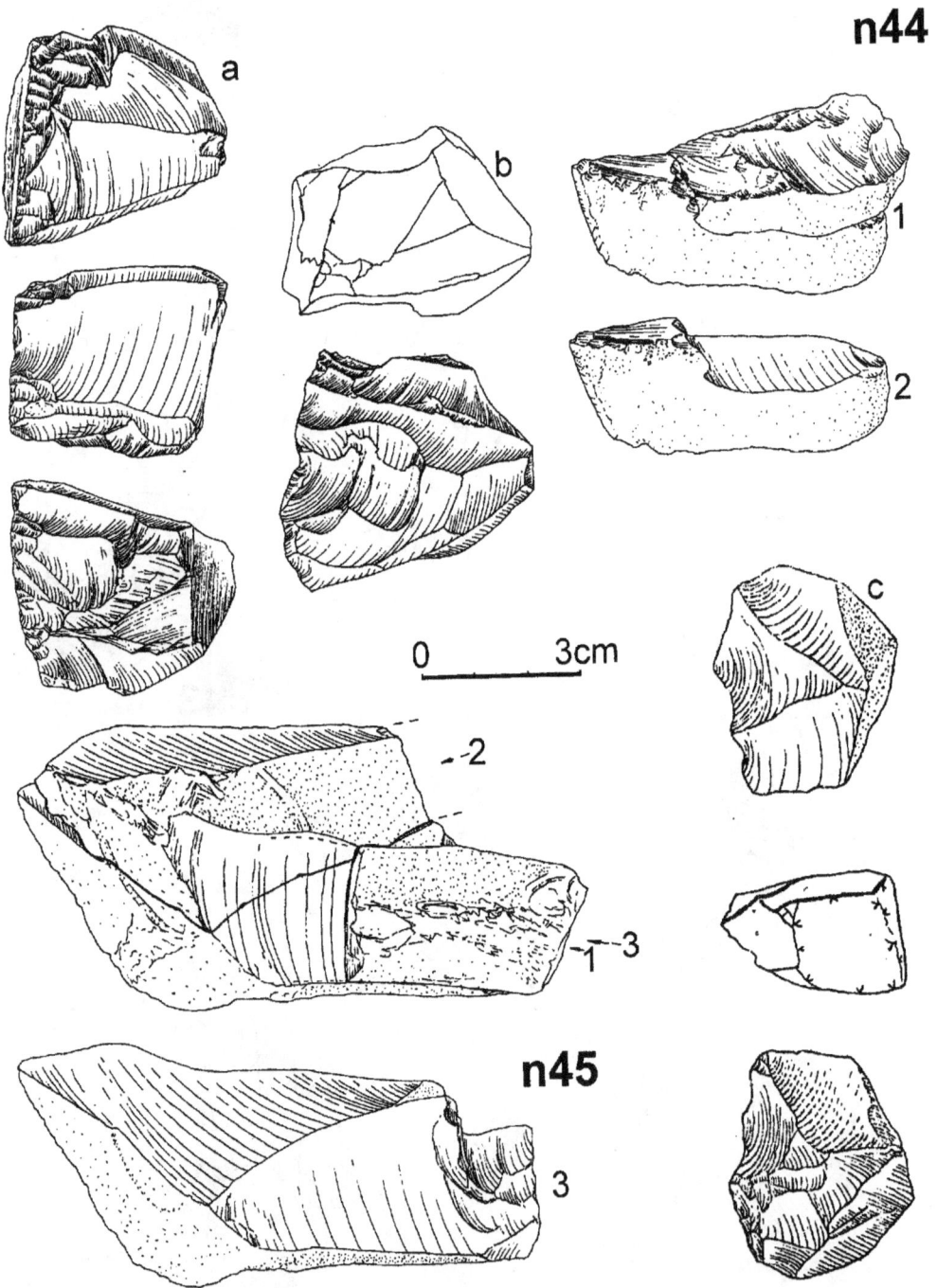

Figure 6.25 Illustrations of refitted artifacts from Tor Faraj: constellations 44 and 45. **n44** and **n45** show unidirectional blade removals with cortex

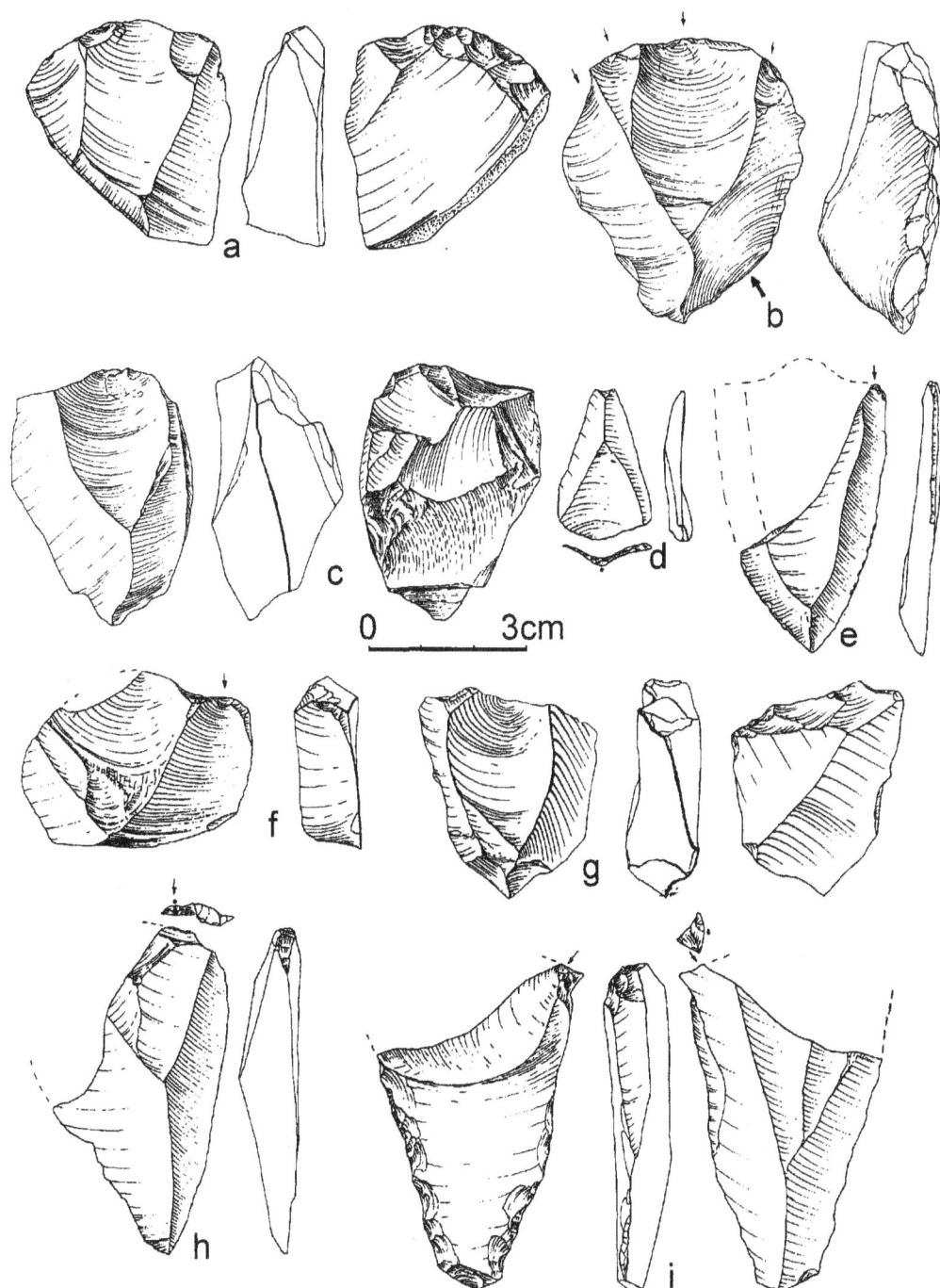

Figure 6.26 Other technologically informative artifacts from Tor Faraj: (a) core on flake; (b, f, g) Levallois point core on flake; (c) small Levallois point core; (d) small Levallois point; (e, h, i) burin-like spalls from Levallois points

Conjoined pieces

A total of 21 flakes and blades were completely and partially reconstructed. These constellations fractured transversely (17 examples) and longitudinally (4 examples) during their removal from the cores.

Methods, techniques, and technologies of the primary flaking processes

The following analysis provides a summary of the primary flaking processes that were undertaken at Tor Faraj and are characteristic of the assemblage. As discussed earlier, our interpretation is based upon more than our refitting study as it involves a general background knowledge of certain technological and typological (morphological) aspects of the assemblage. And while we are aware of the ideas of our colleagues relative to the technology of the assemblage as well as the behavioral organization of the occupants of Tor Faraj, we have attempted to arrive at our conclusions objectively and independently.

The assemblage is characterized by the production of broad-based Levallois points that display unidirectional, convergent, Y-*arrete* patterns, often in association with *chapeau de gendarme* butts and 'Concorde' lateral profiles. We should emphasize that typological and refitting studies are in agreement in showing that the Levallois point method dominated in the primary flaking processes, although other non-Levallois methods were occasionally employed. Thus, our descriptions and analysis will center on the Levallois point method and offer only a brief discussion of non-Levallois processes.

The Levallois primary flaking method was based on the exploitation of two kinds of blanks for core reduction: unmodified flint cobbles and various debitage pieces. The differences in the primary flaking technologies between these two varieties of blanks require that they be analyzed and described separately.

Levallois point method: reduction of chert nodules

Raw material selection

The refitted constellations as well as some cores themselves show that oval-shaped chert nodules, some 6 to 15cm long and relatively narrow (e.g., constellations n1, 5, 9, 11, 12, 19, and 20), were the preferred form of raw material (Fig. 6.27). There is no evidence for the use of tabular cherts at Tor Faraj, although sources on the Ma'an Plateau contain both tabular and nodular cherts (see Henry 1995b; Chapter 3, this volume).

Decortification processes

The initial decortification of the nodules was not haphazard, but clearly an orderly part of core preparation (e.g., constellations n2, 9, 14, 19–20). As part of decortification, a core's striking platform was prepared (Fig. 6.27). This resulted in a significant reduction in the length of flaking surfaces and brought their length:width ratios into rough balance (e.g., constellations n2, 3, 9, 15, 21, 23, 25).

Levallois point preparatory processes

Creation of a Y-*arrete* pattern on a core's flaking surface was central to Levallois point production and at Tor Faraj principally followed a unidirectional convergent technique (Fig. 6.27). Although bidirectional preparation was found to be common to cores on flakes, all of the refitted constellations related to the initial reduction of chert nodules relied on a remarkably standardized flaking order in producing the Y-*arrete* pattern.

This order was initiated by the creation of a central plane (forming surface 'A') of the Y-*arrete* pattern by the removal of usually one central flake struck from a convex-faceted platform of a crude, early-stage core (Fig. 6.27; e.g., constellation n18). Following this removal, the striking platform was reshaped by fine faceting of its shoulders in order to produce the classic *chapeau de gendarme* characteristics. At least two, convergent preparatory removals were then struck from the shoulders of the platform in order to create a unidirectional, convergent 'Y'-*arrete* pattern on the core's flaking surface. The negatives of

Face 1

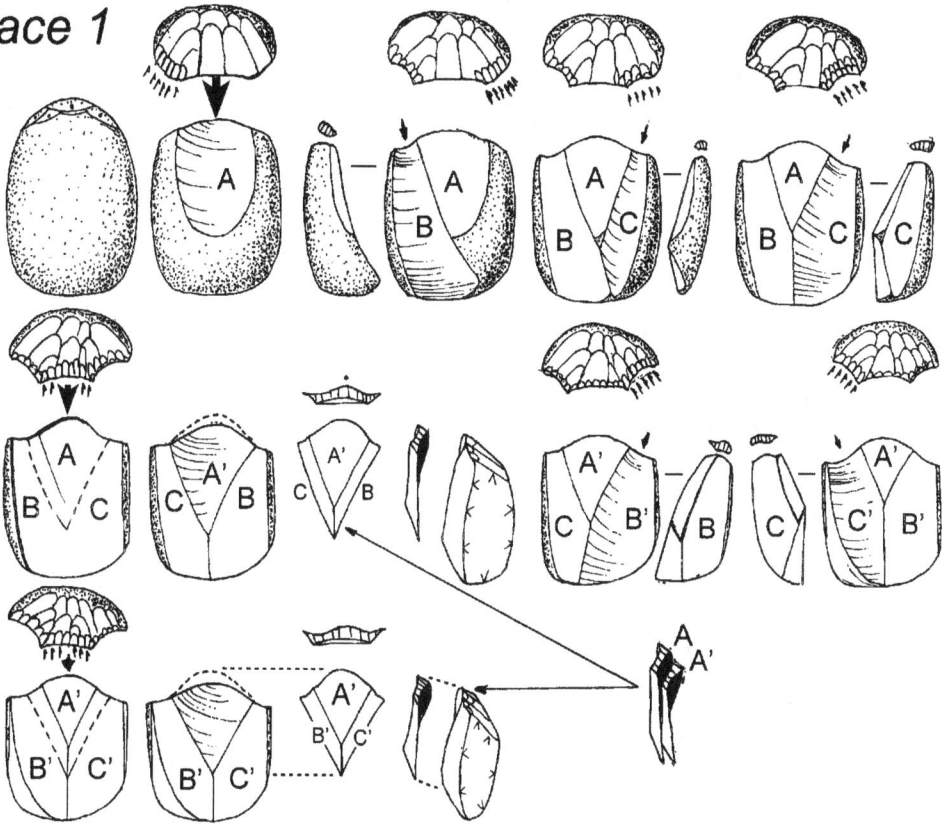

Face 2

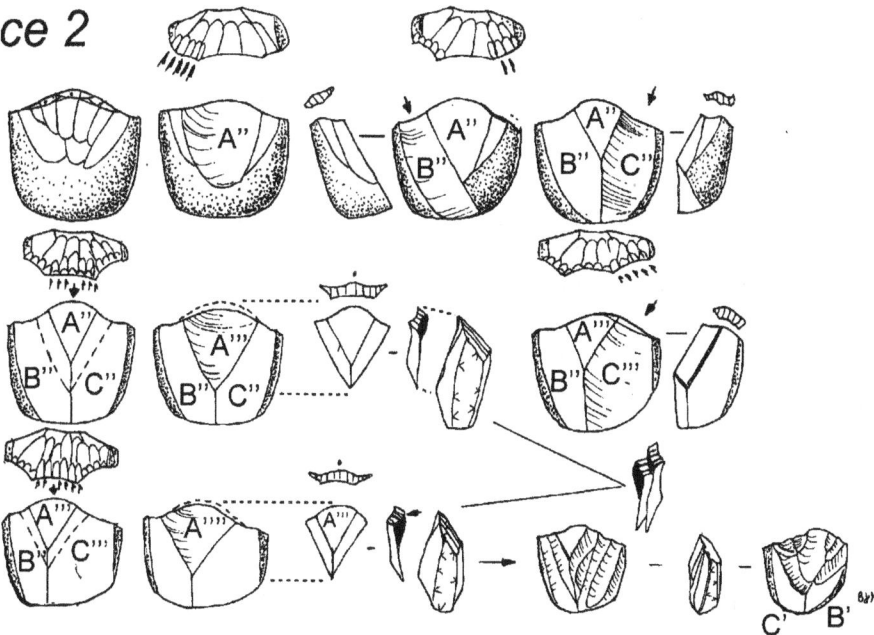

Figure 6.27 Schematic illustration of the reduction sequence(s) reconstructed from the refitting study of Tor Faraj artifacts. Note the efficiency of initial reduction offered by the natural convexity of the chert nodule and the multiple point removals on Face 1 followed by a second set of removals on Face 2

these convergent removals formed sides 'B' and 'C' of the 'Y'-*arrete* pattern. There appears to have been no particular pattern for the order (e.g., right to left) of these removals and they were typically limited to two or three (e.g., constellation n1) and rarely more than four. This highly efficient method of preparing a core's face for the generation of Levallois points also was used in the rejuvenation of the flaking surface for subsequent point removals. In those situations where lateral preparatory flakes could not be successfully removed, the entire working face was struck off in order to clean the face (e.g., constellation n9, item 4). In those situations where the core's face could not be rejuvenated, the core was simply abandoned.

The convergent preparatory removals usually have fine-faceted butts, especially convex ones, and elongated, even-blade, dimensions. The characteristics of convergent preparatory removals appear to have been determined more by technological constraints than by the preferences of the knappers. Finely faceted loci on the shoulders of the platform were necessary for the control of the preparatory removals that followed the lateral edges of the central plane. The elongation of these removals also appear technologically predetermined. Here, it is important to remember the *technological law of Levallois point removal method* with unidirectional convergent technique. It simply holds that the length of the inter-faceting ridge in the Y-*arrete* pattern will be always longer than the length of any subsequent point removed from the same working face. This means that preparations for the delivery of even broad-based points, that are relatively wide to their lengths, require that the preparatory removals be quite elongated, if not of blade proportions. The association then between assemblages, such as Tor Faraj, that have an emphasis on point production and a correlative high blade index is apparent. A similar correlation has been noted by Demidenko and Usik (1994) for the Middle Paleolithic site of Korolevo I, complex 2B in the Ukraine.

Levallois point removal

After the delivery of a point, a core's working face was rejuvenated by the creation of a new Y-*arrete* pattern, but the core's striking platform was retouched only slightly, if at all, before the generation of another point (Fig. 6.27; constellation n1 and 2). Here, it is also noteworthy that 'demi-*chapeau de gendarme*' butts merely represent knapping errors in which point deliveries did not catch both shoulders of the platform (constellation n5).

Another important morphological feature of Levallois points is their 'Concorde' arched profiles. This also has a technological origin in our view. As shown in the refittings, the lateral removals typically form acute angles with the central plane, both laterally and at their convergence (constellations n1, 4, and 6). This, coupled with the natural convexity of the chert nodules, created in points a profile that is strongly arched distally.

Levallois point rejuvenation processes

The great majority of refitted constellations and specimens with evidence associated with point removals trace multiple removals (n1 to 6, 8 and 9, 11 to 13, 21, 23, 25, and 35). In fact, artifactual examples of single removal episodes are quite rare (n7 and 10). Several of the constellations offer an understanding of why cores were abandoned after the delivery of multiple points. Core exhaustion most commonly resulted from the size of the flaking surface becoming so small that continued point production became unfeasible (n23 to 25). But in others, the morphology of the flaking surface (e.g., deep negative of the central plane) evolved in such a way as to make continued point production impractical.

Multiple Levallois point production from unidirectionally prepared flaking surfaces was commonly undertaken at Tor Faraj. The initial removal of a point and the attendant creation of a Y-*arrete* represented the first technological step in preparing a core for the production of another point (Fig. 6.27, constellations n1 and 2, 4, 9, 25). Moreover, for the 'cutting' of the central plane, the removal of a single convergent flake often sufficed in contrast to the two or three removals that were normally required for an initial point removal (*cf.*, constellations n1 and 2 with constellations n4 to 6, 9). Although most of the available evidence can only confirm the production of two points, a few constellations confirm the existence of three (n6, 25) and even six (n9) phases of point production.

Apart from actual refitted constellations, convergent flakes and blades often display a scar of a Levallois point that was struck in the previous Levallois point production phase (constellations n1, 6, 9, 11 to 13). Such specimens assist in defining multiple phases of point production in addition to the directionality of preparation. Similarly, many convergent specimens also exhibit cortex along one lateral edge (n1 to 3, 6, 9, 11 to 13, 15, 19 to 20, 23 to 25). Technologically, such removals promoted the convexity of the flaking surface and simultaneously created the Y-*arrete* pattern. Those specimens bearing both a scar of an earlier point removal and lateral cortex confirm the narrowness of the chert nodules used at Tor Faraj (n1, 6, 9, 11 to 13). The specimens as described resemble the *lames et éclats débordants corticaux* described for the Levantine Mousterian of Kebara (Boëda et al., 1990: Fig. 12, 1-2 and Fig. 13, 1-3).

Two other approaches were used to extend the production of points from chert nodules (Fig. 6.27). These involved using the 'reverse' side of the nodule after initial production (n9) or in expanding production with a 'fan-like' array of removals around the nodule (n23).

Beyond tracing the various ways that Levallois points were produced at Tor Faraj, the refit study also informs us about unsuccessful attempts at point removals (Fig. 6.8: n9:4; Fig. 6.12: n18; Figs 6.14 to 6.15). Hinge fractures, with their deep concavities, often spoiled the flaking surfaces of cores and in other cases the small sizes of cores simply precluded additional removals. Evidence of failed attempts at point removal raises an important analytic question. Should such failures be classified as points although they do not fit the morphological and typological definition of Levallois points? In excluding failed point removals from typological counts, the number of phases of point production and point:core ratios are under-represented. Also, indices for Levallois points and flakes are likely to be skewed. In light of this discussion, it is noteworthy that in following a liberal typological classification of Levallois points in this study, a little over 4 percent of the points display attributes (e.g., understruck terminations) indicative of failed removals (Henry, Chapter 3 this volume).

In summary, the Levallois point method as defined here consisted of: (1) preparing a crude or fine convex-faceted striking platform on a chert nodule after an initial decapitation; (2) creating a central plane by the removal of a large flake; (3) reshaping the platform in the form of a *chapeau de gendarme*; (4) removing two to three, obliquely oriented edge-elements, struck from the shoulders of the platform, in order to create the Y-*arrete* pattern; and (5) detaching a Levallois point.

Our refitting study also shows that after the initial removal of a point, most cores were rejuvenated through only minimal modification for additional production of points and that these procedures were very patterned. The steps largely consisted of: (1) reshaping the striking platform into a new *chapeau de gendarme* form with fine faceting; (2) creating a new Y-*arrete* by using the negative of the first point removal as a central plane and cutting this with one to two oblique removals; and (3) striking off a Levallois point. As confirmed in our study, this procedure allowed for the production of as many as seven points from a core and thus clearly fit within Boëda's 'lineal' method.

Reduction of debitage elements: truncated faceted pieces

Beyond the production of Levallois points from cores formed on chert nodules, points were also generated from cores fashioned on flakes, blades, primary elements, and even broken Levallois points. Our refits showing this approach are consistent with the morphological and typological classification of specimens as truncated faceted *pieces* bearing *Nahr Ibrahim retouch* or simply *cores-on-flakes* (Schroeder 1969; Solecki and Solecki 1970; Copeland 1975; Crew 1975; Munday 1976, 1979; Dibble 1984b; Nishiaki 1985; Goren-Inbar 1988). Although researchers have related truncated faceted pieces to use as cores as well as tools (linked to hafting), there has been a tendency to focus on a single functional explanation for the phenomenon. Perhaps a more productive approach is to consider the full range of functions associated with truncated faceted specimens in light of technological, typological, and even edge-wear evidence (see Chapters 4, 8, and 10, this volume). In the context of our refitting study for the Tor Faraj assemblage, most, if not all, of the truncated faceted specimens could be tied to use as cores. These occur in two forms: (1)

cores on debitage elements that display clear negatives of Levallois points (e.g., Figure 6.26: a, b, c, g) and other preparatory steps toward point production (e.g., constellations 35 and 36); and (2) cores that were aborted because of mistakes in primary reduction (e.g., constellations n28, 31 to 33, 36).

Cores

Although the use of cores made on recycled debitage elements appears to have been markedly less common than the use of cores made from chert nodules, the Levallois point method was employed for both. The method, however, was slightly modified when applied to debitage elements principally because they lacked the 'operational space' of the larger cores on nodules. In being no more than 4 to 5cm in length, cores on debitage elements are likely to have produced only a single point and in rare instances two removals.

The small, constricted flaking surfaces of such cores induced knappers to opportunistically select extant features on the cores to achieve the convergent, Y-*arrete* pattern for guiding point removals. Various morphological features were exploited, such as: the position of negatives on a debitage element's dorsal surface (constellations n8 and 34), the convexity of a debitage element's ventral surface (constellation n35 and Fig. 6.26: b, c, g), or even a Y-*arrete* pattern of a Levallois point (constellation n36 and Fig. 6.26: e, f, h, i). In some cases, the creation of a Y-*arrete* pattern on a debitage element required relatively little modification to the specimen. Examples of such limited modification include: altering the striking platform (constellation n8), forming a central plane on an extant convergent faceted surface (constellation n34), using only one or two removals (central and lateral) to create a Y-*arrete* (constellations n31 to 33, 35, 36, Fig. 6.26). And aside from the various ways the unidirectional convergent technique was implemented, a technique involving distal, bidirectional preparation was identified in two constellations (n7 and 8).

Uncompleted or aborted cores

For cores in which reduction was interrupted by unsuccessful preparatory removals, typical truncated faceted flakes or even burin-like pieces were produced (constellations n31 to 33 and 36).

Beyond providing strong evidence for economizing behaviors, the various procedures by which the knappers of Tor Faraj were able to exploit debitage elements as cores for the production of Levallois points underscores both their flexibility and their focus upon delivering a relatively standardized end-product. Although many truncated faceted pieces recovered from Tor Faraj clearly served as cores for the production of small Levallois points, other truncated faceted specimens were tied to a non-Levallois method of primary flaking (e.g., constellation n28) and perhaps to use as truncated tools (e.g., constellation n37).

Non-Levallois method

The refit study also confirmed the presence of a non-Levallois method for producing serial elongated blanks through a unidirectional, parallel/convergent technique. In that there are only a few examples of refitted constellations (n38 and 43) and cores (Fig. 6.25: a, b) representing this technique, it likely formed only a minor part of the overall lithic technology at the site. The technique involved the serial production of elongated flakes and blades from pyramidal-shaped cores fashioned on ovoid chert nodules. The removals used a large part of a core's circumference during a single reduction phase (e.g., n38). Rejuvenation and strengthening of striking platforms were based upon crude faceting of individual striking loci along the margins of a core. Because of this, well-worked cores display crude faceted or even plain platforms (Fig. 6.25: a, b).

Conclusion

The refitting study informs us about the ways in which the occupants of Tor Faraj organized their behaviors in three ways. First, the efficiency of the primary processing of multiple Levallois points from chert nodules and of Levallois points and other elements from cores-on-flakes underscores the emphasis upon economizing behaviors at the shelter. Although this is not surprising, given that the most used chert sources were outside the site's catchment, the methods used in extending the primary production of imported chert confirm the capacity of Levantine Mousterian groups to inhabit chert-poor settings through technological adaptation. The relative proportion of cores-on-flakes in an assemblage is likely to be inversely related to the availability of the chert. At least in southern Jordan and in the Negev (Munday 1976, 1979), truncated faceted pieces represent greater parts of those assemblages that are found more distant from raw material sources.

Second, refitted constellations clearly trace several alternative technological procedures for achieving the most economical production of Levallois points from a limited amount of chert, while at the same time maintaining a rather standardized end-product. This use of alternative production paths to an end-product with a standard design confirms the flexibility of the knappers at Tor Faraj. Moreover, the importation of chert nodules (as opposed to shaped cores) to the site tells us not only that the knappers anticipated a need to import the nodules, but that they understood nodules were more economic than cores for point production in the context of Tor Faraj.

Third, the missing components of refitted constellations indicate that certain elements were removed to other parts of the site or off-site for use or continued reduction. Cores, Levallois points, and other diagnostic elements (e.g., lateral convergent removals) of the different reductive segments of the Levallois point method are rarely found together for refitting. This indicates that primary reduction, use, and maintenance were not undertaken at a single locus within the shelter and, perhaps more importantly, it opens the possibility that specific areas within the shelter were habitually used for certain lithic related activities. This issue of intra-site spatial patterning will be addressed in Chapters 9 and 10 of this volume.

Notes

1. The terminology employed here refers to 'refits,' *sensu lato*, as specimens which have been fit back together. At a more specific level, 'refits' denote those specimens that are primarily re-articulated through the joining of dorsal and ventral surfaces that were separated through knapping as manufactured removals. In contrast, 'conjoins' represent those specimens that primarily are joined along surfaces of flexion fractures that were produced either during manufacture or in post-depositional contexts (Saragusti and Goren-Inbar 1990: 174). In general, the distinction between refits and conjoins follows that which has been employed in zooarchaeology where 'refits' refer to re-articulated bones and 'conjoins' to broken bones that are connected (Todd and Frison 1992; Todd and Stanford 1992).
2. A 'constellation' simply designates a group of artifacts that has been refitted.

7 Middle Paleolithic Plant Exploitation: The Microbotanical Evidence

ARLENE MILLER ROSEN

Phytolith studies at Tor Faraj were conducted after the previous analysis of a pilot sample revealed abundant phytolith remains at the site (Rosen 1995). The aim of this investigation was to reconstruct local vegetation in the site vicinity, garner paleoclimatic information, and attempt to understand the pattern of plant use by the occupants of the shelter. The exposure of a broad horizontal unit across a Middle Paleolithic period living surface presented the unique opportunity to evaluate the phytolith results within their spatial contexts. Thirty phytolith samples were collected across a single horizontal occupation level, including the living surface and some of the associated hearths, in order to understand the site structure and possible patterning of activities involving plant use and discard. Systematic phytolith sampling has previously been undertaken at two Levantine Mousterian rock shelters (Albert *et al.* 1999; Albert and Weiner, 2001); however, in both of these cases samples were collected from a series of vertical columns within the shelter. This study is the first time a horizontal approach to phytolith sampling has been employed at a paleolithic site in the Near East, and it has allowed us to examine the spatial patterning of plant use.

Methods

Twenty-four phytolith samples were collected from the center of excavation squares and another six samples were collected from hearths from Floor II of Layer D_2 (see Table 7.1 and Fig. 7.1). Subsamples consisting of 5 to 10g of sediment were sieved through a 0.125mm mesh and the fine fractions were treated with 1 N HCl to remove pedogenic carbonates. The samples were then washed and clays dispersed by soaking them for 24 hours in distilled water and then treating them with a saturated solution of sodium pyrophosphate. Clays were then pipetted off after settling fine sand and silt for 1 hour in an 8cm-high column of water. Organic matter was removed by burning in a muffle furnace at 500°C for two hours. The remaining sediment was floated in a sodium polytungstate solution adjusted to a density of 2.3 sp. gravity, in order to separate the opaline silica bodies from the quartz and heavy minerals. The suspense was pipetted off, washed, dried, and mounted in Entellan. An average of 350 phytoliths and other particles were counted at 400× using a polarizing microscope. The phytolith data presented here are in relative percents, although the correlation co-efficients were calculated from the numerical counts.

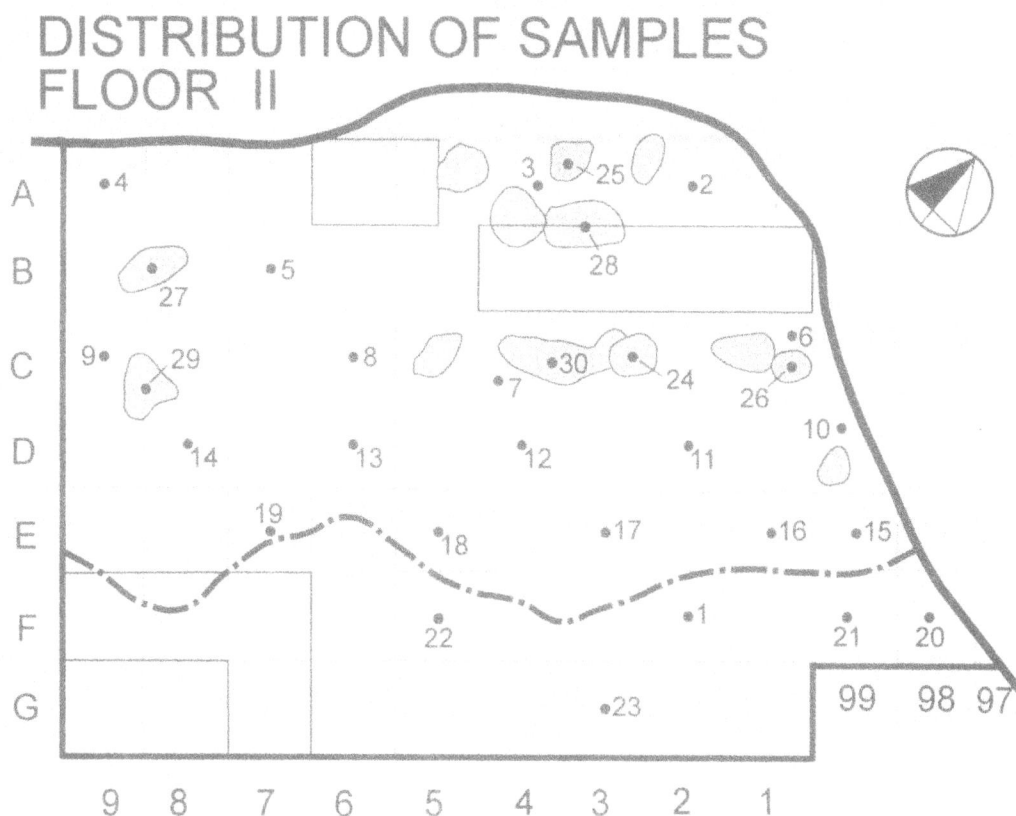

Figure 7.1 Plan map of Tor Faraj showing the locations of samples for phytolith analysis

Results

The samples displayed a surprisingly rich diversity, not only within the silica phytolith assemblage but also in the content of other plant micro-remains including spores, a number of different kinds of starch grains, and calcium oxalate crystals (see Tables 7.2 and 7.3). These remains exhibited a great deal of spatial variability in their distributions across the cave floor. The spores closely resembled those from the genus *Equisetum* (horse-tail rush) (Kapp 1969). Starch grains were abundant at some locations in the cave, and presumably came from a variety of different nuts, tubers, and other plant parts. Although no positive identifications have been made at this time, we are currently assembling a reference collection of starches from local plants in order to assist with these determinations in the future.

The silica bodies occurred in two general categories; first, the single-celled phytoliths which form when a single plant epidermis cell is replaced by silica while still in the living plant. These forms are the traditional phytolith shapes including 'saddles,' 'cones,' 'bilobes' (also known as 'dumbells'), and 'rondels' which are indicative of the monocotyledon families and subfamilies including grasses, sedges, and palms (Mulholland and Rapp 1992). As such, they are also keys to the dominance of C_3 or C_4 grass subfamilies providing information on general environmental conditions in the site vicinity. Plant parts can be distinguished as well from these types, from the epidermal long cells which tend to be smooth-sided in stems and highly wavy or dendritic in the floral parts and seed husks. This distinction provides a tool for the estimation of seasonality with floral and husk phytoliths entering the assemblage in the Levantine late winter and spring (Rosen, 1999a).

Monocot phytoliths also occur as multi-celled forms or 'silica skeletons,' sometimes

Table 7.1 Proveniences of Tor Faraj phytolith samples

Lab sample no.	Site sample no.	Square	Depth	Provenience	Comments
TF-96-1	38	F2	185	Occupation surface	
TF-96-2	47	A2	190	"	
TF-96-3	49	A4	190	"	
TF-96-4	53	A9	190	"	
TF-96-5	55	B7	190	"	
TF-96-6	58	C1	190	"	
TF-96-7	61	C4	190	"	
TF-96-8	63	C6	190	"	
TF-96-9	66	C9	190	"	
TF-96-10	67	D99	190	"	
TF-96-11	69	D2	190	"	
TF-96-12	71	D4	190	"	
TF-96-13	73	D6	190	"	
TF-96-14	75	D8	190	"	
TF-96-15	78	E99	190	"	
TF-96-16	79	E1	190	"	
TF-96-17	81	E3	190	"	
TF-96-18	83	E5	190	"	
TF-96-19	85	E7	190	"	
TF-96-20	87	F98	190	"	
TF-96-21	88	F99	190	"	
TF-96-22	92	F4	190	"	
TF-96-23	93	G3	190	"	
TF-96-24	97	D3a/b	195	Hearth	Feature 14
TF-96-25	100	A4a	175–80	"	Feature 9
TF-96-26	102	C1/D2	200	"	Feature 18
TF-96-27	103	B8a	195	"	Feature 16
TF-96-28	104	A4d/A3c	190	"	Feature 11
TF-96-29	106	C8c	195	"	Feature 17
TF-96-30	108	C4b	195	"	Feature 15

Table 7.2 Phytolith counts and percentages from Tor Faraj

Sample context	TF-96-1 surface		TF-96-2 surface		TF-96-3 surface		TF-96-4 surface		TF-96-5 surface		TF-96-6 surface	
SINGLE-CELLS	No.	%	No.	%	No.	%	No.	%	No.	%	No.	%
Long (leaf/stem)	10	7.8	2	1.1	136	37.8	113	37.5	192	46.2	104	30.5
Long (floral)	0	0.0	0	0.0	18	5.0	7	2.3	13	3.1	14	4.1
Papillae	0	0.0	0	0.0	0	0.0	1	0.3	0	0.0	0	0.0
Hairs	0	0.0	0	0.0	5	1.4	5	1.7	9	2.2	3	0.9
Bulliform	0	0.0	0	0.0	3	0.8	7	2.3	5	1.2	2	0.6
Arrowhead	0	0.0	0	0.0	0	0.0	1	0.3	1	0.2	2	0.6
Ovals	0	0.0	0	0.0	2	0.6	2	0.7	9	2.2	3	0.9
Keystone	0	0.0	0	0.0	0	0.0	0	0.0	1	0.2	0	0.0
Crenates	0	0.0	0	0.0	12	3.3	5	1.7	13	3.1	20	5.9
Bilobes	0	0.0	0	0.0	3	0.8	7	2.3	10	2.4	20	5.9
Polylobate	0	0.0	0	0.0	0	0.0	0	0.0	0	0.0	2	0.6
Short trapezoid	0	0.0	0	0.0	0	0.0	0	0.0	6	1.4	5	1.5
Rondels	0	0.0	0	0.0	17	4.7	22	7.3	38	9.1	23	6.7
Saddles	0	0.0	0	0.0	5	1.4	9	3.0	2	0.5	2	0.6
Cones	0	0.0	0	0.0	4	1.1	1	0.3	2	0.5	1	0.3
Flat tower	0	0.0	0	0.0	0	0.0	0	0.0	0	0.0	0	0.0
Horned tower	0	0.0	0	0.0	0	0.0	0	0.0	0	0.0	0	0.0
Globular form	5	3.9	34	17.9	9	2.5	2	0.7	0	0.0	1	0.3
Platey	79	61.7	69	36.3	39	10.8	16	5.3	17	4.1	26	7.6
Coarse verrucate	0	0.0	0	0.0	1	0.3	0	0.0	0	0.0	1	0.3
Fine verrucate	0	0.0	0	0.0	1	0.3	0	0.0	1	0.2	2	0.6
Smooth sheet	27	21.1	64	33.7	44	12.2	33	11.0	38	9.1	40	11.7
Elongate	7	5.5	12	6.3	5	1.4	13	4.3	8	1.9	13	3.8
Two-tiered	0	0.0	0	0.0	10	2.8	15	5.0	23	5.5	19	5.6
Hollow tube	0	0.0	0	0.0	0	0.0	4	1.3	4	1.0	5	1.5
Rope	0	0.0	2	1.1	0	0.0	1	0.3	0	0.0	1	0.3
Spiked sphere (palm)	0	0.0	0	0.0	1	0.3	1	0.3	0	0.0	2	0.6
Spores	0	0.0	5	2.6	31	8.6	16	5.3	15	3.6	11	3.2
Starches	0	0.0	1	0.5	0	0.0	0	0.0	0	0.0	0	0.0
Polyhedrons	0	0.0	0	0.0	5	1.4	3	1.0	3	0.7	0	0.0
Jigsaw-thin wall	0	0.0	0	0.0	0	0.0	0	0.0	0	0.0	2	0.6
Leaf/stem	0	0.0	1	0.5	7	1.9	17	5.6	6	1.4	17	5.0
Wild grass husk	0	0.0	0	0.0	1	0.3	0	0.0	0	0.0	0	0.0
Cyperus-type	0	0.0	0	0.0	0	0.0	0	0.0	0	0.0	0	0.0
Phragmites	0	0.0	0	0.0	1	0.3	0	0.0	0	0.0	0	0.0
Calcium oxalate	0	0.0	0	0.0	0	0.0	0	0.0	0	0.0	0	0.0
Phoenix leaf(?)	0	0.0	0	0.0	0	0.0	0	0.0	0	0.0	0	0.0
Totals	128		190		360		301		416		341	

Sample Context	TF-96-7 Surface		TF-96-8 Surface		TF-96-9 Surface		TF-96-10 Surface		TF-96-11 Surface		TF-96-12 Surface	
SINGLE-CELLS	No.	%	No.	%	No.	%	No.	%	No.	%	No.	%
Long (Leaf/Stem)	127	31.8	17	5.5	84	21.4	5	2.1	5	1.8	11	6.7
Long (Floral)	17	4.3	49	15.8	10	2.5	5	2.1	24	8.7	1	0.6
Papillae	0	0.0	0	0.0	0	0.0	0	0.0	0	0.0	0	0.0
Hairs	6	1.5	6	1.9	8	2.0	0	0.0	1	0.4	0	0.0
Bulliform	1	0.3	6	1.9	1	0.3	1	0.4	2	0.7	1	0.6
Arrowhead	0	0.0	1	0.3	3	0.8	0	0.0	0	0.0	0	0.0
Ovals	3	0.8	4	1.3	3	0.8	0	0.0	5	1.8	0	0.0
Keystone	0	0.0	3	1.0	0	0.0	0	0.0	2	0.7	0	0.0
Crenates	4	1.0	8	2.6	9	2.3	0	0.0	0	0.0	0	0.0
Bilobes	7	1.8	3	1.0	5	1.3	0	0.0	0	0.0	0	0.0
Polylobate	1	0.3	0	0.0	0	0.0	0	0.0	0	0.0	0	0.0
Short Trapezoid	6	1.5	7	2.3	1	0.3	0	0.0	3	1.1	0	0.0
Rondels	33	8.3	13	4.2	34	8.7	0	0.0	2	0.7	1	0.6
Saddles	0	0.0	2	0.6	4	1.0	0	0.0	0	0.0	0	0.0
Cones	2	0.5	2	0.6	9	2.3	0	0.0	1	0.4	0	0.0
Flat Tower	0	0.0	0	0.0	0	0.0	0	0.0	0	0.0	0	0.0
Horned Tower	0	0.0	0	0.0	0	0.0	0	0.0	0	0.0	0	0.0
Globular Form	1	0.3	68	21.9	38	9.7	54	23.1	34	12.3	15	9.1
Platey	12	3.0	27	8.7	43	10.9	71	30.3	92	33.3	95	57.9
Coarse Verrucate	2	0.5	0	0.0	3	0.8	0	0.0	0	0.0	0	0.0
Fine Verrucate	1	0.3	2	0.6	0	0.0	1	0.4	0	0.0	0	0.0
Smooth Sheet	15	3.8	28	9.0	39	9.9	24	10.3	30	10.9	18	11.0
Elongate	7	1.8	10	3.2	13	3.3	5	2.1	5	1.8	1	0.6
Two-Tiered	16	4.0	10	3.2	8	2.0	1	0.4	0	0.0	1	0.6
Hollow Tube	3	0.8	2	0.6	4	1.0	0	0.0	0	0.0	1	0.6
Rope	0	0.0	0	0.0	1	0.3	0	0.0	0	0.0	0	0.0
Spiked Sphere (palm)	36	9.0	3	1.0	1	0.3	0	0.0	1	0.4	2	1.2
Spores	70	17.5	24	7.7	12	3.1	37	15.8	28	10.1	10	6.1
Starches	27	6.8	15	4.8	38	9.7	11	4.7	4	1.4	6	3.7
Polyhedrons	0	0.0	0	0.0	0	0.0	1	0.4	1	0.4	0	0.0
Jigsaw-Thin Wall	0	0.0	0	0.0	0	0.0	0	0.0	0	0.0	0	0.0
Leaf/Stem	2	0.5	0	0.0	13	3.3	17	7.3	30	10.9	0	0.0
Wild Grass Husk	0	0.0	0	0.0	0	0.0	0	0.0	0	0.0	1	0.6
Cyperus-Type	1	0.3	0	0.0	9	2.3	1	0.4	5	1.8	0	0.0
Phragmites	0	0.0	0	0.0	0	0.0	0	0.0	0	0.0	0	0.0
Calcium Oxalate	0	0.0	0	0.0	0	0.0	0	0.0	0	0.0	0	0.0
Phoenix leaf (?)	0	0.0	0	0.0	0	0.0	0	0.0	1	0.4	0	0.0
Totals	400		310		393		234		276		164	

Sample Context	TF-96-13 Surface		TF-96-14 Surface		TF-96-15 Surface		TF-96-16 Surface		TF-96-17 Surface		TF-96-18 Surface	
SINGLE-CELLS	No.	%	No.	%	No.	%	No.	%	No.	%	No.	%
Long (Leaf/Stem)	109	27.8	6	1.1	14	4.2	38	9.7	5	0.9	0	0.0
Long (Floral)	9	2.3	1	0.2	3	0.9	1	0.3	0	0.0	0	0.0
Papillae	2	0.5	0	0.0	0	0.0	0	0.0	0	0.0	1	0.2
Hairs	11	2.8	1	0.2	0	0.0	5	1.3	0	0.0	0	0.0
Bulliform	3	0.8	1	0.2	1	0.3	1	0.3	2	0.4	0	0.0
Arrowhead	8	2.0	1	0.2	1	0.3	3	0.8	1	0.2	0	0.0
Ovals	8	2.0	1	0.2	1	0.3	2	0.5	1	0.2	0	0.0
Keystone	0	0.0	1	0.2	0	0.0	0	0.0	0	0.0	0	0.0
Crenates	2	0.5	0	0.0	0	0.0	0	0.0	0	0.0	0	0.0
Bilobes	4	1.0	0	0.0	0	0.0	0	0.0	0	0.0	0	0.0
Polylobate	0	0.0	0	0.0	0	0.0	0	0.0	0	0.0	0	0.0
Short Trapezoid	2	0.5	0	0.0	0	0.0	1	0.3	1	0.2	0	0.0
Rondels	43	11.0	1	0.2	0	0.0	1	0.3	5	0.9	1	0.2
Saddles	3	0.8	0	0.0	0	0.0	0	0.0	0	0.0	0	0.0
Cones	12	3.1	0	0.0	0	0.0	0	0.0	0	0.0	0	0.0
Flat Tower	0	0.0	0	0.0	0	0.0	0	0.0	0	0.0	0	0.0
Horned Tower	0	0.0	0	0.0	0	0.0	0	0.0	0	0.0	0	0.0
Globular Form	5	1.3	4	0.7	43	12.8	64	16.4	4	0.7	3	0.5
Platey	24	6.1	67	12.0	100	29.7	72	18.5	113	19.9	152	26.0
Coarse Verrucate	1	0.3	0	0.0	1	0.3	1	0.3	0	0.0	0	0.0
Fine Verrucate	0	0.0	0	0.0	3	0.9	0	0.0	1	0.2	0	0.0
Smooth Sheet	45	11.5	94	16.8	67	19.9	129	33.1	145	25.5	229	39.1
Elongate	3	0.8	3	0.5	3	0.9	1	0.3	0	0.0	0	0.0
Two-Tiered	6	1.5	0	0.0	0	0.0	2	0.5	2	0.4	0	0.0
Hollow Tube	8	2.0	0	0.0	0	0.0	0	0.0	4	0.7	0	0.0
Rope	0	0.0	0	0.0	0	0.0	1	0.3	0	0.0	0	0.0
Spiked Sphere (palm)	0	0.0	0	0.0	0	0.0	0	0.0	1	0.2	0	0.0
Spores	24	6.1	264	47.2	30	8.9	4	1.0	106	18.6	80	13.7
Starches	60	15.3	113	20.2	39	11.6	14	3.6	177	31.1	119	20.3
Polyhedrons	0	0.0	0	0.0	2	0.6	5	1.3	0	0.0	0	0.0
Jigsaw-Thin Wall	0	0.0	0	0.0	0	0.0	0	0.0	0	0.0	0	0.0
Leaf/Stem	0	0.0	1	0.2	24	7.1	40	10.3	1	0.2	0	0.0
Wild Grass Husk	0	0.0	0	0.0	0	0.0	0	0.0	0	0.0	0	0.0
Cyperus-Type	0	0.0	0	0.0	4	1.2	4	1.0	0	0.0	0	0.0
Phragmites	0	0.0	0	0.0	1	0.3	0	0.0	0	0.0	0	0.0
Calcium Oxalate	0	0.0	0	0.0	0	0.0	0	0.0	0	0.0	0	0.0
Phoenix leaf (?)	0	0.0	0	0.0	0	0.0	1	0.3	0	0.0	0	0.0
Totals	392		559		337		390		569		585	

Sample Context	TF-96-19 Surface		TF-96-20 Surface		TF-96-21 Surface		TF-96-22 Surface		TF-96-23 Surface		TF-96-24 Surface	
SINGLE-CELLS	No.	%	No.	%	No.	%	No.	%	No.	%	No.	%
Long (Leaf/Stem)	0	0.0	8	1.5	7	3.5	2	0.8	0	0.0	26	10.5
Long (Floral)	0	0.0	0	0.0	0	0.0	0	0.0	0	0.0	0	0.0
Papillae	0	0.0	0	0.0	0	0.0	0	0.0	0	0.0	0	0.0
Hairs	1	0.4	1	0.2	1	0.5	0	0.0	1	0.5	0	0.0
Bulliform	0	0.0	0	0.0	1	0.5	0	0.0	0	0.0	0	0.0
Arrowhead	0	0.0	0	0.0	1	0.5	0	0.0	0	0.0	0	0.0
Ovals	0	0.0	0	0.0	0	0.0	0	0.0	0	0.0	0	0.0
Keystone	0	0.0	0	0.0	0	0.0	0	0.0	0	0.0	0	0.0
Crenates	0	0.0	0	0.0	0	0.0	0	0.0	0	0.0	0	0.0
Bilobes	0	0.0	0	0.0	0	0.0	0	0.0	0	0.0	0	0.0
Polylobate	0	0.0	0	0.0	0	0.0	0	0.0	0	0.0	0	0.0
Short Trapezoid	0	0.0	0	0.0	0	0.0	0	0.0	0	0.0	0	0.0
Rondels	0	0.0	2	0.4	0	0.0	0	0.0	0	0.0	0	0.0
Saddles	0	0.0	0	0.0	0	0.0	0	0.0	0	0.0	0	0.0
Cones	0	0.0	1	0.2	1	0.5	0	0.0	0	0.0	0	0.0
Flat Tower	0	0.0	0	0.0	0	0.0	0	0.0	0	0.0	0	0.0
Horned Tower	0	0.0	0	0.0	0	0.0	0	0.0	0	0.0	0	0.0
Globular Form	9	3.2	40	7.7	2	1.0	0	0.0	1	0.5	37	14.9
Platey	44	15.4	116	22.3	56	28.3	92	35.7	67	31.2	33	13.3
Coarse Verrucate	0	0.0	0	0.0	0	0.0	1	0.4	0	0.0	1	0.4
Fine Verrucate	0	0.0	0	0.0	1	0.5	0	0.0	0	0.0	0	0.0
Smooth Sheet	101	35.4	50	9.6	84	42.4	111	43.0	117	54.4	90	36.3
Elongate	0	0.0	12	2.3	0	0.0	1	0.4	1	0.5	3	1.2
Two-Tiered	0	0.0	0	0.0	0	0.0	0	0.0	0	0.0	1	0.4
Hollow Tube	0	0.0	1	0.2	2	1.0	0	0.0	0	0.0	0	0.0
Rope	0	0.0	0	0.0	0	0.0	3	1.2	0	0.0	0	0.0
Spiked Sphere (palm)	0	0.0	0	0.0	0	0.0	0	0.0	0	0.0	0	0.0
Spores	90	31.6	137	26.3	9	4.5	9	3.5	14	6.5	45	18.1
Starches	40	14.0	106	20.4	12	6.1	6	2.3	0	0.0	11	4.4
Polyhedrons	0	0.0	13	2.5	0	0.0	0	0.0	0	0.0	0	0.0
Jigsaw-Thin Wall	0	0.0	0	0.0	0	0.0	0	0.0	0	0.0	0	0.0
Leaf/Stem	0	0.0	32	6.2	0	0.0	0	0.0	0	0.0	0	0.0
Wild Grass Husk	0	0.0	0	0.0	0	0.0	0	0.0	0	0.0	0	0.0
Cyperus-Type	0	0.0	1	0.2	0	0.0	0	0.0	0	0.0	0	0.0
Phragmites	0	0.0	0	0.0	0	0.0	0	0.0	0	0.0	0	0.0
Calcium Oxalate	0	0.0	0	0.0	21	10.6	33	12.8	14	6.5	1	0.4
Phoenix leaf (?)	0	0.0	0	0.0	0	0.0	0	0.0	0	0.0	0	0.0
Totals	285		520		198		258		215		248	

Sample Context	TF-96-25 Hearth		TF-96-26 Hearth		TF-96-27 Hearth		TF-96-28 Hearth		TF-96-29 Hearth		TF-96-30 Hearth	
SINGLE-CELLS	No.	%	No.	%	No.	%	No.	%	No.	%	No.	%
Long (Leaf/Stem)	27	6.7	63	17.1	97	28.1	143	43.1	76	20.3	179	40.6
Long (Floral)	0	0.0	6	1.6	1	0.3	15	4.5	1	0.3	15	3.4
Papillae	0	0.0	0	0.0	0	0.0	0	0.0	0	0.0	0	0.0
Hairs	0	0.0	2	0.5	2	0.6	3	0.9	5	1.3	5	1.1
Bulliform	0	0.0	0	0.0	3	0.9	5	1.5	6	1.6	4	0.9
Arrowhead	0	0.0	0	0.0	1	0.3	0	0.0	1	0.3	3	0.7
Ovals	0	0.0	1	0.3	2	0.6	1	0.3	3	0.8	8	1.8
Keystone	0	0.0	0	0.0	0	0.0	0	0.0	0	0.0	2	0.5
Crenates	0	0.0	3	0.8	0	0.0	4	1.2	2	0.5	3	0.7
Bilobes	0	0.0	0	0.0	0	0.0	7	2.1	0	0.0	2	0.5
Polylobate	0	0.0	0	0.0	0	0.0	1	0.3	0	0.0	0	0.0
Short Trapezoid	0	0.0	1	0.3	1	0.3	5	1.5	4	1.1	4	0.9
Rondels	0	0.0	7	1.9	0	0.0	13	3.9	4	1.1	12	2.7
Saddles	0	0.0	0	0.0	0	0.0	1	0.3	0	0.0	0	0.0
Cones	0	0.0	3	0.8	2	0.6	2	0.6	2	0.5	15	3.4
Flat Tower	0	0.0	0	0.0	0	0.0	0	0.0	0	0.0	1	0.2
Horned Tower	0	0.0	0	0.0	1	0.3	1	0.3	0	0.0	1	0.2
Globular Form	125	31.0	53	14.4	44	12.8	9	2.7	42	11.2	11	2.5
Platey	91	22.6	53	14.4	54	15.7	40	12.0	59	15.7	40	9.1
Coarse Verrucate	0	0.0	0	0.0	0	0.0	1	0.3	2	0.5	0	0.0
Fine Verrucate	0	0.0	1	0.3	1	0.3	1	0.3	1	0.3	1	0.2
Smooth Sheet	64	15.9	106	28.7	67	19.4	38	11.4	76	20.3	55	12.5
Elongate	3	0.7	1	0.3	0	0.0	0	0.0	1	0.3	0	0.0
Two-Tiered	1	0.2	0	0.0	0	0.0	7	2.1	1	0.3	4	0.9
Hollow Tube	1	0.2	1	0.3	4	1.2	4	1.2	7	1.9	5	1.1
Rope	0	0.0	0	0.0	2	0.6	0	0.0	1	0.3	0	0.0
Spiked Sphere (palm)	0	0.0	0	0.0	0	0.0	0	0.0	0	0.0	0	0.0
Spores	0	0.0	4	1.1	1	0.3	0	0.0	37	9.9	10	2.3
Starches	4	1.0	2	0.5	4	1.2	0	0.0	19	5.1	13	2.9
Polyhedrons	18	4.5	7	1.9	9	2.6	1	0.3	7	1.9	2	0.5
Jigsaw-Thin Wall	0	0.0	0	0.0	0	0.0	0	0.0	0	0.0	1	0.2
Leaf/Stem	62	15.4	53	14.4	49	14.2	28	8.4	17	4.5	44	10.0
Wild Grass Husk	0	0.0	0	0.0	0	0.0	2	0.6	0	0.0	0	0.0
Cyperus-Type	7	1.7	2	0.5	0	0.0	0	0.0	1	0.3	0	0.0
Phragmites	0	0.0	0	0.0	0	0.0	0	0.0	0	0.0	1	0.2
Calcium Oxalate	0	0.0	0	0.0	0	0.0	0	0.0	0	0.0	0	0.0
Phoenix leaf (?)	0	0.0	0	0.0	0	0.0	0	0.0	0	0.0	0	0.0
Totals	403		369		345		332		375		441	

Table 7.3 Percentages for selected groupings of phytoliths and starch grains

Lab no.	Unit	Context	Monocots	Dicots	Multi-cell	Seed husks	Phoenix	Starch
TF-96-01	F2	Occ. Surf.	7.8	86.7	0	0	0	0
TF-96-02	A2	Occ. Surf.	1.1	87.9	0.5	0	0	0.5
TF-96-03	A4	Occ. Surf.	56.9	28.9	2.5	5	0.3	0
TF-96-04	A9	Occ. Surf.	59.8	21.9	5.6	2.3	0.3	0
TF-96-05	B7	Occ. Surf.	72.4	19	1.4	3.1	0	0
TF-96-06	C1	Occ. Surf.	58.9	26.1	5	4.1	0.6	0
TF-96-07	C4	Occ. Surf.	51.8	11.8	0.8	4.3	9	6.8
TF-96-08	C6	Occ. Surf.	39	43.5	0	15.8	1	4.8
TF-96-09	C9	Occ. Surf.	43.5	33.3	5.6	2.5	0.3	9.7
TF-96-10	D99	Occ. Surf.	4.7	64.5	7.7	2.1	0	4.7
TF-96-11	D2	Occ. Surf.	16.3	56.5	12.7	8.7	0.4	1.4
TF-96-12	D4	Occ. Surf.	8.5	78.7	0.6	0.6	1.2	3.7
TF-96-13	D6	Occ. Surf.	55.1	20.7	0	2.3	0	15.3
TF-96-14	D8	Occ. Surf.	2.3	29.5	0.2	0.2	0	20.2
TF-96-15	E99	Occ. Surf.	5.9	63.5	6.6	0.9	0	11.6
TF-96-16	E1	Occ. Surf.	13.3	68.7	11.3	0.3	0	3.6
TF-96-17	E3	Occ. Surf.	2.6	46.6	0.2	0	0.2	31.1
TF-96-18	E5	Occ. Surf.	0.3	65.6	0	0	0	20.3
TF-96-19	E7	Occ. Surf.	0.4	54	0	0	0	14
TF-96-20	F98	Occ. Surf.	2.3	39.6	6.3	0	0	20.4
TF-96-21	F99	Occ. Surf.	5.6	72.2	0	0	0	6.1
TF-96-22	F4	Occ. Surf.	0.8	79.1	0	0	0	2.3
TF-96-23	G3	Occ. Surf.	0.5	86	0	0	0	0
TF-96-24	D3a/b	Hearth	10.5	65.3	0	0	0	4.4
TF-96-25	A4a	Hearth	6.7	69.7	17.1	0	0	1
TF-96-26	C1/D2	Hearth	23.3	57.7	14.9	1.6	0	0.5
TF-96-27	B8a	Hearth	31.9	48.1	14.2	0.3	0	1.2
TF-96-28	A4d/A3c	Hearth	60.5	28.9	9	4.5	0	0
TF-96-29	C8c	Hearth	27.7	48.3	4.8	0.3	0	5.1
TF-96-30	C4b	Hearth	57.6	25.2	10.2	3.4	0	2.9

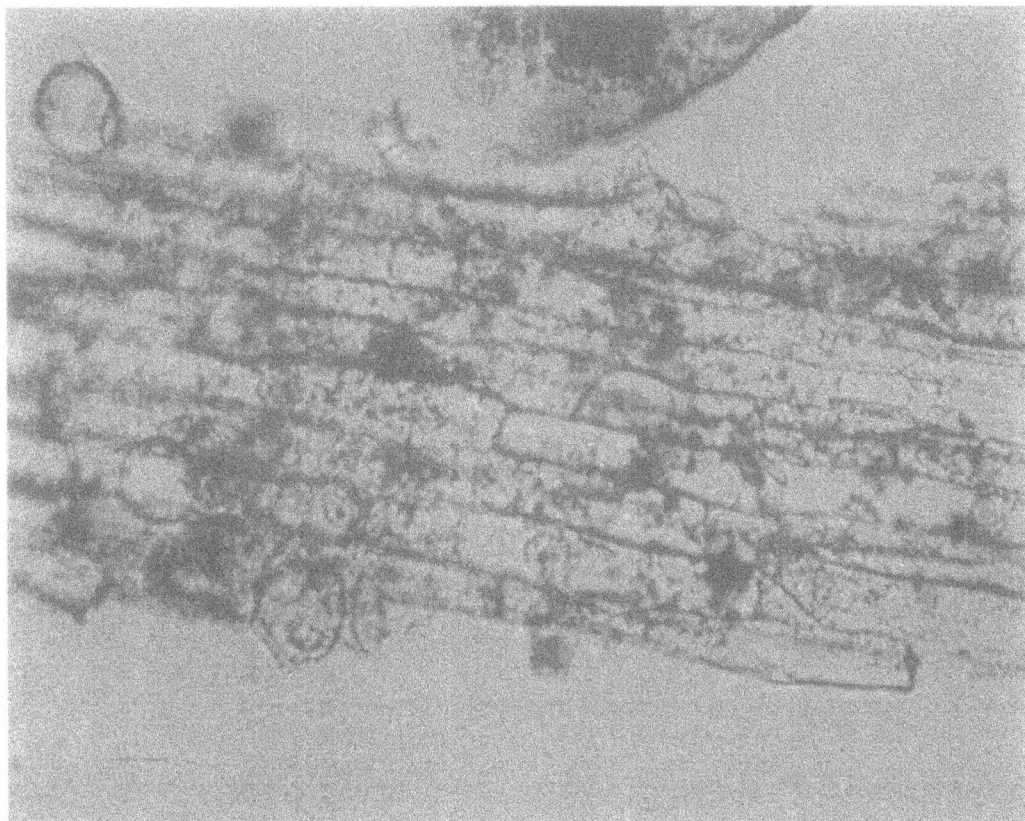

Figure 7.2   Phytolith of an unknown monocotyledon stem from Sample TF-96-11. Scale bar (lower left) = 10 micrometers

attaining sizes in the hundreds of micrometers. These types occur primarily in silica-rich growing environments, especially within geographic regions with high evapo-transpiration rates (Rosen 1999b). Since silica skeletons are casts of numerous adjacent plant epidermal cells, these assemblages of different cell types often allow identification at the genus and sometimes species level. They are also easily identifiable to plant part, assisting in reconstructions of activity areas and seasonality.

Dicotyledons (woody plants) in this region are generally less diagnostic, although recent research on these plant types is helping to characterize more phytolith forms from eastern Mediterranean trees and shrubs (Albert *et al.* 1999; Albert and Weiner, 2001). At the present time, however, we usually can only determine that the form came from either the wood and bark of a woody plant or on the other hand the leaf of these plants.

Paleoenvironmental implications

Today the site of Tor Faraj is located at 900masl at the edge of a piedmont near the boundary between the Irano-Turanian steppe and the Saharo-Iranian desert zone (Henry 1995c). Some general trends in the distribution of phytolith types suggest much moister environmental conditions at the time of occupation than at present. These trends support similar patterns detected by the pilot sample (Rosen 1995). The two major grass subfamilies represented here are the pooids (or festucoids—mostly C_3 grasses) and the panicoids (primarily C_4 grasses). The pooids which generally favor cooler and moister growing conditions than the panicoids (over 300mm rainfall per annum) are by far the dominant forms (see Fig. 7.3). The distributions of the pooids and panicoids co-vary over the living surface, with a correlation coefficient value of 0.79, implying that they were brought into the cave and used in similar

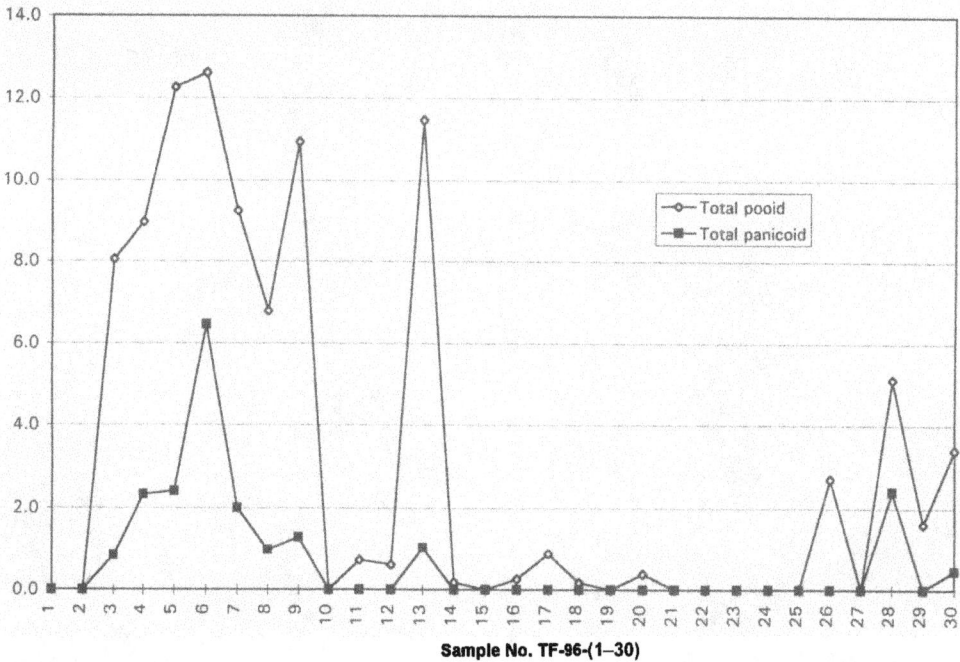

Figure 7.3 Percentages of pooid and panicoid grass phytoliths at Tor Faraj

locations, perhaps in the proportions in which they were found in the environs of the cave. A more mesic environment is further supported by the phytoliths from plants such as *Phragmites sp.* (common reeds) and *Cyperus sp.* (marsh rushes) which grow in standing water, and the fossil spores of *Equisetum sp.* (horse-tail rush) which also favors moist growing conditions. The presence of date palm (*Phoenix dactylifera*) phytoliths suggests active springs in the vicinity of the site during the Mousterian occupation. This contrasts markedly with the water sources available in the site vicinity today which are exclusively derived from seasonal run-off and short-term pooling on bedrock within the nearby wadis. Additionally, the abundance of phytoliths from dicotyledons also implies a source of trees or shrubs in proximity to the site at the time of occupation.

Plant use at Tor Faraj

It is clear from the microbotanical results that a wide variety of different plants were exploited by the Mousterian occupants of the Tor Faraj shelter. The date phytoliths (Fig. 7.1) mark the earliest example of the use of date palms worldwide. Previously, the earliest archaeological occurrences of dates came from

sixth and fifth millennia BC sites in Egypt, Iran, and Pakistan, and are presumed to represent collection from the wild (Zohary and Hopf 1994: 160). The palm phytoliths from Tor Faraj are identical to modern reference samples of *Phoenix dactylifera* (Rosen 1992, Fig. 7.4). However, these silica bodies occur in both the leaves as well as the fruit of the palm (Cummings 1992) and it is unclear if the dates themselves were consumed or the leaves of the tree were used for a variety of other purposes. However, it is difficult to imagine that foragers in a semi-arid environment would have refrained from exploiting the date fruit if it were readily available. *Equisetum sp.* (horse-tail rush) also has various uses and its spores occur in a number of the samples at the site. Because of the high proportions of silica bodies within the shoots, it functions as an effective sandpaper for smoothing wood. It is unlikely that it was used in this fashion at Tor Faraj simply because the distribution of *Equisetum* spores varies considerably from the phytoliths of wood. However, the great difference between the amount of phytoliths produced in *Equisetum* and the small amount from wood could invalidate this kind of comparison. Alternatively, the plant might have been

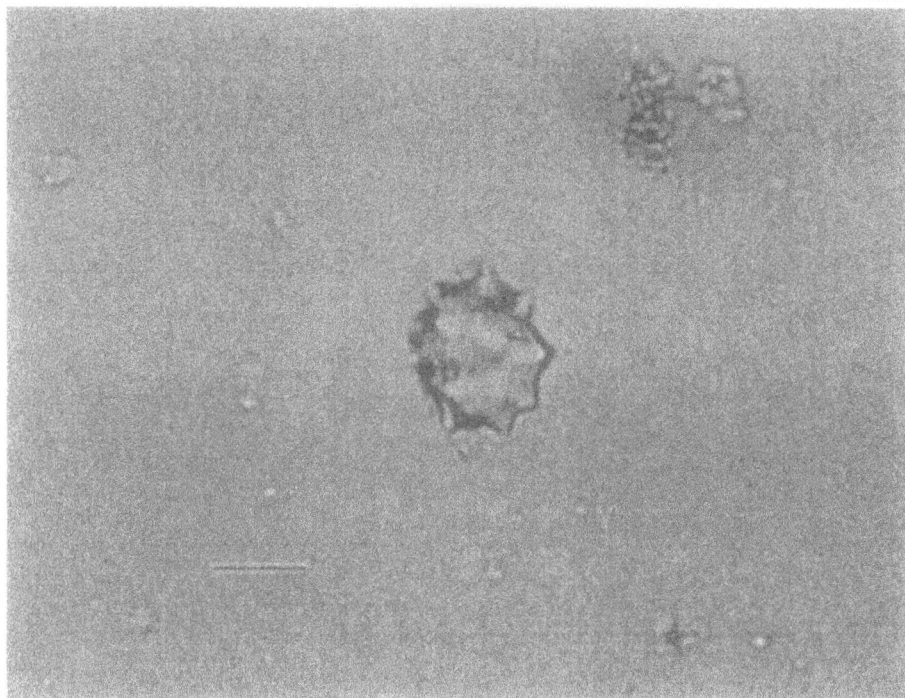

Figure 7.4 Phytolith from a date palm (*Phoenix dactylifera*) photographed from Sample TF-96-7. Scale bar (lower left) = 10 micrometers

collected for food. Although horse-tail rushes are not a common plant food due to occasional difficulties in digestion, there are many ethnographic examples of their exploitation as a food source. The cone-bearing shoots, peeled stems, roots, and tubers are all potentially edible (Harrington 1967).

Another non-phytolith particle found in these sediments were starch grains. Several different forms of such grains occurred within a number of samples from the site and it is likely that they are indicative of nuts, roots, and tubers brought into the shelter. One form of the starches is identical to those that were derived from reference samples of pistachio. There is a reasonably high correlation between the occurrence of starch grains and those of spores (Pearson's $r = 0.75$) suggesting some relationship between the two. Perhaps some of them come from the *Equisetum* itself, and others were possibly stored or collected in horse-tail mats or containers.

The advantage of comparing samples from a single horizontal exposure on an occupation surface is evident from the relationships between the spatial distributions of different plant types. Single-celled phytoliths from monocotyledons are distributed in different locations around the shelter from phytoliths of dicotyledonous plants. This suggests two different functions for these general plant types. The phytoliths from grasses are primarily found well within the dripline of the cave close to the back wall, and in spaces between the hearths (Fig. 7.5). This kind of distribution would be consistent with the use of these grasses for bedding or flooring material. In contrast, the phytoliths from woody plants cluster primarily toward the outer boundary of the shelter (Fig. 7.6) and in hearths (not represented in Fig. 7.6, but see Table 7.3). The dicot phytoliths from the outer boundary of the site occur beyond the dripline of the shelter. It would be tempting to suggest that this represents the disintegration of a brush enclosure fence, but the concentration of silica phytoliths in woody plants of this region is usually very low, unless concentrated into ash deposits (Albert and Weiner 2001). However, it is also unlikely that this concentration of dicot phytoliths represents waste from hearths that was dumped outside of the dripline, since hearth ash in the shelter also contained lithic debris, and there is little such debris in the

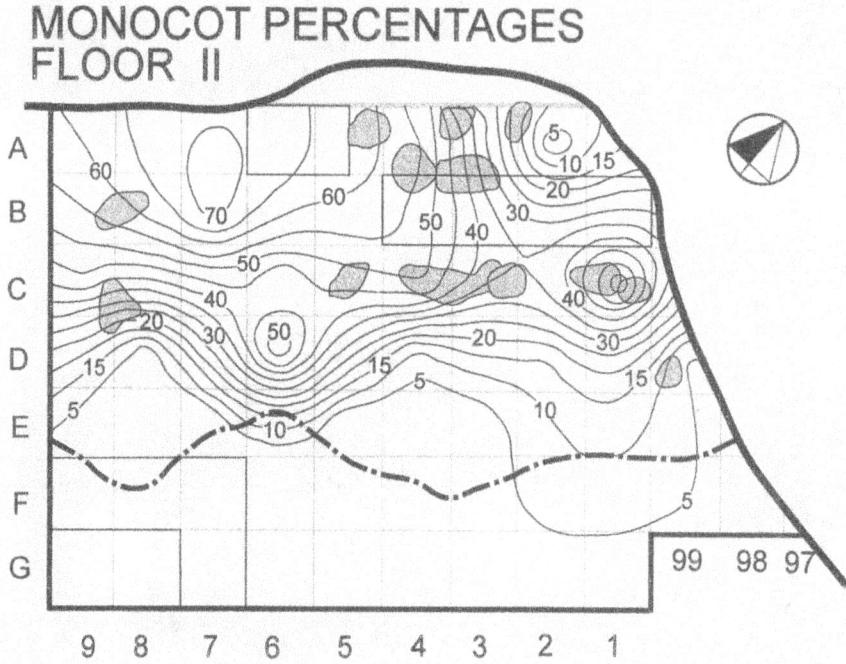

Figure 7.5 Distribution of phytoliths from monocotyledons across Floor II (hearth data not included) at Tor Faraj

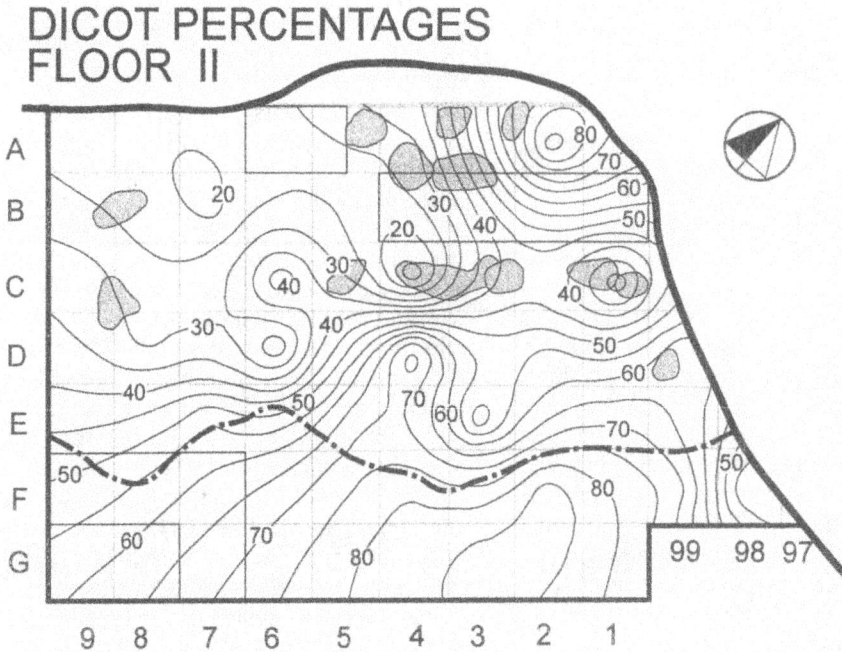

Figure 7.6 Distribution of dicotyledon phytoliths across Floor II (high dicot percentages from hearths not included) at Tor Faraj

area of dicot concentration outside of the shelter (see Chapters 5 and 10, this volume). Perhaps a reasonable explanation for these dicot concentrations beyond the dripline is the seasonal burning of brush outside of the cave, either to clear away natural shrubs blocking the entrance of the shelter or to clear away dried shrubs deliberately placed there to shield the entrance during previous occupations.

Within the category of single-celled phytoliths there is a small but quite significant proportion of dendritic long-cells derived from the floral parts or seed husks of grasses (Fig. 7.10). These indicate two things. One is the probable occupation of Tor Faraj during months in which the grasses flower and produce seeds (roughly from February to May) and, second, it is likely that these seed husks, and presumably the seeds themselves, were purposely collected for food consumption. Evidence for this comes from their placement within the cave and their distribution with respect to other plant parts. If the seeds entered the cave as floral parts attached to grass stems brought in for other purposes, then the husks should occur in the same

locations as the stem and leaf silica skeletons which are found together with the single-celled phytoliths from pooid and panicoid grasses (Fig. 7.7). In fact, phytoliths from the grasses within the hearths do indeed come from both husks as well as stems of the plants. However, this is not the case with the phytoliths from the occupation surfaces. The highest percentages of husk phytoliths within the cave (samples TF-96-8 and TF-96-11) are located in places with relatively low proportions of other plant parts, suggesting that the husks and seeds were separated from the other plant parts for specific purposes (see Fig. 7.10). The largest husk percentage is located close to the central hearth area, a locality that also contains a number of date phytoliths, and may indicate an area of food preparation or consumption (see Figs 7.9 and 7.10).

Conclusion

To summarize some of the results obtained from this study, the phytoliths from Tor Faraj indicate a moister environment around the

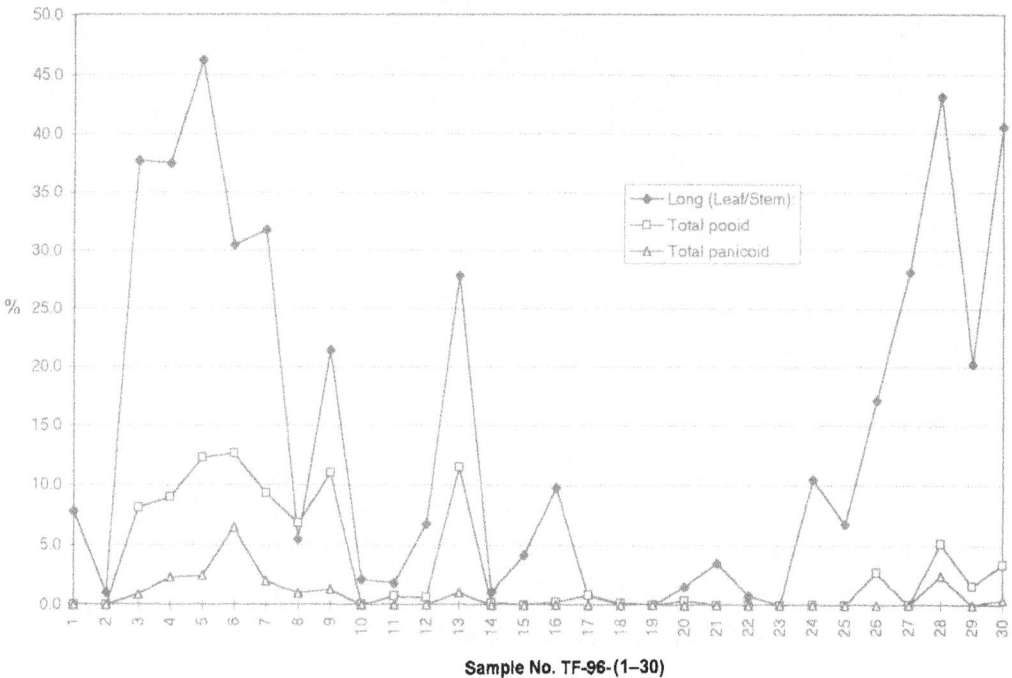

Figure 7.7 Phytolith percentages of pooid, panicoid, and long cells from stems and leaves of plants, showing the plant parts from which these phytoliths were derived at Tor Faraj

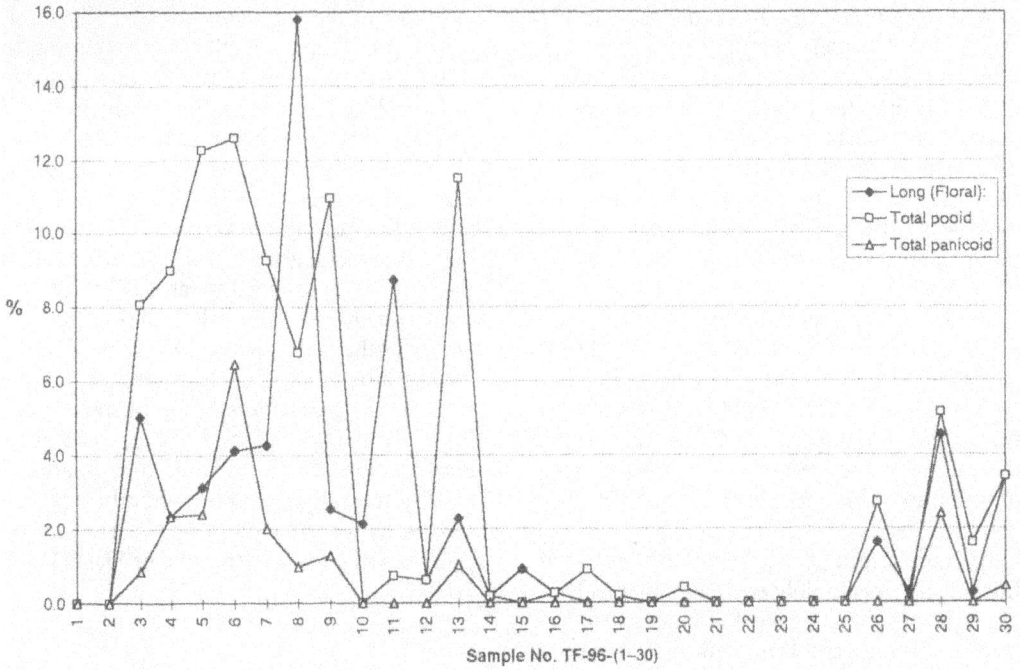

Figure 7.8 Phytolith percentages of dendritic (floral/seed husk) long-cells showing that the distribution of these differs from those of the other grass phytoliths on occupation surfaces but not in hearths at Tor Faraj

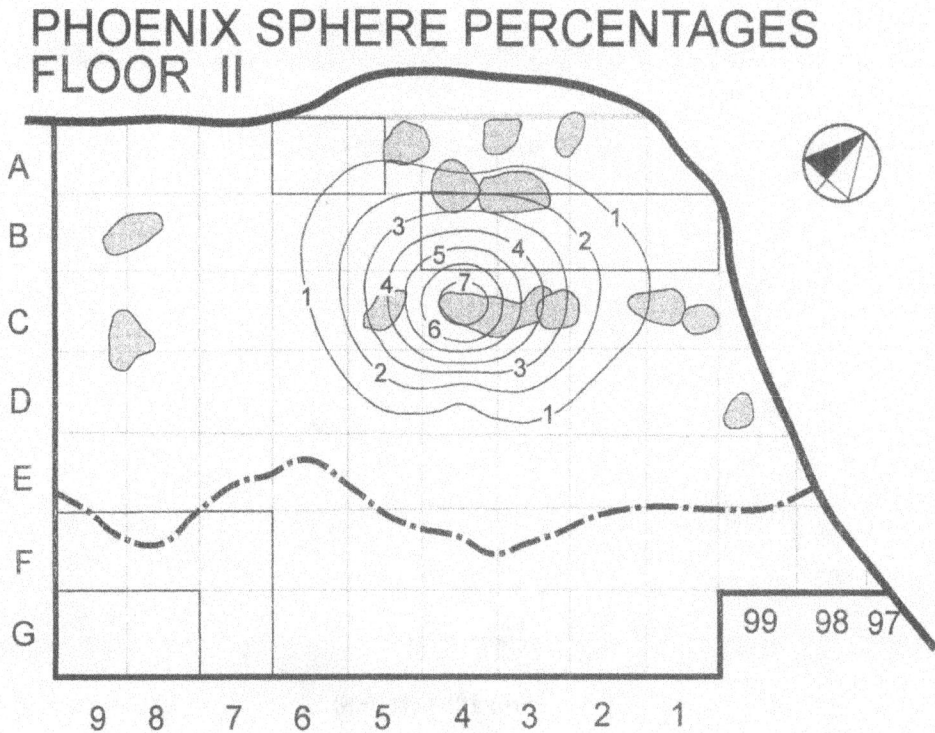

Figure 7.9 Distribution of phytoliths from date palms (*P. dactylifera*) across Floor II at Tor Faraj

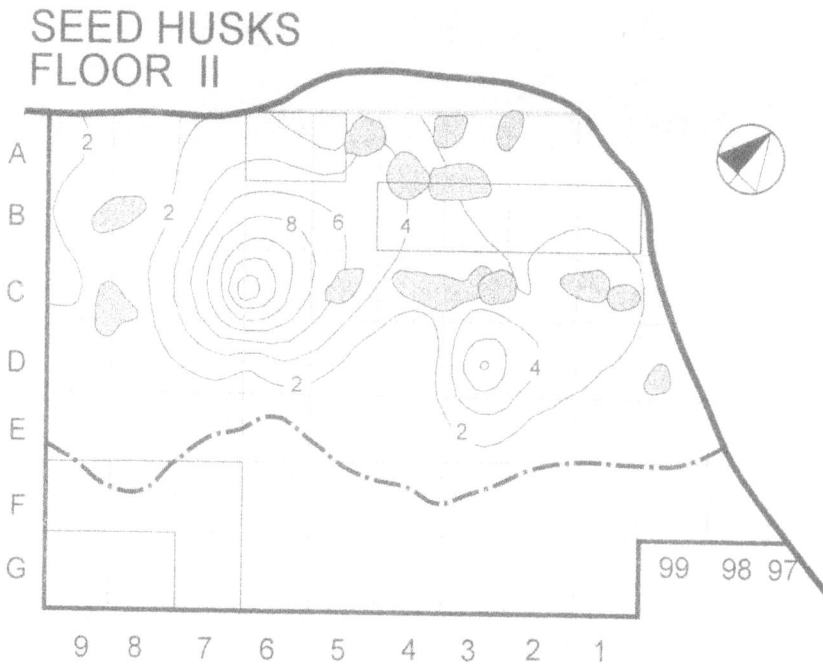

Figure 7.10 Distribution of phytoliths from seed husk phytoliths across Floor II at Tor Faraj

vicinity of the shelter than at present. They also suggest there were abundant sources of standing water and springs at the time of occupation. Some of the plants exploited by the Mousterian inhabitants of the cave as possible food sources include horse-tail rushes, dates, wild grass seeds, and pistachio nuts. They also used a variety of woody plants for fuel as well as common reed (*Phragmites sp*) and rushes (*Cyperus sp*). The distribution of these plants over the living surface shows that grasses were spread on the shelter floor near the back wall and center of the cave, and in a space between hearths. These grasses are well within the dripline of the shelter, a pattern consistent with the possibility of prepared sleeping areas. Grass seeds and date (fruit?) were concentrated near a centrally located hearth, suggestive of a food preparation or consumption area. Finally, high concentrations of dicot phytoliths at the outer edge of the site, beyond the dripline, suggest a locality where either natural shrubs or an intentionally placed brush windbreak were repeatedly (perhaps seasonally) burnt.

The sample collection strategy at Tor Faraj focused on an attempt to look at the variability of plant remains across a single occupation surface at the site. This has allowed us the unique opportunity of examining research questions related to the spatial distribution of plant-use within the shelter. Although in the present study relative percentages of phytoliths were used, future work using absolute phytolith counts per volume of sediment will improve the accuracy of the results. The horizontal approach to sample collection adds a new dimension to phytolith studies at paleolithic sites and greatly supplements information on the spatial distribution of other types of data.

Acknowledgments

I would like to thank Don Henry for providing the samples and the opportunity to conduct the phytolith research at Tor Faraj. This chapter benefited from discussions and comments provided by Linda Scott Cummings, Don Henry, Hal Hietala, Steve Rosen, Wilma Wetterstrom, and Henry Wright. Laboratory equipment used in these analyses was provided by grants from the CARE Archaeological Foundation and the National Center for Cooperation Between the Sciences and Archaeology, Weizmann Institute, Israel.

8 Formation Processes and Paleosurface Identification

HAROLD J. HIETALA

The validity of spatial pattern interpretations, whether the data derive from caves, rock-shelters or open-air sites, strongly depends on two primary conditions. The first condition generally requires minimal movement, through natural processes, of the cultural materials. Of equal importance, the second requires temporal consistency in site structure (Binford 1981; Schiffer 1987). That is, spatially organized behavior potentially represented by material culture elements must be reasonably consistent in time in order to interpret spatial patterning associated with the material culture remains. A single episodic occupation might give rise to plausible interpretations if the material residue represents the remains of archaeologically visible activities undertaken by the inhabitants of the site over a short period of time. On the other hand, many repeated occupations of a single site over a long period of time will probably result in a palimpsest of different spatial distributions that are impossible to untangle and interpret. It is optimal for spatial interpretive possibilities if cultural material residues resulting from brief episodic occupations are represented by separate and distinct stratigraphic levels. In the absence of distinct stratigraphy associated with repeated episodic occupations, it is incumbent upon the archaeologist to demonstrate the plausible existence of undisturbed paleosurface 'living floors' before behavioral interpretations of spatially distributed cultural material residues can be attempted. Here a 'living floor' is defined as a representation in three-dimensional space of artifacts, ecofacts, and features that are not only post-depositionally undisturbed but also represent material culture from temporally consistent spatially organized behavior.

Minimal criteria for establishing the existence of a living floor are discussed by Petraglia (1993) and Dibble et al. (1997). They argue that post-depositional movement through natural agencies must be eliminated as a factor for the spatial positioning of material culture artifacts, but in addition give several criteria that should be used when attempting to identify undisturbed paleosurfaces. These include the general nature of the geological deposits in which the artifacts and features are embedded with demonstrations that the artifacts, in general, have not naturally been removed from or positionally altered on the site. Specific factors involve hearth conditions, artifact freshness, three-dimensional artifact refit distributions, artifact distributions relative to size and direction, internal compositions of lithic assemblages, and spatial positioning of artifacts in three-dimensional space. The lack of environmentally induced geological disturbance by itself, of course, does not facilitate interpretations of spatial patterns since a palimpsest of successive episodic occupations located three-dimensionally in unstratified sediments might 'smear' the nature of individual occupations if the data are collapsed onto a presumed two-dimensional occupation surface. That is, if activities undertaken by the inhabitants of the site are sufficiently different to induce temporally inconsistent site structure, then it is not reasonable to assume that spatial clusters or patterns are associated with consistent spatially organized behavior. Thus, material culture resulting from a sequence of repeated and undisturbed episodic occupations, without discrete stratigraphic separation, should show consistent spatial patterning of artifacts, ecofacts, and features, or at least the lack of significant smearing, if it is thought to represent the remains of distinct cultural activities that are spatially organized and therefore identified with a presumed living floor. The above considerations, in any case, obviously depend on an accurate portrayal of cultural and a-cultural data elements in three dimensions.

The three-dimensional context of information, at Tor Faraj, was controlled through the use of a laser theodolyte and data collector (Sokkia Set 6 Total Station). Individual large artifacts, more than 30mm in maximum dimension, were horizontally mapped in an x-y coordinate system with the vertical dimension either mapped in place or at the bottom of arbitrary 5cm field levels. Artifacts obtained through dry screening of the sediments (see Chapter 3) were assigned a unit-level designation in the field. In addition, each large artifact was assigned a unique specimen number associated with its field unit and level designations. In some cases, bags were incorrectly labeled in the field but a comparison of artifact three-dimensional coordinates to their field unit and level designations eliminated these errors. In these cases, the corresponding artifacts (primarily chips) retrieved through screening were appropriately reassigned to new proveniences. Ecofacts and features were also located in three dimensions. The analyses below are generally restricted to artifacts, ecofacts, and hearths between 160 and 195cm below datum, as recorded by the laser theodolyte.

Depositional considerations

The general prehistoric stratigraphy of Tor Faraj (see Chapter 3 for details) can be simplistically summarized as a process in which rocks falling from the retreating brow of the rockshelter led to a concentration of rocks along the margin of the dripline (see Fig. 3.7). Aeolian sediments entrapped behind the roof-fall created nearly level bedding planes in which the artifacts then became embedded. Level 175, and above, post-dates a major brow collapse in the south corner of the site. The brow collapse event (see Chapter 3) marks a structural change in the spatial organization of the site occupants, relative to the positioning of activities. Minimally, the roof-fall area in the south corner of the shelter was differentially utilized prior to and subsequent to the roof-fall event. This is particularly important for the establishment of living floors since levels above 175 should therefore not be combined with levels below 175 for spatial analytic purposes. As will be shown below, other areas were also affected by the major roof-fall event. Nevertheless, it needs to be established that living floors are associated with material culture in the levels above 175 as well as the levels below 175. Since the roof-fall event created different depositional environments for the preservation of cultural materials, it is appropriate to investigate the nature of the lithic material at Tor Faraj.

If all artifacts were uniformly exposed to the environment over protracted periods of time, evidence of significant artifact weathering would be expected in most areas of the site. This seems not to be the case since 77 percent of all artifacts were either unpatinated or lightly patinated (see Table 8.1 for frequency information and Fig. 8.1 for spatial configurations). In general these were resting flat, suggesting rapid coverage and no post-depositional movement (see Chapter 3). A major exception occurs in the south corner of the site (Fig. 8.1) in layer D1 sediments associated with the major brow collapse of the rockshelter roof. Rows D to G and columns 6 to 9 of the excavation (Fig. 8.1) roughly bound the south corner of the site. Artifacts recovered from this area were frequently heavily patinated and resting on end or edge (see Chapter 3). Within layer D1, approximately three-fifths (60.5 percent) of the artifacts were heavily patinated while only one-fifth (18.1 percent) were heavily patinated in the other sedimentary layers (Table 8.1). In addition, over half (340 of 603 or 56.4 percent) of all heavily patinated artifacts occur in the south corner even though it only includes one-quarter (646 of 2620 or 24.6

Table 8.1 Percentage of artifact patination by site quadrant and sedimentary layer

Degree of patination	Site quadrant				Entire site	Layer	
	West	North	East	South		D1	Other
None or light	582	544	585	306	2017	120	1897
Heavy	82	78	103	340	603	184	419
Total	664	622	688	646	2620	304	2316
Percentage heavy	12.3	12.5	15.0	52.6	23.0	60.5	18.1

Note: West quadrant bounded by excavation rows A–C and columns 6–9 (see Fig. 8.1); north quadrant bounded by excavation rows A–C and columns 1–5 and 97–9 (Fig. 8.1); east quadrant bounded by excavation rows D–G and columns 1–5 and 97–9 (Fig. 8.1); south quadrant bounded by excavation rows D–G and columns 6–9 (see Fig. 8.1)

percent) of all lithic artifacts. In addition, over half (52.6 percent) of all artifacts in the south corner of the site are heavily patinated compared to no more than 15 percent in other areas of the site (Table 8.1). It seems as though artifacts, from other areas, were discarded in the rocky matrix associated with the roof-fall area. Also, there is some evidence that smaller elements (chips, for example) may have migrated to the lower depths of the rocky matrix associated with the roof-fall zone (see Chapter 5). Clearly, many artifacts from the brow collapse area were exposed to the environment over a long enough time to create heavy patination while artifacts in the remainder of the excavated portion of the site were generally sitting flat on near level bedding planes and were, most often, rapidly covered with aeolian sediments. The spatial distribution of heavily patinated artifacts (Fig. 8.1) demonstrates that heavily patinated artifacts primarily occur in the south corner of the site. Vertically, the relative frequencies of heavily patinated artifacts (Table 8.2) range from a low of 7.4 percent in Level 195 (preceding the brow collapse) to a high of 31.8 percent in Level 165 (following the brow collapse). In general, the condition of the artifacts suggests that significant weathering occurred behind the dripline (Fig. 8.1a) but especially in the brow collapse area in the south corner of the site. Although these data strongly inform on the nature of artifactual weathering, they say little about the possibilities of post-depositional spatial repositioning, in space and time.

A specific line of evidence for investigating the possibility of natural post-depositional artifact movement involves artifact size distributions. If, for example, artifacts were subject to significant fluvial action, then small artifacts (chips) might be expected to occur in larger frequency downslope within the site or be washed off the site, partially or entirely. The latter is certainly not the case since the ratio of small artifacts (chips) to large artifacts (more than 30mm in maximum dimension) is approximately 78 percent for the site as a whole, consistent with values from generally undisturbed sites (Henry, personal communication). More specifically, the ratio of chips to large artifacts suggests a remarkable homogeneity in variation from level to level where the values (Table 8.2) range from a low of 74.1 percent in Level 190 to a high of 80.4 percent in the adjacent Level 185. Broken piece percentages also support the observation of structural homogeneity, from level to level, since the percentage of broken pieces is approximately 43 percent for the site as a whole and varies from a low of 38.9 percent in Level 160 to a high of 46.2 percent in the adjacent Level 165 (Table 8.2). We are more interested, however, in the possibilities of horizontal artifact movement. The presumed presence of a slight paleosurface dip (estimated paleosurface slope of approximately 1 percent (see Chapter 3) from the back of the rockshelter to the front may be used to investigate whether or not chips are more frequent downslope. With chip movement through fluvial action, higher frequencies of chips would be expected close to the dripline of the rockshelter, and away from the back

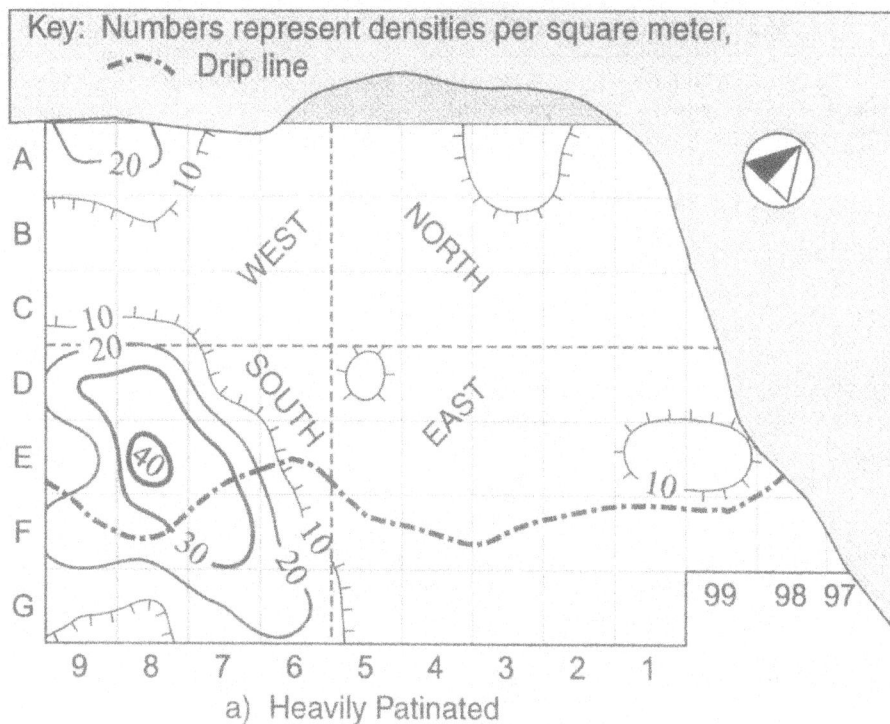

a) Heavily Patinated

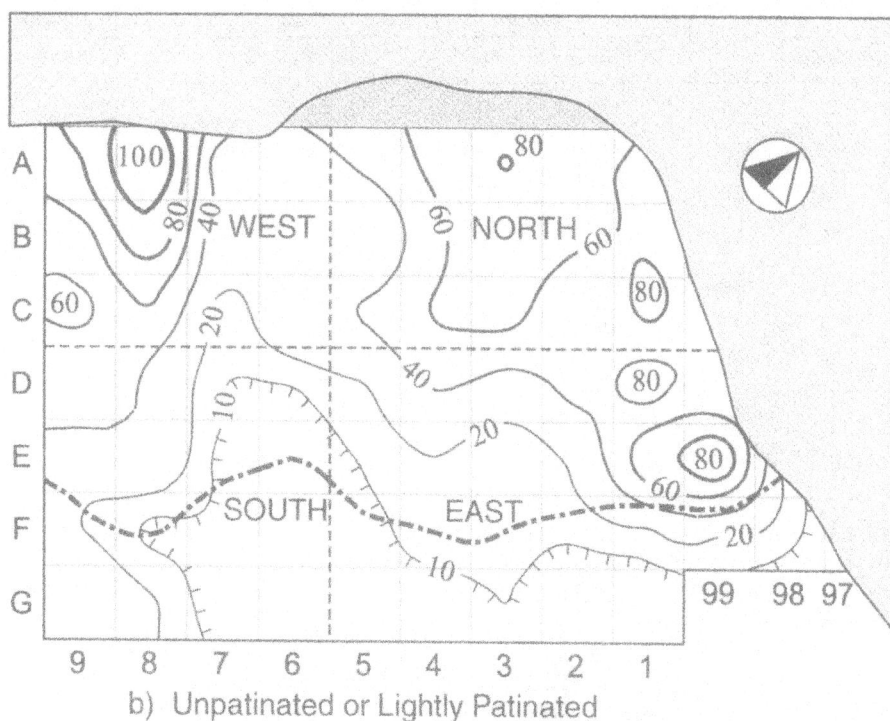

b) Unpatinated or Lightly Patinated

Figure 8.1 Spatial frequencies of large artifacts by degree of patination at Tor Faraj: **a**, heavily patinated; **b**, unpatinated or lightly patinated. *Note*: In Figure 8.1 the numbers represent densities per square meter and Table 8.1 includes the summary sample size data

Table 8.2 Chip and broken piece percentages within levels

Level	Chips	Total large pieces	% Heavy patination	Broken pieces	% Chips*	% Broken pieces**
160	873	247	31.8	96	77.9	38.9
165	1324	340	30.1	157	79.6	46.2
170	1316	405	20.2	175	76.5	43.2
175	1268	320	NA	NA	79.8	NA
180	1258	316	29.8	137	79.9	43.4
185	1580	386	21.9	165	80.4	42.7
190	1232	430	17.6	197	74.1	45.8
195	NA	462	7.4	206	NA	44.6
Overall					78.4	43.0

*The percentage of chips is relative to the count of chips and total large pieces.
**The percentage of broken pieces is relative to the count of total large pieces

Table 8.3 Chip frequencies and percentages by site quadrant within levels

	Site quadrant area							
	West		North		East		South	
Level	Count	%	Count	%	Count	%	Count	%
160	74	8.4	364	41.7	194	22.2	241	27.6
165	216	16.3	543	41.1	513	38.8	49	3.7
170	432	32.8	436	33.2	397	30.2	51	3.9
175	155	12.2	559	44.1	434	34.2	120	9.5
180	296	23.5	495	39.3	375	29.8	92	7.3
185	413	26.1	649	41.1	459	29.1	59	3.7
190	355	28.8	616	50.0	259	21.0	2	0.2

Note: See Table 8.1 for definitions of the quadrants

wall. The spatial distributions of chips in levels 160 through 190 (Fig. 8.2) demonstrate that this is clearly not the case. It is clear that there are always heavy concentrations of chips along the back wall in the north and west areas of the site and along the side wall in the east area (see Fig. 8.2). It may be noted that not all areas of each level have major concentrations of chips (Fig. 8.2). Counts of chips by area (Table 8.3) show that the area with the highest chip frequencies, for all levels, is always the north area where the dominant cluster is against the back wall. The secondary, tertiary, and least influential areas, relative to chip abundance, are generally the east, west, and south areas respectively. The southern area is seemingly rich in chips only for Level 160 although small concentrations occur in Levels 175 and 180. These latter concentrations may be associated with a downward movement of chips in the roof-fall matrix (see Chapter 5). Differences and similarities of the chip distributions will be returned to later when occupational structure is discussed. For now, it seems clear that chips do not seem to have been displaced through fluvial action since, in general, the chip concentrations in the different levels are not only disassociated with the presumed downslope areas of the site but, in addition, are positioned in three or four spatially separated localities. These localities, with the exception of the one in Level 160 (Fig. 8.2a) in the south corner, will be seen later to be primarily associated with hearth locations. Finally, if fluvial action had been an important force in the three-dimensional positioning of artifacts, which it clearly does not seem to be, then one might additionally expect large artifacts (> 30 mm in maximum dimension) to have directional tendencies associated with their long axes. This again is not the case. In fact, the directional tendencies appear to be more or less random in all directions (see Fig. 10.1). The presence of a single modal direction (north) is of no great consequence since it does not appear to be large enough to be significant. Consequently it seems safe to conclude that the action of fluvial forces had little or no effect in the positioning of the artifacts in space and that there is no evidence to support a premise of artifact post-depositional movement. If anything, these data, as will be shown later, strongly support the notion that artifact locations, laterally in space, are due to cultural forces alone.

The refitting of artifacts also provides another avenue of investigation to support the idea that the forces primarily responsible for the three-dimensional spatial positioning of artifacts are primarily cultural. Little post-depositional movement seems to have occurred since only 5 percent of the refitted constellations of artifacts have elements that are horizontally more than 15cm apart and only 2 percent of the refits are separated by as much as 15cm vertically (see Chapter 10 for details). Of importance here is that refits are restricted to Levels 160 to 170 or Levels 180 to 195 with no refits between the lower and upper levels. This lends emphasis to the notion that the lower levels might represent one occupational period and the upper levels another.

The above observations taken together, suggest that artifacts were not subject to significant post-depositional movement by natural forces. In fact, the above data point toward cultural action as a determining force

involved in the spatial positioning of material culture elements at Tor Faraj.

Artifact, feature, and rock distributions

Prior to combining individual levels as representations of living floors, it must be established that the three-dimensional distributions of artifacts, features, and natural materials are consistent with certain expectations. Features, for example, should be locationally consistent in levels presumably associated with living floors. In addition, the individual levels should minimally provide data leading to an observation that cultural activities responsible for the spatial arrangements of artifacts are not dissimilar in the separate levels. These types of observations are more likely to be established in a site that is only occupied a small number of times, over a short period of time, by individuals behaving in the same way in specific spatial loci of the site. This, of course, is the advantage of a rockshelter in that the back wall, dripline, and natural exposure locationally constrain behavior. Hearths, for example, are generally not placed at the dripline or immediately adjacent to the back wall of a rockshelter. Importantly, cultural activities are oftentimes tied to hearth locations and differentially constrain the locations of other behavior, including lithic reduction activities and even leisure time activities. Specifically, the nature of artifactual spatial distributions, as they relate to cultural and natural features, allows probable inferences in the domain of prehistoric organized behavior.

Hearths represent major cultural features at Tor Faraj. Since cultural activities are likely to be tethered to hearths and related to the back wall, roof-fall, and dripline of the rockshelter, it is of some interest to study hearth distributions in three dimensions (Binford 1996). Three-dimensional distributions of rocks are also important since large angular rocks well within the dripline of the shelter should not naturally be there (see Chapter 10 for further details). In addition, three-dimensional distributions of debitage and tools further contribute to our understanding of the depositional sequence and the nature of repeated occupations.

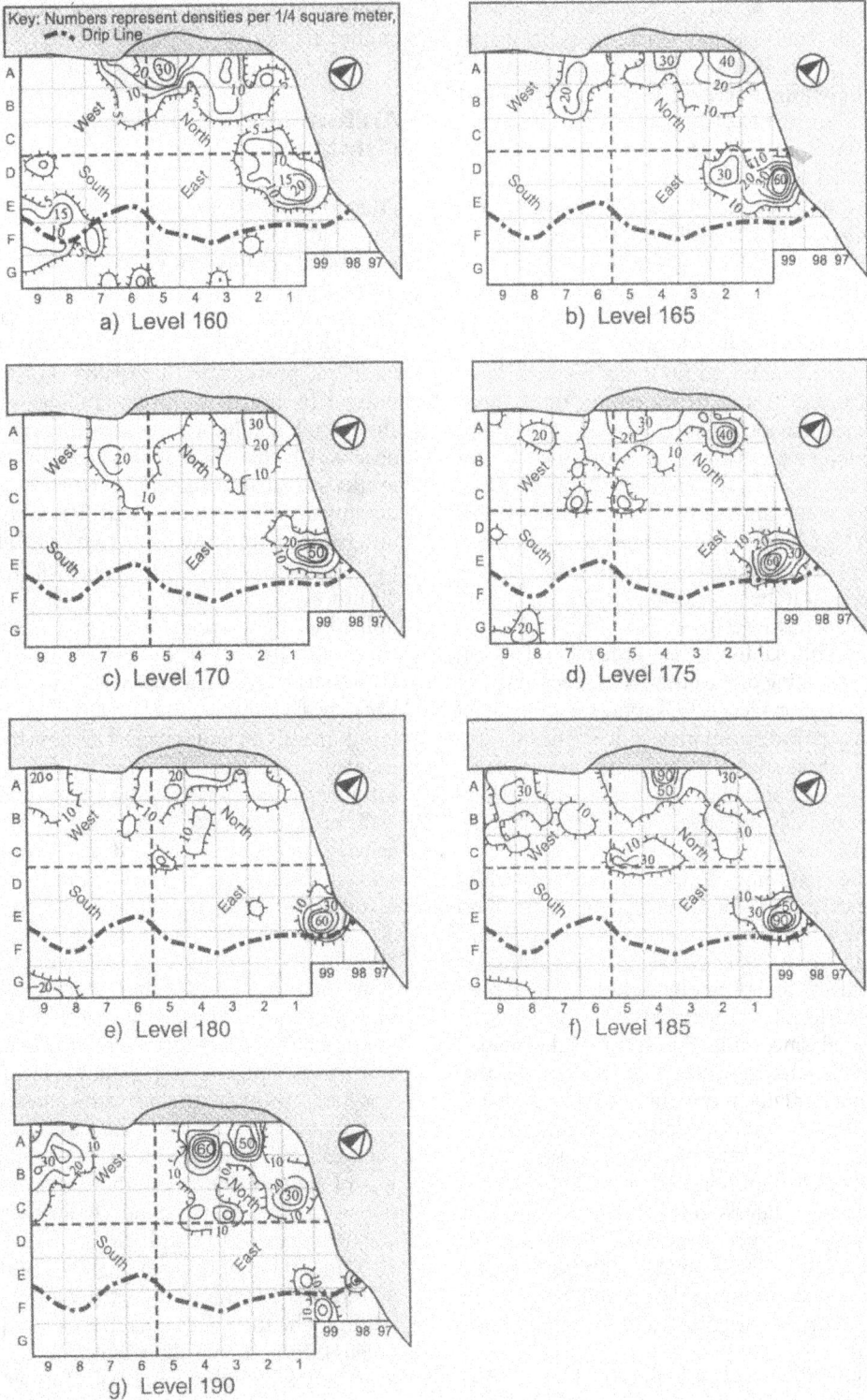

Figure 8.2 Spatial frequencies of chips by level at Tor Faraj: **a**, Level 160; **b**, Level 165; **c**, Level 170; **d**, Level 175; **e**, Level 180; **f**, Level 185; **g**, Level 190. *Note*: In Figure 8.2 the numbers represent densities per 1/4 square meter and Table 8.2 includes the summary sample size data

Table 8.4 Frequencies and global percentages for selected material classes

| | Material artifact category | | | | | | | |
| | Rocks | | Hearths | | Debitage | | Tools | |
Level	Count	%	Count	%	Count	%	Count	%
160	48	15.1	0	0.0	196	8.6	43	7.8
165	45	14.2	1	5.6	269	11.7	61	11.1
170	55	17.3	4	22.2	313	13.7	81	14.8
175	16	5.0	1	5.6	256	11.2	53	9.7
180	25	7.9	3	16.7	256	11.2	60	10.9
185	30	9.4	3	16.7	333	14.5	44	8.0
190	56	17.6	4	22.2	310	13.5	110	20.1
195	43	13.5	2	11.1	360	15.7	96	17.5

Note: The global percentages are relative to combined Levels 160-95

Rock and hearth distributions

The highest frequencies of rocks (Table 8.4) occur in Levels 160 to 170 and 190 to 195 with the lowest frequency in Level 175. The distribution is clearly bimodal (Fig. 8.3a) with levels 160 to 170 representing one interval of high frequencies and Levels 180 to 195 the other. Hearths, on the other hand, show the highest frequencies (Table 8.4) in Levels 170 and 190 with a low frequency in Level 175 where only one hearth is present. Again the distribution is bimodal (Fig. 8.3b) with one mode in Level 170 and moderate to high frequencies in Levels 180 to 195. It should be noted that the level to which a hearth is assigned is based upon the elevation at the bottom or middle of the hearth (Table 3.2). The hearth assigned to Level 175 was found in the vertical interval 170 to 175cm below datum and is likely associated with cultural materials in the upper levels, as will be further discussed below. The frequency bar graphs of both hearths and rocks, by level, show that Level 175 is uniformly low while the adjacent levels above and below Level 175 generally have higher frequencies. The numbers of hearths and rocks by level (Fig. 8.4a) show a major dip or trough in their absolute frequencies at Level 175 with modal frequencies above and below at Levels 170 and 190 respectively. Together, these data demonstrate a bimodal distribution with one interval of high frequencies in Levels 160 to 170 and another in Levels 180 to 195.

The association of hearths and rocks by depth is illustrated in Figure 8.5a where the north-south profile plot show rocks concentrated close to the dripline of the shelter (excavation rows D, E, F, and G) while the hearths are primarily concentrated closer to the back wall of the shelter (excavation rows A, B, and C). The concentration of rocks is highest in the uppermost levels (160 to 170) associated with rows D to G where there is a near absence of hearths. The analogous east-west profile plot (Fig. 8.5b) demonstrates that rocks have their heaviest concentrations in excavation columns 6 to 9, particularly for Levels 160 to 170. The profile plots together, not unexpectedly, demonstrate a conspicuous absence of hearths in the southern corner of the excavation where rocks predominate in the uppermost levels. Hearths, on the other hand, are concentrated most heavily in excavation columns 1 to 5, closer to the back wall and side wall of the shelter. The vertical distributions of hearths in the north-south profile (Fig. 8.5a) may suggest a paleosurface corresponding to the bottom of the hearths; running from the back of the rockshelter to the front of the rockshelter with a slight dip. If this is the case, then the hearth in Level 175 probably associates with a paleosurface in the upper levels. It might be noted that the vertical

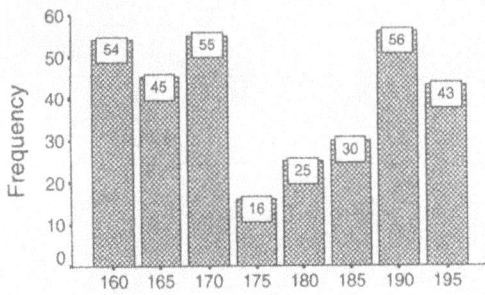

a) Rock Frequencies by Level

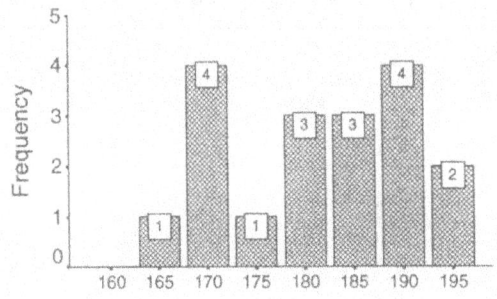

b) Hearth Frequencies by Level

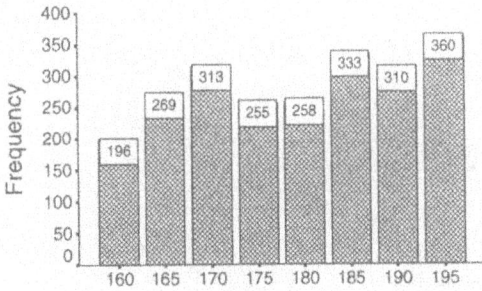

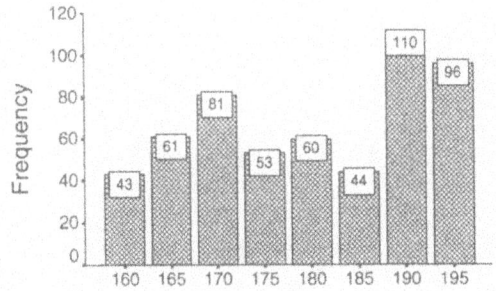

c) (debitage)

d) (tools)

Figure 8.3 Counts of rocks, hearths, debitage, and tools at Tor Faraj: **a**, rocks; **b**, hearths; **c**, debitage; **d**, tools. Note: Figure 8.3 specifically gives the raw counts and Table 8.4 also includes the summary sample size data

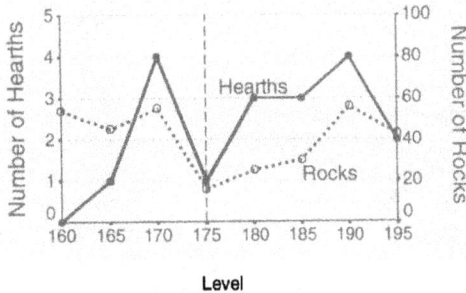

a) **Hearth and Rock Counts**

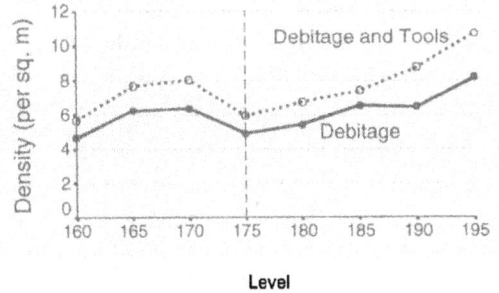

b) **Debitage-Tool Densities**

Figure 8.4 Rock-hearth counts and debitage-tool densities by level at Tor Faraj: **a**, rocks and hearths; **b**, debitage and tools. Note: Table 8.4 includes the summary sample size data for the raw counts and/or densities per square meter

hearth distributions in the east–west profile (Fig. 8.5b) is suggestive of a paleosurface running parallel to the back wall of the shelter. Horizontal associations between hearths and rocks are shown in Figure 8.6 where the centers of rocks are plotted for each of the levels. Clearly hearths and rocks are segregating although there are some rocks close to a

few hearths. Some of the rocks, interior to the dripline and close to hearths may be manuports (see Chapter 10 for further details). A meter or more separates most hearths although some hearths cluster close to one another in several levels. Specifically, two hearths in Level 170 (Fig. 8.6c) are immediately adjacent to each other, two hearths in

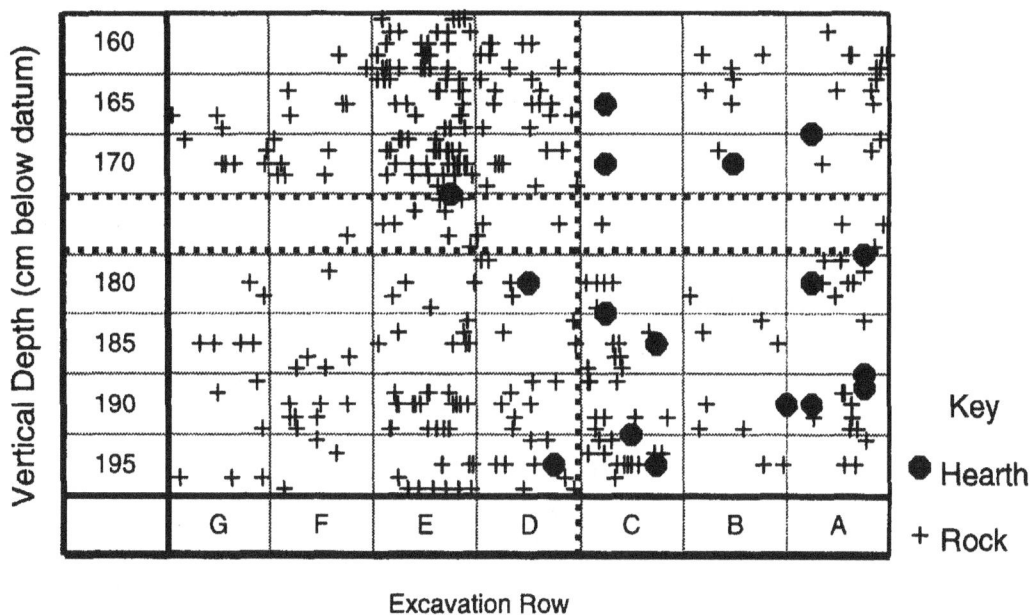

a) North - South Profile (northwest-southeast)

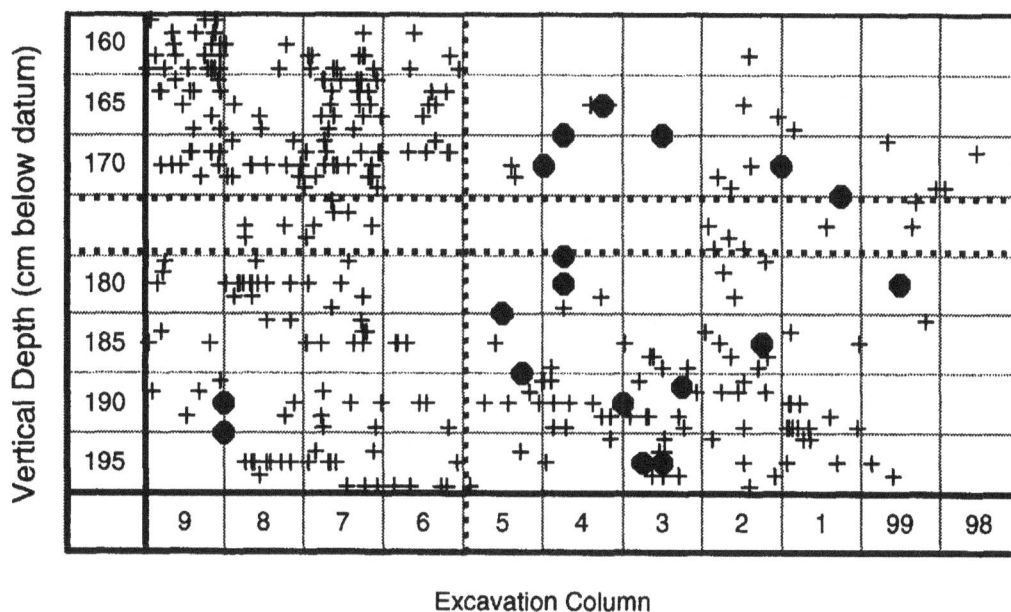

b) East - West Profile (northeast-southwest)

Figure 8.5 North–south and east–west profile plots of rocks and hearths at Tor Faraj: **a**, north–south; **b**, east–west. *Note:* Figure 8.5 is a point plot of hearths and rocks and Table 8.4 includes the summary sample size data

Level 180 are partially in Unit A4 (Fig. 8.6e), four hearths are assigned to Level 190 (Fig. 8.6g) where two are partially in Unit A3 and the other two are partially in Units B8 and C8, and, finally, two hearths in Level 195 are overlapping in Unit C3. Most often, these nearby hearths are not overlapping in vertical provenience and likely represent two successive hearths in almost the same location by the same inhabitants of the shelter. In fact, hearths are consistently placed in the same locations regardless of vertical provenience since all are within one meter of five different units (A3, A4, C8, C4, and C1). Two major hearth patterns emerge with hearths either close to the back wall in a tight spatial cluster or further from the back wall on a line running roughly parallel to and midway between both the back wall and the dripline. These sets of hearths may well have different functions. Finally, the hearth distributions by depth below datum may suggest a shorter time depth or lower intensity of repeated occupations for Levels 160 to 170, relative to Levels 180 to 195, since a maximum of six hearths are associated with the upper levels while a minimum of twice that number are associated with the lower levels. As will be seen, total artifact frequencies in the upper and lower levels also support this proposition.

Debitage and tool distributions

Debitage and tool frequencies also show patterns suggestive of higher artifact concentrations in Levels 160 to 170 and Levels 180 to 195. Debitage, for example, has higher frequencies (Table 8.4) in Levels 170, 185, and 195 with marginally lower frequencies in Levels 175 and 180. Although the evidence is weaker, the suggested distribution is still bimodal (Fig. 8.3c), with Levels 160 to 170 representing one modal interval and Levels 185 to 195 the other, if Levels 175 and 180 are assumed to be levels separating and defining the modes of occupation prior to and following the major roof collapse in the southwestern corner of the site. One problem with using frequencies, or even relative frequencies in this case, however, is the inability to identify accurately occupational intensity. A better measure of occupational intensity is artifact density, the average number of artifacts per cubic meter of excavation.

This measure is much improved when the average is based only on the units with recovery of cores, tools, or debitage. Empty units simply bias down the average by including areas of the site for which cultural material deposition did not occur. Debitage densities per level when graphically portrayed (Fig. 8.4b) show a clear bimodal pattern with higher debitage densities above and below Level 175. Specifically, as with rocks and hearths, Levels 160 to 170 represent one modal distribution and Levels 180 to 195 another. Tools present a similar distribution in that the highest frequency levels are 170, 190, and 195 (Table 8.4) with lower frequencies between Levels 170 and 190. The distribution is again bimodal (Fig. 8.3d) although Levels 180 and 185 are slightly problematical. It should be clearly noted that although the tool percentage in Level 185 appears to be low, the tool and debitage density when combined (Fig. 8.4b) yields the same bimodal pattern exhibited for rocks, hearths, and debitage alone. That is, debitage and tools together present a similar bimodal pattern as determined earlier with one modal interval corresponding to Levels 160 to 170 and the other to Levels 180 to 195.

Nevertheless, in order to collapse the data from Levels 160 to 170 into one presumed living floor and Levels 180 to 195 into another, it is still necessary to demonstrate that lateral patterning remains relatively consistent for the levels associated with the presumed floors.

Spatial patterning as a function of vertical depth

Although it was earlier established that chip distributions are relatively undisturbed by natural agencies, it seems relevant to investigate their spatial arrangements by level to see if there appears to be consistency of patterning and, if so, how that patterning might manifest itself by vertical provenience. Distributions of large debitage will be used later to firm up and define specific vertically consistent areas of the site for both the lower and upper levels.

Chip distributions

Fortunately, chip counts were available for the

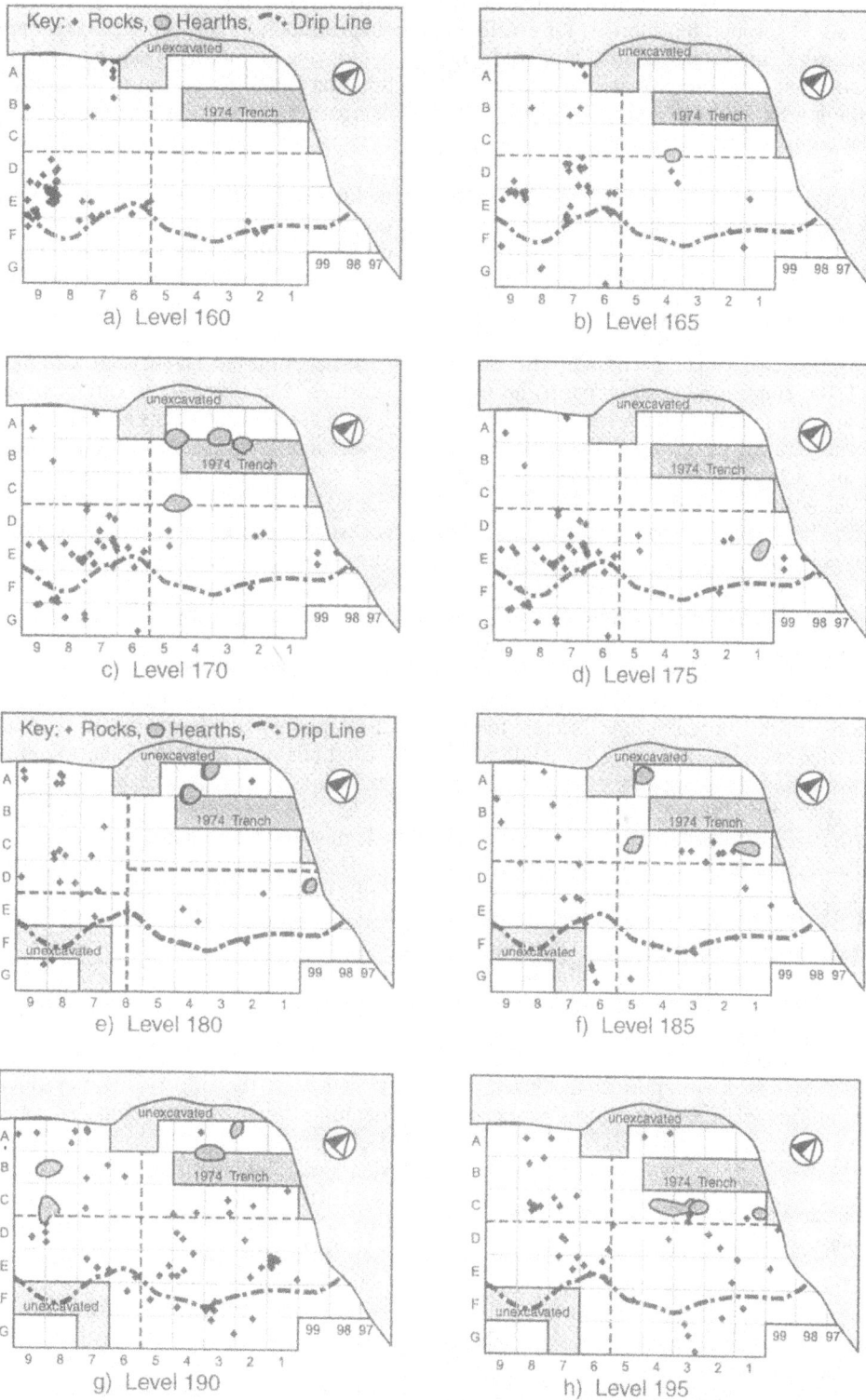

Figure 8.6 Point plots of rocks and hearth distributions by level at Tor Faraj: **a**, Level 160; **b**, Level 165; **c**, Level 170; **d**, Level 175; **e**, Level 180; **f**, Level 185; **g**, Level 190; **h**, Level 195. *Note*: Figure 8.6 is a point plot of hearths and rocks and Table 8.4 includes the summary sample size

trench sounding in 1984 (not 1974), located in Units B1 through B4, allowing for excellent topographic map realizations, rendered by Winsurf, but were unfortunately not available for the lowest level (195cm below datum). A visual comparison of the spatial distributions (Fig. 8.2) shows three or four separate and distinct spatial loci associated with high concentrations of chips in each of the levels. There are some differences that should be noted in the lower and upper levels of the site. First, it may be noted that chip concentrations in the south sector are somewhat confounded by the major roof-fall event. On the other hand, the concentration of chips in the west area appears to exist for all levels although the densities are higher in the lower levels (Figs 8.2f and 8.2g) where they are associated with the easternmost hearths in Level 190 (Fig. 8.6g). The north and east areas of the site seem to show complex patterns segregating the back wall and side wall areas. Specifically, the upper levels seem to show a major but spatially restricted concentration in the north area associated with hearths along the back wall (see Figs 8.2 and 8.6). A larger concentration, in the spatial sense, seems to be associated with hearths along the midline of the site (row C) and appears to be stronger in the lower levels, where most of the midline hearths occur. Hearths adjacent to the side wall are associated with chip concentrations in both the upper and lower levels. A small spatial concentration, in the lower and upper levels, appears to be just inside the dripline of the site and close to the side wall, making it a unique locus. Since chips are undoubtedly the residue of flint-knapping activities and will remain in place if not moved by natural or cultural factors, it is important to look at the distributions of debitage classes associated with lithic reduction activities.

Debitage distributions and formal area definitions

The formal definition of four areas each in the lower and upper levels were strongly influenced by the distributions of primary flakes and core trimming elements for the combined upper levels (160 to 170) and the combined lower levels (180 to 195). Figure 8.7 shows these distributions clearly where the concentrations alluded to in the discussion of chip distributions are visually apparent. These concentrations were then arbitrarily separated by drawing boundary lines between them. The boundary lines were further modified by comparing them to the individual distributions of all debitage by level. Although this may seem to be a method specifically designed to fulfill one's expectations, it clearly would not work if the spatial distributions did not possess a remarkable degree of consistency from level to level. Also, it is merely an analytic approximation since the inhabitants of the site certainly did not partition out the space of the rockshelter into loci associated with unrelated activities. Nevertheless, it certainly helps to have these concentrations aligned with hearth distributions and distances from the back wall and the dripline of the shelter since one premise, still to be investigated, is that the rockshelter inhabitants organized their behavior about these natural and cultural features. Figure 8.8 shows the resulting areal definitions with all point-plotted artifacts and hearths for Levels 160 to 170 (later to be termed Floor I) and Levels 180 to 195 (later to be termed Floor II). The four areas, for both the upper and lower levels, contain the definitions of areas A, B, C, and D illustrated in Figure 10.4 as defined from chip distributions and interpreted by Henry (1998a, Chapter 10 this volume).

The large lithic elements related to lithic reduction activities are cores, core trimming flakes, primary elements, and truncated-faceted pieces. The distributions (Fig. 8.9) of these specific elements, by level, clearly show a conformance of the individual distributions, by level, to the postulated areas. It may be noted that Level 175 does not clearly conform to either of the upper or lower floor areal definitions but seems somewhat mixed. In fact, Level 175 may be excluded from floor definitions for this reason alone. Blades and flakes, their Levallois equivalents, and burin spalls constitute the debitage elements not tied to early phases of lithic reduction activities. Their distributions by level (Fig. 8.10) show a strong conformance to the patterns exhibited by the early lithic reduction elements. It is of some interest to note the circular nature of the east pattern (Area C) about the hearth location associated with the upper levels and the analogous pattern for the hearth location in the lower levels. It is also of

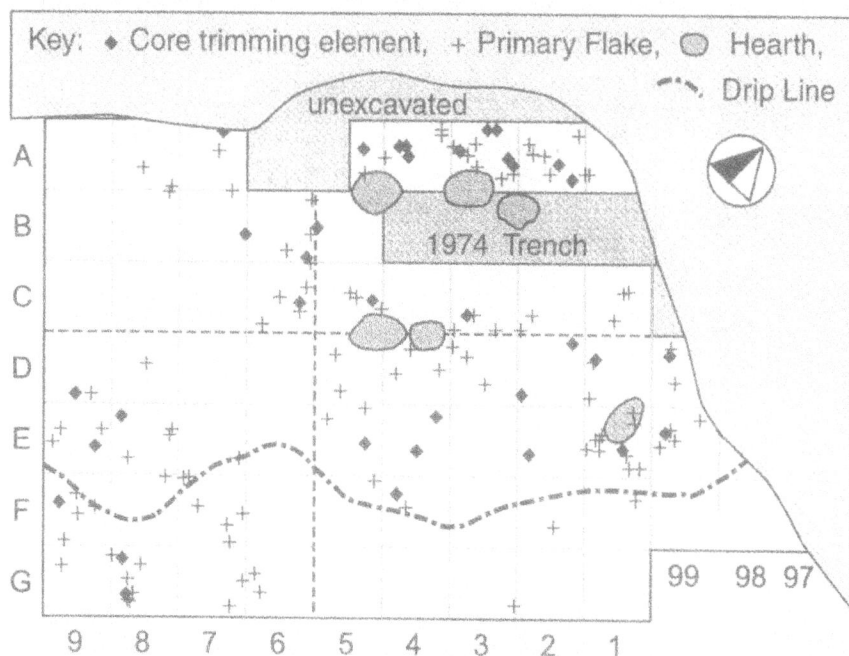

a) Primary and core trimming elements for combined levels 160-170

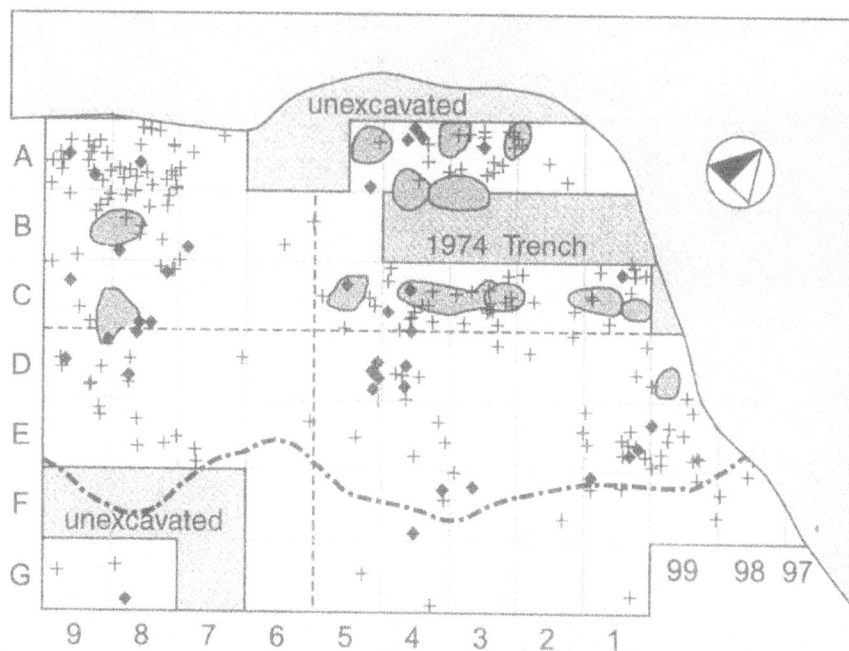

b) Primary and core trimming elements for combined levels 180-200

Figure 8.7 Point plots of primary and core trimming elements at Tor Faraj: **a**, Levels 160 to 170; **b**, Levels 180 to 195. *Note*: Figure 8.7 is a point plot of primary and core trimming elements and Table 8.6 includes the summary sample size data by level

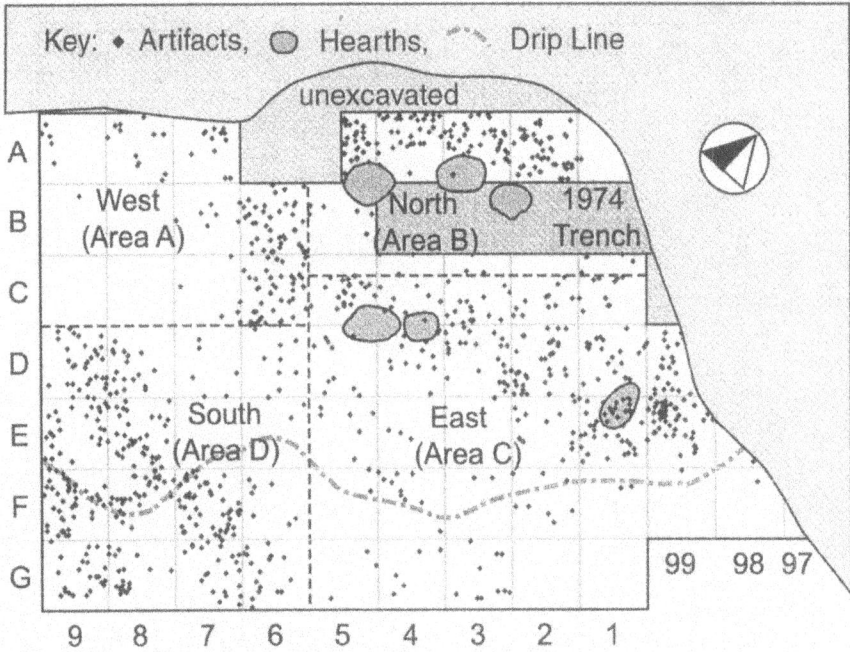

a) **Areal Definitions for Levels 160-170**

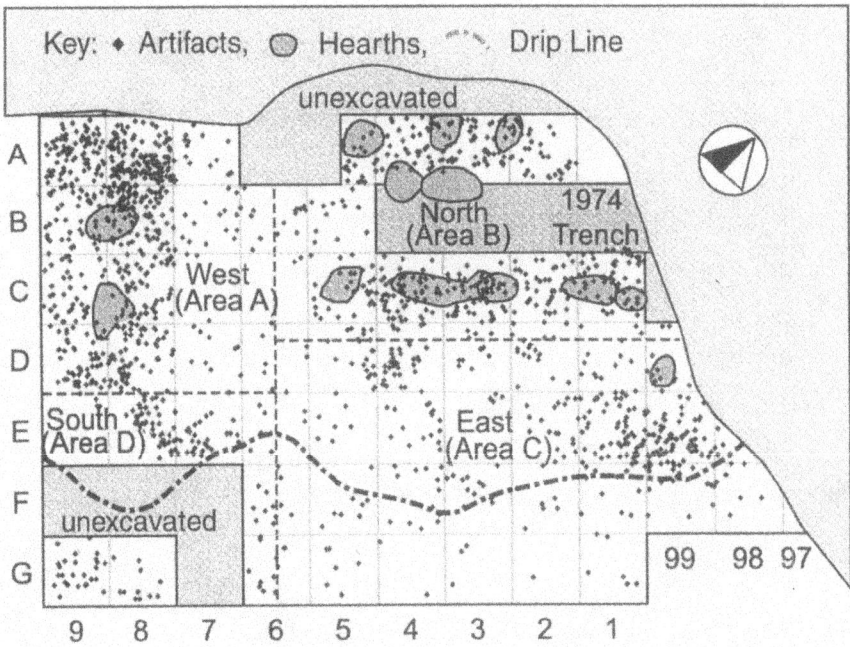

b) **Areal Definitions for Levels 180-195**

Figure 8.8 Areal definitions for Levels 160 to 170 and Levels 180 to 195 showing the spatial locations of all artifacts at Tor Faraj: **a**, Levels 160 to 175; **b**, Levels 180 to 195. *Note:* Figure 8.8 is a point plot of all artifacts and is used only to illustrate the areal definitions. Total sample sizes are given in the text

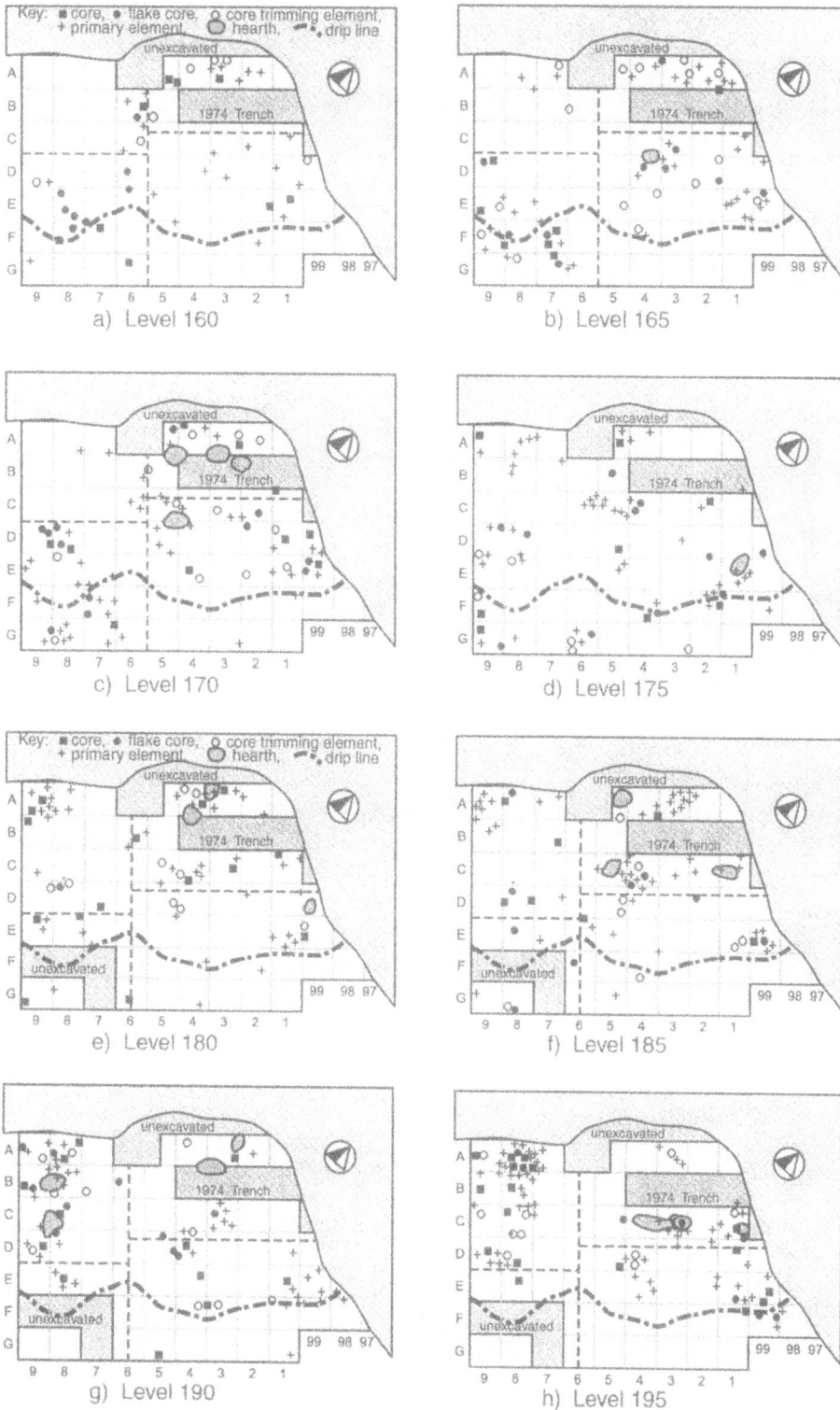

Figure 8.9 Debitage reduction element scatter diagrams at Tor Faraj: **a**, Level 160; **b**, Level 165; **c**, Level 170; **d**, Level 175; **e**, Level 180; **f**, Level 185; **g**, Level 190; **h**, Level 195. *Note*: Table 8.6 includes the summary sample size data of debitage reduction elements

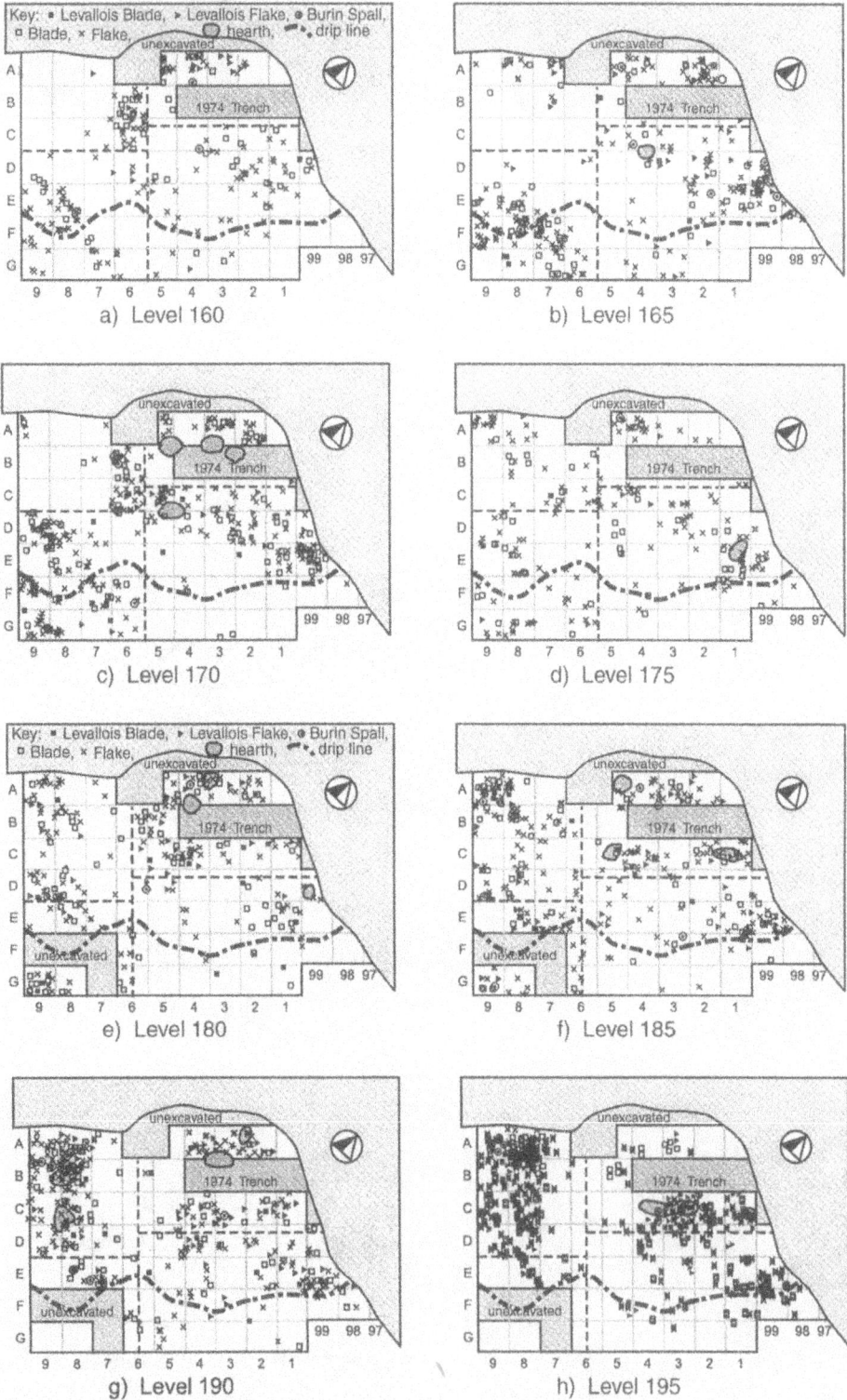

Figure 8.10 Flakes, blades, Levallois pieces, and burin spall distributions at Tor Faraj: **a**, Level 160; **b**, Level 165; **c**, Level 170; **d**, Level 175; **e**, Level 180; **f**, Level 185; **g**, Level 190; **h**, Level 195. *Note*: Table 8.6 includes the summary sample size data for the point plots of ordinary debitage, Levallois debitage, and burin spalls

some interest to note the consistency of patterning in the west (Area A) for the lower levels associated with the hearth locations in Level 190. The strong consistency of these patterns may suggest that tools will also be associated with these patterns. Since tool counts are generally small relative to the spatial area of each level, it seems appropriate to investigate the tool distributions in conjunction with the distribution of cores and unretouched debitage. The distributions of generic cores, tools, and debitage (Fig. 8.11) show that tools are consistently distributed with the other artifact classes in space for both of the presumed living floors. It may be noted, for example, that the proportional occurrence of individual artifact classes within areas may be different from level to level. This would be a natural expectation if the degree to which certain behaviors, spatially restricted to different loci, varied from one occupation to another. Certainly, people do not spend a constant percentage of time involved with the production of specific aspects of their material culture nor do they consistently produce exactly the same material culture inventory with every visitation to a particular site. Some aspects of the material culture inventory, however, might produce a constant proportional occurrence for a given area regardless of the visitation. Since core reduction activities are relatively easy to monitor, it is of interest to see if cores are consistently produced within specific areas of a site regardless of vertical depth. In this regard, the focus will be separate for the lower levels and the upper levels since it has already been established that Levels 160 to 170 have a common spatial pattern that is different from the common spatial pattern for Levels 180 to 195. The consistency of vertical patterning for debitage and tool classes, also of some interest, is discussed later.

Cores

The formal core class was augmented by including cores-on-flakes (equivalently, truncated faceted or Nahr Ibrahim pieces) as cores (Chapter 4). Interestingly, the summary data by count and relative frequency (Table 8.5a) show that the east area (Area C), containing the hearths midway to the dripline in the upper levels (160 to 170), has a reasonably high percentage of cores (27.3 percent).

Spatially, the cores (including cores-on-flakes) in the east area are in direct association with the hearths. The south area (Area D) has an even higher percentage of cores (54.5 percent) and is in direct association with the rocky matrix in the roof-fall with 71 percent showing evidence of heavy patination. The distributions of cores and truncated faceted pieces by area and level in the upper levels yield a p-value of .323 (Table 8.5a) for testing the null hypothesis of equal level-wise proportions by area and thus do not demonstrate major distributional differences by level. This suggests that the cores represent, at least in the east area (Area C), a major locus of lithic reduction. A conclusion that this area represented a lithic reduction area was also reached in Chapter 5, where chips were analyzed relative to their potential for identifying the lithic reduction sequence. The analysis in Chapter 5 also provided evidence that the south area (Area D) was a likely dumping area, consistent with the very high percentage of heavily patinated cores found in this area. This is also reinforced by large number of cores in Area D for each of the upper levels whereas Figure 8.2 clearly shows that only Level 160 has a high percentage of chips in this area. Also Area D does not possess any hearths, a corollary of lithic reduction in the other areas.

Table 8.5 also provides the data to show that cores (including cores-on-flakes) are also proportionally distributed by area in Levels 180 to 195 (p-value = .183). The highest percentages of cores are found in the west area (Area A) with 44.9 percent of all cores. Area D (the south area) has the lowest percentage of cores (11.5 percent) with the reminder split between Areas B and C. Spatially, the cores in the lower levels are in direct association with hearths with the exception of cores of those found in Area D. This area was also identified as a discard area in Chapter 3. Areas B (the north area) and C (the east area) also seem to represent lithic reduction areas consistent with conclusions suggested in Chapter 3.

Certainly, the core distributions in Levels 160 to 170 support the contention that the levels can be collapsed and interpreted as an archaeological living floor, hereafter tentatively referred to as Floor 1. Levels 180 to 195 data also support the contention that they may be combined to create a second living floor,

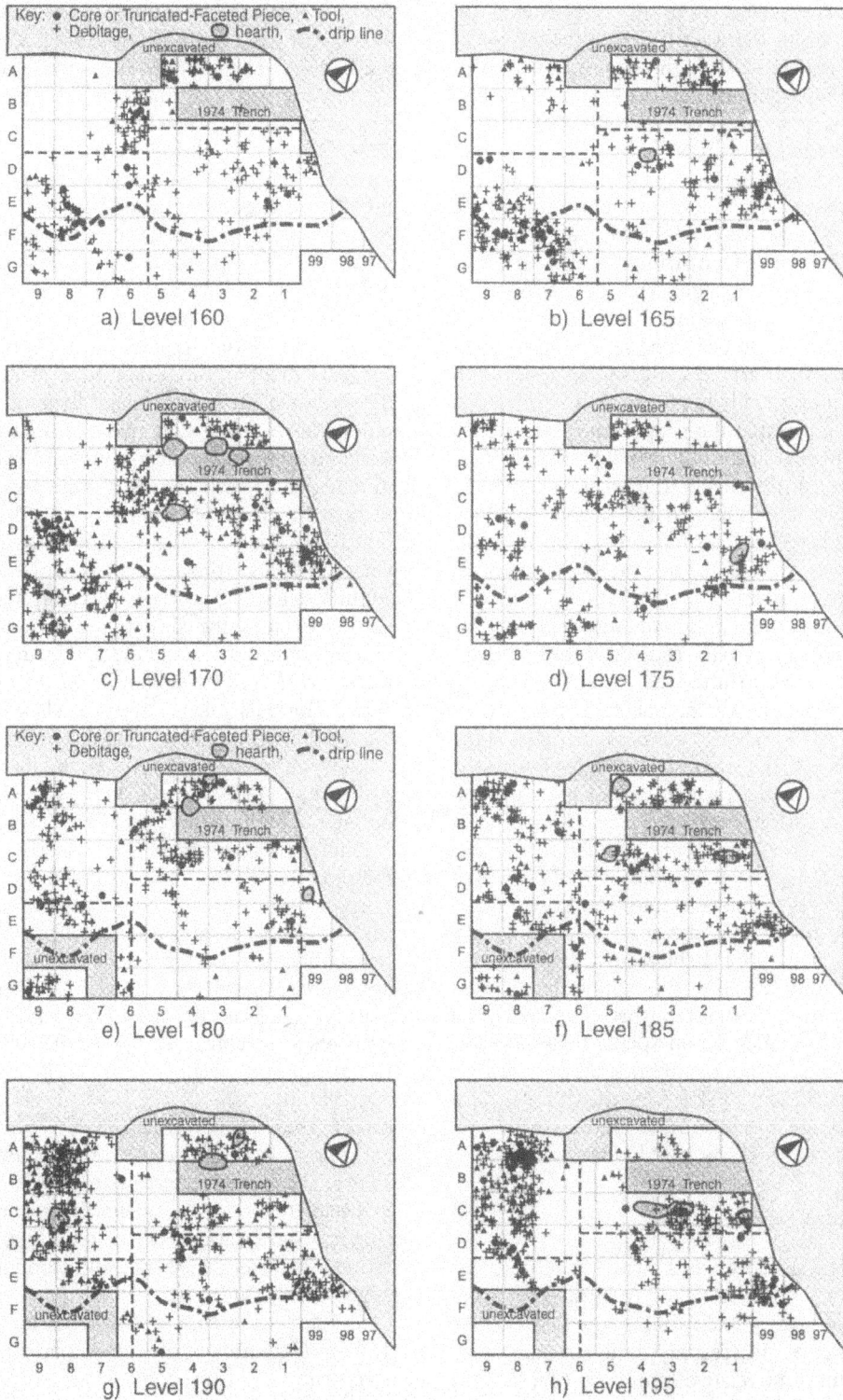

Figure 8.11 Spatial distributions for generic cores, debitage, and tools at Tor Faraj: **a**, Level 160; **b**, Level 165; **c**, Level 170; **d**, Level 175; **e**, Level 180; **f**, Level 185; **g**, Level 190; **h**, Level 195. *Note*: Tables 8.4 to 8.9 include summary sample size data for the point plots of generic cores, debitage, and tools

Table 8.5 Core percentages by defined areas within specified grouped levels: **a**, Levels 160-70; **b**, Levels 180-95

a. Levels 160-70: Likelihood Ratio Statistic = 7.94; df = 6; Monte Carlo *p*-value = .323

| Level | Total core count | Defined areal concentration | | | | | | | |
| | | Area A (west) | | Area B (north) | | Area C (east) | | Area D (south) | |
		Count	%	Count	%	Count	%	Count	%
160	17	2	11.8	3	17.6	2	11.8	10	58.8
165	17	0	0.0	2	11.8	5	29.4	10	58.8
170	21	0	0.0	3	14.3	8	38.1	10	47.6
Floor I	55	2	3.6	8	14.5	15	27.3	30	54.5

Notes: Includes cores-on-flakes

Area A (west) bounded by rows A-C and columns 6-9 (see Fig. 8.8a);
Area B (north) bounded by rows A-C$_{25}$ and columns 1-5 and 97-9 (Fig. 8.8a);
Area C (east) bounded by rows C$_{25}$ -G and columns 1-5 and 97-9 (Fig. 8.8a);
Area D (south) bounded by rows D-G and columns 6-9 (see Fig. 8.8a)

b. Levels 180-95: Likelihood Ratio Statistic = 13.9; df = 9; Monte Carlo *p*-value = .183

| Level | Total core count | Defined areal concentration | | | | | | | |
| | | Area A (west) | | Area B (north) | | Area C (east) | | Area D (south) | |
		Count	%	Count	%	Count	%	Count	%
180	15	4	26.7	6	40.0	1	6.7	4	26.7
185	16	6	37.5	3	18.8	4	25.0	3	18.8
190	23	12	52.2	3	13.0	7	30.4	1	4.2
195	24	13	54.2	4	16.7	6	25.0	1	4.2
Floor II	78	35	44.9	16	20.5	18	23.1	9	11.5

Notes: Includes cores-on-flakes

Area A (west) bounded by rows A-D and columns 6$_5$-9 (see Fig. 8.8b);
Area B (north) bounded by rows A-D$_{25}$ and columns 1-6$_5$ and 97-9 (Fig. 8.8b);
Area C (east) bounded by rows D$_{25}$-G and columns 1-6$_5$ and 97-9 (Fig. 8.8b);
Area D (south) bounded by rows E-G and columns 6$_5$-9 (see Fig. 8.8b)

hereafter tentatively referred to as Floor II. It is of some interest to investigate more formally the integrity of these proposed floors relative to the material culture afforded by other artifact types and classes.

Debitage classes

At the outset, it should be pointed out that frequencies of debitage classes by level are perfectly consistent with each other. Table 8.6 gives the proportion of each class-type by level where a *p*-value of 0.231 results for an Exact Chi-Square Test of equal proportions. This result is all the more interesting when it is noted that the sample size for this test numbers 2293 artifacts. Although the proportions are certainly constant across levels, the same cannot be said for the areal proportions within levels. Table 8.7 shows that Area A in level 165 only possesses 8 percent of the debitage relative to 19 percent and 16 percent in Levels 160 and 170. Also, Area B has only 11 percent of the debitage in Level 170 versus 18 to 20 percent in the other two levels. It is this type of difference that disallows the

Table 8.6 Debitage class frequencies and percentages within levels

| | Level (depth below datum in cm) | | | | | | | | |
	160	165	170	175	180	185	190	195	Total
Core trimming element	6	14	11	6	9	8	7	8	69
	3.1%	5.2%	3.5%	2.3%	3.5%	2.4%	2.3%	2.2%	3.0%
Primary element	21	36	42	43	42	47	33	61	325
	10.7%	13.4%	13.4%	16.8%	16.4%	14.1%	10.6%	16.9%	14.2%
Flake	112	132	155	144	122	178	174	187	1204
	57.1%	49.1%	49.5%	56.3%	47.7%	53.5%	56.1%	51.9%	52.5%
Blade	43	54	71	42	52	59	61	69	451
	21.9%	20.1%	22.7%	16.4%	20.3%	17.7%	19.7%	19.2%	19.7%
Levallois flake	11	21	27	14	22	28	24	17	154
	5.6%	7.8%	5.4%	5.5%	8.6%	8.4%	7.7%	4.7%	6.7%
Levallois blade	1	6	14	6	8	7	8	11	61
	.5%	2.2%	4.5%	2.3%	3.1%	2.1%	2.6%	3.1%	2.7%
Burin spall	2	6	3	1	1	6	3	7	29
	1.0%	2.2%	1.0%	.4%	.4%	1.8%	1.0%	1.9%	1.3%
Total	196	269	313	256	256	333	310	360	2293
	100%	100%	100%	100%	100%	100%	100%	100%	100%

Note: Likelihood ratio statistic = 49.3; df = 42; Monte Carlo exact test p-value = .231

Table 8.7 Debitage percentages by defined areas within specified grouped levels

a. Levels 160-70: Likelihood Ratio Statistic = 25.1; df = 6; Monte Carlo p-value = .000

| | | Defined areal concentration | | | | | | | |
| | | Area A (west) | | Area B (north) | | Area C (east) | | Area D (south) | |
Level	Total count	Count	%	Count	%	Count	%	Count	%
160	196	38	19.4	35	17.9	70	35.7	53	27.0
165	269	21	7.8	53	19.7	109	40.5	86	32.0
170	313	49	15.7	35	11.2	114	36.4	115	36.7
Floor I	778	108	13.9	123	15.8	293	37.7	254	32.6

b. Levels 180-95: Likelihood Ratio Statistic = 66.5; df = 9; Monte Carlo p-value = .000

| | | Defined areal concentration | | | | | | | |
| | | Area A (west) | | Area B (north) | | Area C (east) | | Area D (south) | |
Level	Total count	Count	%	Count	%	Count	%	Count	%
180	256	74	28.9	96	37.5	47	18.4	39	15.2
185	333	114	34.2	110	33.0	70	21.0	39	11.7
190	310	131	42.3	72	23.2	86	27.7	21	6.8
195	360	176	48.9	82	22.8	87	24.2	15	4.2
Floor II	1259	495	39.3	360	28.6	290	23.0	114	9.1

Note: See Table 8.5a for definitions of the areal concentrations in Levels 160-70 and Table 8.5b for definitions of the areal concentrations in Levels 180-95

exactness of constant proportionality by area. A similar statement can be made for the levels within the second proposed floor. The same results do not occur, however, for individual debitage classes. Table 8.8 summarizes the p-values for testing equal areal proportions by level for all debitage classes. It should be noted that core trimming elements (an indicator of early lithic reduction) has p-values of .57and .13 for testing areal equiprobabilities by level. For Levels 160 to 170, the high probability areas were Areas B and C, each with 36 percent of the core trimming elements, suggesting perhaps that these areas, with hearths along the back wall, side wall, and central midline (Fig. 8.7a), were involved with initial core reduction. Areas A and C had higher percentages in Levels 180 to 195 (34 percent each). Also, Area B had 28 percent of the core trimming elements in Floor II. These areas all have associated hearths and may have been involved with the early part of the lithic reduction sequence. The only area without moderate to high percentages of core trimming elements in Floor I and II were Areas A and D in Floor I and Area D in Floor II. These are the only areas in Floors I and II without hearths. The only categories that do not support the areal equiprobability hypothesis are flakes for both floors and primary ele-

ments for Floor II. It should be mentioned that some of the types have small sample numbers and that it would be extremely difficult to reject the hypothesis if there is only a modicum of support for the equiprobability hypothesis. Nevertheless, there is substantial evidence that not only are the levels similarly patterned, relative to the postulated floors, but they also seem to possess the same types of material culture in different loci of the floors. These facts give great support for the existence of living floors at Tor Faraj.

Tools

The above arguments for debitage classes apply reasonably well for tools. Table 8.9 provides tool type frequencies and percentages by level. It can be seen that the tool inventory for each level is variable. Tools are not as consistent as debitage from level to level. Even though there are only 416 tools, the hypothesis of equal proportions of tool types by level is overwhelmingly rejected (p-value = .001). It may be noted that the proportions of unretouched Levallois points and notches by themselves may be responsible for this result. It is clear that there are significantly higher proportions of Levallois points in the Floor I levels. It is not surprising

Table 8.8 Exact hypothesis test p-values for equal areal proportions

Debitage type	Combined levels		Tool type	Combined levels	
	160–70	180–95		160–70	180–95
Primary elt.	.075	.001	Lev. point. (ret.)	1.000	.004
Core trim. elt.	.571	.131	Lev. pt. (unret.)	.345	.556
Blade	.053	.103	Side-scraper	.503	1.000
Flake	.022	.000	End-scraper	.333	1.000
Lev. blade	.357	.083	Burin	.654	.803
Lev. flake	.342	.099	Trunc. piece	1.000	1.000
Burin spall	.150	.597	Notch	.332	.000
Core	.073	.309	Denticulate	1.000	1.000
Trunc. fac. pc.	.193	.101	Retouched pc.	.983	.000
			Varia	1.000	.573

Note: p-values of 1.000 can occur when all elements belong to one and only one area; p-values of 0.000 can occur when all elements belong to different areas by level

Table 8.9 Tool type frequencies and percentages by level

	Level (depth below datum in cm)							
	160	165	170	180	185	190	195	Total
Lev. point ret.	2	1	4	2	2	10	2	23
	5.9%	1.9%	5.6%	4.4%	5.4%	10.3%	2.6%	5.5%
Lev. point unret.	12	13	18	10	5	11	8	77
	35.3%	24.1%	25.4%	22.2%	13.5%	11.3%	10.3%	18.5%
Side-scraper	1	2	1	1		2	5	12
	2.9%	3.7%	1.4%	2.2%		2.1%	6.4%	2.9%
End-scraper		1	2			1	1	5
		1.9%	2.8%			1.0%	1.3%	1.2%
Burin	6	3	9	12	2	13	9	54
	17.6%	5.6%	12.7%	26.7%	5.4%	13.4%	11.5%	13.0%
Truncated piece	1		1	2	1			5
	2.9%		1.4%	4.4%	2.7%			1.2%
Notch	1	5			7	7	10	30
	2.9%	9.3%			18.9%	7.2%	12.8%	7.2%
Denticulate		3		2	2	3		10
		5.6%		4.4%	5.4%	3.1%		2.4%
Retouched piece	11	26	34	15	17	46	41	190
	32.4%	48.1%	47.9%	33.3%	45.9%	47.4%	52.6%	45.7%
Varia			2	1	1	4	2	10
			2.8%	2.2%	2.7%	4.1%	2.6%	2.4%
Total	34	54	71	45	37	97	78	416
	100%	100%	100%	100%	100%	100%	100%	100%

Note: Likelihood Ratio Statistic = 97.4; df = 54; Monte Carlo Exact Test p-value = .001

Table 8.10 Tool percentages by defined areas within specified grouped levels

a. Levels 160-70: Likelihood Ratio Statistic = 11.3; df = 6; Monte Carlo p-value = .099

		Defined areal concentration							
Level	Total count	Area A (west)		Area B (north)		Area C (east)		Area D (south)	
		Count	%	Count	%	Count	%	Count	%
160	34	6	17.6	10	29.4	9	26.5	9	26.5
165	54	5	9.3	5	9.3	18	33.3	26	48.1
170	71	5	7.0	9	12.7	27	38.0	30	42.3
Floor I	159	16	10.1	24	15.1	54	34.0	65	40.9

b. Levels 180-95: Likelihood ratio statistic = 39.6; df = 9; Monte Carlo p-value = .000

		Defined areal concentration							
Level	Total count	Area A (west)		Area B (north)		Area C (east)		Area D (south)	
		Count	%	Count	%	Count	%	Count	%
180	45	9	20.0	22	48.9	9	20.0	5	11.1
185	37	8	21.6	7	18.9	16	43.2	6	16.2
190	97	37	38.1	22	22.7	31	32.0	7	7.2
195	78	46	59.0	17	21.8	13	16.7	2	2.6
Floor II	257	100	38.9	68	26.5	69	26.8	20	7.8

Note: See Table 8.5a for definitions of the areal concentrations in Levels 160-70, and Table 8 5b for definitions of the areal concentrations in Levels 180-95

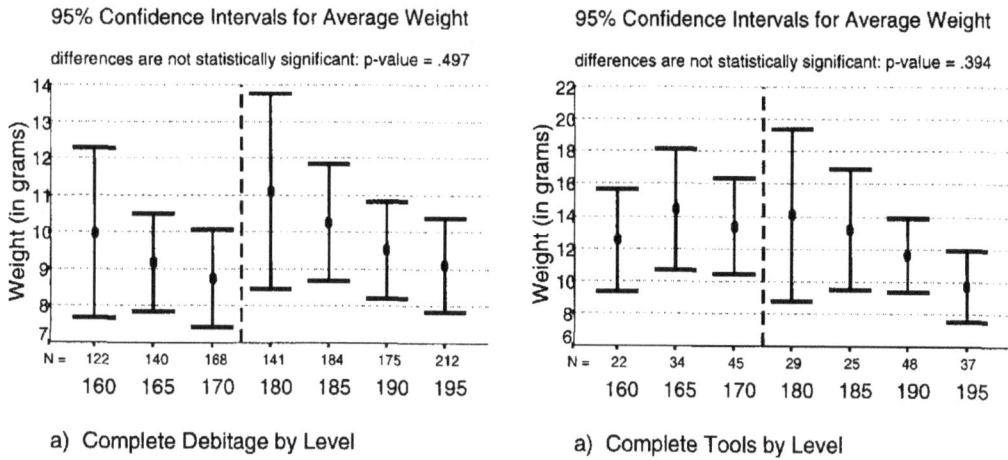

95% Confidence Intervals for Average Weight
differences are not statistically significant: p-value = .497

a) Complete Debitage by Level

95% Confidence Intervals for Average Weight
differences are not statistically significant: p-value = .394

a) Complete Tools by Level

Figure 8.12   Debitage and tool size by level at Tor Faraj: **a**, complete debitage; **b**, complete tools

at all that overall hypotheses of equal areal proportions for all tools is not consistent for Floors I and II (Table 8.10). Although tool type proportions vary across levels (Table 8.9) and areal proportions of all tools are highly variable (Table 8.10), our main concern is with individual tool types by area within the levels for the proposed floors. Hypotheses of areal equiprobability by level were tested for each of the proposed floors with resulting p-values given in Table 8.8. Here it is noted that the only tool classes leading to a rejection of the hypothesis (at the .05 level of significance) are retouched Levallois points, notches, and retouched pieces for Floor II. Overall, there is substantial support, among tools, for the living floor proposition. To conclude this exercise in the justification of living floors at Tor Faraj, it may be of interest to look at the size of artifacts by level and the diversity of tools and debitage by level.

Debitage and tool size

Artifact size is measured for all complete artifacts by artifact weight in grams. Confidence intervals (95 percent) for all complete debitage and all complete tools (Fig. 8.12) show that outside of Level 160 for tools, the average complete piece size is larger in the level associated with the top of the floor and smaller in the level associated with the bottom of the floor. Level 160 for tools may fail to fit this pattern due to a

different inventory of tools relative to the other levels in Floor I; Level 160 has fewer unretouched Levallois points and more burins than the other two levels. In general, however, the trend may suggest that smaller tools and debitage filter downward somewhat in the soft fine-grained sediments of layer C. Nevertheless, the floors seem to be intact in that the tools did not filter down below the earliest probable level associated with the floors. In all honesty, this result might be purely associated with chance since an application of the analysis of variance to test hypotheses of equal mean weights for complete tools, on the one hand, and complete debitage, on the other, totally supports the null hypothesis. This is clear from Fig. 8.12 since the 95 percent confidence intervals clearly overlap for all levels. Nevertheless, it is an interesting trend that is statistically without merit.

Debitage and tool diversity

Debitage and tool diversity may be measured through debitage and tool richness and Simpson's index of tool diversity. Table 8.11 shows that debitage has equal richness values (8) for all levels and the diversity indices hardly vary at all. This is not surprising since the debitage inventories by level are completely consistent with each other. Tools, on the other hand, vary in richness from seven in Level 160 to nine in Level 190. It should be

Table 8.11 Simpson's debitage and tool diversity measures by level

a. Debitage

	Level						
	160	165	170	180	185	190	195
Evenness	0.310	0.341	0.337	0.350	0.322	0.316	0.332
Diversity index	0.644	0.709	0.700	0.728	0.670	0.657	0.690
Richness	8	8	8	8	8	8	8
Sample size	205	276	323	271	340	323	377

b. Tools

	Level						
	160	165	170	180	185	190	195
Evenness	0.388	0.340	0.334	0.375	0.358	0.334	0.330
Diversity index	0.756	0.707	0.695	0.779	0.745	0.733	0.689
Richness	7	8	8	8	8	9	8
Sample size	34	54	71	45	37	97	78

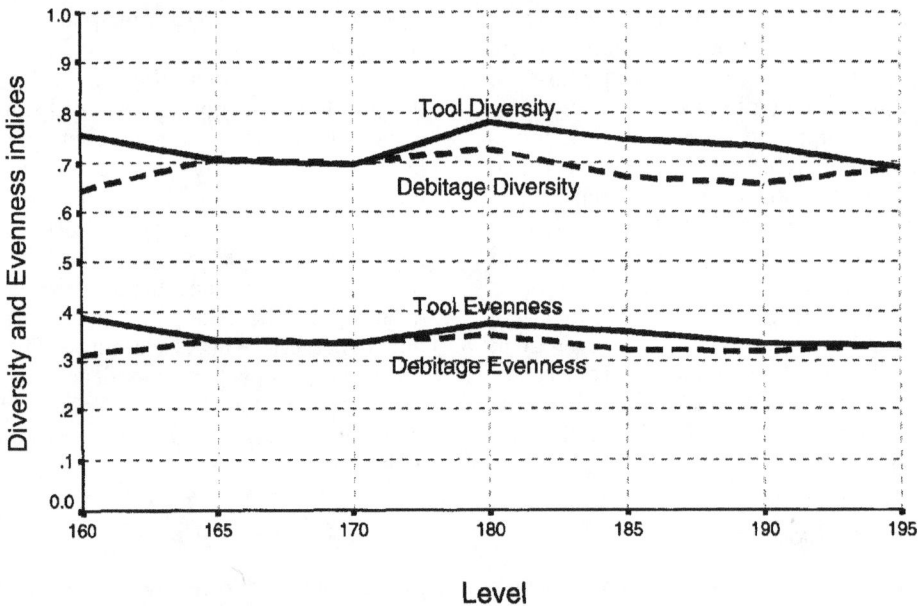

Figure 8.13 Diversity and evenness indices for tools and debitage by level at Tor Faraj. *Note*: Figure 8.13 is a plot of indices from Table 8.11 which includes the summary sample size data

noted that Level 160 has only 34 tools while Level 190 has 97 tools. Richness is known to be a function of sample size. Larger sample sizes invariably are associated with more tool types (richness). The diversity measure for tools range from a low of .689 in Level 195 to a high of .779 in Level 180. The measure of evenness (also related to diversity) also shows little variation from level to level. There clearly is little difference in either tool diversity or debitage diversity as can be readily seen (Fig. 8.13) when evenness and diversity are plotted across levels for complete debitage and complete tools.

Conclusion

The existence of two separate living floors at Tor Faraj has been amply demonstrated using many lines of evidence ranging from simple investigations of post-depositional movement to complex investigations regarding the consistency of artifact patterning in three-dimensional space. Conceptually tying the nature of patterning to natural and cultural features made the effort easier. In addition, the change in internal site structure necessitated by the chance roof-fall event gave some meaning to Area D in the southern corner of the site. How the patterns vary from Floor I to Floor II and possible interpretations of these patterns is the subject of the following chapter.

Site Structure and Material Patterning in Space on the Tor Faraj Living Floors

HAROLD J. HIETALA

The existence of viable living floors at Tor Faraj (Chapter 8) has been sufficiently demonstrated with Levels 160 through 170 defining the latest occupation floor (Floor I) and Levels 180 through 195 defining a slightly earlier occupation floor (Floor II). Fortunately, the spatial positioning of roof-fall, dripline, back wall, and hearths serve as natural and cultural features about which the patterning of artifacts and ancillary scientific information can be archaeologically interpreted for the upper and lower floors. An analysis of the upper floor (Levels 160 to 170) is limited to the spatial patterning of lithic information, tied to the natural and cultural features, and is consequently more restricted relative to potential behavioral interpretations. Nevertheless, the data from Floor I are quite capable of producing reasonable conclusions regarding the material structure of its associated occupation(s). The lower floor, on the other hand, has chemical, phytolith, and use-wear information associated with the lithic patterns in space. Floor II, therefore, not only provides data for the understanding of site structure but also allows stronger conclusions regarding the behavioral nature of the site occupants.

Floor I analysis

Four distinct areas in the west, north, east, and

south of the excavated portion of Tor Faraj were defined for Floor I (Fig. 8.8a) based on the three-dimensional spatial patterning of lithic artifacts (see Chapter 8). These areas, hereafter, are referred to as areas A, B, C, and D consistent with an earlier, preliminary analysis of the living floors at Tor Faraj (Henry 1998a). It is clear that these have different combinations of natural and cultural features associated with them. Area A (west) has a small amount of roof-fall (Fig. 8.6a-c), is adjacent to the back wall, and is close to two hearths, one each in Areas B and C. Area B, tucked into an alcove in the northern wall of the shelter, has essentially no rocks (Fig. 8.6a-c) and has three hearths organized along a linear pattern parallel to the back wall. These hearths are approximately 1.5 meters from the back wall and spaced less than one meter from each other. Area C (east) has two adjacent hearths in the central portion of the shelter and another along the side wall near the dripline. This area also has a few rocks (Fig. 8.6a-c) and includes the longest portion of the dripline in the excavated portion of the site. Finally, Area D (south) is primarily noted for the presence of a major roof-fall concentration within its boundary with the dripline running midway through it and does not possess any hearths.

Four of the six hearths (Fig. 8.6c) were assigned to the same vertical provenience (170cm below datum) and are possibly associated with a single group of individuals visiting the site. Three of the six hearths (Fig. 8.8a) are in close proximity to the back wall in Area B while one of the other three, in Area C, is close to the side wall. Each hearth location corresponds to one of two spatial patterns. The first is the tight linear pattern close to and parallel to the back wall in Area B. The second is a more dispersed pattern in Area C, between the back wall and dripline, with one hearth near the side wall and dripline and the other two distant from the shelter walls in the middle of the shelter. The hearth adjacent to the side wall has vertical provenience 170 to 175cm below datum but is considered part of Floor I due to the likely slope of the paleosurface (see Chapter 8).

The density map of total artifacts (Fig. 9.1a) across the site suggests, as a general pattern, the existence of four major high density clusters, one for each of the four areas mentioned above. The high-density peaks are all greater than 40 artifacts per m^2 with intervening lower densities generally less than 20 artifacts per m^2. It should also be noted that the high-density peaks are all approximately within one meter of hearths with the exception of the concentration in the roof-fall area. Specifically the density peak in Area A is in Unit C6 adjacent to the hearth in Unit C5. The density peak in Area B is in Unit A2 adjacent to the hearths in Units A3 and B2 and the density peak in Area C is in Unit E99 adjacent to the hearth in Unit E1. It may also be noted that the density peaks in Areas B and C are between the hearths and the wall of the shelter. It is possible that the inhabitants of the site were involved in specialized activities in these areas close to the wall of the rockshelter.

The hearth and total artifact distribution suggests that Floor I may be the result of a small number of occupational episodes where it is posited that the occupants engaged in similar activities at different occupational loci. It is of considerable interest to ascertain if the inhabitants of the floor left evidence of interpretable behavior based, in part, on spatial patterning of their lithic remains. Unfortunately, Area D artifacts were frequently on edge and heavily patinated. The spatial densities of heavily patinated artifacts (Fig. 9.2a) show that most of them are located in the roof-fall area with only small numbers in the other areas of the site. This area is almost

certainly a discard area for lithics no longer considered desirable by the occupants of the site (see Chapters 5 and 8). If one calculates heavy patination percentages for cores, debitage, and tools for all artifacts farther from the front of the rockshelter than the midline of row E (see Fig. 9.1a and Fig. 9.2a), it is found that 77.3 percent of all cores, 47.2 percent of all debitage, and 53.7 percent of all tools are heavily patinated with an overall heavy patination percentage of 50.1 percent. On the other hand, the overall heavy patination percentage for artifacts inside this imaginary line is only 15.8 percent. Nevertheless, the primary dumping area is Area D.

In looking for interpretable spatial patterns associated with the other areas of the site, however, it seems reasonable to start with initial core reduction activities since some elements of this phase are likely to be left in place.

Initial core reduction activities

Lithic elements generally associated with initial core reduction activities are the cores themselves (although they may have been subsequently moved or discarded), core trimming elements (less likely to be spatially repositioned by the inhabitants), and primary elements. Included within the larger core class are cores-on-flakes (also known as truncated-faceted pieces or Nahr Ibrahim elements); hereafter *cores-on-flakes* will be abbreviated as *flake cores* without confusing them with traditional Middle Paleolithic cores. It is easily demonstrated that the two categories of cores are equiproportionally located (Table 9.1a; $p = .106$) in the same areas of Floor I. It should be noted that core and flake core proportions are expected to be the same in specific areas of the site if this hypothesis is true. This hypothesis is statistically investigated using the likelihood ratio chi-square statistic and employing the exact test p-value for testing the hypothesis. When the exact test (calculated in SPSS) could not be easily exploited, due to time constraints or insufficient computer memory, the exact test was simulated by SPSS using 10,000 simulations with 99 percent confidence. That cores and flake cores occupy the same spatial loci is evident from their combined density map (Fig. 9.3a) and their point locations (Fig. 8.9a–c) where it is

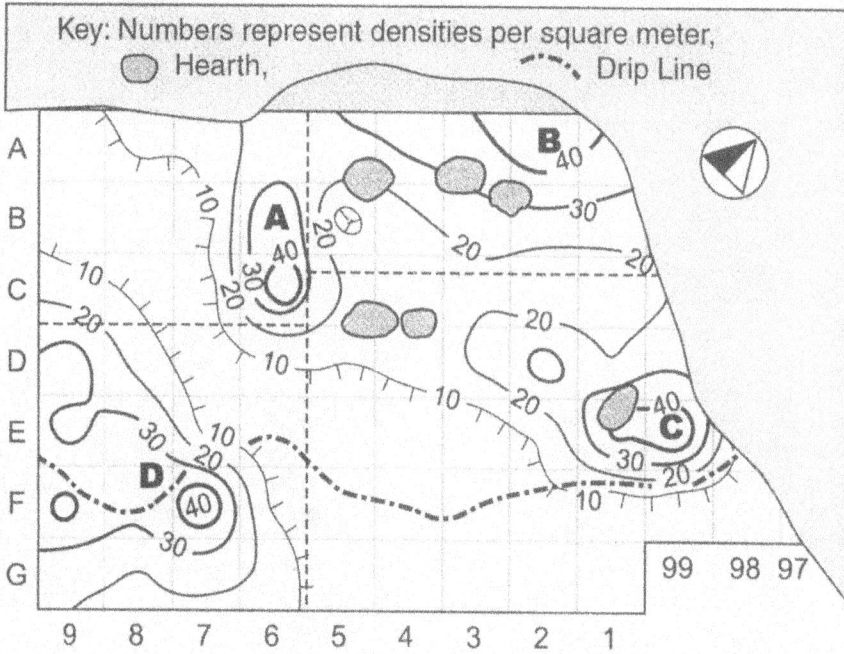

a) Floor I

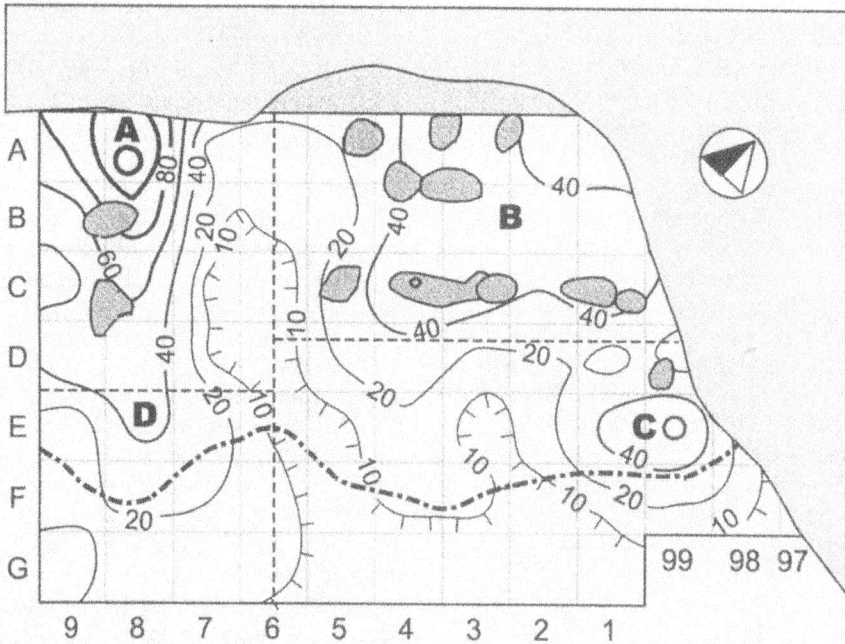

b) Floor II

Figure 9.1 Spatial frequencies of all artifacts by floor at Tor Faraj: **a**, Floor I; **b**, Floor II. *Note*: In Figure 9.1 the numbers represent densities per square meter. Total sample sizes are given in the text

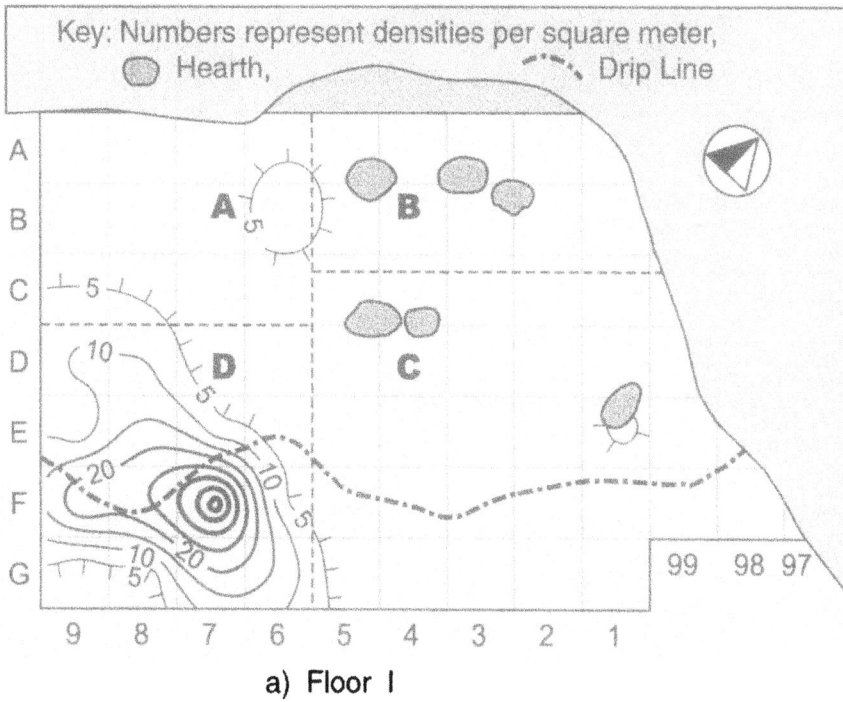

a) Floor I

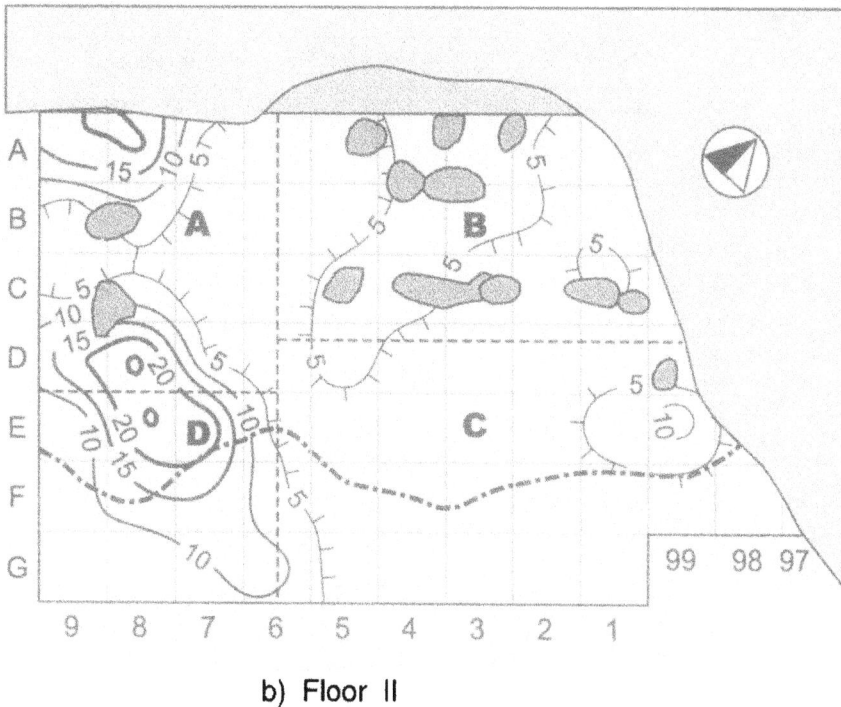

b) Floor II

Figure 9.2 Spatial frequencies of heavily patinated artifacts by floor at Tor Faraj: **a**, Floor I; **b**, Floor II. *Note:* In Figure 9.2 the numbers represent densities per square meter. Total sample sizes are given in the text and in Table 8.2

Table 9.1 Percentages and frequencies within core groups and areas by floor

a.

	Area A (west)		Area B (north)		Area C (east)		Area D (south)		Class total	
	Count	Row %	Count	Row %	Count	Row %	Count	Row %	Count	Row %
Cores	1	3.4	1	3.4	9	31.0	18	62.1	29	100
Flake cores	1	3.8	7	26.9	6	23.1	12	46.2	26	100
Subtotal	2	3.6	8	14.5	15	27.3	30	54.5	55	100

Note: Likelihood Ratio Statistic = 6.71; df = 3; Exact Text *p*-value = .106

b.

	Area A (west)		Area B (north)		Area C (east)		Area D (south)		Subtotal	
	Count	Col %	Count	Col %	Count	Col %	Count	Col %	Count	Col %
Cores	1	50.0	1	12.5	9	60.0	18	60.0	29	52.7
Flake cores	1	50.0	7	87.5	6	40.0	12	40.0	26	47.3
Area total	2	100	8	100	15	100	30	100	55	100

c.

	Area A (west)		Area B (north)		Area C (east)		Area D (south)		Class total	
	Count	Row %	Count	Row %	Count	Row %	Count	Row %	Count	Row %
Cores	10	38.5	7	26.9	6	23.1	3	11.5	26	100
Flake cores	25	48.1	9	17.3	12	23.1	6	11.5	52	100
Subtotal	35	44.9	16	20.5	18	23.1	9	11.5	78	100

Note: Likelihood Ratio Statistic = 1.12; df = 3; Exact Test *p*-value = .781

d.

	Area A (west)		Area B (north)		Area C (east)		Area D (south)		Subtotal	
	Count	Col %	Count	Col %	Count	Col %	Count	Col %	Count	Col %
Cores	10	28.6	7	43.8	6	33.3	3	33.3	26	33.3
Flake cores	25	71.4	9	56.3	12	66.7	6	66.7	52	66.7
Area total	35	100	16	100	18	100	9	100	78	100

Note: **a**. Floor I: percentages relative to core classes; **b**. Floor I: percentages relative to site areas; **c**. Floor II: percentages relative to core classes; **d**. Floor II: percentages relative to site areas

seen that most of them are located in Area D. In fact, the roof-fall zone (Table 9.1a) includes slightly more than half of all cores (54.5 percent) and Area C slightly more than a quarter (27.3 percent). The multiple hearth back wall area includes 14.5 percent, while Area A has fewer cores (3.6 percent). Nevertheless, the spatial map for all cores (including flake cores) is locationally consistent with the four general clusters earlier recognized from total artifact distributions (Fig. 9.1a). A very minor discrepancy between the two patterns exists in Area B where the total artifact density peak (Fig. 9.1a) exists in the neighborhood of Units A2/3 while the total core density peak (Fig. 9.3a) occurs in the neighborhood of Units A3/4. The roof-fall zone has the same cluster pattern for total artifacts and total cores and corroborates the 'dumping area' hypothesis since 70.0 percent (21 of 30) of all cores and flake cores were heavily patinated in this area compared to 12 percent (3 of 25) in the other three areas. In addition, 87.5 percent (21 of 24) of the heavily patinated cores occur in Area D.

Of interest is the central area of the site around the central hearths (Fig. 9.3a), where cores were absent. Cores exhibit a clear spatial pattern where the highest concentrations are between hearths and the shelter wall or in the roof-fall area. None were found in association with the hearths in the central area of the shelter. Abundant lithic material in this central area (Fig. 9.1a) suggests that the occupants of the site moved cores (perhaps into the so-called dump zone). Cores were certainly moved during their useful life spans and Area C (Fig. 9.3a) was probably involved in initial core reduction activities. The distribution of cores (including flake cores) along with core trimming elements and primary elements, however, might shed more light on this problem. It is known that other two components of the initial core reduction stage, core trimming elements and primary flakes, are equiproportionally distributed across Areas A, B, C, and D (Fig. 9.4, Table 9.2a: p-value = .136). Perhaps, core trimming elements, and to a lesser extent primary flakes, are not moved or tossed into the dumping area as often as cores. This may suggest that these elements remain more often than not in their production location and are good indicators of locations where initial core

reduction took place. The equiproportional hypothesis for initial core reduction elements fails (p-value = .002) due to extreme differences in the proportional occurrence of cores and core trimming elements in area D (Table 9.2a). Also, a much higher percentage contribution (Table 9.3a) of cores, 54.5 percent, than of primary and core trimming elements, 26.2 percent, occurs in Area D. If Areas A, B, and C only are compared, a satisfactory result ensues (p-value = .157). Thus, this difference related to Area D is one of proportion and not one of kind.

The initial core reduction elements show four Floor I concentrations similar to that noticed earlier for cores (Fig. 9.3a). Specifically, the cluster centroids are in Units B6, A3, E1, and F7 associated, clockwise, with Areas A, B, C, and D, respectively. With the exception of the roof-fall area, all density peaks, however small, are in the near vicinity of hearths. The cluster in Area A has a peak density of more than five elements per m^2, out of 18 total elements (Table 9.3a), remains highly dispersed but is within a meter of a back wall hearth in Area B. The cluster in Area B has a peak density of more than 11 elements per m^2, out of 35 total, and has the pattern of a large amorphous medium-high density cluster associated with all of the hearths close to the back wall. Finally, Area C represents, as with cores alone, a smaller but more tightly defined cluster (more than nine elements per m^2 out of 68 total) and has a smaller but more concentrated high-density peak associated with the hearth close to the dripline and side wall of the shelter. Area B and C each possess 35.5 percent of all core trimming elements (Table 9.2a) with the remainder equally split between Areas A and D. Also, Area C has the highest frequencies (outside of Area D) of cores, core trimming elements, and primary elements. This supports the conclusion that Area C is strongly associated with initial core reduction activities. Areas A and B are represented by initial core reduction elements but in much lower frequency, relative to Area C. Area A is the weakest of the three areas in initial core reduction elements. Tables 9.3a–b illustrate the differences in the composition of initial core reduction elements. It is easily noted that Area C (Table 9.3a) has the highest percentage of primary and core trimming elements (40.8 percent) and the highest

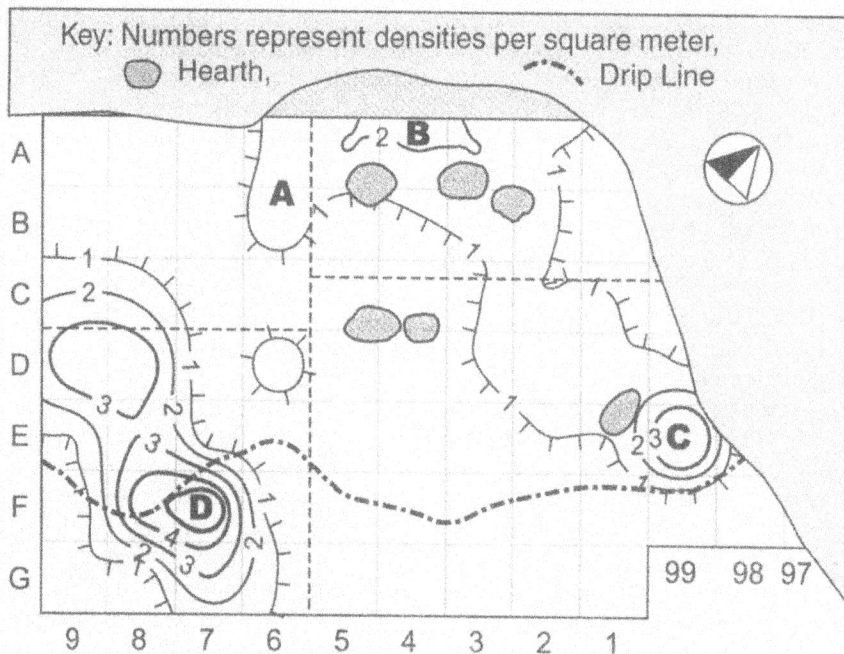

a) Floor I

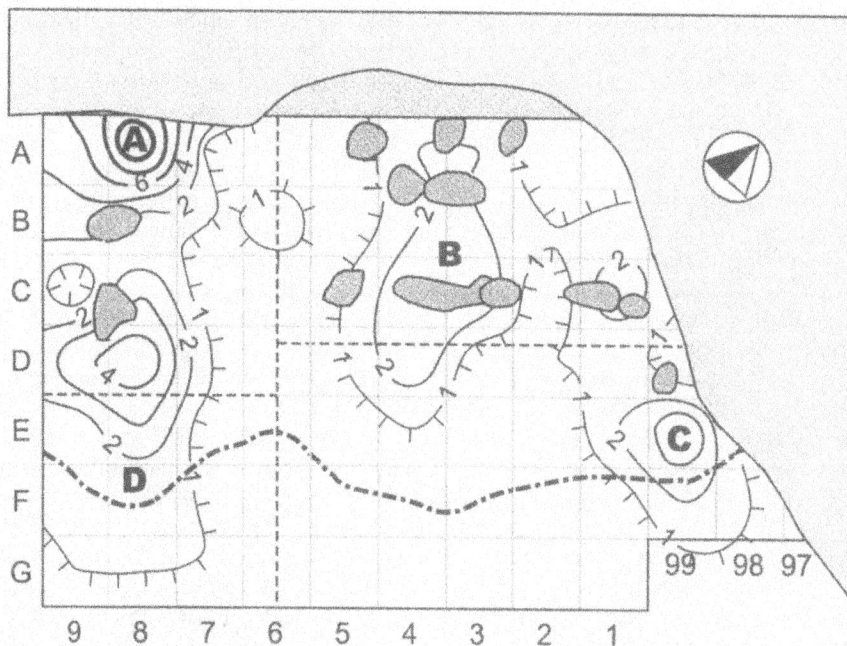

b) Floor II

Figure 9.3 Spatial frequencies of cores and cores-on-flakes by floor at Tor Faraj: **a**, Floor I; **b**, Floor II. *Note*: In Figure 9.3 the numbers represent densities per square meter, and summary sample size data are given in Table 9.1

Table 9.2 Debitage class frequencies and percentages by area for Floors I and II

Note: **a** Floor I: Levels 160-70 (p-values in parentheses for Area D are excluded); **b** Floor II: Levels 180-95 (p-values in parentheses are for Area D excluded)

a.

	Area A (west)		Area B (north)		Area C (east)		Area D (south)		Class total	
	Count	Row %	Count	Row %	Count	Row %	Count	Row %	Count	Row %
Core or flake core	2	3.6	8	14.5	15	27.3	30	54.5	55	100
Core trimming element	4	12.9	11	35.5	11	35.5	5	16.1	31	100
Primary element	12	12.1	16	16.2	42	42.4	29	29.3	99	100
Flake	47	11.8	59	14.8	144	36.1	149	37.3	399	100
Blade	27	16.1	21	12.5	72	42.9	48	28.6	168	100
Levallois flake	13	26.5	10	20.4	13	26.5	13	26.5	49	100
Levallois blade	3	14.3	3	14.3	6	28.6	9	42.9	21	100
Burin spall	2	18.2	3	27.3	5	45.5	1	9.1	11	100
Total	110	13.2	131	15.7	308	37.0	284	34.1	833	100

Notes: All categories: Likelihood Ratio Statistic = 44.1; df = 21; Monte Carlo Exact Test p-value = .003 (.231)
Initial red'n: Likelihood Ratio Statistic = 27.5; df = 9; Monte Carlo Exact Test p-value = .002 (.157)
Later red'n: Likelihood Ratio Statistic = 16.3; df = 9; Monte Carlo Exact Test p-value = .066 (.134)
Cores and flake cores: Likelihood Ratio Statistic = 6.71; df = 3; Exact Test p-value = .106 (.081)
Primary and CTEs: Likelihood Ratio Statistic = 5.80; df = 3; Exact Test p-value = .136 (.174)
Flakes and blades: Likelihood Ratio Statistic = 6.16; df = 3; Exact Test p-value = .106 (.348)
Levallois debitage: Likelihood Ratio Statistic = 2.57; df = 3; Exact Test p-value = .463 (.704)
Lev. vs. non-lev. elts: Likelihood Ratio Statistic = 6.85; df = 3; Exact Test p-value = .080 (.041)

b.

	Area A (west)		Area B (north)		Area C (east)		Area D (south)		Class total	
	Count	Row %	Count	Row %	Count	Row %	Count	Row %	Count	Row %
Core or flake core	35	44.9	16	20.5	18	23.1	9	11.5	78	100
Core trimming element	11	34.4	9	28.1	11	34.4	1	3.1	32	100
Primary element	62	33.9	68	37.2	44	24.0	9	4.9	183	100
Flake	271	41.0	182	27.5	150	22.7	58	8.8	661	100
Blade	106	44.0	47	19.5	57	23.7	31	12.9	241	100
Levallois flake	25	27.5	36	39.6	18	19.8	12	13.2	91	100
Levallois blade	14	41.2	13	38.2	5	14.7	2	5.9	34	100
Burin spall	6	35.3	5	29.4	5	29.4	1	5.9	17	100
Total	530	39.6	376	28.1	308	23.0	123	9.2	1337	100

Notes: All categories: Likelihood Ratio Statistic = 41.9; df = 21; Monte Carlo Exact Test p-value = .006 (.012)
Initial red'n: Likelihood Ratio Statistic = 19.6; df = 12; Monte Carlo Exact Test p-value = .089 (.184)
Later red'n: Likelihood Ratio Statistic = 32.2; df = 9; Monte Carlo Exact Test p-value = .000 (.001)
Cores and flake cores: Likelihood Ratio Statistic = 1.12; df = 3; Exact Test p-value = .781 (.596)
Primary and CTEs: Likelihood Ratio Statistic = 1.92; df = 3; Exact Test p-value = .618 (.428)
Flakes and blades: Likelihood Ratio Statistic = 8.02; df = 3; Exact Test p-value = .046 (.087)
Levallois debitage: Likelihood Ratio Statistic = 3.13; df = 3; Exact Test p-value = .390 (.449)
Lev. vs. non-Lev. elts: Likelihood Ratio Statistic = 11.5; df = 3; Exact Test p-value = .010 (.004)

Table 9.3 Percentages within reduction sequence groups and areas by floor

Note: **a** Floor I: percentages relative to artifact reduction sequence groups; **b** Floor I: percentages relative to site areas; **c** Floor II: percentages relative to artifact reduction sequence groups; **d** Floor II: percentages relative to site areas

a.

	Area A (west)		Area B (north)		Area C (east)		Area D (south)		Group total	
	Count	Row %	Count	Row %	Count	Row %	Count	Row %	Count	Row %
Cores and flake cores	2	3.6	8	14.5	15	27.3	30	54.5	55	100
Primary and core trimming elements	16	12.3	27	20.8	53	40.8	34	26.2	130	100
Flakes and blades	74	13.1	80	14.1	216	38.1	197	34.7	567	100
Levallois debitage	16	22.9	13	18.6	19	27.1	22	31.4	70	100
Subtotal	108	13.1	128	15.6	303	36.9	283	34.4	822	100

b.

	Area A (west)		Area B (north)		Area C (east)		Area D (south)		Subtotal	
	Count	Col %	Count	Col %	Count	Col %	Count	Col %	Count	Col %
Cores and flake cores	2	1.9	8	6.3	15	5.0	30	10.6	55	6.7
Primary and core trimming elements	16	14.8	27	21.1	53	17.5	34	12.0	130	15.8
Flakes and blades	74	68.5	80	62.5	216	71.3	197	69.6	567	69.0
Levallois debitage	16	14.8	13	10.2	19	6.3	22	7.8	70	8.5
Area total	108	100	128	100	303	100	283	100	822	100

c.

	Area A (west)		Area B (north)		Area C (east)		Area D (south)		Group total	
	Count	Row %	Count	Row %	Count	Row %	Count	Row %	Count	Row %
Cores and flake cores	35	44.9	16	20.5	18	23.1	0	11.5	78	100
Primary and core trimming elements	73	34.0	77	35.8	55	25.6	10	4.7	215	100
Flakes and blades	377	41.8	229	25.4	207	22.9	89	9.9	902	100
Levallois debitage	39	31.2	49	39.2	23	18.4	14	11.2	125	100
Subtotal	524	39.7	371	28.1	303	23.0	122	9.2	1320	100

d.

	Area A (west)		Area B (north)		Area C (east)		Area D (south)		Subtotal	
	Count	Col %	Count	Col %	Count	Col %	Count	Col %	Count	Col %
Cores and flake cores	35	6.7	16	4.3	18	5.9	9	7.4	78	5.9
Primary and core trimming elements	73	13.9	77	20.8	55	18.2	10	8.2	215	16.3
Flakes and blades	377	71.9	229	61.7	207	68.3	89	73.0	902	68.3
Levallois debitage	39	7.4	49	13.2	23	7.6	14	11.5	125	9.5
Area total	524	100	371	100	303	100	122	100	1320	100

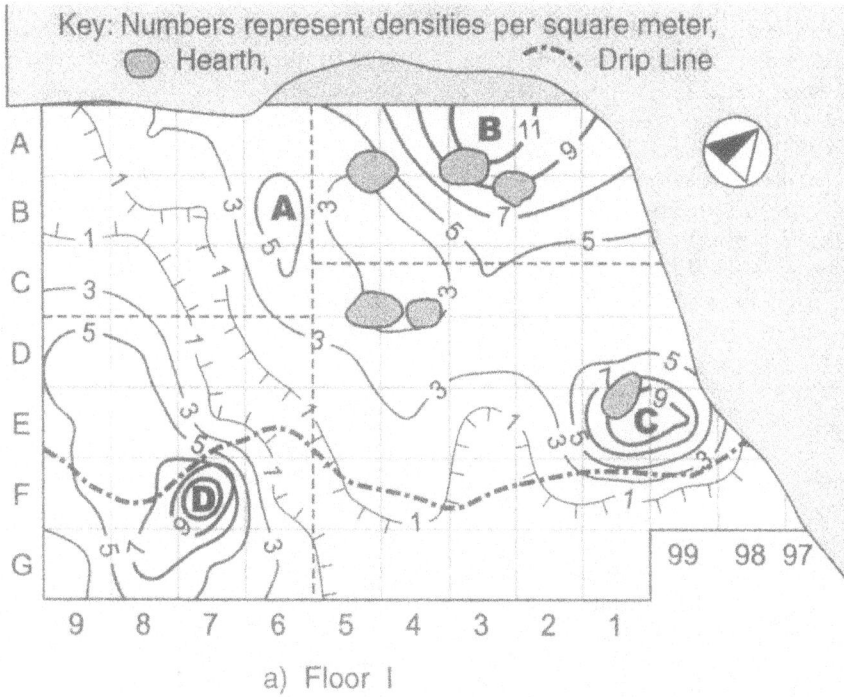

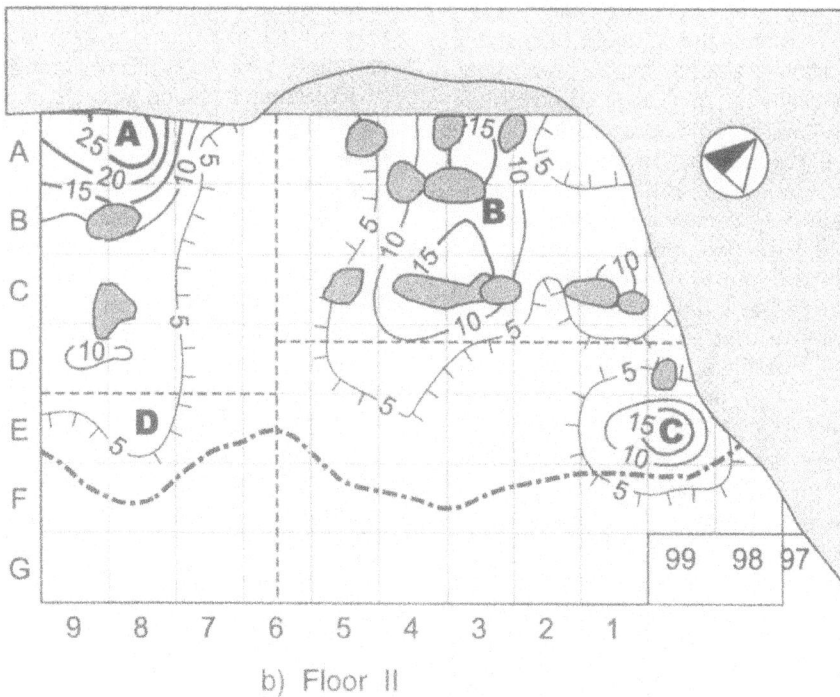

Figure 9.4 Spatial frequencies of initial core reduction elements by floor at Tor Faraj: **a**, Floor I; **b**, Floor II.
Note: In Figure 9.4 the numbers represent densities per square meter, and sample size data are given in Tables 9.2 and 9.3

percentage of cores (outside of Area D). In fact, Area C is also highest in total debitage, outside of Area D. Area C is almost certainly a major area of debitage production. Areas B and C, on the other hand, have almost the same percentages (Table 9.3b) of initial core reduction elements relative to their total assemblages. The primary difference between Areas B and C is in the intensity to which initial core reduction activities took place. The study in Chapter 5 (based on chips alone), also supports these general observations.

Middle phase core reduction activities

Flakes, blades, Levallois flakes, and Levallois blades correspond to debitage elements removed from a core following the phase of initial core reduction. It is therefore useful to compare the frequencies of these debitage types across the areas of the site. In this case, the flake and blade classes are combined into a single category of non-Levallois debitage since their areal proportions (Table 9.2a) are alike ($p = .106$). The Levallois debitage classes are also combined into a single category of Levallois debitage since their areal proportions are statistically alike ($p = .463$). Although the raw percentages (Table 9.2a) indicate more Levallois flakes in Area A and more Levallois Blades in Area D, the differences are insignificant, since the sample sizes are small. The secondary reduction phase elements, all Levallois and non-Levallois flakes and blades, are in fact equiproportionally distributed (p-value = .066) across the four areas. Based on this result, it might be expected that Levallois debitage and non-Levallois would occupy the same spatial loci in roughly the same relative frequencies. In fact, these expectations are only partially met. The distribution of all flakes and blades (Fig. 9.5a) and the distribution of all Levallois flakes and blades (Fig. 9.6a) warrant two general observations. First, both distributions demonstrate four major clusters with the three in Areas A, B, and D at the same loci defining the general overall patterns discussed previously. Second, Area C does not possess the same pattern identified previously for other artifact classes. Area C, for Levallois debitage, will be returned to following a brief discussion of the first point.

The major centroids for all areas, excluding Levallois debitage in Area C, are located in Units C6, A2/3, E99, and D7 for Areas A, B, C, and D, respectively. All these clusters exhibit the same patterns discussed earlier; A is a midline cluster situated in close proximity to the midline hearths in Area C and B is a back wall cluster amorphously distributed between the back wall hearths and the back wall itself. The cluster pattern in Area C, relative to non-Levallois flakes and blades, also conforms to the previously discussed patterns for total artifacts and initial core reduction elements. It may be noted that the toss and dump area has the same general pattern although Levallois debitage might be deposited here less frequently (Figs 9.5a and 9.6a). In general, the pattern exhibited for non-Levallois debitage is in strict conformance with the previously discussed patterns. This is not surprising since flakes and blades (Table 9.3b) make up the bulk of the total assemblage (69.0 percent of all debitage and cores). It should also be noted that Areas C and D, together, possess the greater majority of flakes and blades (72.8 percent–Table 9.3a). Specifically, Areas A and B have approximately 13 to 14 percent each of all flakes and blades while the percentages for Areas C and D range from 35 to 38 percent. It should be noted, thus far, that cores, initial core reduction elements, and flakes and blades all have each produced consistent spatial patterning. The patterns are consistent relative to relationships between clusters and hearths, the positioning of clusters relative to hearths, walls and dripline of the shelter, and, most significantly, the positioning of the cluster centroids. Variation between clusters has been limited to abundance and relative frequency differences.

Levallois debitage, on the other hand, shows a significant variation on the previous theme (cf. Figs 9.1a and 9.6a). The major exception to the previous patterns is in Area C where the dominant concentration of Levallois debitage (Fig. 9.6a) is centered in Unit D2, between the side wall hearth and the hearths in the center of the shelter. It is possible that the central hearths had functions separate from the back wall and side wall hearths. Note also that Area C minor concentrations occur in the corresponding locations of major concentrations for the other comparative debitage group (cf. Units E99 and D2 in Figs 9.5a and 9.6a). It should also be noted that a lower concentration of Levallois pieces, relative to

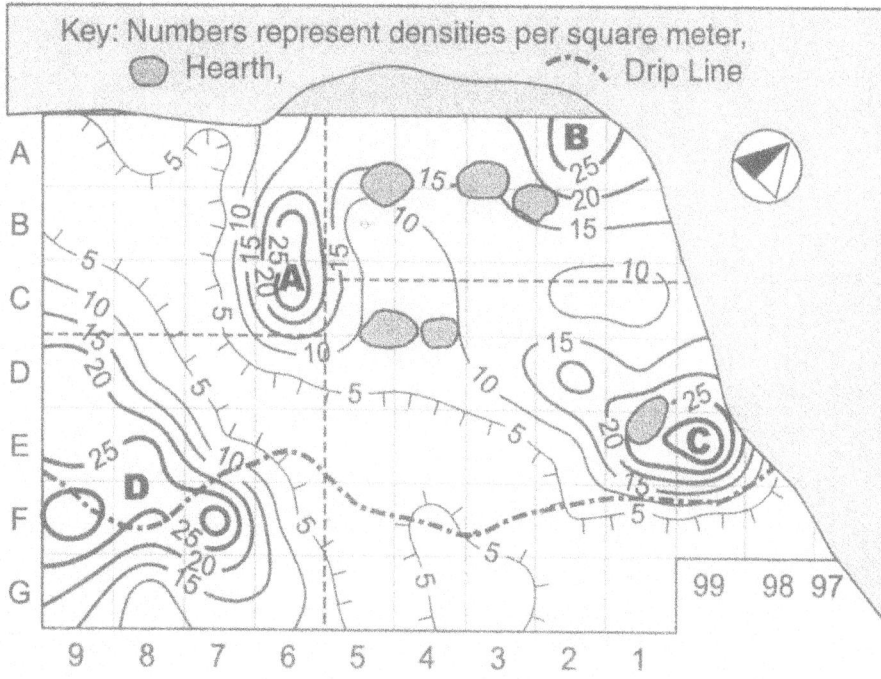

a) Floor I

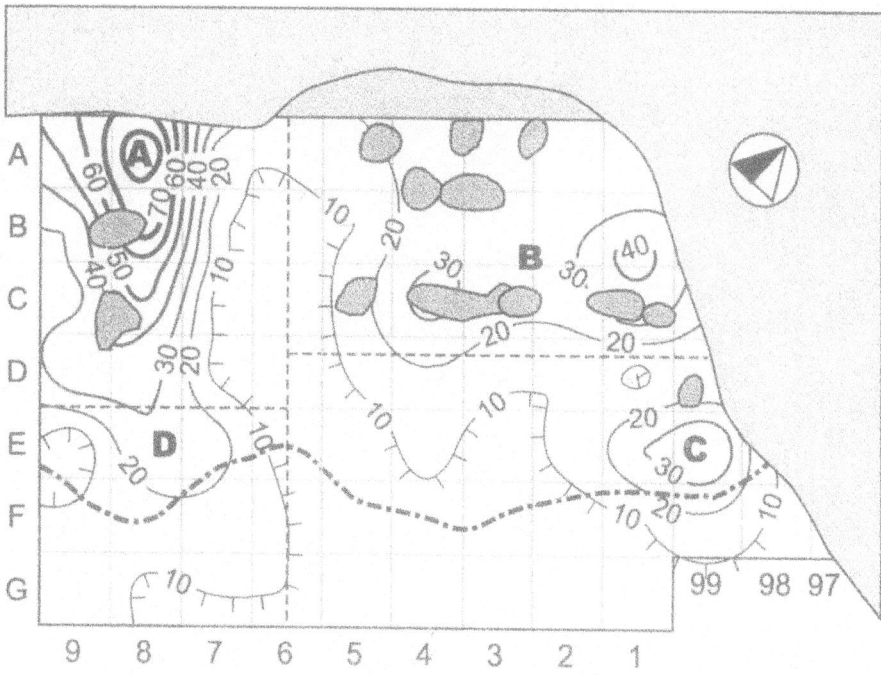

b) Floor II

Figure 9.5   Spatial frequencies of all non-Levallois debitage by floor at Tor Faraj: **a**, Floor I; **b**, Floor II. *Note:* In Figure 9.5 the numbers represent densities per square meter, and sample size data are given in Tables 9.2 and 9.3

Key: Numbers represent densities per square meter, Hearth, Drip Line

a) Floor I

b) Floor II

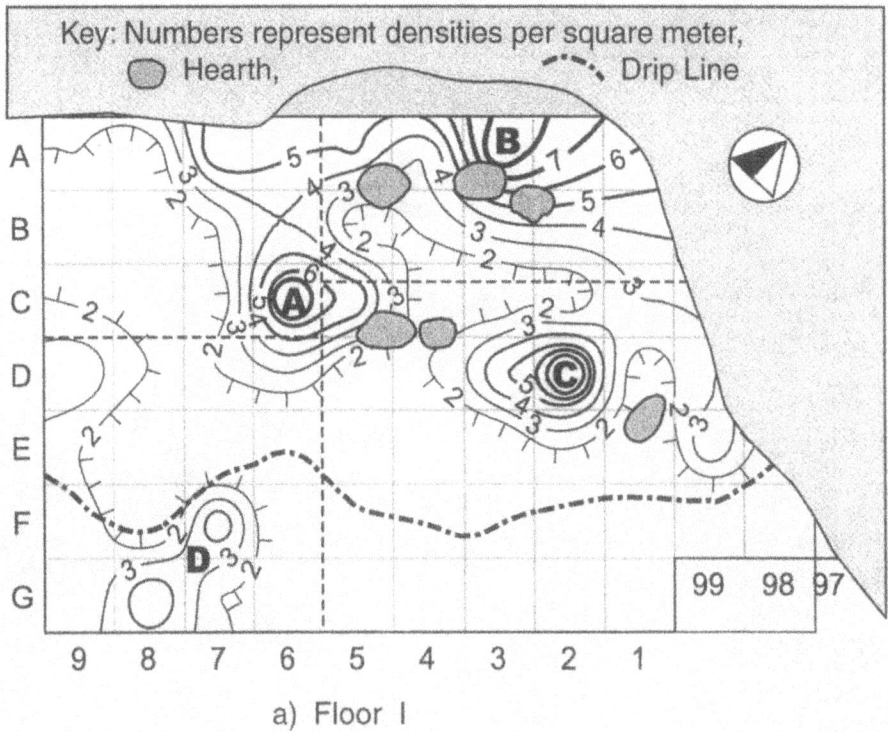

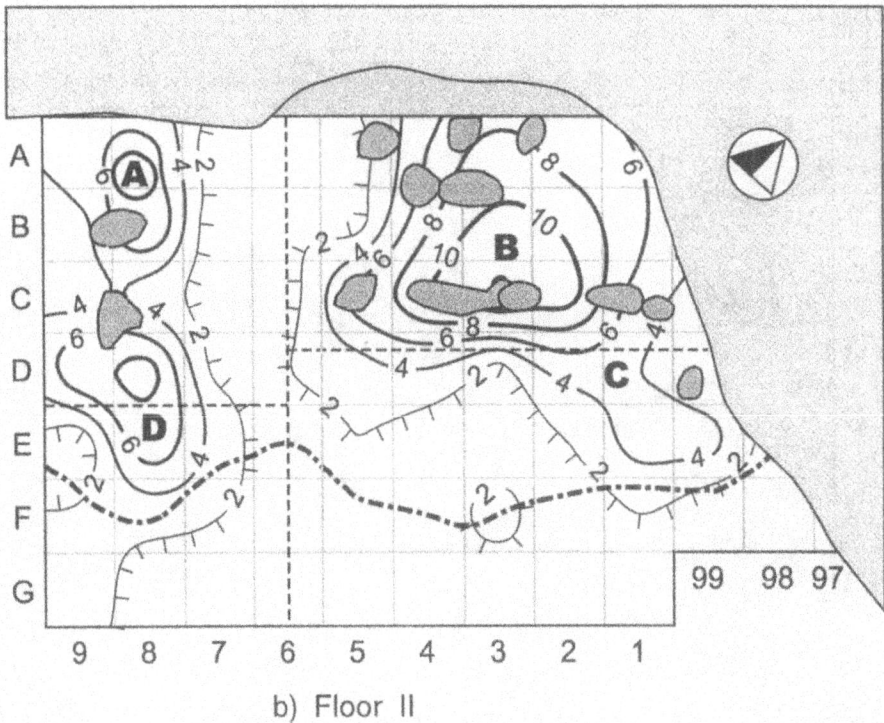

Figure 9.6 Spatial frequencies of all Levallois debitage by floor at Tor Faraj: **a**, Floor I; **b**, Floor II. *Note*: In Figure 9.6 the numbers represent densities per square meter, and sample size data are given in Tables 9.2 and 9.3

non-Levallois pieces, is apparent along the dripline (*cf.* Figs 9.5a and 9.6a). This may be the result of an emphasis placed on the production of Levallois points by the inhabitants of the site. Although there are spatial differences within the areas for debitage classes, it is thought that any differences between areas are primarily related to differential dumping of core and debitage elements into Area D. This is supported (Table 9.2a: *p*-value = .231) by the hypothesis of equiproportionality across Areas A, B, and C for all core and debitage classes. In general, the back wall and side wall concentrations seem to be somewhat involved at all stages of core reduction and are adjacent to hearths. The midline concentrations, on the other hand, seem to be poorer in their representation of cores (a possible reflection of core movement), show elements of initial and middle phases of core reduction and are richer in Levallois debitage. It should be clear, at this point, that several interpretations are possible. The spatial distributions of tools should help to clarify the situation.

Locations of tools

Levallois points, representing a late stage of the core reduction process, might be relevant to questions concerning their production and use locations. It is not unusual for Middle Paleolithic peoples expediently to produce tools, as they are needed, leaving them at the location where they were used (Hietala 1983; Marks 1983a). As will be seen later, tools were extensively used at Tor Faraj so it is of critical concern to note their spatial patterns, if any. Both retouched and unretouched Levallois points (Table 9.4a) were combined into a single category since they strongly co-vary, proportionally, by area (*p* = .938). The only area without a significant presence of points is the roof-fall area where only 12 percent (Fig. 9.5a) are located. Otherwise, Area C has approximately twice as many Levallois points as Areas A and B (42 percent compared to 20 percent and 26 percent). The density distribution of Levallois points (Fig. 9.7a) shows a new distributional form entirely. There are two major clusters, one centered at A3 in Area B and the other at C5 in Area C. Both of these clusters are immediately adjacent to hearths. The cluster in Area C, in the middle of the

shelter, is immediately adjacent to the other three areas and consequently contributes to the numerical frequencies for all areas. Also, a small cluster occurs in Area A (Unit A7), immediately adjacent to the back wall of the shelter, and the hearth along the side wall does not seem to be strongly associated with Levallois points. As will be shown later, there are points in low density associated with the side wall hearth. It can be concluded, however, that heavy densities of Levallois points occur along the back wall of the shelter and in the middle of the shelter. Elsewhere, the density of Levallois points is low.

Although the numerical frequencies (Table 9.4a) suggest twice as many Levallois points in Area C as in Areas A and B, the surfer map (Fig. 9.7a) does not realistically translate this information. In this case, the numerical frequencies are false indicators of cluster locations and cluster densities based on the arbitrariness of the definitions used to define the areas of the floor (Chapter 8). It should be recalled that the four areas were defined largely on the basis of the distributions of all artifacts (Figs 8.8a and 9.1a). There is a clear lack of conformance between the distributions suggested by Figures 9.1a and 9.7a. Perhaps, in retrospect, the hearth placements, in conjunction with the overall density distribution, should have been used for defining the concentration areas. It was thought at the time that the concentrations of lithics should simply define the areas to avoid tying the data to the hearths. In any case, it really does not matter since the spatial distributions are undoubtedly the result of many forces, some of which are acting in concert with one another and others in opposition to one another. The notion of unambiguous, non-overlapping, activity areas is a poorly chosen concept foreign to the behavior of individuals undergoing a series of socially complex activities associated with the demands of procuring a living in an equally complex landscape. In this case, the distributions of flakes and blades, on the one hand, and Levallois points, on the other, present spatial clusters that are quite different. Other tool types might also shed some light on the complexity of the spatial information presented on Floor 1 of Tor Faraj.

The spatial interaction between Levallois points and other tools is interesting since most

Table 9.4 Tool type frequencies by area for Floors I and II

Note: **a** Floor I: Levels 160–70 (*p*-values in parentheses for Area D are excluded); **b**. Floor II: Levels 180-95 (*p*-values in parentheses for Area D are excluded)

a.

	Area A (west)		Area B (north)		Area C (east)		Area D (south)		Total	
		Row		Row		Row		Row		Row
	Count	%	Count	%	Count	%	Count	%	Count	%
Lev. point ret.	2	28.6	2	28.6	2	28.6	1	14.3	7	100
Lev. point unret.	8	18.6	11	25.6	19	44.2	5	11.6	43	100
Side-scraper			1	25.0			3	75.0	4	100
End-scraper					1	33.3	2	66.7	3	100
Burin	1	5.6	3	16.7	8	44.4	6	33.3	18	100
Truncated piece							2	100	2	100
Notch	1	16.7			1	16.7	4	66.7	6	100
Denticulate			1	33.3	1	33.3	1	33.3	3	100
Retouched piece	4	5.6	6	8.5	20	28.2	41	57.7	71	100
Varia					2	100			2	100
Total	16	10.1	24	15.1	54	34.0	65	40.9	159	100

Notes: All tool types Likelihood Ratio Statistic = 52.4; df = 27; Monte Carlo Exact Test *p*-value = .002 (.818)
　　　Levallois points: Likelihood Ratio Statistic = .710; df = 3; Exact Test *p*-value = .938 (.853)
　　　All other tools Likelihood Ratio Statistic = 20.2; df = 21; Monte Carlo Exact Test *p*-value = .543 (.791)

b.

	Area A (west)		Area B (north)		Area C (east)		Area D (south)		Group total	
		Row		Row		Row		Row		Row
	Count	%	Count	%	Count	%	Count	%	Count	%
Lev. point ret.	4	25.0	3	18.8	9	56.3			16	100
Lev. point unret.	5	14.7	21	61.8	8	23.5			34	100
Side-scraper	2	25.0			2	25.0	4	50.0	8	100
End-scraper	1	50.0	1	50.0					2	100
Burin	15	41.7	12	33.3	7	19.4	2	5.6	36	100
Truncated piece	1	33.3	1	33.3	1	33.3			3	100
Notch	13	54.2	1	4.2	6	25.0	4	16.7	24	100
Denticulate	2	28.6	2	28.6	2	28.6	1	14.3	7	100
Retouched piece	52	43.7	25	21.0	34	28.6	8	6.7	119	100
Varia	5	62.5	2	25.0			1	12.5	8	100
Total	100	38.9	68	26.5	69	26.8	20	7.8	257	100

Notes: All tool types: Likelihood Ratio Statistic = 66.9; df = 27; Monte Carlo Exact Test *p*-value = .000 (.000)
　　　Levallois points: Likelihood Ratio Statistic = 8.73; df = 2; Exact Test *p*-value = .021 (.021)
　　　All other tools: Likelihood Ratio Statistic = 30.8; df = 21; Monte Carlo Exact Test *p*-value = .116 (.343)

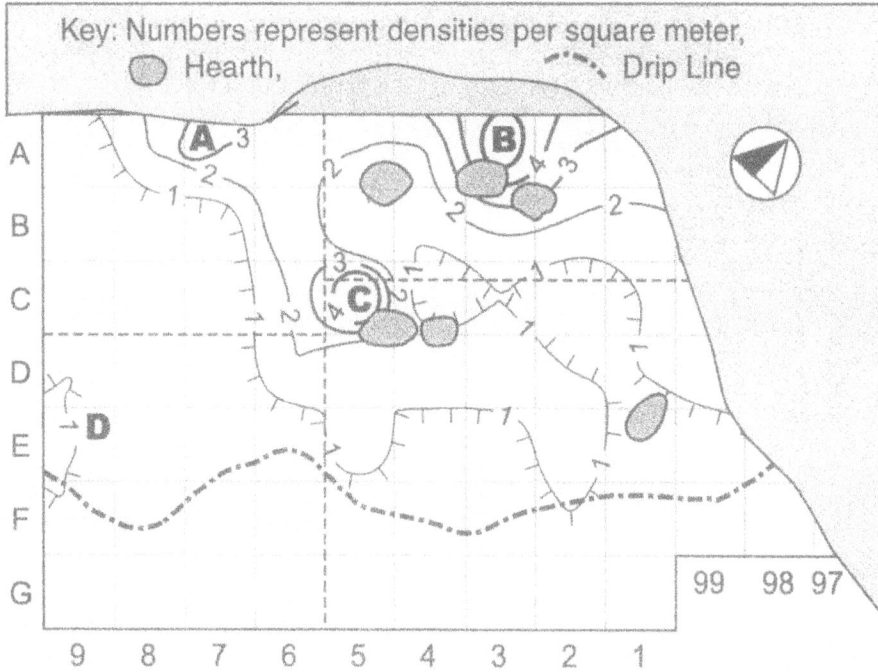

a) Floor I

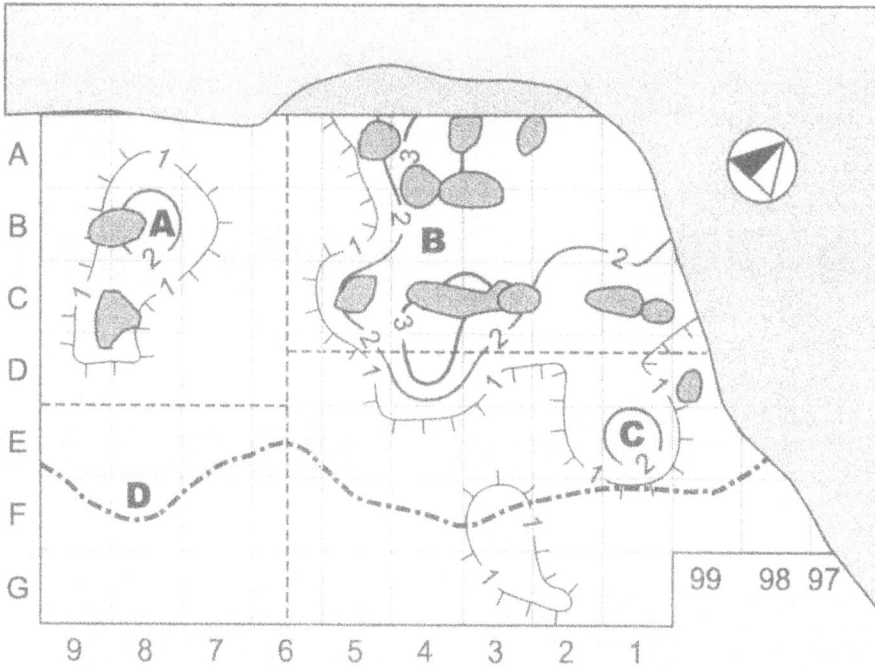

b) Floor II

Figure 9.7 Spatial frequencies of all Levallois points by floor at Tor Faraj: **a**, Floor I; **b**, Floor II. *Note*: In Figure 9.7 the numbers represent densities per square meter, and sample size data are given in Tables 9.4 and 9.5

of the other tool classes are spatially segregating from Levallois points. Table 9.4a illustrates, for example, that few Levallois points find their way into the discard zone (Area D) but that a minimum of 33 percent of all other tool classes do. Overall (Table 9.5a), 12.0 percent of Levallois points are in Area D compared to 54.1 percent for all other tools. Levallois points were certainly a valuable commodity of the inhabitants of the site. While only one-third of the burins and denticulates are found in the roof-fall area, approximately 60 percent or more of the other tool types find their way into the dump pile. This may, or may not, have something to do with the value that the inhabitants of the site placed on individual artifacts associated with Middle Paleolithic tool types, a modern creation.

In any case, Levallois points must be differentially distributed from the other tool types. Overall, all tools overwhelmingly reject the proposition of areal equiproportionality (Table 9.4a: p-value = .002). Excluding Area D from the calculation changes the p-value to a perfectly acceptable one (.000 to .818). Also, all of the tools (excepting Levallois points) strongly support the proposition of areal equiproportionality (p=.543) for all four areas. Retouched pieces, the most numerous tool type, is a typical representative of the other tools. This tool type is represented by 57.7 percent (41 of 71 total) of its members in Area D (Table 9.4a) with only 43.3 percent (30 of 71 total) in the other three areas. It can be spatially seen (Fig. 9.9a) that there is essentially only one cluster (in the roof-fall area) with the remaining retouched pieces spottily identified in the remainder of the excavated area. A scatter diagram is best for seeing small-scale and small sample size variation. In this case (Fig. 9.9a), it can be seen that there is not a strong relationship between the positioning of hearths and the location of retouched pieces.

Burins, on the other hand, when investigated as a single category of spatial information, are equally uninformative. But, when combined with burin spalls, they inform positively on the proposition that they are made on the spot (Fig. 9.10a), when needed, are used and then oftentimes left behind. This is also supported by the observation that 33.3 percent of the burins (Table 9.4a) are found in Area D while only 9.1 percent of the burin spalls (Table 9.2a) are found there. Also, it

may be noticed, in general, that burins and burin spalls align themselves very nicely with the positions of the hearths.

Finally, a point plot of Levallois points and notched pieces (Fig. 9.11a) shows their virtually complete segregation but more importantly shows the nature of the point distribution as it relates to the position of hearths. Outside of the major roof-fall area, primarily used as a discard area, it can be seen that most of the points are in close proximity to hearths. Specifically, Area C has a major cluster of points about its central hearths and a lighter, more dispersed distribution in the vicinity of the side wall hearth. Area B has a strong cluster between the back wall hearths and the back wall itself. Area A has a few points, some adjacent to the back wall and some close to the central and back wall hearths. Note how the areal frequencies of Levallois points would substantially change in Table 9.4a if the four areas were redefined to reflect the reality of their concentrations rather than the reality of all artifacts. Nevertheless, the frequencies of other tool types would also change in the same directions, consistent with patterns observed in Table 9.5a and 9.5b. Specifically, Levallois points and other tools are strongly segregating (Table 9.5a) and the 'Levallois point' to 'other tool' ratio is highest in Areas A and B and smaller in Area C. Clearly, Levallois points are not found as often in initial core reduction areas as they are in other areas but they are, in general, still found in association with hearths. Spatially, unretouched Levallois points and retouched Levallois points do not even differ at the very local level (Fig. 9.12a). Finally, it should be noted that Levallois debitage clusters (Fig. 9.6a) are found in Units 1 and 2 meters from the central hearths (in Units C6 and D2). However, a conspicuously large number of Levallois points are found in adjacent units or between the two Levallois debitage clusters, in or adjacent to the central hearths. This suggests that Levallois points may have been used in different locations than where they were produced.

Summary for Floor I

The data from Floor I support several conclusions regarding the nature of site structure in

Table 9.5 Percentages and frequencies within tool groups and areas by floor

Note: **a** Floor I: percentages relative to tool groups; **b** Floor I: percentages relative to site areas; **c** Floor II: percentages relative to tool groups; **d** Floor II: percentages relative to site areas

a.

	Area A (west)		Area B (north)		Area C (east)		Area D (south)		Group total	
	Count	Row %	Count	Row %	Count	Row %	Count	Row %	Count	Row %
Levallois points	10	20.0	13	26.0	21	42.0	6	12.0	50	100
Other tools	6	5.5	11	10.1	33	30.3	59	54.1	109	100
Subtotal	16	10.1	24	15.1	54	34.0	65	40.9	159	100

b.

	Area A (west)		Area B (north)		Area C (east)		Area D (south)		Subtotal	
	Count	%	Count	%	Count	%	Count	%	Count	%
Levallois points	10	62.5	13	54.2	21	38.9	6	9.2	50	31.4
Other tools	6	37.5	11	45.8	33	61.1	59	90.8	109	68.6
Area total	16	100	24	100	54	100	65	100	159	100

c.

	Area A (west)		Area B (north)		Area C (east)		Area D (south)		Group total	
	Count	Row %	Count	Row %	Count	Row %	Count	Row %	Count	Row %
Levallois points	9	18.0	24	48.0	17	34.0			50	100
Other tools	91	44.0	44	21.3	52	25.1	20	9.7	207	100
Subtotal	100	38.9	68	26.5	69	26.8	20	7.8	257	100

d.

	Area A (west)		Area B (north)		Area C (east)		Area D (south)		Subtotal	
	Count	%	Count	%	Count	%	Count	%	Count	%
Levallois points	9	9.0	24	35.3	17	24.6			50	19.5
Other tools	91	91.0	44	64.7	52	75.4	20	100	207	80.5
Area total	100	100	68	100	69	100	20	100	257	100

the upper levels of Tor Faraj. First and foremost is that the material culture as represented through lithics is, in general, firmly tied to the locations of the hearths. Second, there is strong evidence that at least one hearth locus (side wall hearth) was strongly involved with the initial reduction of cores. This is seen through the strong presence of initial core reduction elements. Third, that cores were moved in their lifetimes is seen through the heavy discard rate into Area D and the presence of strong debitage production in Area A. The production of Levallois debitage in Area A and in a locus of Area C between the side wall and central hearths also suggests a movement of cores directed toward the production of tools (specifically Levallois points). Fourth, there is strong evidence that opportunistic lithic reduction, use, and discard occurred; the distributions of burins and burin spalls provide evidence for one example. Some artifacts were preferred over others with undesirable elements, perhaps use exhausted, discarded in the roof-fall zone. Fifth, there is strong evidence that one area (Area B) was involved with all stages of lithic reduction including the production of tools (Levallois points) in the near vicinity of hearths. It may be noted that this area was not weak in any of the lithic categories represented by more than a few pieces. Sixth, Levallois points are generally found in the vicinity of hearths and some may have been produced in other locations. Evidence is provided by the distributions of Levallois points, on the one hand, and Levallois debitage, on the other, around the central hearths. In general, strong evidence exists for a structured set of activities tethered to the hearths. Ancillary information would certainly help for improved behavioral interpretations. Fortunately, such information does exist for Floor II.

Floor II analysis

Floor II consists of the collapsed Levels 180 to 195 where four areas (Fig. 8.8b) were defined for the occupation surface based on the distributions of initial core reduction elements and all artifacts (Fig. 9.1b). Again, the four areas differ dramatically in their relationships to the different natural and cultural features.

Area D is still a zone associated with roof-fall (rocks), and the dripline, without the presence of a hearth. Area A is associated with numerous rocks (Fig. 8.6e–h) and two hearths, one within 1.5m of the back wall and another at the midline. Area B, the largest activity area, includes numerous hearths, five of which are close to the back wall and five others midway between the back wall and the dripline. Two of the midline hearths are also close to the side wall. It also contains a few tabular pieces of rock, which must have been manuports since there is no other mechanism to explain how they might have gotten there. Finally, Area C has large numbers of rocks, possesses a single hearth in its corner close to the side wall and has the dripline running midway through it.

The distribution of all artifacts (Fig. 9.1b) clearly supports the areal definitions. It should be noticed, however, that Area A has peak artifact densities, up to 120 artifacts per square meter, and then the concentration simply drifts toward the dripline with much lower densities in Area D. The high-density cluster in Area A is between the hearths and the back wall. Note that there is a band of very low density separating Areas A and D from Areas B and C. This band is reasonably well defined by column 6 of the excavated units. Area C has a small side wall cluster of approximately 60 artifacts per square meter between its side wall hearth and the dripline. Most of Area C, particularly along the dripline, has small numbers of artifacts. Area B, on the other hand, is associated with numerous hearths and has broadly spread concentrations with a large area including between 40 and 60 artifacts per square meter. All the hearths in Area B have reasonable artifact concentrations associated with them. Throughout Floor II, it should be noted that each of the major density peaks is either on or adjacent to a hearth. Based on total artifact density, Area D does not seem to include a cluster of its own, unlike Floor I. It should be remarked, however, that the occupations at Tor Faraj associated with Floor II preceded the major brow collapse. Nevertheless, the second living floor is still related to roof-fall in the sense that sediments were entrapped behind the rocks, allowing the formation of nearly level surfaces upon which the occupants engaged in activities of various sorts (Chapter 8). Like Floor I, the hearths present two general patterns: hearths close to and paralleling the back wall and hearths paralleling and adjacent to the midline of the shelter. The hearths along the midline break into three subsets: close to the side wall, in the center of the shelter, and far from the side wall. One hearth is, as in Floor I, near the side wall and close to the dripline.

Heavy patination also seems to be less extreme in Floor II, in contrast to Floor I. The peak heavily patinated artifact densities (Fig. 9.2b) are far less than their corresponding total artifact densities (Fig. 9.1b) in all but area D, where the peak is substantially smaller than the corresponding peak for Floor I (Fig. 9.2a). Note that Areas A and D form two clusters based on heavy patination densities. Overall, 19.8 percent of all artifacts were heavily patinated in Floor II compared to 27.7 percent in Floor I. The primary discard area in Floor II is expected to be Area D, as it was in Floor I. This expectation is seemingly met since 64.0 percent of all debitage, 50.0 percent of all tools, and, in general, 60.1 percent of all artifacts in Area D are heavily patinated. In addition, it will be noticed that the only artifactual cluster that occurs in Area D is the one associated with heavily patinated artifacts. In actuality, the area close to and beyond the dripline is probably a discard area for artifacts. If one calculates heavy patination percentages for cores, debitage, and tools for all artifacts farther from the front of the rockshelter than the midline of row E (see Figs 9.1b and 9.2b), it is found that 13.3 percent of all cores, 31.9 percent of all debitage, and 32.2 percent of all tools are heavily patinated with an overall heavy patination percentage of 31.1 percent. On the other hand, the overall heavy patination percentage for artifacts inside this imaginary line only has a heavy patination percentage of 16.8 percent.

The analytical method used in the discussion of Floor I will be paralleled here in the analysis of Floor II.

Initial core reduction activities

Combining cores and flake cores into a single category for spatial analytic purposes is even more strongly justified in Floor II. The Floor II core and flake core percentages by area are very much alike (Table 9.1c) where the p-value (0.781) strongly supports the hypothesis of areal equiproportionality. Unlike Floor

I which had roughly a 50-50 split between cores and cores-on-flakes (Table 9.1b), there are two flake cores for each core in Floor II (Table 9.1d). This may represent a greater intensity of occupation for Floor II relative to Floor I. The frequency density distribution of the combined core group (Fig. 9.3b) suggests two clusters in Area A, two in Area B, and one in Area C. The dominant cluster in Area A, centered at Unit A8, is located between the back wall hearth and the back wall itself while the minor cluster, centered at Unit D8, is found between the midline hearth and the dripline. The largest cluster in Area B, centered approximately at B/C-3/4, is generally associated with the back wall and central hearths while the smallest cluster, centered at C1, is directly associated with the side wall hearths. Finally, the single cluster in Area C, centered at Unit E99, is adjacent to the side wall hearth but between it and the dripline. Numerically, Area A has the largest number of combined cores (35 for 44.9 percent of the total) while areas B and C have about 22 percent each (Table 9.1c). Note that the major cluster in Area B contributes a few cores to Area C and thus the Area B clusters, in reality, have more cores than are represented by the areal counts (see Fig. 8.9e-h). Area D, the dump zone, is the weakest area relative to core abundance.

The distribution of initial core reduction elements shows a pattern largely in support of the areal definitions and the distribution of cores discussed above. The clusters in Area A (Fig. 9.4b) have the same centroids as the core clusters (Fig. 9.3b) although the size of the minor cluster is much smaller. There are two clusters in Area B (one centered in Unit A3 and the other at C3). The two clusters together form a much larger cluster, embracing the back wall and central hearths. As in the core cluster for this area, some of the initial core reduction elements overlap into Area C. Finally, there are two side wall clusters with size and shape characteristics virtually identical to the core clusters. Primary flakes and core trimming elements are equiproportionally distributed by area (Table 9.2b: p-value = .618). More importantly, all the initial core reduction elements support the proposition (p-value = .089). Numerically, three observations may be noted from the frequencies and percentages of artifacts by area (Table 9.3c, d).

First, the numbers and percentages of initial core reduction elements in Area D are far lower than the post-roof-fall values (*cf.* Table 9.3a to Table 9.3c). Second, the relative composition of initial core trimming elements in Areas A, B, and C are very similar. Third, the intensity of initial core reduction seems to be strongest in Area A and weakest in Area C. This is not surprising given the nature of the clusters. Although numerical data for the side wall cluster in Area B is not given, it should be reasonably clear that its percentage composition is very similar to the Area C side wall cluster composition although its numerical abundance will be much smaller (see Fig. 8.9e–h). In general, all the clusters indicate the presence of initial core reduction with differences only in the intensity of the activity.

Middle Phase core reduction activities

Although blades and flakes are not equi-proportionally distributed across the four areas (Table 9.2b), the *p*-value (.046) is not only influenced by the large sample size (902 total), but is also influenced by Area D to some extent. Removing Area D from the calculation improves the *p*-value to .087, an acceptable value, given the very large sample size. Thus flakes and blades can reasonably be combined into a single group. The Levallois debitage classes can also be combined into a single group (Table 9.2b) since the hypothesis of areal equiproportionality (*p*-value = .390) is easily accepted.

The frequency density distribution of flakes and blades combined (Fig. 9.5b) shows a pattern almost identical to the pattern exhibited by the total artifact distribution. Again, this is not surprising since flakes and blades (Table 9.3d) account for two-thirds (68.3 percent) of all cores and debitage. The only distributional difference noted is in Area B where two subclusters are exhibited for Units C4 and B/C1. These subclusters are associated with the largest of the central hearths and the side wall hearths. It is not surprising that Area A again is dominant with 41.8 percent of all flakes and blades with approximately 24 percent each in Areas B and C.

The frequency density distribution of the Levallois debitage category (Fig. 9.6b), like Floor I, introduces a new pattern. Area A now has two equally dominant clusters, each of

which is smaller in size, adjacent to, and partially includes its respective hearth. Also, there is only one major cluster in Area B and it is centered on Unit C3, directly associated with the two central hearths partially within it. This cluster radiates outward in all directions until it essentially contains all hearths in Areas B and C. Frequencies of over six Levallois pieces per m² are prevalent in most of Area B and all hearths except two, in this area, are inside or partially inside the 6 per m² contour line. The two hearths outside this line are within 1m of it. Finally, the single hearth in Area C is only weakly associated with the production of Levallois debitage. That Levallois and non-Levallois debitage are differentially distributed across the four areas is suggested by a strong rejection (*p*-value = .010) of the hypothesis of areal equipropor-tionality (Table 9.2b). This is also noted since Area B, an apparent center of Levallois debitage production, not only contains the highest percentage (39.2 percent) of Levallois debitage elements (Table 9.3c) but also contains the highest (13.2 percent) Levallois debitage composition percentage (Table 9.3d). The major concentration is centered at Unit C3 where approximately 12 Levallois pieces per m² were produced. It should be noted that this is a central hearth location, as opposed to a back wall location. It is probable, as was the case for Floor I, that high Levallois point frequencies will be found adjacent to the high-density loci of Levallois debitage.

Locations of tools

The frequencies of unretouched and retouched Levallois points by area (Table 9.4b) show that unretouched Levallois points are dominant in Area B (61.8 percent) while retouched Levallois points are dominant in Area C (56.3 percent). Thus the two types are not equiproportionally distributed across Areas A, B, and C (*p*-value = .021); there are no Levallois points in Area D. Unfortunately, it is again the arbitrary nature of defining the four areas of the site that has led to this result. It will be shown below that a slight redefinition of the areas to make them consistent with the Levallois point clusters will mitigate this problem to the extent that the Levallois points indeed become equiproportional across the areas. The slight redefinition takes into consideration the dipping of the Area B Levallois point cluster into Area C discussed below.

The frequency density distribution (Fig. 9.7b) of Levallois points clearly shows three clusters of Levallois points. There is a cluster of Levallois points in Area A, centered at Unit B8 that includes both hearths in this area. A comparison with the frequency density distribution of Levallois debitage (Fig. 9.6b) shows that the Levallois point cluster fits neatly between the centroids of the debitage clusters. A tiny cluster occurs in Area C, in Unit E1 offset from the generalized Levallois debitage cluster originating in Area B. A large amorphous cluster occurs in Area B, centered at two subclusters in Units C4 (central hearths) and A4 (back wall hearths). The peak density units are within a half-meter of seven of the ten hearths in Area B. All hearths are within the two Levallois points per m^2 contour line, with the exception of the side wall hearths, which are a half-meter from this line. More importantly, the peak density units for Levallois points (Fig. 9.7b) are offset from the peak densities for Levallois debitage suggesting that Levallois points were made close to where they were used. It is important to note that the Levallois point cluster extends toward the dripline into Area C. It will be shown later that there are three retouched Levallois points in Unit D4 just adjacent to the line separating Areas B and C. If these three points are re-allocated to Area B, the p-value for the hypothesis of areal equiproportionality changes from .021 (reject the hypothesis) to .356 (accept the hypothesis). As it turns out, retouched Levallois points will still be patterned in an interesting way.

Tools other than Levallois points (Table 9.4b) support the hypothesis of areal equiproportionality (p-value = .116). The dominant tool type is retouched pieces accounting for 46.3 percent (119 of 257 total) of all tools. Its frequency density distribution is typical of other tools. Retouched pieces have a completely different density distribution (Fig. 9.8b) from Levallois points where it can be seen that two primary concentrations are identified. The strongest cluster is Area A centered on the hearth in Unit B8. Another strong concentration occurs in Area C centered again at Unit E1 and adjacent to a side wall hearth. The other retouched pieces are diffusely scattered in Area B. The frequency distribution by area

(Table 9.4b) shows that 21.0 percent of the retouched pieces are in Area B. This compares very unfavorably with the 48.0 percent figure for Levallois points but is very consistent with the figure of 21.3 percent for all other tools (Table 9.5c). Other tools dominate the area composition percentages (Table 9.5d) with 91 percent in Area A and 75.4 percent for Area B but only 64.7 percent in Area B. The reallocation of only three retouched Levallois points from Area C to Area B changes these figures to 78.8 percent in Area C and 62.0 percent in Area B. Since the Levallois point distribution seems to be strongly associated with hearths and since Levallois points and retouched pieces seem not to be strongly associated, it might be expected that retouched pieces are not so strongly associated with hearths. A point plot (Fig. 9.9b) confirms the expectation that retouched pieces are not especially clustered about hearths.

Burins show another tool type pattern. Again, as in Floor I, the distribution of burins and burin spalls (Fig. 9.10b) confirms the expectation that they not only are hearth associated but also co-vary together in the same locations.

The spatial distribution of Levallois points and notched pieces (Fig. 9.11b) demonstrates that notches and denticulates are, as in Floor I, segregating from Levallois points and are primarily located in Area A. A number of them are in the vicinity of the dripline. The dripline zone of Area D is an area of artifact discard since approximately half of all the artifacts in this area are heavily patinated. Finally, there are points and notches in Area C that are not near the hearth but are instead near the dripline. Also, the spatial distribution of retouched and unretouched Levallois points (Fig. 9.12b) demonstrates first that retouched Levallois points are not positioned near the back wall, but instead are mostly located near hearths away from the back wall. Second, it demonstrates that most points are in the vicinity of hearths with the exception of a few that may well be in a discard area along the dripline of the shelter.

Ancillary information concerning the distribution of phosphates, phytoliths, and use-wear should greatly assist the interpretation of the above lithic patterns which are generically similar to those found for Floor I.

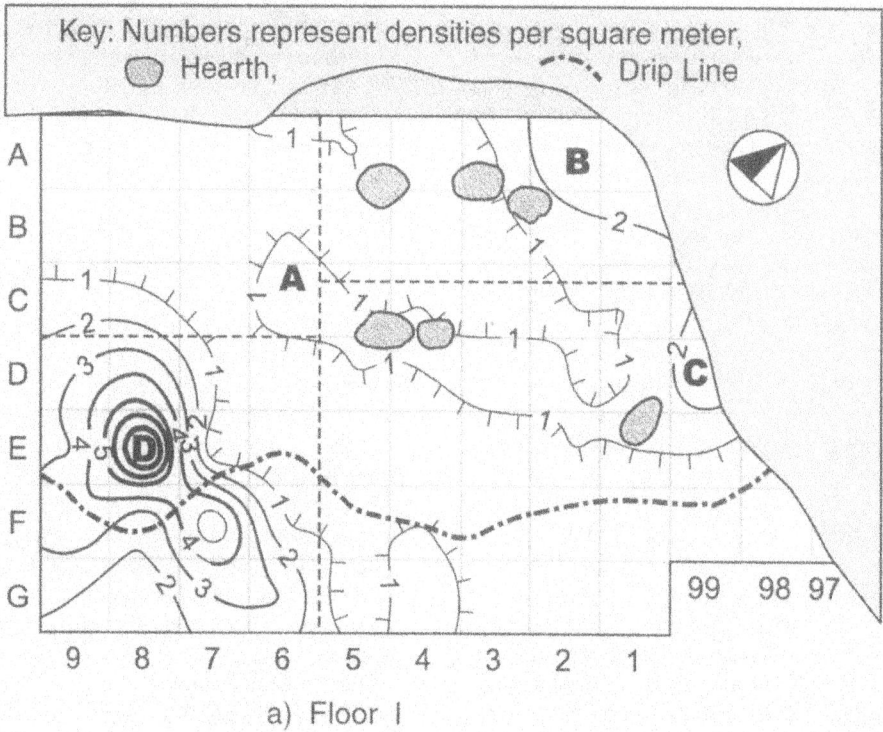

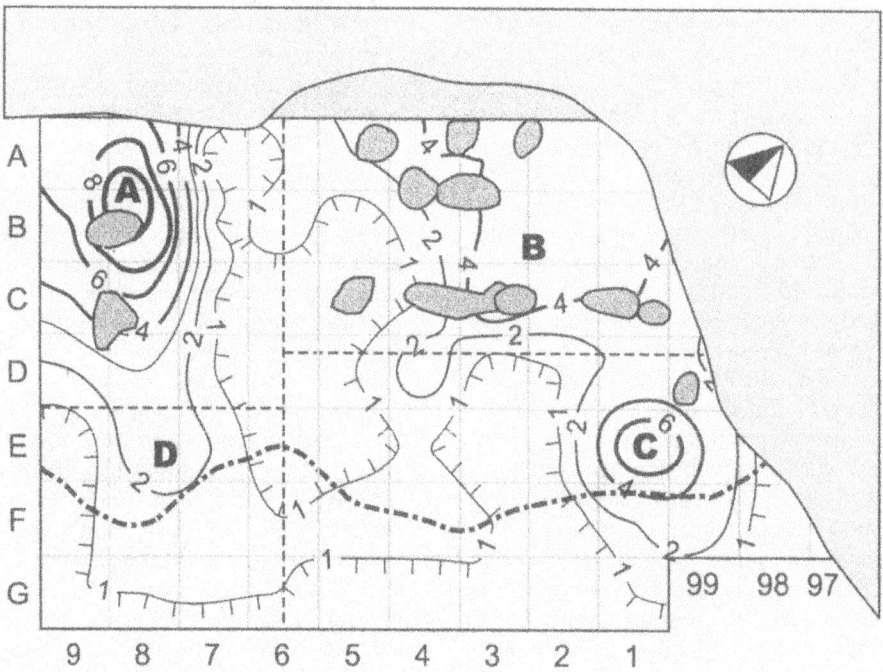

Figure 9.8   Spatial frequencies of retouched pieces by floor at Tor Faraj: **a**, Floor I; **b**, Floor II. *Note*: In Figure 9.8 the numbers represent densities per square meter, and sample size data are given in Tables 9.4 and 9.5

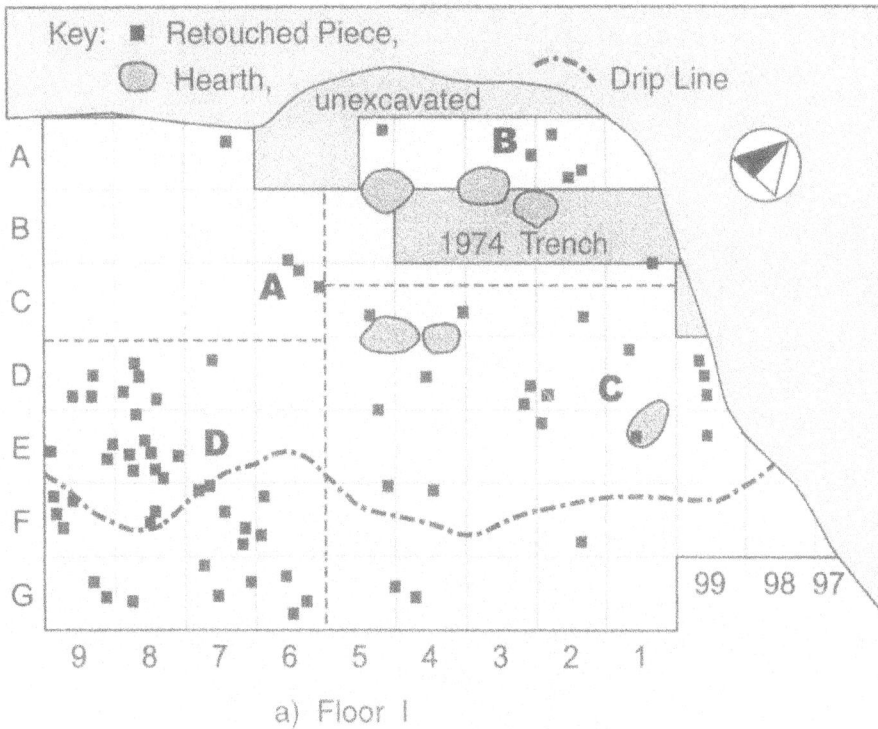

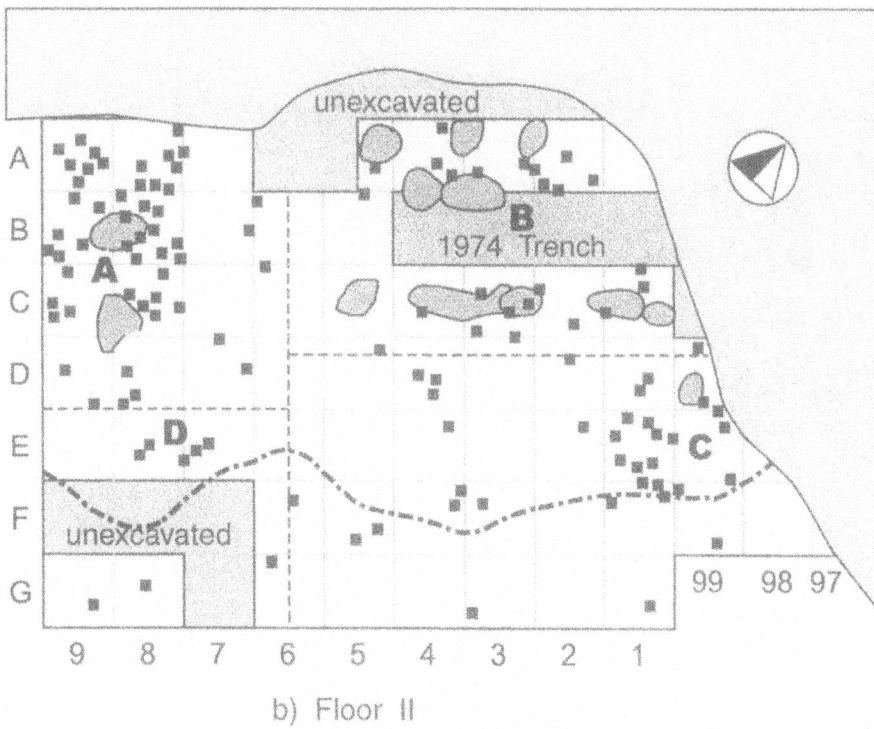

Figure 9.9 Point plots of retouched pieces by floor at Tor Faraj: **a**, Floor I; **b**, Floor II. *Note*: The summary counts of retouched pieces are given in Tables 9.4 and 9.5

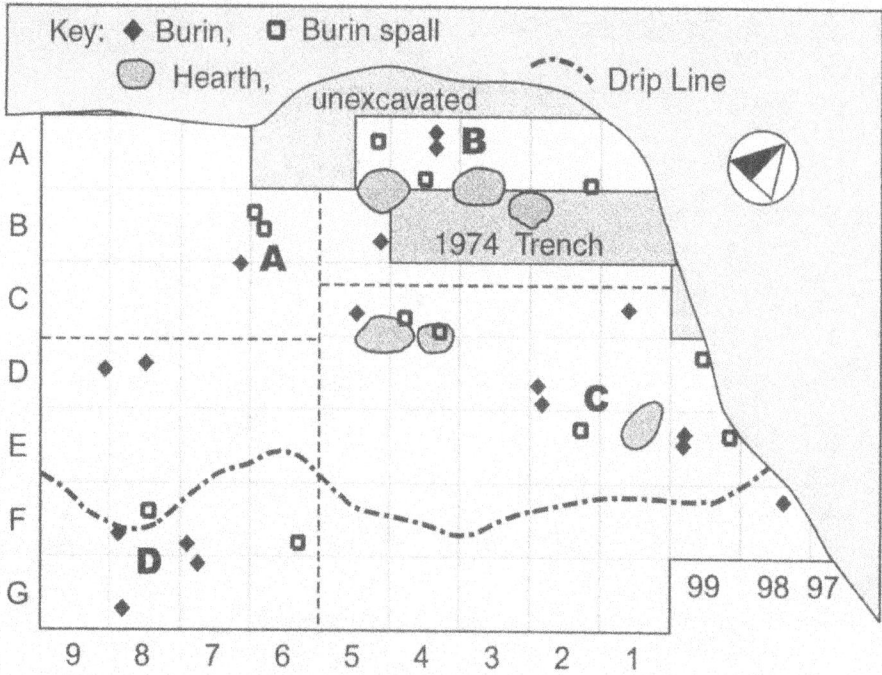

a) Floor I

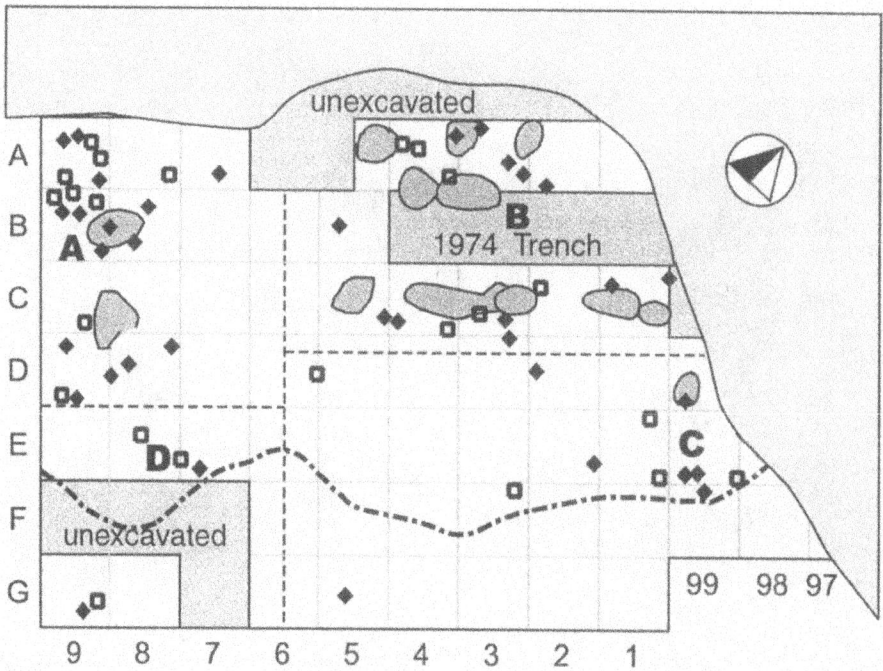

b) Floor II

Figure 9.10 Point plots of burins and burin spalls by floor at Tor Faraj: **a**, Floor I; **b**, Floor II. *Note*: The summary counts of burins and burin spalls are given in Tables 9.2 and 9.4

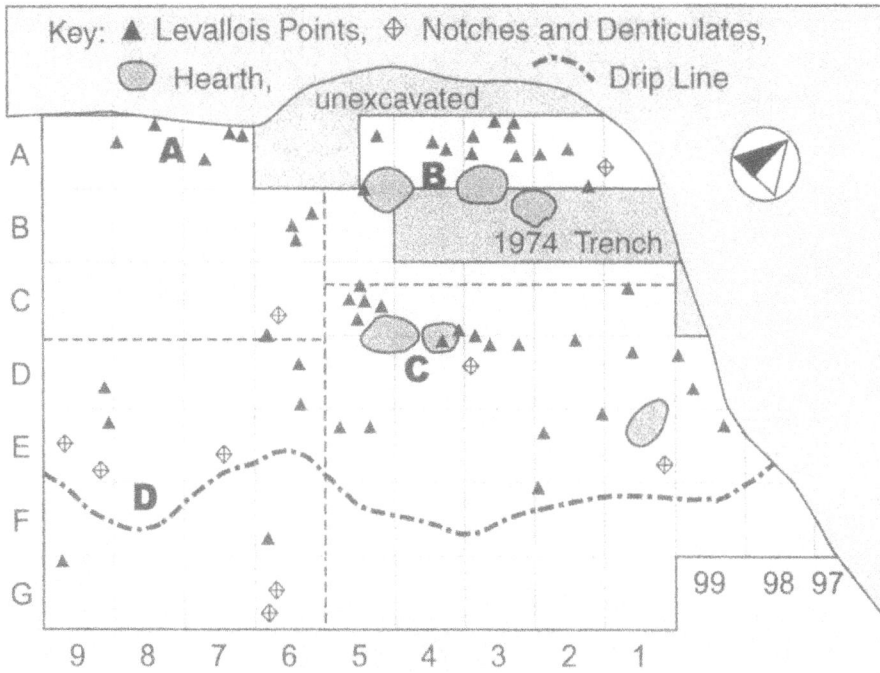

a) Floor I

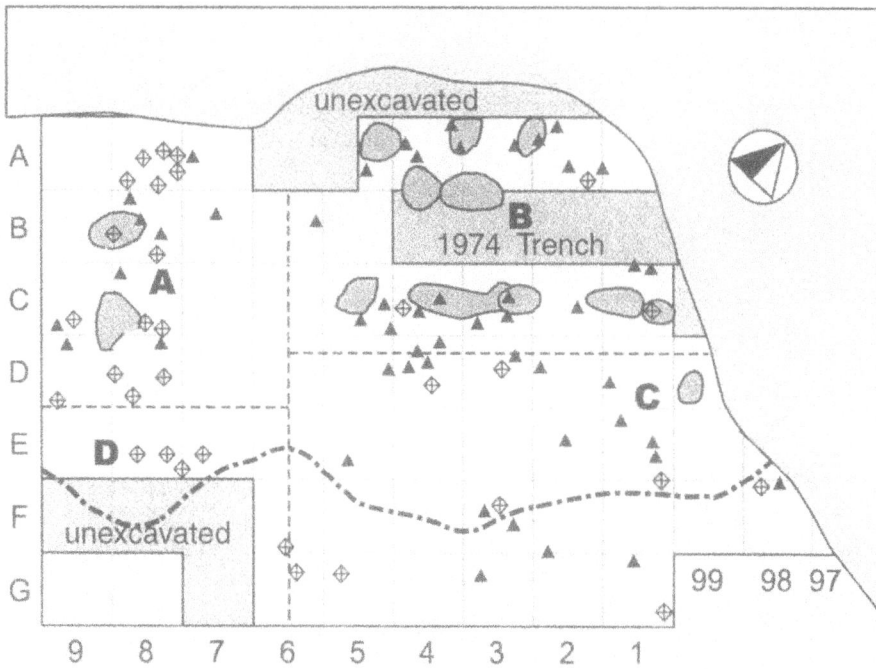

b) Floor II

Figure 9.11 Point plots of Levallois points and notched pieces by floor: **a**, Floor I; **b**, Floor II. *Note:* The summary counts of Levallois points and notched pieces are given in Tables 9.4 and 9.5

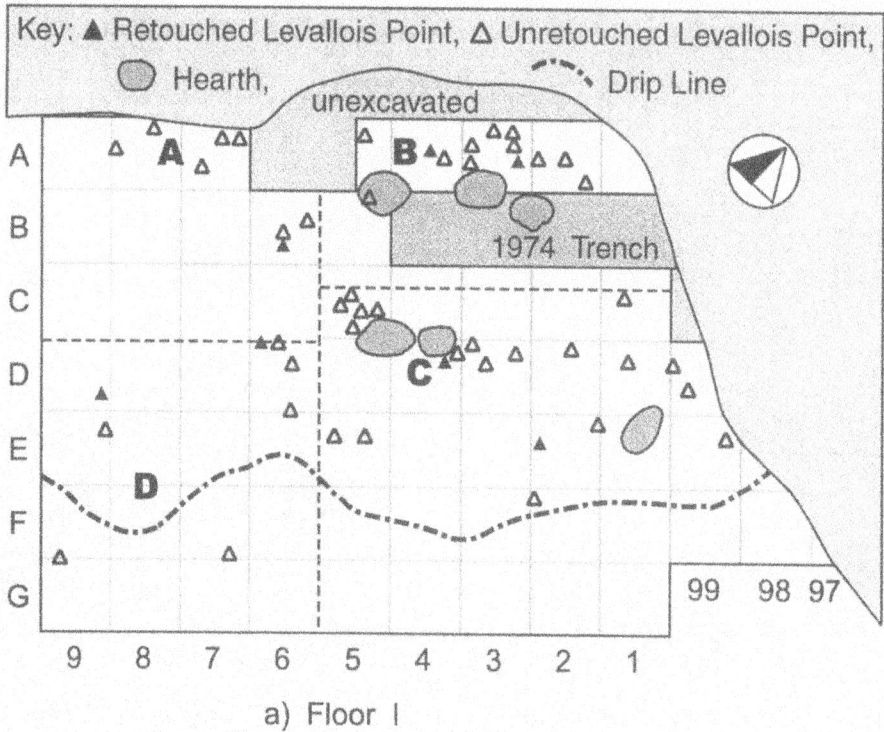

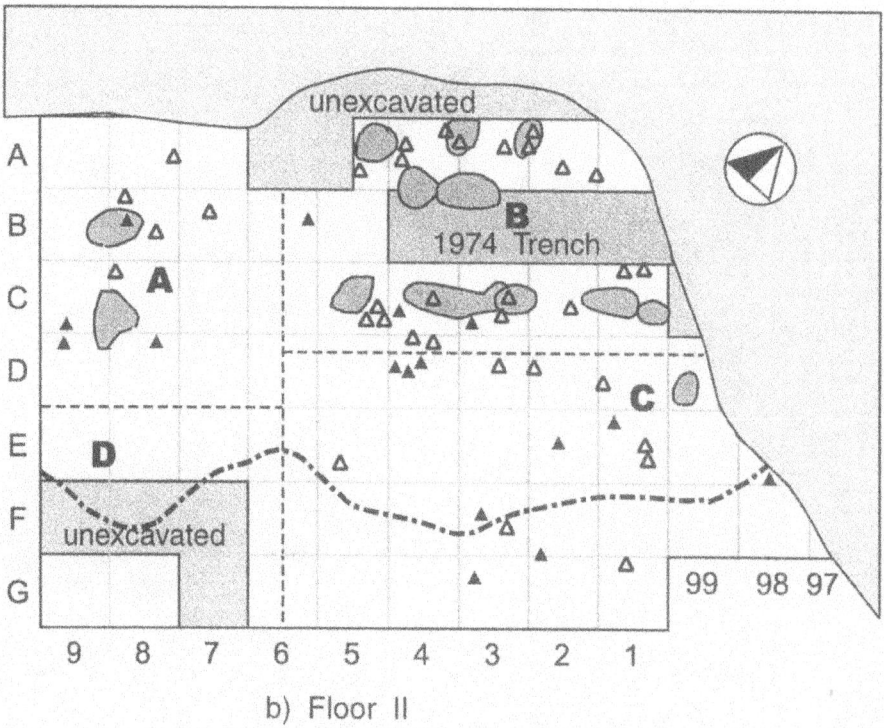

Figure 9.12 Point plots of unretouched and retouched Levallois points at Tor Faraj: **a**, Floor I; **b**, Floor II. *Note*: The summary counts of unretouched and retouched Levallois points are given in Tables 9.4 and 9.5

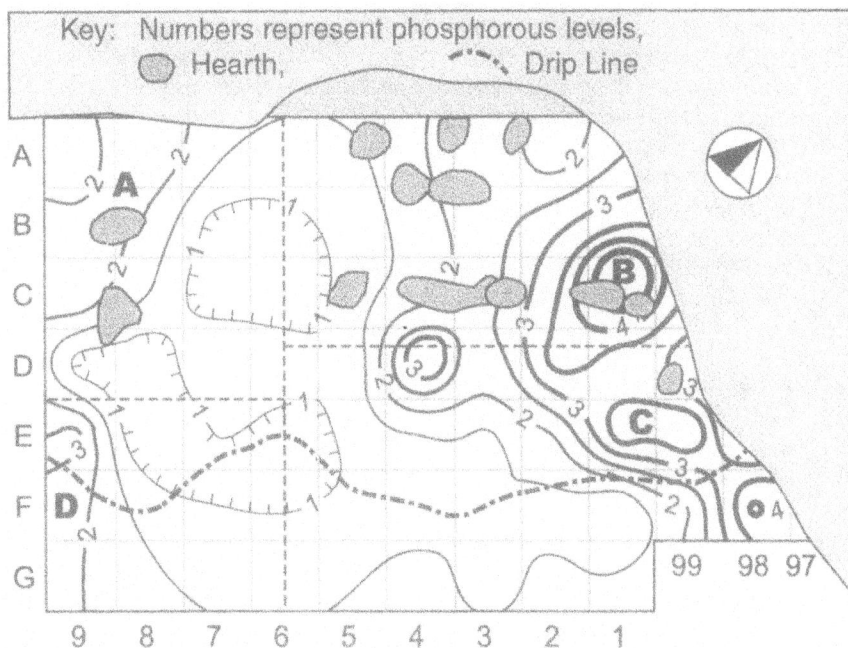

Figure 9.13 Spatial distribution of phosphorous levels for Floor II at Tor Faraj

Phosphate distributions

Sediment samples for chemical analyses were obtained at systematic intervals in level 190cm below datum. The density map for phosphate analyses performed on these samples (Fig. 9.13; Appendix D) clearly shows that the levels of phosphorus are very low in the corridor with very low artifact densities between Areas A and D, on the one hand, and Areas B and C, on the other. Higher phosphorous levels are apparent only on each side of this corridor. On the other hand, the phosphorus readings seem to be high in all the areas associated with numerous artifacts (cf. to Fig. 9.1b). The readings also are consistently very high only in the vicinity of the side wall hearths in Areas B and C. More will be said about a possible interpretation in the wear pattern section below.

Phytolith distributions

Phytolith analyses (Chapter 7) were performed on a series of 30 samples drawn both systematically (spanning the extent of site occupation) and purposively from Level 190cm below datum. These samples were analyzed and the percentages of phytolith classes were plotted to give percentage density maps across Floor II of Tor Faraj. This resulted in a series of maps for phoenix spheres (date palm), seed husks, total starch, spores, silica skeletons, monocots (grasses), and dicots (woody plants) (Figs 7.4, 7.5, 7.8, and 7.9). Rosen drew the following conclusions from her study: (1) the date palm and seed husk data associated with the central hearths in Area B are thought to be associated with food preparation; (2) phytoliths from grasses (monocots), found close to the back wall in spaces between the hearths, are interpreted as use of grasses for bedding material; and (3) phytoliths from woody plants (dicots) were generally found in high frequencies between the central hearths and the outer boundary of the shelter. It is likely that these deposits represent waste from hearths dumped near the dripline or possibly represent brush remains. It will be shown below that some of these conjectures are at least partially supported by use-wear studies of the artifacts.

Use-wear studies

Dr. Laura Longo performed use-wear studies on 286 lithic artifacts from Level 185cm below datum. This sample size resulted from a preliminary screening for artifacts with likely indicators of potentially useful wear pattern results. The resulting sample constituted the greater majority (66.7 percent) of the artifacts in Level 185. Since approximately 22 percent of the artifacts in this level were heavily patinated and most of these were in a toss zone or behind the dripline, the sample is virtually a 100 percent sample of artifacts initially thought to be fresh enough to warrant wear pattern analysis (Hietala and Longo 1996).

The analyses resulted in classifying the artifacts into: (1) those that were environmentally too degraded for use-wear analysis; (2) those for which the artifacts were not used or the wear was indeterminate; and (3) those that were used. The artifacts that were definitely used were then further classified, if possible, into categories representing the hardness of the material that was worked. In addition, the lithics were also binomially classified into categories representing applications to plant materials or animal products. Artifacts representing combinations of hardness or worked material were classified into the dominant category in order to facilitate this analysis. The results presented here are a simple extension

of those presented at the 1996 UISPP meetings by this author and Dr. Longo. Debitage and tools were not used at the same rate with tools being used slightly more frequently (66.7 percent) than debitage (46.7 percent).

Use-wear, hardness of material, and worked material

The initial stage of the use-wear analysis (Table 9.6) involved classifying the artifacts into those that were environmentally too degraded for further study (31), those that were not used or were indeterminate (136), and those that were definitely used (119). It is easy to show that 27.8 percent (119 out of 429 total) of all artifacts in Level 185 were certainly used (46.7 percent of the artifacts in this sample that were not too environmentally degraded to study). Of the artifacts that were definitely used by the inhabitants of Floor II, 88.3 percent were in areas A or B (Table 9.6). A point plot (Fig. 9.14) shows that the distribution of artifacts correspond to the areal definitions discussed earlier. In addition, it is seen that used artifacts are generally in or adjacent to hearths. Also note the presence of environmentally degraded artifacts along the dripline.

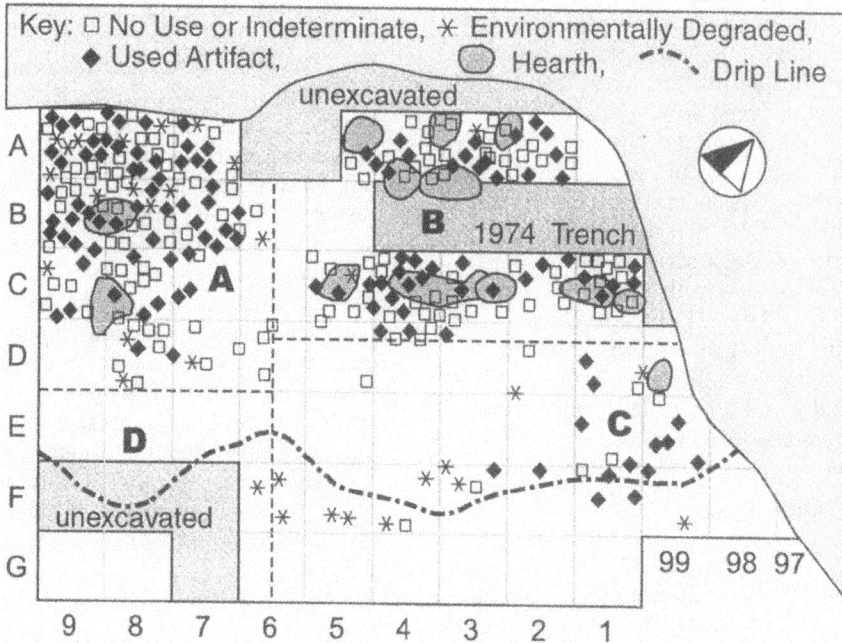

Figure 9.14 Point plots of artifacts by generic use-wear at Tor Faraj

Table 9.6 Artifact counts by use condition, hardness, and worked material by area

Note: **a** generic artifact use condition for Level 185 artifacts; **b** hardness of used raw material for Level 185 artifacts; **c** generic classes of processed raw material for level 185 artifacts

a.

		Defined areal concentration				
		Area A (west)	Area B (north)	Area C (east)	Area D (south)	Total
Environmentally degraded	Count	17	2	10	2	31
	Percentage	54.8	6.5	32.3	6.5	100.0
Not used/indeterminate	Count	65	63	8		136
	Percentage	47.8	46.3	5.9		100.0
Used	Count	61	44	14		119
	Percentage	51.3	37.0	11.8		100.0
Total	Count	143	109	32	2	286
	Percentage	50.0	38.1	11.2	.7	100.0

Note: Use condition: Likelihood Ratio Statistic = 36.3; df=6; Exact Test p-value = .000

b.

Hardness of raw material		Defined area concentration			
		Area A (west)	Area B (north)	Area C (east)	Total
Soft	Count	7	10	4	21
	Percentage	33.3	47.6	19.0	100.0
Medium	Count	25	24	7	56
	Percentage	44.6	42.9	12.5	100.0
Hard	Count	6	6	1	13
	Percentage	46.2	46.2	7.7	100.0
Total	Count	38	40	12	90
	Percentage	42.2	44.4	13.3	100.0

Note: Hardness: Likelihood Ratio Statistic = 1.48; df=4; Exact Test p-value = .839

c.

Worked material		Defined area concentration			
		Area A (west)	Area B (north)	Area C (east)	Total
Plant	Count	17	20	3	40
	Percentage	42.5	50.0	7.5	100.0
Animal	Count	19	19	7	45
	Percentage	42.2	42.2	15.6	100.0
Total	Count	36	39	10	85
	Percentage	42.4	45.9	11.8	100.0

Note: Worked material: Likelihood Ratio Statistic = 1.49; df = 2; Exact Test p-value = .485

Of the 119 artifacts known to have been used, 90 provided evidence of the hardness of the worked material (Table 9.6b). The majority (56) were classified as having worked medium hard material. A hypothesis test of equal proportions of material type worked by area is clearly correct ($p = .839$). As can be calculated, 23.3 percent of the materials processed were soft, 62.2 percent medium, and 14.4 percent hard. This is true of all areas. A spatial plot of artifact distribution by hardness of worked material (Fig. 9.15a) seems to suggest that worked soft materials take place along the back wall of the shelter in both Areas A and B.

Of the used artifacts, 85 were further amenable to classification relative to plant or animal use. Again the hypothesis of equal proportions by area holds ($p = .485$) with 47.1 percent applied to plants and 52.9 percent applied to animals. The spatial plot (Fig. 9.15b) suggests that both plant and animal processing takes place in the vicinity of hearths. A greater amount of plant processing, however, might take place near the back wall of the shelter.

Materials processed and interpretations

The processing of materials shows (Table 9.7a and Fig. 9.16) that plant materials and grass and green wood were processed near hearths close to the back wall while wood materials were processed near hearths further out toward the dripline. In addition, butchering and hide processing took place near the central hearths while bone and antler processing took place near hearths closer to the back wall. There is no evidence at all for butchering near the back wall in Area B. Instead, there seems to be evidence of bone and antler work there. In Area A, there seems to be more plant material and grass cutting nearer to the back wall with a greater emphasis on wood cutting near the midline. Butchering seems to take place in Area A and near the central hearths in Area B. Hide processing seems to occur everywhere although it may be slightly more prevalent away from the walls of the shelter. It should be clear that although there are no areal differences in materials processed or the kinds of activities taking place, there do seem to be differences that are associated with distances from the wall of the shelter. If 'close to the rockshelter wall' is interpreted as

approximately a meter or so from the back wall or side wall, then more interesting patterns emerge. Specifically, it can be observed that plant cutting, grass cutting, green wood cutting, and bone and antler processing are more frequent close to the wall of the rockshelter (Table 9.8a). Elsewhere, wood cutting, butchering, and hide processing are more prevalent. The hypothesis that these activities are equiproportional is very marginally accepted (p-value = .053). The summary table (Table 9.8b) emphasizes that plant, grass, and green wood cutting as well as bone and antler work take place much more often near the wall of the shelter. Also, butchering, hide processing, and wood processing take place much more often away from the back and side walks. The hypothesis of equiproportionality is soundly rejected (p-value = .006). It should also be noted that the diversity of activities near the wall of the rockshelter is much greater than the diversity of activities further away from the wall. This is visually obvious from the column percentages in Tables 9.8a and 9.8b.

It was mentioned earlier that some of Arlene Rosen's conjectures based on phytolith analyses are borne out from the wear pattern study. Certainly, her point about grass phytoliths near the back wall is amply borne out by the wear pattern study. Her conjecture about plant processing relative to food preparation near the central hearths is likely consistent with butchering if we assume that the butchered remains were then cooked. If cooking takes place, then food preparation is also taking place. The conjecture about woody plants near the dripline makes perfect sense if the dripline marks a boundary for dumped materials. Although this proposition does not have a wear pattern analogue, it does have an analogue associated with dumped lithic materials. Finally, the distribution of phosphorus seems to be high where activities were taking place. Is it possible that the level of high phosphorus readings near the side wall are indicating a food consumption area?

Summary for Floors I and II

The data from Floor II support several conclusions regarding the nature of site

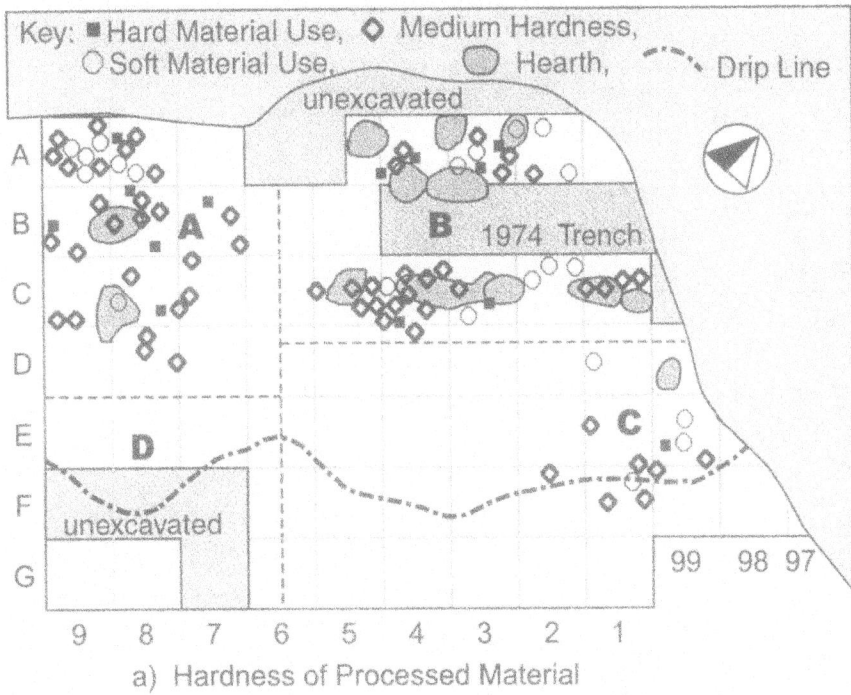

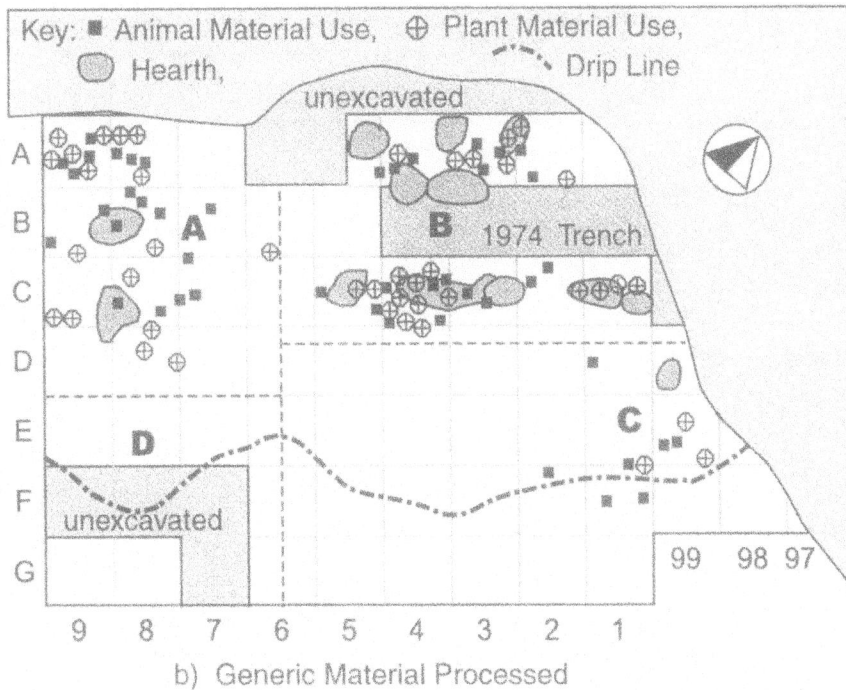

Figure 9.15 Point plots of artifact use-wear by material and hardness classes at Tor Faraj: **a**, hardness of processed material; **b**, generic material processed. *Note:* The data are summarized relative to the sample sizes presented in Table 9.6

Table 9.7 Wear pattern study results by area

Note: **a** percentage of wear pattern interpretation across areas of the site; **b** percentage of wear pattern interpretation within areas of the site. Likelihood Ratio Statistic = 11.2; df = 18; Exact Test *p*-value = 0.885

a.

Processed material interpretations	Area A (west) Count	Area A (west) Row %	Area B (north) Count	Area B (north) Row %	Area C (east) Count	Area C (east) Row %	Total Count	Total Row %
Plant cutting	1	25.0	3	75.0			4	100
Grass cutting	2	50.0	2	50.0			4	100
Green wood cutting	4	50.0	3	37.5	1	12.5	8	100
Wood cutting	8	38.1	11	52.4	2	9.5	21	100
Impact fracture			1	100			1	100
Butchering	6	54.5	3	27.3	2	18.2	11	100
Hide processing	6	35.3	9	52.9	2	11.8	17	100
Bone scraping	1	20.0	3	60.0	1	20.0	5	100
Bone incising	1	100					1	100
Antler grooving			1	100			1	100
Total	29	39.7	36	49.3	8	11.0	73	100

b.

Processed material interpretations	Area A (west) Count	Area A (west) Col %	Area B (north) Count	Area B (north) Col %	Area C (east) Count	Area C (east) Col %	Total Count	Total Col %
Plant cutting	1	3.4	3	8.3			4	5.5
Grass cutting	2	6.9	2	5.6			4	5.5
Green wood cutting	4	13.8	3	8.3	1	12.5	8	11.0
Wood cutting	8	27.6	11	30.6	2	25.0	21	28.8
Impact fracture			1	2.8			1	1.4
Butchering	6	20.7	3	8.3	2	25.0	11	15.1
Hide processing	6	20.7	9	25.0	2	25.0	17	23.3
Bone scraping	1	3.4	3	8.3	1	12.5	5	6.8
Bone incising	1	3.4					1	1.4
Antler grooving			1	2.8			1	1.4
Total	29	100	36	100	8	100	73	100

Table 9.8 Artifact wear pattern inferences by distance from rockshelter wall

a. All data: Likelihood Ratio Statistic = 16.9; df = 8; exact test *p*-value = .053

Artifact wear pattern inferences	Near shelter wall						Total	
	Close to wall of rockshelter			Interior or midline				
	Row			Row			Row	
	Count	%	Col %	Count	%	Col %	Count	%
Plant cutting	3	75.0	8.6	1	25.0	2.7	4	100
Grass cutting	4	100	11.4				4	100
Green wood cutting	6	75.0	17.1	2	25.0	5.4	8	100
Wood cutting	6	28.6	17.1	15	71.4	40.5	21	100
Butchering	4	36.4	11.4	7	63.6	18.9	11	100
Hide processing	7	41.2	20.0	10	58.8	27.0	17	100
Bone scraping	3	60.0	8.6	2	40.0	5.4	5	100
Bone incising	1	100	2.9				1	100
Antler grooving	1	100	2.9				1	100
Total	35	48.6	100	37	51.4	100	72	100

b. Summary table: Likelihood Ratio Statistic = 13.3; df = 3; Exact Test *p*-value = .006

	Near shelter wall						Total	
	Close to wall of rockshelter			Interior or midline				
	Row			Row			Row	
	Count	%	Col %	Count	%	Col %	Count	%
Plant, grass, and green wood cutting	13	81.3	37.1	3	18.8	8.1	16	100
Bone and antler scraping, incising, and grooving	5	71.4	14.3	2	28.6	5.4	7	100
Butchering and hide processing	11	39.3	31.4	17	60.7	45.9	28	100
Wood cutting and whittling	6	28.6	17.1	15	71.4	40.5	21	100
Total	35	48.6	100	37	51.4	100	72	100

Note: 'Close to rockshelter wall' is defined as between the hearths and the back wall in Area A, between the trench and the back wall in Area B, within the side wall hearth concentration in Area B, and within 1m, approximately, of the side wall in Area C

a) Plant Materials and Interpreted Processing

b) Animal Products and Interpreted Processing

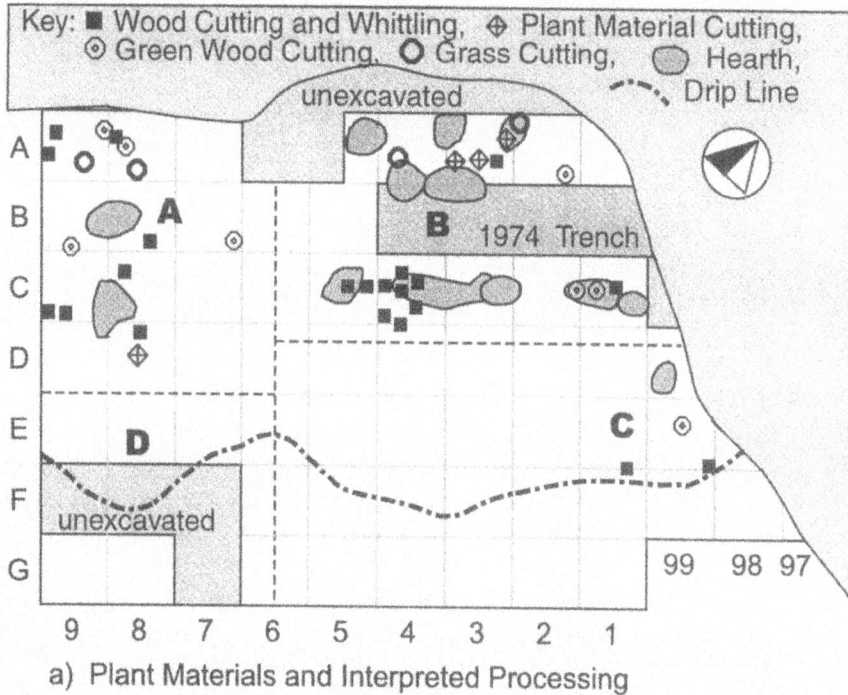

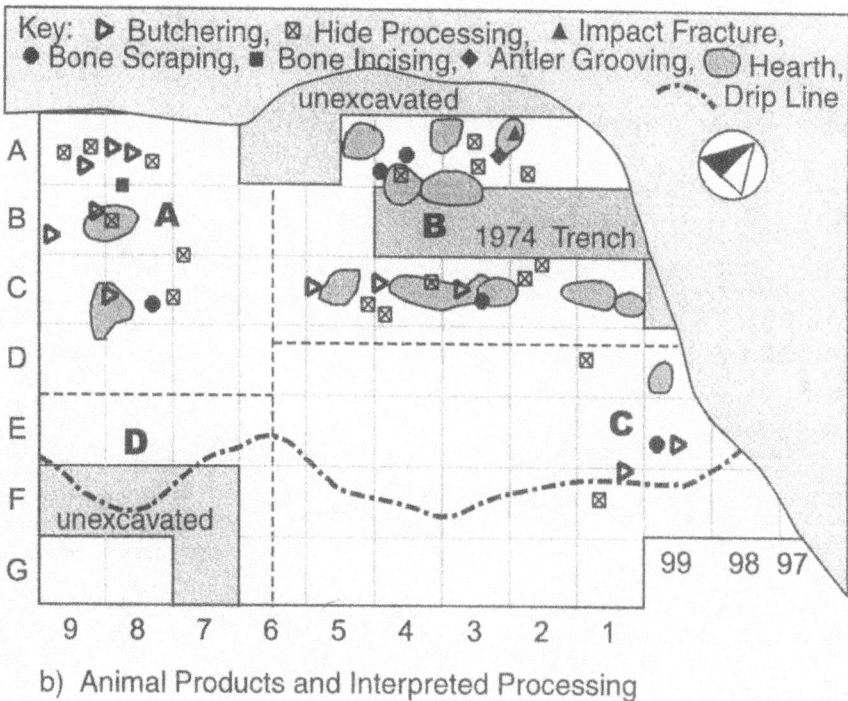

Figure 9.16 Point plots of artifact use-wear with material and processing interpretations at Tor Faraj: **a**, plant materials and interpreted processing; **b**, animal products and interpreted processing. *Note:* The data are summarized relative to the sample sizes presented in Tables 9.7 and 9.8

structure in the lower levels of Tor Faraj. Certainly, as with Floor I, it is well established that material culture, as represented through lithics, is firmly tied to the locations of the hearths. The variability in locations as they are represented by differing stages of the lithic reduction process is as clear in Floor II as it was in Floor I. Certainly, there are a few locations that seem to possess all the material elements associated with initial core reduction up and through the production of flakes and blades. As with Floor I, however, it seems as though the production of Levallois debitage is offset from these areas. The presence of Levallois points becomes more concentrated about the hearths but they are still offset from the Levallois debitage production areas. Certainly, cores would have to be moved during their lifetimes for this to happen. Again, the distribution of burins and burin spalls provides evidence that opportunistic lithic reduction, use, and discard occurred. As with Floor I, some artifacts were preferred over others with undesirable elements, perhaps use-exhausted, discarded. Area A was certainly involved in all stages of lithic reduction, including the production of tools (Levallois points) in the near vicinity of hearths. It may be noted that this area was not weak in any of the lithic categories represented by more than a few pieces.

It may also be concluded that some areas are more diverse than others. Certainly, Area A is very diverse in the kinds of lithic reduction taking place. It is probably not an accident that this area is also very diverse relative to inferences garnered from the wear pattern study. On the other hand, some areas are less diverse than others. It seems clear that the side wall location in Area C does not manifest itself strongly in all elements of lithic reduction. Of course, it is also more restricted in the kinds of inferences about activities based on wear pattern studies. It should be mentioned here that the diversity of inferred behavior near the wall of the shelter does not necessarily take place everywhere near the shelter wall. On the other hand, lower inferred behavioral diversity away from the shelter wall, however, does seem to have meaning in that it implies lower lithic diversity.

Finally, hearths near the back wall were involved with plant processing and bone and antler work. This area also possesses phytoliths associated with grasses. It does not seem too far out of the question to conclude that this was an area to warm by the fires, sleep, and pursue leisure time activities, such as the processing of antler. The central hearths have indications of plant processing for food preparation from the phytoliths, extensive activity involved with wood cutting and both plant and animal processing, including butchering activities. These are all consistent with a multi-purpose series of hearths used for cooking, warming, and gathering around. The lithic patterns, it may be recalled, are all associated with these hearths. It is also true that the dripline area and roof-fall area were probably associated with the discard of unwanted materials, including the possible dumping of ash from the hearths. Finally, there seems to be some evidence, however weak, that woody materials (brush) were associated with the toss zone near the dripline. In sum, there is ample evidence that the occupants of Tor Faraj organized themselves and structurally responded to life, in and about a rockshelter, in a manner equivalent to that of modern humans.

Summary

10 Behavioral Organization at Tor Faraj

DONALD O. HENRY

The excavation of Tor Faraj centered on defining the ways in which the Middle Paleolithic occupants of the shelter organized their behaviors in conjunction with seeking to understand the degree to which their behavioral organization resembled that followed by modern humans. The search for behavioral organization involved three, sequential research tasks. First, it was necessary to establish that discrete paleosurfaces or *living floors* could be detected within the deposit of the shelter. Upon confirming the presence of two stratified floors, a second task involved examining the spatial distributions of natural and cultural features, artifacts, and other associated data in an effort to define the site structures of the two floors. Subsequently, these structures were compared and shown to parallel one another closely. This common site structure suggests that during different Middle Paleolithic encampments in the shelter, the occupants organized their behaviors in much the same way. Finally, an effort was made to decode and interpret the site structure relative to understanding the behavioral organization followed by the occupants of Tor Faraj. This decoding process relied heavily upon inferences inspired by ethnographic analogies and logical assumptions about creature comfort (e.g., protection from the elements and exposure to sunlight) in different parts of the shelter. It should be stressed here, however, that these inferences were subsequently evaluated in light of expectations within other primary data-sets generated by the excavation.

Site structure

Site structure consists of the spatial distributions and relationships of features, artifacts, and other evidence associated with archaeological sites. Archaeologists view the content of site structure as the static residuals of the behaviors which they hope to reconstruct. For the sites of prehistoric foragers, this has been approached at two levels. Traditionally, studies focused on reconstructing those behaviors specific to a site; a kind of paleoethnography. Clark's (1971) study of Mesolithic Star Carr and Leroi-Gourhan's (1972) seminal work at the Magdalenian site of Pincevent typified such an approach. In referring to this approach as an 'episodic paradigm,' Petraglia (1987: 13-14) also notes the emphasis that Leroi-Gourhan and his students placed on studying individualistic prehistoric behaviors and even thoughts through the archaeologic record. More recently, largely led by Binford's (1978, 1983a, 1996) research, studies have taken a more general perspective, centering upon cross-cultural, time-transgressive factors that condition a site's structure. Factors such as the duration of residence, the number of residents, the social composition of the occupants, the economic activities undertaken, and so forth are examined in the context of the various components of a site's structure. This processual paradigm also involved the implicit recognition of non-cultural, natural agencies that shaped the archaeological record and attendant site structure (Straus 1979, 1997; Binford 1981,1996; Petraglia 1987).

Definition of a living floor

A fundamental, initial step to examining site structure involves establishing the spatial integrity of the behavioral residuals that form the structure. If these residuals of prehistoric behavior have experienced significant post-depositional disturbances and are not in their primary contexts, a study of their structure is really meaningless. Serving as natural sediment traps, rockshelters and caves seemingly would represent ideal settings for artifacts and other evidence to be preserved in their primary contexts. In reality, however, protected sites are subject to a wide range of processes, both natural and cultural, that lead to post-depositional spatial distortion (Straus 1979, 1997; Petraglia 1987, 1993; Bar-Yosef 1993). Recognizing this, some scholars argue that protected sites are actually less suitable than open-air occurrences for intra-site spatial studies. In recent reviews of the issue, Dibble et al. (1997) and Petraglia (1993) suggest a series of observations that assist in establishing the presence of a living floor or paleo-surface. These relate to the nature of the sedimentary processes, condition of artifacts, the ratio of small to large flakes (debris to debitage/tool categories), the spatial distributions of behaviorally meaningful artifacts, the distributions of artifacts in three-dimensional space, the distribution of refits, and the orientation of the long axes of elongated artifacts. In addition to the observations proposed by Dibble et al. (1997) and Petraglia (1993), several other indicators for the presence of living floors were identified within the Tor Faraj deposit.

Sedimentary processes

The processes by which sediments accumulated at Tor Faraj were conducive to the preservation of behavioral residues in their primary context. In many of the limestone caves of the Levant, the formation of solution cavities and fluvial action led to the post-depositional distortion of beds, making large-scale intra-site spatial studies impractical (Bar-Yosef 1993). At Tor Faraj, a predominantly dry shelter, the differential weathering of sand-stone layers created an overhang and a progressive retreat of the shelter into the cliff face. Although there is some evidence of water having been discharged from the crevasse in the northeastern corner of the Tor Faraj, this apparently was a low energy flow, a seep, leaving behind carbonate laminae within a narrow zone that extended no more than 50cm from the bedrock that forms the back of the shelter. The accumulation of fine sand and silt in the shelter was principally the result of wind-borne sediments becoming entrapped behind the roof-fall that formed across the shelter's mouth.

The bedding planes displayed by aeolian sediments, carbonate laminae, and disintegrated roof-fall trace a nearly level-bedded stratigraphy running parallel to the back wall and beds inclined from 0 to 5° running perpendicular to this line. Hearths and ash lenses furnish additional confirmation of a nearly level to very gently sloping floor from the back to the front of the shelter. The contacts between the fine sand-silt deposits of Layers C and D_2 are conformable, suggesting that their deposition was not separated by an extended period of surface stability or erosion. The laminae tracing the pulses of sedimentation within layers are typically fine-grained and do show some cross-bedding. But, in lacking the coarse-grain, lag deposits associated with extensive winnowing and long diastems, the deposit appears unlikely to have been exposed to extensive wind erosion.

Other agents of post-depositional disturbance

Bioturbation is especially common to protected sites in the Near East because such settings naturally attract burrowing animals (ibid.). Numerous small rodent and 'bug runs' were observed in the upper part of the deposit and a viper was 'excavated' from one of these, but the density of such runs declined noticeably with depth. Perhaps it is only with the modern use of the shelter by Bedouin for grain storage that rodents were attracted in large numbers. In any event, the fragile hearths and ash lenses would not have remained intact had the deposit been subjected to extensive bioturbation. The preservation of these delicate features also indicates that the deposit was not disturbed by human activities linked to successive encampments. Intensively occupied shelters often display a stratigraphic smearing of individual occupational surfaces and a mixing of the residuals of the palimpsest of encampments. It is clear that the hearths and ash lenses of Tor Faraj simply would not have stood up under such conditions.

Stratigraphic distribution of artifacts

The stratigraphic distribution of artifacts within the Tor Faraj deposit displays a pronounced bimodality with a trough in the 175cm Level and peaks at the 170cm and 195cm Levels (Fig. 8.4). Although Level 175 was never sterile of artifacts, its artifact density declined noticeably from the overlying Level 170cm. Moreover, during excavation, it seemed that it was really the lower part of Level 175cm and the beginning of Level 180cm where the deposit was especially scarce in artifacts.

Stratigraphic distribution of hearths

In forming a bimodal distribution with peaks in Levels 170cm and 190cm, the stratigraphic distribution of hearths parallels that seen for artifacts in general (Fig. 8.3). Of the 19 hearths recorded in the excavation, only one (Hearth 8) falls within the 170 to 175cm interval (Level 175cm). This also is the hearth closest to the mouth of the shelter and the dripline. This position may have been somewhat elevated in absolute elevation below datum relative to the floor of the shelter further behind the dripline, because of the sedimentation coming from over the brow of the shelter. Thus Hearth Feature 8 may be representative of the paleosurface exposed in Level 180cm of Floor II.

Stratigraphic densities of rocks

The stratigraphic distribution of rocks (as recorded by their bottom elevations) shows a distinct bimodality that again closely parallels that seen with the distributions of artifacts and hearths. Levels 170cm and 190cm display peaks in rock distributions, whereas Level 175cm shows a low point (Fig. 8.3). As one might expect from a planar perspective, the density of rocks is greatest along and outside of the dripline, especially in the area of brow

collapse in the southwest corner of the excavation block, but there are substantial numbers of rocks, even quite large ones, 2 to 3m inside the dripline. Most of the rocks coming from the roof of the shelter are derived from the retreating outside margin of the brow. The ceiling in the interior of the shelter shows a different weathering process that involves the exfoliation of fine particles and thin plates of sandstone rather than the breaking away of large slabs along bedding planes. This is important for it indicates that the rocks on the floor of the shelter, that are located well behind the dripline, were deposited there by human transport rather than natural agencies. Thus rock density is a measure of both the rate of sediment (and rock) deposition within the shelter and the intensity by which Tor Faraj was occupied.

Orientation of artifacts

In an effort to assess the degree to which natural forces may have affected the distribution of artifacts, the orientations of artifacts were recorded along their long axes in the direction of their smallest ends. This procedure was also undertaken with natural sandstone fragments from Floor II. If postdepositional erosion played a role in the movement of specimens, artifacts and rocks would be expected to display orientations disproportionately skewed toward the source of flow or perpendicular to the direction of flow. This would of course be upslope in the case of sheet erosion or fluvial processes (Schick 1986: 162; Schiffer 1987; Petraglia 1993: 101–2; Dibble *et al.* 1997). A minor 'spike' in the orientations of artifacts from Tor Faraj does point upslope, toward the back of the shelter, but this accounts for only 17.8 percent of the specimens and other orientations are relatively balanced in their representation (Fig. 10.1). Petraglia (1993: 101-2) viewed a similar orientation pattern (with spikes of 17 to 19 percent) at Abri Dufaure as evidence for an intact, undisturbed deposit. The pattern of orientation for rocks at Tor Faraj, however, shows a bimodal distribution skewed more strongly along a line perpendicular to the upslope axis. Schick (1986: 136-7) found such bimodal orientations of large artifacts (> 8cm long axis) to be associated with fluvial disturbance. The apparent

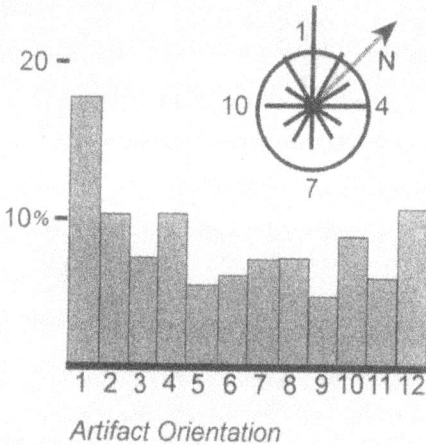

Artifact Orientation

Figure 10.1 Histogram showing the directional distributions of plotted artifact orientations

contradiction between the artifact and rock data from Tor Faraj likely comes from the fact that the artifacts were largely recovered from the protected area behind the dripline, whereas the large majority of the rock data were obtained outside the dripline. Overall, the orientation data indicate that the deposit behind the dripline is in primary context with only minor post-depositional disturbance from low energy sheet-wash. In contrast, the area outside the dripline has experienced greater natural post-depositional disturbance.

Artifact refit study

Another means of evaluating the amount of post-depositional disturbance at Tor Faraj is through examining the spatial distributions of refitted artifacts. Beyond the artifacts that were refitted from those recovered from the Bedouin backdirt, 247 artifacts with precise provenience (recovered from Levels 160 to 195cm) were refitted into 87 constellations. On average, these were separated by slightly more than 1m horizontal distance and 7.5cm vertical distance. Perhaps a more telling statistic, relative to the stratigraphic integrity of the deposit, is that only five (5.7 percent) of the constellations contain artifacts that are separated by more than 15cm. And within these five constellations, there are only five artifacts (2 percent of the refitted artifacts) that show vertical separations exceeding 15cm. Upon closer inspection, three of these five artifacts (in constellations 18, 24, and 43) are

recorded 20 to 30cm above the others in their constellations and in stratigraphic positions just 5cm below the disturbed Layer B. In short, there is a good chance that these were walked into the top of Layer C from the overlying Bedouin backdirt forming Layer B, thus creating the reverse stratigraphy of the refits. Even if this explanation is incorrect, however, the exceedingly small proportion of artifacts that were refitted beyond the vertical spread of 15cm shows that the deposit has experienced little post-depositional disturbance.

The refits can also inform us about the integrity of Floors I and II. There are five constellations (and five artifacts) that show a connection between the two floors and three of these are thought to come from the Bedouin backdirt, as discussed earlier. The two constellations that are believed to be *in situ* and that link the floors come from the bottom of Floor I (Level 170cm) and the top of Floor II (Level 180cm). From another perspective, the refits that cross-over Floors I and II constitute only 2.2 percent of the constellations and 0.8 percent of the refitted artifacts. The stratigraphic distribution of refitted artifacts also provides support for the observation that Floor I extends into the upper part of Level 175cm. Of the eight constellations (and eight artifacts) that link Level 175cm to other levels, all connect Level 175cm to higher levels within Floor I; none links Level 175cm to the lower levels of Floor II.

Spatial associations of behavioral residue

In addition to forming the foundation for the examination of site structure, spatial distributions of behavioral residues also furnish a means of establishing the integrity of living floors. If such a floor exists, it should display behaviorally meaningful data that are non-randomly distributed (Dibble *et al.* 1997). As explored in Chapters 4, 6, 8, and 9, there are several lithic data-sets (chips, cores, Levallois points, side-scrapers, and notches) at Tor Faraj that exhibit strong patterns of spatial distribution which make sense only as a consequence of human behavior. When viewed in the context of the spatial distributions of hearths, phytoliths, and phosphorus concentrations, it is apparent that the spatial patterns seen in lithic artifact categories resulted principally from the behaviors of the occupants of the shelter and not from natural forces.

The components of site structure

Largely following Leroi-Gourhan's research, studies of site structure have traditionally recognized two broad categories of evidence recovered from an archaeological site: features (e.g., hearths, pits, post molds, burials) and the spatial distributions of artifacts (inclusive of ecofacts). These two categories of evidence differ in two important ways. First, features can only exist in primary context, whereas artifacts may have been moved from their primary point of discard. And, second, the locations of features appear to condition the locations of those behaviors that produce and distribute artifacts. This primacy of features, in framing the locations of human behaviors, is emphasized by Binford (1983a: 145) when he argues that such features (facilities in his terms) provide the framework around which activities are organized. Thus, from an analytic perspective, studies of site structure have traditionally focused on the locations of features relative to distributions of artifacts and this has especially been so for hearths (Leroi-Gourhan 1972, 1984; Binford 1978, 1983a, 1996; Kind 1985; Gamble 1986, 1991).

In regard to sheltered occupations, however, a third category of evidence needs to be considered when studying site structure. This involves the natural composition of such a site and how this may have influenced the locations and the varieties of human behavior. As recently noted by Straus (1979; 1997: 6) in his review of the prehistoric use of Spanish rockshelters, the walls, roofs, rockfall blocks, talus slopes, and other physical features served to structure and organize human occupations. With this in mind, rather than beginning with the locations of cultural features in a study of site structure of a protected occupation, we should probably begin with an examination of the site's physical features and natural composition.

The physical features of Tor Faraj

The most important characteristics of the morphology of a protected site that condition its human use include: (1) the gradient and composition of the floor or living surface; (2) the exposure to sunlight; (3) the protection from precipitation; (4) the shielding from wind; and (5) the amount of moisture in the protected area. It is also important to keep in mind that these characteristics may change through the duration of the occupation of a site as a result of the morphological evolution of a cave or shelter (Straus 1997).

At Tor Faraj, the physical evolution of the shelter appears to have been subtle and the changes that occurred would have had little effect on the human use of the site during the period represented by excavation. The overhang appears to have migrated only slightly since the Middle Paleolithic occupation as shown by the correspondence of the modern dripline and the roof-fall (Layer D_1) in which Floor 1 artifacts are imbedded. Although the accumulation of the cultural deposit would have reduced the floor to ceiling clearance by several meters during the full course of the prehistoric occupation, this would have had little bearing on the positioning of activities within the shelter, given that the ceiling provided 10 to 13m clearance even at the end of the occupation interval.

The modern slope of the floor of Tor Faraj from back to front is about 8 percent and paleosurfaces along this line appear to have been *ca.* 5 percent. Fine sands and silt filled the shelter except where roof-fall has accumulated along the dripline in the central part (SW corner of excavation block). Therefore, with the exception of the area of roof-fall, most of the shelter would have provided a nearly level, comfortable occupation floor for prehistoric encampments.

Oriented from the shallow recess on its eastern end, the shelter opens to the south. The roof of the shelter extends out from the back wall for some 5 to 6m for most of its length of *ca.* 24m. A terrace provides an additional 5 to 6m wide, gently sloping occupation floor running parallel to, but outside the dripline. In vertical profile the shelter's brow rests *ca.* 13m above the floor and even at the shelter's back wall, its ceiling is still some 10m high. The area available for occupation at Tor Faraj is *ca.* 216m^2 and the protected area is *ca.* 136m^2.

The high ceiling and southern exposure of Tor Faraj provide substantial indirect light and direct sunlight during much of the day. In

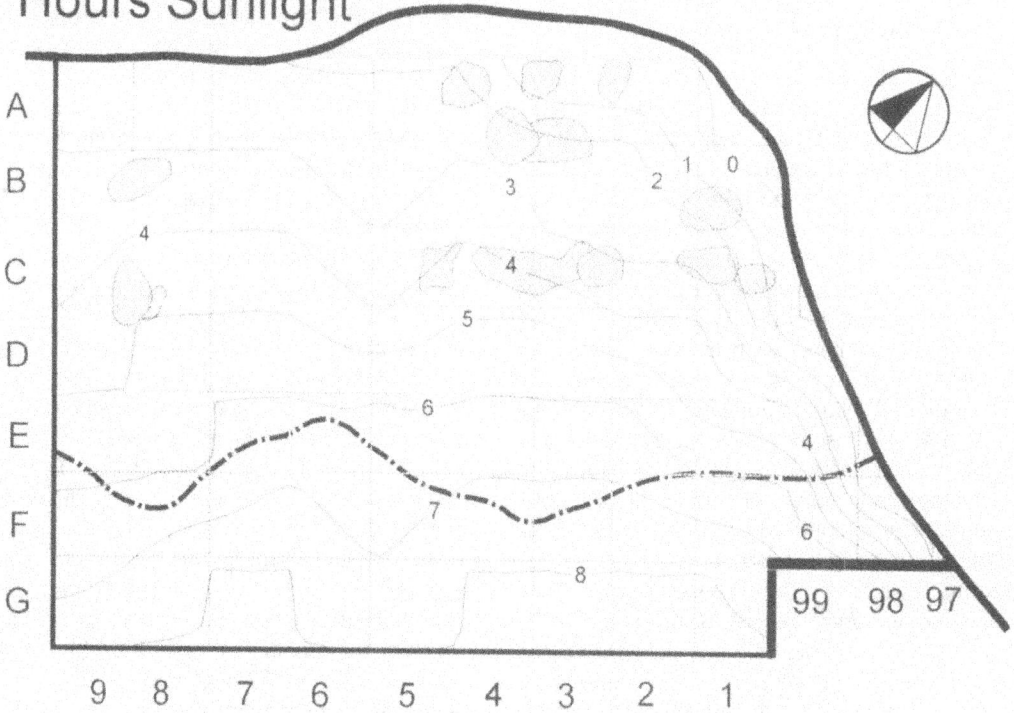

Figure 10.2 Plan of Tor Faraj showing the length of time (in hours) various parts of the shelter are exposed to sunlight in July. Note that with the shift of sun to the south for winter sunset, the northern wall of the shelter would receive much greater afternoon sunlight

early July of 1994, the recording of the sun/shadow line on the floor of the shelter showed that little of the protected area received direct sunlight before late morning, and after reaching the point of maximum sunlight around noon, the site was mostly in shadow again by 4pm (Fig. 10.2). But this was a summer sunlight record, not the winter season, the suspected season of occupation of Tor Faraj. An attempt to obtain a winter record through direct readings failed because of cloudy days in January 1998, but an estimate of winter sunlight conditions can be made by calculating the shift in the position of the sun. With a winter sunset located maximally 47° south of the summer solstice, afternoon sunlight is not only extended, but the sunlight-shadow line of the shelter is oriented differently with a stronger north-south axis. This is important, for unlike the summer sunlight, winter afternoon sunlight bathes the north wall of the shelter. On sunny days this serves as a solar

furnace. The red sandstone, heated during the day, radiates heat during the evening hours when the temperature drops. Thus, based upon available sunlight, the most preferred protected location within the shelter would have been in the area near the wall just east of the alcove.

Another major consideration for organizing behaviors in a rockshelter is protection from wind, especially in open, arid regions such as southern Jordan. As previously discussed (Chapter 2), the accumulation of aeolian sands during the Middle Paleolithic points to winds blowing from the east and south as opposed to the modern prevailing winds from the northwest. This would have meant that winds would have come up the canyon from the east rather than down-canyon from the west, as they do today. The area of greatest protection from drafts would have been along the north wall in the shallow recess of the shelter.

In reviewing the physical features of Tor Faraj from the perspective of how these would have shaped its use by Middle Paleolithic groups, it is apparent that the natural composition of the shelter would have placed only general constraints on how its occupants would have organized their activities. Unlike many protected sites, Tor Faraj offered a large, relatively level, soft-sediment-filled, and well-lighted sheltered area. This also was accompanied by a large, relatively level terrace. The area of rock-fall along the dripline would have constrained some activities, but it also would have provided a low windbreak and a ready source for large blocks to be used as tables or anvils within the protected area. Beyond the obvious importance of the area behind the dripline offering protection from the elements, the area located in the shallow alcove on western end of the northern wall would have been especially attractive for the warmth furnished by direct sunlight and radiant heat as well as protection from the wind. Another aspect of the natural positioning of Tor Faraj is the view that it provides of the plain of the Hisma Basin and the lower reaches of the Wadi Aghar. From the shelter, Mousterian hunters would have been able to monitor herd animals grazing in the Hisma Basin and seeking water from sandstone potholes that line the bed of the Wadi Aghar.

The cultural features

Hearths were the only cultural features recorded at Tor Faraj. They were defined mainly by ash and charcoal fines, although some also displayed burnt sandstone and chert artifacts and fire-reddened sediment. Most of the hearths were oval or round in form and small (mean 57cm diameter). Many of the hearths exhibited 2 to 3 successive concentric zones of ash, typically ranging from darker to lighter hues. In cross-section, most revealed a shallow depression averaging about 6cm in maximum thickness. Although many of the hearths contained some burnt sandstone, none were rock-lined.

Of the 19 hearths, six were recorded for Floor I and 13 for Floor II (Table 3.2; Fig. 10.3). The spatial distribution of hearths for each of the floors shows a very similar pattern. In addition to all of the hearths falling behind the dripline, they are concentrated in the area

of the shallow alcove located at the juncture of the north and west walls. This area, bounded by grid Units A1-C1-C5-A5, represents only 15m^2 (*ca.* 23 percent of the excavated block), yet it holds *ca.* 79 percent of the hearths. Also, both of the floors show a single outlying hearth located along the north wall, just inside the dripline. Two other outliers appear in Floor II, south and west of the main concentration. A closer look at the distribution of hearths in the alcove area shows a line of hearths that generally follows the wall and a centrally placed set of hearths in Units C3-C5. The hearth-line also can be seen to connect to the two outliers (Units D99 and E1) located along the wall near the dripline.

The distribution of hearths offers clues to site structure in defining several spatial patterns in the relationship of cultural and natural features at Tor Faraj. The Mousterian occupants of the shelter placed their hearths behind the dripline in the protected area of the shelter, although they could also have built hearths on the terrace. This is, in fact, the overwhelming pattern among groups inhabiting protected sites. A cross-cultural survey of archaeological and ethnographic sheltered sites shows that less than 2 percent have hearths outside the dripline (Appendix C). Some of the reasons for this are obvious. Hearths need to be protected from precipitation and they generate stronger heat sinks when located under an overhang and close to the walls of a shelter. Also, they provide a better light source with a ceiling for reflection. At an even more restricted level within the protected area of Tor Faraj, however, the shelter's natural features seem to have again played a role in shaping the occupant's decisions about hearth placement. The concentration of hearths in the shallow alcove is associated with that part of the shelter that would have been heated by direct afternoon sunlight and the radiant heat from the shelter's south-facing wall during the night. And perhaps most importantly, the alcove would have been protected from wind.

Within the alcove area, hearths are positioned within a band following the wall. In his excavation of Gatecliff Shelter, Thomas (1983: 524-6) observed a similar phenomenon which he explored by comparing the distances between hearths, walls, and dripline. Through seven stratified horizons at the site, Thomas (*ibid.*) compared the distances between 36 hearths, the changing back wall position, and the nearly constantly positioned dripline. What he found was a strong statistical relationship between the distances between hearths and the back wall of the shelter, but a much weaker relationship between hearths and their distances to the dripline. Even though the floor area of the shelter changed through time, in concert with the changing configuration of the back wall, a hearth-line was established about 4m from the wall during successive occupations. From this, Thomas (*ibid.*: 525) concluded that the hearth positioning created a relatively warm and smoke-free area for working and sleeping. In exploring the notion of a constantly positioned hearth-line in sheltered sites, the much larger cross-cultural sample (Appendix C) shows hearths to be located nearer to shelter walls than shown at Gatecliff, i.e., 1.3m from the nearest wall, 2.2m from the back wall, and 2.2m from the dripline. Although the absolute distances differ from those recorded at Gatecliff Shelter, like the Gatecliff data, the distance to the nearest wall appears to be the strongest predictor of hearth positioning for the cross-cultural sample as indicated by the smaller standard deviation (1.3) when compared to the standard deviations of 2.2 for back wall and dripline distances.

When the data from Tor Faraj are compared to the cross-cultural sample, the hearth to nearest wall distance averages only 1.8m, i.e., 0.5m less than that of the cross-cultural sample. Hearth to back wall and dripline distances of 2.3m and 3.5m, respectively, register slightly above those of the cross-cultural sample. Clearly, a distance of 1.8m between hearth and wall would not provide adequate space for many activities, but what about sleeping? When the cross-cultural sample is restricted to only those hearths adjacent to bedding or sleeping areas, there is a substantial reduction in the space between hearth and wall, registering only 1.3m. These data imply that more than one 'hearth-line' may be defined for shelter occupations: a line for sleeping hearths that falls within a band of 1 to 2m from the nearest wall and another line of hearths used for domestic or communal activities that is situated some 2 to 4m from the nearest wall. The hearth distribution from Tor Faraj appears to agree with this twin

hearth-line pattern in that 12 (63 percent) of the hearths fall within a band positioned between 0.8 to 1.5m from the nearest wall and the rest, ranging from 1.6 to 3.6m from the nearest wall, are concentrated along a line located *ca.* 3m from the nearest wall.

Another dimensional attribute of hearths that has received attention is that associated with the distances between hearths themselves. Gamble (1986, 1991: 12) has observed that hearths recorded in ethnographic and archaeological encampments, set in various environments across the world, tend to be spaced about 3m apart. He also notes that this spacing holds for both open and sheltered sites. In summarizing the detailed data on hearth distributions provided by Nicholson and Cane's (1991) ethnographic work in Australia's Western Desert, Gamble (1991) points to the possibility that hearth spacing may also vary with hearth function. As noted by Nicholson and Cane (1991: 330) for open sites, sleeping hearths tend to be more tightly spaced than those used for cooking and conversation. The cross-cultural rockshelter sample assembled for this study largely agrees with Gamble's '3m rule' with a mean distance of 2.4m from center to center of the nearest hearths. The next nearest hearth (3.3m) and the third nearest hearth (3.7m) also cluster in the 3m range. When restricting the sample to those hearths associated with sleeping areas, the distances between the nearest hearths average 2.4m, identical to the global mean, with a large standard deviation (1.8m). This indicates that, at least with the data at hand, hearth spacing is not a useful predictor of hearth function.

A much stronger relationship, however, is seen between the spacing of hearths and the number of hearths in an encampment; as the numbers of hearths in a site increase, the space separating them progressively declines. For shelters containing only two hearths, mean spacing is *ca.* 3.3m, whereas for those shelters with 11 hearths, mean spacing registers only 1.4m. Two factors may account for the inverse relationship between the spacing and numbers of hearths. From a behavioral perspective, increasing numbers of occupants (and hearths) in a shelter, with its restrictive space, may give rise to a kind of hearth packing. In an archaeological context, the indirect relationship between the spacing and number of hearths could simply be the result of overlapping occupations, the palimpsest phenomenon. When the cross-cultural data are broken into archaeological and ethnographic sub-samples, the archaeological hearths are shown to be more tightly spaced than the ethnographic ones, but both sub-samples retain the trend of tighter spacing with greater numbers. This would suggest that both factors, the palimpsest phenomenon and occupant packing, account for the inverse relationship between hearth spacing distance and numbers.

A review of the cross-cultural data also shows the density of hearths in shelters to be greater for archaeological (1 hearth/14.7m^2) than ethnographic (1 hearth/23.6m^2) occupations. Again, this most likely points to the effect of the palimpsest phenomenon. Additional comparisons of archaeological with ethnographic occupations show that although the mean numbers of hearths is only slightly greater for archaeological sites (4.7 compared to 4.2), none of the ethnographic occupations contains more than six hearths in contrast to as many as 11 for archaeological sites. This implies that when archaeological horizons display more than six hearths, there is a strong likelihood that more than one occupational episode is represented.

In comparing the distances separating hearths at Tor Faraj, the floors conform to the trend observed in the cross-cultural sample, i.e., less space separating greater numbers of hearths. The six hearths identified in Floor I are separated by mean distance of 1.3m, whereas the 13 hearths of Floor II are spaced only 1m apart on average. Given the cross-cultural data, the absolute numbers of hearths for the floors at Tor Faraj suggest that Floor I is likely to represent one to two discrete occupational episodes, whereas Floor II may represent some two to four individual episodes of residence at the shelter.

In summary, the hearth features at Tor Faraj are all located behind the dripline and concentrated in an area that should have received warmth from sun and protection from wind. The positioning of the hearths creates two hearth-lines, one following a swath located 0.8 to 1.5m from the wall and another positioned 1.6 to 3.6m from the wall. The inter-hearth distances at Tor Faraj average 1 to 1.3m, some 35 to 40cm less than those recorded for floors with similar numbers of hearths in the cross-cultural samples and 70 to 100cm less than the global cross-cultural sample.

The site structure defined by the hearths implies that more than a single occupational episode is likely to have produced the behavioral residuals encompassed by each of the floors at the shelter. But this structure also suggests that discrete occupational episodes were likely restricted to no more than two for Floor I and four for Floor II. The redundance in the positioning of hearths between and within floors also implies that the groups residing in the shelter organized their behaviors similarly. At a more detailed scale, patterns in the distribution of the hearths at Tor Faraj point to two hearth-lines. The hearth-line positioned close to the wall of the shelter resembles ethnographic hearth-lines associated with sleeping areas, whereas the hearth-line more centrally located in the shelter more closely parallels ethnographic hearths tied to communal areas for cooking, other domestic tasks, and conversation.

The spatial distributions of artifacts and related evidence

An understanding of the spatial patterning of artifacts at Tor Faraj is based principally on the distributions of chipped stone specimens, although phytoliths and geochemical data furnish significant additional information on the locations of plant remains and organic residue. Unfortunately, bone was not preserved in the deposit except for a few rare fragments found associated with the carbonate deposit near the back wall of the shelter.

Chips

Small flakes (< 30mm long axis) represent by far the largest artifact category at Tor Faraj. Over 9000 were recovered from Floors I (3531) and II (5771) during the 1993-94 excavation. In adding the chip counts from corresponding levels excavated in the old 1983–84 trench, Floors I (3918) and II (6604) were enlarged to contain 10,522 specimens. Unlike the larger artifacts, that were piece-plotted with the laser theodolyte, chips were collected in quarter-meter units (quadrants) in 5-cm-thick levels.

Beyond the practical and statistical advantage of yielding very large samples for defining distributions, chips are more likely to define the precise locus of the activity which produced them than are larger artifacts. Their small size would have precluded them from being reworked or recycled, as often occurred with larger specimens, and this would have reduced the likelihood that they would have been moved about an occupation floor. And because of their small size, most chips would not have been regarded as bothersome litter prompting removal from work or activity areas, the *drop zone* defined by Binford (1983a). Some chips, however, may have been removed along with ash in the cleaning of firepits and swept up with larger artifacts in clearing areas for sitting and sleeping.

In order to identify the distribution of chips, a contour map was generated for each floor with *Surfer* 7 (Golden Software, Inc.) based on the chip counts of each quadrant which were point-plotted in the center of the quadrant. The resulting contours show four concentrations (Areas A, B, C, D) that largely are positioned in the same places within the shelter for both floors (Fig. 10.3). The portions of the excavation that show especially low densities of chips are found outside the dripline and across the central part of the excavation block behind the dripline.

Despite their overall similarity, Floors I and II do show subtle differences in their chip distributions (Fig. 10.3). Area A was more pronounced in Floor II than in overlying Floor I and its center moved northeastward (*ca.* 2m) from its Floor II position by Floor I times. While this apparent shift may be influenced in part by the exclusion of the disturbed units (B9, B8, C9, C8) from Floor II, this would not explain the low density also seen in the undisturbed deposit of Units A9 and A8. Area B shrank in size from Floor II to Floor I and there was a concomitant reduction in the number of concentration peaks from three to one. Area C shifted slightly to the west and back from the dripline from its Floor II placement. Area D, well defined, although marginally positioned outside the dripline in Floor II, had become diffuse, and barely recognizable in Floor I. The migrations of Area C and Area D for distances of 0.5 to 1m toward the back wall and inside the dripline may reflect a slight retreat of the brow that

formed the Layer D₁ roof-fall which separated Floors I and II.

Armagan's attribute study of small debris (Chapter 5, this volume) also reveals differences between the activity areas relative to lithic processing and formation processes. Greater emphasis on hard-hammer percussion and initial lithic processing are indicated for Area D of both floors and Area A of Floor II. Soft-hammer percussion and final processing dominate the other activity areas. Whereas high densities of burnt artifacts corroborate the locations of hearths identified as features in excavation, burnt material along with other attributes suggest that Area D may also have served as a location for dumping ash from hearth cleanings.

Debitage

This, the second largest artifact category, includes over 2600 specimens that were piece-plotted. The distribution of debitage strongly resembles that shown by chips for each floor, but there are differences (Fig. 9.1). The most striking of these relates to an extension of debitage from Area A toward the dripline in Floor II and a much more pronounced presence of artifacts in Area D in Floor I. As described in Chapter 9, the different classes of debitage (e.g., blades, flakes, primary elements, core trimming elements) conform to the spatial distributions of debitage as a whole.

Cores and cores-on-flakes (truncated faceted pieces)

Although cores, *sensu lato*, include only 123 plotted specimens, they show an interesting spatial pattern differing somewhat from debitage as a whole (Fig. 10.4). In Floor II, cores fashioned from nodules are conspicuously absent from that portion of Area B that rests along the back wall although this area is rich in other artifacts. For the rest of Floor II, cores-on-nodules largely co-vary spatially with the concentrations of chips and other artifacts. In Floor I, the pattern in Area B is repeated in that only two cores were recorded along the back wall. And again cores largely co-occur with the other artifact concentrations, although they are proportionately more highly represented in Areas C and D. When the

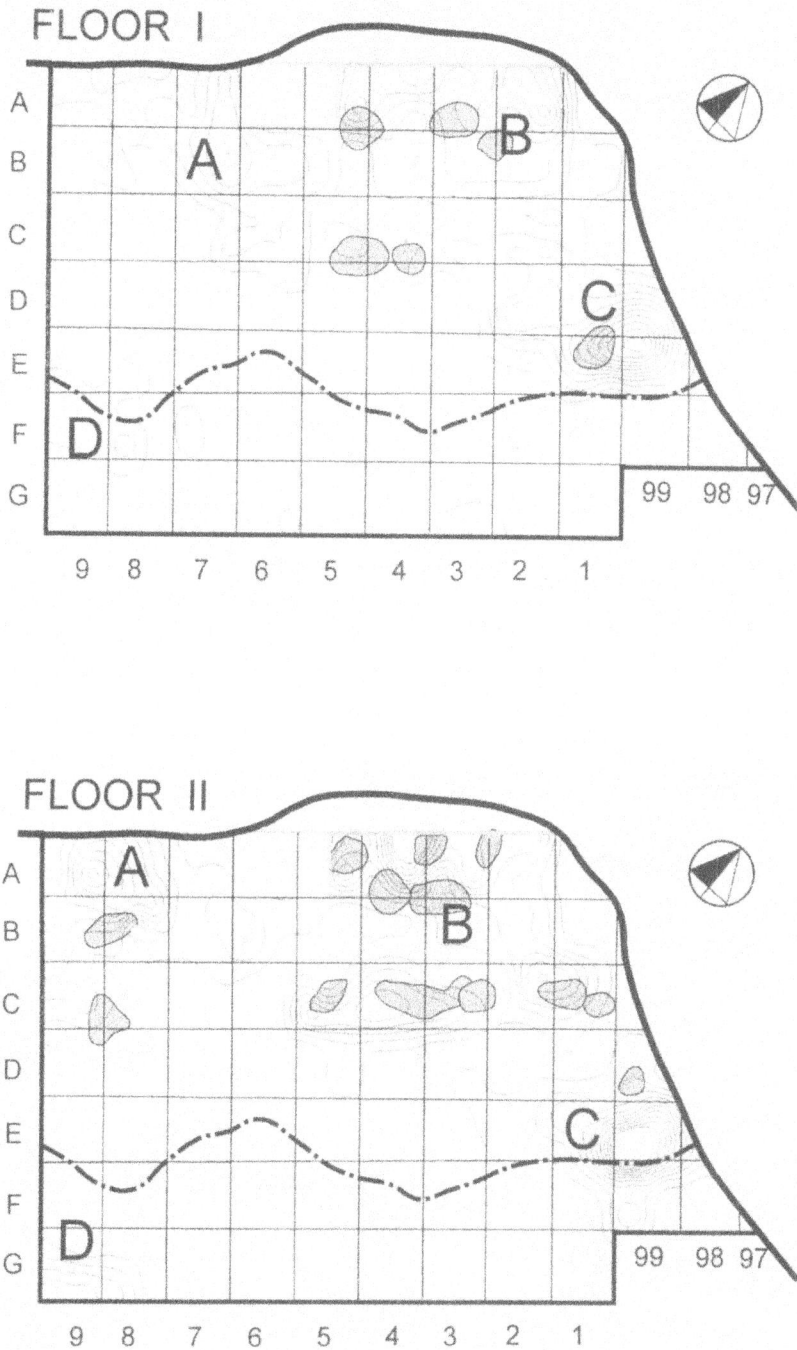

Figure 10.3 Plan of Tor Faraj showing the distributions of hearths and chip concentrations for **a**, Floor I ($n = 3918$); and **b**, Floor II ($n = 6604$). The density contours are drawn at intervals of 20 specimens

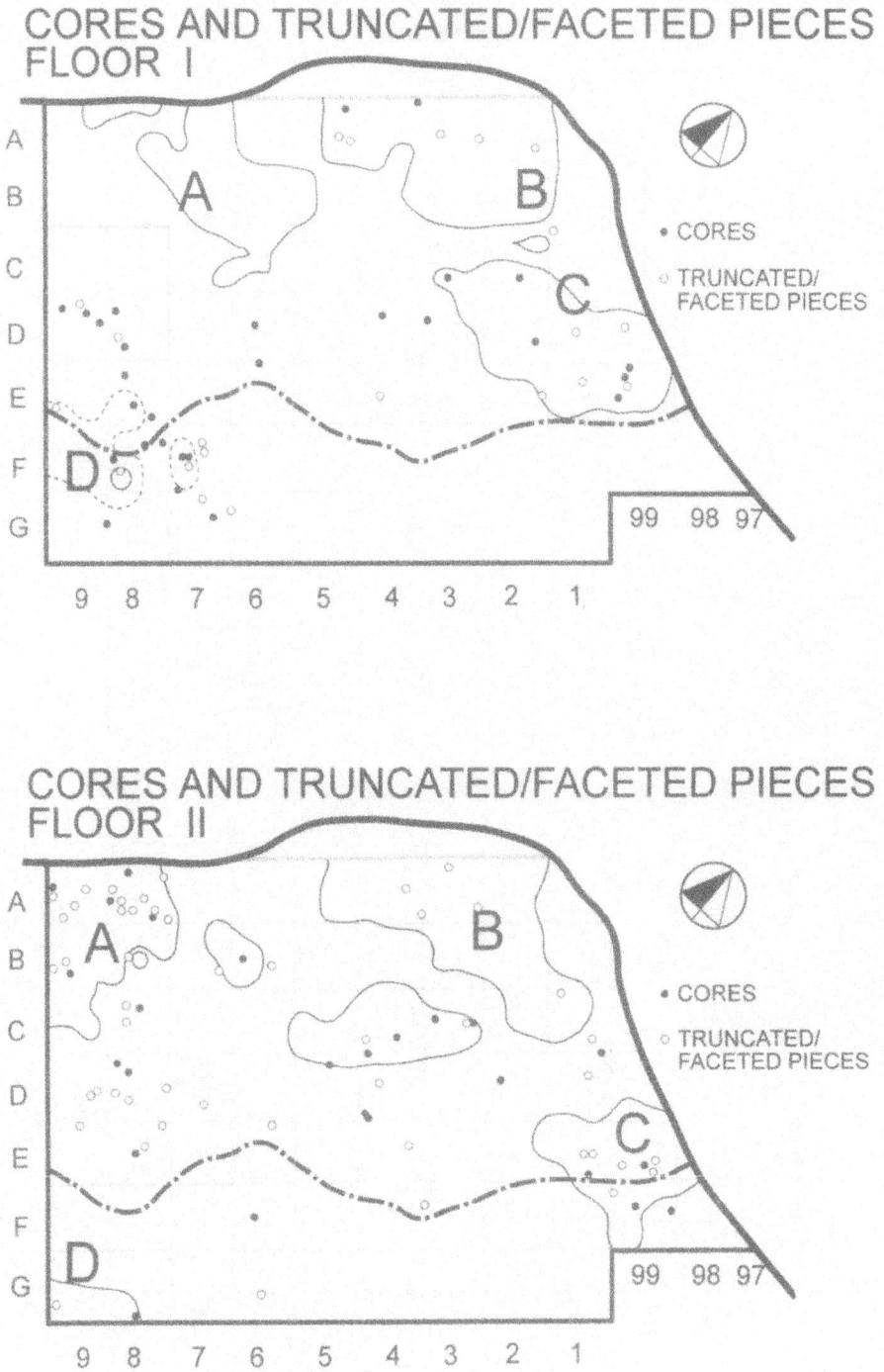

Figure 10.4 Plan of Tor Faraj showing the distributions of cores-from-nodules and cores-on-flakes (truncated faceted pieces). Cores: Floor I ($n = 28$), Floor II ($n = 25$); truncated/faceted pieces: Floor I ($n = 21$), Floor II ($n = 49$)

distributions of cores-on-flakes are examined, they show a clear correlation with the spatial patterns of cores-on-nodules (Fig. 10.4). An exception to this is found in cores-on-flakes being recovered from both floors along the back wall in Area A. Proportionately, Areas A and C show the highest representation of truncated faceted specimens.

Tools

This category, consisting of 495 plotted specimens, displays spatial distributions for each of the floors that strongly match the distributions of debitage, but at the more specific level of tool class, Levallois points, side-scrapers, and notches show distinctive spatial patterns.

Levallois points

Retouched and unretouched Levallois points are concentrated in the alcove of the shelter for both floors (Fig. 10.5). In Floor II they are largely confined to Area B, being poorly represented in Areas A and C, and entirely absent from Area D. Floor I shows a slightly different pattern with points again being concentrated in Area B, but a small point concentration also appears in the open space separating Areas A, B, and C.

Notches

The class consists of only 27 specimens, yet their distributions are strongly patterned, especially for Floor II (Fig. 10.6). In Floor II, notches are concentrated within a roughly 2-meter-wide zone stretching from the back wall in Area A to the dripline. Although only five specimens were plotted for Floor I, four of these appear in Area D. This distribution also parallels that seen in Floor II where notches were concentrated along the south-western edge of the excavation block.

Side-scrapers

The tool class includes only a few specimens, but in both floors these are mostly confined to Area D and the southwestern portion of the excavation block (Fig. 10.6). In their virtual absence from Areas A, B, and C, side-scrapers display a spatial pattern strongly resembling that of notches.

Use-wear study

Laura Longo's use-wear analysis of artifacts recovered from Level 185 of Floor II identified 119 specimens that showed microscopic evidence of having been utilized (Chapter 9). Most of these (*ca.* 80 percent) were associated with activity areas A and B, but this apparent association may be partly skewed by the fact that those artifacts too weathered for microscopic analysis largely came from Areas C and D along the dripline.

The study revealed subtle differences in use-wear attributes between hearth centered areas across Floor II, but the overarching findings imply that there existed a rough balance in the processing of plant and animal materials dominated by those of medium hardness. The working of grass and green wood (inclusive of reeds and rushes) was most strongly tied to the hearth-line near the back wall of the shelter, as was hide procesing, bone, and antler work. In contrast, the centrally located hearths of Area B appear to have been used more for wood work and butchering. Butchering is also the dominant activity in Area A.

Phytoliths

In addition to furnishing important information on the wide variety of plants that were exploited at Tor Faraj, Arlene Rosen's microbotanical study traces the distribution of plant remains across the floor of the shelter (Chapter 7, this volume). Twenty-four sediment samples collected from the centers of excavation units and another six samples gathered from hearths of Floor II yielded a rich and diverse silica phytolith assemblage. Spores and different types of starch grains were also identified.

The spatial distributions of phytoliths of date palm (*Phoenix dactylifera*), seed husks, grasses (monocots), and woody plants (dicots), along with the spores of horse-tail rush (*Equisetum sp.*) and starch grains, provide important evidence of plant related activities in the shelter. Phytoliths of date palms and those of seed husks are concentrated in Area B around the hearths of Features 4, 15, and 14. Rosen argues that this may represent a location where date fruit and plant seeds were prepared and consumed. Starch grains are

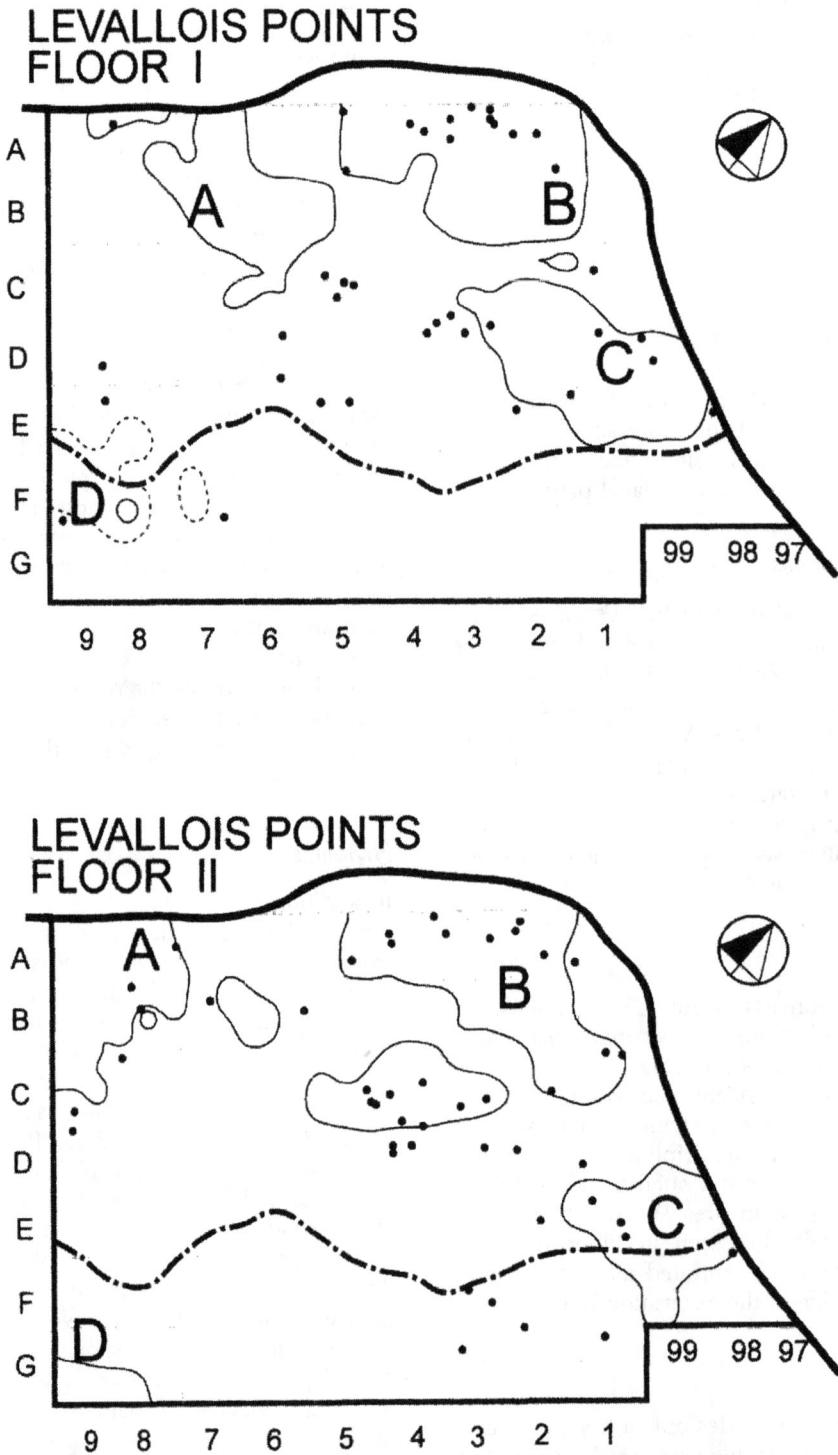

Figure 10.5 Plan of Tor Faraj showing the distributions of Levallois points. Floor I ($n = 38$); Floor II ($n = 47$)

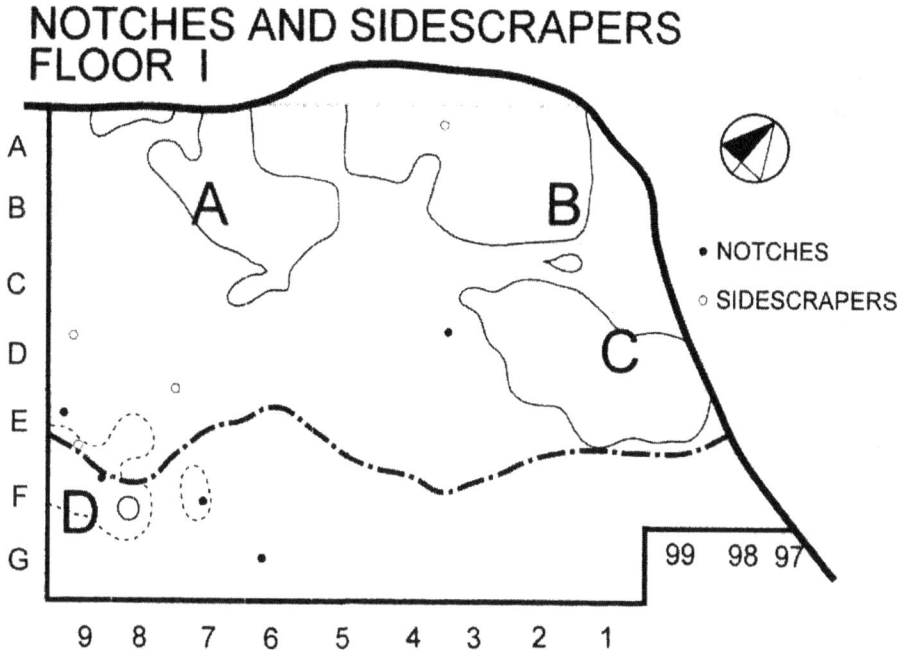

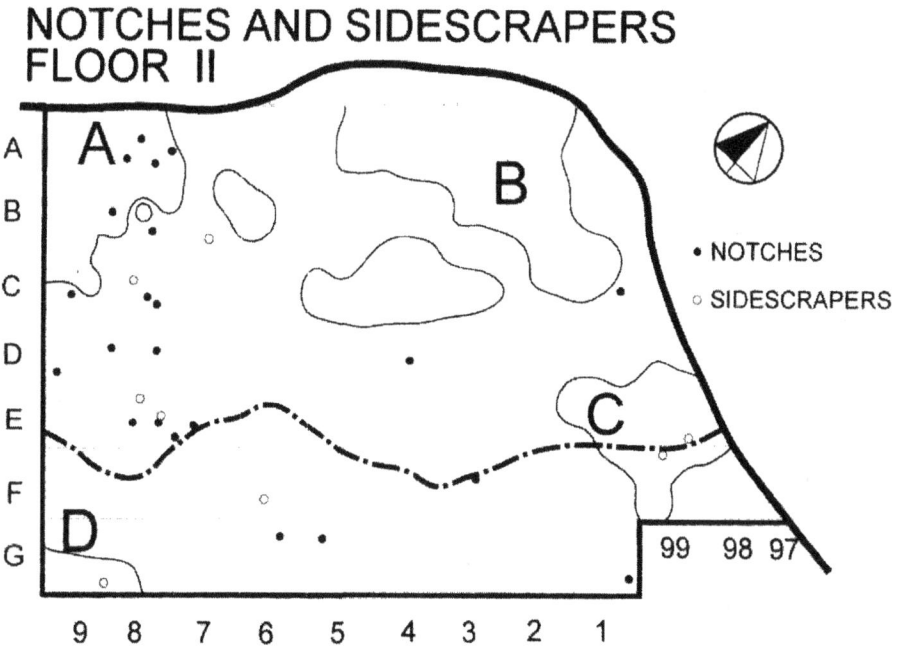

Figure 10.6 Plan of Tor Faraj showing the distributions of side-scrapers and notches. Side-scrapers: Floor I (n = 4), Floor II (n = 8); notches: Floor I (n = 5), Floor II (n = 22)

largely confined to three concentrations form-ing a swath that stretches from west of Area C to north of Area D. Only the western-most concentration is in immediate proximity of a hearth. In her study, Rosen suggests that the starch grains are likely derived from nuts, roots, and tubers brought into the shelter. She found one form of the starches to be identical to reference samples of pistachio. The starch grains also show a reasonably strong spatial correlation with the spores of horse-tail rush, prompting Rosen's observation that the rushes may have been used for making mats or containers, or that the tubers of rushes themselves were a source of some of the starch grains.

Phytoliths of woody plants (dicots) and grasses (monocots) also display very distinct spatial patterns. The dicot phytoliths are concentrated along and outside of the dripline and in a small pocket in the eastern end of the shelter's alcove. In contrast, the monocot phytoliths are restricted to the protected zone of the shelter where they occur inside the dripline, along the back wall between Areas A and B, and on the eastern edge of Area B. These locations along the back wall of the shelter, positioned between hearths, are con-sistent with the notion that the high densities of grass phytoliths may be derived from bedding. Experimental studies have shown that high densities of phytoliths of woody plants are normally restricted to ash deposits as is shown in Rosen's data from the hearths at Tor Faraj. In the absence of hearths, the concentration of dicot phytoliths along the dripline could have resulted from the dump-ing of ash collected from hearth cleanings, but other evidence indicates that this was not the case, at least not entirely. The small debris study did indicate that Area D served as an ash dump, but Area D is situated at the extreme western end of the dripline and corresponds to relatively low densities of dicot phytoliths. Similar artifactual evidence of ash dumping was not detected further east along the dripline where the highest dicot densities occur. Rosen suggests that the concentration of dicot phytoliths may have resulted from the seasonal burning of natural shrubs or brush used in the construction of a wind-break along the dripline.

Phosphorous

Fifty sediment samples were collected from Levels 180 and 185 of Floor II for analysis of their phosphorous and zinc content (Harris, Appendix D). Geochemical studies have shown phosphorus to provide a residual signature of organic materials in archaeo-logical deposits (Sjöberg 1976; Craddock et al. 1985; Bethel and Máté 1989; Lillios 1992). There also is some suggestion that zinc may furnish a parallel indicator for bone (Akridge 1994). But when the phosphorus and zinc values from the Tor Faraj deposit were compared, they were not found to co-vary and further analysis of the zinc data was not pursued. When the phosphorus (P) values are examined across Floor II, using a contour map generated with Surfer 7 (Golden Software, Inc.), high concentrations of P are shown along a swath extending from beyond the dripline into the alcove following the northern wall of the shelter (Fig. 9.13). Low P values dominate the central and much of the south-western portion of the floor. At a more detailed scale, peaks in the concentration of P occur in activity Areas B and C and co-occur spatially with hearths. An exception to this pattern is seen in a P peak that rests against the back wall and just beyond the dripline of the shelter.

Integrated site structure

The site structure of Tor Faraj is derived from the contextual relationship of natural features, cultural features, artifacts, and associated plotted data (e.g., phytoliths and phosphor-ous). Examination of the site's structure leads to several significant observations.

Natural features

The shelter, with its large protected area behind the dripline and extensive terrace, furnished a sizeable area in which groups could establish their encampments. But the natural features of Tor Faraj also would have made the alcove area the most attractive for intensive use because of its protection from the elements and its exposure to afternoon sunlight during the cold season.

Cultural features and hearths

Hearths, confined to the protected area of the shelter, are clustered in the alcove through successive occupations. Their distribution also reveals dual hearth-lines: one following the back wall of the shelter and another clustered in the center of the alcove. Metrical analysis of the hearths also define patterned regularities for the spacing between hearths and distances from the hearths to the back wall. The dual hearth-lines and metrical patterns strongly match those observed for shelter occupations of foraging groups in ethnographic and archaeological contexts.

Artifact and associated data distributions

The spatial patterns of various artifact categories, microbotanical data, and phosphorous concentrations are overwhelmingly tethered to hearths. Spatial plots for the largest of these groups (chips) define four activity areas (A, B, C, and D). These areas appear to have been positioned largely in the same locations within the shelter for successive, discrete occupational episodes.

- *Area A.* Of the four activity areas, Area A displays the greatest intra-area differences between floors. The center of the chip concentration defining Area A drifts about 2m to the northeast from Floor II to Floor I times. And while the area contains two hearths in Floor II, none were found in the area in Floor I. Lithic technology appears to have shifted from an emphasis on initial processing in Floor II to final processing by Floor I times as evidenced by changes in small debris attributes and the relative proportions of cores. For Floor II, relatively high frequencies of side-scrapers and notches are present, but these disappear in Floor I. Paleobotanic data for the area consist principally of grass phytoliths that cluster along the back wall, extending eastward to Area B. The grass may represent the bedding of a sleeping location. The use-wear study indicates that various tasks were undertaken in Area A, but butchery and working green wood and/or grasses predominated.
- *Area B.* For both floors, Area B in the alcove appears to have been the focal location for the most intensive use of the shelter and also the locus for the greatest range of activities. In Floor II, Area B contained most of the hearths of the floor and was dominated by final processing activities as shown in the small debris analysis and debitage reduction study (Table 10.1). Cores (both those on nodules and flakes) and cortical elements occur in low frequencies. In contrast, end-of-stream products represented by Levallois elements, especially Levallois points, are concentrated in the alcove area. Interestingly, side-scrapers and notches are under-represented here. The pattern seen in the cluster of hearths and the lithic related activities is repeated during Floor I times. A review of the lithic indices traces a very similar profile for the area in both floors (Table 10.1). Phytoliths of date palm (*Phoenix dactylifera*) and seed husks cluster around the hearths centered in the alcove and imply that food processing was undertaken there. Results of the use-wear study show plant cutting, wood working, and hide processing to have been focal activities for the activity area. And at a more detailed scale, spatial plots of studied specimens suggest that butchering activities took place around the central hearths, while bone and antler work are associated with the hearth-line following the back wall. Also, concentrations of grass phytoliths along the back wall near the eastern and western ends of the alcove may reflect locations for bedding and sleeping locations.
- *Area C.* The area shows striking redundancy between Floors I and II in the numbers and locations of hearths and in the lithic indices. And in many ways, Area C represents a kind of extension of Area B, but more peripherally situated with less intensive utilization. Perhaps Area C's location so close to the dripline would have made it less attractive under certain conditions. The configuration of Area C's lithic assemblage strongly resembles that of Area B, but with a greater emphasis upon initial processing as expressed in higher densities of cores. The high values of phosphorus, that form a swath along the northern wall of the shelter in Areas B and C, point to the frequent processing and discard of organic remains in both areas. Area C, however, does not exhibit phyto-

Table 10.1 A comparison of the four activity areas by living floor relative to the composition of the data-sets present

	Area A	Area B	Area C	Area D
Floor I				
Hearths	0	5	1	0
Lithic processing	Final	Final	Final	Initial
Cores	None	Low	Moderate	High
Levallois points	Low	High	High	Low
Side-scrapers	0	1	0	3
Notches	0	0	1	3
Floor II				
Hearths	2	10	1	0
Lithic processing	Initial	Final	Final	Initial
Cores	High	Low	Moderate	High
Levallois points	Moderate	High	High	None
Side-scrapers	2	1	1	4
Notches	9	2	2	7
Use-wear, predominant material processed	GGW, A	P, W, H, BA	MH	W
Phytoliths				
Grass	+	+	–	–
Wood	–	+	+	+
Seed husks	–	+	–	–
Dates	–	+	–	–
Starch	–	–	+	+
Phosphorus	low	high	high	low

Key for materials processed: A-animal; BA-bone and antler; GGW-grass and green wood; H-hide; MH-meat and hide; P-plant; W-wood

liths suggestive of intensive plant processing, at least in close proximity of the hearth. This interpretation is partially supported by the results of the use-wear study that shows less plant processing than for Area B, but a greater emphasis on meat processing.

- *Area D.* Located along the dripline and distant from the back wall of the shelter, Area D is stratigraphically redundant, but when compared across each floor it stands apart from the other activity areas along most lines of evidence. The area encompasses the densest part of the roof-fall which includes massive sandstone slabs as well as smaller rubble. Because of its position in the roof-fall, Area D appears to have experienced a slower rate of deposition than the others, as indicated by a higher rate of artifact patination. The area also lacks hearths and displays the lowest density of artifacts of the three activity areas. Although some initial processing appears to have taken place here, as evidenced by both small debris attributes

and the concentration of cores, final processing activities apparently were rarely undertaken. Levallois elements, especially Levallois points, are absent or present in very low frequencies. In the absence of hearth features, the relatively high frequency of small debris attributes linked to burning implies that Area D may also have served as a location for dumping the ash-fills of hearths. Beyond the dicot phytoliths of woody plants, perhaps reflecting the remains of a brush enclosure along the mouth of the shelter, plant remains occur in low frequencies in the area. The use-wear study of artifacts from Area D, hampered by a high incidence of patination, indicates a rough balance between the processing of plant and animal materials. Although the combined evidence suggests that the area was rarely used for more than initial lithic production activities and as a spot for dumping ash from hearth cleaning, it does contain exceptionally high proportions of side-scrapers and notches.

Simple versus complex site structure

In comparing the behavioral organization of archaic and modern foragers, researchers have focused on the relative complexity of site structures (Binford 1983a, 1996; Simek 1987; Marks 1988b; Stringer and Gamble 1993; Mellars 1996; Henry 1998a, Kaufman 1999). The *simple* site structure of archaic occupations is generalized as displaying: (1) an intensive activity area tied to a central hearth or a few redundant activity areas tied to a small number of hearths; and (2) evidence of temporally continuous and spatially overlapping activities. In contrast, the *complex* structure of the occupations of modern foragers is described as exhibiting: (1) discrete, nonredundant activity areas in which most, but not all, are tied to hearths; and (2) evidence of temporally segmented and spatially segregated activities.

Structural complexity at Tor Faraj

At Tor Faraj, both floors reveal distinct activity areas, most of which are tethered to hearths. Area B, situated in the shallow alcove of the shelter, appears to have been the most intensively used part of the shelter and the focus of domestic activities related to food preparation, cooking, and sleeping. Additionally, use-wear evidence points to the area as a location for the working of hide, wood, bone, and antler. Activity Areas A and C, located peripheral to the alcove along the wall of the shelter, reflect less intensive use and they are associated with more limited ranges of activities. Area A, as expressed for Floor II, was a spot used for core preparation and removals, butchery, and working grass and green wood. During the Floor I occupation, Area A was less intensively used and the emphasis on lithic work had shifted to final processing. While Area C yields evidence indicative of lithic related activities that strongly resemble those associated with the adjacent Area B, other activities tied to the area appear to differ considerably from those reconstructed for the alcove. Food plant remains are uncommon to the area and use-wear analysis shows little evidence for plant processing there as well. Finally, Area D stands apart from the other activity areas across most lines of evidence. It lacked hearths and was the least intensively utilized. Apparently, it served principally as a primary lithic processing area and as a spot for dumping hearth fills.

Temporal segmentation and spatial segregation of activities

Lithic signatures expressed in the debitage, small debris, and refit studies indicate that some initial processing was undertaken in most locations of the shelter, but these activities appear to have been habitually concentrated in the southwestern portion, Areas A and D. It is in this part of the shelter where chert nodules were preliminarily trimmed and shaped for the removals of Levallois elements, especially Levallois points. In judging from the refit study, this process most likely resulted in a series of point removals given the little amount of core preparation to the face and platform required between removals. While evidence in the form of small debris, cores, and primary elements tie this area to initial processing, the end-products of the reduction (i.e., Levallois elements and Levallois points) are actually located on the opposite side of the shelter in Areas B and C. And it is in these areas within and adjacent to the alcove that we see a shift in lithic technology toward final processing activities linked to edge retouch and a dominance of soft-hammer percussion. These areas also show the greatest intensity and diversity of use-wear.

These data then suggest that the inhabitants of the shelter discriminated between tasks associated with the initial production of Levallois points, their principal tool blank, and the use, maintenance, and rejuvenation of the points. Moreover, they appear to have conceptualized the division of these tasks as different production stages which they, in turn, segregated into different parts of the shelter. While this may not seem extraordinary, as it parallels the ways in which modern foragers often organize their camp activities, it differs from our prevailing view of how archaic foragers organized their behaviors. This view holds that tasks are likely to have been conceptually unbroken and largely associated with *ad hoc* behaviors. Cores would have been shaped, blanks removed, and then used, all in the same spot, as part of a continuous, unbroken conceptual scheme devoted to a specific, situational need.

Another data-set from Tor Faraj even more fully underscores the ways in which the inhabitants of the shelter segregated their activities. As discussed earlier, cores fashioned from chert nodules and those made from thick flakes (truncated faceted specimens) were found to display a very strong spatial co-variation. In recalling the results of technological (Chapter 3) and refit (Chapter 6) studies, the truncated faceted specimens were linked to an economizing effort associated with recycling large, thick flakes that had been previously generated from nodular cores. From the perspective of lithic reduction, the flakes would have been produced as later removals and they would likely have been distributed over much of the shelter. But when recycled as cores, however, they were conceptually 'relabeled' and spatially repositioned to the areas where initial processing was undertaken. This observation is especially important for I think it shows how a certain part of the shelter was seen as a place for undertaking initial manufacturing tasks regardless of whether chert nodules were obtained from near their sources, distant from the site, or from flakes that were collected from across the floor of the shelter for recycling as cores. While the alcove area was clearly another place for certain designated activities, the natural, physical features of the shelter would likely have conditioned these and influenced their placement. The natural features of the shelter seem less likely to have played a role in the positioning of Areas A and D, other than their placement largely behind the dripline.

Other dimensions of site structure: drop–toss and exogene cave models

Beyond the complexity of site structure, researchers have also focused on the contextual relationships of features and certain kinds of artifact distributions. Drawing from ethnoarchaeological evidence, Binford (1978, 1983a) has observed a relationship between the sizes of artifacts and their distributions in concentric zones encircling a hearth. He identified an interior *drop zone* consisting of

small residues of hearth-side activities and an exterior *toss zone* comprising larger, bulkier materials that are removed from the intensively used area around the hearth because of their interference with seating and other hearth-side activities. In comparing the size and weight distributions of artifacts recorded at Tor Faraj to the Drop-Toss Model, drop zones are evident as can be seen in the chip concentrations tied to most of the hearths. For Floor II, a peak density of chips is found within a meter of all 11 hearths and in Floor I chip concentrations rest within a meter of four of the six hearths. But the Tor Faraj data offer no clear evidence for the presence of a toss zone. Larger and heavier artifacts are somewhat concentrated in Areas A and D, but this mainly is because cores (being the largest and heaviest artifact category) cluster in these areas of primary processing. Moreover, the small debris data indicate that the cores were not tossed there, but were, in fact, initially processed and dropped there.

Given Thomas' (1983) research into the drop-toss phenomenon at Gatecliff Shelter, it may not be surprising that the artifact distributions recorded at Tor Faraj fail to conform to the expected pattern. In studying artifact distributions for successive floors in the shelter, Thomas found a toss zone of heavier, larger artifacts to radiate from the hearth area in the direction of the mouth and beyond the dripline of the shelter, rather than all around the hearth as in the Drop-Toss Model. Thus, Thomas' Exogene Cave Model suggests that foragers, occupying protected sites, dispose of unwanted items differently than those encamped in the open. In protected sites, large, bothersome items are removed from the intensively utilized areas about hearths, directionally, toward the mouth of the shelter. Anecdotal, ethnographic evidence is consistent with the model, showing foragers occupying shelters regularly to use the area beyond the dripline as a dump. When the size and weight distributions of artifacts from Tor Faraj are examined, however, they show no evidence of such behaviors. Transects from the back wall to and beyond the dripline show relatively uniform distributions.

The lack of fit between the Tor Faraj data and the artifact distribution models developed by Binford and Thomas raises several questions. The most direct interpretation is that the archaic inhabitants of Tor Faraj were more tolerant of large artifacts within their zones of intensive activity. But before assuming that they were bad housekeepers, some other factors responsible for the lack of agreement between the artifact distributional data and the models need examination. First, we need to consider how big objects must be for them to be viewed as annoyances in activity areas around hearths. It is likely that, unless they impede comfortable seating or get in the way of other hearth-side activities, they are tolerated. At Tor Faraj, most of the chipped stone artifacts simply may not have been large enough to have been considered nuisances. Cores (the most massive chipped stone artifact category), for example, average only $50 \times 55 \times 24$mm; about the size of a hen's egg bisected longitudinally. Both the Drop-Toss and Exogene Cave Models were based upon a considerably larger threshold for items that were tossed. Although larger artifacts are not available at Tor Faraj for checking this idea, the sandstone rubble scattered across the floor indicates that it may have been cleared from the areas of intensive activity. The spatial plots for sandstone across the two floors at Tor Faraj show a void of rubble around the hearth clusters in the intensively used alcove area (Area B). Also, smaller pockets without sandstone occur around the hearths in Areas A and C.

Decoding site structure and the palimpsest phenomena

Perhaps the greatest challenge to understanding the prehistoric behaviors that were responsible for creating the structure of a site relates to teasing apart specific occupational episodes. In this study, we formally evaluated through various lines of evidence the degree to which the shelter's fill had experienced post-depositional disturbance, both natural and cultural. All indicators pointed to the deposit being largely undisturbed (except for the recent Bedouin construction activities) and the occupation residue of the two living floors having contextual integrity.

The depositional environment of Tor Faraj and the relatively low intensity of Middle Paleolithic use of the shelter allowed for the formation of living floors with features, artifacts, and related evidence preserved in their primary context. Although two distinct floors were isolated for the examination of their site structure, we are still stuck with the vexing question of what these floors represent in terms of the numbers of specific occupational events. For site structure studies, this relates to the problem associated with the palimpsest phenomenon, but at a more refined scale and within thinner slices of time. If we are accurately to decode a site's structure in terms of behavioral meaning, it is essential that we have some understanding of the number of occupational episodes that were responsible for generating our findings. While a complete answer to the question is not possible at Tor Faraj, there are some clues that provide, at least, a partial understanding of the dynamic nature of the prehistoric occupations of the shelter.

A comparison of the numbers and densities of hearths at Tor Faraj with similar data from shelter occupations in ethnographic contexts indicates that Floor II most likely reflects two to three distinct occupations, while Floor I is probably an expression of one to two occupational events (Table 10.2). A review of hearth data associated with cross-cultural, ethnographic occupations of shelters shows a mean of 4.2 hearths/occupation, a hearth density of 1 hearth/23.6m², and a maximum of six hearths per occupation. A direct comparison with the Tor Faraj data is complicated by the fact that the excavation block accounts for only 38 percent of the overall protected area (the area behind dripline) of the shelter, but even within this block most of the hearths are clustered in a small portion of the shelter in the alcove.

The relative spacing of hearths also offers a means of teasing apart specific occupational episodes at Tor Faraj. In Binford's (1996: 230) studies of 'hearth-centered' behaviors, he found that in addition to the regular patterns that delimited drop and toss zones, a 'circle defined by the area occupied by seated persons surrounding the hearth' regularly measured 1.76m in radius from the center of a hearth. Such a circular zone set aside for hearth-side activities would strongly influence the spacing of hearths relative to other hearths and also to the back walls of shelters. This activity zone may largely explain the regularity

Table 10.2 Predictions of the number of occupations that would have been represented by the hearths for each living floor at Tor Faraj based upon hearth data from ethnographically described shelter occupations

At Tor Faraj	Ethnographic	Predicted for Tor Faraj
Hearth density		
Excavated area (52m^2)	1 hearth/23.6m^2	2.2 hearths
Total sheltered area (136m^2)	1 hearth/23.6m^2	5.8 hearths
Maximum number of hearths **per occupation**		
Floor I - 6 hearths	6 hearths	Minimum of 1 occupation
Floor II - 13 hearths	6 hearths	Min. of 2-3 occupations
Mean number of hearths per occupation		
Floor I - 6 hearths	4.2 hearths	1-2 occupations
Floor II - 13 hearths	4.2 hearths	3-4 occupations
Density of hearths Floor I		
Excavated area - 6 hearths	est. 2.2 hearths	2-3 occupations
Total sheltered - 6 hearths	est. 5.8 hearths	1-2 occupations
Floor II		
Excavated area -13 hearths	est. 2.2 hearths	5-6 occupations
Total sheltered - 13 hearths	est. 5.8 hearths	2-3 occupations

in hearth spacing, as noted by Gamble (1991) with his '3m rule,' although ethnographic data suggest that the absolute distances between hearths may also be conditioned by other factors. The number of residents in a camp (Hassan 1981: 72) and hearth function, e.g., cooking versus sleeping (Nicholson and Cane 1991), have been observed to influence hearth to hearth distance. And as discussed earlier, the distance between hearths in ethnographic occupations appears to be inversely related to the number of hearths. However, even in light of these conditioning factors, the distances between hearths regularly fall in the 2 to 3m range.

In an effort to compare these ethnographic regularities in hearth spacing to the hearths exposed in the Tor Faraj living floors, circles of 1.8m, representing the hearth-side activity zone, were centered on each of the hearths (Fig. 10.7). In assuming that only a single hearth should command an activity zone, other hearths falling within a zone are presumed to represent a different occupational event.

Examination of the six hearths of Floor I shows Hearths 2 and 6 to fall within other hearth-side zones. This suggests that they represent a specific occupational event distinct from that of Hearths 3, 21, 8, and 7. Further review of the hearth pattern shows Hearths 3, 21, and 7 to be positioned roughly equidistant from each other at a distance of about 2m from the centers of the hearths; just beyond the hearth-side zone of adjacent hearths (Fig. 10.7). Moreover, Hearths 3, 21, and 8 show their hearth-side zone to end precisely with the back wall of the shelter. These patterns suggest that the six hearths of Floor II reflect two specific occupational events with Hearths 3, 21, 8, and 7 seeing synchronous use, while Hearths 2 and 6 were used at another time or times. The precise length of time separating the use of the hearths is impossible to establish. The close proximity of the anomalously positioned hearths with patterned ones, however, may simply represent subtle repositions of hearths during a single interval of encampment in the shelter.

A similar analysis was undertaken for the hearths of Floor II, but after they were separated stratigraphically into upper (Levels 180-90) and lower (Levels 190-200) groups (Fig. 10.7). The upper group shows Hearths 4,

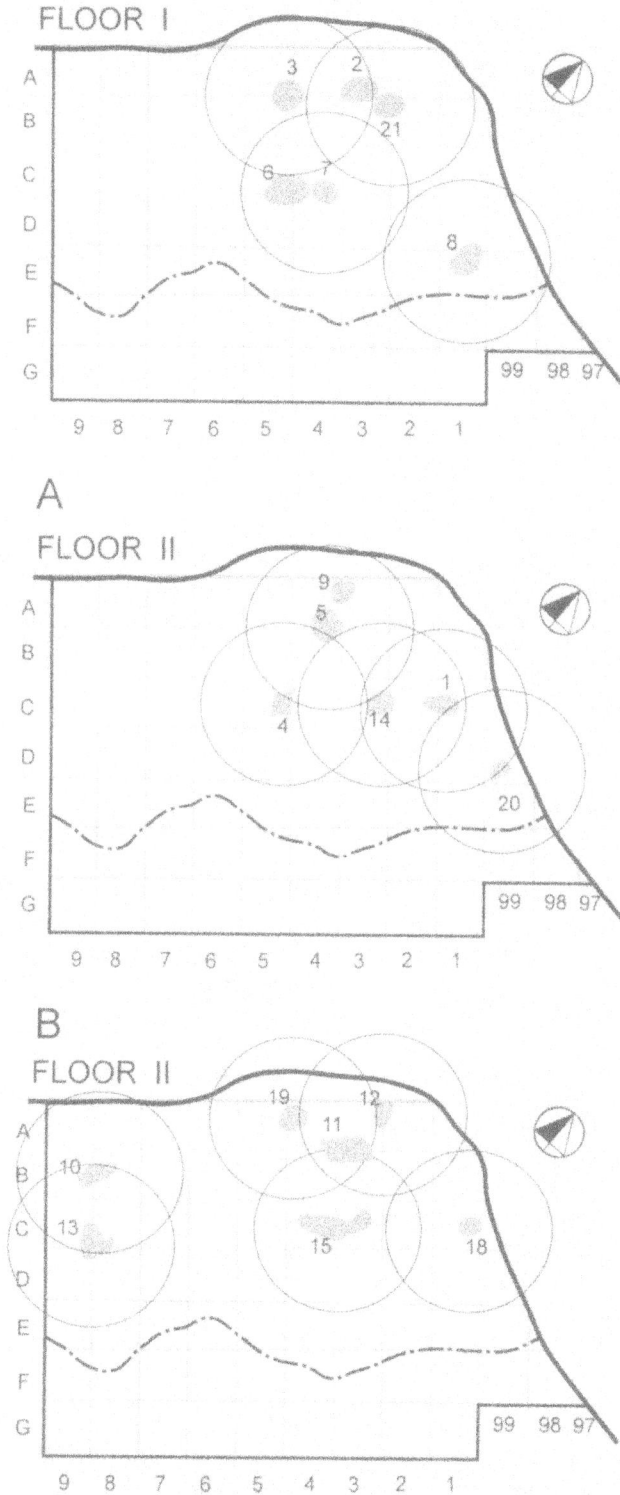

Figure 10.7 Plan of Tor Faraj showing the distributions of hearths and their hearth-side activity zones (1.75m radius from hearth center) for Floor I; **A**, upper Floor II; and **B**, lower Floor II

5, 14, 1, and 20 to be roughly equidistant and again positioned at or near the limits of the hearth-side zones of adjacent hearths. As seen in Floor I, hearths near the back wall are also positioned roughly equidistant between adjacent hearths and the wall (e.g., Hearths 5 and 1). Hearth 9 clearly stands out as an anomaly to the overall pattern. The lower group again shows remarkable consistency in hearth spacing. Only one, Hearth 11, is irregularly positioned relative to the adjacent Hearths 19 and 12. And as seen in the hearth patterns of Floor I and upper Floor II, most of the hearths are spaced about 2m apart.

Relative to the numbers of discrete occupational events, the hearth patterns suggest that Floor I was formed by one to two episodes and Floor II was produced by two to three such events. The uncertainty about the exact numbers of occupational events mainly stems from how the atypically positioned hearths are interpreted. If the four irregularly placed hearths reflect subtle repositions of nearby ones, Floor I would reflect a single episode of encampment in the shelter and Floor II, two such occupations.

The numbers, densities, and spatial patterns of hearths at Tor Faraj then are generally in agreement in indicating one to two episodes of occupation for Floor I and two to three such occupations for Floor II.

Reconstructing the occupations

The combined evidence from the excavation suggests that Late Levantine Mousterian groups occupied the shelter during the late winter to spring. The recovery of phytoliths from seed husks and the floral parts of plants indicates use of the shelter between February and May. This would have been the time of the greatest available water in the Wadi Aghar and the southern exposure of the shelter also is consistent with its use in the cold season. Mousterian groups most likely inhabited Tor Faraj as part of their annual cycle of transhumance in which they moved from the Ma'an Plateau to the Rift Valley (Henry 1994, 1995b). After inhabiting the relatively warm environs of the Rift Valley during the coldest part of the winter, Mousterian foragers would have progressively moved to higher elevations as they followed the peak of the growing season.

Conceivably, the shelter could have been used during both their downslope and upslope migrations. The presence of chert from the Rift Valley in low (5 percent), but consistent percentages, however, implies that Tor Faraj was typically inhabited as part of the upslope segment of transhumance. When camping at the shelter, groups are likely to have recharged their chert supply mainly from the local Humeima and Ma'an Plateau sources. Although the Ma'an Plateau source is at a distance similar to that of the Rift Valley, it offers greater ease of access. Additionally, the simple energetics involved in carrying heavy loads would have favored downslope returns from the Ma'an Plateau over upslope ones from the Rift Valley for elevation intervals of *ca.* 600m either way. Therefore, the presence of the Rift Valley chert in the shelter is best explained by it being imported as part of regularly scheduled residential moves rather than through special collection forays.

Numbers of occupants

A review of several different approaches to estimating prehistoric populations suggests that Tor Faraj was inhabited by some 12 to 15 occupants during any one encampment at the shelter (Table 10.3). Methods of prehistoric population estimation, largely relying upon comparative ethnographic data, are hindered by limited evidence and numerous conditioning factors. This is compounded in the context of sheltered settings because comparative data are extremely rare (Binford 1996). And, in addition, there are indications that some of the relationships that hold in open-air encampments are reversed in sheltered settings because of the spatial constraints on floor space. The number of persons encamping at Tor Faraj was estimated on the basis of the floor area of the site (Hassan 1981: 71), the average distances between hearths (*ibid.*: 72), the numbers of hearths (Nicholson and Cane 1991: 326) and the size of the bedding areas (Nicholson and Cane 1991: 336; Binford 1996: 239). Also, in an attempt to test the accuracy of the specific approaches, each of the methods was applied to ethnoarchaeological examples with known populations; the Vedda Rockshelter, Bendiyagalge, Ceylon (Seligmann and Seligmann 1911; Binford 1996) and the

Yungubalibanda Shelter 6 in Australia (Nicholson and Cane 1991).

Population estimates of foraging groups based upon site area have been developed through various equations (Hassan 1981: 66-72), but recent studies show that such empirical relationships may lack cross-cultural integrity for a variety of reasons (Whitelaw 1983; Nicholson and Cane 1991). Moreover, given the spatial constraints of shelter occupations, they are likely to exhibit a relationship between occupation area and population that differs from that of open sites. In an effort to check the applicability of the population estimate procedures described by Hassan (1981: 71) to shelter sites, data from ethnographic shelter occupations were considered. Given the similar sizes of the protected areas of the two ethnographic shelters (*ca.* 32m^2), they yielded a population estimate of seven to ten persons when, in fact, six and 12 occupants were reported for the shelters (Table 10.3). Although this shows that the technique lacks precision, it also suggests that the range of the estimate is reasonably close to the actual numbers of persons residing in the shelters. A factor that may be skewing the relationship between occupation space and numbers of persons in the two ethnographic

examples is body size. The six boys and men using Yungubalibanda Shelter are likely to have required more space per person than the four adults and eight children residing in the Vedda shelter. The estimates for Tor Faraj are computed by two different assumptions. One is that the site area consisted of the total protected area of Tor Faraj (*ca.* 136m^2) and the other is that the site area is defined by that portion of the shelter that was confirmed to have been occupied through excavation (*ca.* 67m^2). These assumptions, which are likely to bracket the range of values possible for the occupation, yield estimates ranging from about 10 to 19 persons (Table 10.3).

Population estimates developed from distances between hearths were made by Hassan (1981: 72) from Yellen's (1977) data for open-air sites. Hassan (1981) observed that such distances increase directly with the numbers of camp residents. However, as discussed earlier, in shelter occupations with their constraints on space, the distances between hearths appear to decline with increased number of occupants. At the Vedda Rockshelter, the mean spacing (1.2m) of those hearths behind the dripline yields a population estimate of *ca.* two persons when, in fact, the shelter held 12 people. When this

Table 10.3 A comparison of the estimated and the observed populations for two ethnographically reported shelters, Yungubalibanda Shelter 6 (Nicholson and Cane 1991) and Vedda Rockshelter, Bendiyagalge (Binford 1996; Seligmann and Seligmann 1911), and Tor Faraj based upon four different methods of population estimation

	Population: Estimated and Observed				
	Tor Faraj	Yungubalibanda Shelter 6		Vedda Shelter Bendiyagalge	
Basis of estimate	(Estimated)	Estimated reported		Estimated reported	
Site area					
Excavated	15–19	7–10	6	7–10	12
Protected	10–13				
Mean distance between					
hearths	8	3	6	2	12
Number of hearths	9	5	6	9	12
Size of sleeping area	10	3	6	9	12

Note: The mean distance between hearths approach furnishes the least accurate estimates

procedure is applied to the Yungubalibanda Shelter data, the mean hearth spacing (1.5m) produces an estimated population of three persons compared to the reported six residents of the shelter.

In their ethnoarchaeological study of Australian Bushmen open camps, Nicholson and Cane (1991: 326) noted a very strong correlation between the numbers of hearths and residents. In using their data on those shelter occupations where they report the number of residents, in conjunction with parallel data for the Vedda Shelter, a similarly strong correlation (R value of .795) can be seen.

Nicholson and Cane (*ibid.*: 336) also examined the sizes of sleeping areas in open-air camps and found most (66 percent) to consist of areas for a single person that commanded about 0.94m². Sleeping areas for 2 (0.83m²/person), 3 (0.32m²/person), and 4 (0.42m²/person) persons were less common and utilized relatively less space per person. Overall, the 25 persons in the study enjoyed about 0.68m²/person for sleeping. If this global average is used to estimate the numbers of persons at Tor Faraj based upon the sizes of the areas proposed for bedding (6.75m²), as defined by the distribution of grass phytoliths, then some ten people would have encamped in the shelter. In applying the same approach to the Vedda shelter, an estimate of nine persons is generated.

A comparison of the results produced by the alternative models of population estimation to the actual Yungubalibanda and Vedda Shelter data shows three of the models to yield reasonable estimates, falling with 75 to 83 percent of the actual population, while the hearth spacing model furnishes a poor fit (Table 10.3). When these approaches are applied to Tor Faraj, it would seem that the results based upon numbers of hearths and size of the sleeping areas should best be viewed as slightly under-representing the numbers of Middle Paleolithic inhabitants of the shelter. And in basing the population estimate on site area, a value somewhere between the estimates for the total protected area and the excavated area is probably close to the actual numbers of occupants. In view of these alternative approaches, it would seem that some 12 to 15 persons are most likely to have inhabited Tor Faraj.

Length of occupation

How long did groups camp in the shelter? Whatever the absolute length of time was that groups spent in shelter, the three major occupations appear to have been of about the same duration. If artifact density and numbers of hearths are a measure of length of residence, then the durations of the encampments were roughly the same for Floor I and the two episodes of occupation for Floor II. But how long did groups use the shelter in an absolute sense? Chert usage may provide a means of getting at this vexing question.

If the weights of all artifacts (including chips) are calculated, Floor I contained about 17kg of chert and Floor II contained 27kg, about equally divided between this floor's upper and lower occupations. As described earlier, chert was introduced to the shelter primarily in the form of fist-sized nodules that average about 300g each. Therefore, the total artifact weights indicate that about 57 nodules were consumed by the occupants of Floor I and about 45 nodules were used for each of the occupations of Floor II.

In recalling the lithic technology and refit studies, lithic reduction at Tor Faraj focused almost solely on the production of Levallois points and as many as six Levallois points were produced for each nodular core that was processed. Additional points were generated from recycled cores-on-flakes, but because of their small sizes, these rarely resulted in more than a single point. When the numbers of nodular cores are compared to the numbers of points, we see a point:core ratio of about 2:1. But when cores-on-flakes are also considered, the ratio falls to about 1:1. This discrepancy between the potential numbers of points that could have been produced from cores and the numbers of points found in the shelter relative to cores can be explained in two ways. The loss of points by hunters, while away from the shelter, most likely accounts for the largest part of the discrepancy. Some points were recycled into other tool types and this also would reduce the point:core ratio. Given the potential point:core production of 7:1 and the observed (after loss) point:core ratio of 1: 1, an actual production ratio of 4–5:1 seems reasonable. This would mean that some 75 to 80 percent of those points produced in the shelter were lost, damaged, or recycled. In light of the fragility of stone points, as evidenced by ethnographic accounts (Ellis 1997: 56-8) and experimental results (Odell and Cowan 1986), the need to produce large numbers of points is understandable. If we assume a 'consumption' of some ten points per day for each knapper and the presence of two to three knappers for the group, some three to eight nodules per day would have been used. This would have depleted the raw material of Floor I in 8 to 14 days and Floor II in 6 to 11 days.

Activities and use of space in the shelter

Hearth positioning and general artifact distributions indicate that the occupants of the shelter positioned their activities in generally similar ways during their stays at Tor Faraj. The most intensive use of the shelter was centered in Area B located in the alcove. Hearths, habitually clustered near the mouth of the alcove, were associated with plant food preparation and maintenance tasks linked to working hide, wood, bone, and antler. A large sandstone slab, positioned by the hearth cluster in Floor II, may well have served as a platform for undertaking some of these tasks. Some initial lithic production was carried out here, but final processing involving edge modification, use, and rejuvenation of tools was the focus of the flaked stone work. Further back in the alcove, a hearth-line paralleling the wall is flanked by two pockets of grass phytoliths thought to represent bedding. While these are interpreted as sleeping areas, the concentrations of chips and Levallois points, along with the results of use-wear analysis, show that some maintenance activities were also undertaken between the bedding spots. The very low density of cores is consistent with the results of the small debris study in showing that little initial core shaping and blank production were undertaken near the back of the alcove.

Activity Areas A and C are peripherally positioned to the alcove along the back wall of the shelter and they appear to flank the two sleeping locations. Both areas are associated with fewer hearths than occur in the alcove and neither of the areas is linked to food preparation or cooking, at least as evidenced by paleobotanic remains. In many ways, Areas

A and C appear as outliers to the alcove, connected to it by the bedding. However, while Area C generally mimics the maintenance and final lithic processing tasks evident in Area B, Area A differs considerably with its focus on initial processing and butchery.

Area D straddles the dripline well removed from the shelter's back wall. It stands apart from the other activity areas in lacking hearths, but apparently serving as a spot used for dumping ash from hearth cleanings. The concentration of cores and the small debris attributes also indicate that it was an area of intensive initial processing, at least during Floor I times.

A composite view of the positioning of activities in the shelter shows a centrally located area for food preparation, cooking, and general domestic tasks that was situated at the mouth of the alcove. This position, well back from the dripline, would have offered good protection from eastern winds and precipitation in addition to providing late afternoon sunlight. But, perhaps more importantly, in locating the central hearth cluster about 3m from the nearest wall of the shelter, the occupants allowed room for the formation of a swath of sleeping spots and accompanying hearths between the central hearths and the shelter's back wall. Such positioning also allowed for those engaged in sleeping and other tasks along the back wall hearth-line nearly equal access to the central hearth-cluster. Such access may have had as much to do with ease of conversation as physical movement between the central hearths and the outliers. Other activity patterns that cross-cut the activity areas of the shelter have to do with the production and use of Levallois points and the presence of notches and side-scrapers. That part of the shelter stretching from Areas A to D was targeted for core shaping and delivery of Levallois points. But the points appear to have been used, maintained, stored, and discarded to a markedly greater extent in Activity Areas B and C. A similar activity area dichotomy is suggested by the distributions of side-scrapers and notches as they are almost exclusively found in Areas A and D. Although we are unable to link the side-scrapers and notches to specific functions, their distributions furnish additional evidence that many of the activities undertaken in Areas A and D differed from those in the alcove.

Social composition of the groups

The interpretation of the accumulated data suggests that 12 to 15 persons used the shelter for stays of one to two weeks during three major episodes of occupation, but how were the groups composed socially? If they were organized along the lines of modern foragers, the shelter may have been used by a residential unit of two to three families or perhaps by a sex-specific, task unit such as a hunting or collecting party. Given the suspected size of the groups residing in the shelter, their lengths of residence, and their diversity of activities, it seems unlikely that they represented specific task groups, however. A variety of extractive and maintenance activities linked to both plant and animal products points more strongly to the use of the shelter by foragers engaged in a wide range of domestic tasks by both males and females. But what if the social organization of the Middle Paleolithic occupants of Tor Faraj consisted of small residential units that lacked the kind of family group recognition which is common to modern foragers?

This difference in social organization is precisely what Binford (1996: 234) questions:

> What may be quite different between fully modern humans and ancient hominids is the social organization and, therefore, the way that social groups are segmented. These characteristics in turn affect how such segments are articulated to one another in carrying out daily tasks and in shifting residential camp sites during subsistence activities.

Binford's emphasis on the importance of family unit recognition within modern foraging groups parallels the arguments of others who have stressed that, at a larger social scale, the emergence of inter-group social networks or alliances signaled the transition to modern culture (Whallon 1989; Stringer and Gamble 1993; Gamble 1994). Although few dispute the significance of social networks in hominid evolution, several scholars question the notion that such networks appeared only with the beginning of the Upper Paleolithic (Roebroeks et al. 1988; Féblot-Augustins 1993; Hayden 1993; also see Kaufman 1999: 65-70 for an exhaustive review). The identification of such networks has relied upon evidence for symboling and importation of distant raw materi-als, but when these attributes are evaluated in archaeological contexts, they rarely provide unambiguous tests for the presence of modern social networks. The material manifestations of symboling, for example, are not universal among modern hominids, so how can their rarity or absence be used to discount symboling by archaic groups (Marshack 1989)? And while importation of distant raw materials has been shown in archaic contexts (see review in Mellars 1996: 141-68), in reality, there are so many other factors (e.g., settlement permanence, extractive techniques, technological constraints) beyond social alliances that condition raw material exploitation, it is probably not a reliable attribute of modern social organization.

In contrast to other proposed attributes of human modernity, patterns in site structure, thought by Binford (1996: 234) to define family (or sleeping-eating) units, appear to be universally present among modern foragers regardless of other factors. And from the perspective of social evolution, it seems likely that family unit recognition would have been required before larger-scale, inter-group social alliances could be formed. The most visible archaeological signature of family units in site structure should include sleeping areas and hearths that are much alike in scale and layout. In his description, Binford (ibid.: 234) notes that:

> the internal partitioning of habitation space into different modular units that are each essentially alike, have similar facilities, and are simultaneously occupied by a separate 'family' or sleeping-eating unit is a diagnostic characteristic of fully modern man.

Plans of ethnographic and archaeological occupations of shelters (Fig. 10.8), that exhibit residues of hearths and sleeping areas, illustrate the segmented, modular layout described by Binford (ibid.). Sleeping areas occur along the back walls of shelters accompanied by nearby 'sleeping' hearths. Another key element in the site structure of such occupations is the presence of a hearth (or hearth cluster) positioned further away from the back wall and near the center of the protected living space of the shelter. In serving as the focal point for group or communal activities, as opposed to the more private space of the

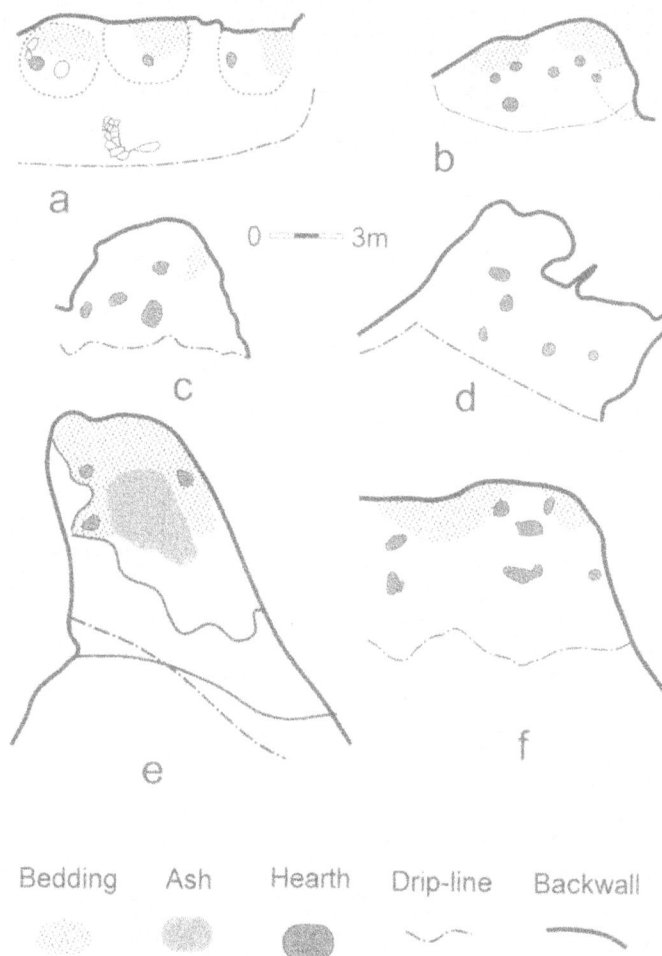

Figure 10.8 Comparison distributions of hearths, ash, and bedding at Tor Faraj f, with ethnographic and archaeological examples associated with modern foragers: **a**, Big Elephant Cave, Africa (Clark and Walton 1962); **b**, Vedda Rockshelter, Bendiyagalge, Ceylon (Seligmann and Seligmann 1911; Binford 1996); **c**, Yungubalibanda Shelter 6, Australia (Nicholson and Cane 1991); **d**, Gatecliff Shelter, Horizon 9, Nevada USA (Thomas 1983); **e**, De Hangen Cave, South Africa (Parkington and Poggenpoel 1971, Parkington and Mills 1991)

sleeping areas, these hearths are typically centrally positioned, placed nearly equidistant from the 'family' modules. The spatial layout and positioning of sleeping modules relative to communal areas within an encampment therefore mirror the social distances between family or sleeping-eating units and the group as a whole.

When the hearth plans of Tor Faraj are compared to these patterns, we see strong parallels. What conforms to an ethnographically defined line of sleeping hearths follows a swath located 1 to 2m away from the back wall. Moreover, in each of the Tor Faraj occupations, a centrally located hearth or hearth cluster, corresponding to the ethnographic communal hearth, is positioned near the mouth of the alcove. Beyond the pattern shown in the positioning of the hearths, the grass phytoliths found in two pockets along the back wall in Floor II are consistent with the notion that the hearth-line warmed these areas for sleeping. Also, associated artifacts and use-wear data indicate that the 'sleeping' areas likely served to define personal space for maintenance activities related to bone and antler work. The paleobotanic and use-wear data from Floor II also points to the centrally

data in Middle Paleolithic sites prompted Pettitt (1997: 208) to conclude that any patterning that is present 'can be explained by recourse to nothing more than simple human biomechanics, and, in enclosed sites, displays a simple spatial organization that does not differ from non-human carnivores.' This simple spatial organization is seen by Pettitt (*ibid.*: 215, 218, 219) to consist of *living* and *disposal/processing* zones for which he finds parallels in the use of caves by bears and hyenas. His view of archaic site structure involves very small residential groups who organized their space into a core activity or living area, largely defined by lithic processing, and peripheral areas that were used for dumps, butchery, and other 'messy' activities, including defecation. Although he emphasizes the parallels drawn from his analysis of archaic occupations and non-human carnivore sites, his dichotomous site structure is so general that it would also largely fit the intra-site patterns left by modern foragers. There is an important difference in Pettitt's notion of a simple site structure and the more complex structures of modern foragers, however. This rests in the presence of activity areas, in camps of modern foragers, that are placed peripheral to the central living space for reasons other than simply distancing these areas from the main part of the camp because of associated noxious odors and insects. The use of such places for specialized work or rest, in fact, constitutes the *extensive* activity areas noted by Binford (1983a) and Simek (1987) as hallmarks of modern foraging camps. And it is the evidence for these kinds of activities that sets the Tor Faraj occupation apart from the site structure viewed as *typical* of Middlle Paleolithic encampments.

Unlike the simple site structure thought to characterize most Middle Paleolithic occupations elsewhere, Tor Faraj displays multiple hearths consisting of a central hearth or hearth-cluster and peripheral hearths. The activity areas associated with the focal hearth, peripheral hearths, and spots lacking hearths also show the extensive activities and intra-site diversity common to modern forager base camps. An especially important feature at Tor Faraj is a line of hearths thought to be tied to sleeping areas positioned along the back wall of the shelter. Another difference between the Tor Faraj hearths and those believed typical of

other archaic encampments rests in their consistent positioning during successive episodes of occupation, a pattern generally lacking in the Middle Paleolithic of Europe (Mellars 1996: 309).

The degree to which the intra-site patterns at Tor Faraj fit the Drop-Toss and Exogene Cave Models largely reflects the pragmatic decisions on hearth placement made by the shelter's occupants and the hearth-side space required by the human body. Although such regularity in spacing and positioning of hearths and related hearth-side activities offers a means of teasing apart the discrete occupational episodes that often are blurred, even in fine resolution, living floor contexts (i.e., the palimpsest phenomenon), such regularity tells us little, at least directly, about behavioral organization. Similarly, one might argue that intra-site variability keyed to specific manufacturing locations and bone discard areas simply results from *ad hoc* choices on lithic processing locations and practical decisions concerning refuse disposal (*ibid.*: 309-11; Pettitt 1997).

But the intra-site patterns at Tor Faraj seem to suggest more than expedient and pragmatic decisions regarding behavioral organization. These intra-site patterns imply that the residents of the shelter habitually and formally segregated their behaviors. This appears to have involved conceptually labeling specific parts of the shelter as places where certain activities would be undertaken. We see during successive occupations a consistency in the layout for hearths and, with minor exceptions, a regular positioning of activities in the shelter (Fig. 10.9). The concentration of primary processing activities in the southwestern part of the shelter (Areas A and D) and final processing in the northeastern portion in the alcove and along the back wall (Areas B and C) implies a formal segregation of behaviors. The spatial linkage between cores fashioned from nodules and those formed on previously generated flakes is particularly significant for it suggests that the residents of the shelter conceptually labeled Areas A and D for primary processing. Despite the fact that cores-on-nodules and those on flakes came from different 'immediate' raw material sources, were worked at different stages in the reduction stream, and were processed with different techniques, the activity appears

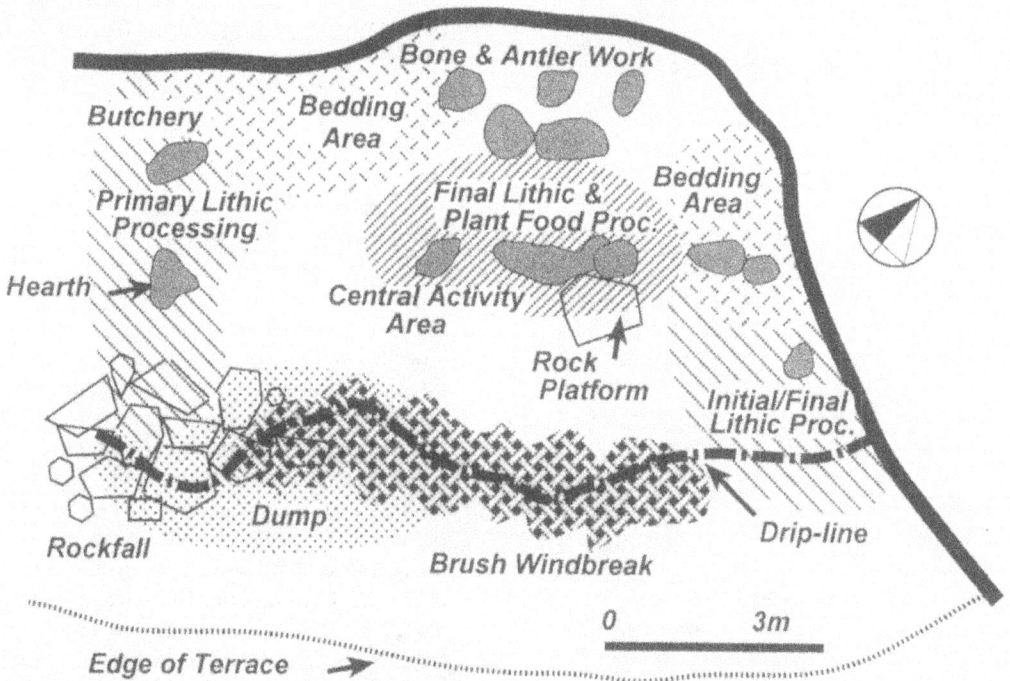

Figure 10.9 Composite reconstruction of activity areas at Tor Faraj. Note the probable traffic corridor defined by low artifact densities between the dripline and the central activity area

to have had a common conceptual label and as such was undertaken at a common locus. Other activities linked to communal tasks (central hearth Area B), sleeping (Areas A and B), and dumping (Area D) also appear to have had conceptual labels as evidenced by the regularity in their segregation and positioning across the shelter.

Some of the task areas undoubtedly were placed in specific parts of the shelter for very pragmatic reasons having to do with the nature of the activity and the local conditions of differents part of the shelter. Using the edge of the terrace beyond the dripline as a dump or the zone running along the wall for sleeping are good examples of such pragmatically determined spatial use of the shelter. But other activity areas appear to have been created by the occupants of the shelter in order to segregate spatially those specific behaviors simply in order to acquire work space. The concentration of primary processing, regardless of whether this involved initial cobble reduction or recycled cores-on-flakes, in Areas A and D is hard to explain as a result of pragmatic decisions. Moreover, the use of a

specific place in the shelter for core preparation and blank production at two quite different intervals (i.e., cobble and recycled flake) in a lithic reduction stream confirms that the place was not defined by *ad hoc* behavior. Instead, it is clear that such a place was conceptually labeled as a spot where a certain kind of task would be habitually undertaken.

Another aspect of the site structure of Tor Faraj is the apparent presence of sleeping areas and associated hearths. These, radiating from a central activity area, are especially important for they may give us some insight into the social organization of the groups that inhabited the shelter. If, as suspected, the hearths supported modular sleeping–eating areas along the back wall of the shelter, they likely signify the existence of social sub-sets (e.g., family units) within the larger foraging groups. This, as noted by Binford (1996: 234), has been unknown in the Middle Paleolithic and earlier (but see Yellen 1996).

While the broader inferences drawn from the evidence discussed here may be arguable, this is not the case with the site structure of

Tor Faraj which shows clear, irrefutable differences with those site structures described as *typical* of the Middle Paleolithic. Moreover, the site structures defined for the successive occupations of Tor Faraj strongly resemble those reported for numerous shelter occupations associated with modern humans in both archaeological and ethnographic contexts. If site structure mirrors behavioral organization, then we have to assume that the Middle Paleolithic occupants of the shelter were organizing their activities essentially along modern lines.

Other researchers also have identified modern elements of behavioral organization in the Middle Paleolithic, but generally in the context of inter-site patterns (Marks and Freidel 1977; Marks 1988b; Roebroecks *et al.* 1988; Féblot-Augustins 1993; Kaufman 1999). If this is indeed the case, the notion that a fundamental cognitive shift, accompanied by major changes in behavioral organization, was responsible for the replacement of archaic by modern populations needs reconsideration.

APPENDIX A

Alphabetical Listing of Attribute Definitions Used for the Tor Faraj Small Lithic Debris Study

TERESA L. ARMAGAN

Artifact class For this study there were four attribute states: complete, broken, shatter, and other. A specimen was considered a complete flake if it had one discernible ventral side with a definable bulb. A broken flake also had one discernible ventral side and could be proximal, distal, medial, or lateral. Shatter had no single discernible ventral side and could be quite angular and blocky. The 'other' category was for artifacts that were not the products of knapping technology, e.g., potlids.

Bulbar scarring Here a bulbar scar is one which comes down from the platform. This should not be confused with an eraillure scar which can form anywhere on the bulb and which can move across the flake in any direction. The latter were found to have quite mixed results within and between various loading techniques. Bulbar scarring was measured here as present or absent.

Cortex amount This has three attribute states: none, mixed, and all. If the artifact has any cortex at all—without the dorsal surface being completely covered with cortex—it is considered mixed. If the entire dorsal surface is covered with cortex, it is in the category of all cortex.

Cortex type The attribute states for this category are *in-situ* limestone and river-worn gravel. *In-situ* limestone is defined as the chalky surface that surrounds the exterior of the flint found in its natural state. River-worn gravel is the naturally roughened surface of flint that has been worn by natural elements. It may or may not have a different color from the rest of the flint.

Crushing–platform/bulbar Although crushing was found to have power of discrimination between hard-hammer and soft-hammer percussion for the Hayden and Hutchings (1989) study, Patterson (1982b) and Henry *et al.* (1976) found no real difference. There was, however, a difference shown between direct percussion and pressure flaking (Sollberger and Patterson 1976). Here platform and bulbar crushing were measured separately to observe trends, but measured for the same states, presence or absence. A platform, and likewise a bulb, was considered crushed if all or part of it had been pulverized.

Dorsal scar count This attribute is measured only for those artifact classes other than shatter. Attributes states include one, two, multiple, and cortex. These states are self-explanatory in general, but there are two items to note. If the dorsal side of a specimen has both cortex and dorsal scars, the number of scars is recorded, rather than being recorded as cortex. If a specimen is broken and has only one or two scars, the scar count is recorded as indeterminate unless it is obvious that there could not have been more scars. Scars are counted only if they are longer than 2 mm (to preclude smaller scars from platform preparation).

Flake types Throughout the experiments listed in the small debris literature, it is noted that multiple loading techniques can produce similar flake types. There are, however, two types of flakes identified as coming specifically from soft-hammer percussion: the distinctive expanding billet (DEB) flake and the 'r' flake (Hayden and Hutchings 1989).

DEB flake: A DEB flake (Fig. A.1) has a proportionally small platform, greater curvature of the ventral surface, proportional thinness, and expanding margins that are fairly symmetrical for at least half the flake (*ibid.*: 245). An artifact is considered to be expanding only if both of its lateral sides extend out from the platform. Arbitrarily I chose to set the designation of presence at a platform-width-to-width ratio of at least 1:1.5, measured perpendicularly from the flaking axis to each lateral side (Fig. A.2). An artifact was considered to be a DEB flake when it exhibited all of the above characteristics.

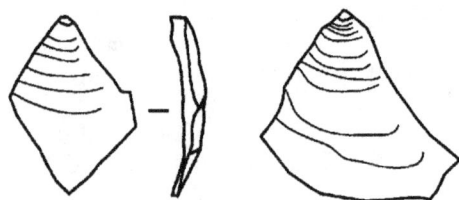

Figure A.1 Examples of distinctive expanding billet (DEB) flakes. Flake schematics have been drawn with the platform up to show the small platform size. Other characteristics of a DEB flake are the thinness of the flake, its curvature along the ventral surface, and that it is bilaterally symmetrical for at least half the flake (Figure has been tailored after *ibid.*: 246, Fig. 6)

'r' Flake: An 'r' flake (Fig. A.3) has a larger proportional platform area (comparable to that of flakes from hard-hammer percussion),

Flaking Axis

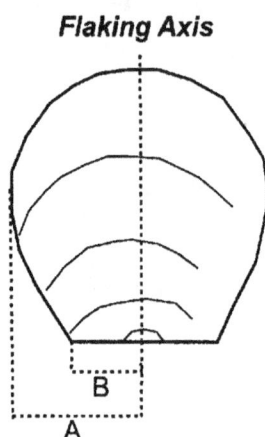

Figure A.2 Measurement of flake margin expansion. The platform-width-to-width ratio was measured by dividing length A by length B for both the right and left lateral sides. If the measurement for either side was less than 1.5, the piece was said to lack expanding margins

Figure A.3 Examples of 'r' flakes. Flake schematics have been drawn with the platform up to show the large platform size. Most characteristic, however, is the 'r' shape (reversed here) that it has in its lateral profile. Note that there is no bulb of percussion protruding from the edge of the platform along the ventral surface (Figures have been tailored after *ibid.*: 251, Fig. 11)

'a very broad fracture front,' without a restrictive bulb, and a peculiar shape something like the Arabic letter 'r' (*ibid.*: 250). An artifact was considered to be an 'r' flake when it exhibited all of these characteristics.

Lipping The two attribute states used for this study were lipped and unlipped. The bulb was defined as lipped if one's fingernail would catch on a protuberance at the junction of the ventral surface with the platform. This excluded, however, those instances where one's fingernail would catch on a protuberance caused by an inclusion or crushing. In such a case, the artifact was considered unlipped.

Loading technique   There are three loading techniques that are being investigated: (1) hard-hammer percussion; (2) soft-hammer percussion; and (3) pressure flaking. Each one of these techniques is defined by the attribute states that are listed for it within the main text in the subsection entitled Loading technique hypotheses (Chapter 5).

Multiple bulbs   This was measured as presence/absence. A flake has multiple bulbs of percussion if more than one bulb has developed off the striking platform.

Patination degree   The three attribute states used here are no patination, light patination, and heavy patination. An artifact is considered lightly patinated if it is at least lightly coated with white or gray spots on its surfaces or has a visible coating on the edges and ridges of the piece. A piece is considered highly patinated if all or part of it is patinated to the point that the original raw material is difficult or impossible to identify.

Platform cortex   Although not included in the studies listed in Table 5.3, it is included here because, based on inference from the attribute cortex amount, it should also give an indication of lithic reduction stage. This attribute is measured as present/absent.

Platform facets   This attribute has the following states: single, dihedral, multiple, and cortex. A single faceted platform is simply a flat plane (with possibly some cortex on it). A dihedral platform is one with two facets. The multiple category is for platforms with three or more facets. Platforms with only cortex and no facets are put into the cortex category.

Point of impact features   This attribute was measured in terms of presence or absence. Point of impact features are observed at the top of the bulb of percussion at the platform. They may include a very small concentric ring at the point of impact of the bulb, the top of a well-defined hertzian cone, or the point where a tiny portion of the raw material at the junction of the platform and the bulb is almost to the point of breaking off or is slightly crushed.

Raw material   There were eight raw material categories after Henry (1995b: 114-19). Raw material number 6 was for miscellaneous flint types and for material so patinated and/or burnt that the original material is unrecognizable. Flake types were identified by comparing each artifact's color, pattern, inclusions, cortex, luster, texture/grain size, and translucence to samples of each raw material type.

Reduction sequence   There are two reduction stages that are being investigated: initial processing and final processing. Each of these stages is defined by the attribute states that are listed for it within the main text in the subsection entitled Reduction sequence hypotheses (Chapter 5).

Residual striking platform   This is the amount of platform remaining after a flake has been removed from the parent material. Since it was often difficult to determine how much platform there should have been, this was listed as present if the majority of platform appeared to have been present; absent if a majority of it had been removed.

Size attributes   All caliper measurements were taken to the nearest hundredth of a millimeter with digital Scherr-Tumico calipers that download directly into an IBM-compatible computer.
Length: Artifact length was measured along the flaking axis from the proximal to the distal end. In the case of a broken artifact, measurements were made along the most likely flaking axis. For shatter or other types of specimens, the longest axis was measured.
Width: This attribute was measured along the ventral surface of the artifact, perpendicular to the measurement of length. In the case of shatter and other types of specimens, it was measured on the flatter orientation of the piece, perpendicular to the measurement of length. With all specimens, it was the widest part that was being measured.
Thickness: This was measured perpendicular to length and width measurements on a three-dimensional plane. It was measured at the point of greatest thickness.
Platform width: This was measured generally parallel to the maximum width measurement, along the platform at its widest point.
Platform thickness: This was measured

roughly perpendicular to the maximum platform width from the ventral surface, at the thickest platform dimension.

Platform size to weight ratio: For this attribute, a formula for surface area was used to estimate platform area. This was then divided by the artifact's weight. Area formulas, such as triangle, rectangle, circle, and other (generated on an individual artifact basis), were derived somewhat subjectively by choosing the one that was judged to give the most accurate area estimation based on the platform width and thickness measurements.

Weight: Weight of specimens was measured to the nearest one-thousandth of a gram using an Ohaus precision balance scale that downloads data directly into an IBM-compatible computer.

Overall artifact size: This attribute actually includes all the size attributes, i.e., weight and all linear measurements. Largely it is looked at in terms of weight, length, width, and thickness.

Symmetry While symmetry measurements may seem complicated at first, this was the most objective means I had of measuring what seemed to be an all too subjective attribute in the literature (e.g. Patterson and Sollberger 1978).

Bilateral symmetry: This was measured by bisecting the specimen along the flaking axis and comparing one side to the other along three points: one-fourth of the distance from the proximal to the distal end, half of the distance, and three-fourths of the distance (Fig. A.4). At these three points, the distances from the bisecting line to both lateral edges were measured perpendicular to the length of the artifact. These two measurements were then used to determine the ratio of symmetry at that point by dividing the lower number into the higher number. If all of the points had a ratio between 1.00 and 1.25, then the attribute state of symmetry was said to be good. If any of the ratios fell between 1.26 and 1.50 and did not exceed 1.50, then the symmetry was fair. If any of the ratios exceeded 1.50, then the specimen had poor symmetry.

Cross-sectional symmetry: This was measured in a similar manner to bilateral symmetry, but along a different plane (Fig. A.5). At the three quartiles along the flaking axis,

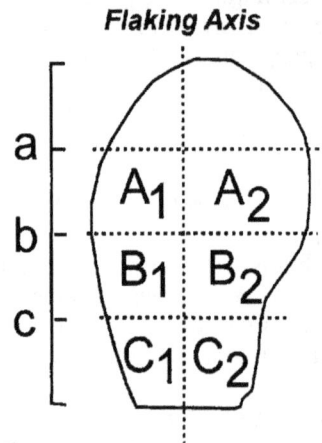

Figure A.4 Measurement of bilateral symmetry. At each quartile in the maximum length of the flake, a, b, and c, the larger of the two width segments is divided by the smaller of the two to get a ratio measurement. For example, A_2 is divided by A_1, B_2 is divided by B_1, and C_1 is divided by C_2

measurements of the specimen's thickness were taken at a distance of one fourth of its width at that point. Note that this distance was measured from the edge of the artifact. Again, if all of the points had a ratio between 1.00 and 1.25, then the attribute state of symmetry was said to be good. If any of the ratios fell between 1.26 and 1.50 and did not exceed 1.50, then the symmetry was fair. If any of the ratios exceeded 1.50, then the specimen had poor symmetry.

Thermal alteration The attributes states used were: no alteration, heat-treated, burnt, and other. An artifact was considered heat treated if the raw material had a higher luster to it than the material would usually have. It also must have an almost greasy quality and more sharply defined areas of color with more vivid red coloring. Also, there must be no evidence of more intensive thermal alteration. The burnt category consists of pot-lidded and heat-crazed specimens. In the 'other' category, some specimens have what appear to be fractures from general thermal stress, such as extreme day/night time temperatures. These fractures have irregular shapes, can be quite wavy along the axis of the break, and have a rough appearance on the break area. Also, there is no bulbar scar or any lipping (such as one might find on a bending fracture).

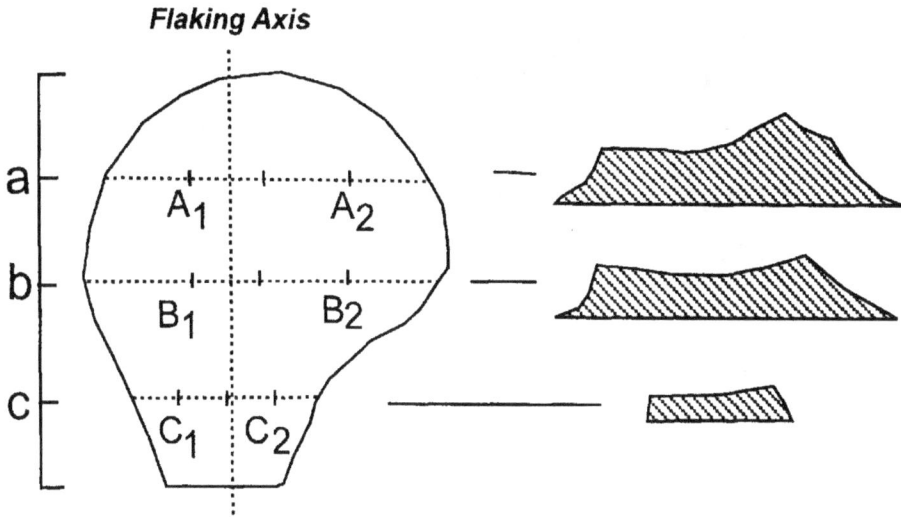

Figure A.5 Measurement of cross-sectional symmetry. Measurements are taken at each quartile in the maximum length of the flake, segments a, b, and c. At each of these three segments, the thickness of each flake is measured at a distance of one-fourth of the total width of the segment. Thickness is obtained from both lateral sides. The larger of the two thickness measurements along the segment is divided by the smaller of the two to get a ratio measurement. For example, A_2 is divided by A_1, B_2 is divided by B_1, and C_1 is divided by C_2

Ventral rippling (radiating Force Lines) These are recorded as present or absent based on whether ripples can be seen on the ventral surface under an incandescent light.

APPENDIX B

Small Lithic Debris Analysis Results Tables

TERESA L. ARMAGAN

Loading techniques attributes

The following attributes were analyzed to determine what loading techniques were used on and across the site of Tor Faraj. The relative position of the subclusters for all attributes can be viewed as points on a continuum of reduction that generally ranges from hard-hammer percussion, through soft-hammer percussion, to pressure flaking. For most attributes, the subclusters from each floor are listed in order of attribute frequency of occurrence or mean relative to loading techniques. For bilateral and cross-sectional symmetries, all subclusters from each floor are listed in order of their relative symmetry indices. This index was devised by summing the frequency of 'good' symmetry artifacts multiplied by three, the 'fair' by two, and the 'poor' by one, resulting in an index score that ranges from 100 points (100 percent poor symmetry) to 300 points (100 percent good symmetry). This index is a somewhat artificial device, but it is useful for getting a general idea of the symmetry of artifacts within each subcluster.

For attributes of nominal data, the relative frequency of occurrence and the number of artifacts used in the evaluation (N) are listed. X^2 tests (using Yate's correction for continuity when necessary) and Fisher's Exact Tests were done in order to detect significant differences between subclusters. For attributes of interval data, the mean, standard deviation (S.D.), and number of artifacts used in the evaluation (N) are listed. In addition, the co-efficient of variation (C.V.) is listed for width, in order to show variability of widths about each subcluster's mean. Analysis of variance tests (and median tests when necessary) were used in order to detect significant differences between subclusters. Statistical significance between the subclusters at the .05 alpha level is noted by an asterisk after each subcluster designation. Statistical significance between floors is noted in a similar fashion. Specific results are given in Armagan (1998: 60-92).

'r' Flakes						
	Subcluster	D1b	D1a	B1	A1	C
	Frequency	0	0	0	2.35	5.08
Floor I	N	36	30	88	85	118

Floor II	Subcluster	D2b	B2	A2	C	D2a	B1
	Frequency	0	0	0	2.08	2.56	2.67
	N	33	42	71	48	39	75

Residual platform						
	Subcluster	B1	C	A1	D1b	D1a
	Frequency	75.29	78.90	82.72	83.33	86.21
Floor I	N	85	109	81	36	29

Floor II	Subcluster	C	A2	D2b	B1	B2	D2a
	Frequency	75.61	79.71	81.25	83.33	88.37	89.47
	N	41	69	32	72	43	38

Bulbar crushing						
	Subcluster	C	B1	D1a	A1	D1b
	Frequency	39.42	39.24	33.33	30.12	26.47
Floor I	N	104	79	27	83	34

Floor II	Subcluster	A2	B2	C	D2a	D2b	B1
	Frequency	36.36	35.71	32.50	31.58	24.14	22.54
	N	66	42	40	38	29	71

Platform crushing						
	Subcluster	C	B1	A1	D1a	D1b
	Frequency	39.42	37.35	35.80	29.63	23.53
Floor I	N	104	83	81	27	34

Floor II	Subcluster	A2	B2	B1	D2b	C	D2a
	Frequency	33.85	33.33	26.76	25.00	24.39	23.68
	N	65	39	71	32	41	38

Lipping						
	Subcluster	A1*	B1	D1b	D1a	C*
	Frequency	23.75	34.52	35.29	38.46	40.00
Floor I	N	80	84	34	26	105

Floor II	Subcluster	B2	D2b	C	D2a	A2	B1
	Frequency	23.81	25.81	32.50	34.21	38.24	38.57
	N	42	31	40	38	68	79

Bulbar scarring						
	Subcluster	D1a	A1	D1b	C	B1
	Frequency	29.63	28.40	26.47	25.00	17.07
Floor I	N	27	81	34	104	82

Floor II	Subcluster	D2a	D2b	C	B2	A2	B1
	Frequency	39.47	33.33	32.50	28.57	27.69	25.71
	N	38	30	40	42	65	70

Point of impact features						
	Subcluster	B1	D1a	C	A1	D1b
	Frequency	10.67	7.69	5.83	3.80	2.94
Floor I	N	75	26	103	79	34

Floor II	Subcluster	D2b*	A2	C	B1	B2*	D2a*
	Frequency	19.35	7.69	7.50	5.71	2.44	.0
	N	31	65	40	70	41	38

Multiple bulbs of percussion	Subcluster	D1a	C	B1	A1	D1b	
	Frequency	18.52	10.58	9.64	6.10	5.88	
Floor I	N	27	104	83	82	34	
Floor II	Subcluster	D2b	D2a	A2	C	B2	B1
	Frequency	13.79	13.16	12.70	10.00	9.52	8.45
	N	29	38	63	40	42	71

Ventral rippling	Subcluster	B1*	D1b*	A1*	D1a*	C*	
	Frequency	85.25	80.00	71.43	68.18	54.88	
Floor I*	N	122	60	112	44	164	
Floor II*	Subcluster	D2a	C	B1	B2	A2	D2b
	Frequency	84.91	84.62	82.29	80.36	80.18	78.79
	N	53	65	96	56	111	66

Length (complete flakes)	Subcluster	C	D1b	B1	A1	D1a	
	Mean	11.19	11.84	12.20	12.95	14.92	
	S.D.	6.13	4.18	6.70	5.37	6.88	
Floor I*	N	48	7	36	40	12	
Floor II*	Subcluster	B1*	C*	D2b	B2	A2*	D2a*
	Mean	11.87	12.50	14.26	15.73	16.54	18.19
	S.D.	5.97	5.94	4.73	6.57	5.77	6.31
	N	28	19	9	12	27	19

Width (complete flakes)	Subcluster	D1a	A1	D1b	B1	C	
	Mean	14.05	12.88	12.43	11.67	10.19	
	S.D.	4.69	5.95	3.55	6.23	4.39	
	N	12	40	7	36	48	
Floor I*	C.V.	33.38	46.20	28.56	53.38	43.08	
Floor II*	Subcluster	A2*	D2a*	B2	D2b	C*	B1*
	Mean	15.70	15.21	14.82	13.41	12.12	11.29
	S.D.	4.99	4.39	8.22	3.07	6.04	6.34
	N	27	19	12	9	19	28
	C.V.	31.78	28.93	55.47	22.89	49.83	56.16

Thickness (all complete flakes)	Subcluster	D1a*	A1	B1	D1b	C*	
	Mean	3.66	2.60	2.39	2.32	2.29	
	S.D.	1.97	1.24	1.33	.52	1.42	
Floor I*	N	12	40	36	7	48	
Floor II*	Subcluster	D2b	A2	B2	D2a	C	B1
	Mean	3.42	3.39	3.20	2.98	2.98	2.65
	S.D.	1.69	1.81	1.95	.93	2.25	1.61
	N	9	27	12	19	19	28

Thickness (complete flakes 4-10mm)	Subcluster	A1	D1a	D1b	B1	C	
	Mean	2.47	2.16	2.04	1.84	1.81	
	S.D.	1.47	.72	.42	.94	.99	
Floor I	N	21	3	3	26	31	
Floor II	Subcluster	D2b	D2a	C	B1	A2	B2
	Mean	4.77	2.22	1.78	1.74	1.41	.90
	S.D.	3.73	.38	.68	1.09	.31	.25
	N	2	3	10	16	4	4

Thickness to length ratio (complete flakes) Floor I	Subcluster	D1a	A1	C	B1	D1b	
	Mean	.2581	.2341	.2139	.2104	.2088	
	S.D.	.1345	.1890	.0962	.0873	.0515	
	N	12	40	48	36	7	
Floor II	Subcluster	D2b	C	B1	A2	B2	D2a
	Mean	.2639	.2359	.2251	.2137	.1996	.1808
	S.D.	.1599	.0991	.1208	.1023	.1180	.0757
	N	9	19	28	27	12	19
Weight (complete flakes) Floor I*	Subcluster	D1a	A1	B1	D1b	C	
	Mean	.750	.455	.419	.349	.338	
	S.D.	.782	.469	.550	.243	.540	
	N	12	40	36	7	48	
Floor II*	Subcluster	A2	B2	D2a	D2b	B1	C
	Mean	.976	.830	.732	.586	.501	.468
	S.D.	1.008	.712	.640	.362	.741	.658
	N	27	12	19	9	28	19
Platform width (all except 'r' flakes) Floor I*	Subcluster	D1a*	B1*	A1*	D1b*	C*	
	Mean	11.45	7.72	7.67	7.26	7.23	
	S.D.	5.29	4.84	4.33	4.59	4.37	
	N	24	77	77	29	90	
Floor II*	Subcluster	A2*	D2a*	B2	D2b	B1*	C+*
	Mean	10.30	9.94	9.48	9.41	8.26	7.71
	S.D.	5.67	5.32	5.75	5.15	5.25	3.42
	N	61	32	33	29	63	33
Platform thickness (all except 'r' flakes) Floor I*	Subcluster	D1a*	D1b	C*	A1*	B1*	
	Mean	3.02	1.89	1.68	1.65	1.61	
	S.D.	1.77	1.18	1.23	.94	1.25	
	N	24	29	90	77	77	
Floor II*	Subcluster	D2b	A2	D2a	C	B2	B1
	Mean	2.65	2.22	2.19	2.18	2.14	1.93
	S.D.	1.64	1.41	1.23	1.79	1.63	1.48
	N	29	61	32	32	33	63
Platform size to weight ratio (all except 'r' flakes) Floor I	Subcluster	C*	D1a*	B1	D1b	A1*	
	Mean	57.32	54.48	39.53	35.89	33.05	
	S.D.	67.08	32.79	34.96	52.98	26.92	
	N	44	11	33	7	38	
Floor II	Subcluster	C*	B2*	B1	A2	D2b	D2a*
	Mean	73.40	52.49	52.14	32.96	32.82	27.52
	S.D.	92.20	42.73	52.19	26.84	25.03	42.35
	N	17	11	25	26	9	17
Bilateral symmetry	Subcluster	D1b*	B1*	D1a*	C	A1*	
	Freq.–Good	5.26	6.56	0	8.75	14.29	
	Freq.–Fair	5.26	19.67	42.86	27.50	36.51	
	Freq.–Poor	89.47	73.77	57.14	63.75	49.21	
	N	19	61	21	80	63	
Floor I	Index	115.79	132.79	142.86	145.00	165.08	

Floor II	Subcluster	B2	A2	D2a	D2b	B1	C
	Freq.–Good	0	8.51	14.29	17.39	12.96	16.67
	Freq.–Fair	19.05	25.53	17.86	13.04	22.22	30.00
	Freq.–Poor	80.95	65.96	67.86	69.57	64.81	53.33
	N	21	47	28	23	54	30
	Index	119.05	142.55	146.43	147.83	148.15	163.33

Cross-sectional symmetry	Subcluster	D1a	B1	C	A1	D1b	
	Freq.–Good	4.35	8.20	12.05	6.15	16.00	
	Freq.–Fair	30.43	26.23	28.92	41.54	24.00	
	Freq.–Poor	65.22	65.57	59.04	52.31	60.00	
	N	23	61	83	65	25	
Floor I	Index	139.13	142.62	153.01	153.85	156.00	

Floor II	Subcluster	B2	A2	D2a	C	D2b	B1
	Freq.–Good	0	11.54	12.90	9.09	14.29	12.73
	Freq.–Fair	23.08	19.23	19.35	27.27	21.43	30.91
	Freq.–Poor	76.92	69.23	67.74	63.64	64.29	56.36
	N	26	52	31	33	28	55
	Index	123.08	142.31	145.16	145.45	150.00	156.36

Lithic reduction stage attributes

The following attributes were analyzed to determine what stages of lithic reduction occurred on and across site Tor Faraj. For each attribute, all subclusters from each floor are listed in order of attribute frequency of occurrence or mean value relative to the initial and final stages. The relative position of subclusters can be viewed as points on a continuum of reduction, which ranges from initial to final lithic processing.

For attributes of nominal data, the relative frequency of occurrence and the number of artifacts used in the evaluation (N) are listed.

X^2 tests (using Yate's correction for continuity when necessary) were done in order to detect significant differences between subclusters. For attributes of interval data, the mean, standard deviation (S.D.), and number of artifacts used in the evaluation (N) are listed. Analysis of variance tests (and median tests when necessary) were used in order to detect significant differences between subclusters. Statistical significance between the subclusters at the .05 alpha level is noted by an asterisk after each subcluster designation. Statistical significance between floors is noted in a similar fashion. Specific results are given in Armagan (1998: 92–108).

Artifact class	Subcluster	D1b*	D1a	B1*	C*	A*	
	Freq. complete	10.9	25.0	26.5	27.6	32.0	
	Freq. broken	85.9	68.8	66.9	67.2	60.8	
	Freq. shatter	3.1	6.3	6.6	5.2	7.2	
Floor I*	N	64	48	136	174	125	

Floor II*	Subcluster	D2b	B2*	A2	C	B1	D2a*
	Freq. complete	12.7	20.3	22.9	24.7	27.5	35.8
	Freq. broken	83.1	74.6	76.3	70.1	69.6	64.2
	Freq. shatter	4.2	5.1	.8	5.2	2.9	.0
	N	71	59	118	77	102	53

Cortex amount (complete, broken, shatter)	Subcluster	D1b	A1	C	D1a	B1
	Freq. none	78.1	81.6	82.8	83.3	86.8
	Freq. mixed	20.3	17.6	16.7	16.7	11.0
	Freq. all	1.6	.8	.6	.0	2.2
Floor I	N	64	125	174	48	136

Floor II	Subcluster	A2	D2b	D2a	B2	B1	C
	Freq. none	74.1	74.6	75.5	78.0	80.4	83.1
	Freq. mixed	25.0	23.9	24.5	22.0	17.6	14.3
	Freq. all	.9	1.4	.0	.0	2.0	2.6
	N	116	71	53	59	102	77

Dorsal scar count	Subcluster	C*	B1	D1b	A1*	D1a*	
	Freq. none	.0	1.3	2.6	.0	.0	
	Freq. 1 scar	20.2	19.7	18.4	8.2	10.0	
	Freq. 2 scars	33.9	23.7	21.1	24.7	13.3	
	Freq. 3 scars	45.9	55.3	57.9	67.1	76.7	
Floor I	N	109	76	38	85	30	

Floor II	Subcluster	C	B1	B2	A2	D2b	D2a
	Freq. none	.0	1.4	2.3	1.3	2.4	.0
	Freq. 1 scar	15.6	15.5	6.8	9.0	7.1	5.0
	Freq. 2 scars	33.3	29.6	27.3	20.5	19.0	22.5
	Freq. 3 scars	51.1	53.5	63.6	69.2	71.4	72.5
	N	45	71	44	78	42	40

Weight (complete, broken, shatter) Floor I*	Subcluster	D1a*	A1*	D1b*	B1*	C*	
	Mean	.742	.516	.429	.366	.312	
	S.D.	.910	.620	.506	.462	.421	
	N	48	125	64	136	174	

Floor II*	Subcluster	D2b*	A2*	D2a*	B2*	C*	B1*
	Mean	.705	.666	.612	.590	.401	.356
	S.D.	.765	.770	.647	.674	.522	.597
	N	71	118	53	59	77	102

Length (complete flakes) Floor I*	Subcluster	D1a	A1	B1	D1b	C	
	Mean	14.92	12.95	12.20	11.84	11.19	
	S.D.	6.88	5.37	6.70	4.18	6.13	
	N	12	40	36	7	48	

Floor II*	Subcluster	D2a*	A2*	B2	D2b	C*	B1*
	Mean	18.19	16.54	15.73	14.26	12.50	11.87
	S.D.	6.31	5.77	6.57	4.73	5.94	5.97
	N	19	27	12	9	19	28

Width (complete flakes) Floor I*	Subcluster	D1a	A1	D1b	B1	C	
	Mean	14.05	12.88	12.43	11.67	10.19	
	S.D.	4.69	5.95	3.55	6.23	4.39	
	N	12	40	7	36	48	

Floor II*	Subcluster	A2*	D2a*	B2	D2b	C*	B1*
	Mean	15.70	15.21	14.82	13.41	12.12	11.29
	S.D.	4.99	4.39	8.22	3.07	6.04	6.34
	N	27	19	12	9	19	28

Thickness (complete flakes) Floor I*	Subcluster	D1a*	A1	B1	D1b	C	
	Mean	3.66	2.60	2.39	2.32	2.29	
	S.D.	1.97	1.24	1.33	.52	1.42	
	N	12	40	36	7	48	

Floor II*	Subcluster	D2b	A2	B2	D2a	C	B1
	Mean	3.42	3.39	3.20	2.98	2.98	2.65
	S.D.	1.69	1.81	1.95	.93	2.25	1.61
	N	9	27	12	19	19	28

Platform width (complete and broken flakes) Floor I*	Subcluster	D1a*	B1*	A1*	C*	D1b*	
	Mean	11.45	7.92	7.79	7.33	7.31	
	S.D.	5.29	5.09	4.45	4.28	4.52	
	N	24	79	80	95	30	
Floor II*	Subcluster	A2*	D2a*	B2	D2b	B1*	C*
	Mean	10.30	9.97	9.48	9.41	8.20	7.84
	S.D.	5.67	5.24	5.75	5.15	5.18	3.45
	N	61	33	33	29	65	34
Platform thickness (complete and broken flakes) Floor I*	Subcluster	D1a*	D1b*	C*	A1*	B1*	
	Mean	3.02	1.95	1.84	1.80	1.61	
	S.D.	1.77	1.21	1.44	1.23	1.25	
	N	24	30	95	80	79	
Floor II*	Subcluster	D2b	C	D2a	A2	B2	B1
	Mean	2.65	2.38	2.25	2.22	2.14	1.96
	S.D.	1.64	2.12	1.26	1.41	1.63	1.47
	N	29	33	33	61	33	65
Platform facet count (complete and broken flakes)	Subcluster	B1*	C*	A1*	D1b*	D1a*	
	Freq. cortex	.0	4.6	7.4	6.9	4.2	
	Freq. 1 facet	60.3	49.4	47.1	37.9	25.0	
	Freq. 2 facets	16.2	19.5	19.1	13.8	12.5	
	Freq. 3 facets	23.5	26.4	26.5	41.4	58.3	
Floor I	N	68	87	68	29	24	
Floor II	Subcluster	C	B1	B2	D2a	D2b	A2
	Freq. cortex	.0	3.3	.0	6.1	3.7	5.8
	Freq. 1 facet	56.3	49.2	45.5	33.3	40.7	44.2
	Freq. 2 facets	18.8	14.8	21.2	24.2	14.8	7.7
	Freq. 3 facets	25.0	32.8	33.3	36.4	40.7	42.3
	N	32	61	33	33	27	52

Debris concentration attributes

The following attributes were analyzed to determine possible explanations for small lithic debris concentrations on and across site Tor Faraj. For each attribute, all subclusters from each floor are listed in order of attribute frequency of occurrence. Since the following attributes do not fall within any kind of reduction continuum, they are presented a little differently from the attributes in the previous two sections. The organizing attribute state for raw material type is the frequency of type 6, the 'other' category that determines weathering processes. Artifact class is organized by the frequency of the attribute state, 'complete.' Thermal alteration, patination degree, cortex amount, and cortex type are organized by the frequency of the attribute state, 'none.' Artifact size attributes are not listed in the tables because they are listed in the above sections. Finally, loading techniques and reduction stages are not included, as they are listed in the text of the chapter in Tables 5.4a, b, and c and 5.5a, b, and c respectively.

Since all attributes listed here are nominal data, χ^2 tests (using Yate's correction for continuity when necessary) were done in order to detect significant differences between subclusters. Statistical significance between the subclusters at the .05 alpha level is noted by an asterisk after each subcluster designation. Statistical difference between the floors is noted in a similar fashion. Specific results are given in Armagan (1998: 109-37).

Note that just because two subclusters are listed next to each other does not mean that they are closer to one another statistically than a subcluster further in the list. Also, generally all artifacts, rather than subsets, were examined for the attributes listed in this section.

Raw materials	Subcluster	D1b*	D1a*	A1*	B1*	C*	
	Freq. Type 1	9.5	22.0	17.2	19.4	25.0	
	Freq. Type 2	4.1	12.0	11.0	24.1	10.3	
	Freq. Type 3	4.1	8.0	7.4	7.1	8.8	
	Freq. Type 4	18.9	12.0	15.3	17.1	18.1	
	Freq. Type 5	9.5	6.0	5.5	.0	2.0	
	Freq. Type 6	45.9	32.0	23.9	16.5	14.2	
	Freq. Type 7	2.7	8.0	5.5	5.3	2.0	
	Freq. Type 8	5.4	.0	14.1	10.6	19.6	
Floor I*	N	74	50	163	170	204	
Floor II*	Subcluster	D2b*	B2*	A2*	C*	B1*	D2a*
	Freq. Type 1	11.7	7.4	10.7	19.8	34.5	22.0
	Freq. Type 2	7.8	8.5	17.6	7.3	16.0	5.1
	Freq. Type 3	11.7	24.5	20.6	35.4	16.0	30.5
	Freq. Type 4	5.2	9.6	13.7	13.5	7.6	11.9
	Freq. Type 5	2.6	.0	3.8	2.1	2.5	3.4
	Freq. Type 6	54.5	34.0	22.1	15.6	14.3	11.9
	Freq. Type 7	5.2	9.6	6.9	5.2	7.6	10.2
	Freq. Type 8	1.3	6.4	4.6	1.0	1.7	5.1
	N	77	94	131	96	119	59
Artifact class	Subcluster	D1b*	B1*	C*	D1a*	A1*	
	Freq. complete	9.5	21.2	23.5	24.0	24.5	
	Freq. broken	74.3	53.5	57.4	66.0	46.4	
	Freq. shatter	2.7	5.3	4.4	6.0	5.5	
	Freq. other	13.5	20.0	14.7	4.0	23.3	
Floor I	N	74	170	204	50	163	
Floor II	Subcluster	D2b*	B2*	C*	A2*	B1*	D2a*
	Freq. complete	11.7	12.8	19.8	20.6	23.5	32.2
	Freq. broken	76.6	46.8	56.3	68.7	59.7	57.6
	Freq. shatter	2.9	3.2	4.2	.8	2.5	.0
	Freq. other	7.8	37.2	19.8	9.9	14.3	10.2
	N	77	94	96	131	119	59
Thermal alteration	Subcluster		C*	D1b	A1*	B1*	D1a
	Freq. none		53.3	55.6	56.5	67.2	71.9
	Freq. burnt		22.2	29.6	25.9	27.0	15.6
	Freq. heat treated		3.0	7.4	3.4	2.2	3.1
	Freq. other		21.5	7.4	14.3	3.6	9.4
Floor I*	N		135	54	147	137	32
Floor II*	Subcluster	B2*	A2*	C*	D2a*	B1*	D2b*
	Freq. none	37.3	38.7	40.3	48.9	54.8	60.0
	Freq. burnt	43.4	31.1	26.4	14.9	26.9	26.7
	Freq. heat treated	2.4	13.2	9.7	31.9	9.7	6.7
	Freq. other	16.9	17.0	23.6	4.3	8.6	6.7
	N	83	106	72	47	93	60

Patination degree						
	Subcluster	D1b*	D1a*	C*	A1*	B1*
	Freq. none	10.8	14.0	25.0	33.1	34.7
	Freq. light	31.1	48.0	54.4	42.3	43.5
	Freq. heavy	58.1	38.0	20.6	24.5	21.8
Floor I	N	74	50	204	163	170

Floor II	Subcluster	D2b*	D2a*	A2*	C*	B2*	B1*
	Freq. none	10.4	16.9	20.6	26.0	28.7	35.3
	Freq. light	10.4	61.0	55.0	45.8	48.9	47.1
	Freq. heavy	79.2	22.0	24.4	28.1	22.3	17.6
	N	77	59	131	96	94	119

Cortex amount						
	Subcluster	D1b*	D1a	A1	C*	B1*
	Freq. none	78.4	82.0	82.2	83.8	88.8
	Freq. mixed	20.3	18.0	16.6	15.7	8.8
	Freq. all	1.4	.0	1.2	.5	2.4
Floor I	N	74	50	163	204	170

Floor II	Subcluster	A2	D2b	D2a	B2	B1	C
	Freq. none	75.2	75.3	76.3	81.9	82.4	85.4
	Freq. mixed	24.0	23.4	23.7	18.1	16.0	12.5
	Freq. all	.8	1.3	.0	.0	1.7	2.1
	N	129	77	59	94	119	96

Cortex type						
	Subcluster	D1b	D1a	A1	C	B1
	Freq. none	78.4	82.0	82.2	83.8	88.8
	Freq. limestone	10.8	6.0	10.4	9.3	4.7
	Freq. gravel	10.8	12.0	7.4	6.9	6.5
Floor I	N	74	50	163	204	170

Floor II	Subcluster	A2	D2a	D2b*	B2	B1	C*
	Freq. none	76.2	76.3	77.3	81.9	83.1	86.3
	Freq. limestone	12.3	11.9	18.7	12.8	10.2	4.2
	Freq. gravel	11.5	11.9	4.0	5.3	6.8	9.5
	N	130	59	75	94	118	95

APPENDIX C

Cross-Cultural Data for Hearths in Rockshelters

Site	Provenience	Area(m)	H-N	Shape	H-Dia	Lgth	Wdth	H-area	Dis-H1	Dis-H2	Dis-H3	Dis-NW	Dis-BW	Dis-DL	Functn	Reference
1 G. Naquitz	B1-14	100	2	round	50			1963	3.5			2.5	2.5	12.4		Flannery 1986
2 G. Naquitz	B1-11	100	2	round	88			6079	3.5			4.6	4.6	9.5		Flannery 1986
3 G. Naquitz	D-22	100	1	round	50			1963				5.4	5.7	8.4		Flannery 1986
4 Gatecliff	Horizon 7, A	72	8	oval		100	150	49063	1	2.8	4	2	3.5	2.5		Thomas 1983
5 Gatecliff	Horizon 7, B	72	8	oval		60	100	20096	2	2	2.8	3.5	5.8	2		Thomas 1983
6 Gatecliff	Horizon 7, C	72	8	round	50			1963	1.5	2	2.5	3.5	3.6	3.8		Thomas 1983
7 Gatecliff	Horizon 7, D	72	8	round	75			4416	2.6	4.6	5	1.5	2	0.6		Thomas 1983
8 Gatecliff	Horizon 7, E	72	8	oval		30	100	13267	1	2	2.3	1.7	1.7	5		Thomas 1983
9 Gatecliff	Horizon 7, F	72	8	oval		30	75	8655	1	2	2.7	1.5	1.5	5.5		Thomas 1983
10 Gatecliff	Horizon 7, H	72	8	oval		35	110	16505	1.5	2	2	1.5	3.5	3.5		Thomas 1983
11 Gatecliff	Horizon 7, I	72	8	round	80			5024	2	2.4	2.5	3.5	2.5	2.5		Thomas 1983
12 Gatecliff	Horizon 8, A	52	11	round	30			707	2	2.1	3.3	2.2	1.2	4.1		Thomas 1983
13 Gatecliff	Horizon 8, B	52	11	oval		30	60	6359	2	2.3	3.5	1.2	0.3	4.1		Thomas 1983
14 Gatecliff	Horizon 8, C1	52	11	round	100			7850	0.8	1	2.3	1.8	2.5	2.3		Thomas 1983
15 Gatecliff	Horizon 8, C2	52	11	round	75			4416	0.8	0.8	0.8	3	3	2		Thomas 1983
16 Gatecliff	Horizon 8, C3	52	11	round	50			1963	0.5	0.8	0.8	1.5	3	1.5		Thomas 1983
17 Gatecliff	Horizon 8, C4	52	11	round	60			2826	0.5	0.5	0.5	2	3.5	1.5		Thomas 1983
18 Gatecliff	Horizon 8, C5	52	11	round	65			3317	0.5	0.8	1.1	2	3.8	1		Thomas 1983
19 Gatecliff	Horizon 8, C6	52	11	round	60			2826	0.8	1	1.1	2.9	3.3	1.8		Thomas 1983
20 Gatecliff	Horizon 8, E	52	11	oval		75	100	24041	2.5	3	3.5	2.5	3.1	3.5		Thomas 1983
21 Gatecliff	Horizon 8, F	52	11	round	50			1963	2.5	3	3	4	6.5	0.8		Thomas 1983
22 Gatecliff	Horizon 8, G	52	11	round	40			1256	2.5	4.4	4.8	0.3	4	1.7		Thomas 1983
24 Gatecliff	Horizon 9, A	48	6	round	40			1256	1.8	4	4.7	2	2	2.3		Thomas 1983
25 Gatecliff	Horizon 9, B	48	6	round	50			1963	1.8	2.8	3		2.8	1.8		Thomas 1983
26 Gatecliff	Horizon 9, C1	48	6	round	35			962	2.8	3.4	4.5		0.3	6		Thomas 1983
27 Gatecliff	Horizon 9, C2	48	6	oval		50	95	16505	1.3	2.5	2.8	2	2.8	3.5		Thomas 1983
28 Gatecliff	Horizon 9, D1	48	6	round	50			1963	1.3	1.5	2.5	3.4	3.8	2.7		Thomas 1983
29 Gatecliff	Horizon 9, D2	48	6	round	50			1963	1.5	2.5	2.9	3.1	5.2	1		Thomas 1983
31 Gatecliff	Horizon 10, A	40	1	round	40			1256				0.8	2.8	3.5		Thomas 1983
33 Gatecliff	Horizon 11, A	36	2	round	50			1963	3.9			2.5	1.5	2.5		Thomas 1983
34 Gatecliff	Horizon 11, B	36	2	round	15			177	3.9			3	3	0.5		Thomas 1983
35 Gatecliff	Horizon 12	42	4	round												Thomas 1983
36 Gatecliff	Horizon 12, A	42	4	round	100			7850	2.7	2.8	5.4		2.3	2		Thomas 1983
37 Gatecliff	Horizon 12, B	42	4	oval		70	140	34619	2.8	2.9	3.8		3	2		Thomas 1983
38 Gatecliff	Horizon 12, C	42	4	round	40			1256	2.5	3.8	5.6		0.1	4.5		Thomas 1983
39 Gatecliff	Horizon 12, D	42	4	round	50			1963	3	5.5	5.6		3			Thomas 1983

Site	Provenience	Area(m)	H-N	Shape	H-Dia	Lgth	Wdth	H-area	Dis-H1	Dis-H2	Dis-H3	Dis-NW	Dis-BW	Dis-DL	Functn	Reference
41	Gatecliff	Horizon 13, A	44	2	oval		50	75	12266	4.3	.	.	2.5	4.5	0		Thomas 1983
42	Gatecliff	Horizon 13, B	44	2	round	100	.	.	7850	4.3	.	.	.	2.5	2		Thomas 1983
44	Gatecliff	Horizon 14, A	38	3	round	50	.	.	1963	2.5	4.9	.	.	1	1		Thomas 1983
45	Gatecliff	Horizon 14, B	38	3	round	45	.	.	1590	2.5	7	.	.	0.6	0.3		Thomas 1983
46	Gatecliff	Horizon 14, C	38	3	round	45	.	.	1590	4.9	7	.	.	1.4	2.8		Thomas 1983
47	Gatecliff	Horizon 15, A	30	3	round	50	.	.	1963	3.3	5.3	.	.	1.8	3		Thomas 1983
48	Gatecliff	Horizon 15, B	30	3	round	50	.	.	1963	2.3	3.3	.	.	3.5	0.2		Thomas 1983
49	Gatecliff	Horizon 15, C	30	3	round	70	.	.	3847	2.3	5.3	.	.	2	0.5		Thomas 1983
50	Australian V Site 1		25	3	round	25	.	.	491	2	3.8	.	1.1	1.9	0.9		Nicholson and Cane 1991
51	Australian V Site 1		25	3	oval		60	100	20096	2	2	.	.	1.9	1.6		Nicholson and Cane 1991
52	Australian V Site 1		25	3	round	40	.	.	1256	2	3.8	.	2	2.1	0.5		Nicholson and Cane 1991
53	Australian V Site 2		14	4	oval		30	100	13267	1	3.6	.	1	1.3	1.5		Nicholson and Cane 1991
54	Australian V Site 2		14	4	oval		30	60	6359	1	3.7	.	1.3	1.6	1.1		Nicholson and Cane 1991
55	Australian V Site 2		14	4	round	30	.	.	707	3.6	3.7	.	3	5	1.6		Nicholson and Cane 1991
56	Australian V Site 2		14	4	round	50	.	.	1963	.	.	.	.	0.3	1		Nicholson and Cane 1991
57	Australian V Site 3		23	2	round	50	.	.	1963	1.2	.	.	.	0.8	1.8		Nicholson and Cane 1991
58	Australian V Site 3		23	2	round	40	.	.	1256	1.2	.	.	.	0.8	2		Nicholson and Cane 1991
59	Australian V Site 4		16	4	round	80	.	.	5024	0.8	2.1	4.2	.	0.6	1.3		Nicholson and Cane 1991
60	Australian V Site 4		16	4	oval		30	80	9499	0.8	1.5	3.6	.	1.2	1.4		Nicholson and Cane 1991
61	Australian V Site 4		16	4	round	30	.	.	707	1.5	2.1	2.7	.	0.4	1.7		Nicholson and Cane 1991
62	Australian V Site 4		16	4	round	40	.	.	1256	2.7	3.6	4.2	0.8	2	0.8		Nicholson and Cane 1991
63	Australian V Site 5		29	2	round	40	.	.	1256	1.4	.	.	0.6	1.4	1.5		Nicholson and Cane 1991
64	Australian V Site 5		29	2	round	50	.	.	1963	1.4	2.1	.	2.1	2.2	1.5		Nicholson and Cane 1991
65	Australian V Site 6		32	4	round	60	.	.	2826	2	2.1	3.8	.	1.8	2.7		Nicholson and Cane 1991
66	Australian V Site 6		32	4	round	100	.	.	7850	2	1.5	2.5	3.1	3.5	1.1		Nicholson and Cane 1991
67	Australian V Site 6		32	4	oval		40	75	10382	1.2	1.5	2.5	1.8	2.1	1.7	s	Nicholson and Cane 1991
68	Australian V Site 7		75	2	round	40	.	.	1256	3.2	.	.	.	0.5	1		Nicholson and Cane 1991
69	Australian V Site 7		75	2	round	60	.	.	2826	3.2	.	.	.	3.5	6.5		Nicholson and Cane 1991
70	Australian V Site 8		24	1	round	35	.	.	962	.	.	.	.	2	2.5		Nicholson and Cane 1991
71	Australian V Site 9		35	2	round	25	.	.	491	4.1	.	.	.	0.3	2		Nicholson and Cane 1991
72	Australian V Site 9		35	2	round	35	.	.	962	4.1	.	.	.	1.1	4		Nicholson and Cane 1991
73	Australian V Site 10		20	1	round	30	.	.	707	.	.	.	.	2	2.1		Nicholson and Cane 1991
74	Felsstalle Rockshelter IIIb		60	2	round	50	.	.	1963	3.5	.	.	.	1.5	1.3		Kind 1984
75	Felsstalle Rockshelter IIIb		60	2	round	33	.	.	855	3.5	.	.	.		1.2		Kind 1984
76	Felsstalle Rockshelter IIa3		60	1	round	40	.	.	1256	.	.	.	.		1.1		Kind 1984
77	Helga-Abri IIIB		.	2	oval		37	75	9847	3.3	.	.	.	1.5	1.7		Hahn 1984
78	Helga-Abri IIIB		.	2	oval		40	100	15386	3.3	.	.	.	1.5	1.3		Hahn 1984
79	Big Elephant Cave		65	3	round	50	.	.	1963	3.3	7.9	.	.	1.5	4.5	s	Clark and Walton 1962
80	Big Elephant Cave		65	3	round	50	.	.	1963	4.6	7.9	.	.	1.8	4.2	s	Clark and Walton 1962
81	Big Elephant Cave		65	3	round	30	.	.	707	4.6	3.3	.	.	1.6	4.3	s	Clark and Walton 1962
82	Vedda Rock Bed Hearth 1, West		26	6	round	40	.	.	1256	1.0	1.1	2.3	.	1.3	1.7	s	Seligmann and Seligmann, 1911; Binford 1996

Site	Provenience	Area(m)	H-N	Shape	H-Dia	Lgth	Wdth	H-area	Dis-H1	Dis-H2	Dis-H3	Dis-NW	Dis-BW	Dis-DL	Functn	Reference
83	Vedda Rock Bed Hearth 2, west	26	6	round	40	.	.	1256	1.0	1.4	1.4		1.2	2.3	s	Seligmann and Seligmann 1911; Binford 1996
84	Vedda Rock Hearth 3, east	26	6	round	30	.	.	707	1.1	1.4	2.0		1.3	2.6	s	Seligmann and Seligmann 1911; Binford 1996
85	Vedda Rock Bed Hearth 4, east	26	6	round	40	.	.	1256	1.0	1.1	2.4		1.6	1.6	s	Seligmann and Seligmann 1911; Binford 1996
86	Vedda Rock Bed Hearth 5, east	26	6	round	30	.	.	707	1.0	1.7	3.1		1.3	1.7	s	Seligmann and Seligmann 1911; Binford 1996
87	Vedda Rock 'Kitchen' hearth	26	6	round	56	.	.	2461	1.0	1.4	2.0		2.3	1.0	s	Seligmann and Seligmann 1911; Binford 1996
88	Papua New Guinea Nip (Site MTE)	187	2	other	.	100	60	600	5.4	.	.		1	5.5		Gorecki 1991
89	Papua New Guinea Luanana (Site JIE)	28	4	oval	.	35	60	2100	2.4	2.5	4.3		1.5	2.5		Gorecki 1991
90	Papua New Guinea Luanana (Site JIE)	28	4	round	30	.	.	707	2.4	2.5	3.5		4.1	0.5		Gorecki 1991
91	Papua New Guinea Luanana (Site JIE)	28	4	oval	.	75	100	7500	2	2.5	2.6		1.6	2		Gorecki 1991
92	Papua New Guinea Luanana (Site JIE)	28	4	oval	.	50	100	5000	2	4.4	5		1	1.1		Gorecki 1991
93	Papua New Guinea Adjiga (Site COM)	90	2	round	80	.	.		3.4	5.5	12	1.2	12	5		Gorecki 1991
94	Papua New Guinea Adjiga (Site COM)	90	2	round	50	.	.		7	12	15	.	0.7	9		Gorecki 1991
95	Papua New Guinea Marindjila (Site C)	169	4	round	50	.	.		3.5	5	7.1	0.7	11	1.5		Gorecki 1991
96	Papua New Guinea Marindjila (Site C)	169	4	round	50	.	.		2.5	3.5	5	3.9	10	1.9		Gorecki 1991
97	Papua New Guinea Marindjila (Site C)	169	4	round	40	.	.		2.5	2.6	5	5.5	8	4.3		Gorecki 1991
98	Papua New Guinea Marindjila (Site C)	169	4	round	60	.	.		2.6	5	7.1	5	6	7		Goreck, 1991
99	De Hangen SE hearth	64	3	round	36	.	.	1017	2.3	6.1	2.3	0.7		6.4	s	Parkington and Poggenpoel 1971
100	De Hangen NE hearth	64	3	round	57	.	.	2550	2.3	5.8	5.8	0.6		8.8	s	Parkington and Poggenpoel 1971
101	De Hangen W hearth	64	3	oval		128	100	12800	5.8	6.1	6.1	1.4		7.8	s	Parkington and Poggenpoel 1971

Notes: Column labels: H-area, hearth area (cm³); Dis-H1, distance to 1st hearth (m); Dis-H2, distance to ... hearth (m) measured from center of hearths; Dis-NW, distance to nearest wall (m); Dis-DL, distance to dripline (m); Functn – S, sleeping

APPENDIX D

Analysis of Sediments for Zinc and Phosphate Ions

THOMAS M. HARRIS

Sediment samples collected from Floor II of Tor Faraj were analyzed for phosphate and zinc ions. It was hoped that the results from these tests would contribute to the knowledge of patterns of human habitation within the shelter. Similar analyses of archaeological sediments have been used to trace areas of organic deposition related to bone discard and midden accumulation (Sjöberg 1976; Craddock *et al.* 1985; Bethel and Máté 1989).

The determination of phosphorus in archaeological sediments has received significant attention. Recent investigators (Lillios 1992) have utilized analytical facilities at the University of Wisconsin-Milwaukee, where a phosphate speciation procedure developed by

Eidt (1984) has been applied to sediment samples from around the world. The Eidt procedure is believed to allow for the determination of four different geochemical forms of phosphate ion in a soil through sequential extraction and spectrophotometric analysis of the extracts. The four forms include base-extractable phosphate (Extract I-A), phosphate adsorbed to calcite (Extract I-B), phosphate adsorbed to hydrous oxides of aluminum and iron (Extract II), and calcium phosphate (Extract III) (Table D.1). The spectrophotometric analysis is based on the formation of the blue-colored phosphomolybdate complex in the solutions derived from these extracts.

Table D.1 Analytical procedure for the determination of phosphate speciation in archaeological sediments

I-A. Exchangeable phosphate
1. Combine 1g of soil (dried and sieved) with 40mL of a solution containing 0.10 M NaOH and 1.0 M NaCl in a 250mL polypropylene centrifuge tube with a screw top. Close the tube and rotate overnight on a laboratory rotator at medium speed.
2. Centrifuge the mixture until the supernatant is clear, then transfer the liquid phase to a clean, dry polyethylene bottle using a disposable polyethylene pipette.
3. Add 50mL of 1.0 M NaCl to the sample, agitate vigorously, and then centrifuge until the supernatant is clear. Remove all of the free liquid phase with a disposable pipette. Discard this liquid.

I-B. Calcite-sorbed phosphate
1. Add 50mL of a solution containing 0.22 M sodium citrate and 0.11 M sodium bicarbonate to the sample. Place the sample tube in a water bath heated to 80°C. Agitate and open the tube to release pressure periodically.

2. After 30 minutes, close the sample tube and centrifuge until the supernatant is clear. Transfer the liquid phase to a clean 100-mL volumetric flask using a disposable polyethylene pipette.
3. Add 1 drop of 3 N FeCl₃ solution to the flask containing the liquid phase, then dilute to volume with distilled water.
4. Add 25mL of 1.0 M NaCl to the sample, agitate vigorously, and then centrifuge until the supernatant is clear. Remove all of the free liquid phase with a disposable pipette. Discard this liquid.

II. *Hydrous metal oxide-sorbed phosphate*
1. Add 50mL of a solution containing 0.22 M sodium citrate and 0.11 M sodium bicarbonate to the sample. Place the open sample tube in a water bath heated to 80°C. Agitate periodically until the sample has reached the temperature of the bath.
2. Add 1g of sodium dithionite to the sample. Agitate periodically.
3. After 15 minutes, close the sample tube and centrifuge until the supernatant is clear. Transfer the liquid phase to a clean 100-mL volumetric flask using a diposable polyethylene pipette.
4. Add 25mL of 1.0 M NaCl to the sample, agitate vigorously, and then centrifuge until the supernatant is clear. Transfer all of the free liquid to the flask of step 3 with a disposable polyethylene pipette.
5. Add 1 drop of 3 N FeCl₃ solution to the flask containing the combined liquid phases, then dilute to volume with distilled water. Transfer this solution to a clean, dry polyethylene bottle and allow it to set for 8 days before analyzing it.
6. Add 25mL of 1.0 M NaCl to the sample, agitate vigorously, and then centrifuge until the supernatant is clear. Remove all of the free liquid phase with a disposable pipette. This liquid may be discarded.
7. Blank: Repeat steps 1, 2, 4, and 5 without a residue from the previous extraction.

III. *Calcium phosphate*
1. Add 40mL of a 1.0 M HCl solution to the sample. Close the tube and rotate for 4 hours on a laboratory rotator at medium speed.
2. Centrifuge the mixture until the supernatant has cleared, then transfer the liquid phase to a clean, dry polyethylene bottle using a disposable polyethylene pipette.

IV. *Phosphate determination*
1. Pipette 2mL of the sample solution to a clean 25-mL volumetric flask. Add 4mL of distilled water to the flask.
2. Pipette 2mL of the ammonium molybdate reagent solution to the flask and mix. Then pipette 6mL of the tin chloride reagent solution and mix. Dilute to volume with distilled water and mix thoroughly.
3. Allow the analytical solution to set for at least 10 minutes before analyzing it. During this time, establish the blank and the standard curve, using blank and standard solutions tailored to the extract of interest. The analytical wavelength used is 725nm.
   Standard: Using an analytical balance with an accuracy of 0.0001g, weigh 0.426g of ammonium monohydrogen phosphate into a small, clean, dry beaker. Dissolve the salt in distilled water. Quantitatively transfer the solution to a 1-L volumetric flask. EachmL of this solution contains 0.1mg of phosphorus.
   Molybdate reagent solution: Using a balance with an accuracy of 0.01g, weigh 15g of ammonium molybdate into a 1-L beaker. Add 300mL of warm distilled water to the beaker and mix until the salt has dissolved. Add 350mL of concentrated hydrochloric acid, mix well, and then add sufficient distilled water to make 1L of solution. Transfer this reagent to a dark glass bottle.
   Stannous chloride reagent solution: Using a balance with an accuracy of 0.01g, weigh 5.3g of tin metal into a small beaker. Add 25mL of concentrated hydrochloric acid. After the tin has dissolved, transfer the solution to a dark glass bottle. Immediately prior to use, pipette 1mL of the concentrated solution into a 400mL beaker. Add 330mL of distilled water. Use this solution for no more than 8 hours.

There is no generally accepted procedure for the determination of zinc in anthropological sediments. For the sake of convenience the extracts obtained for the determination of phosphate were also analyzed for zinc by atomic absorption spectrometry.

Experimental methodology

Details of the sequential chemical extraction are presented as a step-by-step procedure in Table D.1. All chemicals utilized were reagent-grade. High purity water was produced with a Millipore Milli-Q water purification system.

The Eidt methodology (*ibid.*) calls for the use of two different spectrophotometric analyses for phosphate in the various extracts. Extracts I-A and III are analyzed using a 'Murphy–Riley solution'; presumably this refers to the solution first used by Murphy and Riley (1962). Extracts I-B and II are analyzed using the molybdenum blue method (Snell and Snell 1949), which varies only slightly from the Murphy–Riley procedure. The reason for utilizing two different spectrophotometric analyses was not given in any of Eidt's papers.

For the sake of expedience, in the present work the molybdenum blue method was employed with all four extracts. Details of the analysis are also presented in Table D.1. A Hewlett-Packard Model 8452 diode array spectrometer was used for making the spectrophotometric measurements. The analytical wavelength was 726nm. 'Total phosphate' was calculated by summing the amounts found to be present in the individual extracts.

The Extract III for each sediment sample was also analyzed for zinc by atomic absorption spectrometry. A Perkin-Elmer Model 2380 atomic absorption spectrometer with flame atomization was utilized. Instrumental parameters included an analytical wavelength of 213.9nm and a slitwidth of 0.7nm. The instrument was calibrated with a 1.00ppm zinc solution, prepared by dilution of a 1000ppm stock solution (Fisher Scientific), and 2 percent nitric acid served as the diluent. The sample extracts were relatively dilute in zinc, so it was not necessary to dilute them prior to analysis for zinc. On the other hand, these low concentrations prohibited intentional dilution with 2 percent nitric acid, which is commonly employed to reduce matrix interferences. Thus, the results from this analysis have to be interpreted with this issue in mind.

Results and discussion

A total of 50 samples were extracted and analyzed. Because of the large investment in time associated with the sequential extraction procedure, no more than eight of the samples were extracted in duplicate. The appearance of each extract was noted. A dark color, indicative of the presence of dissolved organic matter, appeared in only one extract (Extract I-A) of one of the 50 different sediment samples. Thus, efforts to exclude organic matter that had been present on the floor of the shelter from the sediment samples, which were acquired from much deeper layers, appear to have been successful.

The results of the phosphate speciation analysis are presented in Table D.2. The amounts of 'total phosphate' are larger, by a factor of approximately five, than values reported in previous studies (Eidt 1977; Lillios 1992). With few exceptions the greatest amount of phosphate was observed in Extract III (Fig. D.1). In almost all of the samples this fraction constituted 50 to 80 percent of the total phosphate. In previous studies by Eidt (1977) and others (Lillios 1992), higher values for this extract were found to be characteristic of 'residential' sites. However, in those studies the amount of phosphate in Extract III was typically no larger than the amounts in Extract I (combined) or Extract II. Eidt (1977) has suggested that phosphate shifts from the geochemical form accessed in Extract I to the form accessed in Extract II over long periods of time (i.e., hundred of years). One might imagine that transformation to the form accessed in Extract III occurs over even longer periods of time.

Table D.2 Results of phosphate and zinc analyses

Sample No.	Ex I-A P (mg/g)	Ex I-A Zn (mg/g)	Ex I-B P (mg/g)	Ex I-B Zn (mg/g)	Ex II P (mg/g)	Ex II Zn (mg/g)	Ex III P (mg/g)	Ex III Zn (mg/g)	Total P (mg/g)	Total Zn (mg/g)
25	0.00	0.0012	0.15	0.011	0.35	0.035	3.96	0.035	4.5	0.082
29	0.00	0.0012	0.30	0.011	0.00	0.025	1.58	0.018	1.9	0.056
30	0.04	0.0004	0.00	0.027	0.25	0.053	2.54	0.040	2.8	0.121
31	0.00	0.0004	0.00	0.018	0.45	0.048	1.38	0.017	1.8	0.084
32	0.18	0.0004	0.30	0.019	0.55	0.042	1.62	0.013	2.7	0.075
33	0.02	0.0004	0.65	0.015	0.65	0.054	2.54	0.011	3.9	0.081
34	0.02	0.0004	0.25	0.014	1.00	0.049	1.70	0.023	3.0	0.087
35	0.06	0.0004	0.40	0.016	1.80	0.041	0.88	0.014	3.1	0.071
36	0.00	0.0016	0.50	0.007	0.80	0.025	0.84	0.016	2.1	0.050
37	0.00	0.0008	0.25	0.007	0.20	0.026	1.96	0.017	2.4	0.051
38	0.00	0.0004	0.60	0.008	0.85	0.027	2.06	0.023	3.5	0.058
39	0.00	0.0012	0.15	0.006	0.15	0.025	4.88	0.021	5.2	0.053
40	0.04	0.0008	0.20	0.012	0.85	0.045	3.36	0.034	4.5	0.091
41	0.06	0.0008	0.25	0.009	0.95	0.032	2.26	0.030	3.5	0.072
42	0.04	0.0008	0.30	0.008	0.75	0.033	1.72	0.023	2.8	0.065
43	0.04	0.0004	0.30	0.013	1.10	0.050	1.18	0.016	2.6	0.080
44	0.02	0.0004	0.40	0.008	1.10	0.032	0.62	0.016	2.1	0.056
45	0.00	0.0004	0.55	0.013	0.80	0.026	0.62	0.015	2.0	0.054
46	0.06	0.0008	0.55	0.008	0.55	0.024	1.54	0.020	2.7	0.053
47	0.12	0.0008	0.85	0.005	1.00	0.022	2.52	0.018	4.5	0.046
48	0.02	0.0008	0.15	0.005	0.15	0.020	2.60	0.014	2.9	0.040
49	0.02	0.0008	0.05	0.006	0.15	0.023	3.10	0.011	3.3	0.041
50	0.52	0.0012	0.00	0.017	0.25	0.041	3.66	0.080	4.4	0.139
51	0.12	0.0008	0.10	0.008	0.20	0.032	2.10	0.022	2.5	0.063
52	0.12	0.0004	0.80	0.007	0.45	0.021	3.52	0.019	4.9	0.047
53	0.06	0.0004	0.35	0.010	0.64	0.019	0.98	0.014	2.0	0.043
54	0.10	0.0004	0.05	0.008	0.35	0.033	1.36	0.014	1.9	0.056
55	0.10	0.0004	0.00	0.010	0.00	0.029	1.78	0.016	1.9	0.055
56	0.06	0.0008	0.05	0.007	0.15	0.025	0.50	0.016	0.8	0.049
57	0.04	0.0012	0.05	0.007	0.50	0.020	0.74	0.039	1.3	0.067
58	0.14	0.0008	0.60	0.006	0.35	0.017	2.36	0.044	3.5	0.068
59	0.00	0.0004	0.20	0.007	1.45	0.021	3.82	0.036	5.5	0.064
60	0.04	0.0008	0.55	0.008	0.80	0.036	1.96	0.018	3.4	0.063
61	0.04	0.0008	0.80	0.006	0.75	0.024	1.40	0.020	3.0	0.050
63	0.02	0.0008	1.50	0.008	1.00	0.022	1.48	0.031	4.0	0.062
64	0.00	0.0008	0.45	0.008	0.45	0.028	0.70	0.017	1.6	0.054
65	0.02	0.0012	0.40	0.009	0.70	0.022	1.02	0.020	2.1	0.052
66	0.02	0.0008	0.25	0.013	0.00	0.024	0.24	0.030	0.51	0.068
67	0.00	0.0004	0.20	0.007	0.50	0.024	2.70	0.024	3.40	0.055
68	0.02	0.0020	0.30	0.006	0.45	0.018	4.12	0.024	4.89	0.050
69	0.00	0.0020	0.50	0.007	0.95	0.018	1.96	0.020	3.41	0.047
70	0.00	0.0004	0.30	0.038	0.40	0.056	0.98	0.034	1.68	0.128
71	0.06	0.0008	0.30	0.011	0.30	0.026	1.36	0.017	2.02	0.055
72	0.06	0.0004	0.75	0.010	0.85	0.023	1.64	0.015	3.30	0.048
73	0.06	0.0004	0.20	0.010	0.55	0.017	1.06	0.012	1.87	0.040
74	0.20	0.0004	0.50	0.007	0.70	0.023	1.54	0.010	2.94	0.040
75	0.12	0.0004	0.35	0.006	0.50	0.021	1.68	0.010	2.65	0.038
76	0.02	0.0008	0.45	0.005	0.70	0.024	1.24	0.022	2.41	0.051
77	0.00	0.0004	0.20	0.006	0.80	0.015	1.80	0.027	2.80	0.048

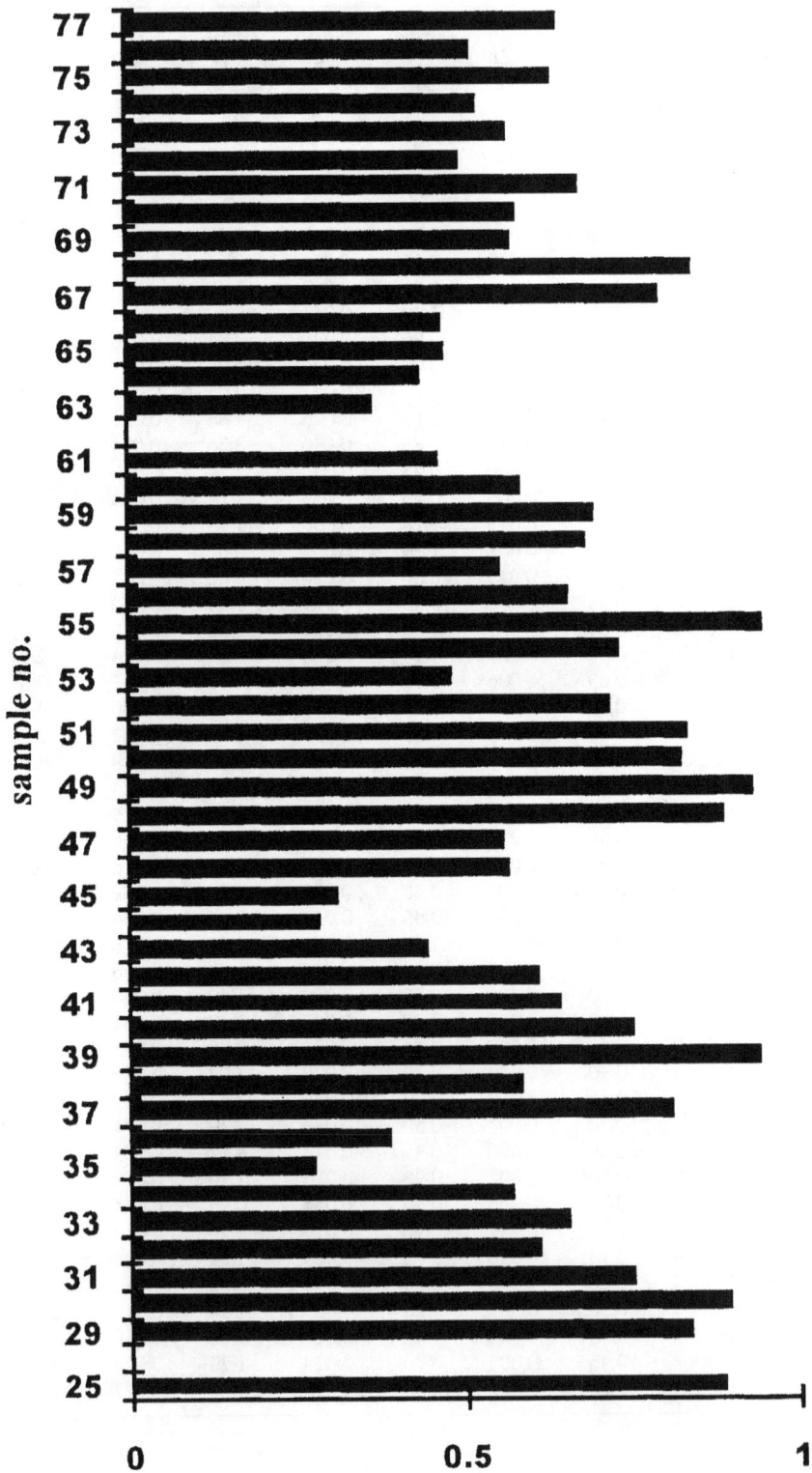

Figure D.1 Fraction of total phosphate found in Extract III

Table D.3 Results of spike tests

Sample No.	Ex I-A (0.40 mg)	Ex I-B (0.25 mg)	Ex II (0.25 mg)	Ex III (0.10 mg)
30			0.38	
40			0.39	
50			0.39	
57	0.43	0.41		
58	0.41	0.54		
64	0.42	0.49		
65	0.42	0.45		
70			0.37	0.11
71				0.11
72				0.10
73				0.10
74				0.10
75				0.10

Note: All values are in units of mg. Actual spike amounts are given in parentheses

As noted above, Eidt's procedure called for the use of the Murphy-Riley procedure for the spectrophotometric determination of phosphate in Extract I-A and Extract III. However, to expedite analysis in the present study, these extracts were analyzed by the molybdenum blue spectrophotometric method instead. Spike tests performed by adding known amounts of phosphate to several examples of Extract I-A and Extract III (Table D.3) indicated that the molybdenum blue analysis provides accurate results with these extracts. Thus, it is difficult to imagine why Eidt (1984) specifies the use of the Murphy-Riley reagent for determining phosphate in these two extracts. It was noted that the time required to achieve a maximum absorbance at 726nm in the case of Extract III was longer than three hours. To eliminate this issue as a potential source of error, standard solutions were prepared at the same time as the sample solutions, so that the 'age' of both sets of solutions was identical.

Eidt's (ibid.) procedure does call for use of the molybdenum blue method for Extract I-B and Extract II. Interestingly, it was with these two extracts that significant inaccuracy was encountered in the performance of spike tests. Spike tests with sample extracts yielded values greater than those anticipated (Table D.3). However, absorbance values obtained when standard solutions were prepared with appropriate amounts of these extractants were more than 50 percent lower than those obtained

with the solutions employed for Extract I-A and Extract III. Taken together, these observations suggest that a component of these extraction solutions, citrate ion, reduces the absorptivity of the molybdenum blue complex, perhaps by interfering with its formation. However, when the extraction solution is placed in contact with a sediment sample, this interfering component is apparently consumed or otherwise inactivated with respect to interfering with the complexation. This type of matrix interference is very difficult to overcome. Fortunately, the amounts of phosphate in Extract I-B and Extract II were relatively small, such that these errors do not affect the total phosphate quantity to a debilitating extent.

Results from duplicate extractions are presented in Table D.4. The repeatability of the extraction that yields Extract III, and its subsequent analysis by the molybdenum blue procedure, is acceptable. Of course, poor repeatability may be expected with a heterogeneous material such as an anthropogenic sediment.

The results of the analysis for zinc also appear in Figure D.2. The largest amount of zinc was more often found in Extract II, rather than Extract III. Zinc ions are known to adsorb strongly to the surface of hydrous ferric oxide (Gadde and Laitinen 1974), which is believed to undergo reductive dissolution in Extract II. On the other hand, since zinc phosphate is much less soluble than calcium

Table D.4 Results of duplicate extractions

Sample No.	Ex I-A (mg/g)	Ex I-B (mg/g)	Ex II (mg/g)	Ex III (mg/g)
50	0.026/0.000		0.005/0.010	0.183/0.195
51	0.006/0.003	0.002/0.005	0.004/0.014	0.105/0.089
52	0.006/0.001	0.016/0.021	0.009/0.028	0.176/0.156
53	0.003/0.006		0.013/0.019	0.049/0.059
54	0.005/0.002		0.007/0.020	0.068/0.067
55	0.005/0.002		0.000/0.014	0.089/0.089
57	0.002/0.005	0.001/0.008		0.037/0.029
64	0.000/0.005	0.009/0.020		0.035/0.064
65	0.001/0.005	0.008/0.017		0.051/0.079

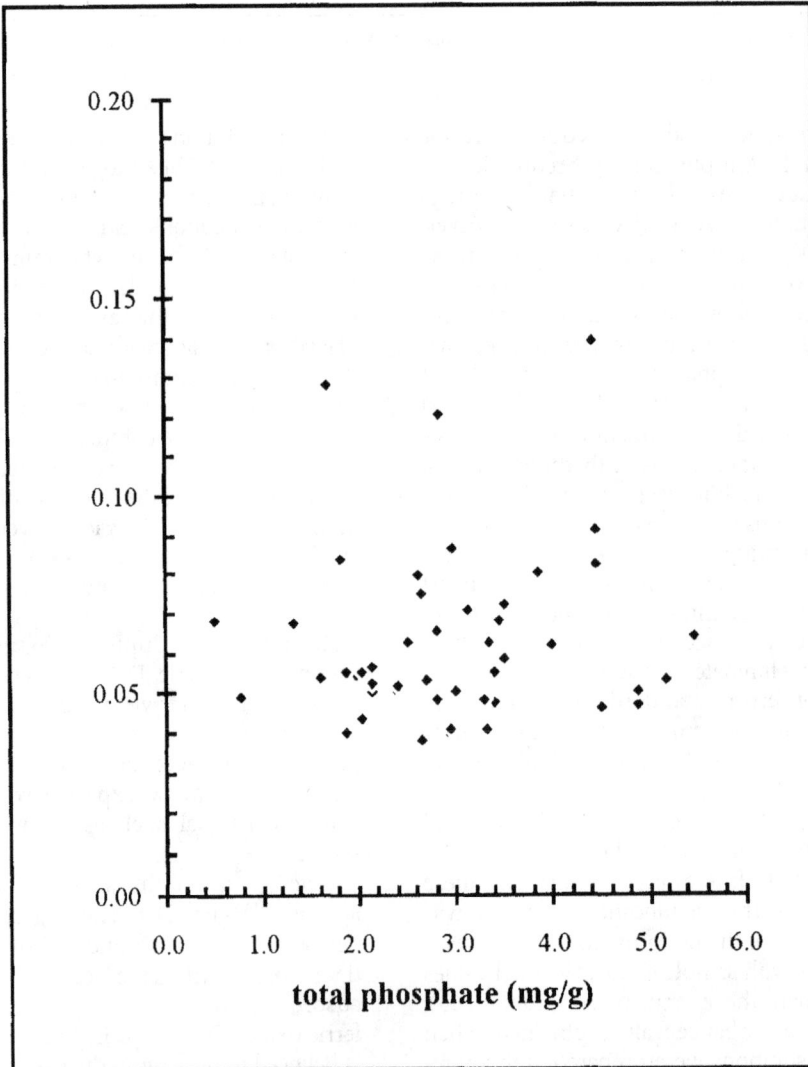

Figure D.2 Relationship between total phosphate and total zinc

phosphate (*ibid.*), zinc should also be associated through surface adsorption with the calcium phosphate that survives this extraction, but is believed to dissolve in Extract III. This issue deserves to be studied with the aid of synthetically produced materials.

The total phosphate content of the sediment samples is plotted against the total zinc content in Figure D.2. There is no obvious correlation between these two parameters.

Conclusion

The sequential extraction procedure for phosphate ion developed by Eidt (1984), modified slightly with respect to the subsequent spectrophotometric analysis of the extracts, was used in the analysis of sediments from Tor Faraj. The sequential extracts were also analyzed for zinc ion by atomic absorption spectrophotometry. The samples exhibited a wide range of total phosphate values. With few exceptions, the greatest amount of phos-

phate was observed in Extract III. These results are consistent with Eidt's hypothesis that phosphate ion is gradually converted to calcium phosphate over long periods of time.

To expedite analysis in the present study, all four of the sequential extracts were analyzed by the molybdenum blue spectrophotometric method. Spike tests indicated that this method provides accurate results with Extract I-A and Extract III. However, significant inaccuracies were encountered with Extract I-B and Extract II. A complex matrix interference can be attributed to the presence of citrate ion in the corresponding extractants.

The zinc content of these sediments samples was uniformly low. The largest amount of zinc was more often found in Extract II, indicating an adsorptive role for hydrous ferric oxide, which is believed to undergo reductive dissolution in Extract II. The total phosphate and total zinc values for the samples considered in this study do not correlate.

References

Addington, L. R. (1986) *Lithic Illustration*. Chicago: University of Chicago Press.

Ahler, S. A. (1989a) Experimental knapping with KRF and midcontinent cherts: overview and applications. In D. S. Amick and R. P. Mauldin (eds.), *Experiments in Lithic Technology*, pp. 199–234. Oxford: BAR International Series 528.

Ahler, S. A. (1989b) Mass analysis of flaking debris: studying the forest rather than the tree. In D. O. Henry and G. H. Odell (eds.), *Alternative Approaches to Lithic Analysis*, pp. 85–118. Washington, DC: Archaeological Papers of the American Anthropological Association No. 1.

Akazawa, T. (1979) Middle Paleolithic assemblages from Douara Cave. *Bulletin of the Museum of the University of Tokyo* 16: 1–30.

Akazawa, T. (1987) The ecology of the Middle Paleolithic occupation at Douara Cave, Syria. *Bulletin of the University Museum*, University of Tokyo 29: 155–66.

Akazawa, T., (1988) Ecologie de l'occupation de la grotte de Douara, Syrie, au Paléolithique Moyen. *L'Anthropologie* 92: 883–900.

Akazawa, T., Muheisen, S., Dodo, Y., Kondo, O., Mizoguchi, Y., Abe, Y., Nishiaki, Y., Ohta, S., Oguchi, T., and Haydal, J. (1995) Neanderthal infant burial from the Dederiyeh Cave in Syria. *Paléorient* 21: 77–86.

Akridge, G. (1994) The Sloan Site revisited: a preliminary report of two soil samples. *Field Notes, Newsletter of the Arkansas Archaeological Society* 260: 5–10.

Albert, R. M., Lavi, O. *et al.* (1999) Mode of occupation of Tabun Cave, Mt Carmel, Israel during the Mousterian period: a study of the sediments and phytoliths. *Journal of Archaeological Science* 26: 1249–60.

Albert, R. M. and Weiner, S. (2001) Study of phytoliths in prehistoric ash layers using a quantitative approach. In J. D. Meunier, F. Colin, and L. Faure-Denard (eds.), *The Phytoliths: Applications in Earth Science and Human History*. Aix en Provence: CEREGE.

Aldus Corporation (1991) *Aldus Freehand Users Manual*, version 3.0. Seattle: Aldus.

Altena, C. O. van Regteren (1962) Molluscus and echinoderms from Palaeolithic deposits in the rock shelter of Ksar 'Akil, Lebanon. *Zoologische Mededelingen* 38: 87–99.

Amick, D. S. and Mauldin, R. P. (1989) Comments on Sullivan and Rozen's 'Debitage analysis and archaeological interpretation.' *American Antiquity* 54: 166–8.

Amick, D. S., Mauldin, R. P., and Tomka, S. A. (1988) An evaluation of debitage produced by experimental bifacial core reduction of a Georgetown chert nodule. *Lithic Technology* 17: 26–36.

Andrefsky, W. Jr. (1986) A consideration of blade and flake curvature. *Lithic Technology* 15: 48–54.

Arensburg, B. and Belfer-Cohen, A. (1998) Sapiens and Neanderthals: rethinking the Levantine Middle Paleolithic hominids. In T. Akazawa, K. Aoki, and O. Bar-Yosef (eds.), *Neandertals and Modern Humans in Western Asia*, pp. 311–22. New York: Plenum Press.

Arensburg, B., Schepartz, L. A., Tiller, A.-M., Vandermeersch, B., and Rak, Y. (1990) A reappraisal of the anatomical basis for speech in Middle Palaeolithic hominids. *American Journal of Physical Anthropology* 88: 137–46.

Armagan, T. (1998) Small Debris Analysis of Site J430: Tor Faraj in Southern Jordan. Unpublished MA thesis. Department of Anthropology, University of Tulsa, Tulsa, Oklahoma.

Baruch, U. (1994) The Late Quaternary pollen record of the Near East. In O. Bar-Yosef and R. S. Kra (eds.), *Late Quaternary Chronology and Paleoclimates of the Eastern Mediterranean*, pp. 103–20. Tucson, AZ: Radiocarbon, Department of Geosciences, The University of Arizona.

Baruch, U. and Bottema, N. (1991) Palynological evidence for climatic changes in the Levant *ca.* 17,000–9,000 B.P. In O. Bar-Yosef and F. R. Valla (eds.), *The Natufian Culture in the Levant,* pp. 11-20. Ann Arbor, MI: International Monographs in Prehistory.

Bar-Yosef, O. (1987) Pleistocene connections between Africa and southwest Asia: an archaeological perspective. *The African Archaeological Review* 5: 29-38.

Bar-Yosef, O. (1989) Upper Pleistocene cultural stratigraphy in southwest Asia. In E. Trinkaus (ed.), *The Emergence of Modern Humans: Biocultural Adaptations in the Later Pleistocene*, pp. 154-80. Cambridge: Cambridge University Press.

Bar-Yosef, O. (1992) Middle Paleolithic human adaptations in the Mediterranean Levant. In T. Akazawa, K. Aoki, and T. Kimura (eds.), *The Evolution and Dispersal of Modern Humans in Asia*, pp. 189-216. Tokyo: Hokusen-Sha.

Bar-Yosef, O. (1993) Site formation process from a Levantine viewpoint. In P. Goldberg, D. T. Nash, and M. D. Petraglia (eds.), *Formation Processes in Archaeological Context*, pp. 13-32. Madison, WI: Prehistory Press.

Bar-Yosef, O. (1994) The contributions of southwest Asia to the study of the origin of modern humans. In M. H. Nitecki and D. V. Nitecki (eds.), *Origins of Anatomically Modern Humans*, pp. 24-66. New York: Plenum Press.

Bar-Yosef, O. (1995) The origins of modern humans. In T. E. Levy (ed.), *The Archaeology of Society in the Holy Land*, pp. 110-23. London: Leicester University Press.

Bar-Yosef, O. (1998) The chronology of the Middle Paleolithic of the Levant. In T. Akazawa, K. Aoki, and O. Bar-Yosef (eds.), *Neanderthals and Modern Humans in Western Asia*, pp. 39-56. New York: Plenum Press.

Bar-Yosef, O. (2000) The Middle and Early Paleolithic in southwest Asia and neighboring regions. In O. Bar-Yosef and D. Pilbeam (eds.), *The Geography of Neanderthals and Modern Humans in Europe and the Greater Mediterranean*, pp. 107-56. Cambridge, MA: Peabody Museum Bulletin 8, Peabody Museum of Archaeology and Ethnology, Harvard University.

Bar-Yosef, O. and Dibble, H. (1995) Preface. In H. Dibble and O. Bar-Yosef (eds.), *The Definition and Interpretation of Levallois Technology*, pp. ix-xiii. Madison, WI: Prehistory Press.

Bar-Yosef, O. and Kuhn, S. L. (1999) The big deal about blades: laminar technologies and human evolution. *American Anthropologist* 101: 322-38.

Bar-Yosef, O. and Meignen, L. (1992) Insights into Levantine Middle Paleolithic cultural variability. In H. Dibble and P. Mellars (eds.), *The Middle Paleolithic: Adaptation, Behavior, and Variability*, pp. 163-82. Philadelphia, PA: The University Museum, University of Pennsylvania.

Bar-Yosef, O. and Pilbeam, D. (2000) Afterword. In O. Bar-Yosef and D. Pilbeam (eds.), *The Geography of Neanderthals and Modern Humans in Europe and the Greater Mediterranean*, pp. 183-7. Cambridge, MA: Peabody Museum Bulletin 8, Peabody Museum of Archaeology and Ethnology, Harvard University.

Bar-Yosef, O. and Vandermeersch, B. (1981) Notes concerning the possible age of the Mousterian layers in Qafzeh cave. In J. Cauvin and P. Sanlaville (eds.), *Préhistoire du Levant*, pp. 281-6. Paris: C.N.R.S.

Bar-Yosef, O., Vandermeersch, B., Arensburg, B., Belfer-Cohen, A., Goldberg, P., Laville, H., Meignen, L., Rak, Y., Speth, J. D., Tchernov, E., Tillier, A.-M., and Weiner, S. (1992) The excavations in Kebara Cave, Mt. Carmel. *Current Anthropology* 33: 497-550.

Baumler, M. and Downum, C. (1989) Between micro and macro: a study in the interpretation of small-sized lithic debitage. In D. Amick and R. Mauldin (eds.), *Experiments in Lithic Technology*, pp. 101-16. Oxford: BAR International Series 528.

Bednarik, R. G. (1992) Palaeoart and archaeological myths. *Cambridge Archaeological Journal* 2: 27-57.

Belfer-Cohen, A. and Goren-Inbar, N. (1994) Cognition and communication in the Levantine Lower Paleolithic. *World Archaeology* 26: 144-57.

Belfer-Cohen, A. and Hovers, E. (1992) In the eye of the beholder: Mousterian and Natufian burials in the Levant. *Current Anthropology* 33: 463-71.

Bergman, C. A. (1987) *Ksar Akil, Lebanon: A Technological and Typological Analysis of the Later Palaeolithic Levels of Ksal Akil.* Oxford: BAR International Series 329.

Bethel, P. and Máté, I. (1989) The use of soil phosphate analysis in archaeology: a critique. In J. Henderson (ed.), *Scientific Analysis in Archaeology and in Its Interpretation*, pp. 1-29. Oxford: Oxford University Committee for Archaeology, Monograph No. 19.

Bickerton, D. (1981) *Roots of Language.* Ann Arbor, MI: Karoma.

Bickerton, D. (1990) *Language and Species.* Chicago: University of Chicago Press.

Binford, L. R. (1973) Interassemblage variability: the Mousterian and the functional argument. In C. Renfrew (ed.), *The Explanation of Cultural Change*, pp. 227-54. London: Duckworth.

Binford, L. R. (1978) Dimensional analysis of behavior and site structure: learning from an Eskimo hunting stand. *American Antiquity* 43: 330-61.

Binford, L. R. (1979) Organization and formation processes: looking at curated technologies. *Journal of Anthropological Research* 35, 255-73.

Binford, L. R. (1980) Willow smoke and dogs' tails: hunter-gatherer settlement systems and archaeological site formation. *American Antiquity* 45: 4-20.

Binford, L. R. (1981) Behavioral archaeology and the 'Pompeii premise'. *Journal of Anthropological Research* 37: 195-208.

Binford, L. R. (1983a) *In Pursuit of the Past.* New York: Thames and Hudson.

Binford, L. R. (1983b) Working at archaeology: the Mousterian problem—learning how to learn. In L. R. Binford (ed.), *Working at Archaeology,* pp. 65-9. New York: Academic Press.

Binford, L. R. (1984) *Faunal Remains from Klasies River Mouth.* New York: Academic Press.

Binford, L. R. (1985) Human ancestors: changing view of their behavior. *Journal of Anthropological Archaeology* 4: 292-327.

Binford, L. R. (1987) Searching for camps and missing the evidence? Another look at the Lower Paleolithic. In O. Soffer (ed.), *The Pleistocene Old World: Regional Perspectives,* pp. 17-31. New York: Plenum Press.

Binford, L. R. (1989) Isolating the transition to cultural adaptations: an organizational approach. In E. Trinkaus (ed.), *The Emergence of Modern Humans: Biocultural Adaptations in the Later Pleistocene,* pp. 18-41. Cambridge: Cambridge University Press.

Binford, L. R. (1991) When the going gets tough the tough get going: Nunamiut local groups, camping patterns and economic organization. In C. S. Gamble and W. A. Boismier (eds.), *Ethno-archaeological Approaches to Mobile Campsites,* pp. 25-138. Ann Arbor, MI: International Monographs in Prehistory, Ethnoarchaeological Series 1.

Binford, L. R. (1992) Hard evidence. *Discover,* February: 44-51.

Binford, L. R. (1996) Hearth and home: the spatial analysis of ethnographically documented rock shelter occupations as a template for distinguishing between human and hominid use of sheltered space. In N. J. Conard and F. Wendorf (eds.), *Middle Paleolithic and Middle Stone Age Settlement Systems,* pp. 229-39. Forlì, Italy: A.B.A.C.O. Edizioni.

Boëda, E. (1982) Etude expérimentale de la technologie des pointes Levallois. *Studia Praehistoricale Belgica* 2: 23-56.

Boëda, E. (1986) Approche technologique du concept Levallois et évaluation de son champ d'application: étude de trois gisements saaliens et weichséliens de la France septentrionale. Unpublished PhD dissertation. Paris: Université de Paris X.

Boëda, E. (1995) Levallois: a volumetric construction, methods, a technique. In H. L. Dibble and O. Bar-Yosef (eds.), *The Definition and Interpretation of Levallois Technology,* pp. 41-68. Madison, WI: Prehistory Press.

Boëda, E., Geneste, J. M., and Meignen, L. (1990) Identification de chaînes opératoires lithiques du Paléolithique ancien et moyen. *Paléorient* 2: 43-80.

Boëda, E. and Muhesen, S. (1993) Umm El Tlel (El Kowm, Syrie): Etude préliminaire des industries lithiques du Paléolithique moyen et supérieur 1991-1992. In J. Cauvin (ed.), *Cahiers de l'Euphrate,* pp. 47-92. Paris: Editions Recherche sur les Civilizations.

Boquet-Appel, J.-P. and Demars, P. Y. (2000) Neanderthal contraction and modern human colonization of Europe. *Antiquity* 74: 544-52.

Bordes, F. (1961) *Typologie du Paléolithique Ancien et Moyen.* Bordeaux: Delmas.

Bordes, F. (1972) *A Tale of Two Caves.* New York: Harper and Row.

Bordes, F. (1980) Le débitage levallois et ses variantes. *Bulletin de la Société Préhistorique Française* 77: 45-9.

Bottema, S. and van Zeist, W. (1981) Palynological evidence for the climatic history of the Near East 50000-6000 B. P. In J. Cauvin and P. Sanlaville (eds.), *Préhistoire du Levant,* pp. 115-32. Lyon: Maison de l'Orient, CNRS.

Bourguignon, L. (1996) Un Moustérien tardif sur le site d'Umm el Tlel (Bassin d'El Kowm, Syrie)? Exemples des niveaux II Base et III 2A. In E. Carbonell and M. Vaquero (eds.), *The Last Neanderthal: The First Anatomically Modern Humans,* pp. 317-36. Tarragona: Universitat Rovira i Virgili.

Boutié, P. (1981) *L'industrie moustérienne de la grotte de Kebara, Mount Carmel Israel.* Musée National d'Histoire Naturelle, Musée de L'Homme Mémoire 10. Paris: CNRS.

Boutié, P. (1989) Etude technologique de l'industrie Moustérienne de la grotte de Qafzeh (près de Nazareth, Israël). In O. Bar-Yosef and P. Vandermeersch (eds.), *Investigations in South Levantine Prehistory: Préhistoire du Sud-Levant,* pp. 213-29. Oxford: BAR International Series 497.

Bräuer, G. (1992) The origins of modern Asians: by regional evolution or by replacement. In T. Akazawa, K. Aoki, and T. Kimura (eds.), *The Evolution and Dispersal of Modern Humans in Asia,* pp. 401-13. Tokyo: Hokusen-Sha.

Brown, L. (1982) Struthioniformes. In L. Brown, E. Urban, and K. Newman (eds.), *The Birds of Africa,* Vol. 1. London: Academic Press.

Bull, P. A. and Goldberg, P. (1985) Scanning electron microscope analysis of sediments from Tabun Cave, Mount Carmel, Israel. *Journal of Archaeological Science* 12: 177-85.

Butzer, K. W. (1982) *Archaeology as Human Ecology: Method and Theory for a Contextual Approach.* Cambridge: Cambridge University Press.

Byrd, B. (1998) Spanning the gap between the Upper Paleolithic and the Natufian: the Early and Middle Epipaleolithic. In D. O. Henry (ed.), *The Prehistoric Archaeology of Jordan,* pp. 64-82. Oxford: BAR International Series 705.

Cahen, D. and Keeley, L. H. (1980) Not less than two, not more than three. *World Archaeology* 12: 166-80.

Cahen, D., Keeley, L. H., and Van Noten, F. L. (1979) Stone tools, toolkits and human behavior in prehistory. *Current Anthropology* 20: 661-83.

Cahen, D. and Moeyersons, J. (1977) Subsurface movements of stone artefacts and their implications for the prehistory of Central Africa. *Nature* 266: 812-15.

Carr, C. (1984) The nature of organization of intrasite archaeological records and spatial analytical approaches to their investigation. In M. B. Schiffer (ed.), *Advances in Archaeological Method and Theory*, Vol. 7, pp. 103-222. New York: Academic Press.

Cashdan, E. (1992) Spatial organization and habitat use. In E. A. Smith and B. Winterhalder (eds.), *Evolutionary Ecology and Human Behavior*, pp. 237-66. New York: Aldine de Gruyter.

Chase, P. G. (1989) How different was Middle Palaeolithic subsistence? A zooarchaeological perspective on the Middle to Upper Palaeolithic transition. In P. Mellars and C. Stringer (eds.), *The Human Revolution: Behavioral and Biological Perspectives on the Origins of Modern Humans*, pp. 321-37. Princeton, NJ: Princeton University Press.

Chase, P. G. and Dibble, H. L. (1987) Middle Paleolithic symbolism: a review of current evidence and interpretations. *Journal of Anthropological Archaeology* 6: 263-96.

Chomsky, N. (1986) *Knowledge of Language: Its Nature, Origin, and Use.* New York: Praeger.

Clark, G. A. and Lindly, J. M. (1989) Modern human origins in the Levant and western Asia. *American Anthropologist* 91: 962-85.

Clark, G. A., Schuldenrein, J., Donaldson, M. L., Schwarcz, H. P., Rink, W. J., and Fish, S. K. (1997) Chronostratigraphic contexts of Middle Paleolithic horizons at the 'Ain Difla rockshelter (WHS 634), west-central Jordan. In H.-G. Gebel, Z. Kafafi, and G. O. Rollefson (eds.), *The Prehistory of Jordan, II: Perspectives from 1997*, pp. 77-100. Berlin: ex oriente.

Clark, J. D. and Walton, J. (1962) A late stone age site in the Erongo mountains, south west Africa. *Proceedings of the Prehistoric Society* 28: 1-16.

Clark, J. E. (1986) Another look at small debitage and microdebitage. *Lithic Technology* 15: 21-33.

Clark, J. G. D. (1971) *Excavations at Star Carr: An Early Mesolithic Site at Seamer Near Scarborough, Yorkshire.* Cambridge: Cambridge University Press.

Copeland, L. (1975) The Middle and Upper Palaeolithic of Lebanon and Syria in the light of recent research. In F. Wendorf and A. E. Marks (eds.), *Problems in Prehistory: North Africa and the Levant*, pp. 317-50. Dallas, TX: Southern

Methodist University Press.

Copeland, L. (1983a) Levallois/non-Levallois determinations in the early Levant Mousterian: problems and questions for 1983. *Paléorient* 9: 21-38.

Copeland, L. (1983b) The Paleolithic industries at Adlun. In D. Roe (ed.), *Adlun in the Stone Age*, pp. 89-366. Oxford: BAR International Series 159.

Copeland, L. (1998) The Middle Paleolithic flint industry of Ras el-Kelb. In L. Copeland and N. Moloney (eds.), *The Mousterian Site of Ras el-Kelb, Lebanon*, pp. 73-175. Oxford: BAR International Series 706.

Copeland, L. and Hours, F. (1983) Le Yabroudien d'El Kowm (Syrie) et sa place dans le Paléolithique du Levant. *Paléorient* 9: 21-38.

Corruccini, R. S. (1992) Metrical reconsideration of the Skhul IV and IX and Border Cave crania in the context of modern human origins. *American Journal of Physical Anthropology* 87: 433-45.

Cotterell, B. and Kamminga, J. (1979) The mechanics of flaking. In B. Hayden (ed.), *Lithic Use-Wear Analysis*, pp. 97-112. New York: Academic Press.

Cotterell, B. and Kamminga, J. (1987) The formation of flakes. *American Antiquity* 52: 675-708.

Cowgill, G. L. (1982) Clusters of objects and associations between variables: two approaches to archaeological classification. In R. Whallon and J. A. Brown (eds.), *Essays on Archaeological Typology*, pp. 30-55. Evanston, IL: Center for American Archaeology Press.

Crabtree, D. E. (1970) Flaking stone with wooden implements. *Science* 169: 146-53.

Craddock, P. T., Gurney, D., Pryor, F., and Hughes, M. J. (1985) The application of phosphate analysis to the location and interpretation of archaeological sites. *Archaeological Journal* 142: 361-76.

Crelin, E. S. (1987) *The Human Vocal Tract: Anatomy, Function, Development, and Evolution.* New York: Vantage.

Crew, H. (1975) An evaluation of the relationship between the Mousterian complexes of the eastern Mediterranean: a technological perspective. In F. Wendorf and A. E. Marks (eds.), *Problems in Prehistory: North Africa and the Levant*, pp. 427-37. Dallas, TX: South Methodist University Press.

Crew, H. (1976) The Mousterian site of Rosh Ein Mor. In A. E. Marks (ed.), *Prehistory and Paleoenvironments in the Central Negev, Israel.* Vol. 1: 75-111. Dallas, TX: Department of Anthropology, ISEM, Southern Methodist University.

Cummings, L. S. (1992) Illustrated phytoliths from assorted food plants. In G. J. Rapp and S. C. Mulholland (eds.), *Phytolith Systematics: Emerging Issues*, pp. 175-92. New York: Plenum Press.

Cziesala, E., Eickhoff, S., Arts, M., and Winter, D. (eds.) (1990) The big puzzle: international symposium of refitting stone artifacts. In *Studies in Modern Archaeology*. Bonn: Holos.

Deacon, T. W. (1989) The neural circuitry underlying primate calls and human language. *Human Evolution* 4: 367–401.

Debénath, A. and Dibble, H. L. (1994) *The Handbook of Paleolithic Typology*. Vol. I, *The Lower and Middle Paleolithic of Europe*. Philadelphia: The University Museum Press.

Demidenko, Yu. E. and Usik, V. I. (1991) On the end-scrapers fragmentation in the Upper Paleolithic. *Acta Archaeologica Carpathica* (*Krakow*) 30: 5–16 (in Russian).

Demidenko, Yu. E. and Usik, V. I. (1993a) Leaf points of the Upper Palaeolithic industry from the 2nd complex of Korolevo II and certain methodical problems in description and interpretation of the category of Palaeolithic tools. *Préhistoire Européenne*, 4: 49–62.

Demidenko, Yu. E. and Usik, V. I. (1993b) On the *lame à crête* technique in the Paleolithic. *Préhistoire Européene* 4: 33–48.

Demidenko, Yu. E. and Usik, V. I. (1993c) On the Levallois technique in the Upper Palaeolithic. In J. Pavuk (ed.), *Actes du XII Congrès International des Sciences Préhistoriques et Protohistoriques*, pp. 239–42. Bratislava: Institut Archéologique de l'Académie Slovaque des Sciences.

Demidenko, Yu. E. and Usik, V. I. (1993d) The problem of changes in Levallois technique during the technological transition from the Middle to Upper Palaeolithic. *Paléorient* 19: 5–15.

Demidenko, Yu. E. and Usik, V. I. (1994) On the Levallois point technology in the Middle Paleolithic (on the materials of Korolevo I site-complex 2B in the Ukrainian Transcarpathians). *Archaeological Almanac* 3 (Donetsk): 35–46.

Demidenko, Yu. E. and Usik, V. I. (1995) Establishing the potential evolutionary technological possibilities of the 'point' Levallois-Mousterian: Korolevo I site-complex 2B in the Ukrainian Transcarpathians. In H. I. Dibble and O. Bar-Yosef (eds.), *The Definition and Interpretation of Levallois Technology*. Madison, WI: Prehistory Press, Monographs in World Archaeology 23: 439–54.

Dennell, R. (1985) *European Economic Prehistory: A New Approach*. London: Academic Press.

D'Errico, F., Zilhao, J., Julien, M., Baffier, D., and Pelegrin, J. (1998) Neanderthal acculturation in western Europe? *Current Anthropology* 39: S1–S22.

Dibble, H. L. (1984a) Interpreting typological variation of Middle Paleolithic scrapers: function, style, or sequence of production. *Journal of Field Archaeology* 11: 431–6.

Dibble, H. L. (1984b) The Mousterian industry from Bisitun Cave (Iran). *Paléorient* 10: 23–34.

Dibble, H. L., Chase, P. G., McPherron, S. P., and Tuffreau, A. (1997) Testing the reality of a 'living floor' with archaeological data. *American Antiquity* 62: 629–51.

Duarte, C., Mauricio, J., Pettitt, B., Souto, P., Trinkaus, E., Plicht, H. V., and Zilhão, J. (1999) The early Upper Paleolithic human skeleton from the Abrigo do Lagar Velho (Portugal) and modern human emergence in Iberia. *Proceedings of the National Academy of Sciences, USA* 96: 7604–9.

Dunnel, R. C. and Stein, J. K. (1989) Theoretical issues in the interpretation of microartifacts. *Geoarchaeology* 4: 31–42.

Ebert, J. I. and Camilli, E. (1993) Lithic distributions and their analytical potential: an example. *Lithic Technology* 18: 95–105.

Eidt, R. C. (1977) Detection and examination of anthrosols by phosphate analysis. *Science* 197: 327–1333.

Eidt, R. C. (1984) Theoretical and practical considerations in the analysis of anthrosols. In G. Rapp, Jr., G. Gifford, and J. A. Gifford (eds.), *Archaeological Geology*, pp. 155–90. New Haven, CT: Yale University Press.

El-Eisawi, D. M. (1985) Vegetation in Jordan. In A. Hadidi (ed.), *Studies in the History and Archaeology of Jordan*. Vol. 2, pp. 67–78. Amman: Department of Antiquities of Jordan.

Ellis, C. J. (1986) Factors influencing the use of stone projectile tipes: an ethnographic perspective. In H. Knecht (ed.), *Projectile Technology*, pp. 37–74.

Ellis, C. J. (1997) Factors influencing the use of stone projectile tips: an ethnographic perspective. In H. Knecht (ed.), *Projectile Technology*. New York: Plenum Press.

Emery-Barbier, A. (1988) Analyses polliniques du Quaternaire Supérieur en Jordanie Méridionale. *Paléorient* 14: 111–17.

Emery-Barbier, A. (1995) Pollen analysis: environmental and climatic implications. In D. O. Henry (ed.), *Prehistoric Cultural Ecology and Evolution. Insights from Southern Jordan*, pp. 375–84. New York: Plenum Press.

Engen, S. (1978) *Stochastic Abundance Models, with Emphasis on Biological Communities and Species Diversity*. London: Chapman and Hall.

Ensor, H. B. and Roemer, E. Jr. (1989) Comments on Sullivan and Rozen's debitage analysis and archaeological interpretation. *American Antiquity* 54: 175–8.

Evenari, M., Shanan, L., and Tadmor, N. (1971) *The Negev: The Challenge of a Desert*. Cambridge, MA: Harvard University Press.

Farizy, C. and David, F. (1992) Subsistence and behavioral patterns of some Middle Palaeolithic local groups. In H. L. Dibble and P. A. Mellars (eds.), *The Middle Palaeolithic: Adaptation, Behavior, and Variability*, pp. 87–96.

Philadelphia, PA: University of Pennsylvania, University Museum Monographs No. 72.

Farrand, W. R. (1979) Chronology and paleoenvironments of Levantine prehistoric sites as seen from sediment studies. *Journal of Archaeological Science* 6: 369-92.

Féblot-Augustins, J. (1993) Mobility strategies in the late Middle Palaeolithic of central Europe and western Europe: elements of stability and variability. *Journal of Anthropological Archaeology* 12: 211-65.

Fish, P. R. (1978) Consistency in archaeological measurement and classification: a pilot study. *American Antiquity* 43: 86-9.

Fish, P. R. (1979) The interpretive potential of Mousterian debitage. Tempe, PA: Arizona State University Anthropological Research Papers No. 16.

Fish, P. R. (1981) Beyond tools: Middle Paleolithic debitage analysis and cultural inference. *Journal of Anthropological Research* 37: 374-86.

Fladmark, K. R. (1982) Microdebitage analysis: initial considerations. *Journal of Archaeological Science* 9: 205-20.

Flannery, K. (1986) Spatial analysis of Guila Naquitz living floors: an introduction to Part VI. In K. Flannery (ed.), *Guila Naquitz*, pp. 319-30. New York: Academic Press.

Fleisch, S. J. (1970) Les habitats du Paléolithique moyen à Naamé, (Liban). *Bullétin du Musée de Beyrouth* 23: 25-98.

Fodor, A. (1983) *The Modularity of Mind*. Cambridge, MA: MIT Press.

Gadde, R. R. and Laitinen, H. A. (1974) Studies of heavy metal absorption by hydrous iron and manganese oxides. *Analytical Chemistry* 46: 2022-6.

Gamble, C. S. (1986) *The Palaeolithic Settlement of Europe*. Cambridge: Cambridge University Press.

Gamble, C. S. (1991) An introduction to the living spaces of mobile peoples. In C. S. Gamble and W. A. Boismier (eds.), *Ethnoarchaeological Approaches to Mobile Campsites*, pp. 1-24. Ann Arbor, MI: International Monographs in Prehistory, Ethnoarchaeological Series 1.

Gamble, C. S. (1994) *Timewalkers: The Prehistory of Colonization*. Cambridge, MA: Harvard University Press.

Gargett, R. (1989) The evidence for Neanderthal burial. *Current Anthropology* 30: 157-90.

Gargett, R. (1999) Middle Paleolithic burial is not a dead issue: the view from Qafzeh, Saint-Cézaire, Kebara, Amud and Dederiyeh. *Journal of Human Evolution* 37: 27-90.

Garrard, A. (1982) The environmental implications of a reanalysis of the large mammal fauna from the Wadi el-Mughara caves, Palestine. In J. Bintliff and W. Van Zeist (eds.), *Palaeoclimates, Paleoenvironments and Human Communities in the Eastern Mediterranean Region in Later Prehistory*, pp. 185-7. Oxford: BAR International Series 133.

Garrod, D. A. E. and Bate, D. M. (1937) *The Stone Age of Mount Carmel*. Oxford: Clarendon Press.

Geneste, J.-M. (1985) Analyse Lithique d'Industries Moustériennes du Périgord: Une Approche Technologique du Comportement des Groupes Humains au Paléolithique Moyen. PhD thesis. Bordeaux: Université de Bordeaux.

Geneste, J.-M. (1988) Les industries de la Grotte Vaufrey: technologie du débitage, économie et circulation de la matière première lithique. In J.-P. Rigaud (ed.), *La Grotte Vaufrey: paléoenvironnement, chronologie, activités humaines*, pp. 441-517. Paris: Mémoires de la Société Préhistorique Française 19.

Gibson, K. R. (1988) Brain size and the evolution of language. In M. E. Landsberg (ed.), *The Genesis of Language: A Different Judgement*, pp. 149-72. Berlin: Mouton de Gruyter.

Gibson, K. R. (1990) New perspectives on instincts and intelligence: brain size and the emergence of hierarchical mental constructional skills. In S. T. Parker and K. R. Gibson (eds.), *Language and Intelligence in Monkeys and Apes: Comparative Developmental Perspectives*, pp. 97-128. Cambridge: Cambridge University Press.

Gibson, K. R. (1993) Tool use, language and social behavior in relation to information processing capacities. In K. R. Gibson and T. Ingold (eds.), *Tools, Language and Cognition in Human Evolution*, pp. 251-69. Cambridge: Cambridge University Press.

Gifford-Gonzalez, D. P., Damrosch, D. B., Damrosch, D. R., Pryor, J., and Thunen, R. L. (1985) The third dimension in site structure: an experiment in trampling and vertical dispersal. *American Antiquity* 50: 803-18.

Gilead, I. (1988) Le site Moustérien de Fara II (Néguev septentrional, Israël) et le remontage de son industrie. *L'Anthropologie* 92: 797-808.

Gilead, I. and Grigson, C. (1984) Farah II: a Middle Palaeolithic open air site in the Northern Negev, Israel. *Proceedings of the Prehistoric Society* 50: 71-97.

Gladilin, V. N. (1976) *The Problems of the Early Paleolithic of Eastern Europe*. Kiev (in Russian).

Gladilin, V. N. (1989) The Korolevo Palaeolithic site: research, methods, stratigraphy. *Anthropologie* (Brno) XXVII/2-3: 93-103.

Gladilin, V. N. and Demidenko Yu. E. (1989) Upper Palaeolithic stone tool complexes from Korolevo. *Anthropologie* (Brno) XXVII/2-3: 143-78.

Gladilin, V. N. and Demidenko, Yu. E. (1990) On the origins of Early Upper Paleolithic industries with leaf points in the Carpatho-Balkan region. In J. K. Kozlowski (ed.), *Les industries à pointes* foliacées du Paléolithique supérieur européen, Krakow 1989, pp. 115-24. Liège: ERAUL.

Goldberg, P. (1981) Late Quaternary stratigraphy of Israel: an eclectic view. In J. Cauvin and P. Sanlaville (eds.), Préhistoire du Levant, pp. 55-66. Lyons: Maison de l'Orient, CNRS.

Goldberg, P. (1983) The geology of Boker Tachtit, Boker, and their surroundings. In A. E. Marks (ed.), Prehistory and Paleoenvironments in the Central Negev, Israel, pp. 39-62. Dallas, TX: Department of Anthropology, ISEM, Southern Methodist University.

Goldberg, P. (1984) Late Quaternary history of Qadesh Barnea, northeastern Sinai. Zeitschrift für Geomorphologie N.F. 28: 193-217.

Goldberg, P. (1986) Late Quaternary environmental history of the Southern Levant. Geoarchaeology 1: 225-44.

Goldberg, P. and Bar-Yosef, O. (1998) Site formation processes in Kebara and Hayonim Caves and their significance in Levantine prehistoric caves. In T. Akazawa, K. Aoki, and O. Bar-Yosef (eds.), Neanderthals and Modern Humans in Western Asia, pp. 107-26. New York: Plenum Press.

Goreck, P. (1991) Horticulturalists as hunter-gatherers: rock shleter usage in Papua New Guinea. In C. S. Gamble and W. A. Boismier (eds.), Ethnoarchaeological Approaches to Mobile Campsites, pp. 237-62. Ann Arbor: International Monographs in Prehistory, Ethnoarchaeological Series I.

Goren, N. (1979) An Upper Acheulean industry from the Golan Heights. Quatär 29-30: 105-31.

Goren-Inbar, N. (1988) Too small to be true? Reevaluation of cores on flakes in Levantine Mousterian assemblages. Lithic Technology 17: 1, 37-44.

Goren-Inbar, N. (1990) The exploitation of raw material at the Mousterian site of Quneitra. In N. Goren-Inbar (ed.), Quneitra: A Mousterian Site on the Golan Heights, pp. 150-66. Monographs of the Institute of Archaeology, The Hebrew University. Jerusalem: Qedem.

Goren-Inbar, N. and Belfer-Cohen, A. (1998) The technological abilities of the Levantine Mousterians: cultural and mental capacities. In T. Akazawa, K. Aoki, and O. Bar-Yosef (eds.), Neanderthals and Modern Humans in Western Asia, pp. 205-21. New York: Plenum Press.

Gowlett, J. A. (1984) Mental abilities of early man: a look at some hard evidence. In R. A. Foley (ed.), Hominid Evolution and Community Ecology, pp. 167-92. London: Academic Press.

Grayson, D. and Delpech, F. (1994). The evidence for Middle Paleolithic scavenging from couche VIII, Grotte Vaufrey (Dordogne, France). Journal of Archaeological Science 21: 359-75.

Gregory, R. L. (1984) Mind in Science. London: Penguin Books.

Grün, R., Schwarcz, H. P., and Stringer, C. B. (1991) ESR dating of teeth from Garrods Tabun Cave collection. Journal of Human Evolution 20: 231-48.

Gvirtzman, G., Shachnai, E., Bakler, N., and Ilani, S. (1985) Stratigraphy of the kurkar group (Quaternary) of the coastal plain of Israel. Geological Survey of Israel. Current Research. Vol. 1983/1984: 70-82.

Hahn, J. (1984) Spatial organization and occupation of the Helga-Abri, near Schelklingen, Swabian Jura. In H. Berke, J. Han, and C. J. Kind (eds.), Upper Paleolithic Settlement Patterns in Europe, pp. 79-88. Tubingen: Verlag Archaeologica Venatoria, Institut für Urgeschichte, Der Universität Tubingen.

Halford, G. (1987) A structure-mapping approach to cognitive development. International Journal of Psychology 22: 609-42.

Hall, S. (1996) Late Quaternary Geology of the Al Quwayra Area, Southern Jordan: An Overview. Unpublished manuscript.

Harlan, J. R. (1988) Natural resources. In B. MacDonald (ed.), The Wadi el Hasa Archaeological Survey 1979-1983, West-Central Jordan, pp. 40-7. Waterloo, ON: Wilfrid Laurier University Press.

Harrington, H. D. (1967) Edible Native Plants of the Rocky Mountains. Albuquerque, NM: University of New Mexico.

Hassan, F. A. (1981) Demographic Archaeology: An Approach to Population Prehistory. New York: Academic Press.

Hassan, F. A. (1995) Late Quaternary geology and geomorphology of the area in the vicinity of Ras en Naqb. In D. O. Henry (ed.), Prehistoric Cultural Ecology and Evolution: Insights from Southern Jordan, pp. 23-31. New York: Plenum Press.

Hayden, B. (1987) From chopper to celt: the evolution of resharpening techniques. Lithic Technology 16: 33-43.

Hayden, B. (1993) The cultural capacities of Neanderthals: a review and re-evaluation. Journal of Human Evolution 24: 113-46.

Hayden, B. and Hutchings, W. K. (1989) Whither the billet flake? In D. S. Amick and R. P. Mauldin (eds.), Experiments in Lithic Technology, pp. 235-57. Oxford: BAR International Series 528.

Henry, D. O. (1982) The prehistory of southern Jordan. Journal of Field Archaeology 9: 417-44.

Henry, D. O. (1983) Adaptive evolution within the Epipaleolithic of the Near East. In F. Wendorf and A. E. Close (eds.), Advances in World Archaeology, pp. 99-160. London: Academic Press.

Henry, D. O. (1986) Prehistory and Paleoenvironments of Jordan: an overview. Paléorient 12: 5-26.

Henry, D. O. (1988) Summary of research: pre-historic and paleoenvironmental research in the northern Hisma. In H. G. Gebel and A. N. Garrard (eds.), *The Prehistory of Jordan in 1986*, pp. 7-37. Oxford: BAR International Series 705.

Henry, D. O. (1989a) Correlations between reduction strategies and settlement patterns. In D. O. Henry and G. H. Odell (eds.), *Alternative Approaches to Lithic Analysis*, Archaeological Papers of the American Anthropological Association Number 1, pp. 138-55. Washington, DC: American Anthropological Association.

Henry, D. O. (1989b) *From Foraging to Agriculture: The Levant at the End of the Ice Age*. Philadelphia, PA: University of Pennsylvania Press.

Henry, D. O. (1992) Transhumance during the late Levantine Mousterian. In H. L. Dibble and P. Mellars (eds.), *The Middle Palaeolithic: Adaptation, Behavior, and Variability*, pp. 143-62. Philadelphia, PA: University of Pennsylvania University Museum Monographs No. 72.

Henry, D. O. (1994) Prehistoric cultural ecology in southern Jordan. *Science* 265: 336-41.

Henry, D. O. (1995a) The influence of mobility levels on Levallois point production, Late Levantine Mousterian, Southern Jordan. In O. Bar-Yosef and H. Dibble (eds.), *The Definition and Interpretation of Levallois Technology*, pp. 185-200. Madison, WI: Prehistory Press.

Henry, D. O. (1995b) Late Levantine Mousterian patterns of adaption and cognition. In D. O. Henry (ed.), *Prehistoric Cultural Ecology and Evolution*, pp. 107-32. New York: Plenum Press.

Henry, D. O. (1995c) The Middle Paleolithic sites. In D. O. Henry (ed.), *Prehistoric Cultural Ecology and Evolution*, pp. 49-84. New York: Plenum Press.

Henry, D. O. (ed.) (1995d) *Prehistoric Cultural Ecology and Evolution: Insights from Southern Jordan*. New York: Plenum Press.

Henry, D. O. (1997) Cultural and geologic successions of Middle and Upper Paleolithic deposits in the Jebel Qalkha area of southern Jordan. In H. Gebel, Z. Kafafi, and G. Rollefson (eds.), *The Prehistory of Jordan II: Perspectives from 1996*, pp. 69-76. Studies in Early Near Eastern Production, Subsistence, and Environment 4. Berlin: ex oriente.

Henry, D. O. (1998a) Intrasite spatial patterns and behavioral modernity: indications from the Late Levantine Mousterian rockshelter of Tor Faraj, southern Jordan. In T. Akazawa, K. Aoki, and O. Bar-Yosef (eds.), *Neanderthals and Modern Humans in Western Asia*, pp. 127-42. New York: Plenum Press.

Henry, D. O. (1998b) The Middle Paleolithic of Jordan. In D. O. Henry (ed.), *The Prehistoric Archaeology of Jordan*, pp. 23-38. Oxford: BAR International Series 705.

Henry, D. O., and Garrard, A. N. (1998) Tor Hamar: an epipaleolithic rockshelter in southern Jordan. *Palestine Exploration Quarterly* 120: 1-25.

Henry, D. O., Hall, S., Hietala, H., Demidenko, Yu E., Usik, V., Rosen, A., and Thomas, P. (1996) Middle Paleolithic behavioral organization: 1993 excavation of Tor Faraj, southern Jordan. *Journal of Field Archaeology* 23: 31-53.

Henry, D. O., Hassan, F. A., Henry, K. C. and Jones, M. (1983) An investigation of the prehistory of southern Jordan. *Palestine Exploration Quarterly* 115: 1-24.

Henry, D. O., Haynes, C. V., and Bradley, B. (1976) Quantitative variations in flaked stone debitage. *Plains Anthropologist* 21: 57-61.

Henry, D. O., Kerry, K, Brauer, H., Beaver, J. and White, J. (2001) Survey of prehistoric sites, Wadi Araba, southern Jordan. *Bulletin of the American Schools of Oriental Research* 323: 1-19.

Henry, D. O. and Miller, G. H. (1992) The implications of amino acid racemization dates of Levantine Mousterian deposits in southern Jordan. *Paléorient*, 18, 2: 45-52.

Hietala, H. J. (1983) Boker Tachtit: intralevel and interlevel spatial analysis. In A. E. Marks (ed.), *Prehistory and Paleoenvironments of the Central Negev, Israel*. Vol. III, pp. 217-81. Dallas, TX: Department of Anthropology, ISEM, Southern Methodist University.

Hietala, H. J. (ed.) (1984) *Intrasite Spatial Analysis in Archaeology*. Cambridge: Cambridge Press.

Hietala, H. J. and Longo, L. (1996) Investigations of early human behavior through functional and spatial analyses of lithics at Tor Faraj in southern Jordan. Paper delivered at Workshop 5, Middle Paleolithic and Middle Stone Age settlement Systems of the XIII Congrès International des Sciences Préhistoriques et Protohistoriques (UISPP), Forlì, Italy.

Hietala, H. and Stevens, D. (1977) Spatial analysis: multiple procedures in pattern recognition studies. *American Antiquity* 42: 539-59.

Higgs, E. S. and Jarman, M. R. (1975) Palaeoeconomy. In E. S. Higgs (ed.), *Palaeoeconomy*, pp. 1-8. Cambridge: Cambridge University Press.

Higgs, E. S. and Vita-Finzi, C. (1972) Prehistoric economies: a territorial approach. In *Papers in Economic Prehistory*, pp. 27-36. Cambridge: Cambridge University Press.

Hofman, J. L. and Enloe, J. G. (eds.) (1992) *Piecing Together the Past: Applications of Refitting Studies in Archaeology*. Oxford: BAR International Series 578.

Horowitz, A. (1976) Late Quaternary paleoenvironments of prehistoric settlements. In A. E. Marks (ed.), *Prehistory and Paleoenvironments in the Central Negev, Israel*. Vol. 1, pp. 57-68. Dallas, TX: Department of Anthropology, ISEM, Southern Methodist University.

Horowitz, A. (1979) *The Quaternary of Israel*. New York: Academic Press.

Hovers, E. (1990) The exploitation of raw material at the Mousterian Site of Quneitra. In N. Goren-Inbar (ed.), *Quneitra: A Mousterian Site on the Golan Heights*, pp. 150–66. Monographs of the Institute of Archaeology, The Hebrew University. Jerusalem: Qedem.

Hovers, E. (1997) Variability of Levantine Mousterian Assemblages and Settlement Patterns: Implications for the Development of Human Behavior. PhD dissertation. Jerusalem: The Hebrew University.

Hovers, E. (1998) The lithic assemblages of Amud Cave: implications for understanding the end of the Mousterian in the Levant. In T. Akazawa, K. Aoki and O. Bar-Yosef (eds.), *Neanderthals and Modern Humans in Western Asia*, pp. 143–63. New York: Plenum Press.

Howell, F. C. (1998) Evolutionary implications of altered perspectives on homini demes and populations in the Later Pleistocene of western Eurasia. In T. Akazawa, K. Aoki, and O. Bar-Yosef (eds.), *Neanderthals and Modern Humans in Western Asia*, pp. 5–27. New York: Plenum Press.

Hublin, J.-J., Spoor, F., Braun, M., Zonneveld, F., and Condemi, S. (1996) A late Neanderthal associated with Upper Paleolithic artefacts. *Nature* 381: 224–6.

Hull, K. L. (1987) Identification of cultural site formation processes through microdebitage analysis. *American Antiquity* 52: 772–83.

Ibrahim, K. M. (1990) *Wadi Gharandal 3050III*. Amman, Jordan: Natural Resources Authority, Geological Directorate, Hasemite Kingdom of Jordan, Royal Geographic Centre.

Jelinek, A. J. (1981) The Middle Paleolithic in the Southern Levant from the perspective of the Tabun Cave. In J. Cauvin and P. Sanlaville (eds.), *Préhistoire du Levant*, pp. 265–80. Paris: CNRS.

Jelinek, A. J. (1982) The Tabun Cave and Paleolithic man in the Levant. *Science* 216: 1369–75.

Jelinek, A. J. (1992) Problems in the chronology of the Middle Paleolithic and the first appearance of early modern *homo sapiens* in southwest Asia. In T. Akazawa, K. Aoki, and T. Kimura (eds.), *The Evolution and Dispersal of Modern Humans in Asia*, pp. 253–75. Tokyo: Hokusen-Sha.

Jelinek, A. J. (1994) Hominids, energy, environment and behavior in the Late Pleistocene. In M. H. Nitecki and D. V. Nitecki (eds.), *Origins of Anatomically Modern Humans*, pp. 67–92. New York: Plenum Press.

Kalin, J. (1981) Stem point manufacture and debitage recovery. *Archaeology of Eastern North America* 9: 134–75.

Kapp, R. O. (1969) *How to Know: Pollen and Spores*. Dubuque: Brown.

Kaufman, D. (1999) *Archaeological Perspectives on the Origins of Modern Humans: View from the Levant*. London: Bergin and Garvey.

Keckler, A. (1994) *Surfer for Windows*. Golden: Golden Software.

Kerry, K. W. and Henry, D. O. (2000) Conceptual domains, competence, and *chaîne opératoire* in the Levantine Mousterian. In L. E. Stager, J. A. Greene, and M. D. Coogan (eds.), *The Archaeology of Jordan and Beyond: Essays in Honor of James A. Sauer*, pp. 238–54. Winona Lake: Eisenbrauns.

Kind, C.-J. (1984) The Felsstalle, a rockshelter near Ehingen-Mühlen, Alb-Donau-Kreis (Southwest Germany) with particular emphasis on the occupational structures from the Magdalenian horizon IIIb. In H. Berke, J. Hahn, and C.-J. Kind (eds.), *Upper Paleolithic Settlement Patterns in Europe*, pp. 89–97. Tübingen: Archaeologica Venatoria 7.

Kind, C.-J. (1985) *Die Verteilung von Steinartefakten in Grabungsflächen: Ein Modell zur Organisation alt und Mittelsteinzeitlicher Siedlungsplätze*. Tübingen: Archaeologica Venatoria 7.

Klein, R. G. (1994) The problem of modern human origins. In M. N. Nitecki and D. V. Nitecki (eds.), *Origins of Anatomically Modern Humans*, pp. 3–17. New York: Plenum Press.

Klein, R. G. (2000) Archaeology and the evolution of human behavior. *Evolutionary Anthropology* 9: 17–36.

Krings, M., Geisert, H., Schmitz, R. W., Krainitzki, H., and Pääbo, S. (1999) DNA sequence of the mitochondrial hypervariable region II from the Neanderthal specimen. *Journal of Human Evolution* 96: 5581–5.

Krings, M., Stone, A., Schmitz, R. W., Krainitske, H., Stoneking, M., and Pääbo, S. (1997) Neanderthal DNA sequences and the origin of modern humans. *Cell* 90: 19–30.

Kuhn, S. L. (1991) 'Unpacking' reduction: lithic raw material economy in the Mousterian of west-central Italy. *Journal of Anthropological Archaeology* 10: 76–106.

Kuhn, S. L. (1995) *Mousterian Lithic Technology: An Ecological Perspective*. Princeton, NJ: Princeton University Press.

Kuhn, S. L., Stiner, M. C., and Güleç, E. (1999) Initial Upper Paleolithic in south-central Turkey and its regional context: a preliminary report. *Antiquity* 73: 505–17.

Kuijt, I., Prentiss, W. C., and Pokotylo, D. L. (1995) Bipolar reduction: an experimental study of debitage variability. *Lithic Technology* 20: 116–27.

Kuijt, I. and Russell, K. W. (1993). Tur Imdai rockshelter, Jordan: debitage analysis and historic Bedouin lithic technology. *Journal of Archaeological Science* 20: 667–80.

Laville, H., Rigaud, J.-P., and Sackett, J. (1980) *Rock Shelters of the Périgord: Geological Stratigraphy and Archaeological Succession*. New York: Academic Press.

Lee, C. M. (1987) 'A Functional Analysis of Levallois Points from Two Middle Paleolithic Sites in South Jordan: Results and Interpretations'. Unpublished MA thesis. Department of Anthropology, University of Tulsa, Tulsa, Oklahoma.

Leroi-Gourhan, A. (1972) Annexe IV, vocabulaire. In A. Leroi-Gourhan and M. Brézillon (eds.), *Fouilles de Pincevent: essai d'analyse ethnographique d'un habitat magdalénien (la section 36).* Paris: CNRS.

Leroi-Gourhan, A. (1980) Les analyses polliniques au Moyen Orient. *Paléorient* 6: 79–91.

Leroi-Gourhan, A. (1984) *Pincevent: campement magdalénien de chasseurs de Rennes.* Paris: Ministère de la Culture.

Leroi-Gourhan, A. and Brézillon, M. (1966) L'habitation magdalénienne N 1 de Pincevent Près Monterau (Seine-et-Marne). *Gallia Préhistoire* 9: 263–385.

Leroi-Gourhan, A. and Brezillon, M. (1972) Fouilles de Pincevent. *Essai d'analyse ethnographique d'un habitat magdalénien (la section 36).* Paris: CNRS.

Lieberman, D. (1998) Neanderthal and early modern human mobility patterns: comparing archaeological and anatomical evidence. In T. Akazawa, K. Aoki, and O. Bar-Yosef (eds.), *Neandertals and Modern Humans in Western Asia,* pp. 263–76. New York: Plenum Press.

Lieberman, D. E. (1993). Mobility and Strain: The Biology of Cementogenesis and Its Application to the Evolution of Hunter-Gatherer Seasonal Mobility in the Southern Levant During the Quaternary. PhD dissertation. Harvard University. Ann Arbor: University Microfilms.

Lieberman, D. E. and Shea, J. J. (1994) Behavioral differences between archaic and modern humans in the Levantine Mousterian. *American Anthropologist* 96: 300–32.

Lieberman, P. (1975) *On the Origin of Language: An Introduction to the Evolution of Human Speech.* New York: Macmillan.

Lieberman, P. (1984) *The Biology and Evolution of Language.* Cambridge, MA: Harvard University Press.

Lieberman, P. (1992) On Neanderthal speech and Neanderthal extinction. *Current Anthropology* 33: 409–10.

Lillios, K. T. (1992) Phosphate fractionation of soils at Agroal, Portugal. *American Antiquity* 57: 495–506.

Lindly, J. and Clark, J. (1987) A preliminary lithic analysis of the Mousterian site of 'Ain Difla (WHS 634) in the Wadi Ali, west-central Jordan. *Proceedings of the Prehistoric Society* 53: 279–92.

Magne, M. P. R. (1989) Lithic reduction stages and assemblage formation processes. In D. S. Amick and R. P. Mauldin (eds.), *Experiments in Lithic Technology,* pp. 15–31. Oxford: BAR

International Series 528.

Marks, A. E. (1981) The Middle Paleolithic of the Negev, Israel. In J. Cauvin and P. Sanlaville (eds.), *Préhistoire du Levant,* pp. 287–98. Paris: CNRS.

Marks, A. E. (1983a) The sites of Boker Tachtit and Boker: a brief introduction. In A. E. Marks (ed.), *Prehistory and Paleoenvironments of the Central Negev, Israel.* Vol. III, pp. 15–37. Dallas, TX: Department of Anthropology, ISEM, Southern Methodist University.

Marks, A. E. (ed.) (1983b) *Prehistory and Paleoenvironments in the Central Negev, Israel.* Vol. III. Dallas, TX: Department of Anthropology, ISEM, Southern Methodist University.

Marks, A. E. (1988a) The curation of stone tools during the Upper Pleistocene: a view from the Central Negev, Israel. In H. L. Dibble and A. Montet-White (eds.), *Upper Pleistocene Prehistory of Western Eurasia,* pp. 275–85. Philadelphia, PA: The University Museum, University of Pennsylvania.

Marks, A. E. (1988b) Early Mousterian settlement patterns in the central Negev, Israel: their social and economic implications. In M. Otte (ed.), *L'Homme de Néanderthal.* Vol. 6: *La subsistance,* pp. 115–26. Liège: ERAUL.

Marks, A. E. (1992a) Typological variability in the Levantine Middle Paleolithic. In H. Dibble and P. Mellars (eds.), *The Middle Paleolithic: Adaptation, Behavior, and Variability,* pp. 127–42. Philadelphia, PA: The University Museum, University of Pennsylvania.

Marks, A. E. (1992b) Upper Pleistocene archaeology and the origins of modern man: a view from the Levant and adjacent areas. In T. Akazawa, K. Aoki, and T. Kimura (eds.), *The Evolution and Dispersal of Modern Humans in Asia,* pp. 229–52. Tokyo: Hokusen-Sha.

Marks, A. E. and Freidel, D. (1977) Prehistoric settlement patterns in the Avdat/Aqev area. In A. E. Marks (ed.), *Prehistory and Paleoenvironments in the Central Negev, Israel.* Vol. II, pp. 131–59. Dallas, TX: Department of Anthropology, ISEM, Southern Methodist University.

Marks, A., and Monigal, K. (1995) Modeling the production of elongated blanks from the Early Levantine Mousterian at Rosh Ein Mor. In H. Dibble and O. Bar-Yosef (eds.), *The Definition and Interpretation of Levallois Technology,* pp. 267–78. Madison, WI: Prehistory Press.

Marks, A. E., Shokler, J., and Zilhao, J. (1991) Raw material usage in the Paleolithic. In A. Montet-White and S. Holen (eds.), *Raw Material Economies Among Prehistoric Hunter-Gatherers,* pp. 127–41. Lawrence, KS: University of Kansas.

Marks, A. E. and Volkman, P. (1983) Changing core reduction strategies: a technological shift from the Middle to the Upper Pleistocene in the

Southern Levant. In E. Trinkhaus (ed.), *The Mousterian Legacy: Human Biocultural Change in the Upper Pleistocene*, pp. 13-34. Oxford: BAR International Series 164.

Marks, A. E. and Volkman, P. (1986) The Mousterian of Ksar Akil: levels XXIV through XXVIIIb. *Paléorient* 12: 5-20.

Marks, A. E. and Volkman, P. (1987) Technological variability and change seen through core reconstruction. In G. de Sieveking and M. H. Newcomer (eds.), *The Human Uses of Flint and Chert*, pp. 11-20. Cambridge: Cambridge University Press.

Marshack, A. (1989) Comment. *Current Anthropology* 30: 332-5.

Marshack, A. (1996) A Middle Paleolithic symbolic composition from the Golan Heights: the earliest known depictive image. *Current Anthropology* 37: 357-65.

Martell, A. E. and Sillen, R. M. (1976) *Critical Stability Constants*. Vol. 4. New York: Plenum Press.

Martinson, D. G., Pisias, N. G., Hays, J. D., Imbrie, J., Moore, J. T. C., and Shackleton, N. J. (1987) Age dating and the orbital theory of the Ice Ages: development of a high resolution 0 to 300,000-year chronostratigraphy. *Quaternary Research* 27: 1-29.

Mauldin, R. P. and Amick, D. S. (1989) Investigating patterning in debitage from experimental bifacial core reduction. In D. S. Amick and R. P. Mauldin (eds.), *Experiments in Lithic Technology*, pp. 67-88. Oxford: BAR International Series 528.

McCown, T. D. (1937) Mugharet es-Skhul: description and excavations. In D. A. E. Garrod and D. M. A. Bate (eds.), *The Stone Age of Mount Carmel*, pp. 91-107. Oxford: Clarendon Press.

McCown, T. D. and Keith, A. (1939) *The Stone Age of Mount Carmel II: The Fossil Human Remains from the Levalloiso-Mousterian*. Oxford: Clarendon Press.

McHugh, W. P. and Mitchum, B. A. (1981) 'Quantitative characteristics of debitage from heat treated chert,' by L. W. Patterson. *Plains Anthropologist* 26: 327-31.

Meignen, L. (1995) Levallois lithic production systems in the Middle Paleolithic of the Near East: the case of the unidirectional method. In H. L. Dibble and O. Bar-Yosef (eds.), *The Definition and Interpretation of Levallois Technology*, pp. 361-79. Madison, WI: Prehistory Press.

Meignen, L. (1998) Hayonim Cave lithic assemblages in the context of the Near Eastern Middle Paleolithic: a preliminary report. In T. Akazawa, K. Aoki, and O.Bar-Yosef (eds.), *Neandertals and Modern Humans in Western Asia*, pp. 165-80. New York: Plenum Press.

Mellars, P. (1996) *The Neanderthal Legacy: An Archaeological Perspective from Western Europe*. Princeton, NJ: Princeton University Press.

Mellars, P. (1998) Comments: Neandertal acculturation in western Europe? *Current Anthropology* 39: S25-26.

Mellars, P. and Tixer, J. (1989) Radiocarbon accelerator dating of Ksar Aquil (Lebanon) and the chronology of the Upper Paleolithic sequence in the Middle East. *Antiquity* 63: 761-8.

Mercier, N., Valladas, H., Froget, L., Joron, J.-L., Vermeersch, P. M., Van Peer, P., and Moeyersons, J. (1999). Thermoluminescence dating of a Middle Palaeolithic occupation at Sodmein cave, Red Sea Mountains (Egypt). *Journal of Archaeological Science* 26: 1339-46.

Mercier, N., Valladas, H., Valladas, G., Reyss, J. L., Jelinek, A., Meignen, L., and Joron, J. L. (1995) TL dates of burnt flints from Jelinek's excavations at Tabun and their implications. *Journal of Archaeological Science* 22: 495-510.

Metcalfe, D. and Heath, K. M. (1990) Microrefuse and site structure: the hearths and floors of Heartbreak Hotel. *American Antiquity* 55: 781-96.

Mithen, S. (1994) From domain specific to generalized intelligence: a cognitive interpretation of the Middle/Upper Palaeolithic transition. In C. Renfrew and E. B. Zubrow (eds.), *The Ancient Mind*, pp. 29-39. Cambridge: Cambridge University Press.

Mulholland, S. C. and Rapp, G. J. (1992) A morphological classification of grass silica-bodies. In G. J. Rapp and S. C. Mulholland (eds.), *Phytolith Systematics: Emerging Issues*, pp. 65-89. New York: Plenum Press.

Munday, F. C. (1976) Intersite variability in the Mousterian of the central Negev. In A. E. Marks (ed.), *Prehistory and Palaeoenvironments in the Central Negev, Israel*. Vol. I: *The Avdat/Aqev Area*, Part 1, pp. 113-40. Dallas, TX: Department of Anthropology, ISEM, Southern Methodist University.

Munday, F. C. (1977), Nahal Aqev (D35): a stratified, open-air Mousterian occupation in the Avdat/Aqev area. In A. E. Marks (ed.) *Prehistory and Paleoenvironments in the Central Negev, Israel*. Vol. II. Dallas, TX: Department of Anthropology, ISEM, Southern Methodist University.

Munday, F. C. (1979) Levantine Mousterian technological variability: a perspective from the Negev. *Paléorient*, 5: 87-104.

Murphy, J. and Riley, J. P. (1962) A modified single solution method for the determination of phosphate in natural waters. *Analytical Chimica Acta* 27: 31-6.

Neuville, R. (1951) *Le Paléolithique et le mésolithique du désert de Judée*. Paris: Masson et Cie, Editeur.

Newcomer, M. H. (1975) 'Punch technique' and Upper Paleolithic blades. In E. Swanson (ed.), *Lithic Technology, Making and Using Stone Tools*, pp. 97-102 and plates ii-iii. The Hague: Mouton Publishers.

Newcomer, M. H. and Sieveking, G. de G. (1980) Experimental flake scatter-patterns: a new interpretive technique. *Journal of Field Archaeology* 7: 345-52.

Nicholson, A. and Cane, S. (1991) Desert camps: analysis of Australian Aboriginal proto-historic campsites. In C. S. Gamble and W. A. Boismier (eds.), *Ethnoarchaeological Approaches to Mobile Campsites*, pp. 263-354. Ann Arbor, MI: International Monographs in Prehistory, Ethnoarchaeological Series 1.

Nishiaki, Y. (1985) Truncated-faceted flakes from Levantine Mousterian assemblages. *Bulletin* (The University of Tokyo) 4: 215-26.

Nishiaki, Y. (1989) Early blade industries in the Levant: the placement of Douara IV industry in the context of the Levantine Early Middle Paleolithic. *Paléorient* 15: 215-29.

Nishiaki, Y. and Copeland, L. (1992) Keoue Cave, Northern Lebanon, and its place in the context of the Levantine Mousterian. In T. Akazawa, K. Aoki, and T. Kimura (eds.), *The Evolution and Dispersal of Modern Humans in Asia*, pp. 107-27. Tokyo: Hokusen-Sha.

Norusis, M. J. (1990) *SPSS Introductory Statistics Student Guide*. Chicago: SPSS.

O'Connell, J. (1987) Alyawara site structure and its archaeological implications. *American Antiquity* 52: 74-108.

Odell, G. H. (1989) Experiments in lithic reduction. In D. S. Amick and R. P. Mauldin (eds.), *Experiments in Lithic Technology*, pp. 163-98. Oxford: BAR International Series 528.

Odell, G. H. and Cowan, F. (1986) Experiments with spears and arrows on animal targets. *Journal of Field Archaeology* 13: 194-212.

Ogilvie, M., Curran, B., and Trinkaus, E. (1989) Incidence and patterning of dental enamel hypoplasia among the Neandertals. *American Journal of Physical Anthropology* 79: 25-41.

Ohnuma, K. (1988) *Ksar Akil, Lebanon: A Technological Study of the Earlier Upper Paleolithic Levels at Ksar Akil. Vol. 3, Levels XXV-XIV*. Oxford: BAR International Series 426.

Ohnuma, K. and Bergman, C. A. (1990) A technological analysis of the Upper Palaeolithic Levels (XXV-VI) of Ksal Akil, Lebanon. In P. Mellars (ed.), *The Emergence of Modern Humans*, pp. 91-138. Edinburgh: Edinburgh University Press.

Osborn, G. and Duford, J. M. (1981) Geomorphical processes in the Inselberg region of southwestern Jordan. *Palestine Exploration Quarterly* 1-17.

Parkington, J. and Mills, G. (1991) From space to place: the architecture and social organization of Southern African mobile communities. In C. S. Gamble and W. A. Boismier (eds.), *Ethnoarchaeological Approaches to Mobile Campsites*, pp. 355-70. Ann Arbor, MI: International Monographs in Prehistory, Ethnoarchaeological Series 1.

Parkington, J. and Poggenpoel, C. (1971) Excavations at de Hangen. *South African Archaeological Bulletin* 26: 3-36.

Patterson, L. W. (1979) Quantitative characteristics of debitage from heat treated chert. *Plains Anthropologist* 24: 255-9.

Patterson, L. W. (1982a) The importance of flake size distribution. *Contract Abstracts and CRM Archeology* 3: 70-2.

Patterson, L. W. (1982b) Replication and classification of large size lithic debitage. *Lithic Technology* 11: 50-8.

Patterson, L. W. (1990) Characteristics of bifacial-reduction flake-size distribution. *American Antiquity* 55: 550-8.

Patterson, L. W. and Sollberger, J. B. (1978) Replication and classification of small size lithic debitage. *Plains Anthropologist* 23: 103-12.

Petraglia, M. D. (1987) *Site Formation Process at the Abri Dufaure: A Study of Upper Paleolithic Rockshelter and Hillslope Deposits in Southwestern France*. Ann Arbor, MI: University Microfilms International.

Petraglia, M. D. (1993) The genesis and alteration of archaeological patterns at the Abri Dufaure: an Upper Paleolithic rockshelter and slope site in southwestern France. In P. Goldberg, D. T. Nash, and M. D. Petraglia (eds.), *Formation Processes in Archaeological Context*, pp. 97-112. Madison, WI: Prehistory Press.

Pettitt, P. B. (1997) High resolution Neanderthals? Interpreting Middle Paleolithic intrasite spatial data. *World Archaeology* 29: 208-24.

Prentiss, W. C. and Romanski, E. J. (1989) Experimental evaluation of Sullivan and Rozen's debitage typology. In D. S. Amick and R. P. Mauldin (eds.), *Experiments in Lithic Technology*, pp. 89-99. Oxford: BAR International Series 528.

Purdy, B. (1975). Fractures for the archaeologist. In E. Swanson (ed.), *Lithic Technology: Making and Using Stone Tools*, pp. 133-41 and plates xi-xvii. The Hague: Mouton Publishers.

Quam, R. M. and Smith, F. H. (1998) A reassessment of the Tabun C2 mandible. In T. Akazawa, K. Aoki, and O. Bar-Yosef (eds.), *Neandertals and Modern Humans in Western Asia*, pp. 405-21. New York: Plenum Press.

Raab, L. M., Cande, R. F., and Stahle, D. W. (1979) Debitage graphs and archaic settlement patterns in the Arkansas Ozarks. *Midcontinental Journal of Archaeology* 4: 167-82.

Rabb'a, K. (1988) *Al Quwayra 3049 I*. Amman, Jordan: Natural Resources Authority, Geological Directorate, Hasemite Kingdom of Jordan, Royal Geographic Centre.

Ragir, S. (1972) A review of techniques for archae-ological sampling. In M. Leone (ed.), *Contemporary Archaeology*, pp. 178-92. Carbondale, IL: Southern Illinois University Press.

Rak, Y. (1990) On the differences between two pelvises of Mousterian context from Qafzeh and Kebara Caves, Israel. *American Journal of Physical Anthropology* 81: 323-32.

Rak, Y. (1998) Does any Mousterian Cave present evidence of two hominid species? In T. Akazawa, K. Aoki, and O. Bar-Yosef (eds.), *Neandertals and Modern Humans in Western Asia*, pp. 353-66. New York: Plenum Press.

Rak, Y., Kimbel, W. H., and Hovers, E. (1994) A Neandertal infant from Amud Cave, Israel. *Journal of Human Evolution* 26: 313-24.

Roebroeks, W., Kolen, J., and Rensink, E. (1988) Planning depth, anticipation and the organiza-tion of Middle Paleolithic technology: the 'archaic natives' meet Eve's descendants. *Helinium* 28: 17-34.

Rolland, N. (1981) The interpretation of Middle Paleolithic variability. *Man* 16: 15-42.

Rolland, N. and Dibble, H. (1990) A new synthesis of Middle Paleolithic variability. *American Antiquity* 55: 480-99.

Ronen, A. (1984) *Sefunim Prehistoric Sites, Mount Carmel, Israel*. Oxford: BAR International Series 230.

Rosen, A. M. (1992) Preliminary identification of silica skeletons from Near Eastern archaeological sites: an anatomical approach. In G. J. Rapp and S. C. Mulholland (eds.), *Phytolith Systematics: Emerging Issues*, pp. 129-47. New York: Plenum Press.

Rosen, A. M. (1993) Microartifacts as a reflection of cultural factors in site formation. In P. Goldberg, D. T. Nash, and M. D. Petraglia (eds.), *Formation Processes in Archaeological Context*, pp. 141-8. Madison, WI: Prehistory Press.

Rosen, A. M. (1995) Preliminary analysis of phytoliths from prehistoric sites in southern Jordan. In D. O. Henry (ed.), *Prehistoric Cultural Ecology and Evolution: Insights from Southern Jordan*. New York: Plenum Press.

Rosen, A. M. (1999a) Phytolith analysis in Near Eastern Archaeology. In S. Pike and S. Gitin (eds.), *The Practical Impact of Science on Aegean and Near Eastern Archaeology*, pp. 86-92. London: Archetype Press.

Rosen, A. M. (1999b) Phytoliths as indicators of prehistoric irrigation farming. In P. C. Anderson (ed.), *Prehistory of Agriculture: New Experimental and Ethnographic Approaches*, pp. 193-8. Los Angeles: UCLA Institute of Archaeology.

Rozen, K. C. and Sullivan, A. P. III (1989a) Measure-ment, method, and meaning in lithic analysis: problems with Amick and Mauldin's middle-range approach. *American Antiquity* 54: 169-75.

Rozen, K. C. and Sullivan, A. P. III (1989b) The nature of lithic reduction and lithic analysis: stage typologies revisited. *American Antiquity* 54: 179-84.

Sanlaville, P. (1981) Stratigraphie et chronologie du Quartenaire marin du Levant. In J. Cauvin and P. Sanlaville (eds.), *Préhistoire du Levant*, pp. 21-31. Paris: CNRS.

Saragusti, I. and Goren-Inbar, N. (1990) Conjoinable pieces from the lithic assemblage of Quneitra, Area B. In N. Goren-Inbar (ed.), *Quneitra: A Mousterian Site on the Golan Heights*, pp. 173-88. Monographs of the Institute of Archaeology, The Hebrew University. Jerusalem: Qedem.

Schick, K. D. (1986) *Stone Age Sites in the Making: Experiments in the Formation and Transformation of Archaeological Occurrences*. Oxford: BAR International Series 319.

Schick, T. and Stekelis, M. (1977) Mousterian assemblages in Kebara Cave, Mount Carmel. In B. Arensburg and O. Bar-Yosef (eds.), *Eretz-Israel*. Vol. 13, pp. 97-149. Jerusalem: The Israel Exploration Society.

Schiffer, M. B. (1983) Toward the identification of formation processes. *American Antiquity* 48: 675-706.

Schiffer, M. B. (1987) *Formation Processes of the Archaeological Record*. Albuquerque: University of New Mexico Press.

Schroeder, B. (1969) The Lithic Industries from Jerf Ajila and Their Bearing on the Problem of the Middle to Upper Paleolithic Transition. PhD dissertation. New York: Columbia University.

Schuldenrein, J. and Clark, G. A. (1994) Landscape and prehistoric chronology of west-central Jordan. *Geoarchaeology: An International Journal* 9: 31-55.

Schwarcz, H. P., Blackwell, B., Goldberg, P., and Marks, A. E. (1979) Uranium series dating of travertine from archaeological sites, Nahal Zin, Israel. *Nature* 277: 558-60.

Schwarcz, H., Buhay, W., Grün, R., Valladas, H., Tchernov, E., Bar-Yosef, O., and Vandermeersch, B. (1989) ESR dating of the Neanderthal site, Kebara Cave, Israel. *Journal of Archaeological Science* 16: 653-69.

Schwarcz, H. P., Goldberg, P., and Blackwell, B. (1980) Uranium series dating of archaeological sites in Israel. *Israel Journal of Earth Sciences* 29: 157-65.

Schwarcz, H. P. and Rink, W. J. (1998) Progress in ESR and U-series chronology of the Levantine Paleolithic. In T. Akazawa, K. Aoki, and O. Bar-Yosef (eds.), *Neandertals and Modern Humans in Western Asia*, pp. 57-67. New York: Plenum Press.

Scott, T. R. (1977) The Harifian of the central Negev, Israel. In A. E. Marks (ed.), *Prehistory and Paleoenvironments in the Central Negev, Israel*.

Vol. II, pp. 271-322. Dallas, TX: Department of Anthropology, ISEM, Southern Methodist University.

Seligmann, M. D. and Seligmann, B. (1911) *The Vedas.* Cambridge: Cambridge University Press.

Sellet, R. (1995) Levallois or not Levallois: does it really matter? Learning from an African case. In H. L. Dibble and O. Bar-Yosef (eds.), *The Definition and Interpretation of Levallois Technology,* pp. 25-39. Madison, WI: Prehistory Press.

Sharon, G. and Goren-Inbar, N. (1998) Soft percussor use at the Gesher Bebnot Ya'aqov Acheulian site, Jerusalem. *Journal of the Israel Prehistoric Society* 28: 55-80.

Shea, J. J. (1989) A functional study of the lithic industries associated with hominid fossils in the Kebara and Qafzeh Caves, Israel. In P. Mellars and C. Stringer (eds.), *The Human Evolution,* pp. 611-25. Edinburgh: Edinburgh University Press.

Shea, J. J. (1991) The Behavioral Significance of Levantine Mousterian Industrial Variability. Vols I and II. PhD. dissertation. Cambridge, MA: Harvard University.

Shea, J. J. (1995) Lithic microwear analysis of Tor Faraj rockshelter. In D. O. Henry (ed.), *Prehistoric Cultural Ecology and Evolution: Insights from Southern Jordan,* pp. 85-105. New York: Plenum Press.

Shea, J. J. (1998) Neandertal and early modern human behavioral variability: a regional-scale approach to lithic evidence for hunting in the Levantine Mousterian. *Current Anthropology* 39 (Supplement): S48-S78.

Shea, J. J. (2001) Early modern humans and Neandertals in the Levant. *Near Eastern Archaeology* 64: 38-64.

Shehadeh, N. (1985) The climate of Jordan in the past and present. In A. Hadidi (ed.), *Studies in the History and Archaeology of Jordan II,* pp. 25-38. Amman: Department of Antiquities.

Shott, M. J. (1994) Size and form in the analysis of flake debris: review and recent approaches. *Journal of Archaeological Method and Theory* 1: 69-110.

Simek, J. F. (1987) Spatial order and behavioural change in the French Paleolithic. *Antiquity* 61: 25-40.

Simek, J. F. (1992) Neanderthal cognition and the Middle to Upper Paleolithic transition. In G. Bräuer and F. H. Smith (eds.), *Continuity or Replacement: Controversies in Homo Sapiens Evolution.* Rotterdam, Brookfield: A. A. Balkema.

Simmons, T. (1994) Origins of anatomically modern humans. In M. H. Nitecki and D. V. Nitecki (eds.), *Origins of Anatomically Modern Humans,* pp. 201-26. New York: Plenum Press.

Simms, S. R. and Heath, K. M. (1990) Site structure of the Orbit Inn: an application of ethnoarchaeology. *American Antiquity* 55: 797-813.

Sjöberg, A. (1976) Phosphate analysis of anthropic soils. *Journal of Field Archaeology* 3: 447-54.

Smith, W. G. (1984) *Man, the Primeval Savage.* London: E. Stanford.

Snell, F. D. and Snell, C. T. (1949) *Colorimetric Methods of Analysis,* 3rd edn. Vol. 2. Princeton, NJ: van Nostrand.

Soffer, O. (1989) The Middle to Upper Palaeolithic transition on the Russian Plain. In P. Mellars and C. Stringer (eds.), *The Human Revolution: Behavioral and Biological Perspectives on the Origins of Modern Humans,* pp. 714-42. Princeton, NJ: Princeton University Press.

Soffer, O. (1994) Ancestral lifeways in Eurasia—the Middle and Upper Paleolithic records. In M. H. Nitecki and D. V. Nitecki (eds.), *Origins of Anatomically Modern Humans,* pp. 101-19. New York: Plenum Press.

Solecki, R. L. and Solecki, R. S. (1970) A new secondary flaking technique at Nahr Ibrahim cave site. *Bulletin du Musée de Beyrouth* 23: 137-42.

Sollberger, J. B. and Patterson, L. W. (1976) Prismatic blade replication. *American Antiquity* 41: 517-31.

Speth, J. D. (1972) Mechanical basis of percussion flaking. *American Antiquity* 37: 34-60.

Speth, J. D. (1974) Experimental investigations of hard-hammer percussion flaking. *Tebiwa* 17: 7-36.

Speth, J. D. and Tchernov, E. (1998) The role of hunting and scavenging in Neanderthal procurement strategies: new evidence from Kebara Cave (Israel). In T. Akazawa, K. Aoki, and O. Bar-Yosef (eds.), *Neanderthals and Modern Humans in Western Asia,* pp. 223-39. New York: Plenum Press.

Spurrell, F. C. J. (1880a) On implements and chips from the floor of a Palaeolithic workshop. *Archaeological Journal* 37: 249-99.

Spurrell, F. C. J. (1880b) On the discovery of the place where Palaeolithic implements were made at Crayford. *Quarternary Journal of the Geological Society* 36: 544-9.

Stahle, D. W. and Dunn, J. E. (1982) An analysis and application of the size distribution of waste flakes from the manufacture of bifacial stone tools. *World Archaeology* 14: 84-97.

Stahle, D. W. and Dunn, J. E. (1984) *An Experimental Analysis of the Size Distribution of Waste Flakes from Biface Reduction.* Fayetteville: Arkansas Archaeological Survey Technical Paper No. 2.

Stiner, M. C. (1994) *Honor Among Thieves: A Zooarchaeological Study of Neanderthal Ecology.* Princeton, NJ: Princeton University Press.

Straus, L. G. (1979) Caves: a paleoanthropological resource. *World Archaeology* 10: 331-9.

Straus, L. G. (1997) Convenient cavities: some human uses of caves and rockshelters. In C. Bonsall and C. Tolan-Smith (eds.), *The Human Use of Caves*. Oxford: BAR International Series 667.

Stringer, C. B. and Gamble, C. (1993) *In Search of the Neanderthals: Solving the Puzzle of Human Origins*. London: Thames and Hudson.

Sullivan, A. P. III and Rozen, K. (1985) Debitage analysis and archaeological interpretation. *American Antiquity* 50: 755-79.

Suzuki, H. and Takai, F. (1970) *The Amud Man and His Cave Site*. Tokyo: University of Tokyo Press.

Taborin, Y. (1993) Shells of the French Aurignacian and Perigordian. In H. Knecht, A. Pike-Tay, and R. White (eds.), *Before Lascaux: The Complex Record of the Early Upper Paleolithic*, pp. 211-29. Boca Raton, FL: CRC Press.

Tague, R. (1992) Sexual dimorphism in the human bony pelvis, with a consideration of the Neandertal pelvis from Kebara Cave, Israel. *American Journal of Physical Anthropology* 88: 1-21.

Tattersall, I. and Schwartz, J. H. (1999) Hominids and hybrids: the place of Neanderthals in human evolution. *Proceedings of the National Academy of Sciences, USA 96*, 7117-19.

Tchernov, E. (1992) Biochronology, paleoecology, and dispersal events of hominids in the southern Levant. In T. Akazawa, K. Aoki, and T. Kimura (eds.), *The Evolution and Dispersal of Modern Humans in Asia*, pp. 149-88. Tokyo: Hokusen-Sha.

Tchernov, E. (1994) New comments on the biostratigraphy of the Middle and Upper Pleistocene of the southern Levant. In O. Bar-Yosef and R. S. Kra (eds.), *Late Quaternary Chronology and Paleoclimates of the Eastern Mediterranean*, pp. 333-50. Tucson, AZ: Radiocarbon, Department of Geosciences, The University of Arizona.

Tchernov, E. (1998) The faunal sequence of the Southwest Asian Middle Paleolithic in relation to hominid dispersal events. In T. Akazawa, K. Aoki and O. Bar-Yosef (eds.), *Neandertals and Modern Humans in Western Asia*, pp. 77-90. New York: Plenum Press.

Thomas, D. H. (1983) *The Archaeology of Monitor Valley: Gatcliff Shelter*. Anthropological Papers, 59(1). New York: American Museum of Natural History.

Thomas, D. H. (1986) *Refiguring Anthropology: First Principles of Probability and Statistics*. Prospect Heights, IL: Waveland Press.

Tillier, A.-M., Arensburg, B., Rak, Y., and Vandermeersch, B. (1988) Les sépultures néandertaliennes du Proche Orient: état de la question. *Paléorient* 14: 130-4.

Todd, L. and Frison, G. (1992) Reassembly of bison skeletons from the Horner Site: a study in anatomical refitting. In J. Hofman and J. Enloe (eds.), *Piecing Together the Past: Applications of Refitting Studies in Archaeology*, pp. 63-82. Oxford: BAR International Series 578.

Todd, L. and Stanford, D. (1992) Application of conjoined bone data to site structural studies. In J. Hofman and J. Enloe (eds.), *Piecing Together the Past: Applications of Refitting Studies in Archaeology*, pp. 21-35. Oxford: BAR International Series 578.

Tomka, S. A. (1989) Differentiating lithic reduction techniques: an experimental approach. In D. S. Amick and R. P. Mauldin (eds.), *Experiments in Lithic Technology*, pp. 137-61. Oxford: BAR International Series 528.

Towner, R. H. and Warburton, M. (1990) Projectile point rejuvenation: a technological analysis. *Journal of Field Archaeology* 17: 311-21.

Trinkaus, E. (1983) Neandertal postcrania and the adaptive shift to modern humans. In E. Trinkaus (ed.), *The Mousterian Legacy*, pp. 165-200. Oxford: BAR International Series 164.

Trinkaus, E. (1984) Western Asia. In F. H. Smith and F. Spencer (eds.), *A World Survey of the Fossil Evidence of Modern Humans*, pp. 251-93. New York: Alan R. Liss, Inc.

Trinkaus, E. (1989) The Upper Pleistocene transition. In E. Trinkaus (ed.), *The Emergence of Modern Humans: Biocultural Adaptations in the Later Pleistocene*, pp. 42-66. Cambridge: Cambridge University Press.

Trinkaus, E. (1993) Comment. *Current Anthropology* 34: 620-2.

Trinkaus, E. (1995) Neanderthal mortality patterns. *Journal of Archaeological Science* 22: 121-42.

Trinkaus, E., Ruff, C. B., and Churchill, S. E. (1998) Upper limb versus lower limb loading patterns among Near Eastern Middle Paleolithic hominids. In T. Akazawa, K. Aoki, and O. Bar-Yosef (eds.), *Neandertals and Modern Humans in Western Asia*, pp. 391-404. New York: Plenum Press.

Trinkaus, E. and Thompson, D. (1987) Femoral diaphyseal histophometric age determinators for the Shanidar 3, 4, 5, and 6 Neandertals and Neandertal longevity. *American Journal of Physical Anthropology* 84: 249-60.

Usik, V. I. (1989) Korolevo-transition from Lower to Upper Palaeolithic according to reconstruction data. *Anthropologie* (Brno) XXVII 2/3: 179-212.

Valladas, H., Mercier, H., Joron, J.-L., and Reyss, J.-L. (1998) GIF laboratory dates for Middle Paleolithic Levant. In T. Akazawa, K. Aoki, and O. Bar-Yosef (eds.), *Neandertals and Modern Humans in Western Asia*, pp. 69-75. New York: Plenum Press.

Van Peer, Ph. (1991) Interassemblage variability and Levallois styles: the case of the Northern

African Middle Palaeolithic. *Journal of Anthropological Archaeology* 10: 107–51.

Van Peer, Ph. (1992) *The Levallois Reduction Strategy*. Madison, WI: Prehistory Press.

Van Peer, Ph. (1995) Current issues in the Levallois problem. In H. L. Dibble and O. Bar-Yosef (eds.), *The Definition and Interpretation of Levallois Technology*, pp. 1–9. Madison, WI: Prehistory Press.

Van Peer, Ph. (1998) The Nile Corridor and the Out-of-Africa model: an examination of the archaeological record. *Current Anthropology* 39: 115–40.

Vandermeersch, B. (1981) *Les Hommes fossiles de Qafzeh (Israël)*. Paris: CNRS.

Vandermeersch, B. (1992) The Near Eastern hominids and the evolution of modern humans in Asia. In T. Akazawa, K. Aoki, and T. Kimura (eds.), *The Evolution and Dispersal of Modern Humans in Asia*, pp. 29–38. Tokyo: Hokusen-Sha.

Vermeersch, P. M., Paulissen, E., Stokes, S., Charlier, C., van Peer, P., Stringer, C., and Lindsay, W. (1998) A Middle Palaeolithic burial of a modern human at Taramsa Hill, Egypt. *Antiquity* 72: 475–84.

Villa, P. (1982) Conjoinable pieces and site formation processes. *American Antiquity* 47: 276–90.

Vita-Finzi, C. and Higgs, E. S. (1970) Prehistoric economy in the Mount Carmel area of Palestine: site catchment analysis. *Proceedings of the Prehistoric Society* 36, 1–37.

Volkman, Ph. W. (1983) Boker Tachtit: core reconstructions. In A. E. Marks (ed.), *Prehistory and Paleoenvironments in the Central Negev, Israel*. Vol. III, pp. 127–90. Dallas, TX: Department of Anthropology, ISEM, Southern Methodist University.

Waters, M. R. (1992) *Principles of Geoarchaeology: A North American Perspective*. Tucson, AZ: The University of Arizona Press.

Weinstein-Evron, M. (1988) Middle Paleolithic sequence from the Hula Valley, Israel. In M. Otte (ed.), *L'Homme de Neandertal*. Vol. 2, pp. 207–22. Liège: ERAUL.

Wenban-Smith, F. F. (1989) The use of canonical variates for determination of biface manufacturing technology at Boxgrove Lower Paleolithic Site and the behavioral implications of this technology. *Journal of Archaeological Science* 16: 17–26.

Whallon, R. (1989) Elements of cultural change in the later Palaeolithic. In P. Mellars and C. Stringer (eds.), *The Human Revolution: Behavioral and Biological Perspectives on the Origins of Modern Humans*, pp. 433–54. Princeton, NJ: Princeton University Press.

White, R. (1989) Production complexity and standardization in early Aurignacian bead and pendant manufacture: evolutionary implications.

In P. Mellars and C. Stringer (eds.), *The Human Revolution: Behavioral and Biological Perspectives on the Origins of Modern Humans*, pp. 366–90. Princeton, NJ: Princeton University Press.

White, R. (1998) Comments: Neandertal acculturation in western Europe? *Current Anthropology* 39: S30–32.

Whitelaw, T. (1991) Some dimensions of variability in the social organization of community space among foragers. In C. S. Gamble and W. A. Boismier (eds.), *Ethnoarchaeological Approaches to Mobile Campsites*, pp. 139–88. Ann Arbor, MI: International Monographs in Prehistory, Ethnoarchaeological Series 1.

Whitelaw, T. M. (1983) People and space in hunter-gatherer camps: a generalising approach in ethnoarchaeology. *Archaeological Review from Cambridge* 2: 48–66.

Wilkins, W. K. and Wakefield, J. (1995) Brain, evolution and neurolinguistic preconditions. *Behavioral and Brain Sciences* 18: 161–226.

Wiseman, M. F. (1993) Lithic blade elements from the southern Levant: a diachronic view of changing technology and design process. *Journal of the Israel Prehistoric Society* 25: 13–102.

Wolpoff, M. (1996) *Human Evolution*. New York: McGraw-Hill.

Wood, W. R. and Johnson, D. L. (1978) A survey of disturbance processes in archaeological site formation. In M. B. Schiffer (ed.), *Advances in Archaeological Method and Theory*. Vol. 1, pp. 315–81. New York: Academic Press.

Wynn, T. (1979) The intelligence of later Acheulean hominids. *Man* 14: 379–91.

Wynn, T. (1985) Piaget, stone tools and the evolution of human intelligence. *World Archaeology* 17: 32–43.

Wynn, T. (1991) Tools, grammar and the archaeology of cognition. *Cambridge Archaeological Journal* 1: 191–206.

Wynn, T. (1993) Layers of thinking in tool behavior. In K. R. Gibson and T. Ingold (eds.), *Tools, Language and Cognition in Human Revolution*, pp. 389–405. Cambridge: Cambridge University Press.

Wynn, T. (1995) Handaxe enigmas. *World Archaeology* 27: 10–24.

Yellen, J. E. (1977) *Archaeological Approaches to the Present*. New York: Academic Press.

Yellen, J. E. (1996) Analysis of a Middle Stone Age 'pavement' at Katanda 9, Semliki River, Zaire. In N. J. Conard and F. Wendorf (eds.), *Middle Paleolithic and Middle Stone Age Settlement Systems*, pp. 313–18. Forlì: A.B.A.C.O. Edizioni.

Yellen, J. E., Brooks, A. S., Cornelissen, E., Klein, R. M., Mehlman, M., and Stewart, K. (1995) A Middle Stone Age worked bone industry from Katanda, Upper Semliki River (Kivu) Zaire. *Science* 268: 553–6.

Yevtushenko, A. I. (1998) Kabazi V: introduction and excavations. In A. E. Marks and V. P. Chabai (eds.), *The Paleolithic of Crimea: The Middle Paleolithic of Western Crimea*, Vol. 1, ERAUL 84, pp. 273-85.

Ziaei, M., Schwarcz, H., Hall, C., and Grün, R. (1990) Radiometric dating of the Mousterian site of Quneitra. In N. Goren-Inbar (ed.), *Quneitra: A Mousterian Site on the Golan Heights*, pp. 232-5. Jerusalem: Qedem. Monographs of the Institute of Archaeology, The Hebrew University.

Zohary, D. (1962) *Plant Life of Palestine*. New York: The Ronald Press Company.

Zohary, D. (1973) *Geobotanical Foundation of the Middle East*. Amsterdam: Swets and Zeitlinger.

Zohary, D. and Hopf, M. (1994) *Domestication of Plants in the Old World*. Oxford: Clarendon Press.

Zubrow, E. (1989) The demographic modelling of Neanderthal extinction. In P. Mellars and C. Stringer (eds.), *The Human Revolution: Behavioural and Biological Perspectives on the Origins of Modern Humans*, pp. 212-31. Edinburgh: Edinburgh University Press.

Index

Page numbers in *italics* refer to figures and tables

bioturbation 238
blade production
    debitage 29, 61-4, 67-8, 70-2, 246
    early 26-7
    laminar system 14
    Levallois and notched 77, 80, 81
    Levallois technique 12
    refitted 82, 107-17, 114-15, 122, 126-9,
        127-8, 135, 137, 139, 140, 142, 143-6, 150-3
    retouched 79, 82
    site structure 205-6, 208, 211, 218, 233
    spatial distribution 184, 188, 192-3
    tool blanks 74, 74-5, 76, 85
    transitional 28
boars 24
Boker Tachtit 13, 22, 26, 29, 108, 146
bone 228, 230-1, 232, 245, 249, 263, 265
bone tools 10, 10-11
Border cave 4, 27
Bordesian systematics 72, 74
Bos 46
bows and arrows 11
bulbar scars 67-8, 70, 91, 92-3, 271, 274, 277-8
bulliform (phytoliths) 159
burials 25, 241
burins
    C-type assemblages 14
    manufacture 74, 76
    refitted 110, 135, 143, 144, 149, 154
    retouched 29, 82, 85
    spatial distribution 64, 188, 188, 192-4, 205,
        212, 214, 216, 219, 222, 233
burning 98-101, 102-6, 246
Bushmen open camps 262

C-type assemblages 13, 14, 15, 19, 20, 22-3, 29, 43
calcareous sandstone 40
calcic paleosols 38-9
calcium oxalate (phytoliths) 159
calcium phosphate 294, 296
Calligonum comosum 36
Cambrian sandstones 37, 47, 49
camels 22-3
canes 42
carbonate
    cement 40
    deposits 39-40, 59, 238, 245
    laminae 238
    nodules 40
carinated pieces 109-10
Carmel, the 12, 14
Carpathian-Balkan region 107
cedar trees 35-6
Cedrus libani 35
Celtis sp. 24
Cenomanian cherts 47
    see also cherts
Cenomanian limestone 47
cereals 24

Ceylon 260, 261, 265
chaîne opératoire 27-8, 61, 69
Chalcolithic period 39, 41
chamfered blades 28
    see also blade production
chapeau de gendarme butts 17, 26, 64, 73, 113,
        116-19, 126, 129, 143-50, 145, 150-7
charcoal fines 243
Châtelperronian tradition 6, 8
cherts
    distribution 260, 262
    first appearance 7-11
    location 9, 25, 28, 37, 47, 49, 59, 61-3, 66-7,
        260
    production 61, 63, 67, 70-1, 83-5, 102-3,
        106, 255-6
    refitted 108-9, 112, 115, 117, 122, 124,
        126-7, 129, 150-5, 151
chips (small artifacts) 14, 174, 176-7, 178, 182,
        184, 189, 208, 240, 245-6, 247, 253, 256-7,
        263, 265
chronometric techniques 17, 19, 21
chukar 46
citrate ion 294
Clactonian notches 80
cleaning 103
cluster centroids 87, 208, 217
coarse verrucate (phytoliths) 159
cognition 3, 5-6, 8-10
collecting strategy model 45
Combe Grenal 4, 8-9
concave-faceted fine butt 129
concorde profiles 17, 73, 113, 150, 152
cones (phytoliths) 159
conjoined pieces 150
constellations 113-55, 115, 120-1, 123-5, 127-8,
        130-1, 134, 136-7, 140-2, 144-5, 147-8
continuity model 3
convergent blades 134, 135, 142
convergent cores 68, 113, 117, 150
convergent facet patterns 68-9, 71
convergent scar patterns 117, 119, 122, 132
converging forms 30, 68, 126, 129-30, 131,
        152-3
convex-faceted crude butt 132
convex-faceted fine butt 113, 116-17, 119, 122,
        126, 129, 135, 137, 139
core faces 68, 71, 72, 85, 119, 122, 132-5, 142,
        153-4, 248
core shaping
    debitage 64, 67
    location 47, 203, 205-7, 208, 211, 216-18, 233
    method 14, 61, 67, 96
    origins 25-6
    refitted 109-12, 119, 122, 126-31, 131, 132,
        136-42, 139, 143, 146, 149, 150-4
    spatial distribution 184, 185, 189, 190-3, 193,
        202-3, 240, 246, 253-7, 254,
        262-3, 267-8

plants and trees (Latin names), *cont.*
  festucoids *see* grasses
  Haloxylion articulata 36
  Laurus nobilis 35
  monocot phytoliths, *see* grasses
  panicoids 165-6, 169
  see also grasses
  Pistacia atlantica 35-6
  pistachia vera L. 24, 47-8, 167, 171, 252
  pooids 165-6, 169, *see also* grasses
  Quercus calliprinus 35
  Retama raetam 36
  Zizyphus spina-christi 36
  Zygophyllum dumasum 36
platey (phytoliths) *159*
platform
  cortex 273
  facets 69, 97, 117, 122, 273
  regularization 14, 277
  shapes 69, 91, *93*, 282
Pleistocene Age 3, 5, 14, 22, 28-9, 33, 36-8, 40, 43
pluvial conditions 43
point bases 79
point production 12, 14, 29, 61-2, 73-4, 77, 112-13, 118-19, 122, *123*, 126, *134*, 255, 263
pointed distal shapes 68-9, *70*, 71
pollen 21, 37, 40, 42
polyhedrons (phytoliths) *159*
polylobates (phytoliths) *159*
pooids (grasses) 165-6, 169; *see also* grasses
Portugal 4
Precambrian rocks 108
pressure flaking 89-91, *93*, 95
primary reduction 111, *192-203*, 205-6
prismatic cores 26
proto Cro-Magnon 5
punctiform butt 129

Q1 Red Sand 38-9, *38*, 41
Q2 Yellow Silt 38-9, *38*
Q3 Red Sand *38*, 41, 58
Q4 Yellow Silt *38*, 41
Qafzeh caves 4, *13*, 14, 18-19, 22-3, 25, 27, 84
Qafzeh-Skhul skulls 5
Quercus calliprinus 35
Quneitra *13*, 14, 17, 23-6
Quweira 34

r flakes 91, *92-3*, 272, 277, 279
radiometric assays 26
Ras el Kelb 14-17
Ras en Naqb Escarpment 34-6, *34-5*, 40, 43
red ochre 25
Red Sea *13*, 28
reeds 42, *159*, 166, 171
refitted artifacts 107-55, *114-16*, *118*, *120-1*, *123-5*, *127*, *130*, *132*, *133*, *135*, *136-8*, *140-2*, *144-5*, *147-8*, 150, 152, 154, 177, 240, 255, 262
replacement model 3-5

residual striking platform 273, 277
Retama raetam 36
retouched tools 84
  blades *78-81*, 110
  flakes *78*, 81
  pieces *74*, 80, 82-3, *83*, 129, *193-4*, 195, *212*, *214*, 219, *221*, 255
  points 79, 195, 224
  rejuvenation flakes 75
  side scrapers 79
retouched truncated faceted flake 78
rhino 23
rhyolite rocks 37
Rift Valley, *see* Wadi Araba
rondels (phytoliths) *159*
rope (phytoliths) *159*
Rosen, Arlene Miller 156-71
Rosh Ein Mor *13*, 14, 17, 21, 23, 146
rushes 42

Sabiha Formation *38*, 41
saddles (phytoliths) *159*
sage 36
Sahara 27, 36
Saharo-Arabian dune fields 37
Saharo-Iranian desert zone 165
Sahba 14
Salib Arkose 49
saltwood 36
sand
  Member I 40
  Member II 40
Saragusti 24
Saudi Arabia 34
saxual shrub 36
scar pattern 28, 110-13, 115-16, 119, 132
seed husks *160*, 171, *225*, *254*, 260
Sefunim 17
sessile animals 23-4
sheep 46
sheet erosion 239
shells 7, 25, 30
short trapezoid (phytoliths) *159*
side-scrapers 9, 14, 17, *64*, *74-5*, 80, *81*, *83*, *193-4*, *212*, 240, 249, 251, 253-4, *254*, 263
silica skeletons 156, 165-6, 169, 225
silicified limestone 47
Sinai Desert 23, 29
siqs 37
Skhul 4, *13*, 14, 18, 19, 25, 27
smooth sheet (phytoliths) *159*
sodium polytungstate 156
sodium pyrophosphate 156
Sodmein Cave *13*, 28
soft-hammer percussion 14, 67, 89, 90-1, *93*, 95, 99, *101*, 103-6, 246, 255, 271-3, 276
Sokkia Set 6 Total Station, *see* laser theodolyte
South Africa 265
Southern Rift Valley, *see* Wadi Araba

www.ingramcontent.com/pod-product-compliance
Lightning Source LLC
Chambersburg PA
CBHW081428270326
41932CB00019B/3125